THE INTERNATIONAL PROTECTION OF LABOR:
INTERNATIONAL LABOR ORGANIZATION, HISTORY AND LAW

THE MACMILLAN COMPANY
NEW YORK · BOSTON · CHICAGO · DALLAS
ATLANTA · SAN FRANCISCO

MACMILLAN & CO., LIMITED
LONDON · BOMBAY · CALCUTTA
MELBOURNE

THE MACMILLAN CO. OF CANADA, LTD.
TORONTO

THE INTERNATIONAL PROTECTION OF LABOR

INTERNATIONAL LABOR ORGANIZATION,
HISTORY AND LAW

BY

BOUTELLE ELLSWORTH LOWE, A.M., Ph.D.

Sometime President of Language Institute, New York City, Principal of Hackensack Summer School, Head of Department of History and Social Studies, Hackensack High School, Professor of Economics and Social Science, Junior College of Bergen County, Hackensack, N. J. Author of "Representative Industry and Trade Unionism of an American City," "International Aspects of the Labor Problem," "International Education for Peace," etc.

NEW EDITION
Revised and Enlarged

New York
THE MACMILLAN COMPANY
1935

PRINTED IN UNITED STATES OF AMERICA

COPYRIGHT, 1921 AND 1935
BY BOUTELLE ELLSWORTH LOWE

Set up and electrotyped. Published October, 1921
Revised Edition, August, 1935.

BARAT COLLEGE

FOREWORD

By the action of Congress and the President, the United States became a member of the International Labor Organization on August 20, 1934. By all who have been interested in the establishment of international standards to safeguard the rights of workers, employers, and the general public, this action on the part of the United States will be regarded as a most important step in promoting friendly co-operation among nations. The International Labor Organization is essentially the work of men whose principal interest is the establishment of social justice. It is not "a creation of socialists". The president of the Commission which drafted the Constitution of this Organization at the Peace Conference of Paris was Samuel Gompers, a lifelong opponent of socialism.

In the first edition of this book, the story of the international labor movement ended with the Second Session of the International Labor Conference at Genoa in 1920. This edition continues the account through the Eighteenth Session at Geneva in 1934.

The origin of the writer's interest in labor problems dates back to a year of graduate work in Economics and History at the University of Rochester in 1912. Believing that economic legislation in the field of international affairs would be better understood by one familiar with international law, he undertook its study at Columbia University. It was while he was engaged in this study that he began to write concerning what is now the historic movement for international labor legislation. His attention was first called to this subject by a chance reference to it in a library file. The documents to which this find directed not only awakened interest but also led to the decision to make as thorough a study of international labor legislation as possible. Some sources for this study were obtainable in English, *e.g.*: the *English Bulletin* and other publications in English of the International Labor Office of the International Association for Labor Legislation; articles in the *American Labor Legislation Review* and other materials on

FOREWORD

file at the office of the American Association for Labor Legislation; and also miscellaneous articles in magazines and government bulletins. However, all attempts to find some connected account or history in English of this European movement for co-operation among nations in the legal regulation of labor conditions proved fruitless. Of such histories in French, notably those of L. Chatelain and E. Mahaim, authors respectively of *La Protection internationale ouvrière* (Paris, 1908) and *Le Droit international ouvrier* (Paris, 1913), the study was undertaken with considerable pains to improve reading ability in French. This investigation, involving the use of foreign sources to which these and other works directed, led to the conviction that the efforts to promote international labor legislation were not only worthy but also promised great possibilities for the future welfare of society, and that the United States ought to try to find some way by which it could become a party to such treaties as the Bern Conventions of 1906.

Believing that there would be some Americans who might seek, as the writer had done, to find some connected story of this movement in English, and that there would be many whose interest would be aroused were such a history available, the writer undertook to prepare such an account together with the collection and translation, when necessary, of important documents bearing upon it. This work, which was completed before the spring of 1918, was substantially the same as that published in the first edition of this book with the exception of the Introduction and those parts dealing with developments subsequent to 1917.

A contribution of this nature is small and insignificant as compared with that of those men, including many Americans, who had the privilege of actively participating in the promotion of this kind of legislation. There were American representatives at the Congresses of Zurich and Brussels in 1897, at the Conference of Paris in 1900, and at subsequent meetings of the International Association for Labor Legislation. This representation included delegates sent by the Government of the United States, which, in 1902-03, also began to contribute to the treasury of the International Labor Office at Basel. The American Association for Labor Legislation, a branch of the International Association, came into existence in 1905, and, since that time, has made notable contributions to international co-operation and the improvement of labor conditions in America.

Thus it is evident that many Americans had given serious thought and attention to the problem of the international regulation of labor conditions, a fact which might lead some to misinterpret the intent of the reviewer in certain statements in the *New York Herald* of February 19, 1922, to the effect that: "The United States is generally supposed to be backward in taking official part in the international regulation of labor conditions... We were so isolated that we assumed we were on another planet. Hence it follows that although there are many studies in French and German, Mr. Lowe was the first American to give it serious attention." The writer was "first" in a very minor and unimportant sense only. In so far as he knows, his was the first preparation, in manuscript form, for the publication of a book in English for general readers including an unequivocal advocacy of official American participation in the movement for international labor legislation by adhesion, on the part of the United States Government, to international labor conventions such as those of Bern; and his Doctor's dissertation, *International Aspects of the Labor Problem* (October, 1918), was also, in so far as he knows, the first connected story, published in English, tracing the history of this movement and the growth of the idea.* This history was drawn from French, German, and English sources which were clearly indicated in the footnotes. The discussion of America's relation to this movement was not included in the thesis

*In a letter of October 30, 1918, addressed to a publisher, Professor J. B. Moore wrote: "There is, I believe, no comprehensive work in English on the subject covered by Dr. Lowe's manuscript. More or less has been published on the continent of Europe, chiefly in French and in German, on the international aspects of the labor problem, but in so far as I am aware they do not fully exhibit, as Dr. Lowe has done, the legislative developments in this country which may enable the United States to do more than it has heretofore done towards treating labor problems in an international way."

For recommending the publication of the manuscript, the writer was deeply indebted to Professors J. B. Moore, E. C. Stowell, E. R. A. Seligman, E. T. Devine, and T. I. Parkinson, of Columbia University, Mr. H. N. Shenton of the Council of National Defense, Washington, D. C., Mr. R. S. Rounds of the American Bar Association, and many others who gave encouragement.

FOREWORD

which represented only a part of the materials that had been originally prepared. The complete work did not appear until the publication of the first edition of this book in 1921. At the time the writer was keenly disappointed by his failure to bring about its complete publication in 1918. This was due to various difficulties. That failure, however, proved to be of no importance as developments at the Peace Conference of Paris in 1919 focused attention upon the subject and led to the publication of articles and books devoted to it. Since the United States did not ratify the Treaty of Versailles or join the International Labor Organization, the desirability of American participation in the formulation and ratification of international labor conventions continued to be an open question. Although our country has now joined this Organization, it remains to be seen to what extent it will be possible for it to apply such conventions or the principles contained in them. For a federal state, whose power to enter into international labor agreements is held to be limited because of its constitutional system, special provisions have been made by the Constitution of the International Labor Organization whereby a draft convention may be treated as a recommendation only.

March 24, 1935.   B. E. L.

PREFACE TO THE FIRST EDITION

In 1918 the writer published a Doctor's dissertation on the *International Aspects of the Labor Problem,* after collecting copies of international labor treaties and proposals for such treaties and translating those which had not already been translated into English. Although more or less had been published on the continent of Europe in French and German on the movement for international labor legislation, this subject had received little attention from American or English writers. In 1919 the writer sent to the United States Bureau of Labor Statistics a report including the collection of copies of labor treaties and proposals for such treaties, which led to the publication by that Bureau in 1920 of Bulletin No. 268 (Miscellaneous Series), entitled, *Historical Survey of International Action Affecting Labor.*

Previous to the World War the United States was thought by many to be fully a generation behind Europe with respect to various phases of labor legislation. Certain it is that the United States was among the most backward of great nations in taking part officially in the international regulation of labor conditions. It is the purpose of this book to describe the movement for international labor legislation, to present the labor agreements that have resulted therefrom, and to endeavor to show the legislative developments that may enable the United States to do more than it has heretofore done toward treating labor problems in an international way.

The *Introduction* is topical and briefly outlines the four phases of international action which have affected labor and which have contributed to the movement for international labor legislation (see p. xv). It also contains a more detailed outline of the proceedings of the International Labor Organization.

The Movement for International Labor Legislation in the chronological order of the events that contributed to it up to the time of the war, and in its relation to America and to the formation of the International Labor Organization of the League

PREFACE TO THE FIRST EDITION

of Nations directly after the war, is discussed in Part I (see p. 1).

International Labor Legislation, or, in other words, the polypartite and bipartite labor treaties that had been ratified and brought into actual operation as a result of the movement for international labor legislation, as well as the proposals made for such treaties, up to the time of the war, are treated in Part II (see p. 111) and in Appendices I (see p. 169) and II (see p. 233). A table of contents for Appendix I is given on pp. 171, 172, and for Appendix II on pp. 235-237.

The Supplement (see p. 399) includes a copy of the Covenant of the International Labor Organization of the League of Nations as contained in the Peace Treaty of 1919, as well as copies of the recommendations and draft conventions adopted by the Conference of the International Labor Organization.

The Bibliography (see p. 331) has a table of contents on pp. 332, 333, covering publications in German, French, English, Italian, Spanish, Swedish, Hungarian, Danish, Dutch, and Finnish.

A short Bibliography of most recent publications in English is given on p. 330.

A Key to the abbreviations used in the citation of references in this book and particularly in the Bibliography, will be found on p. 334.

An Index to Parts I and II is contained on pp. 390-398.

A Concise Table of Contents for the entire book is given on p. xi.

Tables of congresses and treaties are given on pp. xii-xiv.

The writer wishes to express his appreciation of the readiness of Dr. John B. Andrews, Secretary of the American Association for Labor Legislation, to place source material at his disposal and of the helpful suggestions of Hon. John Bassett Moore, of the Chair of International Law, at Columbia University.

New York City,   BOUTELLE ELLSWORTH LOWE.
March 24, 1921.

CONTENTS

Chapter   *Page*
INTRODUCTION xv
    International Socialist Movement xvi
    International Trade-Union Movement xxi
    International Activities of Social Reformers, and of Private and
        Semipublic Associations xxv
    Intergovernmental Action Respecting Labor................... xxxii
    The General Conference of the International Labor Organization (1919-1934) xxxviii
    The Entrance of the United States into the International Labor
        Organization lxix

PART I.
THE EARLY MOVEMENT FOR INTERNATIONAL LABOR LEGISLATION AND ITS RELATION TO THE UNITED STATES
   I. The Movement Defined 3
  II. Genesis of the Movement 11
 III. International Labor Conferences 31
 IV. *Pro et Contra* 66
  V. The Relation of America...................................... 79
 VI. The Movement in Perspective 95

PART II.
EARLY INTERNATIONAL LABOR LEGISLATION
   I. Conventions Signed at Bern 112
  II. Protective Labor Treaties 137
      Appendix I. 169
         Labor Law Internationally Adopted—Contents................ 171
      Appendix II. 233
         Labor Resolutions Internationally Subscribed—Contents........ 235
      Index 390

BIBLIOGRAPHY
Short Bibliography (1918-1934)..................................... 330
Bibliography (showing the early development of the international labor
    movement up to the beginning of the World War)............. 331
Contents 332
Key to Bibliography 334

SUPPLEMENT
INTERNATIONAL LABOR ORGANIZATION

Labor Section (Part XIII) of the Peace Treaty of 1919............. 401
Draft Conventions and Recommendations of the International Labor
    Organization, 1919-1934 412
Contents 399

CONTENTS

TABLES OF CONGRESSES

INTERNATIONAL CONGRESSES OF SOCIALISTS (1864-1881)

International Workingmen's Association and the First International
1864 ....xvi, 14
Congress of Geneva, 1866 15
Congress of Lausanne, 1867 16
Congress of Brussels, 1868 16
Congress of Basel, 1869 16
Congress of The Hague, 1872 16
Congress of Geneva, 1873 16
Congress of Brussels, 1874 16
Congress of Bern, 1876 16
Congresses of Verviers and Ghent, 1877............................. 16
Congress of Chur, 1881 16

SOCIALIST AND LABOR CONGRESSES (1883-1888)

Congress of Paris, 1883 ....xvi, xxi, 16, 24
Congress of Paris, 1886 ....xvi, xxi, 16, 24
Congress of London, 1888 ....xvi, xxi, 16

INTERNATIONAL CONGRESSES OF SOCIALISTS (1889-1912, 1919, 1920)

Congress of Paris and the Second International, 1889..........xvii, 16, 27
Congress of Brussels, 1891 ....xvii, 16, 34
Congress of Zurich, 1893 ....xvii, 16, 34
Congress of London, 1896 ....16, 34
Congress of Paris, 1900 16
Congress of Amsterdam, 1904 16
Congress of Stuttgart, 1907 ....xxii, 16
Congress of Copenhagen, 1910 16
Congress of Basel, 1912 ....xvii, 16
Congress of Bern, 1919 xix
Congress of Geneva, 1920 xx

WAR-TIME SOCIALIST CONGRESSES

Congress of Copenhagen, 1915 (Neutral Powers).................... xviii
Congress of Vienna, 1915 (Central Powers)........................ xviii
Socialist and Labor Conferences of London, 1915, 1917, 1918 (Allies) xviii
Congress of Zimmerwald, 1915 (International) xviii
Congress of Kienthal, 1916 (International) xviii
Congress of Stockholm, 1917 (International) xix

CONGRESSES OF THE THIRD INTERNATIONAL

Congress of Moscow, 1919 xx
Congress of Moscow, 1920 xx

MISCELLANEOUS

Congresses of Socialist Women, 1907, 1910........................ xviii
Congress of Socialist Students, 1919............................. xx
Pan-American Socialist Congress, 1919............................ xx

xii

CONTENTS

TABLES OF CONGRESSES—*Continued*

INTERNATIONAL CONGRESSES OF TRADE-UNIONS

The international trade-union movement .... xxi-xxv, 16, 17
Congresses of Paris, 1883 and 1886, and of London, 1888.... xvi, xxi, 16, 21
Congress of Zurich, 1897 .... 35, 247
Congresses of the International Federation of Trade Unions, 1901-1919 xxii
Seventeenth Miners' International Congress, 1906................... 46
Congress of San Salvador, 1911................................... xxiv
Congress of Leeds, 1916 xxiii
Congress of Bern, 1917 xxiv
Congress of Laredo, 1918 xxiv
First International Congress of Working Women, 1919.............. xxv
Congress of Mexico City, 1921.................................... xxiv

INTERNATIONAL CONGRESSES OF SEMIPUBLIC AND PRIVATE ASSOCIATIONS

Congress of Brussels, 1897 .... xxv, 36, 248
Congress of Paris, 1900 .... xxvi, 38
International Association for Labor Legislation.......... xxvi, 39, 40, 249
    First Delegates' Meeting, Basel, September 27, 28, 1901........ 41, 252
    Second Delegates' Meeting, Cologne, September 23, 24, 1902... 42, 254
    Commission Meeting at Basel, September 9-11, 1903.......... 43, 255
    Third Delegates' Meeting, Basel, September 26, 27, 1904........ 44, 258
    Fourth Delegates' Meeting, Geneva, September 27-29, 1906..... 47, 264
    Fifth Delegates' Meeting, Lucerne, September 28-30, 1908...... 57, 269
    Sixth Delegates' Meeting, Lugano, September 26-28, 1910...... 59, 281
    Seventh Delegates' Meeting, Zurich, September 10-12, 1912.... 61, 300
International Congresses on Unemployment, 1906-1913........ xxx, 53, 322
Congresses of the International Federation for the Observance of Sunday, 1876-1915 .... xxviii, 54
Congresses and Conferences of the Permanent International Committee on Social Insurance, 1889-1912.................. xxviii, xxix, 103
Third International Congress on the Cultivation of Rice, 1906........ 56
International Congresses on Occupational Diseases, 1906-1910.... xxix, xxx
International Home Work Congresses, 1910-1912............ xxx, xxxi, 61

OFFICIAL INTERNATIONAL LABOR CONFERENCES

Conference of Berlin, 1890 .... xxxiii, 31, 244
Conference of Bern, 1905...................... xxxiv, 46, 112, 174-175
Conference of Bern, 1906...................... xxxiv, 47, 119, 175-180
Second International Peace Conference at The Hague, 1907.......... 56
Conference of Bern, 1913...................... xxxiv, 64, 131, 318-321
Peace Conference, 1919...................... xxxvii, 105, 106, 401-412

THE GENERAL CONFERENCE OF THE INTERNATIONAL LABOR ORGANIZATION

Sessions: First through the Eighteenth, 1919-1934................ xxxviii
Members of the International Labor Organization................ lxxiii

CONTENTS

BIPARTITE LABOR TREATIES IN CHRONOLOGICAL ORDER

Pages

Franco-Italian Treaty, April 15, 1904...........................137, 180
Swiss-Italian Treaty, July 13, 1904...............................142, 194
German-Italian Treaty, Dec. 3, 1904..............................142, 195
Treaty between Germany and Austria-Hungary, Jan. 19, 1905.....143, 195
Accident Insurance Treaty between Luxemburg and Belgium,
    April 15, 1905...144, 195
German-Luxemburg Accident Insurance Treaty, Sept. 2, 1905......145, 197
Franco-Italian Treaty, Jan. 20, 1906.................................. 146
Franco-Belgian Accident Insurance Treaty, Feb. 21, 1906..........146, 200
Supplementary Convention between Luxemburg and Belgium,
    May 22, 1906..144, 197
Franco-Italian Accident Insurance Treaty, June 9, 1906............148, 184
Franco-Luxemburg Accident Insurance Treaty, June 27, 1906.....149, 203
German-Netherlands Accident Insurance Treaty, Aug. 27, 1907....150, 205
Franco-British Accident Insurance Treaty, July 3, 1909............151, 208
Hungarian-Italian Accident Insurance Treaty, Sept. 19, 1909......152, 210
Supplementary Agreement between France and Belgium,
    March 12, 1910..147, 201
Franco-Italian Treaty, June 10, 1910..............................153, 189
Franco-Italian Treaty, Aug. 9, 1910.................................. 156
German-Swedish Treaty, May 2, 1911.......................... 156, 215
Franco-Danish Treaty, Aug. 9, 1911..............................157, 215
German-Belgian Accident Insurance Treaty, July 6, 1912..........159, 217
German-Italian Workmen's Insurance Treaty, July 31, 1912........160, 221
German-Spanish Accident Agreement Respecting Sailors,
    Feb. 12, 1913...163, 227
Treaty between the United States and Italy, Feb. 25, 1913........164, 228
Franco-Swiss Insurance Agreement, Oct. 13, 1913................165, 229
Supplementary Treaty between the German Empire and the
    Netherlands, May 30, 1914....................................151, 208
Italian-German War Arrangement, May 12-21, 1915.................. 166

INTRODUCTION

The international protection of labor is a name for the movement which has resulted in the adherence of nations to treaties and conventions protecting workers. These agreements tend to establish international standards for the regulation of industry. The international activities of socialists, trade-unionists, social welfare workers, and governments constitute respectively the political, economic, scientific, and official phases of international action which has affected this movement. In its origin and early development it derived very much of its energy from the agitation of socialists. However, to influence existing governments to sign labor treaties was only an item upon the socialist program. The theory of socialism has been to change the principles underlying the present political and social order. Like the socialists, the trade-unionists have advocated international labor legislation, but their influence in this respect was less than that of socialists until the war. In its international aspects as well as in its national aspects, trade-unionism has been chiefly concerned with the economic improvement of the working classes and in strengthening labor in its collective bargaining with employers. It was the social welfare workers, organized in private and semi-public associations and aided by the co-operation of interested governments, who devised the efficient organization that led to the actual adoption of international labor laws.

During the war, however, propaganda of trade-unionists and socialists for international labor legislation and for the incorporation in the Peace Treaty of guarantees for the maintenance of proper labor standards became more pronounced than that of any other groups. A result of the war in its relation to the movement for international labor legislation was the creation of an International Labor Organization in conjunction with the League of Nations, by which governments assumed the official direction of this movement. Following is a brief historical summary of the four phases of international action which have contributed to the movement for international labor legislation.

International Socialist Movement.[1]

In 1838 the Communist League was founded in London for the purpose of bringing about the overthrow of the existing form of society by means of the international organization of workers in all countries. The League gained considerable publicity through the appearance in 1848 of "the manifesto of the Communist Party" written by Karl Marx and Frederick Engels.

Fourteen years after the dissolution of this League, the International Workingmen's Association was founded at London (1864). The organization represented originally a movement of trade-unionists for the economic emancipation of the workers. It contained, however, another group which advocated political domination by the working classes; and, as a result of the influence exerted by this group under the guidance of Karl Marx during the first three congresses, the Association was converted into a socialist organization which is known as the First International. Ten international congresses are identified with this movement from 1864 to 1881. The Association continued active until 1872, when, through the loss of the confidence of its English members because of its supposed connection with the insurrection of the Paris Commune and through the dissension of Marxists and Bakunists within its ranks, it gradually lost its vigor and finally disappeared.

Congresses representing socialists and trade-unionists were convoked at Paris in 1883 and 1886, and at London in 1888. Both of the Congresses held at Paris advocated international labor legislation.

Because of differences which had arisen and which a special conciliatory Congress called by the Social Democratic group of the German Reichstag at The Hague, Feb. 4, 1889 (see p. 243),

[1] Cf. Bulletin of the United States Bureau of Labor Statistics, No. 268, Miscellaneous Series, pp. 34-64.

INTRODUCTION

had failed to settle, the Marxists and Possibilists convened separate congresses in Paris, July 14, 1889. Before the end of their session a rapprochement between these two factions was reached and they agreed to hold their next meeting at Brussels in 1891. The coming together of these socialist groups marks the formation of what is known as the Second International. The Marxists advocated labor treaties for the international application of the protective labor principles embodied in their resolutions for the prohibition of the work of children under fourteen years of age, and of night-work in general; an eight-hour day; weekly rest; conservation of health *etc.*[2]; and they appointed five delegates to use their influence in behalf of such legislation at an international labor conference which had been proposed by the Government of Switzerland. The Possibilists also favored international labor laws.

International labor legislation constituted the principal topic of discussion at the second Congress of the new International held at Brussels in August, 1891, and it was again discussed and advocated by the Congress of Zurich in 1893. Up to the time of the World War the Second International had held eight regular congresses, and one special peace conference in 1912.

In 1900 the International Socialist Bureau was established at Brussels as a result of the Congress held at Paris in that year. Its purpose was to gather and publish information on the problems of socialism and to report on the status of the socialist movement. Its official publication was entitled the *Periodical Bulletin of the International Socialist Bureau.* Each country was allotted two representatives in the membership of the Bureau while members of the Socialist Interparliamentary Commission were made alternate delegates with the privilege of taking part in its meetings. It was decided that the number of votes allowed to each country in the deliberations of the Bureau should be determined by the importance of the country in the socialist movement. By 1910 this organization had held twelve meetings, in which international labor legislation was one of a score or more of the topics considered. The World War caused the seat

[2] See p. 27.

of the International Socialist Bureau to be transferred from Brussels to The Hague for the duration of the war.

The Socialist Interparliamentary Commission was established in 1904, and its purpose was to enable the parliamentary representatives of socialists in different countries to co-operate for the realization of the aims of socialism. Each nation represented in the International Socialist Bureau was permitted to have one representative in the Interparliamentary Commission and to cast the number of votes warranted by its importance. Before the end of 1910 this Commission had held five conferences.

Socialist women have convened international conferences from time to time, for example at Stuttgart in 1907, and at Copenhagen in 1910. Moreover the Young Socialists organized internationally and in 1910 affiliated with the International Socialist Bureau.

After the outbreak of the war,[3] the socialists of neutral countries met in Copenhagen in 1915 to denounce the war and to discuss means of obtaining peace. Socialists of the Central Powers met at Vienna in the same year for a similar purpose. Socialist and labor conferences were held by socialists representing the Allies at London in 1915, 1917, and 1918. Peace terms were discussed, and in 1918, the Congress went on record as favoring the establishment of a league of nations, the abolition of secret diplomacy and imperialism, and the reduction of armaments. It also discussed international means of combatting unemployment.

The first war-time international conference of socialists representing both sides in the war was held at Zimmerwald, Switzerland, in 1915, with representatives present from France, Italy, Bulgaria, Holland, Roumania, Poland, Sweden, Norway, Denmark, and Germany. The second international meeting was held at Kienthal, Switzerland, in 1916. Italy, Sweden, Russia and Germany were represented. These conferences were principally concerned with the action to be taken by the working classes in behalf of peace. The manifesto of the Kienthal Congress, con-

[3] For wartime conferences compare Ayusawa, *International Labor Legislation*, Chapter IV.

taining the signatures of Lenin of Russia, Bouderon of France, and Ledebour of Germany, called for revolution and refusal to support the war. The strength of the left wing or antiparliamentary socialists was increasing. The radicalism of this group led to the establishment of a rival International at Moscow in 1919, known as the Third International.

A war-time international socialist conference occurred at Stockholm in 1917. Delegates arrived from France, Belgium and Germany, but the intervention of the Allies resulted in the holding of an informal meeting only, under the chairmanship of Branting, the leader of the Swedish party. Another international assemblage of socialists was held at Stockholm in the Fall of the same year.

After the signing of the armistice an important international meeting of socialists was convened at Bern in February, 1919. Twenty-five countries were represented including Germany Austria, Holland, Great Britain, France, Canada, and Argentina. A league of nations and the labor section of the Peace Treaty were prominent among the topics which were considered. The assembly favored a league of nations representing not only governments but peoples, the international control of oceans and highways of transportation, a world system for the distribution of raw materials and food, and gradual disarmament. The various measures advocated as proper subjects for protective labor laws included the establishment of employment bureaus and systems of social insurance; the adoption of the eight-hour day for adults, and the six-hour day for children between sixteen and eighteen years of age; the prohibition of night-work of women; the recognition of the necessity of weekly rest of thirty-six consecutive hours, and the institution of compulsory elementary education and free higher education. A commission was appointed for the restoration of the Second International.

This commission convoked conferences at Amsterdam in April, 1919, and at Lucerne in August, 1919. To the latter meeting delegates came from Belgium, Great Britain, France, Holland, and Germany. The minority group of the Russian socialists was also represented. The questions discussed were largely political.

Representatives of the discontented antiparliamentary socialists, called the socialist left wing, assembled at Moscow in March, 1919, on the invitation of the Russian communist party. Among the countries from which accredited delegates came to the gathering of this Communist or Third International were Roumania, Germany, Ukrania, Finland, Bulgaria, Norway, Sweden, Hungary and Armenia. There were other socialists present from the United States, Turkey, Jugo-Slavia, Persia, Korea, France, Switzerland, Holland, Bohemia, Great Britain, Serbia, Spain, and Denmark. This group called for the forcible overthrow of the capitalistic régime. Its manifesto was signed by Lenin, Trotzky, Zinovieo, Tchicherin and Fritz Plattan, and represents the form of socialism that secured the domination of Soviet Russia. The next meeting of the Third International was held at Moscow in July, 1920.

In the same month the Second International called a meeting at Geneva (July 31). The important parties left in the Second International were the Majority Social Democratic Party of Germany, the British Labor Party, the Belgian Labor Party, the Social Democratic Labor Party of Holland, the Austrian Social Democratic Party, the Majority Socialist Parties of Sweden and Denmark, the Polish Socialist Party, and the Finnish Social Democratic Party. The Geneva Congress voted to transfer the International Bureau from Brussels to London.

In 1919 French Socialist students issued a manifesto that caused the creation of the *Comité Internationale des Étudiants Socialistes,* with its headquarters in Geneva. In December of that year this body called an international meeting at Geneva to create an International Federation of Socialist and Communist Students. Sharp divergence of opinion, however, caused the formation of two separate bodies, the "Communist International Students' Federation," which affiliated with the Third International, and the "Independent Students' International," the aim of which was to unite all socialist and communist students for the peaceful realization of the principles of socialism.

The international socialist movement in the Western Hemisphere has also been growing. In 1919 a Pan-American Socialist

INTRODUCTION

Congress was held at Buenos Aires with representatives from Argentina, Bolivia, Chile, Peru, Paraguay, and Uruguay. This group sympathized with the radical left-wing socialists of Europe; it represented a step toward greater unity among socialist groups of South America. The demands of the Congress of Buenos Aires included a forty-four hour week; the compulsory education of children under sixteen years of age; the prohibition of child labor; a minimum wage and the abolition of the trucking system; the establishment of labor exchanges, *etc.* It caused the establishment of the American Labor and Socialist Secretariat at Buenos Aires.

International Trade-Union Movement

The International Workingmen's Association originated as a trade-union organization but became the Socialist International. After the disappearance of the First International, the trade-union element can be distinguished from the socialist element in the international congresses which, as has been mentioned above, were held at Paris in 1883 and 1886, and at London in 1888. Demands for international factory legislation were made at both of the Paris conferences. In 1897 the executive committee of the Swiss Workers' League called the Congress of Zurich the purpose of which was to promote labor legislation. This meeting urged the Swiss Federal Council to bring about the establishment of an international labor office. An international meeting of trade-unionists was held at Paris in 1900. The creation of an international secretariat was discussed and a resolution favoring the curtailment of the hours of labor was unanimously adopted.

After approximately the year 1900, the international trade-union movement became more clearly distinguished from the international socialist movement with which originally it had been incorporated. Delegates at labor congresses are often party socialists and trade-unionists at the same time. In many instances the leaders have been the same in both groups, and trade-unions —even non-socialist unions—have been represented at socialist congresses. This co-operation between trade-unionists and socialists was emphatically endorsed at the socialist Congress of Stuttgart in 1907.

Since 1900 and up to the time of the war, the principal activities of international trade-unions were confined mostly to purely trade-union affairs. They have sought through international federation to unify their standards. Unionism is organized internationally in two forms, viz.., by trades and by federations.

International Trades Secretariats.—The single trades or crafts of different countries are united under international trades secretariats, as the offices of the international secretaries are called. Among the most prominent of these international craft organizations may be mentioned the International Federation of Miners (see p. 46) which was organized in 1890; the International Federation of Transport Workers, the origin of which may be traced back to an international gathering of railroad workers at Zurich in 1893; and the International Federation of Metal Workers organized in 1900. Before the war thirty-two crafts had such international organizations. Their secretaries held a joint meeting in Zurich for the first time, in 1913. The purpose was to promote greater unity in the trade-union movement and more co-operation between the international trades secretariats and the International Secretariat.

International Secretariat.—The second form of international trade-union organization is the International Federation of Trade Unions, of which the central office known as the International Secretariat, was permanently organized in 1901. Until 1913 it was known as the International Secretariat of the National Trade-Union Centers. The International Federation of Trade Unions represents: (1) the national federations of various countries, as for example, the American Federation of Labor which is made up of different trade organizations, (2) the federations of single trades, such as the International Federation of Textile Workers. The International Federation has held congresses at Copenhagen (1901), Suttgart (1902), Dublin (1903), Amsterdam (1905), Christiania (1907), Paris (1909), Budapest (1911), and Zurich (1913). Its first conference after the war was held at Amster-

INTRODUCTION

dam in August, 1919. At this meeting the old organization was abolished and a new International Federation of Trade Unions was formed with its International Secretariat located at Amsterdam. This assembly was dissatisfied with the labor clauses of the Peace Treaty as not providing adequate means for the protection of labor's interests, but it nevertheless decided to support the International Labor Organization of the League of Nations because it believed that this Organization might ultimately become the basis of a league representing peoples as well as governments.

Prior to the war, the American Federation of Labor joined the International Secretariat, but the tendency of the officers of the International Federation of Trade Unions in 1920 to favor socialistic propaganda prejudiced American workers against it. Hence the American Federation did not affiliate with the new International Federation.

International Labor Conferences.—A proposal of the American Federation of Labor, made in 1914 after the commencement of the war, to hold an international labor conference at the same time and place as that at which the peace conference would be held, attracted considerable attention and was endorsed by the Canadian Trades Union Congress and the French *Confédération Général du Travail.* This proposal led to a meeting of representatives of French, Belgian, British, and Italian trade-unions in Paris. Here it was decided to call an Allied trade-union conference to consider labor problems in relation to the war. The conference was held at Leeds in July, 1916.[1] This meeting declared that the peace terms should "insure to the working class

[1] For a discussion of this conference and other war-time conferences of labor, see Carol Riegelman's contribution (Vol. I, pp. 55-79) to *The Origins of the International Labor Organization* (1934), of which Dr. James T. Shotwell is editor. This work is published in two volumes for the Carnegie Endowment for International Peace in the series *The Paris Peace Conference: History and Documents* of which Dr. James Brown Scott is general editor.

"*The Origins of the International Labor Organization* is a documentary history presenting as complete a collection as is now available of the texts which are basic to the story, and a series of studies, narrative, analytic, or interpretative, prepared for the most part by those who shared in the work of the Commission on International Labor Legislation of the Peace Conference." (p. xxv)

"The story stops at the close of the first International Labor Conference, that which met in Washington in November, 1919." (p. xxiii)

of all countries a minimum of guarantees...concerning the right of coalition, emigration, social insurance, hours of labor, hygiene and protection of labor," and that an international commission should be created to secure the enforcement of the proposed laws. It also emphasized the importance of an international labor office and suggested that "the office established by the International Association for Labor Legislation may be put into use for the carrying out of this program."

The Swiss Federation of Labor convoked a conference at Bern, October 1, 1917, representing labor organizations of Denmark, Bulgaria, Bohemia, Hungary, Austria, Germany, Norway, Sweden, the Netherlands, and Switzerland. It demanded the enforcement of labor laws and proposed that the International Association for Labor Legislation be recognized in the Peace Treaty as the agency for the promotion and enforcement of labor legislation, and also that representation in the International Labor Office be given to the International Federation of Trade Unions.

The international labor movement in America was no longer confined to the United States and Canada. In November, 1911, a Central American Labor Congress was held in San Salvador. In November, 1918, the American Federation of Labor and Mexican labor unions convened at Laredo, Texas, the first Pan-American Labor Conference with representatives from the United States, Mexico, Colombia, Guatemala, Costa Rica, and Salvador. The purpose of the Pan-American Federation of Labor was declared to include the "establishment of better conditions for the working people who emigrate from one country to another" and the utilization of "every lawful and honorable means for the purpose of cultivating the most favorable and friendly relationship between the labor movements and the peoples of the Pan-American Republics." Another meeting was held in Mexico City during the week of January 10, 1921, and Mr. Samuel Gompers was re-elected president of the Pan-American Federation of Labor.

The American Federation of Labor at its convention in Atlantic City on June 20, 1919, endorsed almost unanimously the Covenant of the League of Nations and the labor clauses of the Peace Treaty after a long debate.

INTRODUCTION

The first International Congress of Working Women was called by the National Women's Trade Union League of America at Washington, October 28—November 6, 1919. This conference passed resolutions concerning each item of the agenda of the Washington Labor Conference of the League of Nations and submitted recommendations to the Washington Conference concerning the amendment of Article 389 of the Peace Treaty with respect to the representation accorded to countries in the General Conference of the International Labor Organization of the League. The proposed amendment required that each nation represented in the General Conference should appoint "two delegates representing the government, one of whom shall be a woman; two delegates representing labor, one of whom shall be a woman; and two delegates representing the employers."

International Activities of Social Reformers, and of Private and Semipublic Associations.

Efforts of Individuals.—Many persons in the capacity of social reformers or private citizens have exerted a great influence upon the movement for international labor legislation. Its pioneer advocate, Robert Owen (1771-1858) belonged to this class as did his contemporaries, Daniel Legrand (1783-1859) and Jérome Blanqui (1798-1854). Names of men connected with the early history of the movement are Villermé, Hahn, Audiganne, Braber, Bluntschli, Wagner, Brentano, Wolowski, Dumas, Schoenberg, Thiersch, Adler, Albert de Mun, Vaillant and others. Through the efforts of many of these men* the principle of international labor legislation was pressed upon the attention of governments.

Congresses Called upon the Initiative of Private Persons.—In 1897 a meeting was called at Brussels by persons interested in

*Audiganne in 1856 published a book advocating laws for the international regulation of industry. Schoenberg in 1871 took up the discussion of international labor legislation in his *Arbeitsamter.* Thiersch, a theologian, petitioned the German Emeror to convoke an international labor conference. The work of the other men is discussed in connection with events mentioned in following chapters or footnotes. *Cf.* Ayusawa, *International Labor Legislation,* pp. 25-29.

the international labor movement (see p. 248). Although some men who had been delegates at the official Berlin Conference of 1890 were present, the Congress of Brussels had no official status. Its secretary was Professor Ernest Mahaim of the University of Liége, Belgium, who became one of the foremost leaders of the movement. As a result of this meeting, committees were formed to consider means of bringing about the establishment of an international labor office. The organization of an international labor office had been proposed to the Swiss Federal Council in 1889 and had been considered by the Berlin Conference of 1890, by the Congress of Zurich of 1897, and by other labor conferences. Moreover the Swiss Government had undertaken in 1896 to ascertain the attitude of several European countries toward the project with the result that two powers responded favorably, two thought the time inopportune, while the others were either opposed or undecided.

The work of the committees mentioned above led to the calling of a meeting under the direction of Professors Cauwés and Jay at the time of the Paris Exposition in 1900. It was at this International Labor Congress of Paris that the International Association for Labor Legislation was organized including a private International Labor Office established in 1901 and national sections (see pp. 249-252).

International Association for Labor Legislation.—The duties of the Labor Office included studying the development of labor legislation, publishing the results of its studies, and receiving and transmitting information pertaining to the creation and enforcement of international labor conventions. Each national section of the International Association strove for improved working conditions in its own country and at the same time supported the efforts of the Association which continued to work for international labor legislation as socialists, trade-unionists, government officials and private individuals had done before its formation. Under its scientific management the various efforts put forth in behalf of international legislation were co-ordinated and directed into channels that produced practical results. Governments were led to sign bipartite and polypartite labor treaties

INTRODUCTION

making international labor legislation no longer a mere theory but also a fact. Between 1900 and 1912 the Association held seven regular international meetings of delegates (see Exhibits 11, 12, 14-18, pp. 252-316).

In June 1918 the International Labor Office without the approval of the members of the Association requested that a program of international labor legislation be incorporated in the Treaty of Peace and that the International Labor Office be made a part of the organization of the proposed League of Nations. This request was fulfilled by the Labor Covenant (Part XIII) of the Peace Treaty which made an official International Labor Office a part of the International Labor Organization of the League of Nations.

The American section of the International Association is known as the American Association for Labor Legislation (see p. 323). At the annual meeting of the American Association in Richmond, Virginia, December 28, 1918, the following resolution was adopted with reference to international labor protection:

WHEREAS, Maladjustments from which wage-earners suffer, such as inadequate wages, excessive hours of work, unemployment, and industrial accident and disease, are not confined to any one country; and

WHEREAS, These international evils know no frontiers, and national action against them needs to be supplemented and fortified by common agreement on minimum standards of labor conditions below which no person should be required or permitted to work; therefore, be it

RESOLVED, That the American Association for Labor Legislation urge that in international agreements there be incorporated minimum protective labor guarantees, including:

(1) The principle of the living wage.

(2) Three-shift system in continuous industries and one day's rest in seven in all occupations.

(3) Regulation of working hours for women and young persons, and prohibition of night-work by them.

(4) Prohibition of child labor.

(5) Establishment of public employment offices and use of public work to prevent unemployment during the period of demobilization and other comparatively slack times.

(6) Safety and sanitary devices in industry, and in transportation by land and water, including international use of automatic couplers on railroad trains, and the extension of the Seamen's Act.

(7) Comprehensive systems of social insurance against accident, sickness, unemployment, old age, invalidity, and death.

(8) Provisions for collection and publication of comparable labor statistics through the International Association for Labor Legislation and for the enforcement of international labor regulations through a League of Nations.

There are other semi-public and private associations* which have labored for improvement in certain phases of industrial life and in many instances have co-operated with the International Association for Labor Legislation. Some of these societies were formed long before the International Association for Labor Legislation. The following are cited as typical examples of such organizations:

International Federation for the Observance of Sunday.—In 1876 the International Federation for the Observance of Sunday was organized at the Congress of Geneva which was called by a committee of the Evangelical Alliance and was attended by over four hundred delegates from Switzerland, France, England, Holland, Austria-Hungary, Germany, the United States, Norway, Roumania, Spain, Belgium, and Italy. Emperor William I. of Germany was officially represented by one of his ambassadors. Various industrial, social, philanthropic and labor organizations sent delegates. The question of the proper observance of Sunday was approached mainly from the religious standpoint, but the importance of Sunday rest from the standpoint of the needs of the workers has also been recognized and emphasized in various international conferences, notably those of 1900 and 1906 (see p. 54). Congresses on the observance of Sunday have been held at the following places: Geneva (1876); Bern (1879); Paris (1881); Brussels (1885); Paris (1889); Stuttgart (1892); Chicago (1893); Brussels (1897); Paris (1900); St. Louis (1904); Milan (1906); Frankfort on the Main (1907); Edinburgh (1908); Geneva (1911); Oakland, California (1915).

Permanent International Committee of Social Insurance.— This body was organized primarily for the technical study of the problems of social insurance. Its discussions have been published and from these much of value in the principles and practise of social insurance has been derived (see pp. 100, 143).

At the first International Congress on Labor Accidents held at Paris in 1889, a permanent committee was formed to continue

*Cf. U. S. Bulletin, *opp. cit.*, pp. 83-115.

INTRODUCTION

the movement for social insurance. Under the direction of this committee, now known as the Permanent International Committee of Social Insurance, congresses have been held at Bern (1891); Milan (1894); Brussels (1897); Paris (1900); Düsseldorf (1902); Vienna (1905); Rome (1908). To the Congress of Rome in 1908, official delegates were sent by twenty-five countries and nearly 1400 persons attended representing Argentina, Uruguay, the United States, Australia, Austria, Belgium, Canada, Nicaragua, Guatemala, Holland, Hungary, Italy, Japan, Luxemburg, Greece, Norway, New Zealand, Portugal, Roumania, Russia, Serbia, Spain, Sweden, Switerland, China, Denmark, Finland, France, Germany and Great Britain. It was decided at the Congress of Rome to hold the general congresses at longer intervals and to organize national committees to meet more frequently for the purpose of discussing special topics. Under this plan committee conferences were held at The Hague in 1910 and at Dresden in 1911, and a meeting of members of the Permanent International Committee and the national committees, together with other specialists, was held at Zurich in 1912.

International Congress on Occupational Diseases.—The first International Congress on Occupational Diseases was held at Milan in June, 1906. On this occasion an association was formed under the name of Permanent International Commission for the Study of Occupational Diseases.

The purpose of the organization was* "to hold international and national congresses for the study of occupational diseases; to study and assemble material on industrial and social hygiene; to institute at Milan a bibliographical service for the use of all interested in the study of occupational diseases; to publish a bibliographical magazine in French; to call the attention of authorities to the results of researches in industrial hygiene; and to make recommendations to learned societies thereon; and to bring to the public attention of governments, universities, hospitals, *etc.*, the efforts being made in this connection." This organization has formed national committees in various countries

*Ibid., p. 109.

including Switzerland, Holland, Austria, Hungary, France, the United States, Bulgaria, Canada, Spain, Great Britain, Greece and Italy. Italian physicians and scientists have been the leaders in this organization. Its headquarters were located at Milan, Italy. The second international meeting was held at Brussels in 1910.

International Association on Unemployment.—The Italian Society, Umanitaria, held the first International Congress on Unemployment at Milan in 1906 (see p. 53).

In 1910 an International Association on Unemployment was organized at Paris. The headquarters of the Association were located at Ghent. The aim of the organization was to bring about the adoption of the measures most effective in preventing unemployment. For this purpose, it adopted the following methods:** "(1) The organization of a permanent national office to centralize, classify, and hold at the disposition of those interested the documents relating to the various aspects of the struggle against unemployment in different countries; (2) the organization of periodical international meetings, either public or private; (3) the organization of special studies on certain aspects of the problem of unemployment and the answering of inquiries on these matters; (4) the publication of essays and of a journal on unemployment; (5) negotiations with private institutions or the public authorities of each country with the object of advancing legislation on unemployment and obtaining comparable statistics and possibly agreements or treaties concerning matters of unemployment."

National sections of the International Association on Unemployment were organized in sixteen countries before the end of 1913 (see p. 322). The International Committee of the Association held meetings at Ghent in 1911 and at Zurich in 1912. The first general assembly of the Association was convened at Ghent in 1913.

International Home Work Organization.—The permanent bureau of the International Congress of Home Work was created in 1910 by the Brussels Congress on Home Work. Resolutions

***Ibid.*, pp. 111, 112.

INTRODUCTION

were passed calling for* "compulsory registration by contractors or subcontractors of all home workers, with the books relating to wages and description of work open at all times to the labor inspectors; establishment by joint committees for a limited period of time, of a minimum wage applicable to all average workers, the decisions of these committees to be enforced by a superior council; establishment of a standard of healthfulness in the different trades in order to determine the industries which should be either regulated or suppressed; prohibition of work of children under fourteen years of age and instruction of children up to this age." The permanent bureau was located at Brussels and it convened the second International Congress on Home Work at Zurich in 1912. The countries sending official delegates were: Portugal, Norway, Holland, Luxemburg, Japan, Italy, Hungary, Belgium, Chile, Denmark, France, Saxony, Sweden, the United States, Roumania, and Russia. The Congress divided into four sections each of which prepared resolutions on special topics assigned to it. The resolutions contained a "proposed act to regulate paid home work" for legislative adoption by the different countries. This act prescribed the conditions under which home workers should be registered by the employers and the regulations necessary for the protection of the home worker and the ultimate consumer of his product. The resolutions provided for protection from industrial poisoning; the prohibition of the manufacture of foodstuffs and tobacco by home workers; the compulsory notification of contagious diseases, and the precautions to be taken where such occur in home work shops, and a special system of inspection for home work. Also provision was made for fixing wage rates through special wage boards or through existing industrial councils.

The Congress urged that support be given to the trade-union movement among home workers and advised co-operation with consumers' leagues in "spreading the principles adopted by the Congress."

Growth of Internationalism, 1890-1900.—The period from 1890 to 1900 was one of extraordinary activity in the development of international organizations relating to all sorts of movements,

*Ibid., p. 114.

of which the international labor movement was but one. As examples of international movements, some of which were organized previous to 1890 and all of which held meetings prior to 1900, may be mentioned the International Congress of Hygiene and Demography; the International Prison Commission; the Universal Postal Union; the International Co-operative Alliance; the International Railway Conference; the International Actuarial Conference; and the International Congress of Women. In Paris in 1900 during the World's Fair occurred an International Socialist Congress; the formation of the International Association for Labor Legislation; the International Congress for the Teaching of the Social Sciences; the International Congress of Ornithology; the International Congress of Navigation; the International Congress on Work or Assistance in Time of War; the International Co-operative Alliance; the International Congress of Aboriculture; the International Society of Physicists; the International Railway Congress; the International Actuarial Congress; the International Congress of Comparative Legislation; the International Congress on Chronometry; the International Congress on Private International Law; and many other international assemblages.

Intergovernmental Action Respecting Labor

The first official move for the realization of international labor legislation was made in 1855 by the Swiss Canton of Glarus which sent a communication to the Council of Zurich suggesting the international control of certain labor conditions. In 1876 the subject of international labor legislation was discussed by Colonel Frey before the Swiss Parliament and in 1880 he made a motion before the National Council directing the Federal Council to enter into negotiations with other countries with a view to establishing international factory laws. In 1881 the motion was favorably considered by the National Council and the Federal Council began soon after to ascertain the attitude of several other governments toward the project (see p. 19). The replies were not sufficiently encouraging to cause Switzerland to take any further action in the matter at that time. In 1887 and 1888 (see pp. 240-243)

INTRODUCTION

the Federal Council made another attempt to interest other countries and upon receiving a more favorable response than in 1881, it proceeded to prepare for an official international labor congress to be held at Bern. The congress was cancelled, however, to give place to the Conference of Berlin (1890) which was called by the German Government.

In 1884 Count Albert de Mun discussed international labor legislation before the French National Assembly and in the next year leading French deputies including Proudhon, Camelinat, Boyer, Hugues, Basley, and Gilly responded by placing before the committee of the Chamber of Deputies a bill (see p. 239) relating to international labor law and favoring the action of the Swiss Government.

In 1871 Bismarck proposed to a representative of Austria that agreements fixing certain standards of social legislation be concluded between Germany and Austria. This proposed course of action was considered a few years later at a conference, but no such agreements between the countries were reached.

In 1885 Baron von Hertling championed the cause of international labor legislation in the Reichstag, but Bismarck was wholly opposed to the movement as being impracticable. In 1886 the Social Democratic Party proposed that the Reichstag adopt a resolution (see p. 240) calling upon the Chancellor of the Empire to convoke an international conference to formulate an international labor agreement. In 1889 labor disturbances threatened Germany, and the Imperial Government, as mentioned above, convened the first official international labor Conference at Berlin in 1890.

Conference of Berlin, 1890.—International labor legislation was discussed and resolutions (see pp. 244-248) were adopted by the delegates of the governments represented. This Conference did not have any direct practical results. It increased the general interest in the movement, however, and had an indirect influence in the formation of the International Association for Labor Legislation in 1900. Between 1890 and 1905 various unofficial labor congresses were held before the next strictly official labor conference was convened.

THE INTERNATIONAL PROTECTION OF LABOR

Conferences of Bern, 1905 *and* 1906.*—As a direct result of the efforts of the International Association for Labor Legislation, an official Conference was called by Switzerland at Bern in 1905. It drew up draft copies (see pp. 174, 175) of international labor conventions which were amended and approved by the second official Conference of Bern in 1906. When ratified by the various countries, these two conventions (see pp. 175-180) concerning respectively the prohibition of the use of white phosphorus in the manufacture of matches and the prohibition of night-work for women in industrial employment became the first two polypartite labor treaties ever adopted. Some bipartite labor treaties had been adopted previous to this. Thus *The Movement for International Labor Legislation* (see Part I of this book) resulted in the creation of *International Labor Legislation* (see Part II). The United States was not a signatory to either of the Conventions.

In 1906 Great Britain attempted to bring about the formation of a permanent commission to gather information and in a general way to superintend the enforcement of international labor laws as well as to investigate matters in dispute (see pp. 118, 119, 122, 316-318). Although the British proposal was not adopted, it forms the basis in the history of international labor legislation for the labor clauses of the Peace Treaty which confer upon the International Labor Organization means for securing the enforcement of international labor conventions.

Conference of Bern, 1913.—The International Association for Labor Legislation prepared a program to serve as a guide in the creation of two more draft conventions for international adoption and the Swiss Government again took the initiative in calling an official conference. The delegates met at Bern in 1913 and, taking the program proposed by the Association as a basis, drew up and adopted two draft conventions concerning respectively the prohibition of night-work for young persons employed in industrial occupations and the limitation of day-work for women and young persons employed in such occupations (see pp. 318-321). A diplomatic conference for the official adoption of these conventions was scheduled for Sept. 3, 1914, but because of the

---

*See Part II, Chapter I, entitled "Conventions Signed at Bern."

INTRODUCTION

World War the conference was not held and no formal treaties resulted.

Bipartite Labor Treaties.—The International Association for Labor Legislation exerted an important influence in bringing about the formation of bipartite labor treaties. The question of a protective labor treaty between France and Italy was discussed by delegates from the two countries at the Second Delegates' Meeting at Cologne in 1902; and in 1904 the first bipartite labor treaty, drawn up by the French statesman, Arthur Fontaine, in conjunction with the Italian statesman, Luzatti, was ratified by their governments. This Treaty dealt with insurance and protection of foreign workers and with national laws regulating the conditions of labor. It was the first instance in which the movement for international labor legislation resulted in the actual adoption of a labor treaty as the Bern Conventions were not drafted and formally ratified until later. It should be noted that polypartite treaties such as the Bern Conventions make for greater uniformity of labor standards and are more difficult to create than bipartite treaties.

Agreements concerning the migration or recruitment of alien labor were entered into between Great Britain and France under date of October 20, 1906; between Transvaal and Portuguese Mozambique under date of April 1, 1909; between the United States and Japan under date of April 5, 1911; and between Spain and the Republic of Liberia under date of May 22/June 12, 1914.

By far the largest number of bipartite labor treaties concerned the equality of treatment of alien and native workmen with respect to the labor laws of the country giving employment. Several such treaties were savings bank agreements which permitted the transfer of deposits from the savings banks of one country to those of the other country without charge. Other treaties dealt with social insurance and accident insurance, making applicable to resident alien workers the laws of the country of employment, or granting to non-resident dependents of alien workers the benefits of the laws of the country of employment. Social insurance agreements and accident insurance agreements were adopted by the following countries (see Part II, Chapter II, entitled "Protective Labor Treaties"):

THE INTERNATIONAL PROTECTION OF LABOR

France and Italy, April 15, 1904 (for text of Treaty see pp. 180-184).
Switzerland and Italy, July 13, 1904 (p. 194).
Germany and Italy, December 3, 1904 (p. 195).
Germany and Austria-Hungary, January 19, 1905 (p. 195).
Luxemburg and Belgium, April 15, 1905 (pp. 195-197).
Germany and Luxemburg, September 2, 1905 (pp. 197-200).
France and Belgium, February 21, 1906 and March 12, 1910 (pp. 200-202).
Luxemburg and Belgium, May 22, 1906 (p. 197).
France and Italy, June 9, 1906 (pp. 184-188).
France and Luxemburg, June 27, 1906 (pp. 203, 204).
Germany and the Netherlands, August 27, 1907 and May 30, 1914 (pp. 205-208).
France and the United Kingdom, July 3, 1909 (pp. 208-210).
Hungary and Italy, September 19, 1909 (pp. 210-214).
France and Italy, August 9, 1910 (p. 156).
Germany and Sweden, May 2, 1911 (p. 215).
Germany and Belgium, July 6, 1912 (pp. 217-221).
Germany and Italy, July 31, 1912 (pp. 221-227).
Germany and Spain, November 30th, 1912/Feb. 12, 1913 (p. 227).
Italy and the United States, February 25, 1913 (p. 228).
France and Switzerland, October 13, 1913 (p. 229).

A Treaty between France and Italy, June 10, 1910 (pp. 189-194), provided for reciprocal protection of children with respect to the labor and educational laws of each country, and a Treaty between France and Denmark, August 9, 1911 (pp. 215-217) subjected to arbitration disputes relating to their labor laws.

A convention was concluded at Paris, August 9, 1917, between France and the Republic of San Marino in order to insure to workers of the two countries compensation for injuries resulting from industrial accidents. An agreement was drawn up between Norway, Denmark and Sweden, February 12, 1919, respecting reciprocity in the matter of accident insurance. On September, 30, 1919, France and Italy signed a new labor Treaty* which provided that the workers of either country, when employed in the other, should receive the same treatment as nationals with respect to labor conditions and social insurance benefits. The Treaty specified such reciprocity with reference to wages and working and living conditions, stabilization of labor markets, social insurance, acquisition of land, charitable aid, arbitration boards and labor laws, protection of children and adults, workers' taxes, and seamen and fishermen.

*For the text of the Treaty, see the "Monthly Labor Review," (United States Bureau of Labor Statistics), Feb. 1920, pp. 47-53.

INTRODUCTION

International Labor Organization of the League of Nations.—
On January 18, 1919, the Peace Conference formally opened, and at its second plenary session a commission was created to study international labor legislation. Samuel Gompers was the president of this Commission which submitted its report to the Peace Conference dated March 24, 1919. This report recommended the inclusion in the Peace Treaty of labor clauses creating an International Labor Organization in conjunction with the League of Nations (see p. 101 *et seq.*). This recommendation was adopted and the labor clauses (see p. 401 *et seq.*) constitute what is popularly termed the "Labor Charter" (Part XIII of the Peace Treaty).

Every member of the League of Nations subscribed to the following nine fundamental principles:

FIRST.—The guiding principle above enunciated that labor should not be regarded merely as a commodity or article of commerce.

SECOND.—The right of association for all lawful purposes by the employed as well as by the employers.

THIRD.—The payment to the employed of a wage adequate to maintain a reasonable standard of life as this is understood in their time and country.

FOURTH.—The adoption of an eight-hours day or a forty-eight hours week as the standard to be aimed at where it has not already been attained.

FIFTH.—The adoption of a weekly rest of at least twenty-four hours, which should include Sunday wherever practicable.

SIXTH.—The abolition of child labor and the imposition of such limitations on the labor of young persons as shall permit the continuation of their education and assure their proper physical development.

SEVENTH.—The principle that men and women should receive equal remuneration for work of equal value.

EIGHTH.—The standard set by law in each country with respect to the conditions of labor should have due regard to the equitable economic treatment of all workers lawfully resident therein.

NINTH.—Each State should make provision for a system of inspection in which women should take part, in order to ensure the enforcement of the laws and regulations for the protection of the employed.

Without claiming that these methods and principles are either complete or final, the High Contracting Parties are of opinion that they are well fitted to guide the policy of the League of Nations; and that if adopted by the industrial communities who are members of the League, and safeguarded in practice by an adequate system of such inspection, they will confer lasting benefits upon the wage-earners of the world.

THE INTERNATIONAL PROTECTION OF LABOR

The General Conference of the International Labor Organization

First Session, Washington, D. C., October 29—November 29, 1919.—On August 11, 1919, President Wilson cabled an official invitation to thirty-four countries to send representatives to the First Session of the General Conference of the International Labor Organization. The United States was not represented by official delegates at this meeting and consequently cast no votes as it had not signed the Peace Treaty nor become a member of the Labor Organization. The Conference invited employers and workers of the United States to send delegates. Employers did not respond to the invitation. Mr. Samuel Gompers was appointed to represent the workers. Hon. William B. Wilson, Secretary of Labor of the United States, was made president of the Conference. The countries represented by delegates were: Argentina, Belgium, Bolivia, Brazil, Canada, Chile, Czechoslovakia, China, Cuba, Colombia, Denmark, Ecuador, Finland, France, Great Britain, Greece, Guatemala, India, Italy, Japan, Holland, Nicaragua, Norway, Paraguay, Persia, Peru, Poland, Portugal, Rumania, Salvador, Siam, Serbs-Croats-Slovenes, South Africa, Spain, Sweden, Switzerland, Haiti, Panama, Uruguay, and Venezuela.

The Washington Conference adopted six draft conventions and six recommendations.*

The first draft convention "limiting the hours of work in industrial undertakings to eight in the day and forty-eight in the week" applied to persons "employed in any public or private industrial undertaking, or in any branch thereof, other than an undertaking in which only members of the same family are employed." The eight-hour limit could be exceeded on some days by not more than one hour, if there occurred a corresponding decrease in the number of hours required on other days, thus making possible a forty-eight-hour week with a Saturday half-holiday. For persons employed in shifts the day might be extended beyond eight hours provided the average number of hours over a period of three weeks did not exceed forty-eight hours per week. Exceptions were allowed for accidents, emergencies, or *force ma-*

---

*For copies of the draft conventions and recommendations, see the Supplement (p. 400).

INTRODUCTION

jeure, in so far as necessary to avoid serious interference with the ordinary work of the undertaking. A special exception also was allowed in continuous industries provided that the working hours did not exceed fifty-six hours in the week on the average. Other exceptions were allowed so as to make the convention sufficiently elastic for application to the various industries of the different countries. It required each employer to post notices stating the conditions of employment in his industry. Each signatory agreed to apply the convention to its colonies, protectorates, and possessions, with necessary exceptions. Ratifications were to be registered with the Secretary-General of the League of Nations. The agreement permitted denunciation after the expiration of ten years from the date on which the convention first came into force. By 1934 this convention had been ratified by sixteen countries[1] and four other states* had registered ratifications with conditional or delayed application.

The second draft convention concerned unemployment and required that each signatory should communicate to the International Labor Office, as often as once in every three months, all available information concerning unemployment and the measures contemplated for combatting it. Another provision stated that "each member which ratifies this convention shall establish a system of free employment agencies under the control of a central authority," co-ordinated with the International Labor Office, while a third article provided for an agreement upon terms whereby nationals of one of the contracting parties working in the territory of the other could be admitted equally with citizens of that state to the benefits of unemployment insurance. This convention was ratified (by 1934) by thirty nations.[2]

[1] Argentina, Belgium, Bulgaria, Chile, Colombia, Czechoslovakia, Dominican Republic, Greece, India, Lithuania, Luxemburg, Portugal, Rumania, Spain, Uruguay, Nicaragua.
*Austria, France, Italy, Latvia.
[2] In the case of this draft convention and all other conventions mentioned in following pages, the number of states which have ratified is given as of Sept. 1, 1934, unless otherwise indicated. The thirty countries which ratified the convention on unemployment are: Argentina, Austria, Belgium, Bulgaria, Chile, Colombia, Denmark, Estonia, Finland, France, Germany, Great Britain, Greece, Hungary, India, Irish Free State, Italy, Japan, Luxemburg, Netherlands, Nicaragua, Norway, Poland, Rumania, South Africa, Spain, Sweden, Switzerland, Uruguay, Yugoslavia.

Besides this draft convention a recommendation concerning unemployment was adopted to the effect that the establishment of private employment agencies charging fees should be prohibited; that those already established should be required to obtain government licenses and should be abolished as soon as possible; that the recruitment of bodies of laborers in one country with a view to their employment in another country should be permitted only by mutual agreement between the countries; that each member of the International Labor Organization should establish an effective system of unemployment insurance; and that each member should reserve as much public work as practicable for periods of unemployment.

The second recommendation advised each member reciprocally to grant to alien workers the benefits of protective labor laws and the right of lawful organization as enjoyed by its own workers.

The draft convention concerning the employment of women before and after childbirth was the first labor convention applicable to commercial undertakings as well as industrial enterprises. According to its provisions a woman should not be allowed to work within six weeks following her confinement and she should be privileged to leave work six weeks before confinement and to receive adequate benefits during these periods together with proper protection against any unjust dismissal by her employer. Moreover, half an hour twice each day must be allowed to such women for the purpose of nursing their children. This convention was ratified by sixteen states.[3]

The draft convention concerning the employment of women during the night was adopted to supersede the Bern Convention of 1906; but actually it constituted an extension of that Convention which provided a rest period of at least eleven consecutive hours including the interval between ten o'clock in the evening and five o'clock in the morning. The main provisions of the Bern Convention remained unaltered (see Chapter I of Part II). The clause of the old Convention limiting its application to undertak-

[3] Childbirth: Argentina, Brazil, Bulgaria, Chile, Colombia, Cuba, Germany, Greece, Hungary, Latvia, Luxemburg, Nicaragua, Rumania, Spain, Uruguay and Yugoslavia.

INTRODUCTION

ings employing more than ten men or women was removed so as to make the new convention apply to all industrial undertakings excepting only those in which only members of the same family are employed. The definition of "industrial undertakings" was restated so as to make it applicable to all industrial undertakings within the sphere of application of other conventions. This convention was ratified by thirty countries.[4] At the Eighteenth Session in 1934 this convention was revised so as to include a clause restricting its operation as follows: "This Convention does not apply to women holding responsible positions of management who are not ordinarily engaged in manual work." A further item of revision was the addition of the following provision to the definition of "night": "where there are exceptional circumstances affecting the workers employed in a particular industry or area, the competent authority may, after consultation with the employers' and workers' organizations concerned, decide that in the case of women employed in that industry or area, the interval between eleven o'clock in the evening and six o'clock in the morning may be substituted for the interval between ten o'clock in the evening and five o'clock in the morning."

The third recommendation was for the prevention of anthrax and the fourth for the protection of women and children against lead poisoning. The latter urged the exclusion of women and young persons under eighteen years of age from employment in certain processes using lead compounds. Where such employment occurs, the regulations necessary to prevent poisoning were prescribed.

The fifth recommendation advocated the establishment of efficient factory inspection and government service for safeguarding the health of workers; and the sixth recommendation advised each member of the International Labor Organization to adhere to the Bern Convention prohibiting the use of white phosphorus

[4] Night-work of women: Albania, Argentina, Austria, Belgium, Brazil, Bulgaria, Chile, Colombia, Cuba, Czechoslovakia, Estonia, France, Great Britain, Greece, Hungary, India, Irish Free State, Italy, Lithuania, Luxemburg, Netherlands, Nicaragua, Portugal, Rumania, South Africa, Spain, Switzerland, Uruguay, Venezuela and Yugoslavia.

in the manufacture of matches in case it had not already done so.*

By the terms of the fifth draft convention, "children under the age of fourteen years shall not be employed or work in any public or private industrial undertaking, or in any branch thereof, other than an undertaking in which only members of the same family are employed." Special exceptions to this were allowed for Japan and India. The convention required employers to keep a register of all employees under the age of sixteen. Twenty-six countries ratified this convention.[5]

The sixth draft convention concerned the night-work of young persons in industry and prohibited the employment during the night of young persons under eighteen years of age. The Bern draft convention of 1913 (see pp. 318-320, also, p. 131 *et seq.*), which constituted the basis for the formation of this convention, had fixed the age limit at sixteen instead of eighteen. The Washington convention made exceptions for steel works, glass works, paper and raw sugar manufactories, and gold mining reduction work, in which young persons over the age of sixteen could be employed. The term "night" was defined as signifying "a period of at least eleven consecutive hours, including the interval between ten o'clock in the evening and five o'clock in the morning." Special exemptions were allowed for Japan and India. The prohibition of night-work for young persons over sixteen years of age could be suspended in case of serious emergencies. There were also special provisions applying to workers in coal and lignite mines and bakeries. This convention was ratified by thirty states.[6]

* Previous adherents: Canada, Denmark, France, Germany, Great Britain and Ireland, Italy, Luxemburg, Netherlands, New Zealand, Norway, South Africa, Spain, Switzerland. Subsequent adherents up to the spring of 1934: Australia, Austria, Belgium, Bulgaria, China, Czechoslovakia, Estonia, Finland, Hungary, India, Japan, Persia, Poland, Rumania, Sweden, Turkey, Yugoslavia.

[5] Minimum age in industry: Albania, Argentina, Belgium, Brazil, Bulgaria, Chile, Colombia, Cuba, Czechoslovakia, Denmark, Dominican Republic, Estonia, Great Britain, Greece, Irish Free State, Japan, Latvia, Luxemburg, Netherlands, Nicaragua, Poland, Rumania, Spain, Switzerland, Uruguay and Yugoslavia.

[6] Night-work of young persons in industry: Albania, Argentina, Austria, Belgium, Brazil, Bulgaria, Chile, Cuba, Denmark, Estonia, France, Great Britain, Greece, Hungary, India, Irish Free State, Italy, Latvia, Lithuania, Luxemburg, Netherlands, Nicaragua, Poland, Portugal, Rumania, Spain, Switzerland, Uruguay, Venezuela and Yugoslavia.

INTRODUCTION

Second Session, Genoa, June 15—July 10, 1920.—The General Conference of Genoa was devoted exclusively to the consideration of protection for seamen.

The first recommendation favored the adoption of the eight-hour day and forty-eight-hour week in so far as possible in the fishing industry, and the second recommendation urged the same measures for workers employed in inland navigation. The third recommendation asked each member of the International Labor Organization to codify seamen's laws and regulations. The fourth recommendation urged the adoption of unemployment insurance for seamen.

A draft convention fixed fourteen as the minimum age for the admission of children to employment at sea. Twenty-eight countries ratified this.[7]

Another draft convention provided unemployment indemnity for seamen to be paid by the employer in case of the loss or foundering of a ship. Members ratifying the convention engaged, wherever possible, to apply it to colonies, protectorates and possessions with necessary modifications. It was ratified by twenty-one states.[8]

The third draft convention was adopted with a view to establishing facilities for finding employment for seamen. Employment agencies charging fees for profit were prohibited unless licensed by the government. The establishment of free public employment bureaus for seamen was required. Committees representing shipowners and seamen were to give advice concerning the administration of these bureaus. Freedom of choice of ship must be allowed to seamen and the benefits of employment agencies must be accorded to the seamen of all countries adhering to the convention where industrial conditions are approximately the

[7] Minimum age for employment at sea: Argentina, Belgium, Bulgaria, Canada, Colombia, Cuba, Denmark, Dominican Republic, Estonia, Finland, Germany, Great Britain, Greece, Hungary, Irish Free State, Italy, Japan, Latvia, Luxemburg, Netherlands, Nicaragua, Norway, Poland, Rumania, Spain, Sweden, Uruguay and Yugoslavia.

[8] Unemployment indemnity in case of shipwreck: Argentina, Belgium, Bulgaria, Canada, Colombia, Cuba, Estonia, France, Germany, Great Britain, Greece, Irish Free State, Italy, Latvia, Luxemburg, Nicaragua, Poland, Rumania, Spain, Uruguay and Yugoslavia.

same. Furthermore the convention required that all available information concerning seamen's employment be communicated to the International Labor Office. Twenty-three nations registered their ratifications of this convention.[9]

A proposed convention establishing an eight-hour day and a forty-eight hour week for maritime workers in general failed at the Conference of Genoa to obtain the two-thirds vote necessary for its adoption although the majority of governments voted with the workers' representatives in favor of it. Experience in the meetings of the General Conference at Washington and Genoa showed that the fear that governments would vote solidly with employers was unfounded. Government delegates frequently were divided in their vote and tended to support workers' delegates quite as much as employers' delegates in the various issues that arose.

In August, 1920, the International Seafarers' Federation held a meeting in Brussels at which, because of the failure of the Conference of Genoa to adopt the above-mentioned convention, it was decided to commence in every country agitation for an eight-hour day and a forty-eight-hour week at sea with a forty-four hour week in port and to ask Mr. Thomas, who was then the director of the International Labor Office, to co-operate in bringing about a conference between shipowners and seamen in order to reach a satisfactory agreement on this issue. In the event of failure to reach a settlement the Congress decided that a general strike should be called. The action of the Federation in referring the matter to the International Labor Office was another evidence of the confidence of labor in the International Labor Organization. A convention of this nature, however, has not as yet been adopted.

Third Session, Geneva, October 25—November 18, 1921.*— Since the Conference of Genoa, all sessions of the General Con-

[9] Employment for seamen: Argentina, Australia, Belgium, Bulgaria, Colombia, Cuba, Estonia, Finland, France, Germany, Greece, Italy, Japan, Latvia, Luxemburg, Nicaragua, Norway, Poland, Rumania, Spain, Sweden, Uruguay and Yugoslavia.

* For more detailed discussions of the Sessions of the International Labor Conference, see the *International Labour Review,* a monthly publication of the International Labor Office.

INTRODUCTION

ference have been held at Geneva. The 118 delegates at the Third Session came from 39 states; 69 of them represented governments, 24 the employers, and 25 the workers; 230 technical advisers accompanied them. If each state were to send a complete delegation consisting of two representatives of the government, one representative of workers and one of employers, the number of government delegates would equal the total number of employers' and workers' delegates. The fact that some states send incomplete delegations has placed government representatives in the majority and this has constituted one of the serious problems of the Conference up to the present time.

Agricultural problems received a large measure of attention at this session in spite of the fact that the idea of regulating labor conditions in this field had encountered considerable opposition.

A recommendation regarding unemployment in agriculture was adopted. It proposed that governments undertake measures to encourage the adoption of better technical methods for the cultivation of idle and partially idle land. It also proposed the adoption of measures to encourage further settlement on the land and to facilitate the transportation of unemployed farm workers as well as to provide workers in seasonal agricultural enterprises with supplementary employment.

Another recommendation concerning childbirth urged that the same protection be afforded to mothers in agricultural employment as is given to them in industrial and commercial undertakings.

Two other recommendations dealt with the night-work of women and children respectively in agriculture. For women a night rest of not less than nine hours was proposed and, for child workers under fourteen, a rest period of not less than ten consecutive hours. For young persons between the ages of fourteen and eighteen a rest period of at least nine consecutive hours was recommended.

Vocational agricultural instruction was the subject of a recommendation encouraging the wide development of this branch of technical education and urging members to furnish information concerning the measures taken for this purpose.

A recommendation concerning the home conditions of agricultural workers aimed at improvement in matters of morality and hygiene. It dealt with such items as the heating of rooms, the providing of separate beds, the separation of the sexes, and the facilities necessary for personal cleanliness.

A final recommendation pertaining to agriculture asked the members to extend to this class of workers the same benefits of social insurance against old-age, invalidity, and sickness that had been provided for industrial and commercial wage-earners.

A draft convention concerning the age for the admission of children to agricultural work set fourteen as the minimum. This does not apply to work that may be performed outside regular hours of school attendance and that does not interfere with school work. Under certain conditions the hours for vocational instruction may be arranged so as to permit employment in light farm work particularly in the harvest season. Seventeen states ratified the convention.[10]

Another draft convention gave to small tenant farmers and agricultural wage-earners the same rights of association and combination as those accorded to industrial workers. This was ratified by twenty-seven members.[11]

The Conference adopted a convention providing that the benefits of accident compensation laws should be extended to agricultural workers. Of this nineteen members registered their ratifications.[12]

The convention concerning white lead prohibited its use, with certain exceptions, in interior work but permitted its use, under proper regulations, for outdoor work. Children under eighteen years of age and women were excluded from industrial painting

[10] Minimum age in agriculture: Austria, Belgium, Bulgaria, Czechoslovakia, Dominican Republic, Estonia, Hungary, Irish Free State, Italy, Japan, Luxemburg, Nicaragua, Poland, Rumania, Spain, Sweden and Uruguay.

[11] Rights of combination in agriculture: Austria, Belgium, Bulgaria, Chile, China, Colombia, Czechoslovakia, Denmark, Estonia, Finland, France, Germany, Great Britain, India, Irish Free State, Italy, Latvia, Luxemburg, Netherlands, Nicaragua, Norway, Poland, Rumania, Spain, Sweden, Uruguay and Yugoslavia.

[12] Accident compensation for agricultural workers: Belgium, Bulgaria, Chile, Colombia, Denmark, Estonia, France, Germany, Great Britain, Irish Free State, Italy, Latvia, Luxemburg, Netherlands, Nicaragua, Poland, Spain, Sweden and Uruguay.

INTRODUCTION

involving its use. Statistics of morbidity and mortality relevant to this problem were to be compiled. Twenty-two states ratified unconditionally and one state conditionally.[13]

A recommendation on weekly rest in commercial establishments defined such rest as a period of twenty-four consecutive hours one day in seven. It recommended that the whole staff of an establishment be given this rest simultaneously when possible. A draft convention concerning weekly rest for industrial workers used a similar definition stating that, wherever possible, it shall be so fixed as to coincide with the customs of the country or district. Situations requiring exceptions to the law were provided for together with measures to obtain compensatory periods of rest. Twenty-four countries adhered to this convention.[14]

Another draft convention forbade the employment on board ship of persons under the age of eighteen as trimmers or stokers. Exceptions were provided for certain cases where this regulation seemed unwise or impractical. Twenty-eight nations ratified it.[15]

The final draft convention of the session provided that persons under eighteen employed at sea shall be compelled to have a medical certificate and be subject to an annual medical examination. This did not apply to the fishing industry. The ratifications of twenty-six states were registered with the Secretary-General of the League of Nations.[16]

Fourth Session, October 18—November 3, 1922.—The agenda proposed revision of Part XIII of the Treaty of Versailles with

[13] Use of white lead in painting: Austria, Belgium, Bulgaria, Chile, Colombia, Cuba, Czechoslovakia, Estonia, Finland, France, Greece, Hungary (conditional), Latvia, Luxemburg, Nicaragua, Norway, Poland, Rumania, Spain, Sweden, Uruguay, Venezuela and Yugoslavia.

[14] Weekly rest in industry: Belgium, Bulgaria, Chile, China, Colombia, Czechoslovakia, Estonia, Finland, France, Greece, India, Irish Free State, Italy, Latvia, Lithuania, Luxemburg, Nicaragua, Poland, Portugal, Rumania, Spain, Sweden, Uruguay and Yugoslavia.

[15] Minimum age for trimmers or stokers: Belgium, Bulgaria, Canada, Colombia, Cuba, Denmark, Estonia, Finland, France, Germany, Great Britain, Greece, Hungary, India, Irish Free State, Italy, Japan, Latvia, Luxemburg, Netherlands, Nicaragua, Norway, Poland, Rumania, Spain, Sweden, Uruguay and Yugoslavia.

[16] Medical examination of young persons employed at sea: Belgium, Bulgaria, Canada, Colombia, Cuba, Estonia, Finland, France, Germany, Great Britain, Greece, Hungary, India, Irish Free State, Italy, Japan, Latvia, Luxemburg, Netherlands, Nicaragua, Poland, Rumania, Spain, Sweden, Uruguay and Yugoslavia.

THE INTERNATIONAL PROTECTION OF LABOR

a view to the reform of the constitution of the Governing Body of the International Labor Office. Much dissatisfaction had been expressed by some states with the section of the constitution that provided permanent seats on the Governing Body for the eight states of chief industrial importance.

A new text for Article 393 of Part XIII of the Treaty was adopted.

CONSTITUTION OF THE GOVERNING BODY ACCORDING TO

	THE ORIGINAL TEXT	THE NEW TEXT
States of chief industrial importance	8 persons	8 persons
Other states	4	8
Employers' representatives	6	8
Workers' representatives	6	8
Total membership	24	32

The original text did not specify what proportion of the members of the Governing Body should represent non-European countries. The new text specified that of the sixteen members representing governments at least six must be representatives of non-European states and that of the eight employers' representatives at least two must represent non-European countries. Likewise of the eight workers' representatives at least two must belong to non-European states. Before an amendment of this nature can take effect it must be ratified by "the States whose representatives compose the Council of the League of Nations and by three-fourths of the Members." The ratifications required to make this amendment effective were completed in 1934.*

At the Fourth Session four women were present as members of the French, Danish, Norwegian, and Uruguayan delegations. It was reported that the Permanent Court of International Justice had established the competence of the International Labor Organization to deal with the regulation of agricultural labor. No draft conventions were adopted. One recommendation was adopted. It stipulated the nature of information and the frequency of its

*For a discussion of the structure of the International Labor Organization, see the latter part of Chapter VI of Part 1.

communication to the International Labor Office concerning migration, repatriation, and transit of emigrants.

Fifth Session, October 22—29, 1923.—At this meeting of the General Conference there was adopted a recommendation specifying general principles for the organization of systems of inspection for the protection of workers. This recommendation dealt with the sphere of inspection, the functions and powers of inspectors, and the organization of the staff. It laid down principles to the end that greater safety from accidents or diseases might be secured for workers; that inspectors should be properly qualified and trained for their work; that high standards and methods of inspection be secured through the co-operation of employers and workers; and that reports of inspectors conform to proper standards.

Sixth Session, June 16—July 5, 1924.—A new method of procedure was put into operation for the first time. Draft conventions were provisionally adopted and left for final adoption at the Seventh Session. In the meantime governments could offer criticisms and amendments through the International Labor Office. This was called the "second reading" procedure.

One recommendation was given final approval. It treated of the development of facilities for the proper utilization of workers' spare time and sought to guard against encroachment upon it by supplementary employment, insufficient wages, lack of proper sanitary precautions, and lack of precautions against gambling, venereal disease, tuberculosis, and the misuse of alcohol. It commended the increase of the number of healthy dwellings at low rentals in garden cities and the development of home interests (gardens, allotments, poultry keeping) and recreational and educational institutions for the advantageous use of leisure time. Emphasis was placed upon the importance of preserving the workers' freedom and independence in the use of such institutions and the co-ordinating of local action for the attainment of these ends.

Seventh Session, May 19—June 10, 1925.—Of 46 countries represented, 17 sent incomplete delegations. Final action upon one recommendation and three draft conventions, which were drawn up at the Sixth Session, had been postponed until the Seventh Session in accordance with the plan of "second reading."

The recommendation and one draft convention dealt with the same topic; *viz.*, equality of treatment for national and foreign workers as regards workmen's compensation for accidents. The other two draft conventions were concerned with night-work in bakeries and the weekly suspension of work for twenty-four hours in glass manufacturing processes where tank furnaces are used. The convention affecting glass works was rejected as controversy and difference of opinion arose over certain proposed changes in the text. The convention regarding bakeries was adopted with modifications. The convention and recommendation on equality of treatment were approved practically without change. The Session considered it inadvisable to continue the procedure of double reading and proceeded to the final adoption of some new recommendations and draft conventions.

One of the new conventions provided that, in case of personal injury due to an industrial accident, the worker, or his dependents, should receive compensation. By the exceptions allowed, states could exclude from such benefits certain groups of workers including casual workers, outworkers, and members of an employer's family. The convention did not apply to agriculture but specified that the former convention concerning workmen's compensation in agriculture remained in force. This convention concerning compensation for industrial accidents was ratified by sixteen countries.[17]

Two recommendations pertaining to accident compensation were adopted—the one suggested methods of determining the amount of such compensation and favored vocational training for injured workers to fit them for some new field of useful work. The other recommendation had to do with the tribunals that have jurisdiction in disputes on workmen's compensation. It outlined measures by which employers' and employees' representatives could assist in the reaching of equitable decisions in such cases.

The other draft convention, which received original consideration and final approval at this Session, stated that compensation should be paid to the victims of occupational diseases. The

[17] Compensation for industrial accidents: Belgum, Bulgaria, Chile, Colombia, Cuba, Hungary, Latvia, Luxemburg, Mexico, Netherlands, Nicaragua, Portugal, Spain, Sweden, Uruguay and Yugoslavia.

INTRODUCTION

diseases specifically mentioned were those resulting from lead poisoning, mercury poisoning, and anthrax infection. Twenty-eight states ratified this convention.[18] A revision of the convention in 1934 added to the list of occupational diseases. When it is said that draft conventions have received original consideration at any session of the General Conference, the fact must not be overlooked that, during the preceding year or years, the International Labor Office has carried on a very thorough preparation of the subjects. It sends questionnaires to the various governments and on the basis of their replies it prepares a report which includes drafts of texts that are considered likely to be acceptable. The results of this preparation are placed at the disposal of the Conference.

In a recommendation concerning compensation for occupational diseases, each member of the Organization was urged to adopt a simple procedure by which the list of diseases considered occupational in its national legislation may be revised. This aimed at the extension of the schedule so as to include all such diseases of importance.

As has been stated above, the Conference approved the draft convention which accorded equality of treatment to national and foreign workers in respect of accident insurance "without any condition as to residence." Thus nationals of all members of the International Labor Organization which have ratified this convention would be entitled to this equality of treatment when employed as foreigners in the country of any of the aforesaid members. Thirty-three states ratified this.[19] A recommendation concerning this subject asked the states which ratified this convention to adopt certain specified measures to facilitate its application.

[18] Compensation for occupational diseases: Austria, Belgium, Bulgaria, Chile, Colombia, Cuba, Czechoslovakia, Denmark, Finland, France, Germany, Great Britain, Hungary, India, Italy, Irish Free State, Japan, Latvia, Luxemburg, Netherlands, Nicaragua, Norway, Portugal, Spain, Sweden, Switzerland, Uruguay and Yugoslavia.

[19] Equality of treatment in compensation for accidents: Austria, Belgium, Bulgaria, Chile, China, Colombia, Cuba, Czechoslovakia, Denmark, Estonia, Finland, France, Germany, Great Britain, Hungary, India, Irish Free State, Italy, Japan, Latvia, Luxemburg, Mexico, Netherlands, Nicaragua, Norway, Poland, Portugal, South Africa, Spain, Sweden, Switzerland, Uruguay and Yugoslavia.

The draft convention concerning night-work in bakeries forbade such work not only for employees but also for proprietors. However it did not apply to the wholesale manufacture of biscuits. The term "night" included a period of at least seven consecutive hours falling sometime between 10 p. m. and 5 a. m. as might be determined by agreement between employers' and workers' organizations with the approval of the government. Necessary exceptions were provided for. This convention was ratified by ten countries.[20]

Eighth Session, May 26—June 5, 1926.—The Conference decided that at its Eighth and Ninth Sessions in 1926, it would return to the original plan of single discussion and final adoption of draft conventions and recommendations. In accordance with this decision the Eighth Session proceeded to the final consideration and adoption of one new draft convention and an accompanying recommendation.

The convention was on the subject of the means of simplifying the inspection of emigrants on board ship. By its terms the inspector was, as a general rule, to be appointed by "the government of the country whose flag the vessel flies," except where otherwise provided for by agreement between such country and one or more other governments "whose nationals are carried as emigrants on board the vessel." Each of these other governments might also occasionally send a representative to accompany its nationals but he would act as an observer and not be allowed to encroach upon the duties or authority of the official inspector. Three countries ratified this convention conditionally and sixteen unconditionally.[21]

The recommendation provided that, "where fifteen or more women or girls unaccompanied by a responsible person are carried as emigrants," a properly qualified woman be appointed to supervise and assist such emigrants.

At this Session the General Conference decided to give a trial

[20] Prohibition of night-work in bakeries: Bulgaria, Chile, Colombia, Cuba, Estonia, Finland, Luxemburg, Nicaragua, Spain and Uruguay.

[21] Simplification of inspection of emigrants on board ship: Albania, Australia, Austria, Belgium, Bulgaria, Colombia, Czechoslovakia, Finland, France (conditional), Great Britain (conditional), Hungary, India, Irish Free State, Japan, Luxemburg, Netherlands, Nicaragua, Sweden (conditional) and Uruguay.

INTRODUCTION

at its Tenth Session in 1927 to a plan of "double discussion" as a substitute for the rejected procedure of second reading. As previously stated, the plan of second reading was abandoned at the Seventh Session because under it governments had submitted so many criticisms and contradictory amendments as to make it necessary for the Conference to repeat many of the discussions of the previous Session. Moreover, under the plan, one draft convention had failed of adoption. Under the newly proposed procedure of double discussions the International Labor Office would submit its usual report on the items of the agenda including draft questionnaires. The Conference would then consider each topic and decide whether it was suitable for a draft convention or a recommendation. It would also decide the main points on which governments were to be consulted by questionnaire through the International Labor Office. Through the Tenth, Eleventh and Twelfth Sessions, the Conference undertook to determine the final nature of each questionnaire, but at the Twelfth Session it was decided to modify this procedure at future sessions by leaving the drafting of the questionnaire to the International Labor Office; that is, the Office would submit its usual preliminary report on each item of the agenda but this would not necessarily include any draft questionnaires. The Conference would then follow its customary method of considering these topics, deciding the points upon which the governments were to be consulted but not attempting to draft the questionnaires for this purpose; instead, it would be left to the International Labor Office to draft the questionnaires on the basis of the decisions reached by the Conference at its first discussion of the subjects. The questionnaires as drawn up by the Office would then be sent to the governments and their replies would be submitted by the Office to the next session of the Conference with tentative drafts of the proposed conventions and recommendations. At this, the second and last stage of the double discussion procedure, the Conference would undertake the final consideration and adoption of such draft conventions and recommendations.

Ninth Session, June 7—24, 1926.—This Session was devoted entirely to maritime questions which are considered to be of such nature as to make it advisable to treat them separately from other labor questions. The two draft conventions which were approved at this meeting dealt with seamen's articles of agreement and repatriation of seamen. Neither of these conventions applied to ships of war, government vessels not engaged in trade, pleasure yachts, fishing vessels, *etc.*

As to what the nature of articles of agreement between the shipowner and the seaman should be, the convention stated general principles which are widely recognized in national legislation. On certain points it included detailed stipulations that were inserted at the request of seamen for the better protection of their interests. Examples of this were Article 13 dealing with the conditions under which a seaman, who finds it essential to his interests to take his discharge, may furnish a competent substitute, and the clause of Article 6 regarding annual leave with pay after one year's service when such leave is provided for by national law. In general the methods, by which the principles of this convention were to be put into practise, were left to the determination of each government concerned. The Convention was ratified by eighteen countries.[22]

The purpose of the convention on repatriation was to determine the method of applying the principle that seamen, who are put on shore in a foreign country, have the right to be repatriated. The conditions under which foreign seamen, who have been engaged in a country other than their own, have the right to repatriation, were to be determined by national legislation, or, in the absence of such legislation, by the seamen's articles of agreement. As to who should bear the cost of repatriation, national law was to determine; but it was stipulated that such expense was not to be charged to the seaman in cases of shipwreck, unavoidable illness, injury sustained in service, or discharge for which he should not be held responsible. Sixteen states ratified the convention.[23]

[22] Seamen's articles of agreement: Belgium, Bulgaria, Colombia, Cuba, Estonia, France, Germany, Great Britain, India, Irish Free State, Italy, Luxemburg, Mexico, Nicaragua, Poland, Spain, Uruguay and Yugoslavia.

[23] Repatriation of seamen: Belgium, Bulgaria, Colombia, Cuba, Estonia, France, Germany, Irish Free State, Italy, Luxemburg, Mexico, Nicaragua, Poland, Spain, Uruguay and Yugoslavia.

INTRODUCTION

The recommendation concerning repatriation urged the national governments to provide for the repatriation of masters and apprentices "who are not covered by the terms of the Draft Convention on the repatriation of seamen."

The recommendation concerning the inspection of the conditions of work of seamen dealt with the scope of such inspection, its organization, reports of the inspection authorities, the qualifications, rights, powers, and duties of inspectors, and the cooperation of shipowners and seamen with the inspection authorities to the end that the laws governing seamen's work might be properly enforced. In 1923 the International Labor Conference had adopted a recommendation of principles pertaining to factory inspection, but the conditions of factory labor are so different from those under which seamen work that a separate treatment of inspection principles for the latter was considered advisable.

Tenth Session, May 25—June 16, 1927.—At this Session the plan of double discussion was put into operation. It was decided that the topic of sickness insurance for workers had received its first discussion at the Seventh Session and so the Conference proceeded to the final discussion and adoption of two draft conventions and one recommendation concerning it. Topics on the agenda for first discussion were freedom of association and minimum wage-fixing machinery. In these first discussions difficulties were encountered which raised serious doubts concerning the expediency of having so large a group attempt to frame questionnaires.

Both draft conventions concerning sickness insurance allowed exceptions to be made for those parts of a country where scattered population and insufficient means of communication made the application of the conventions impossible. Countries taking advantage of this exception were required to notify their intention when they submitted their ratifications to the Secretary-General of the League of Nations. The inclusion of exceptions of this nature in a convention is permitted by the third paragraph of Article 405 of the Peace Treaty. The privilege had not been used in this way, however, since the Washington Conference. A resolution was adopted requesting the International Labor Office to study the most effective methods of overcoming the difficulties that hinder the organization of a system of compulsory sickness insurance in countries that comprise large and very thinly populated areas or where means of communication are inadequate due to geographic conditions.

According to the terms of the convention on sickness insurance for workers in industry and commerce and domestic servants, each ratifying state undertook to set up a compulsory system of such insurance. The convention applied to "manual and non-manual workers, including apprentices, employed by industrial undertakings and commercial undertakings, out-workers and domestic servants." It stated certain exceptions that might be made to this where such were deemed to be necessary. It did not apply to seamen and sea fishermen. In case of illness the insured person would be entitled to a cash benefit for at least the first twenty-six weeks of incapacity and proper medical attention. Conditions under which cash benefits might be withheld were specified. Contributions to the financial resources of the system were to be made by the insured persons and their employers and also, where national laws so provided, by the government. This convention was ratified by sixteen members.[24] The draft convention concerning agricultural workers provided a system of compulsory sickness insurance similar to that afforded to industrial workers. Separate draft conventions are drawn up for these different classes of workers in order that states, which might be unwilling to accept a single convention covering both groups, may adopt one of them. By September 1, 1934, eleven states had ratified the draft convention concerning sickness insurance for agricultural workers.[25]

The recommendation concerning sickness insurance contained principles which were not specifically stated in the draft conventions but which would facilitate the operation of any such insurance system. The draft conventions laid down general rules and

[24] Sickness insurance for industrial workers: Austria, Bulgaria, Chile, Colombia, Czechoslovakia, Germany, Great Britain, Hungary, Latvia, Lithuania, Luxemburg, Nicaragua, Rumania, Spain, Uruguay and Yugoslavia.

[25] Sickness insurance for agricultural workers: Austria, Bulgaria, Chile, Colombia, Czechoslovakia, Germany, Great Britain, Luxemburg, Nicaragua, Spain and Uruguay.

INTRODUCTION

the recommendation suggested measures that would assist in improving existing conditions. The recommendation dealt with the scope of sickness insurance, the benefits to be paid, means of preventing sickness, the organization of insurance, financial resources, settlement of disputes, and exceptions for sparsely settled territories. Seamen and sea fishermen were excluded from consideration. The thought was expressed in the convention concerning industry that provision for their insurance against sickness might be made at a later Session of the Conference.

Eleventh Session, May 30—June 16, 1928.—Of 46 states that were represented, 11 sent incomplete delegations. To only one previous meeting, that of 1925, had so large a number of members sent delegations. The delegates at the Eleventh Session represented 25 European countries, 14 Latin-American states, 4 Asiatic states, and 3 British Dominions (Australia, Canada, South Africa). The 342 persons who were officially accredited to the Conference included 81 government delegates and 82 government advisers, 35 employers' delegates and 53 advisers, 34 workers' delegates and 57 advisers.

The Conference adopted a draft convention and a recommendation concerning minimum wage fixing machinery. The preliminary discussion of this subject had occurred at the preceding Session. The convention provided that each ratifying state should create means whereby minimum wage rates can be fixed for workers in certain trades (particularly in home working trades) in which machinery does not exist for the effective regulation of wages by collective agreement and in which wages are exceptionally low. Each country was left free to determine the nature of the wage fixing machinery and the methods to be used in its application. It must, however, make annual reports to the International Labor Office listing the trades to which the terms of the convention have been applied and indicating the methods and results of the procedure. The recommendation suggested principles that would assist in the efficient formulation and administration of minimum wage fixing machinery. The draft convention was ratified by sixteen countries.[26]

[26] Minimum wage fixing machinery: Australia, Chile, China, Colombia, France, Germany, Great Britain, Hungary, Irish Free State, Italy, Mexico, Nicaragua, Norway, South Africa, Spain and Uruguay.

THE INTERNATIONAL PROTECTION OF LABOR

Twelfth Session, May 30—June 21, 1929.—One state failed to send a workers' delegate and 13 others sent only government delegates. This Conference had the largest attendance of delegates and advisers of any that had as yet been held; altogether 402 persons were officially accredited to it, and 50 countries were represented. As mentioned before, this Session decided that in the future it should be left to the International Labor Office to make the final draft of questionnaires which were to be sent to governments. The subjects before the Conference for second discussion were the prevention of accidents in industry and the protection against accidents of workers engaged in loading and unloading ships. Two draft conventions resulted, the one concerning the marking of the weight on heavy packages transported by vessels and the other on the safety of dockers. Four recommendations were approved. The questions on the agenda for first discussion were those of forced labor and hours of work of salaried employees.

A recommendation concerning the prevention of industrial accidents advocated research as to the causes of accidents including physical, physiological and psychological factors and preparation of adequate accident statistics for the International Labor Office. It suggested methods to promote the collaboration of state inspectors and employers' and workers' representatives for the prevention of accidents and stressed the importance of education and the "safety first" movement. It stated that an adequate standard of safety must rest on effective national legislation. Plans relative to the construction or substantial alteration of industrial establishments should be such as to properly meet safety requirements in accordance with legislation and in compliance with the orders of authorities who are competent to superintend such work. Finally it was recommended that accident insurance companies give due consideration in the fixing of premiums to the safety precautions taken by industrial enterprises. Such enterprises were held to include mining, manufacturing, construction, transportation, and agriculture.

In order to prevent accidents as a result of the use of hoisting machines of insufficient strength the draft convention on the

INTRODUCTION

transportation of heavy packages by ship obligated the states which ratified it to require that the weight of any packages of one thousand kilograms or more be plainly marked on the outside before loading. Two states ratified this conditionally and twenty-five unconditionally.[27]

A recommendation concerning the responsibility for the protection of power-driven machinery would make it obligatory to equip any machine of this type with the safety appliances required by law before it is installed for use within the territory of any member of the International Labor Organization.

The purpose of the convention affecting the loading and unloading of ships was to establish uniform standards among maritime countries in the matter of properly protecting those engaged in this type of work whether on shore or on shipboard. It did not apply to ships of war and states might exempt certain other classes of vessels. Owners of ships already constructed were allowed four years from the date of ratification within which to comply with the provisions concerning "construction or permanent equipment," provided that the convention's terms in this respect were applied in so far as was practicable during this grace period. This convention was revised in 1932. In original form it was ratified by four states and in revised form by four states up to September 1, 1934.[28] The original convention ceased to be open for ratification from October 30, 1934. Ratification of the revised convention involves *ipso jure* the denunciation of the old convention, from the date of coming into force of the revised convention (October 30, 1934).

The Conference adopted a recommendation urging that states, after they had ratified the convention affecting dockers and had drawn up their regulations in pursuance of it, should enter into

[27] Marking the weight of heavy packages transported by vessels: Australia, Belgium, Chile, China, Czechoslovakia, Denmark (conditional), Estonia, Finland, Germany, India, Irish Free State, Italy, Japan, Luxemburg, Mexico, Netherlands, Nicaragua, Norway, Poland, Portugal, Rumania, South Africa (conditional), Spain, Sweden, Uruguay, Venezuela and Yugoslavia.

[28] Protection of dockers against accidents (original convention): Irish Free State, Luxemburg, Nicaragua and Spain. Revised convention: Italy, Mexico, Spain and Uruguay.

agreement on reciprocity in carrying out the terms and purpose of the convention.

Another recommendation pertaining to the same convention provided for consultation of government authorities with workers' and employers' organizations with reference to the drawing up of regulations for the safety of workers engaged in loading or unloading ships.

Thirteenth Session, October 10—26, 1929.—It was the sole purpose of this Session to examine maritime questions. No draft conventions or recommendations were adopted. Seamen's organizations had urged the Commission on International Labor Legislation, which drafted Part XIII of the Treaty of Peace, to provide for a separate international maritime organization responsible for international legislation on maritime matters to co-operate with the International Labor Organization. This request was not acceded to. Nevertheless, because of the peculiar circumstances to which seafaring labor is subject, the Commission recommended that the International Labor Conference should hold separate sessions for the consideration of labor problems affecting seamen.

The Thirteenth Session examined the following questions: (1) regulation of hours of work on board ship; (2) protection of seamen in case of sickness including the liability of the shipowner toward sick or injured seamen and sickness insurance for seamen (3) promotion of seamen's welfare in ports; (4) the minimum requirement of professional capacity in the case of captains, navigating and engineer officers in charge of watches on board ship. With reference to each of these subjects, conclusions were adopted which were to form the basis for the consultation of governments through the International Labor Office with a view to the future preparation of draft conventions or recommendations.

Fourteenth Session, June 10—28, 1930.—Altogether 365 persons were officially accredited to this Conference, representing 51 states which constituted the largest number as yet represented at any session. The non-European countries included 15 Latin-American states, 5 Asiatic states, 4 British Dominions, and 1 African state. There were 86 government delegates, 35 employers' and 35 workers' delegates, and 209 advisers. The topics for final discussion

INTRODUCTION

were forced labor and hours of work for salaried employees, with reference to which two draft conventions and five recommendations were approved. The question of hours of work in coal mines came before the Conference for discussion for the first time. A draft convention on the subject was submitted, but it was rejected by the Conference.

According to the terms of the draft convention on forced or compulsory labor each ratifying state agreed to suppress the use of this kind of labor within the shortest possible time. It was designed to protect native workers. Each state agreed to apply it to territories under its jurisdiction, but was permitted to make reservations in regard to this in accordance with Article 421 of the Treaty of Versailles. The convention permitted forced labor for public purposes only during a transitional period and subject to certain limitations. After five years from the date of its coming into force, the possibility of the complete abolition of such labor was to be considered. Strict regulations were laid down concerning the use of compulsory labor for the construction of public works. Restrictions were specific as to the persons who might be called upon to render such labor and as to the maximum duration of such work which was not to exceed sixty days in any one period of twelve months. The convention contained provisions concerning the length of the workday, weekly rest, wages, accident and sickness insurance, character of food and habitation, and other conditions subject to which the work must be performed. Forced labor was forbidden in mines and forced porterage was to be abolished as soon as possible. Forced labor for private profit was to be prohibited immediately. For the purposes of the convention, the term "forced labor" did not include compulsory military service involving work of a purely military character, prison labor, work arising from some emergency such as war, fire, flood, famine, epidemics, *etc.*, or work recognized as a normal civic obligation of a self-governing country or community. This convention was ratified by sixteen states.[29] A recommendation concerning indirect compulsion to labor under-

[29] Forced or compulsory labor: Australia, Bulgaria, Chile, Denmark, Great Britain, Irish Free State, Italy, Japan, Liberia, Mexico, Netherlands, Nicaragua, Norway, Spain, Sweden and Yugoslavia.

took to state general principles that would assist states, which ratified this convention, to avoid measures imposing too heavy a burden upon the population involved or constituting indirect compulsion to labor. Another recommendation on the regulation of forced or compulsory labor sought further to guide states in the application of the convention. It stressed the importance of plainly informing the inhabitants concerned of the conditions governing forced labor through printed texts or oral communication where necessary. It advocated the adoption of means to protect the workers against ills which otherwise might arise including alcoholic temptations, the imperiling of the food supply of the community, the unnecessary use of forced labor for the transport of persons or goods, and the illegal employment of women and children.

The draft convention concerning the regulation of hours of work in commerce and offices fixed the maximum hours of employment per week at forty-eight and the normal workday as one of eight hours. The maximum hours per week might be so arranged that hours of work in any one day do not exceed ten hours. The convention applied to commercial and trading establishments, mixed commercial and industrial establishments (unless they are deemed to be industrial establishments), and office work. It did not apply to establishments for the treatment or care of the physically or mentally incapacitated, hotels, boarding-houses, refreshment houses, theaters and places of amusement; except that, in cases where branches of these establishments would, if they were independent undertakings, be included, the convention applied to persons employed in such branches. The competent authority might make exceptions for establishments in which only members of the employer's family were employed, offices for the administration of public authority, managers or persons employed in confidential capacity, outside work of travellers or representatives, and other classes of persons specifically defined in the convention. Further measures were provided to allow for all necessary exceptions and to insure adequate inspection. By September 1, 1934, this convention had been ratified by one state conditionally and by

INTRODUCTION

five others unconditionally.[30] A recommendation concerning hours of work in hotels, boarding-houses, restaurants and similar establishments was approved. The draft convention on hours of work in commerce and offices specifically exempted this class of establishments, but the recommendation urged that a study of work conditions be pursued with a view to the future adoption of a draft convention on hours of work in such establishments. Another recommendation made similar provisions for the study of hours of work in theaters and other places of amusement, and still another, for such a study with reference to establishments for the treatment or care of the sick, infirm, destitute or mentally unfit.

Fifteenth Session, May 30—June 18, 1931.—The problem of limiting hours of work in coal mines advanced to its second and final discussion at this Session which approved the draft convention concerning it. The question of what the age should be for the admission of children to employment in non-industrial occupations received consideration for the first time. Partial revision of the convention concerning the employment of women during the night was attempted, but the revised draft convention that was finally submitted to the Conference failed to obtain the necessary two-thirds majority and so was not adopted.

The convention on hours of work in coal mines applied to coal and lignite mines but contained special provisions relating to the latter. To the open hard coal and lignite mines the provisions of the Washington Convention on hours of work in industrial undertakings were to apply with certain reservations as to overtime. The maximum hours of work in underground hard coal mines were to be seven hours and forty-five minutes per day. Workers were not to be employed on Sundays or legal public holidays save in case of necessary exceptions which were stipulated. A shorter workday was to be provided in workplaces which were unusually unhealthy due to abnormal conditions of temperature or humidity. Under certain specified conditions, public authority might allow a longer workday than seven hours and forty-five minutes. Overtime was limited and was to be paid for at not less than one-and-

[30] Hours of work in commerce and offices: Austria (conditional), Bulgaria, Mexico, Nicaragua, Spain and Uruguay.

a-quarter times the regular rate. The convention could not be construed to make possible the altering of national laws with respect to hours of work so as to reduce the *protective* advantages or guarantees enjoyed by workers. Within at least three years from the coming into force of the convention, its revision was to be considered with a view to the possibility of further reduction in hours of work and overtime.

Sixteenth Session, April 12—30, 1932.—The convention concerning the protection against accidents of workers employed in loading and unloading ships, which was first adopted in 1929, was revised mainly as to points of technical detail so as to make it more acceptable to governments for ratification. The principle of reciprocity, dealt with in the recommendation of 1929, was written into this revised draft convention concerning dockers in 1932; that is, a ratifying member agreed to enter into reciprocal arrangements with other ratifying members after each member had satisfied itself as to the standards of safety established by the other members of the International Labor Organization. A recommendation outlined steps by which these reciprocal arrangements could be expedited and made uniform.

The Conference adopted the draft convention concerning the age for the admission of children to non-industrial employment. This convention applied to cases of employment not dealt with in three previous conventions fixing the minimum age for the employment of children in industrial establishments, in agriculture, and at sea. The competent authority in each country was to determine the lines of division between the type of employment covered by this convention and the other forms of employment covered by the other conventions. In a recommendation it was suggested that light work might be occupations such as "running errands, distribution of newspapers, odd jobs in connection with the practise of sport or the playing of games, and picking and selling flowers or fruits." Article 2 of the convention stipulated: "Children under fourteen years of age, or children over fourteen years who are still required by national laws or regulations to attend primary school, shall not be employed in any employment to which this Convention applies except as hereinafter otherwise provided." Children over twelve years of age might, outside

INTRODUCTION

school hours, be employed on certain forms of light work not prejudicial to their health and education. Such light work was not to exceed two hours on either school days or holidays and in no case was the total number of hours spent at school and on light work to exceed seven per day. Light work was forbidden on Sundays, legal holidays, and during the night. In the interests of art, science or education, certain exceptions might be made by national laws, but no exception was allowed in respect of dangerous employment or employment in circuses, variety shows or cabarets. It was stipulated that in certain forms of employment, including street trading, itinerant occupations, or the use of stalls outside shops, a higher age limit than that stated in the convention should be fixed by national legislation for the admission of young persons. A special exception was made for India where the employment of children under ten was prohibited in general and under fourteen in occupations involving danger to life, health or morals. If India should later make attendance at school compulsory until the age of fourteen, the provisions of the convention would then apply to India on the same terms as to other countries. A recommendation was approved containing definitions, rules and principles to guide national authorities in the interpretation and application of the terms of the convention.

Topics before the Sixteenth Session for a first discussion were: (1) the abolition of fee-charging employment agencies; (2) invalidity, old-age and widows' and orphans' insurance. Forty-nine states were represented but seventeen of them sent only government delegates to the Conference.

Seventeenth Session, June 8—30, 1933.—For the first time the United States sent official delegates to a Conference of the International Labor Organization to observe its work. These delegates later recommended that the United States join this Organization. The Seventeenth Session adopted seven draft conventions and two recommendations.

The draft convention concerning fee-charging employment agencies provided for the abolition of such agencies conducted for profit within three years after the coming into force of the convention. Exceptions could be permitted by national authority in unusual cases. Private agencies, not characterized by the profit motive, were to be subject to strict regulation by the competent authority. A recommendation urged that free public employment agencies, including offices that specialized in particular occupations, be established in place of private agencies; it also specified certain classes of persons who should not be allowed to carry on placing operations.

Six draft conventions were adopted with reference to social insurance. The kinds of insurance dealt with were those pertaining to old-age, invalidity, and survivors. For each of these three categories, two conventions were approved applying to industry and agriculture respectively. The conventions applying to industry covered domestic servants, outworkers, and persons in industrial or commercial undertakings and in the liberal professions. These draft conventions laid down general principles of social legislation which could be applied in harmony with the national laws of the ratifying states. Separate conventions were drawn up for different classes of workers and different types of insurance in order that no state might excuse itself from ratifying a convention on the ground that it included several kinds of insurance one or more of which the state did not recognize in its national legislation.

It was the purpose of these conventions concerning invalidity, old-age, and widows' and orphans' insurance to include all persons ordinarily employed for a wage or salary. Exceptions, applying to a relatively small number of employees, were allowed including workers who earn in excess of a certain maximum, members of the liberal professions, workers who are too old or too young to be insured, members of the employer's family, *etc.* Exceptions of this nature were to be made by a state in its national laws or regulations when it deemed such to be necessary.

In general the cost of the insurance was to be defrayed by contributions from employers, employees, and the government. Employers might be exempted from the levy in case of a national insurance system that was not restricted to employed persons. Insured persons might be exempted from contributing in countries whose regulations did not require such payments at the time of the adoption of the convention. Public authority was to con-

INTRODUCTION

tribute to the financial resources of systems covering employed persons in general or manual workers.

Each of these six draft conventions placed upon each ratifying state the obligation of setting up a compulsory system of insurance, unless, at the time of the first coming into force of the convention, the state had no laws or regulations providing for the compulsory form of the insurance in question. In such a case, an existing non-contributory pension scheme which guaranteed an individual right to a pension, under conditions defined in each of the conventions, was to be deemed to satisfy the requirements of the convention.

The conventions also included clauses relating to equality of treatment in conformity with the general principle, subject to certain stated conditions, that foreign employed persons should be entitled to insurance under the same conditions as nationals.

The conventions concerning invalidity provided that an invalidity pension should be paid to any "insured person who becomes generally incapacitated for work and thereby unable to earn an appreciable remuneration."

The age at which a person should be entitled to receive an old-age pension was to be determined by national laws but the age in no case should exceed sixty-five for employed persons.

Under widows' and orphans' insurance systems pension rights were to be conferred "on widows who have not remarried and the children of a deceased insured or pensioned person."

The recommendation concerning invalidity, old-age, and widows' and orphans' insurance contained general principles that should be observed in the organization of any systems for such insurance. Suggestions were made as to the means of determining the minimum rates of pensions. It was also stated that, when conditions made it advisable to set a minimum age for admission into insurance, "such age should be as close as possible to the age at which compulsory school attendance ceases and at which the choice of an occupation is made"; that "as a general rule the contribution of the insured person should not be higher than the contribution of his employer;" and that "national laws or regulations should provide that insured women are adequately represented on the administrative bodies of invalidity, old-age and widows' and orphans' insurance."

Eighteenth Session, June 4—23, 1934.—There were at this Session 83 government delegates, 29 delegates of employers and 30 of workers, and 205 advisers. The delegations of 22 states were incomplete. The United States was again represented by observers. The Conference adopted four draft conventions and one recommendation.

The convention concerning the employment of women during the night was revised. The nature of this revision has been noted above in the discussion of this convention in connection with the First Session of the General Conference.

Also the convention concerning workmen's compensation for occupational diseases was revised for the purpose of extending the schedule of diseases recognized as occupational. The additions included silicosis, primary epitheliomatous cancer of the skin, pathological manifestations due to radium and X-rays, and poisoning by phosphorus, arsenic, benzene, and the halogen derivatives of hydrocarbons of the aliphatic series.

The draft convention for the regulation of hours of work in automatic sheet-glass works stated that persons so employed should work under a system providing for at least four shifts; that the average hours of work should not exceed forty-two per week (the average to be calculated over a period not exceeding four weeks); and that the length of a spell of work should not exceed eight hours. Exceptions to this could be made in case of accident or *force majeure* or in order to make good the unforeseen absence of one or more members of a shift.

The draft convention ensuring benefit or allowances to the involuntarily unemployed required each ratifying state to maintain an unemployment insurance scheme providing certain cash benefits and allowances which might be remuneration for employment on relief works organized by a public authority. The system might be one of compulsory insurance, voluntary insurance, a combination of both, or any of the foregoing alternatives combined with a complementary assistance scheme. The convention was to apply to all persons habitually employed for wages or salary. Exceptions, however, could be made in specified cases involving servants, homeworkers, members of the employer's family, and certain other classes of workers. Various conditions were stipulated to which the right to receive benefits was made subject. The convention contained a clause on equality of treatment: "Foreigners shall be entitled to benefit and allowances upon the same conditions as nationals: Provided that any Member may withhold from the nationals of any Member or State not bound by this Convention equality of treatment with its own nationals in respect of payments from funds to which the claimant has not contributed."

A recommendation concerning unemployment insurance and various forms of unemployment relief undertook to indicate the principles "which practise shows to be best calculated to promote a satisfactory organization of unemployment insurance and assistance." It favored the creation of compulsory unemployment insurance, provision for the partially unemployed as well as the wholly unemployed, special arrangements necessary for special classes of workers, and suggested rules that should govern qualification, disqualification, *etc.*

The entrance of the United States into the International Labor Organization.—The following Joint Resolution of the Senate and House of Representatives of the Congress of the United States was passed by the unanimous consent of the Senate on June 13, 1934, and by a two-thirds majority of the House on June 15, 1934, providing for membership of the United States in the International Labor Organization:

Whereas progress toward the solution of the problems of international competition in industry can be made through international action concerning the welfare of wage earners; and

Whereas the failure of a nation to establish humane conditions of labor is an obstacle in the way of other nations which desire to maintain and improve the conditions in their own countries; and

Whereas the United States early recognized the desirability of international co-operation in matters pertaining to labor and took part in 1900 in establishing, and for many years thereafter supported, the International Association for Labor Legislation; and

Whereas the International Labor Organization has advanced the welfare of labor throughout the world through studies, recommendations, conferences, and conventions concerning conditions of labor; and

THE INTERNATIONAL PROTECTION OF LABOR

Whereas other nations have joined the International Labor Organization without being members of the League of Nations; and

Whereas special provision has been made in the constitution of the International Labor Organization by which membership of the United States would not impose or be deemed to impose any obligation or agreement upon the United States to accept the proposals of that body as involving anything more than recommendations for its consideration: Therefore be it

Resolved by the Senate and House of Representatives of the United States of America in Congress assembled, That the President is hereby authorized to accept membership for the Government of the United States of America in the International Labor Organization, which, through its general conference of representatives of its members and through its International Labor Office, collects information concerning labor throughout the world and prepares international conventions for the consideration of member governments with a view to improving conditions of labor;

That in accepting such membership the President shall assume on behalf of the United States no obligation under the covenant of the League of Nations (73rd Congress S. J. Res. 131, and H. J. Res. 368).

The above Joint Resolution was transmitted to the Director of the International Labor Office by the American Consul in Geneva.

On June 22, 1934, the International Labor Conference at its Eighteenth Session passed the following resolution unanimously:

The International Labour Conference takes note of the communication of 22 June 1934 addressed to the Director of the International Labour Office by the authorised representative of the Government of the United States of America, heartily welcomes the decision of the Congress of the United States authorising the President to accept on behalf of the Government of the United States Membership on the International Labour Organisation, recalling that it has always been the firm conviction of the Organisation that its ends could be more effectively advanced if the Membership of the Organisation could be made universal, hereby decides to invite the Government of the United States to accept Membership in the International Labour Organisation it being understood that such acceptance involves only those rights and obligations provided for in the constitution of the Organisation and shall not involve any obligations under the Covenant of the League of Nations, and further decides

That, in the event of the Government of the United States accepting Membership, the Governing Body is hereby authorised to arrange with the Government of the United States any questions arising out of its Membership including the question of its financial contribution.

In the following communication of August 20th, which was transmitted to the Director of the International Labor Office, the American Consul in Geneva, Mr. Prentiss B. Gilbert, signified the acceptance by the President of the invitation to the United States to join the International Labor Organization:

INTRODUCTION

Geneva, Switzerland,
August 20, 1934.

Harold Butler, Esquire,
Director of the International Labor Office,
Geneva, Switzerland.

Sir:

In your letter to me of June 22, 1934, you advised that the International Labor Conference had unanimously adopted a Resolution inviting the Government of the United States of America to accept membership in the International Labor Organization and there was transmitted with your letter a copy of the Resolution, which in extending the invitation states 'that such acceptance involves only those rights and obligations provided for in the constitution of the Organization and shall not involve any obligations under the Covenant of the League of Nations.'

I am now writing to say that, exercising the authority conferred on him by a Joint Resolution of the Congress of the United States approved June 19, 1934, the President of the United States accepts the invitation heretofore indicated, such acceptance to be effective on August 20, 1934, and, of course, subject to the understandings expressed in the Conference Resolution, and has directed me to inform you accordingly.

Yours respectfully,

PRENTISS GILBERT.

Changes in the Governing Body of the International Labor Office.—The Governing Body consists of thirty-two persons, sixteen representing governments, eight representing the employers, and eight representing workers. Of the sixteen persons representing governments, eight are appointed by the states of chief industrial importance. The states designated at the Eighteenth Session of the General Conference in June, 1934, as belonging to this group, were: Belgium, France, Great Britain, Italy, Japan, Germany, Canada, and India; but at the Session of the Governing Body in January, 1935, Belgium and Canada were replaced by the United States and Soviet Russia. This action gave to the United States and Russia permanent seats on the Governing Body. Belgium and Canada continued as honorary or deputy members without votes. It was also agreed to give the American delegate representing the American Federation of Labor a full voting membership in the workers' group at all sessions of the Governing Body. The eight representatives of this group, who were elected in June, 1934, before the United States became a member of the International Labor Organization, might take turns in dropping out in order to make possible this full voting membership of a representative of the American workers. Russia was not expected to ask for her voting seat for some time and in the meanwhile Canada could continue to occupy this place.

N. B. At the time of this writing it remained for Congress to make the appropriation necessary to complete American membership in the International Labor Organization.

INTRODUCTION

Members of the International Labor Organization

Albania (joined in 1920)
Argentina
Australia
Austria
Belgium
Bolivia
Brazil
Bulgaria (1920)
Canada
Chile
China
Colombia
Cuba
Czechoslovakia
Denmark
Dominican Republic (1924)
Estonia (1921)
Ethiopia (1923)
Finland (1920)
France
Germany
Great Britain
Greece
Guatemala
Haiti
Honduras
Hungary (1922)
India
Iraq (1932)
Irish Free State (1923)
Italy
Japan
Latvia (1921)
Liberia
Lithuania (1921)
Luxemburg (1920)
Mexico (1931)
Netherlands
New Zealand
Nicaragua
Norway
Panama
Paraguay
Persia
Peru
Poland
Portugal
Rumania
Russia or Soviet Union (1934)
Salvador
Siam
South Africa
Spain
Sweden
Switzerland
Turkey (1932)
United States (1934)
Uruguay
Venezuela
Yugoslavia

INTRODUCTION

Members of the International Labor Organization

Albania (Ceased in 1920)	Italy
Argentina	Japan (1938)
Australia	Latvia
Austria	Lithuania (1921)
Belgium	Luxembourg (1920)
Bolivia	Mexico (1931)
Brazil	Netherlands
Bulgaria (1920)	New Zealand
Canada	Nicaragua
Chile	Norway
China	Panama
Colombia	Paraguay
Cuba	Persia
Czechoslovakia	Peru
Denmark	Poland
Dominican Republic (1924)	Portugal
Estonia (1921)	Roumania
Ethiopia (1923)	Russia or Soviet Union (1934)
Finland (1920)	Salvador
France	Siam
Germany	South Africa
Great Britain	Spain
Greece	Sweden
Guatemala	Switzerland
Haiti	Turkey (1932)
Honduras	United States (1934)
Hungary (1922)	Uruguay
India	Venezuela
Iraq (1932)	Yugoslavia
Irish Free State (1923)	

xiii

PART I

THE EARLY MOVEMENT FOR INTERNATIONAL LABOR LEGISLATION
AND ITS RELATION TO THE UNITED STATES

CHAPTER I.

THE MOVEMENT DEFINED

At the time of the outbreak of the World War in 1914, there was no international law of labor, nor, in fact, had there ever been; because no code of economic principles or legal enactments, for the protection of labor, had ever been so generally accepted as to attain to the authority of international law. That status can be acquired only when, by the common consent of civilized nations, a specific body of protective labor measures is recognized as of universal obligation. Nevertheless there was a system of international labor law that could be said to be in the process of making; for there existed a body of labor legislation, the result of treaties and other international agreements, which bade fair to fulfill at some time the conditions of international obligation.

When, by international convention, ten European countries and thirty-two dependencies had agreed to prohibit the use of the poison, white phosphorus, in the manufacture of matches, and at the same time, twelve Governments and eleven colonies had adhered to an agreement to establish a uniform night's rest of eleven hours' duration for women in industry, it was obvious that certain protective labor measures had reached an advanced stage of international enactment, even if they had not been widely enough accepted or long enough enforced to acquire the prestige of international law in the technical sense of the term.*
The measures referred to are commonly known as the Bern Conventions of 1906. Their event was so satisfactory that proposals were drafted similarly to prohibit the night-work of young persons and limit the day-work of women. In 1913, the year in which tentative outlines to this effect were revised and approved at an intergovernmental conference with the prospect of their incorporation into conventions by an official Diplomatic Assembly in the following year, it did not seem to require any severe

*This was the situation in 1914 before the War.

exercise of the mental powers of the average man or woman to foresee the time when regulations established for the protection of labor should become of such common acceptance and binding authority as to accede to the dignity of international law. And although the war was responsible for a serious break in this as in all fields of international co-operation, the work of the international labor movement, which was among the younger of international movements when the conflict broke and about which less was commonly known, still remained such as to entitle it to a wider recognition than it had received.

To say that there was no international law of labor is not to say that there had been no international law which had directly affected labor or incidentally protected labor. Treaties had not infrequently specified, or identified with international law, rules in respect to the treatment of aliens, sailors, or agents directly concerned with some phase of international intercourse. Maritime codes, regulations governing diplomatic agencies, war codes, all had rules which affected labor or employees in some capacity or other.

But the movement of which we speak, and the laws enacted in pursuance of it, were distinguished by the following characteristics:

1. International protection of labor was the principal motive and aim.
2. Measures enacted were the result of organized propaganda to this end.
3. The laborers first considered and most directly benefited, were employees of industry defined as primarily manufacturing, mining and quarrying; although treaties on social insurance covered workers in still other provinces, including particularly transportation.

Efforts in behalf of laborers within the domain of these spheres had constituted the essential activities of the international protective labor movement. The movement was, however, constantly invading related realms and was not loath to identify itself with any specific international undertaking that might prove a factor in the realization of its aims; as, immigration treaties, congresses of the medical fraternity, Christian organizations, social workers, socialist parties, *etc.*

Agitation for international labor reform has profited much by motives other than that of protecting labor, and some there may be who would characterize this as the lesser and incorrect one by which to distinguish the movement. They would maintain that the accommodation of a nation rather than the laboring portion of a nation, is the essential motive lying underneath and behind protective enactments; that the purpose dear to the heart of each country is the conservation of its own industrial resources necessary to effective competition in world markets and the maintenance of its relative position and industrial prestige. The reform has owed much to this incentive, particularly in its origin. Some believe they have discovered in labor protection a means of eliminating those grievances which precipitate strikes and industrial crises within the nation. The more common trend of argument is as follows: A nation needs industry; industry needs labor; labor must be protected or industry will fail; international competition, becoming daily sharper, tends to drive each nation to grind the working class down under a load of exhausting toil and excessive hours, exploiting men, women, and children, as instruments of cheap and copious production without regard to their rights as human beings. But the inevitable consequence of this is either the destruction or serious impairment of the efficiency of the labor force, by which, in either case, the very foundations of national industry itself are undermined. On the other hand, if a nation places restrictions on industry to protect labor, and other nations do not do likewise, the humane nation is easily outclassed by unscrupulous competitors and falls behind in the industrial race. Tersely stated, the dilemma resolves itself to this: (1) Fail to protect labor and ultimately ruin industry; (2) Protect labor and lose industrial prestige. Even at this, the second should be recognized as the lesser of the two evils; but when the "deluge" can be postponed to the next generation and the profits reaped by this, the temptation is to pin faith to the first horn of the dilemma. And so after studying the difficulty, wiseacres have concluded that the only escape compatible with the maintenance of industrial prestige in international markets and the salvation of national industry is to be found in international labor agreements whose impartial application to the competitors of every country will tend to preserve the relative industrial standing of each in spite of whatever diminution of output such protection may involve.

It is a process of reasoning based upon facts, and which reaches sound conclusions as to what ought to be done in a majority of cases; but it makes industrial efficiency rather than protection of labor the justification and chief end of the protective movement. The results are substantially the same, whichever motive is adopted, until we come to an exigency where it is conceived that the attainment of greater industrial efficiency, even though it be temporary, at the cost of sacrificing labor, is the preferable course to pursue. For example, a nation without protective law might decide to continue thus to take advantage of nations with protective law, and risk the consequences to its laboring population, relying possibly upon an abnormal ability to supply its labor market. Again, there may be cases in which advantage will result from such exploitation during the period of an employer's lifetime, and so from selfish motives, he may be led to obstruct moves that, in effecting the protection of labor, trespass upon his own profits. Thus loyalty to the doctrine of justification by efficiency rather than to justification by protection may become vicious and retard the protection of workers.

Very certain it is that loyalty to labor and to humanity will, in the long run, be found to be entirely compatible with loyalty to national industry; but loyalty to national industry in the short run, may not be compatible with loyalty to labor and humanity; and men are tempted to be swayed by the profits of the short run, especially when that run is co-extensive with their lease on life. Up to this point we have considered the employing class and the working class as having a common national interest connected with their separate group interests. But if we take an entirely different view of the situation and consider the employing class as an international group devoid of national interests or at least placing class above national interests, it still remains true that in the long run the preservation of the health and happiness of the workers by protective law will be highly advantageous to the employer as well as to the best interests of the worker. Therefore, the motive which is safe under all circumstances, and should predominate, is that of protecting labor, which is, after all, the principle that has animated the great leaders of the international labor movement.

The conditions which gave rise to the need for such a movement were economic and constitute a field of history which has been thoroughly treated. However, we make no apology for selecting from facts of common knowledge some of the most striking, with which to sketch a partial picture of the economic origins of today's industrial phenomena, because of their vital connection with the subject matter of our interest.

What is to history a comparatively short time ago, 150 to 200 years, there were in England no factories, no great machines, no steam engines, no hordes of men, women and children crowded within four dingy walls to begin work at the sound of a whistle. The domestic system of manufacture prevailed. The spinning of yarn and thread, the weaving of cloth, the shaping of earthen and metal ware, were all processes carried on in the homes of the townsmen and inhabitants of the rural districts. These products were either sold to the agents of some shipping merchant, or the producer went out to seek his own market. The machinery used was very crude, merely a wooden frame operated by hand or foot power. The craftsman was his own master with regard to rules of production and the ordering of his hours of labor. Master craftsmen, journeymen, and apprentices belonged to the same social class and every worker had the promise of becoming a master in his own trade some day. Then came a momentous change. Between 1750 and 1800, there occurred the most remarkable period of industry-changing devices known to history. In regular succession, Kay brought forth the shuttle drop box (1760); Watt, the improved steam engine (1761-1769); Hargreaves, the spinning jenny (1767); Arkwright, the roller spinner (1769); Crompton, the mule spinner (1779); Cartwright, the power loom (1784); Whitney, the cotton gin (1793); Roebuck, new smelting processes; Lavoisier, important chemical discoveries, *etc.* These inventions revolutionized the whole field of industry: instead of the wooden frame in the home, now the huge machine of iron; instead of supplying power with hand or foot, it now became necessary to place these monsters beside the waterfall, or adjacent to the steam engine where the 100 and 1000 horsepower could be applied; instead of the little family group plying their daily tasks about the home, father, mother and children were obliged to betake themselves to the factory to work twelve, fourteen, or sixteen hours a day under new and strange conditions too often working the havoc of moral and physical degeneration upon their victims.

Viewed in historical perspective, so sudden and unexpected was this transition, so extensive and irresistible the change, that thousands of the laboring masses unable to adjust themselves to the new régime or to compete with factory-made goods, found themselves crushed under what to them was the "Juggernaut" of great machinery and capital. Although certain of the characteristics of war were lacking, this transition has nevertheless been termed a revolution, an industrial revolution, none the less momentous in its consequences than any of the great revolutions of history and entailing in its wake none the less of destruction and misery than any of the wars of the early Britons.

Under the domestic system it had been customary for the family to own a small plot of ground or to use the common pastures and open fields, from which were obtained directly the partial means of its subsistence. But contemporaneous with the industrial revolution, there occurred a widespread agricultural enclosing movement. The homesteads and publicly used lands were consolidated by the gentry and landowning classes into large estates and farms worked on a capitalistic basis. Wretched as had been the condition of the handicraftsman in the domestic stage, it held no comparison to the misery of the new order. Deprived of the ownership and free use of land, face to face with the relentless competition of a new industrial era, they of the domestic system came to realize that they could not hold their own against the factory régime; neither could the laborer any longer look forward to the time when he could be a master in his craft; it was now necessary to have capital to purchase machinery and other appurtenances with which to set up independently in business. That capital the laborer in general could not hope to command. An impassable gulf seemed to be yawning between the employer and the employed. The masses faced the classes in sullen envy and distrust.

Co-eval with the advent of the new order of things went the influence exerted by the epoch-making work of Adam Smith, *The Wealth of Nations* (1776). The physiocrats' doctrine of *laissez faire* was exalted, while the theories of the mercantilists waned. Unprotected by legal enactments and at the mercy of employers who were themselves victims of unrestrained competition, under unjust treatment and unjust laws, under the intense selfishness exhibited by the controlling classes, in the shops and in the factories, employees gradually became educated to the doctrines of collective resistance and collective bargaining. Class consciousness took definite shape. Trade unionism was evolved. Outlawed by governments and oppressed by courts, organizations, spasmodic, secret, timid, nevertheless continued to increase. Nourished by oppression, unionism was but an infant learning to exercise its arms and limbs, but it was an infant of a giant race. Society and government found themselves face to face with phenomena with which they did not know how to deal. Between 1800 and the present time, there has been written in the legislative records of the great industrial nations the history of the struggle to render the large-scale system of production compatible with the welfare of the wage-earner. Laws covering child labor, factory inspection, social insurance, the work of women, the limitation of the workday, occupational diseases, *et cetera*, have rapidly multiplied.

Different countries reflect all the different stages of development of labor regulation, but national and local labor legislation of some kind has become a common factor in the economic life of every civilized community. More or less distinct types of labor laws have had initial development among different national groups. In Great Britain, France, and the United States, protective labor law tended at first to favor women and children; skilled craftsmen have bettered their conditions of employment by collective bargaining and by the exercise of pressure on legislative bodies. Another group of countries was primarily concerned with the general insurance of labor against the risks of industrial life; *i. e.*, accidents, sickness, disease, *etc.* This class of States is represented by Germany, Austria, Hungary, and the Scandinavian powers. Another group has had markedly socialistic tendencies in the administration of labor regulations, as is the case with Australia and New Zealand. These legislations widely divergent in their inception have continued to converge more and more in their adoption of certain fundamental principles. And now the time has come when economists are fully aware that in a world of international markets and international industrial competition, there are conditions of production that can be most effectively controlled in the interest of labor, as well as of others concerned, by international agreements.

CHAPTER II

Genesis of the Movement

Origin of the International Labor Movement [1]

In 1818, when the statesmen of Europe assembled at Aix-la-Chapelle to attempt one of the periodic adjustments of the affairs of that continent, a pioneer in industrial reform addressed to the Congress a petition, unique in its declaration that a prime task for the governments of Europe was the international fixation of the legal limits of the normal workday for the industrial classes of Europe. The person through whom a proposition of this order thus found initial expression before an international assembly, was the noted philanthropist and social worker, Robert Owen;[2] but although standing as he did, the prophet of a new order of diplomacy, the statesmen of that day spared but scant attention to his proposals and gave to them no practical result. After a lapse of several decades, Mr. Owen drew up a declaration entitled: "A LETTER ADDRESSED TO THE POTENTATES OF THE EARTH IN WHOM THE HAPPINESS AND MISERY OF THE HUMAN RACE ARE NOW INVESTED; BUT ESPECIALLY TO AUSTRIA, FRANCE, GREAT BRITAIN, PRUSSIA, RUSSIA, SCANDINAVIA, TURKEY, AND THE UNITED STATES OF NORTH AMERICA; BECAUSE THEIR POWERS ARE NOW AT PEACE WITH EACH OTHER, AND COULD WITHOUT WAR, EASILY INDUCE ALL THE OTHER GOVERNMENTS AND PEOPLE TO UNITE WITH THEM IN PRACTICAL MEASURES FOR THE GENERAL GOOD OF ALL THROUGH FUTURITY," in which among other things he said: ". . . if you will now agree among yourselves to

[1] *Cf.* L. Chatelain, *La Protection internationale ouvrière.* Chapters II and III. E. Mahaim, *LeDroit international ouvrier*, p. 183 *et suiv.*
[2] *Supplementary Appendix to Vol. I. of the Life of Robert Owen.* pp. x-xii, 209-222.

call a congress of the leading governments of the world, inviting those of China, Japan, Burma, *etc.*, and to meet in London in May next, I will, should I live in my present health to that period, unfold to you at that congress the natural means by which you may now, with ease and pleasure, gradually create those surroundings in peace and harmony, which shall have a perpetual good and superior influence upon all of our race." This proposal was not adopted.

Apart from Mr. Owen's own efforts, the idea of international co-operation for the control of industrial conditions was not seconded in any signal manner [3] until a Frenchman, Daniel Legrand by name, a manufacturer of Steinthal, Alsace, also undertook the task of impressing upon men of affairs the urgent need of such co-operation for industrial welfare. Imbued with the idea that in European industry there were conditions which were not susceptible of proper regulation by the individual action of nations, but which would readily lend themselves to such regulation under an accord of the powers, Mr. Legrand addressed various memorials to this effect (1840-1847) to the governments of Europe, memorials which suffered much the same fate as those of Mr. Owen, but which received from their author a vigorous sequel in the form of a letter sent not only to French authorities, but also to the Cabinets of Berlin, St. Petersburg and Turin. This letter was published four times in the years 1853, 1855, 1856, and 1857, respectively. It boldly stated the position that the solution of the problem of according to the laboring classes the moral and material benefits that are desirable, must be found in international labor law, without which industry suffers and the international competition of manufacturers escapes needed limitations; and that moreover things principally to be striven for comprise: ele-

---

[3] *A.d.=Archives diplomatiques,* 1890 (2 Serie), t. XXXVI, p. 36-40.

The idea of international co-operation for the abatement of certain factory evils was expressed by the Frenchman, Villermé, who undertook, under the auspices of the Academy of Social and Political Science, an inquiry into the conditions of the laboring classes in the textile industry, and made his report in 1839. He said, however, that such "disinterestedness" was not to be counted upon, as it was without precedent.

Blanqui in his *Cours d'economie industrielle* (1838-1839) suggested international treaties to regulate conditions of competition. (See Mahaim, E-*Le Droit international ouvrier,* p. 188-189.)

mentary schools; instruction of young workers up to the time of their confirmation; Sunday schools for all ages; protection of the moral and material interests of the labor class by international legislation; the Gospel received into the heart and home of the laborer and his employer; Sunday rest; encouragement of the life and industry of the family by the State and by manufacturers; the extension of the benefits of savings banks to every locality; and old-age pension funds; concurrent with the attainment of all which, it is essential that there be the firm suppression by an international law on industrial labor, of the evils suffered by the laboring people including lack of instruction and education, child labor in factories, excessive labor, night-work, Sunday work, and the absence of proper age limits.

This array of wrongs, according to Mr. Legrand, could be remedied in part at least by the international adoption of provisions such as the following: the total prohibition of the work of male children under ten years of age and of females under twelve; the limitation of their work to six hours in twenty-four until thirteen years of age; the extension of the length of the workday to ten hours upon their attainment of the age of fourteen, with provision for a nooning of at least one hour; the proper certification of the age, school, and employment records of young employees; limitation of the work of adults to twelve hours in twenty-four, none of which labor should be required prior to 5:30 a. m. or subsequent to 8:30 p. m.; the interdiction of Sunday, or night-work for young people under eighteen years of age and for the feminine sex altogether; proper regulation of unhealthy and dangerous trades, *etc.* Most of the reforms advocated by Mr. Legrand have since become the object of international investigation and some of them; *e.g.*, the night-work of women and old-age pensions, of international enactment.

To find the next noteworthy expression of this idea of protecting labor by measures international in scope, we must turn to a Swiss report addressed in 1855 to the Cantonal Council of Zurich by a Commission of the Canton of Glarus.[4] An international *concordat* to regulate the length of the workday, child labor, *etc.*, was suggested by this report, which also remarked the fact that

[4] *Ibid.* t. XXXVI. p. 40-41.

competition between spinners could not be satisfactorily controlled without the creation, by international understandings, of greater uniformity in conditions of production; but since such an idea in that day and age of the world belonged to the category of "vain desires," it remained the duty of the moment to strive for greater uniformity in a sphere more limited. A movement for intercantonal labor legislation which originated in Glarus in 1852 may account for the interest shown by this Canton in the subject of international control.[5]

Soon thereafter (1856), in Belgium, Mr. Hahn introduced the subject of international labor regulation before an international Congress of benevolent societies convened in Brussels, with the result that the idea was discussed and officially endorsed by the Congress.

In the following year (1857) Germany witnessed the approbation of the idea by a Congress at Frankfort. The question succeeded to further publicity in that country in 1858 as a result of the publication of Bluntschli's Dictionary of Political Science, which dealt with the matter of international agreement on labor regulation. In the same year, Bluntschli and Braber, both advocates of doctrines of the socialist professors, broached the question of Sunday rest and came to the conclusion that practical results could be obtained only by an international agreement on the subject. Other German professors to add thought to the movement were Adolph Wagner and Brentano, the former proposing in his work, *Rede über die Sociale Frage,* the protection of labor's class interests by international agreements in such manner as would not be injurious to national industry, while the latter outlined, in his *Handbuch der Politick Oekonomie,* the program of the Christian Socialist Labor Party, championing the prohibition of Sunday labor, the suppression of the factory work of minors and married women, the placing of certain limitations upon the work to be required of a laborer in a day, protection for national labor, and propaganda for the internationalization of protective labor laws.

In 1866, the International Workingmen's Association, known as the International, founded two years previous in London at a

[5] *Ibid.* t. XXXVI. p. 47.

meeting of trade-unionists representing different countries, met at Geneva and formulated a series of resolutions to be thereafter included among the demands of labor. These resolutions embraced a maximum workday of two hours for children between nine and thirteen years of age, of four hours for those between thirteen and fifteen, and of six hours for those between sixteen and seventeen; the prohibition of the night-work of women and of all labor injurious to their health; a maximum workday of eight hours for all laborers and the prohibition of night-work, exclusive of necessary exceptions for certain industries. The Association also proceeded by manifesto to proclaim its conviction of the need for international labor regulation; this it continued to do in subsequent meetings, in which, as also in the Baltimore Convention (1866) of the National Labor Union of America, the idea of international co-operation was approved in a manner very encouraging to proponents of the principle. These early proposals for banning the night-work of women in connection with the recommendation of international co-operation are significant in the light of the international Convention on the subject signed forty years later. Karl Marx delivered the "inaugural address" before the Congress of Geneva and this phase of the international labor movement developed into socialism.[6] The securing of the adoption of international labor legislation by the existing governments became merely an incidental aim of socialism's political program.

[6] In the Bulletin of the *United States Bureau of Labor Statistics, No. 268 (Miscellaneous Series)*, Mr. Leifur Magnusson says: "The political phase of the international labor movement, as stated previously, developed into what is known as socialism. Beginning with the efforts of English and French workers to improve their working conditions, it gradually passed into a movement to change the principles underlying the present organization of society. This is still the theory of those members of the labor movement who have guided and participated in the international congresses. . . . The discussions and resolutions of the congresses, for instance that of Copenhagen, 1910, now deal almost wholly with the problems of reform through labor legislation and trade-union action. The larger political questions of the ballot, disarmament, and universal peace are less prominent than the economic questions of trade-union organization, co-operation, and wealth distribution." p. 64. See also pp. 34-64. For a discussion of the international trade-union movement, see pp. 65-82.

Other congresses called by the Socialist International are as follows: The Congress of Lausanne (1867) at which some concessions were made to the collectivists or state socialists; the Congress of Brussels (1868), where distinctly socialistic principles were adopted; the Congress of Basel (1869), in which Bakunin and other anarchists joined and to which the American National Labor Union[7] sent Mr. A. C. Cameron as the first American delegate to an international labor conference; the Congress of The Hague (1872), on which occasion the anarchists were excluded from the International and its General Council was removed to New York; the Congress of Geneva (1873), where socialists and anarchists held opposition meetings showing the strife that was causing the disruption of the First International; the Congress of Brussels (1874); the Congress of Bern (1876); the Congresses of Verviers and Ghent (1877); and the Congress of Chur (1881), which was the last of the ten congresses having any distinct relation to the original International. A group of socialists held a conference at London in 1871, and some anarchists met at St. Imier in 1872. After the dissolution of the old International, congresses representing both socialists and trade-unionists were held at Paris in 1883 and 1886, and at London in 1888. A second Socialist International was organized at Paris in 1889. It has held congresses at Brussels (1891); at Zurich (1893); at London (1896); at Paris (1900); at Amsterdam (1904); at Stuttgart (1907); at Copenhagen (1910); and at Basel (1912). Its meetings were resumed in February, 1919. American participation in the career of the First International had no important results. It caused a certain degree of co-operation among European labor interests to check the activities of the American Emigrant Company which was engaged in importing into the United States contract laborers to be used to meet employers' needs arising from strikes. As is well known, under the pressure of labor organizations, the Government finally prohibited the immigration of this class of workmen.

Various international trade-unions have also held international congresses, not so much, however, to further the enactment

[7] *Documentary History of American Industrial Society* by Commons and Andrews, Vol. IX, pp. 43-46, 338.

of international laws in general protection of labor as to put forward measures pertaining directly to occupational interests or to political party propaganda. For example, since 1890, the miners have held regular international congresses, a number of which have been under the domination of radical socialists. It is our purpose to discuss those assemblies and efforts that aim principally at international legislation as a means of properly safeguarding the interests of the laboring class, noting at the same time other meetings and events by which the idea of international protection has been advanced.

In the year after the meeting at Lausanne, a French economist, Louis Wolowski, recognizing in foreign competition a condition compelling the industrial exploitation of children, young people, and women, intimated that unanimity of action to remedy the unfortunate situation, after the example of the measures internationally adopted for the suppression of the slave trade, constituted a consummation devoutly to be desired. So many treaties appeared to him to have been concluded with the aim of killing men that he wished to be able to witness the adoption of similar means to enable mankind to live, although in his estimation the international competition of industry had not as yet reached the dreadful pass of sacrificing human life. In 1873 he submitted his idea of international regulation to the French National Assembly, and in the following year Mr. J. B. Dumas likewise submitted a petition to the same Assembly, embodying a similar appeal.

By the end of the period (1871-1874) Bismarck and the Austrian Government had failed to reach an agreement by negotiation with reference to certain standards of labor legislation.[8] Although an incident of this character might seem to a novice, like the first moves of pawns in a game of chess, of little serious import, it was nevertheless a portent of greater things to come.

The same truth was illustrated by events in Switzerland. Twenty-one years after the seemingly fruitless manifesto from the Swiss Canton of Glarus, previously alluded to, Colonel Frey of the Canton of Bale-Campagne, a Swiss Statesman, known in America as a volunteer in the Civil War, afterwards as Swiss Minister in Washington, and finally as President of the Swiss

[8] *G.B.=Bulletin des Internationalen Arbeitsamtes*, Bd. III, S. IX.

Republic,[9] delivered in 1876, before the legislative Chambers, an address [10] in which he raised the question as to whether it was advisable for Switzerland to pursue the subject of the conclusion of treaties uniformly regulating conditions of labor among the several industrial States, presupposing of necessity sufficient elasticity in such regulation to allow for dissimilar conditions of production among the different countries. He assumed in common with most of the early protagonists of the movement that suppression of industrial competition by international regulation constituted the best method of alleviating the hard lot of labor. Subsequent events proved that this agitation of the question was destined to produce fruitful results.

The subject was next adverted to by French socialists in congress assembled at Lyons, France, where a resolution espousing the cause of international labor legislation was adopted in 1877; this was followed in 1878 by a pronouncement in Germany on the part of Baron von Lohman favorable to international regulation protective of their industry and nationals; in 1879 the Association of Christian Manufacturers of the district of which the capital is Lille, declared to the effect that governments could and ought to regulate the relations of labor, and that by means of international negotiations; the same body, met in Paris, renewed the resolution two years later. In 1880 delegates of the Social Democratic Association in Switzerland announced themselves in favor of international intervention for the protection of labor. Not far from this time, there appeared two diametrically opposite views on the subject emanating from representative German authorities, Gustave Cohn, Professor at the University of Göttingen, and Lorenz von Stein, another advocate of the doctrines of the socialist professors, not all of whom, however, favored international control of labor. Lorenz von Stein defended the idea while Gustave Cohn proceeded to postulate the downright inapplicability of any such regulation by reason of the defects evident in existing labor law, the great diversity in industrial and economic conditions, and finally, the hostility of wageworkers themselves to a régime decreeing restrictions upon their faculty to

[9] Geo. Gifford, *U.S. Consular Reports,* July 1901.
[10] *A. d.* 1890. t. XXXVI. p. 41.

work and prohibiting their women and children from betaking themselves to the mills whenever they please.

In December of the year 1880, a motion was made by Colonel Frey before the Swiss National Council that the Federal Council be invited to enter into negotiations with the principal industrial States for the purpose of bringing about international factory legislation. The next year (1881) this proposal [11] received serious consideration by the National Council without arousing any opposition; it was acquiesced in hesitatingly, however; and it was demanded that the Federal Council be left free to choose the opportune moment for taking action in the matter. The opinion was expressed that satisfactory negotiations could take place only with such states as possessed factory legislation similar to that of Switzerland, *e.g.*, England and France, whereas with a country such as Austria, which possessed little or no similar legislation but whose industrial relation to Switzerland was of great importance, such negotiations must of necessity meet with grave difficulty and delay. The motion, so worded as to leave the time for action wholly to the discretion of the Federal Council, was adopted. In deference to this invitation, the Federal Council soon afterwards addressed to the Swiss Legations at Paris, Berlin, Vienna, Rome, and the Swiss Consulates General at London and Brussels a note calling upon them to procure from reliable sources such confidential information as would make it possible to know what States of Europe could be depended upon to coöperate in the matter of international regulation of labor in factories, and also to obtain the information necessary in order to determine the official proceedings best adapted to this end.

To the interrogations consequently submitted to the various powers, Belgium alone deigned no response. Her evaluation of the project must be measured by her silence.

The reply from France indicated that in general the Government deemed it outside the province of the State to interfere with contracts between employers and employees or to curtail the liberty of labor, and that since such intervention was considered unwarranted nationally, the Government was inclined *a fortiori*

[11] *Ibid.*, t. XXXVI. p. 41. *et suiv.* (This citation deals with both the proposal and the replies.)

to adopt an attitude unfavorable to the international treatment of the matter.

The Imperial Government at Berlin was likewise unprepared to co-operate, as it did not take kindly to the regulation of the matter by the dicta of treaties.

The Italian Minister for Foreign Affairs was curious to know which aspects of such a complex question were to be subjected to the procedure proposed: whether the work of women and children, sanitary conditions in workshops, strikes, large or small-scale industry, or all these phases of the problem combined.

The Austro-Hungarian Government exhibited great reserve with reference to the matter. It stipulated that its participation would be made conditional upon the preliminary receipt and examination of a copy of the measures proposed, upon assent to the same, and upon the certainty of the participation of the other important industrial States; and furthermore upon condition that it might authorize its representatives merely to make note *ad referendum* of the points recommended by the delegates, reserving to the Imperial Royal Government the ultimate decision.

The English Secretary of State for the Home Department was opposed, deeming it impracticable to conclude an international convention on the subject of factory regulation.

Such was the first official attempt on the part of a Government, and such the failure, to attain some practical result international in scope for the protection of labor. Discouraged for a time, Switzerland later returned to grapple with this self-imposed task and with more fortunate results. It is fitting to remark right here that to Switzerland more than to any other State belongs the credit and honor of being the pioneer in blazing a trail for the international regulation and protection of labor.

In 1882 a Congress meeting by order of "Verein für Sozialpolitck" and carrying on its program the subject of international factory regulation, was held at Frankfurt-on-Main. The men delegated to draw up a report on the question were Gustav Cohn, with the tenor of whose views we are already familiar, and Dr. Franck, manufacturer of Charlottenburg, who, on the other hand, preferred, like Lorenz von Stein to add the weight of his opinion in favor of the movement, although he did not believe in unduly limiting the work of women and children who ought to be permitted to add their mite to forestall suffering in the rainy day of industrial crisis. In the same year, the German Catholic Party evinced interventional tendencies, recognizing in the insufficiency of state intervention in industrial relations an argument for joint effort on the part of governments, and it recommended an international conference on the problem.

Not long thereafter (1883), an assembly composed of French, English, Spanish and Italian representatives of labor met in Paris and entertained a motion, introduced by delegates from English trade unions, recommending international legislation. It was averred that in certain countries the organization of labor was rendered impossible by unjust enactments, and hence it became the duty of all to uphold the cause, strive for the ameliorations desired, and oppose laws obstructing national or international legislation for the protection of those too feeble to defend themselves against the abuses of the competitive system. In Switzerland also, there occurred during the course of the year a meeting of labor associations which urged the Helvetian Government to continue its efforts for international law regulatory of factory conditions, and created a commission charged with the prosecution of the movement among the working populations of France and Germany.

On the 25th of January, 1884, the idea of international concord in the administration of labor law obtained its first expression before the French Parliament through the person of Count Albert de Mun whose address was followed by an order of the day inviting the Government to make provision for international legislation unharmful to national industry and yet preserving for each State the means of protecting women and children against industrial evils. At Roubaix, in the same year, an International Labor Congress drafted resolutions relating, among other things, to international legislation for the prohibition of work of children under fourteen years of age, and of night-work; also, for the safeguarding of the health of workmen; and for an international minimum wage and a workday of eight hours.

Discussion of the question was continued in 1885 by Mr. Vaillant before the Municipal Council of Paris. He contended that the means of combatting an international evil ought to be international; that the utility of general laws, already recognized to some degree by treaties of commerce, should be recognized in labor regulation; that each country can supplement international regulation by particular laws adapted to the various phases of moral, material, and industrial development peculiar to itself; that the essential elements of international law, demanded by representatives of the proletariat of all nations, have for a long time been recognized; and that as no country can object to international legislation involving no injury to its relative economic power, so no employers' selfishness can set itself in opposition, since in this question the interests of the laboring class and of the capitalistic class coincide, reaping mutual advantage from the decrease of industrial crises and the enhanced stability of commerce. In consequence there was formulated in the name of the Municipal Council of Paris a *voeu* praying that negotiations be instituted by the French Government as promptly as possible with a view to establish international labor regulation. In recognizing that under an international agreement conditions best regulated locally may remain undisturbed, Vaillant makes a point for the failure to appreciate which, many opponents of the movement, *e.g.*, Mr. Leroy-Beaulieu,[12] have seriously erred in their reasoning. It is of course primarily those phases of industry involved in international competition that are to be subjected to international control.

In December, 1885, French deputies submitted to the committee of the Chamber of Deputies a bill indicating by its terms willingness on the part of the French Government to comply with the overtures of the Swiss Government concerning international labor legislation, and readiness to assume the initiative, in concert with Switzerland, in endeavoring to bring about international law that would have for its aim the abolition of child labor under the age of fourteen, the limitation of the work of women and minors, measures of hygiene and safety, accident insurance, inspection, a normal workday, weekly rest, and an international bureau of labor statistics. One and one-half decades were yet to elapse before the establishment of an extralegal bu-

[12] See L. Chatelain, *La Protection internationale ouvrière*, p. 153-158.

reau of the kind proposed, and even a longer time ere the advent of the accident insurance treaties that now prevail.

While these matters were occupying attention in France, a noted personage had proceeded to act as a damper to the movement in the German Empire. A proposal in favor of protecting labor internationally, made in the Reichstag in January, 1885, aroused Bismarck to the utterance of a disquisition upon the subject. "Impracticable" recapitulates in a word his conclusion. Members of the Social Democratic Party retaliated in the succeeding year. Through the medium of a portion of this Party, a plan was set on foot to have the Reichstag adopt a resolution asking that the Chancellor of the Empire convoke a conference of principal industrial States for the purpose of formulating the uniform basis of an international protective labor agreement. The legal establishment of a ten-hour workday, and the suppression of night-work and of the work of children under fourteen, were the particular measures recommended. The resolution precipitated a heated discussion which served the mission of a publicity campaign, and in conjunction with a notable publication of that period resulted in a repercussion of public opinion in favor of the movement.

That publication was the work of Dr. Georg Adler, fellow of the University of Freiburg, and was entitled: *Die Frage des Internationalen Arbeiterschutzes.* The evils cited by this advocate of international regulation included female and child labor in factories; undue length of the workday; excessive assessments upon the wages of unskilled laborers; unemployment, incompetence, and disability due to accidents for which employers cannot legally be held responsible and also due to disease; premature and necessitous old age; and the sordid and unhealthy homes of workmen. In general, Dr. Adler would favor a method of prohibiting the work of children under thirteen so as not to conflict with a proper degree of schooling or professional training; a ten-hour workday for adults; cessation of work at night, with exceptions; a maximum workday of from five and one-half to six hours for young people from thirteen to sixteen years of age and for married women, which would be productive of the system known as "half-time," by which one shift of such persons is employed in the forenoon and the other in the afternoon exclusively; a maximum workday of ten hours for all young people from thirteen to sixteen years of age employed in domestic industry; inhibition of labor on Sunday with exceptions, and also in certain occupations dangerous to health, and especially of the employment of young people or females in enterprises inimical to their health and morals; and finally for backward countries, a period of transition of a dozen years if need be, for the attainment of the standards set.

Shortly after the appearance of Dr. Adler's work, Prof. Lujo Brentano of the University of Leipzig published an article upon "The International Regulation of Industry." He inquired into the effects of factory legislation upon national industrial competition, discovering, in answer, a resultant moral and physical regeneration of laborers, an increase in wages, an improvement in their ability and the general quality of their work compensating in part at least for whatever diminution of production may be attendant upon such regulation. In inquiring into the degree of uniformity possible in labor regulation between different industrial countries, he finds that it is possible only so far as the diversity of conditions of production, including climate, situation, peculiarities of social or industrial organization, financial resources, *etc.*, of the competing countries permits. In his opinion diplomatic pressure can be usefully exercised only to induce each country to pass national factory legislation compatible with its concrete conditions of production, thus preserving its capacity for competition, but, in defense of the employee, precluding excessive competition with the industries of other countries. For the enforcement of labor laws hypothecated in this plan, he suggests the device of adding to commercial treaties a clause making the enjoyment of their advantages conditional upon the faithful observance of the agreements entered into relative to factory legislation. The *prima facie* impracticability, or at best inferiority, of such a scheme, as compared with methods at present in operation, ought to make unnecessary any comment.

The 23d of August, 1886, an international labor congress, convened at Paris to debate the problems of a normal workday, adopted a resolution urging the workers of the different countries to invite their governments to concert the solution of labor's difficulties through international conventions. At the Congress of Montluçon in 1887, the trade unions of France voted to invite the Government to treat with other powers for international labor legislation. In Switzeralnd in the same year Messrs. Descurtins and Favon preferred a motion [13] before the bureau of the National Council taking into consideration the fact that a great number of states either had or were in the process of acquiring labor legislation similar to that of Switzerland, and consequently inviting the Federal Council to establish intercourse with those states relative to the conclusion of treaties or conventions on the protection of minors, the limitation of the work of women, weekly rest and the normal workday. There was little expectation that such action on the part of the Federal Council at that time would produce immediate tangible results other than the exploitation of the subject in the limelight of European public opinion, but even that was considered to be worth while. In 1888 the Federal Council gave its official countenance to the proposition and declared its intention of presenting at some future date to the States of Europe, in place of a general memorial, a concrete and detailed program. It hoped to realize in part at least the measures recommended in the motion, to which it wished to add the regulation of relations between employers and employees and of hygienic conditions in factories. Any attempt to obtain an international workday was characterized as impracticable for the time being. Attention was also directed to 'the fact that the subject of labor control was not one merely between governments, but one in which the populations of the States concerned had a direct interest and one which would be either advanced or impeded in proportion as these populations co-operated for the success of the movement or failed to do so. In further elucidation of the motion the following points were designated by special report as fundamental to the conclusion of a satisfactory international convention, *viz.*: the determination of a minimum age limit for children working in factories and mines, the prohibition of the night-work of women and minors, of the work of women in certain unhealthy and dangerous industries, of Sunday work, and of too long a

[13] *A.d.* t. XXXVI. 1890, p. 46.

workday for minors. The establishment of a central international office to transmit information with reference to the enforcement of international conventions was also advocated by this report.

In 1889 the Federal Council addressed a Circular Note [14] to the governments of Europe recalling to mind its previous unsuccessful action in 1881, but now anticipating a more fruitful issue of its endeavors by reason of progress made in the supervening period of eight years. The question of concurrent labor legislation under an international compact was again broached. Recognition was given to the impossibility of the complete attainment of the ends in view by a single leap. As a beginning, it was thought that the international regulation of Sunday, female and child labor would be apropos. The convocation of an international conference to adjudicate upon such measures, drafted in advance for the sake of convenience, was recommended as a prerequisite to their incorporation into international conventions. Pursuant to the exchange of ratifications, such conventions would become valid to all intents and purposes as the international law of the powers concerned. It is noteworthy that fifteen years later this was substantially the procedure adopted for the creation of the Bern Conventions. The full program proposed in the Note included the prohibition of Sunday labor and of the employment of young people and women in undertakings dangerous or particularly detrimental to health; the establishment of a minimum age for the admission of children into factories, and of a maximum day's work for young workers; the restriction of night-labor for young people and women; and the mode of executing the conventions concluded. This time Austria-Hungary, France, Luxemburg, Belgium, Holland, and Portugal were favorably inclined; Spain merely acknowledged receipt of the communication; the replies of England and Italy contained reservations; Russia frankly refused to participate, finding ground for excuse in the difficulty of uniform regulation of labor under the diversity of conditions existent in different parts of the Empire. Germany, Denmark, Sweden, and Norway sent no reply.

Switzerland had intended to convene a conference if possible in September 1889, but in view of the replies to her Note, she

[14] *A.d.* 1889, t. XXX. p. 77-79.

decided to postpone it to the following year. She addressed another Note [15] to the ministers of the several powers previously approached, in which she reviewed the replies above cited and gave notice of her intention to transmit a detailed program for the coming meeting, as far in advance as possible, to the powers interested. The program was later submitted in connection with a formal invitation to the conference which was to be non-diplomatic in character, and to be convened Monday, May 5, 1890, at three o'clock in the afternoon in the room of the Council of State of the Federal Palace at Bern, Switzerland. That program was conceived in the form of a long list of questions classified according to the topics already mentioned in a previous Note.

In July, 1889, socialists formed a new International at Paris where were presented resolutions prepared by an international conference held at The Hague, Feb. 28, 1889. The resolutions expressed approbation of the efforts of the Swiss Republic and enjoined the co-operation of the socialist parties and labor organizations. The measures advocated the prohibition of the work of children under fourteen years of age, and of night-work in general; an eight-hour workday; hebdomadal rest; the conservation of health; 'an international minimum wage; a system of national and international inspectors chosen by labor and paid by the State to insure the enforcement of the above; and the extension of their supervision to home industry.

In the following August, the general Council of Bouches-du-Rhone adopted a resolution by which the French Government was invited to take the initiative in international legislation to establish a workday of eight hours.

On Feb. 25, 1890, the Swiss Republic, after its preparation of the long list of questions already alluded to, suddenly in a Circular Letter [16] cancelled the international conference which was to be held at Bern and which was at last to crown with success a series of earnest and disappointing efforts extending over nearly a decade. When, after such an expenditure of time and trouble, the hard soil of international obduracy had at last become softened and it had become evident that the time was ripe to achieve

[15] *A.d.* 1889. t. XXXI, p. 342.
[16] *A.d.* 1890, t. XXXIII. p. 373-374.

the honor of bringing about an official international conference between the great powers of Europe to deal with the question of protecting labor by means of treaties, why did the sturdy Switzer suddenly forego the realization of his hopes? The two following rescripts [17] of the German Emperor issued just twenty-one days (Feb. 4) before the sending of the Swiss Note of cancellation, intimate the reason for the abandonment of the project by Switzerland.

The first rescript addressed to Bismarck was as follows:

"I am resolved to lend a hand to the betterment of the condition of the German workers in proportion to my solicitude occasioned by the necessity of maintaining German industry in such a state that it can meet the competition of the international market and insure thereby its own existence and that of the workers as well. The decadence of German industry, by the loss of foreign outlets, would deprive of their means of subsistence not only employers but also their employees. The difficulties which oppose themselves to the betterment of the condition of our workers and which result from international competition can be, if not surmounted, at least diminished, in no other way than by the international agreement of the countries which dominate the international market.

"Being convinced that the other governments are equally animated with the desire of submitting to a common examination the tentative proposals on the subject concerning which international negotiations have been broached by the workers of these countries, I want my official representatives in France, England, Belgium, and Switzerland to find out whether the governments are disposed to enter into negotiations with us with the aim of bringing about an international agreement on the possibility of givng satisfaction to the needs and desires of the workers which have found expression in the strikes of late years and in other forms of unrest.

"As soon as my proposal shall be accepted in principle, I charge you to convoke all the governments interested in like measure

[17] *A.d.* 1890. t. XXXIII. p. 325-326.

in the labor question, to take part in a conference which shall deliberate upon the questions raised.

"Berlin, February 4, 1890.
"WILLIAM."

The second rescript to Messrs. Berlepsch and Maybach was as follows:

"In mounting the throne, I have made known my resolve to favor the development of our legislation in the direction given it by my late grandfather, who had assumed the task of protecting the less fortunate classes in the spirit of Christian morality.

"The measures that the legislative and administrative authorities have taken with a view to bettering the situation of the workers, while being very valuable and very successful, have not however completely sufficed for the task that I have set myself.

"It will be necessary in the first place to complete the legislation on workmen's insurance. Next we shall have to examine the provisions of the present law on the condition of factory workers in order to give satisfaction to their complaints and aspirations in so far as they are just. The examination of this law should proceed on the principle that it is one of the duties of the government to regulate the duration and nature of work in such manner that the health of the workers, the principles of morality, economic needs of workers and their aspirations toward equality before the law, may be safeguarded.

"In the interest of the maintenance of peace between employers and the working people, it would be advisable to make legal provision for the purpose of insuring the representation of workers by men enjoying their confidence and charged with the responsibility of regulating their common affairs and of defending their interests in the negotiations with employers and with government authorities.

"An institution of this kind will facilitate for workers the free and peaceful expression of their desires and grievances. It will furnish to officials the means of keeping informed in a regular manner on the labor situation and of continuing in contact with the workers.

"I desire that in respect of the economic protection to be accorded laborers the mines of the State may become model institutions. As regards private mines, I desire that organized relations be established between my mining officials and these undertakings with a view to a supervision analagous to factory inspection.

"For the preliminary examination of these questions, I decree that the Council of State shall meet under my presidency and examine them, calling in competent persons whom I shall designate. I reserve to myself the appointment of these persons.

"Among the difficulties in regulating the condition of laborers in the way that I propose, the more considerable are those which result from the necessity of taking care of national industry in its competition with foreign industries. I have accordingly advised the Chancellor of the Empire to suggest to the Governments of the States whose industry with ours holds the universal market, the meeting of a conference to bring about an international regulation, fixing the limits of the work that can be required of laborers. The Chancellor of the Empire will forward copy of my rescript to your address.

"Berlin, February 4, 1890. WILLIAM."

Switzerland desired the success more than the honor of the first great international conference of a diplomatic character which would rivet the attention of the whole world upon the subject of international labor regulation. She acquiesced and cooperated in spite of the unexpected change of affairs which the above rescripts precipitated. Conseqently, as had been anticipated, the conference was held; but as had *not* been anticipated, it was held under the auspices of the German Government and at Berlin, of which more hereafter.

CHAPTER III

INTERNATIONAL LABOR CONFERENCES

AFTER the appearance of Emperor William's rescripts, Bismarck proceeded to communicate to the western European powers, exclusive of Russia, Spain and Portugal, the last two of which were invited later, an invitation to send delegates to a labor conference at Berlin. The subject matter proposed for consideration referred to the work of women, children and young persons, Sunday labor, mining, and lastly the means best adapted to the execution of the measurers adopted. This program was notified to Pope Leo XIII by Emperor William with the request that His Holiness lend his aid and sanction to the project. The Pope's reply [1] heartily endorsed the deliberations of a conference that might tend to relieve the condition of the worker, secure for him a Sabbath day's rest, and raise him above the exploitation of those who without respect to the dignity of his manhood, his morality or his home, treated him as a vile instrument.

Conference of Berlin, March 15-29, 1890

The famous Conference convened March 15, 1890, at two o'clock in the afternoon in the Palace of the Chancellor. Fourteen countries were officially represented: France, Germany, Austria-Hungary,[2] England, Holland, Spain, Switzerland, Norway, Sweden, Portugal, Denmark, Belgium, Italy and Luxemburg. The opening address of the session delivered by Baron Berlepsch,[3] German Minister of Commerce, envisaged the menace that had arisen from industrial competition and justified the attempt to realize an accord between the governments to obviate the common dangers of industrialism internationally unregulated. In

[1] *A.d.* 1890. t. XXXV. p. 18-19.
[2] Austria and Hungary may be counted as separate States in respect of Labor Conferences and Conventions.
[3] *A.d.* 1890. t. XXXIV. p. 270-271.

the protocol finally adopted is to be found the result of the Convention's deliberations.[4] The proposals made therein were for the most part approved unanimously, otherwise by a majority.

As to the regulation of mines, it was held desirable gradually to make twelve years in southern countries and fourteen years in others, the age limit for the admission of children; to exclude the feminine sex entirely; to limit the length of a day's work amidst unhealthful environment impossible of improvement; to guarantee so far as possible the health and safety of miners and adequate state inspection of mines; to qualify as mining engineers only men of experience and duly attested competence; to render relations between operators and employees as direct as possible and conducive to mutual confidence and respect; to institute measures of relief and insurance against the consequences of disease, accident, old age, and death; and measures preventive of strikes. Voluntary direct negotiation between employers and employees was recommended as the preferable solution of industrial crises, with ultimate recourse in case of necessity to arbitration.

The desirability of the prohibition of Sunday labor was adhered to with certain exceptions, *e.g.*: undertakings demanding continuity of production, or furnishing articles of prime necessity and requiring daily manufacture, or in case of enterprises functioning in special seasons or dependent upon the irregular action of natural forces. It was recommended that for such cases the governments provide a common basis of regulation by international agreement; and for the laborers involved, the rule of one free Sunday every other week was suggested.

The resolutions to protect children stood for the exclusion of the two sexes from industrial establishments until ten years of age in meridian countries and until twelve years old in all others, with certain educational requirements prerequisite to such labor. It was further held that under fourteen years of age they ought not to be allowed to work nights nor on Sundays; nor to exceed the limit of six hours of daily work, broken by a rest of at least one-half hour; nor to be admitted to unhealthful or dangerous occupations, save in exceptional cases where special protection is provided.

[4] *A.d.* 1890. t. XXXV. p. 175-178.

INTERNATIONAL LABOR CONFERENCES

The advance in standards for the regulation of the night-work of young persons was shown by a draft convention adopted by the International Labor Conference of the League of Nations at Washington, D. C., 1919, which prohibited the night-work of young persons under eighteen years of age with the exception that young persons over sixteen might be employed in certain continuous industries such as iron and steel mills, glass works, paper factories, etc. In case of occupations particularly dangerous or injurious to health, as likewise in the matters of night, Sunday, and a maximum day's work, the conferees at Berlin directed special attention to the need of safeguarding the interests of boys from sixteen to eighteen years old. The night-work of girls and women was condemned, as it had been repeatedly in previous assemblies. An international Convention to this effect since 1906 is the monument to these efforts. The maximum workday recommended for females was to be of eleven hours' duration interrupted by a rest period of at least one and one-half hours. Among numerous international measures favored for the protection of health was one, not met with heretofore, decreeing that lying-in women should not be readmitted to work within four weeks after delivery.

A sufficient number of officials specially qualified, named by the government, and independent of employers and employees, constituted, according to the stipulations of the protocol, the proper machinery by which to superintend the execution of these measures in each State, and to report upon labor conditions. The compilation of these reports and annual inter-communication of the same by the governments, together with relevant labor statistics, texts of legislative regulations and administrative decrees on the subject, *etc.*, were also advocated.

The immediate result of the Conference of Berlin was disappointing; its real aim, unaccomplished. Like previous and less important congresses, it confined itself merely to the expression of views and desires; no definite international conventions were formulated, or, indeed, outlined. Detractors found in its deliberations further proof of the futility of the movement. But, however unsatisfactory were the results obtained and gloated over by opponents, the Conference was an index of the growing power of an ideal, and served to center attention upon it to an unprecedented degree. It was a step in advance and an important one.

Supervening Events

International labor legislation was the chief topic discussed at the socialist Congress of Brussels, August, 1891.* Switzerland returned to the task of crystallizing opinion in favor of the movement, seemingly taking heart from the fact of the Berlin Conference. Her National Council addressed to the Federal Council a review of the importance of that event, the significance of Switzerland's rôle in the events leading up to it, and a historical exposition of the whole question with an optimistic forecast for the future.

In 1892 the Federal Council introduced, through diplomatic agents at Berlin and Vienna, the subject of an international agreement regulating the industry of mechanical embroidery. The move had been suggested and sanctioned by workers and employers of the industry, but it received a cold reception at the hands of the two powers approached and was dropped. In 1895 the Federal Council was invited by the Federal Chambers to take up again with the powers the general question of international labor regulation, but the Council did not believe the time propitious for a new attempt. Its next step (1896) related to the possible establishment of an international bureau charged with gathering important labor statistics, the study and comparison of industrial legislation, and the dissemination of pertinent information. Features of labor law, similar, dissimilar, or worthy of imitation, might thus be borne home to state and interstate consciousness as in no other manner. The countries approached with this plan were: France, Denmark, Germany, Belgium, Sweden, England, Italy, Spain, Holland, Norway, Russia, and Austria. The replies in general gave plain inplication of reluctance or hostility; and so the project was given up for the time being.

*In this period occurred the socialist Congresses of Zurich, 1893, and of London, 1896.

Congress of Zurich, August, 1897

Then came the first international labor Congress of importance in which the United States of America was recognized as one of the powers represented. It was called by the Swiss Workingmen's Society and was held at Zurich in 1897, the other nations represented being Switzerland, Sweden, Holland, Spain, Luxemburg, Russia, Poland, Germany, England, Austria-Hungary, Belgium, Italy, and France. The program was similar in many respects to that of the Congress of Berlin and still further resembled this more famous predecessor by its failure to get beyond the stage of exchanging opinions and expressing views. The resolutions declared for Sunday rest, an age limit for child labor fixed at fifteen, either a day of eight hours or a week of forty-four hours for women and an eight-hour day for adults in general. In the matter of inspection, it recommended that women inspectors be appointed for works giving employment to that sex, and suggested that a special inspection corps might be instituted for agricultural enterprises employing machinery. Other propositions were discussed and their character is easily recognized. They demanded that official recognition be tendered to the offices of labor organizations; that the right of employees of both sexes and all classes to organize be respected, with violation of the same made punishable; that universal suffrage, equal, direct, and secret, be introduced in electing to all representative bodies so as to enhance the real influence of the labor class in all parliaments; that active propaganda be carried on by trade unions and political organizations through such instrumentalities as conferences, publications, conventions, journals, and most important of all, the action of parliaments; and that international congresses be periodically organized to present to different parliaments concurrently proposals of the same law. The Congress importuned the Swiss Federal Council to reattempt the establishment of international legislation and further to prosecute its scheme of an international labor office; and at the same time evinced the fact that it is possible for radical Socialists and Catholics to make mutual concessions for the sake of harmony. The spirit of co-operation distinguished the deliberations of this meeting.

Congress of Brussels, September 27, 1897

The next conference of note assumed the title: Congress for International Labor Legislation. Many former delegates of the Berlin Conference were present. It could hardly be said, however, to be official in character, as the greater number of members came of their own accord without official or governmental sanction. Some governments sent delegates; Germany, Belgium and France led in respect of the number of such representatives. Like the platform prepared originally by the Swiss for the international conference projected by them and later abandoned to give place to the Conference of Berlin, the order of the day was interrogatory in form. This program asked for information concerning the evolution and modification of labor legislation among the various countries subsequent to the Conference of Berlin, inquired the situation of the different industrial States with reference to certain resolutions of that Conference, and put various other questions as to whether international labor protection is possible and desirable, and if so, in what measure and under what form; what regulation if any, should obtain with reference to small industry and domestic industry; what would be the utility and propriety of the concurrent adoption by all industrial states of the regulations imposed upon dangerous industries by a share of them, and found salutary in effect; what the appropriate means of insuring the better execution of protective labor law, what should be the laws and duties of labor inspectors; and what, the desirability of establishing international reports between labor offices and the compilation of labor statistics international in scope.

That the preparation of such statistics would be of great utility seemed to be the universal sentiment of the delegates; but, although the establishment of an official international bureau for that purpose was advocated, there were some who opposed it in preferment of a private office. In consequence of this divergence of opinion, no decision was reached. The possibility of actual contemporary international regulation of labor seemed by tacit recognition to have suffered general preclusion from the minds of the conferees. It was given comparatively slight attention. The conference was nevertheless another link in a chain of events leading on to the positive realization of international labor law; it accorded a profound treatment to many of the questions in hand, and occasioned the production of a noteworthy monograph upon legislative principles in force, and centered the attention of economists of all parties upon international phases of the labor movement. It also evoked from Mr. Henrotte, Belgian Chief of Labor Inspection, the proposal of the suppression of industrial poisons by international agreement, and the observation that a trial of such legislation might be conveniently made by the international prohibition of the use of white lead and white phosphorus.

After the session, some of the delegates, evidently not satisfied with the convention's work, appointed a committee of three to give to it some more practical result. This committee undertook to prepare the way for the establishment of an international labor association representative of all parties interested in the proper protection of labor, and for this purpose drafted statutes or a tentative constitution for such an organization. It also lent its aid to the collection of copies of protective labor laws and regulations in force, with the result that toward the close of 1898, appeared Volume I of the Belgian publication, *L'Annuaire de la législation du travail,* covering in French, the labor laws promulgated in the year 1897. Among the prominent supporters of this undertaking was Mr. Nyssens, Belgian Minister of Industry.

In 1899 Baron Berlepsch to whom the proposed plan of an international association on labor legislation was familiar, met with economists and men of politics in Berlin to consider the proposition and examine the tentative constitution submitted by the committee. The statutes outlined were generally approved and twenty individuals were delegated to enter into relations with other nations for the creation of other committees in furtherance of the project.

[5] E. B. I. (1-3), App. p. 150. (E. B.=*Bulletin of the International Labor Office.*)

The principles stated in this proposed constitution were closely adhered to in the organization of a labor section in France, which infused more life into the movement by summoning interested parties to another international labor Congress at the time of the Paris Exposition of 1900. In the same year, the French Minister of Commerce, Mr. Millerand, made an unsuccessful attempt to bring about with Belgium negotiations on labor legislation. The incident reveals the status of governmental co-operation in matters pertaining to labor at this stage of the movement.[5]

Congress of Paris July 25-29, 1900

The following States sent delegates to the Congress of Paris: Holland, Russia, United States, Austria, Belgium, and Mexico. Many other countries were represented non-officially by prominent men and women.

The representative of Italy, Signor Luzzatti, uttered on this occasion a significant declaration [6] with reference to labor conditions in his country. Said he:

"I come from a country where industry is only just beginning to develop. I should be thankful if you could, by means of a *compellare intrare*, give us an impetus in the right direction of progress. I should be thankful if you could give to Italian workmen by international legislation that protection which national legislation does not afford them.

"Decisive success can only be attained by way of international legislation. I have often urged the prohibition of night-work in cotton mills; the reply has always been: 'Willingly, but first let it be introduced in the neighboring states which compete with us. Try to bring it about by way of international legislation.'

"I feel no doubt that in future, together with, or indeed supplementary to, our commercial treaties, we shall have labor treaties. In such treaties, we shall include provisions tending to level up conditions of exchange.

"Finally, I feel I must give my opinion that all our attempts will remain lifeless if we are not capable of quickening them with the warmth of human solidarity. Especially in the realm of

[6] *Ibid.*

social questions one is continually constrained to think of the beautiful saying that really fruitful thoughts spring always from the heart."

These remarks found partial fulfillment in a pioneer labor treaty concluded between France and Italy four years later.

The work outlined for the Congress consisted of the consideration of four things: the legal limitation of the length of the workday; the prohibition of night-work; the inspection of labor; and the formation of a union or international association for the legal protection of labor. In the discussions it was denied that any expectation was entertained of realizing by international agreement a Utopia of complete unification of protective law; it was rather expected that greater and greater similarity of such laws would gradually evolve; in determination of a maximum workday, it was declared that the consensus of opinion of past congresses seemed to favor a period of eleven hours under condition of its gradual reduction to ten hours; night-work, with the usual reservations, was severely condemned; labor inspection was defined as an essential institution capable of further development with respect to the establishment of permanent relations between its corps in different countries, and of augmentation notably by the addition of penalties, the specialization of functions, and the inclusion of inspectors representative of the rank and file of labor.

The creation of an official international office was opposed as conducive to complications under the excessive burden of responsibility which would be imposed by the superintendence of political, industrial and commercial relations of international consequence; but a private office being deemed admissible and desirable, the matter was resolved in this latter sense by providing for the formation of the: "International Association for the Legal Protection of Labor." [7]

Thus at last, after twenty years of disappointing attempts to attain some practical result, there was conceived and brought forth a child worthy of the splendid cause whose name it bore—

[7] The Association is frequently termed the "International Association for Labor Legislation."

the International Association for the Legal Protection of Labor was born—destined to grow into the robust organization, which, through its International Labor Office and national sections, gradually extended its influence to every quarter of the globe and became responsible more than any other agency for the strides which were taken toward more effective international co-operation in control and protection of industrial workers. To a commission of six wise men was entrusted the task of carrying out the active organization of the new Association. The body had for its presiding officer a Swiss delegate, Mr. Scherrer, lawyer and former president of the Congress of Zurich; his colleagues were Baron Barlepsch, and Messrs. Cauwès, of the Law Faculty of Paris; Phillippovich, of the University of Vienna; Toniolo, of the University of Pisa, and Mahaim, at the University of Liége.

The Association, as organized, was to be directed by a Bureau chosen by the Committee of delegates representing different national sections [8] which were to be wholly autonomous bodies organized in accordance with the desires of the nationals concerned and having their own separate programs. The only prerequisite to membership in the Association was acceptance of the principles of the legality and efficacy of intervention to regulate the relations of capital and labor. Support was derived from contributions and voluntary state subventions. A permanent International Labor Office with a regular salaried staff was established at Basel, Switzerland. By the Peace Treaty, 1919, an International Labor Office was incorporated in the **International Labor Organization of the League of Nations.**

The Constitution of the Association called for the publication in French, German and English of a periodic review of labor legislation in all countries. The French and German publications date from the year 1902; the English, from 1906; they are respectively entitled: *Bulletin de l'office international du travail, Bulletin des Internationalen Arbeitsamtes,* and *Bulletin of the International Labor Office.* These Bulletins gave, either textually or

[8] Each section was given its own official title; thus the American Section is the "American Association for Labor Legislation."

It should be noted also that governments were invited to designate one delegate each, who had the same rights in the Committee as other members. See Appendix II, Exhibit 10.

in résumé, the laws in force relative to the protection of labor in general, and of women and children in particular. They also contain historical expositions of these enactments as well as copies or digests of official reports and documents concerning their interpretation and execution. Here are to be found the facts, gleaned from all the industrial nations of the world, that made possible the effective comparative study of labor legislation so essential to all attempts to unify it. The Association summarized its aims under five principal headings:

"1. To serve as a bond of union to all who believe in the necessity for Labor Legislation.

"2. To organize an International Labor Office.

"3. To facilitate the study of Labor Legislation in all countries, and to provide information on the subject.

"4. To promote International Agreements on questions relating to conditions of Labor.

"5. To organize International Congresses on Labor Legislation."

The work of this conference had direct and far-reaching consequences. In one country after another, national sections were quickly instituted. The section in Germany bore the title of "Society for Social Reform" and had as one of its principal aims the creation of an Imperial Labor Office. Local sections were established in Berlin, Leipzig, Dresden, and Hamburg. As for Austria, a section was organized in spite of the law prohibiting to societies international relations; while in France, Italy, Holland and Hungary, similar sections were also created. The one in Switzerland boasted two hundred and thirty-eight members; Belgium, on the other hand, had to make up in quality what she lacked in quantity. Her limited membership was co-optated so as to preserve the organization's character of political neutrality.

First Delegates' Meeting of the International Association. Basel, Sept. 27-28, 1901.

These sections, excepting that of Hungary, soon were represented at the inaugural meeting of the Association, known as the "Constituent Assembly of the International Association for the

Legal Protection of Labor." This conference proceeded to define the functions of the International Labor Office in contradistinction to those of the International Association, enumerating among the tasks primarily incumbent upon the former the scientific investigation and comparison of national legislative enactments and the solution of the various problems inherent in dangerous and unhealthful occupations, the night-work of women, and the use of poisons, especially lead and white phosphorus in manufacturing processes. But a few years later, the use of white phosphorus in the manufacture of matches was prohibited by international agreement. It was desired also that the Office pay special attention to employers' liability and methods of insurance against accidents and diseases, especially in their relation to imported labor. A careful study of the acts of these congresses reveals the fact that in their resolutions and discussions have been laid the foundations for every important labor law that has since been internationally enacted. The principle of the equal treatment of foreigners and citizens before the social insurance laws of a realm was destined to have a notable carer.

Another subject touched upon in the discussion of certain of the delegates and destined to assume larger proportions in later years, was that of regulating traffic in young Italian laborers, which was an evil particularly prevalent in France.

Second Delegates' Meeting, Cologne, Sept. 23-24, 1902.

The next year witnessed at Cologne the Second Delegates' Meeting of the Association. Forty-four delegates from twelve national sections besides twenty-one official delegates of eleven European powers, constituted an attendance that was very encouraging in contrast with the official representation accorded by only four powers in the year previous. The Assembly confined its labors chiefly to two topics; *i. e.*, the night-work of women and the use of the poisons, white phosphorus and lead, in industry. The principal obstacle encountered in the diagnosis of the first question was the disagreement as to just what exceptions, if any, to the general prohibition of night-work to females were feasible. In disposing of this matter, the convention resorted to the expedient of appointing a commission to discover if possible by scientific analysis of the variant factors entering into that problem, the measures best adapted to the effective prohibition of such labor and the progressive suppression of exceptions to the same. Similar provision was made for the investigation of measures by which to abolish white phosphorus from industry and suppress, in so far as possible, the use of white lead. As a means to this end, it was resolved to bring pressure to bear upon state and local authorities for the elimination of the use of lead in establishments under their jurisdiction. In the following year occurred the publication of the investigations (Jena, Gustav Fischer) under the titles, *Night-Work of Women in Industry* and *The Unwholesome Industries*.

French and Italian delegates at the meeting entered into informal negotiations upon the subject of a Franco-Italian Labor Treaty,[9] but nothing was definitely decided in the matter at this time.

Commission Meeting at Basel, Sept. 9-11, 1903.

The commission to whom the task of making the above researches had been assigned, met for conference in Basel in 1903. In order to arrive at some real and practical outcome of the much mooted questions of twenty years concerning the night-work of women, it besought the Swiss Federal Council to invoke the nations to acquiescence and participation in another international conference whose aim it should be to see this evil put under the ban of effective international prohibition. This prohibition, in the mind of the committeemen, ought to find exception in case of such unavoidable exigencies as fire, flood, explosion, imminent or unexpected accident, or impending loss of perishable products such as fruit or fish. In dealing with the subject of industrial poisons, the commission made known to the Swiss Federal Council its desire to have it undertake the necessary diplomatic action to occasion an international conference before which might be laid the question of prohibiting by international convention the use of white phosphorus in the match industry. The regulation of the use of white lead and its compounds was deemed a subject also worthy of treatment by such a conference; more-

[9] G. B.-*Bulletin des Internationalen Arbeitsamtes* Bd. III, S. x.

over, it was held to be the place of the national sections to pursue energetically the elimination of the use of lead products in public and private painting works.

The response of the Federal Council to these overtures was cordial and now about fifteen years after the Berlin Conference, it proceeded to extend to the various powers an invitation for another international conference. Their reply was in general very favorable; and thus it came about that the Swiss Circular Letter of Dec. 30, 1904,[10] issued a summons that was destined to congregate behind closed doors the representatives of fifteen European countries for a nine days' consideration (May 8-17, 1905) of the international problems of labor. Several other notable events, however, occurred in 1904, before this conference, the date of which, it will be noticed, was set for the spring of the following year.

On April 15, 1904, France and Italy had signed the first of a series of treaties looking toward reciprocal protection of laborers of the one country within the territory of the other. The example thus set was so generally followed as to create in international diplomacy an important departure, which will receive extended treatment in a following chapter.

Third Delegates' Meeting, Basel, Sept. 26-27, 1904.

In the same year occurred the third general assembly of the International Association, convened at Basel, with ten powers officially represented besides the usual delegations from national sections. The program presented five principal topics for consideration, *viz.*: the material and financial resources of the International Office; the prohibition of industrial poisons; the regulation of the night-work of women and young people; the relation of labor legislation to home labor; and lastly the problems of social insurance. The five questions were assigned to as many different committees, which proceeded to consider and report upon them.

The first committee reported a deficit in the treasury of the International Office, and asked new subsidies from the States to meet the need.

[10] *G. B.* Bd. III, S. 442.

The committee on industrial poisons was elated over the fact that anonymous philanthropists had donated 25,000 francs as prize money to be distributed to those who in competition suggested the best methods of overcoming the dangers of lead poisoning. The committee maintained that the question should be studied with reference to each industrial group by which lead was used, *e. g.*: manufactures of lead colors, painting establishments, makers of certain electrical instruments, the polygraphic industry, plumbing, stone cutters, dyers, *etc.*, in order that there might be worked out for each group the restrictions, regulations, or prohibitions necessary to guard the well-being of the laborer. In the painting industry, for example, it urged severe measures to coerce in all instances possible, the substitution of less harmful materials for lead products. And finally, in concluding its resolutions, it recommended, as a preliminary measure for effective resistance to the employment of industrial poisons in general, a careful classification by experts of all such poisons upon the basis of the seriousness of the disease produced by each and the wide publicity of the list when completed.

The third committee did not fail to find in the theme of nightwork of young people abundant material out of which to construct a laudable program of investigation.

The fourth committee desired each national section to study and report upon certain designated phases of the problems inherent in home labor and its relation to labor legislation. The subject of the investigation of home industries had been suggested at the meeting of the special commission in Basel the year before.

The fifth committee was charged with the examination of the topic of industrial or social insurance. The principles sanctioned by the assembly held that insurance law applicable in a given case ought to be that of the place of the undertaking giving employment, and that distinctions should not be drawn between beneficiaries of social insurance because of their nationality, domicile, or residence. The national sections were asked to furnish the Bureau, before the next general assembly of the Association, reports that would throw light upon the means of putting these principles into operation in each country, and internationally. The position taken by the conference upon this point is noteworthy. Here was bold adherence to the position that the topic of workmen's insurance and the right of the laborer to indemnity if incapacitated by accident, did not confine itself to the domain of private law and so by its very nature exclude itself from international treatment. The question of the equality of foreigners and citizens before insurance law had been for a long time a debated issue: the solution which it was gradually approaching is indicated by the fact that in this same year, 1904, Italy signed three treaties with as many governments, in each of which it was mutually agreed, in respect of accident insurance, to investigate the means of bringing into practice the reciprocal protection of citizens of one country working in territory of the other. That this principle is wholly susceptible of application has been amply proved since by a succession of treaties on the subject.

Before adjourning, the assembly extended to the sections an invitation to include among their studies a special investigation of the question of the limitation of the length of the workday.

Bern Conference, May 8-17, 1905.

In the month of May 1905, occurred the first of the two famous assemblages at Bern, in which a majority of the powers of Europe took practical steps toward the concurrent incorporation of labor law into international conventions. We mention the fact here merely in its chronological order, as a succeeding chapter is devoted to the epoch-making transactions of the assembly and that which was its sequel.

Seventeenth Miners' International Congress. June 5-8, 1906.

Apart from congresses proposedly convoked in behalf of the principle of international protection, the subject has been considered in the international meetings, too numerous for detailed discussion at present, which trade unions, philanthropic societies, political parties, and various other organizations, have been constantly holding. An important example is that furnished by the Seventeenth International Congress of Miners, held in London in 1906.[11] The delegates desired that pressure be brought to bear upon governments so as better to safeguard the life and limb of members of their vocation. Their resolutions indicated their numerous wants, which were in brief: mine inspectors chosen from among the workmen and paid by the State; the prohibition of female work, as well as that of children under fourteen, and of youths under sixteen in underground works; an eight-hour workday for underground operations; a minimum wage and the control of wages by the delivery to the miners of every colliery of a duplicate pay book; old-age pensions at fifty-five; the extension of workmen's insurance to provide unconditionally a sufficient allowance for incapacitated miners and likewise for heirs of workmen who have died.

International Diplomatic Conference at Bern. Sept. 17-26, 1906.

Three months later there was held the second of the Bern Conferences, as a result of which the prohibition of the industrial night-work of women and the interdiction of the use of white phosphorus in the manufacture of matches were enacted into law by a large proportion of the nations of Europe and their dependencies throughout the world.

Fourth Delegates' Meeting. Geneva, Sept. 27-29, 1906.

It had now been two years since the International Association for the Legal Protection of Labor had held an official conference; it convened on Sept. 26, 1906, the fourth assembly of the series at Geneva with seventy-eight delegates present and ten nations officially represented. Since its last meeting four new national sections had been added, making a grand total of twelve such branches of the organization. The additions were:

    (1) British Section established in 1904;

    (2) American Section established in 1906;

    (3) Danish Section established in 1906;

    (4) Spanish Section established in 1906.

The financial status of the Association was found to be excel-

[11] *E. B.* Vol 1, (4-8). pp. 229-230.

lent, expenses being more than met by generous contributions and state subventions. Standing at the head in this respect, as in all phases of the movement, has been Switzerland, which in the years 1904-1907 contributed over seven thousand francs more than its nearest rival, Germany, and over fifteen thousand more than its next nearest rival, France. The following table indicates the amounts contributed by the various States within that time:[2]

	1904 f.	1905 f.	1906 f.	1907 f.	Total f.
Germany	7.386	7.374	9.800	10.000	34.560
Austria	3.000	3.125.65	3.122	5.000	14.247.65
Belgium	....	....	2.000	2.000	4.000
Denmark	....	....	687.29	700	1.387.29
United States	1.033.75	1.000	1.000	1.000	4.033.75
France	5.000	3.750	9.000	9.000	26.750
Hungary	....	4.716.98	3.000	3.000	10.716.98
Italy	1.000	2.000	2.000	2.000	7.000
Luxemburg	400	500	500	500	1.900
Norway	....	....	688.30	700	1.388.03
Holland	4.151.10	4.137.95	4.139.75	4.150	16.578.80
Sweden	....	....	4.035.20	1.000	5.035.20
Switzerland	10.000	10.000	9.999.70	12.000	41.999.70
Total	31.970.85	36.604.58	46.972.24	53.050	169.097.67

The sum of four thousand francs was voted to aid in the publication of an English version of the Bulletin of the International Labor Office. The subsidy was accorded for two years only and on condition that supplementary expense be met by the national sections. Since 1906 the English Bulletin has made its regular appearance concurrently with the French and German editions.

The assembly followed the custom of dividing itself into sections, to each of which some special topic was assigned; the chief subjects designated for consideration were:

(1) Child labor.
(2) Industrial poisons.
(3) Night-work for young persons.
(4) Maximum duration of workday.

[12] See L. Chatelain, *La Protection internationale ouvrière*, p. 153-158.

(5) Home work.
(6) Insurance.

The resolutions adopted by the meeting authorized the Bureau of the Association to tender thanks in the name of the Association to the various governments which signed the Bern Conventions, and to congratulate the Swiss Federal Council upon the notable outcome of its efforts; they also called upon the sections to inform the Bureau as to the measures decreed in each country in execution of labor legislation, and recommended the issuance of a *questionnaire* by the Office to obtain information with which to elaborate a comparative report on the subject; moreover, both the Office and the sections were besought to undertake a similar task in the further investigation of the question of child labor.

Upon the topic of the night-work of young workers, the resolutions specified eight particular points: the general prohibition of such work to young persons under eighteen; its absolute prohibition up to the age of fourteen; exceptions above fourteen in cases of necessity; *e.g.,* in industries where materials are subject to deterioration and loss; its total prohibition in public-houses, hotels, and sales establishments; the provision for a minimum night's rest of eleven hours including in every case the hours from 10 p. m. to 5 a. m.; the permission to make certain reservations in accomplishing the transition from old to new regulations; the desirability of seeing the serious enforcement of inspection; the institution of a commission to investigate the ways and means of realizing the above and to report upon the same within two years, each section having the privilege to nominate two delegates for the commission and to designate such experts from among employers and employees as ought to assist in the deliberations. Of such nature were seven laudable propositions advanced with no suggestion of the means of their execution in evidence, save the eighth, which merely provided for the appointment of a commission further to investigate the matter—being "the substance of things hoped for and the evidence of things not seen." Nevertheless, faith wrought works in the matter as will appear later.

The maximum duration of the workday was deemed to be a subject upon which definite conclusions should be reached for the conservation of the physical well-being and proper moral standards of employees. As a means to this end and to be in a way to pronounce upon the utility of international conventions upon the subject, the Bureau was called upon to institute inquiries upon the length of the workday and the effects realized by its reduction among different peoples.

With regard to home labor, the sections were urged to request measures of their governments with the aim of compelling employers to register home workers connected with their industry and to give precise information as to the scale of wages in operation. Means were then to be adopted to insure wide publicity to such information. The extension of labor inspection and social insurance to home work, the vigorous application of health regulations to unsanitary conditions in which such labor might be found to occur, the effective organization whenever needed of professional unions, social leagues of purchasers, *etc.* —were all measures recommended by the resolutions upon the topic. Further, the Bureau was charged to ascertain, in collaboration with a subordinate commission, the branches and the conditions in each country of industry in the home whose products entered into the competition of the world market, and the divisions of such industry most urgently demanding reform in respect of excessive length of the workday, especially for women and children, insufficient wages, periodic unemployment, and the want of insurance against sickness.

Upon the subject of industrial poisons, the Office was urged to facilitate the execution of the measures recommended at the third assembly of the Association, and to have the sections appoint specialists to make necessary inquiries and prepare, before Jan. 1, 1908, reports on better means of combatting lead poisoning in the manufacture and use of lead colors both in the ceramic and polygraphic industries. These reports were to be sent to the International Office. The national sections were further urged to report before March 1, 1908 on the prohibition of the use of lead colors, indicating for each country whether the interdiction had been pronounced by a law or by an administrative measure and whether it applied only to public works or especially to private works, and also the consequences of such prohibition as well as the results which had been attained by the use of leadless colors. The Bureau was also to appoint a commission of three experts to make out, from the lists furnished by the experts whom the sections had appointed, a final list of the more important industrial poisons classified in the order of the seriousness of the malady they caused. This was in execution of a measure resolved at the assembly two years before; the whole question, aside from the Bern Conventions, seemed to stand just about where it had stood then.

The hope was expressed that the powers not adhering to the Bern Convention prohibiting the use of white phosphorus in the match industry would see their way clear to do so, and the sections were charged to labor with all their might for such prohibition.

The resolution on workmen's insurance stood upon the principle of the equality of foreigners and nationals before the law; the Association intimated its dependence upon the reports of the sections to ascertain to what degree it would be possible to realize this equality in insurance regulation by international agreement. It had already been partially realized by accident insurance treaties between Luxemburg and Belgium (April 15, 1905); France and Belgium (Feb. 21, 1906); France and Italy (June 9, 1906); France and Luxemburg (June 27, 1906); also in voluntary national enactments; *e.g.*, those of the German Federal Council under dates of 1901, 1905, and 1906. The formation of international treaties and conventions, the modification of existing law and the passage of new law, were advanced as possibilities to be duly considered and striven for in so far as they promoted the application of this principle: for its realization in national law would be a step toward its incorporation into international law. Reports were to be made by the sections at the next meeting upon various phases of the subject.

The information furnished the Association by the different national sections especially with respect to the enactment and execution of labor law in pursuance of international agreements, could, under the skillful manipulation of the Bureau, be made to partake of the nature of a sanction; such at least seemed to be the hope of the assembly. The Association did not believe the time had as yet come to launch more international conventions; for, not only had those just signed at Bern yet to be fully tried but the agitation of the foregoing problems had yet to become of sufficient extent and intensity to warrant such a step. The delegates were too wise to forget that history is replete with instances where through ill advised haste devotees have wrought the ruin of some noble cause they sought to serve. Besides, the ground needed to be more carefully prepared, the questions more thoroughly analyzed, the whole movement more genuinely popularized, to make secure and safe another great advance, like that of the Bern Conventions, toward the international regulation of industry and labor—a consummation, as deemed by many of its advocates, of vital import not only to national industrial peace, but also to the international peace of the world.

Results of the International Prize Contest Concerning Lead Poisoning.

Shortly after the adjournment of this assembly occurred the announcement of the results of the prize contest which had been inaugurated by virtue of the contribution by anonymous philanthropists of 25,000 francs to be awarded to those who should produce the best treatises upon the subject of the prevention and suppression of plumbism. Announcement of this contest had been made by the commission on industrial poisons at the third meeting of the Association (1904), and the conditions of competition had been published June 10, 1905. Altogether sixty-three monographs arrived at the Office, some of which proved to be worthy of wide circulation and made valuable contributions to the movement for overcoming the evils resulting from the use of white lead and its compounds in industry. The decision of the judges did not award any prize to two works on the means of avoiding poisoning at the time of the treatment of mineral of lead or of minerals containing lead. It was proposed, however, to purchase a work entitled, *Margenstunde hat Gold im Munde.* Of a dozen works on the means of suppressing the dangers of lead in lead foundries, two were awarded prizes which together amounted to 12,500 francs. These treatises were entitled. *Wo ein Wille ist, ist auch ein Weg,* and *L'Homme n'est past fait pour l'industrie, mais au contraire, l'industrie pour l'homme.* The office proposed the purchase of works on the subject carrying the titles: *Gesundheit ist Reichtum,* and *Die Hygiene sei die Freundin des Gewerbes.* No prize was awarded to any of a dozen works on means of avoiding toxication in the chemical use of lead in the manufacture of lead colors, accumulators, ceruse, and in similar industries. Two works entitled: *Quod felix faustum fortunatumque sit,* and *Die Humanität ein zug unseres Herzens,* received a prize of 937 francs each, from out the number of eight or ten competitors, all of whom treated the general topic of preventing lead poisoning in the industries of whitewashing, painting, varnishing, *etc.* A prize of 1,250 francs went to a work entitled, *Vae soli,* and two other awards of 937 francs each, to two essays entitled *Durch Nacht zum Licht,* and *Eile mit Weile.* These last three prize winners belonged to the category of dissertations which treated of preventive measures in establishments employing great quantities of lead or lead composition; *e.g.,* type foundries. Numerous other contributions were proposed for purchase or given honorable mention. In no case however, did the International Office assume responsibility for the suggestions made or conclusions reached by the authors; it did proceed to give publicity to such of their contributions as were deemed worthy and valuable.

International Congress on Unemployment. Milan, Oct. 1-2, 1906.

The first International Congress on Unemployment,[13] held at Milan, Italy, in 1906, undertook, as its main task, to devise means for rendering unemployment less acute, without attempting to do away with it altogether; and therefore, it omitted in its resolutions to deal with the primary causes of unemployment, and went on to enumerate the most important factors requisite to combat the evil, *e.g.*: the determination of standards by which to regulate hours of work, wages, and contracts of labor; the more equitable distribution of labor within different groups; greater co-operation among all forms of labor; and the application of the doctrine

[16] *E. B.* I, (4-8), p. 322.

of intervention by state and local authorities. To facilitate such intervention, recommendations were made to require of all industries a periodic, statistical report of work and unemployment; to establish an international employment bureau and free public employment agencies in every center of population; to provide either optional or compulsory insurance against unemployment, supported by contributions from the State, employers, and workmen; to accord to labor ready access to credit, particularly for the co-operative acquisition of land; and to furnish, through local branches of the government, subsidies to employment bureaus established by workers. Of these resolutions, the one touching upon an international employment bureau was without doubt most worthy of immediate consideration and potentially capable of most far-reaching and helpful results. The scientific adjustment of the supply and demand of the labor market predicates immediate relief for all parties concerned; *i.e.*, the State overcharged with labor, employers undersupplied, and workingmen unemployed. An International Association on Unemployment was organized in 1910.

Eleventh International Conference on the Weekly Day of Rest. Milan, Oct. 29-31, 1906.

Another international assembly followed close upon the heels of the Congress on Unemployment. This Conference concerned itself with the topic of weekly cessation of toil, laying down, as of general obligation, the observance of Sunday as a day of rest.[14] This would include Sunday rest for newspaper employees, and fifty-two days of rest annually, falling on Sunday as often as possible, for post-office employees. For countries where such regulations do not exist, the following reforms were recommended: only one postal delivery on Sunday, excepting express deliveries; non-delivery of postal, collection, and payment instructions, legal documents, and bankruptcy notices, and postal packets (notification to be given consignees of the arrival of packets containing perishable goods or marked for immediate delivery, leaving it for them to call for such within prescribed

[14] *E. B.* I, (9-12) pp. 604-605; 612-615.

post-office hours); and limitation of the opening of post offices on Sunday to two hours, preferably in the forenoon.

For telegraph, telephone and customs service, the resolutions stipulated a rest of sixty-five days per year for the staff, including thirty-nine Sundays or single days plus two vacations of thirteen consecutive days each; an international agreement permitting the sending of telegrams on Sunday only in special cases, with rates for either telegraphic or telephonic messages on that day made twice as high as on other days; and for occupiers of small offices, a salary sufficient to enable them to hire substitutes for a certain number of Sundays per year; and the adoption, for employees in general, of the principle of at least fifty-two free days annually, one-half of which fall on Sunday.

With reference to railway and merchant service, the last mentioned principle was advocated under the condition that single days of dominical rest would at least be made as numerous as possible. As a means to Sunday rest, the authorities concerned in the different countries were invited to decree the closing of freight stations except for the delivery of live animals; the limitation of the number of freight trains to the necessary minimum and their operation only in pursuance of great pressure of traffic; no obligation on the part of transportation officials to deliver shipments (the consignees being notified and privileged to call for such consignments, especially if of perishable nature); the abrogation of all claims for non-delivery of goods on Sunday; the governmental designation of holidays to be reckoned in lieu of Sundays; the discontinuance of labor pertaining to workshops, street repairs, the construction of large tunnels, and other building operations, except in cases of emergency; the extension of the benefits of holidays, in so far as possible, to employees of the merchant service as well as to dock and harbor hands, even if ships are in port and suspension of their unloading is thereby necessitated.

One of the resolutions also called for Sunday rest in the army and navy to the degree that circumstances would permit, parades being scheduled for other days.

The Conference did not wish to be understood as limiting in any degree the general obligation of Sunday rest, although it dealt with the subject from the industrial standpoint particularly; but instead of thereby implying that its observance was to be made co-terminous with the limits of industry or manual labor merely, it rather emphasized that such rest constituted an obligation co-extensive with every class and order of society; at the same time, it did not fail to recognize that beyond this obligation were duties within which justifiable exceptions fell; to illustrate: in some instances Sunday rest might be impossible where weekly rest would be possible; *e.g.*, on Saturday; in such case, next to the obligation of providing Sunday rest would come the duty of providing for weekly Saturday rest, which, while constituting an exception to the principle of dominical rest, would nevertheless be the next best thing to it, if not equally salutary; it was frankly recognized, however, that circumstances were bound to exist which would preclude any solution of this character, and would thus make necessary the invention of other equivalents of hebdomadal rest.

Third International Congress on the Cultivation of Rice. Pavia, Oct. 27-29, 1906.

At Pavia, Italy, at almost the same time, the Third International Congress on the Cultivation of Rice included in its resolutions the decision that joint committees representing capital and labor were necessary for the settlement of inevitable industrial conflicts. [15]

Second International Peace Conference at The Hague, August, 1907

In the course of the following year, the Portuguese Delegation at the Second International Peace Conference at The Hague proposed to replace Article Sixteen of the Hague Conventions with a new Article, by which, among other things, disputes with respect to the interpretation or application of international labor agreements would in all cases be subject to compulsory arbitration as a last resort; in other words, such agreements would be

[15] *E. B.* I, (9-12) p. 604.

outside the purview of that section (Section 16A, of proposed article replacing Article 16) which in reality made each nation the final judge of what it would submit to arbitration, and which read as follows: ". . . it is the exclusive function of each contracting power to determine whether any difference which has arisen affects their essential interests or their independence and accordingly, whether such dispute is of such a nature that it is excluded from arbitration." [16] The proposal of the Delegation was not adopted.

As long as nations reserve the right on every question to determine whether or not it so affects their national interest or honor as to preclude its arbitration, the way is clear for them to find in every dispute elements that waive the obligation of arbitration; for there can be no difference of opinion important enough to make arbitration desirable that cannot be construed by one of the parties as a menace to its national interests or independence if it has the inclination to do so.[17] But unlike disputations in the realms of politics, labor contentions are not apt to be of a character intrinsically involving fine points of national honor. An agreement between nations to submit, when all other peaceable attempts fail, differences arising out of labor conventions to compulsory arbitration, would certainly be a notable step in advance. The arbitration would be rendered compulsory by the species of the agreement in dispute. Should an award of a tribunal on such a question be found to consign a nation to extinction, is it not reasonable to suppose that the victim would still find just as great opportunity to undertake means for self-preservation as would have been the case had it not submitted the matter to arbitration in the first place?

Fifth Delegates' Meeting. Lucerne, Sept. 28-30, 1908.

The Fifth Delegates' Meeting of the International Association for Labor Legislation was held at Lucerne. Its discussions continued and enlarged upon those of the previous meeting. The fact

---

[16] *E. B.* II, (3), p. 428. (See Scott. *The Hague Peace Conferences,* I, pp. 337, 349, 385.

[17] See J. B. Moore, "The Peace Problem," *The Columbia Univerrity Quarterly,* Vol. XVIII, No. 3, June, 1916, pp. 222-223.

that its deliberations dwelt upon the prohibition of the night-work of young persons and the limitation of the day-work of women is significant since these principles were in a few years (1913) to form the basis of outlines for new international conventions. A new topic specifically introduced was that of recommending and defining an eight-hour shift for workmen in coal mines. The succeeding assembly in 1910 dealt with the same matter and defined the length of such a shift as extending from the time when the first man left the surface to descend into the mine until the time when the first man completed his return to the surface at the conclusion of a day's work.

The resolutions drawn up at the previous meeting in 1906 on home-work were reaffirmed. The wretched conditions environing that work were attributed chiefly to the insufficient wages paid, and it was decided to study the question of the organization of committees on minimum wages or wages boards to solve the difficulty. The question of international negotiations with reference to the regulation of labor in the embroidery trade was also considered, as were the problems of suppressing the use of lead paint in interior finish and restricting the employment of lead glazes in the ceramic industry. Other matters that were discussed included the protection of workers in polygraphic trades and in caissons, the preparation of the list of industrial poisons, and the treatment of foreigners in case of accident. The resolutions on these subjects, on that of child labor and other topics, were confirmed in subsequent assemblies, whose resolutions summed up all of importance included in those of this assembly, added thereto and conduced to more practical results.

Between the years 1907-1909, the international movement seemed to lag. In the year 1906 it had reached a high-water mark, but thereafter practical results failed to follow in as rapid succession. Even the English Bulletin of the International Labor Office seemed to shrink. Signatories of the Bern Conventions were tardy in ratifying them. No important labor treaty was signed in the year 1908. By 1910 however, it had become evident that the Bern Conventions were going to be a success; and all phases of the movement received a vigorous treatment at the Sixth Delegates' Meeting held at Lugano in that year.

INTERNATIONAL LABOR CONFERENCES

Sixth Delegates' Meeting. Lugano, Sept. 26-28, 1910.

Sixteen sections and thirteen States were represented, making an attendance of about one hundred and twenty persons. The delegates of the American Section were Dr. and Mrs. John B. Andrews, Prof. Farnam, Dr. L. K. Frankel, and Dr. Helen L. Sumner. Commissioner Charles P. Neill represented the Federal Government. From Canada there was present Hon. W. L. Mackenzie King, Minister of Labor.

The constitutions of two new sections in Sweden and Norway respectively were approved.

The usual procedure of separating into committees for the consideration of special topics was followed. The discussion of subjects introduced in former assemblies, related in part to industrial poisons, home work, the maximum workday, the principle of the equal treatment of foreigners and citizens in respect of social insurance, the methods of administering labor law, and child labor. Detailed codes regulating the hygienic conditions of work in ceramic industries, printing shops and type foundries and in caisson work, were adopted, together with resolutions advocating wage boards regulative of home work and similar to these provided by the British Act of 1910. The trade of machine-made embroidery where carried on as a home industry, received special attention in matters pertaining to the regulation of working hours. The most important steps taken related to measures for incorporating into international conventions the prohibition of night-work of young persons and a universal ten-hour standard by which to delimit their day work as well as that of women. A Conference to this end met in 1913. The American section was urged not to abate its efforts among the various states to bring about the passage of health and accident insurance laws without the discrimination against alien workers that had unfortunately occurred in several States. The International Office presented proofsheets of its first comparative report on measures adopted in European countries to enforce labor law. As for statutes on child labor, a commission was appointed to prepare a report on the comparative methods of executing the same in the several countries.

Topics newly introduced for consideration included labor holidays, the protection of railway employees and the prevention of accidents, and co-operation with the International Association on Unemployment and the Permanent Committee on Social Insurance. The question of the reduction of the usual twelve-hour day in continuous processes was made a subject for special investigation. At the next Delegates' Meeting in 1912, recommendations on the matter were precise and definite as the result of a conference that had been held shortly before (June, 1912) in London by the commission appointed to investigate the subject. Mr. John Fitch was the American delegate at that conference.

Inasmuch as divers operate in foreign waters and on ships of foreign nations, their trade also was deemed a proper one for international regulation. Investigation of this possibility was provided for; but up to the time of the next meeting (1912), little progress had been made in the matter.

The national sections were to press the prohibition of the use of lead paint and colors in interior work. One consequence of this was that later the Swiss Federal Council was invited to issue a decree prohibiting the use of lead colors in such work, and also the regulation that in commerce all such colors should be plainly marked, "poisonous, containing lead." [18] The Council was further recommended to consider, in any regulations issued for the prevention of occupational diseases, the principles drawn up by the Association for the regulation of hygienic conditions in the ceramic industry, type foundries, printing works and work in caissons. While the Association had not thought that caisson work was a vocation sufficiently affected by international competition to render it a proper subject for international agreement, it had nevertheless drawn up a series of regulations on the subject, of which it urged the adoption by individual States. The Council's reply was slightly tart, though not ungracious. It characterized efforts of this nature as meriting full recognition, and conducive to steady improvement of conditions in general; but it declared that international rivalry in the domain of the several measures recommended, was hardly important enough to give rise to international conventions. Then it reviewed various

[18] *E. B.* VI, (2) pp. 217-219.

Swiss regulations in prevention of occupational diseases, not ignoring defects but at the same time making obvious the marked improvement of conditions in Switzerland, and observing a trifle sarcastically mayhap, that the more unfavorable conditions in other countries were hardly to be considered a fair criterion of the situation in Switzerland. The Council tersely affirmed that sufficient evidence had not as yet been adduced to prove the necessity of abolishing the use of lead colors.

Seventh Delegates' Meeting. Zurich, Sept. 10-12, 1912.

The resolutions of the Seventh Delegates' Meeting at Zurich covered twenty-eight topics. Among the first of these was an expression of welcome to a section newly founded in Finland, and approval of its constitution. The Bureau of the Association was instructed to co-operate with the two International Associations on Unemployment and Social Insurance respectively, and with the Bureau of the International Home Work Congress in promoting social reform. It is interesting to note that within September of this year the four International Associations convened at Zurich within a short time of one another and thus gave rise to what was known as "social week," (Sept. 6-12). Thanks were tendered by the Seventh Delegates' Meeting to the Spanish Government for having prohibited the night-work of women; also, to the Swiss Department of Industry for its intention to recommend to the Swiss Federal Council the convocation of a second international conference on labor legislation (which met in 1913); to the Federal Government of the United States for prohibiting the importation and exportation of poisonous phosphorus matches and imposing a prohibitive tax; to the Government of Mexico for similar action; to the Governments of New Zealand and the Union of South Africa for adhering to the Bern Convention prohibiting the use of white phosphorus in the manufacture of matches; to the Hungarian Government for the enactment of the same prohibition; and to the authors of the official list of industrial poisons, so long (since 1904) the object of earnest desire, now completed and published in English, French, Italian, and Finnish. Plans were made for the appointment by the various governments of an international commission of statistical experts to elaborate the principle to be followed by the States in issuing their statistics and reports on labor legislation so as to make possible the publication every four years of a comparative report on the administration of labor law. The introduction in all industrial countries of the principle of the Saturday half-holiday, as a prerequisite to real Sunday rest, received emphatic endorsement. The delegates desired that for women workers and young persons it should be made the subjct of an international convention, and the subcommission collaborating on the principle of the maximum ten-hour workday, was instructed to consider this proposition as well and to report at the next associational meeting.

Progress in the suppression of the use of lead colors in painting and interior decorating, resulting from the legislative action of several States, was noted with satisfaction. Further investigation of plumbism, especially in the polygraphic and ceramic industries, was contemplated with a view to its suppression, and to the conclusion, in the case of the ceramic business, of an international convention restricting the use of lead. The widespread recognition, in legislation on social insurance, of the principle of the equality of aliens and citizens, so faithfully advocated by previous conferences and now adopted by the legislation of many lands, including states of the American Union, and in many treaties, also proved very gratifying. Other principles favored in this connection were: the reduction of rates of insurance paid to foreigners as against that paid to citizens in proportion only to the State's contributions to the insurance fund; and ultimately the preclusion of all necessity for such discrimination by the conclusion of international treaties; the settlement of the claims of insured parties, whether principals or assigns,[19] whose residence is outside the country of insurance, by the payment of a lump sum or by the transfer of the capital value of the annuity to an institution of the recipient's domicile; and the insurance of foreigners even in case of only temporary sojourn within the country. As at the last conference, the American section was urged to press its exertions in securing in the various

[19] In this volume the term "assign" is used to connote the "dependents," "survivors" or "parties entitled" of an insuree.

states of the Union suitable insurance laws against sickness and accident, not discriminating against foreign labor.

Further modes of procedure were defined in detail to subserve many other desirable ends among which may be mentioned: the eight-hour shift in continuous industry and the realization of the same, especially in steel works, through an international convention; the limitation, by the same means, of work in glass factories to fifty-six hours per week on an average; investigations relative to a hygienic working day in dangerous and unhealthy trades; the better protection of the interests of railroad employees, dock workers, miners, tunnel constructors, quarrymen, *etc.*, on an international basis; the abolition of the custom of exacting fines through deductions in wages as well as of the system of paying in kind or through tickets convertible at the employer's store, commonly known as "trucking"; the establishment of the principle of the refund of compulsory contributions made to pension or thrift funds, in case of the laborer's withdrawal from the engagement that entitled to such benefits; the alleviation, especially through effective administration of minimum rates by wage boards, of the unsatisfactory lot of the home worker; the suppression among workers of ankylostomiasis, anthrax, and mercurial poisoning; proper precautions in handling ferrosilicon; the study of the best methods of compiling morbidity and mortality statistics in different countries so as to arrive at a basis upon which to publish uniform international statistics of mortality by trades; the regulation of home work in the manufacture of Swiss embroidery and the suppression of evils resulting from the invention and continuous operation of automatic embroidery machines in factories of Germany, Austria, Switzerland, France, the United States, Italy, and Russia. These machines had been more widely put into operation since the last Delegates' Meeting and had injected a new factor into the embroidery problem.

Of the above, the subjects newly introduced as separate topics in the Association's program were: the Saturday half-holiday; the protection of dock workers; the truck system and deductions from wages; international statistics of morbidity and mortality among working classes; the handling of ferrosilicon; and the international prevention of anthrax amongst industrial workers and of mercurial poisoning in fur-cutting and hat-making.

The next Meeting of the Association was scheduled for Bern in 1914, a meeting which failed to anticipate the war and which, it is therefore not surprising to remark, was never held.

Conference of Bern. Sept. 13, 1913.

A special Conference at Bern preparatory to the creation of a new series of international conventions, held session in the fall of 1913. These draft conventions were never approved due to the war.* The deliberations of the meeting receive attention in the following chapter, entitled, "Conventions Signed at Bern."

*At the first general meeting of the International High Commission of Pan American States, held at Buenos Aires, April 3-12, 1916, one of the topics discussed was that of internatonal agreements on uniform labor legislation. See *House Document* No. 1788, pp. 5-6, 23-24, 64th *Congress, 2nd Session. Report of the International High Commission.*

See Appendix II, Exhibit 25.

MEMBERSHIP

NATIONAL SECTIONS OF THE INTERNATIONAL ASSOCIATION

(Publication of the Association, No. 8, p. 127)

	Section	1901	1902	1904	1906	1908	1910	1912
1.	German	673	980	1,331	1,635	1,695	1,727	1,586*
2.	Austrian	182	252	251	294	247	242	230
3.	Belgian	66	74	77	78	78	72	72
4.	Danish				97	147	143	140
5.	Spanish				66	103	99	154
6.	American				140	272	1,000	2,500
7.	Finnish							111
8.	French	113	134	290	450	466	515	570
9.	British				67	117	205	298
10.	Hungarian	70	332	335	241	192	201	233
11.	Italian	71	80	80	120	120	172	104
12.	Norwegian						81	146
13.	Dutch	175	178	183	193	200	163	161
14.	Swedish						170	173
15.	Swiss	238	243	476	444	596	573	507
	Direct Members	20	45	57	27	27	31	26
	Total	1,608	2,318	3,080	3,852	4,260	5,394	7,011

* The membership of the German Section was calculated on a different basis for 1912 and is therefore not comparable with earlier years.

CHAPTER IV

Pro et Contra.

Objections.

The movement for the international protection of labor has had its full share of detractors. It is enlightening as well as fair to consider the full weight of the objections they raise.

To Regulate Relations Between Capital and Labor is not Within the Province of the State.

On 10th May, 1881, the Swiss Federal Council proposed to several European States that negotiations be undertaken for the creation of international legislation on factories. France replied that it was not within the province of the State to interfere with contracts between employers and employees, either nationally or internationally, unless possibly in cases of extreme necessity.*

Opposition of Employers.

Employers find in factory restrictions favoring labor many distasteful features. In world markets they are obliged to compete with goods produced by the cheap labor of industry that is unhampered by restrictive labor law. If forced to limit production, as a result of the non-employment of women at night, or by reducing the length of the workday, *etc.*, they fall behind in the industrial race; their business, in which they have invested their capital and maybe the best part of their lives, suffers depression or fails, while the laborers themselves suffer by being deprived of their means of subsistence.

Opposition of Laborers.

Thus the laboring class may see in international regulation a menace to its own prosperity. Even as philanthropic and well-disposed a person as Dr. Franck,** who thought himself in favor of the international movement, recognized the unwisdom of

* See p. 19.
** See p. 20.

unduly limiting the work of women and children, who should be permitted to help the family lay in store against the rainy day of hard times. And yet the first international convention signed at Bern strikes at the right of women to engage in night-work, and pending conventions look toward the ultimate limitation of their day-work. It has been said that laborers prefer to live badly than not at all; but the extension of prohibitions such as the above is cutting the ground of livelihood from right under their feet. When workers prefer to increase the family income and insure better standards of living by extra work, is it not shortsighted and unkind procedure to deny them the privilege?

Differences in Laboring Peoples.

Moreover, is it to be expected that a rule applicable to alert workmen of the temperate zone will be equally applicable to more sluggish and easy-going laborers of the torrid zone? Are industries in Ceylon to undergo the same regulations as industries in Iceland, as international regulation would seem to predicate? Do not children of one land mature much less quickly than those of another, and may not laws suitable in one case be wholly inapplicable in the other? Measures adapted to protect one laboring population may be a menace if applied to the folk of another clime.

Dissimilarity in Geographic Environment.

Climate is of itself a well-nigh insurmountable obstacle to any uniform regulation of industry such as is postulated by the international protective movement. Why, for instance, should night-work be prohibited to women in tropical countries where the only cool period in twenty-four hours extends from sunset to sunrise? Each country must be left to draw up those regulations best adapted to its geographic conditions without trying to adhere to any uniform statutes decreed for all countries of the world alike. Differences in soil, mineral resources, supplies of water and fuel, seasonal changes with their effect on goods handled, and natural conditions in general make for such dissimilarity in manufacturing processes as to defy the realization of uniformity in labor regulation.

Differing Systems of Labor Legislation.

Different States have by a long and slow process of evolution built up systems of labor legislation and administration adapted to their peculiarities of situation, geographic, social, and economic. Is it reasonable to expect a State to overthrow or supersede such a system by the adoption of some international code which may be quite suitable to some other country or group of countries, but is wholly unadapted to its own industrial organization? Some countries, for example the United States, have not in the past seemed to favor uniformity in their own internal administration of labor law; if this remains the case, how much more incongruous is the attempt at uniformity on an international scale?

Constitutional Dissimilitude.

Differing constitutional systems also doom the attempt at international protection of labor to ultimate failure. Labor legislation that is possible under an autocratic rule may be quite impossible under a democratic rule. Moreover, States belonging to the same category according to the classifications of political science may have very diverse methods of administering labor legislation. Adhesion to the Bern Convention prohibiting nightwork for women may present no particular difficulty to the Federal Government of Switzerland; but how is the Federal Government of the United States to become party to that convention and remain loyal to the principle of leaving the regulation of intra-state industry to the legislatures of the individual states of the Union?

But waiving the constitutional difficulties, a country with large capital and well established industry may find itself able to submit to limitations imposed by protective labor law that will spell absolute ruin to the industry of a nation with little capital, or to the infant industry of a young industrial nation. In the weaker country, are not the laboring people to be allowed, by excessive hours of work, to compensate national deficiency of fiscal resources, or lack of industrial longevity? If the less favored country becomes subject to a regulation such as that of the Bern Convention on white phosphorus, it may be forced to substitute a more expensive substance; and consequently, to make up for the extra cost of production, it may be obliged to increase the hours of labor, or if that is forbidden, to require faster and more exhausting work per hour, from which the employees will suffer more than if there had been no so-called protective measure. If the burden is not thus shifted to the laborer, the employer must lose, until possibly the industry ceases to pay and is allowed to disappear to the detriment of every class concerned. Thus do different circumstances conditioning production in the several countries of the globe militate against the advisability of international agreements making for unformity in the protecton of labor.

Difficulties of Enforcing the Law

But even if countries do go through the formalities of signing and ratifying labor agreements, who is to superintend or guarantee their faithful execution? The difficulties which immediately arise over the question of a sanction became only too evident at the Diplomatic Conference of Bern in 1906.* Imagine the harmonious co-operation of an industrial commission of Englishmen, Germans, Italians and Austrians, charged with supervising the enforcement of law in various countries! How could such a commission avoid the transgression of national sovereignty? If the enforcement is left to each State, who is to know whether they will enforce the law or not? What assurance is there that the large State will not yield to the temptation of intermeddling with the affairs of the small State under pretext of checking delinquences on the part of the latter in the observance of its pledges?

Contradictory Interpretations.

For an example of the differences of opinion that may arise in interpreting a treaty, note the quibble raised by certain co-signatories to the Convention prohibiting the use of white phosphorus over the question as to whether the importation of sample matches containing that substance was forbidden.**

* See p. 122.
** See p. 131.

Source of Friction and War

Thus differences in interpretation, laxity in execution, mutual jealousy and suspicion, would constitute an interminable source of friction which might even induce war. Such possibilities constitute their own commentary upon the desirability of international protective labor agreements. . . . And thus the indictment of the objector is closed.

If these difficulties seem to loom so large upon the horizon of possibilities now, how doubly immense must they have seemed to the early proponents of the movement, who had no international labor conventions to which to point as proof positive of the possibility of their existence and the success of their operation. But certain arguments of the objector are already out of date. Such certainly is the asseveration that it is not within the province of the State to intervene between capital and labor in the regulation of industry. Indeed, intervention has been found absolutely necessary and salutary by every great industrial nation of the world.

That employers have found fault with such intervention in many instances is true, but their objecting has been much more strenuous in the national domain of regulation than in the international; and so much the more have they been subjected to State control by the most efficient industrial nations of the world. Germany was an example of such efficiency before the war. Those who are familiar with the history of industry know that employers, under the urge of competition and in devotion to their own profits, have been careless of the rights of labor, and to that degree has the field of industry in which they might exercise their own free will been constantly narrowed by the hands of government. It may be human nature for employers to object, but that is far from proving that it is wise or humane to heed their faultfinding. However innumerable their objections may have been, it is safe to say, as will be demonstrated hereafter, that from the standpoint of pure self-interest, employers will find more to favor in the international control of labor than to object to in national regulation. It is needless to add that unnumbered directors of industry are heartily in favor of protective labor law for the sake of industry as well as of labor.

As for the opposition of labor to protective measures, it is almost non-existent. For half a century labor has been a propelling force behind the protective movement. It believes in "protection from dangerous machinery and occupational diseases; the abolition of child labor; the regulation of the hours of labor for women as shall safeguard the physical and moral health of the community; suppression of the sweating system; reduction of the hours of labor to the lowest practicable point, and that degree of leisure for all which is the condition of the highest life; a release from employment one day in seven; a living wage as the minimum in every industry, and the highest wage that each industry can afford; suitable provision for the old age of workers and for those incapacitated by injury in industry";* "the lifting of the crushing burdens of the poor, and the reduction of the hardships and the upholding of the dignity of labor." The mass of labor is not to be hoodwinked into turning traitor to its own interests. The resolutions (Appendix II) of international congresses representative of labor of all parts of the world are sufficient proof of this.

Wherein International Labor Conventions Have Solved Difficulties Presented by Differences in Race, Geographical Conditions, Constitutional Systems, Labor Legislation, Relative Strength of States, etc.

A false assumption of the opponents of the movement seems to be that international regulation presupposes absolute uniformity of regulation. But this is not true. It makes for uniformity in all cases lending themselves to uniformity; it makes for legitimate exceptions in all other cases. A short answer to the list of objections cited above is that, in spite of all difficulties, international labor conventions have been applied and applied suc-

* Resolutions of Religious Organizations cited in the *Supplement* to *The Typographical Journal*, Oct. 1911, pp. 23-30.

cessfully to peoples differing in race, geographical environment, government, financial resources, and labor legislation. These conventions have encountered practically all the ubiquitous obstacles which the antagonists of the movement have carried in their brief cases for forty years; and only a study of each convention's provisions will reveal why it has survived.

Consider the Bern Convention aiming at the prohibition of night-work for women. It has conduced to the repeal of old or passage of new law among the leading powers of the world, to say nothing of dependencies; and has wrought reform and made for uniformity that never before existed. But we have been told that while this may be well and good for Europe, how unconscionably brutal would be its application to the females of central Africa whom perforce it would compel to labor in the heat of the day rather than the cool of night! But this is not the case. Should the night or some portion of the night be found to be the more healthful time for toil upon the equator, the Convention distinctly leaves a way open whereby that can be allowed; provided, of course, compensatory rest is accorded during the day (See Art. VII).* Thus does it prove that desirable uniformity in the matter of guaranteeing rest during the night, or its equivalent, and dissimilarity of geographic conditions are not incompatible yokefellows. Its adherents now reach from the tropical islands of Fijii and Ceylon to Norway in the longitude of Iceland. Moreover, for slow and sluggish populations or native works that cannot be practically or rightfully subjected to its regulations, ample considerations are provided since a power in notifying the adhesion of a colony may make necessary reservations (Art. VI-VII). For industries in every country demanding special treatment, due exceptions are made, as well as for emergencies or necessities in every industry (Art. III, IV, VIII). The Convention is so constructed as to be reasonably adaptable to every clime and all conditions, and yet to secure the desirable aspects of the reform aimed at.

Differences in government or industrial organization have not presented any impassable barrier. The Bern Conventions have been applied by autocracies, monarchies, and republics with all

*Appendix I, Exhibit 3.

sorts of differing labor law. The relation of the United States is peculiar. After the Convention banning white phosphorus had been adhered to by other leading industrial nations, the American Congress was constrained to introduce prohibitions which were practically equivalent. Hindered by constitutional practises, we attempt to follow a worthy example as best we can; but to continue so to follow, if America prefers the less honorable (but by no means dishonorable) course of following rather than leading, some changes in the theory and practise of American labor administration must occur. The movement presents a problem to America much more than America presents a problem to the movement.

But again we are told that through this movement the weak State may be forced to lock arms with industrial ruin. Is it of no significance that one of the smallest of industrial States has been the leader of the cause? Small countries, weaker financially and industrially than their more powerful contemporaries, have not found in the Bern Conventions any short cut to industrial suicide. Whether small or great, old or young, a country's powers of endurance in the industrial race are guaranteed by the conservation of its labor force even to the third and fourth generation. Real patriotism looks beyond the present moment. The legacy of a healthy ancestry constitutes the moral right of posterity. Protection of labor is essential to national perpetuity plus industrial vitality. Experience has proved that healthy workmen produce more and better goods in a shorter workday than unhealthy workmen in a longer day. In other words, conservation of human resources pays capital as well as labor. But should protective law mean an inevitable loss, both small and large States can much better afford to let capital foot a temporary loss in dollars and cents than to let labor pay the price by the exhaustion and degeneration of its women and children. If, however, a young or weak industrial nation is convinced that immediate adhesion spells ruin, it may await the firmer establishment of its institutions without arousing suspicion; but the large or old industrial State that refuses to adhere may with greater reason be suspected of contemplating temporary profits by taking a discreditable advantage in the world market.

As for the assumption that international labor law will not be enforced if enacted, facts again belie the ill prediction. So far as time has permitted, such law has been enforced with very slight friction or laxity. The war constituted an unavoidable interruption, but no valid argument against the cause. Even had the war led to the denunciation of all the labor conventions or treaties ever ratified, they had lived long enough to propagate their kind. By the international dissemination of relevant facts about the labor situation, by encouraging the comparative study of protective law, and by stimulating to progress in legislation along such lines, the International Association for Labor Legislation with its Bulletins, Office, and national sections, had proved to partake of the elements of a very effective sanction for the law in question. Unlike the Permanent Court at The Hague, it possessed an organization that lacked the official title of permanence but supplied the fact instead. Constantly and uninterruptedly it strove for the realization of the principles for the sake of which it was created.

Thus, however formidable certain objections to the movement may seem, no one of them is insurmountable; and in a vast majority of cases we can leave them to encompass their own undoing by mere self-exinanition. The fact, however, that a man is killed is no proof that his opponent ought to live, although the slaying of an argument does tend to create a presumption in favor of the side that slays. What has been said is by way of refutation; it remains to adduce constructive argument to establish the desirability of the means adopted to protect labor on an international basis.

For the sake of definiteness, we limit the proposition as follows: Resolved, That international conventions constitute the best method of securing certain desirable regulations protective of labor.

I. In the first place, the affirmative of this proposition has been proved by two international Conventions.

A. No sane person familiar with the disease of necrosis of the jawbone, popularly known as "phossy jaw," will deny the indisputable desirability of its prevention. Before the enactment of the Bern Conventions, "phossy jaw" was a prevalent and practicably ineradicable disease directly attributable to the use of white (yellow)phosphorus in the manufacture of matches. It was ineradicable because industry insisted upon the employment of white phosphorus on account of its cheapness, and government gave its sanction in order that national industry might compete successfully with other industrial nations that used the substance, among which were Great Britain, the United States, Hungary, Norway, Italy, *etc.* Although approximately half a dozen States had passed some kind of law prohibiting or restricting the use of the substance, other attempts to eliminate it had failed. But when the possibility of international prohibition was broached, industry and governments gave respectful attention, and co-operated for the elimination of the plague. So powerful did the movement become when made international, in marked contrast to its feebleness nationally, that even the United States, although not a signatory to the Convention, nevertheless took effective steps to abolish the poison. These achievements alone fully vindicate the movement and prove our proposition.

B. The Bern Convention prohibiting the night-work of women worked reform salutary and likewise international in scope. The various national measures taken to limit and prohibit such work constitute their own proof of the widely recognized desirability of such protection. The unprecedented success with which the reform met when it was expressed in the terms of an international convention, is again convincing proof that this is the best method which has ever been discovered to procure the most effective application of certain regulations in protection of labor. In proof of the assertion we cite the history of the case presented in Chapters III (Part I) and I (Part II), and also the arguments as given by the International Labor Office. (App. II, Exhibit 24).

II. In the second place, there still exists a need for protective labor laws which can be most effectively realized only through international co-operation; *e. g.,* laws establishing the principle of release from employment one day in seven, concerning reciprocity of treatment of foreign workers with respect to insurance agreements, concerning the migration or recruitment of alien labor, protecting employees from contracting diseases through handling materials such as white lead, *etc.* For brevity's sake, we will confine ourselves to the desirability of an international convention realizing to a greater extent than heretofore the last of the above-mentioned reforms, which, once established, is again sufficient to prove our proposition.

A. The attempts of nations to prevent industrial disease is proof of a widespread desire for such reform. To verify the statement, there need only be reviewed the labor legislation of England, France, Germany, Italy, and other countries and the recommendations of the Washington Conference of 1919. The mass of facts which have led to the general recognition of the desirability of laws of this character for the sake of the physical welfare of workers, we believe it to be unnecessary to marshal here.

B. The fact that the Washington Conference of the International Labor Organization of the League of Nations drew up recommendations upon this subject with a view to effect being given them by national legislation or otherwise, goes to prove, aside from the fact of the deeply felt need of such legislation, that nations believe international co-operation to be the best and most effective means by which to consummate such reforms. There are various grounds which show their belief to be a sound one.

1. Governments swayed by national self-interest are not prone to expose their industries to the hazard of falling behind in the competition of international markets through the imposition of restrictive laws which competing nations do not adopt.

2. Employers are less willing to risk an increase in the cost of production by the adoption of protective law when it means either a loss of profits or an increase of their commodity's selling price, which may lose for them their relative position in markets captured by business of other countries not subject to equally stringent labor law. Capital may forsake and ruin industry so handicapped.

3. Governments and employers become willing to submit to the restrictions of labor law to whose mutual adoption all competing nations have agreed; for such concurrent action tends to leave the industry of each country in the same relative position in world markets as existed before the law was imposed. Viewed from the standpoint of national industrial prestige and employers' interests, international protective law has a distinguishing advantage over national labor law.

4. Protective laws tend to allay the discontent of labor, there-

by preventing strikes disastrous to industry, national prosperity, and often to the laborers themselves. Indeed international conventions are deemed by many to constitute one of the most effective remedies for civil strife between capital and labor.

5. Moreover, limitation of output by international agreement is an antidote for overproduction and the evils which reaction brings in its train; *i. e.*, the closing of shops, unemployment, paralysis of trade, and in consequence a national crisis.

III. In the third place international law for labor benefits all parties concerned.

A. *The laborer.* If it did not benefit labor it would not be protective. The elimination of "phossy jaw" is a practical illustration in point.

B. *The employer.* Protection means a healthier working force, which, as experience has proved, can produce more and better goods in shorter time, tending thus to compensate for any increased cost of production that protective law may involve. The supply of labor for the future is conserved instead of destroyed or enfeebled, while the menace of strikes is diminished. These among other things, the employer stands to gain without sacrificing his relative position in the world market as has been shown.

C. *The nation.* Industry that thrives and labor that is prosperous will supply to a nation the wherewithals of general prosperity, especially if that nation is "rooted and grounded" in industry.

D. *The world.* In proportion as nations progress or fail to progress in the fine art of co-operation, especially if it be for the welfare of humanity, in that proportion will they hasten or retard the dawn of universal peace. International engagements for the regulation of labor predicate such co-operation, and are therefore directly to the interest and advancement of world-wide peace. This is what Mr. Sarrien of the French cabinet had in mind in 1906 when he spoke in endorsement of the movement.*
Failure to enact international law may become a direct menace to every party above mentioned by tending to discourage protective law in well-disposed nations where it now exists, and reviving international competition in exploitation of women and degeneration of children.

* See p. 118.

IV. As a fourth and final point, we may advert to the fact that experience has proved the entire practicability of the kind of law advocated. If any doubter presumes still to demand evidence in support of this assertion, we invite him to recapitulate the facts we endeavored to set forth in the rebuttal that preceded this brief outline of a constructive argument, then to reread the documents signed at Bern and their subsequent history, and finally to make thorough use of the Bibliography.

CHAPTER V.

THE RELATION OF AMERICA.

In 1910 three things stood out distinctly in the general regulation of labor conditions in Europe:

(1) A clear recognition by governments of the need of protection for industrial populations;

(2) A definite and well organized attempt on the part of governments to meet that need;

(3) International co-operation to supplement national shortcomings.

I. Now imagine forty-eight competing industrial countries in that same year, many of them great and powerful, but fully a generation behind Europe in initiating the protective laws needed by their working classes, where, as followers of the vocation averred, four workmen were killed in mining accidents to every miner fatally injured in Europe;[1] where the horrors of "phossy jaw" were allowed to spread in the midst of working men and women without statutes to eliminate the use of the poisonous phosphorus that caused the disease; where methods used in the making of storage batteries and lead products were far more dangerous, and unnecessarily so, than those used in England or Europe; where the same was true of painting trades when they were compared with the same occupations in England, France, Germany, and the Low Countries;[2] where only twenty-eight of the forty-eight states in question had laws to conserve the health or comfort of factory employees, and only twenty-one provided any protection against dangerous machinery;[3] where not a single one had any adequate regulation for factory illumination in its

---

[1] This and many following facts are taken from statements of various contributors to the *American Labor Legislation Review*. Vols. I-VII. If in any case their statements do not hold good for the year 1910, they do for this approximate period. See *American Labor Legislation Review*, Vol. I, (1) p. 44.
[2] *Ibid*, I, (1) pp. 21-22.
[3] *Ibid*, I, (2) pp. 1-2.

vital relation to the health of the workmen[4]; where only one had a real factory ventilation law[5]; where not a single legislative body had passed a law compelling the effective removal of poisonous gases, fumes and vapors by well defined mechanical appliances[6]; and where no physicians were required by state law to report occupational diseases[7].

Lest the indictment become monotonous, we pause; but it is essential for the sake of comparison that we still add to it some important facts. The night-work of women and children seemed to be steadily increasing[8]; only three States of the forty-eight had any workmen's compensation laws[9]; none had any state insurance against sickness, old age and invalidity, death, or unemployment, and that in the light of the extensive social insurance systems of Europe!

The annual social and economic cost of employees' sickness was estimated at over $770,000,000 while the estimated cases of disease totalled over 13,000,000 causing the loss of over 280,000,000 days of productive work.[10] Preventable ill health was reckoned to entail for the nation an economic waste of at least 193 million dollars each year.[11] The world's record for pre-eminence in the slaying and mangling of men, women, and children in industry was not infrequently conceded to the said territories, whose fatal accidents were variously numbered at from 15,000 to 57,500 *per annum*.[12] It was further calculated that the workmen injured during the same period would be sufficiently numerous to populate a city half the size of greater New York.[13] According to conservative estimates, 4,500,000 employees were regularly engaged in seven-day labor at the same time that Sunday rest, or compensatory rest, prevailed under national law in Italy and France, and the same principle of compensatory rest was embodied in law in various parts of the world, including Argentina,

[4] *Ibid.*, I, (2) pp. 114-115.
[5] *Ibid.*, I, (2) p. 118.
[6] *Ibid.*, I, (2) p. 122.
[7] *Ibid.*, I, (4) p. 107.
[8] *Ibid.*, I, (4) p. 141.
[9] *Ibid.*, I, (1) p. 55.
[10] *Ibid.*, I, (1) p. 127.
[11] *Ibid.*, I, (1) p. 127.
[12] *Ibid.*, IV, (4) p. 562.
[13] *Ibid.*, III, (1) p. 67.

Austria, Bosnia, Herzegovina, Belgium, British India, Canada, Cape of Good Hope, Chili, Denmark, France, Germany, Italy, Portugal, Roumania, Spain, *etc.*[14] Such were forty-eight industrial societies in 1910, inflicting upon employers and employees human and fiscal losses of the character described, and recognized before the bar of world opinion as at least one generation behind the times in any adequate governmental recognition of responsibility for the health and welfare of 33,500,000 workers.

But let us be careful to heed the injunction "to judge not that ye be not judged." Possibly these countries were unenlightened lands? Whatever their standing and however much certain facts in their case may have been unwittingly exaggerated by those who attempted to ascertain the true condition of affairs (many of the calculations are known to be understated), the situation was certainly, to put it mildly, an unfavorable one.

II. But waiving the appalling need in the forty-eight states, let us examine what their governments actually had accomplished by 1910, in the way of protecting labor. To cope with conditions such as theirs, we should expect to find these peoples ardently at work; firstly, gathering vital statistics upon which to base successfully legislation, as have their European contemporaries; secondly, developing the science of precise and appropriate labor law; and thirdly, employing an efficient inspectorate in conjunction with a carefully wrought-out scheme for enforcing the law. What then are the facts in regard to the first premise?

We find that for any considerable amount of the valuable statistics we are seeking, we must look elsewhere than to the reports of their factory inspectors. We know very well that this would not be the case were we investigating similar reports in England, Germany, France, Austria, or Belgium.[15] We discover that if a statistician seeks to evolve order from the chaos of their information on industrial casualties, he must command superhuman powers and find relief in the fact that only fourteen of the states require any systematic reporting of accidents at all.[16] Nevertheless, we should not despair, but look further. For their

[14] *Ibid.,* III, (1) pp. 55-57.
[15] *Ibid.,* I, (1) p. 35.
[16] *Ibid.,* I, (2) p. 2; IV, (4) pp. 563-564.

statistics on occupational maladies, which must form the basis of all intelligent legislation against industrial disease, we will investigate the reports of their physicians. Alas, we recall that not one of the forty-eight require any such reports! Such unthinkable laxity would be beyond all comprehension in the enlightened communities of Europe; for Europe, we must remember, prefers to do her killing in quite another way. And shall we add, that if like Europe these states were to preserve the health of their people in order that the world might witness a more splendid spectacle in the arena of battle, we doubt the ultimate progress that would be made after all?

But shall we hazard further inquiry? Have not the states at least a modern treatise on occupational diseases by a native authority on industrial hygiene? No, not one.[17] And yet England possesses the monumental work of Thomas Oliver on that subject and, since 1855, has been compiling valuable official reports and statistics relating to the health of the English industrial, as compared with which anything that the forty-eight states, individually or collectively, can produce is of humiliating insignificance. But Germany, Austria, and other continental countries, if anything, surpass England in this respect. Dr. Theodore Weyl is the foremost German authority. In 1905 the German Imperial Parliament voted about $80,000 for the analysis of certain mortality and sickness statistics, which authorities recognized as indispensable to the intelligent safeguarding of the nation's health, but with which the famous forty-eight, consistent with their record, had nothing to compare; for, if they had amassed all that they possessed upon the topic of industrial disease, its paucity would have become painfully evident in comparison with the wealth of European information on the subject.

Having thus discovered that by 1910, they had next to nothing upon which to build respectable labor law, it is with considerable misgiving that we approach the investigation of our second premise; *viz.*, the labor statutes that they did possess. The character and extent of legislation they did not possess must have been suggested by facts already stated; and it does not allay our apprehension any to discover that their legislators sometimes

[17] *Ibid.*, I, (1) pp. 129-137.

deemed themselves quite equal to the task of drafting protective labor law over.night. Need it be a cause for surprise if the chief statistician of the New York State Department of Labor, Mr. Leonard W. Hatch, found that the legislatures of these commonwealths managed to produce factory laws which had "not passed beyond a fairly primitive stage."[18] And in view of these facts, would it be strange if yonder in Central Europe some self-righteous pharisee had piously murmured: "By their fruits ye shall know them"? Moreover, some of these legislators discovered that it was much easier to copy a labor law than to create a labor law, and they acted according to the light they had.

Among the defects that may be pointed out in respect of this legislation were: (1) too great generality and vagueness in reference to the provisions to be applied and the establishments involved; (2) great rigidity of detail regarding a few specific processes but lack of definiteness as to the industries' contemplated; (3) a narrow range of application when the intent was perfectly clear. It is therefore obvious that the enforcement of many of the laws depended entirely upon the advent of a very extraordinary inspection corps.

This brings us to the third premise, which concerns the mechanism of their law-enforcing institutions. After careful inquiry we find that in 1910, of these forty-eight industrial States, exactly three had a factory inspection force whose members were obliged to pass a civil service examination to become eligible.[19] In Prussia, we are told, the prospective inspectors pursued three years of technical study including such subjects as mechanics and chemistry, beside one and one-half years of work upon economics and public law. In addition to this, they passed two examinations in a German university. We have, since 1910, been forcibly reminded of the fact that Prussia has the failing of going to extremes. There is a "golden mean", and to err on one side may be just as bad as to go astray on the other. But to return to our subject, the appropriations of the forty-eight States for inspection were in a vast number of cases entirely inadequate, while unsuitable and antiquated methods akin to the "spoils system" were too frequently employed in the appointment of the offi-

[18] *Ibid.*, I, (2) p. 106.
[19] *Ibid.*, I, (1) p. 13.

cials in charge. One great state with more than 70,000 workers had one factory inspector; fourteen others had none whatever for industry employing nearly one-half million people. For an area of over three million square miles and possessed of 7,000,000 employees, there were to be found among the states approximately 425 inspectors. It is said, on reliable authority, that probably in no one state were standards of inspection so high as in England, France, Prussia, Saxony, Russia, Holland, Spain, Finland, Hungary, or Norway. The annual report of the chief factory inspector in one of the great commonwealths constituted exactly fourteen words (July 1, 1911): "I have visited the same factories as last year and find conditions the same."[20]

Such was their efficiency in the enforcement of industrial law. In the hope of discovering a definite and satisfactory attempt to meet labor's need of protection, we have weighed these states three times; firstly, as to their progress in the collection of necessary statistics; secondly, as to the character of their labor laws; and thirdly, as to their enforcement of those laws; and in each instance they have been found wanting.

Furthermore, in addition to, and as a partial explanation of, their great lack, the courts of many of these states held to principles of the common law and constitutional interpretations whereby important protective law was held actually illegal. In adherence to the principle of "freedom of contract," they refused to sanction many such interferences of the state between employers and employees as were necessary to establish **compensation laws, social insurance, limitation of the hours of labor,** *etc.,* preferring to remain in that stage of economic thought which was voiced by France in 1881.[21] If an employee who had become the victim of an accident, wished to obtain redress, he was obliged to sue under a judicial system that seemed to be biased in favor of employers by three widely accepted doctrines: (1) The fellow-servant doctrine, by which it devolved upon the claimant to prove that his injury was not due to any fault of a fellow employee; (2) the doctrine of the assumption of risk, which is to say that an employee by accepting the contract to work, had assumed the

[20] *Ibid.,* III, (1) pp. 23-28.
[21] See p. 20.

risk incident to the business; (3) and the doctrine of contributory negligence to the effect that carelessness of the employee contributory to an accident constituted a defense for the employer. These judge-made doctrines became so palpably unfair that the 80's saw in England the origin of an important movement, whose influence was later felt in the United States, in favor of employers' liability laws to counteract injustices of the system and to make employers liable for damages in cases of accident that they might have prevented.[22] These laws made it possible for the worker to recover damages when he could prove that negligence on the part of his employer was responsible for the accident that gave rise to the injury. The common law theory of liability was not abandoned and the employer was not made liable for accidents due to risks concealed in the business rather than to any fault or negligence. The laws, however, have involved much litigation and have never been deemed a satisfactory solution of the problem.

III. Our next inquiry is with reference to the co-operation of these states in supplementing by mutual agreement their individual shortcomings. They are adjacent one to the other. Evils and losses incident to competition unrestricted by mutual agreement are theirs, and have fallen upon employers as well as upon employees. This is evident from facts already stated. Practically all of the arguments that were found to vindicate international labor law as between the countries of Europe and other parts of the world (Chapter IV) are found to hold equally good, and in most cases doubly so, for these forty-eight states. Diversity of conditions of production among them are great, but not as great as obtains between many of the other countries referred to. Furthermore, the advantages derived from national adhesion to international labor conventions should accrue in equal, if not in greater measure, to a similar industrial co-operation between these states. Producers who suffer an annual loss of millions of dollars partly because of the inadequate protection of labor,[23] ought to realize that this is not good business. When Europe made that discovery, she acted upon it. The working populations

[22] *Amer. Lab. Leg. Rev.*, I, (1) p. 57.
[23] See p. 80.

of these states are shifting constantly from one to the other and give rise to a large percentage of the problems that the nations of Europe, in view of a similar migration of their inhabitants, have found it expedient to solve through treaties.

To what extent then can these states be expected to bring about uniformity of labor law? They form a federal union and have a central government. May not their national Congress enact labor laws applicable to all states? Seemingly not, because the national Constitution may be so interpreted as to prohibit federal control of intra-state industry. By Article I, Section 8, "The Congress shall have power to regulate commerce with foreign nations and among the several states," authority over interstate commerce is delegated to the federal government, but upon the principle that powers not so delegated are reserved to the states, intra-state industry remains a subject for state legislation. Consequently, it may be held that the federal government ought not to ratify a treaty such as the Bern Convention prohibiting night-work for women since its enforcement would involve undue interference with intra-state industry. The same constitutional system prevents the states from entering into international agreements and prohibits them from forming compacts between themselves without the consent of Congress.

These constitutional difficulties, together with a traditional adherence to the *laissez-faire* principle in economic life, obstructed interstate, national and international co-operation for the attainment of uniform labor legislation.

Such were forty-eight industrial countries in 1910, which separately failed to provide proper protection for their working people, and which collectively seemed to favor an interpretation of their constitutional system that not only prohibited their federal government from introducing the protection needed, but also precluded it from becoming party to international guarantees of protection for the laboring peoples of the world* and these forty-

*According to Article VI, Section 2, of the Constitution of the United States, "all treaties made... under the authority of the United States shall be the supreme law of the land." Under this clause it would be possible for the Supreme Court to uphold the provisions of labor treaties even if they involved the national regulation of phases of intra-state industry. This would be a severe limitation of the doctrine of "state rights."

eight states in 1910 constituted the same people who, as the self-avowed defenders of humanity, were in 1918 justly and proudly pouring out their treasure and their blood to rescue from impending disaster the civilization of the world—THE UNITED STATES OF AMERICA.

In the interval between 1910 and 1918 had there been an awakening of public conscience to a greater sense of social responsibility? Such an awakening had occurred, and, in spite of interruptions, it has continued to increase up to the present time. Among factors responsible for this were the progressivism of Theodore Roosevelt and the social philosophy of Woodrow Wilson. Many of the forces contributing to this movement had been set in motion long prior to 1910. Among the evidences of progress were the activities to increase the protection accorded to America's industrial population.

As early as 1902 the International Association for Labor Legislation attempted to bring about the formation of an American branch. This purpose was achieved by the formation of the American Association for Labor Legislation in 1905 and the formal adoption of its Constitution on February 15, 1906.[24] The Association established its headquarters at Albany, N. Y., later moved to Madison, Wisconsin, and finally located at 131 East 23d St., New York City. Its membership grew from twenty-one to over three thousand. Its secretaries have been Dr. Adna F. Weber, Professor John R. Commons, and Dr. John B. Andrews who has held the office since 1909.

This organization exerted an important influence in the field of labor legislation in America. It promoted the compilation of valuable statistics, the passage and enforcement of labor laws, and increased conformity to uniform standards. This necessitated extensive research and the publication of a vast amount of literature. Its official bulletin, published since 1911, is, *The American Labor Legislation Review.*

It formed standing Committees and Subcommittees upon Industrial Hygiene (1908); Brass Poisoning, Nomenclature of Occupations, Workmen's Compensation, Woman's Work (1909);

---

[24] For its Constitution, see App. II, Exh. 23.

Standard Schedules and Tabulations, Enforcement of Labor Law, One Day of Rest in Seven (1911). In 1913 the Committee on Workmen's Compensation was merged with a Committee on Social Insurance. The Association caused the convocation of National Conferences On Industrial Diseases (1910 and 1912), Preventing and Reporting of Industrial Injuries (1911), Social Insurance (1913), Unemployment (1914 and 1915). Also, it sent representatives abroad to international congresses on occupational diseases, unemployment, social insurance, *etc.* Efficiency and uniformity in labor legislation were promoted through the scientific drafting of standard labor laws which the Association presented to state legislatures for approval and adoption. The Legislative Drafting Research Fund of Columbia University cooperated with the Association in this work. An example of this work was the bill protecting tunnel and caisson workers which New Jersey enacted into law in 1914.[25] Another standard bill for the protection of industrial workers from regular seven-day employment was adopted by New York State and Massachusetts in 1913.[26]

In 1910 a memorial was presented to the President of the United States urging the importance of a national investigation of the subject of occupational diseases.[27] The Federal Bureau of Labor extended its operations in the field of industrial hygiene and commenced continuous research with respect to occupational poisons. A campaign to cause the states to require the reporting of occupational diseases was undertaken by the Association with the result that within five years fifteen states had introduced regulations for this purpose, nine of them adopting the standard reporting blank recommended.[28] Within three years a standard form for the reporting of accidents was so widely adopted as to apply to one-half of the factory employees of the United States.

By 1910 no state had succeeded in establishing a permanent workmen's compensation act; the first permanent statute went into effect in New Jersey in 1911. Earlier laws on the subject

[25] *Am. Lab. Leg.* Rev., IV, (4) p. 528.
[26] *Ibid.*, IV, (4) p. 614.
[27] *Ibid.*, I, (1) pp. 125-143.
[28] *Ibid.*, IV, (4) p. 525.

were declared unconstitutional. But before the close of 1915, workmen's compensation laws had been passed by thirty-three legislatures,[29] besides various other social insurance measures such as mothers' pensions enacted into law in fifteen states by 1913[30] and old-age pensions introduced into Alaska and Utah by 1915.[31]

Through the efforts of Professor John R. Commons, the Association had a direct part in the establishment of the single state industrial commission, a plan for administering labor laws which Wisconsin was the first to adopt in 1911.[32] This centralized the administration of accident prevention and compensation laws. The commission issued the rules and committee orders necessary for the proper application and enforcement of the statute law. Other states followed Wisconsin's example.

A complete study of the efforts that led to the noteworthy progress in protective labor legislation in the United States between the years of 1910 and 1918 would have to include not only the work of The American Association for Labor Legislation and of allied social-welfare societies, but also that of labor organizations, among the foremost of which is the American Federation of Labor. Under the leadership of the president, Samuel Gompers, the American Federation of Labor became one of the powerful institutions in American public life. Had it not been for the potent influence of this organization compelling nation-wide attention to the rights and needs of American labor, the American Association for Labor Legislation would have found its task a far more difficult and less successful one. Although we do not attempt to present here the record of the American Federation of Labor, or of other labor organizations, it is not our wish to deny to them one iota of credit due them for their great work of safeguarding the interests of the working people.

That which perhaps constituted the greatest achievement of the American Association from the standpoint of uniform national labor law was the passage of the Esch-Hughes Bill in Congress, April 9, 1912, levying a prohibitive tax on matches containing

---

[29] *Ibid.*, V, (4) p. 637.
[30] *Ibid.*, III, (2) p. 149.
[31] *Ibid.*, V, (4) p. 637.
[32] *Ibid.*, I, (4) pp. 61-69; III, (1) pp. 9-14, 39; III, (4) pp. 473-478.

white phosphorus and prohibiting their exportation or importation. This was the result of a campaign waged by the Association for several years. It is interesting to note that just as nations hesitate to place themselves through advanced social legislation at a disadvantage with competing industrial nations, so have states refused to adopt progressive measures because of their fear of the competition of industries in other states. This was illustrated by the New York State compensation law of 1910 which was limited to industries not affected by interstate competition.[33] For one state to have prohibited the use of white phosphorus in the match industry while other states permitted its use might not only have injured its own manufacturers but have led some of them to move their factories into states with less severe laws.

But when through the exercise of the taxing power the federal government found a way of securing the abolition of the use of white phosphorus in all states, objection became inconsequential. How far would the reform have progressed if it had been left to the individual action of each state? We know this: had there been attained in this particular that which has not been accomplished in respect of any single state labor law; *viz.*, uniformity through the passage of the same law by all the states, the ever possible revocation of the law by one or more legislatures would render the uniformity attained forty-eight times more uncertain than it is at the present time under federal enactment. However, the attempt of the federal government further to extend this use of its taxing power as a means of bringing about social reform proved ineffectual. Congress passed a law in 1919 levying a tax upon all establishments that employed children between fourteen and sixteen at night or more than eight hours a day, but in 1922 the Supreme Court declared this law to be unconstitutional.

America in Relation to World Leadership and Social Legislation

By 1919 it had become evident that the world expected the United States to occupy a new position of leadership in international affairs. At the Peace Conference of Paris American states-

[33] *Ibid.*, I, (1) p. 60.

men played a most important part in shaping the future destinies of mankind. But, in conformity with traditional policies of avoiding what might prove to be entangling alliances, the United States did not ratify the Treaty of Versailles or join the League of Nations. Effort was concentrated upon the return to normalcy and improvement of domestic conditions.

The subsequent era of prosperity deprived social reform of the impetus which depression later developed. The more favorable position which organized labor had attained during the war was lost in large measure in this post-war period. Antiradical feeling and employers' opposition to unionism, as evidenced in the open-shop drive, weakened organized labor. Company unions, sharing of profits through bonuses and employee ownership of stock, various kinds of welfare work, higher nominal wages, and the belief that a new economic era had dawned promising permanent and increasing prosperity—all tended to lull the masses into a feeling of security and contentment. Some progress, however, was made in labor legislation. By 1932 forty-four states had adopted workmen's compensation. Seventeen had systems of old-age pensions of which nine were state-wide and compulsory. Wisconsin had enacted the first state law on unemployment insurance. This law provided for an unemployment reserve fund by requiring the employer to set aside reserves for the protection of his employees for a limited time while involuntarily deprived of work. In 1933 Massachusetts established a Commission on Interstate Compacts for the purpose of meeting similar commissions of other states in an effort to promote uniformity of legislation concerning labor conditions through an interstate compact. Such compacts have been made between states for the purpose of constructing bridges, regulating water rights, and settling boundary disputes. Their more extensive use in the interests of social legislation, subject to Congressional approval,* has been advocated on various occasions in the past. It remains to be seen to what extent this device can or will be used to achieve uniform labor laws.

*Article I, Section 10, of the Constitution of the United States gives this permission in a negative way: "No State shall, without the consent of Congress....enter into any agreement or compact with another State."

THE NEW DEAL AND LABOR

The New Deal has become a means of illustrating the processes described by James Bryce when he said of America:

> The American form of government will go on and live long after most other forms of government have fallen or been changed and the reason is this: In other nations when a new problem comes up it must be tested in a national laboratory, and a solution of the problem must be worked out, and when it is worked out that solution must be applied to the nation as a whole. Sometimes it may be the correct solution and other times it may be the wrong solution. But you in the United States have forty-eight laboratories and when new problems arise you can work out forty-eight different solutions to meet the problem. Out of these forty-eight experimental laboratories some of the solutions may prove unsound or unacceptable, but out of this experimentation history shows you have found at least some remedies which can be made so successful that they will become national in their application.

Many of the principles which the New Deal involves have been tried in one way or another in other countries or in limited areas in this country. The basic principle of government control to meet a crisis is not a new or novel one; it seems new because it has been a control exercised by the national government in spheres that heretofore have been left exclusively to regulation by state authorities. In no field has this assumption of unusual authority at Washington been more strikingly illustrated than in that of industry and labor; in fact, it is this centralized control over an area that includes the entire nation that constitutes the essentially new feature about the New Deal in its relations with labor. The public acceptance of this sudden centralization of power in matters pertaining to our economic life must be attributed to the severity and length of the depression and the widespread belief that the measures undertaken are of remedial and temporary nature.

Under the National Industrial Recovery Act child labor was widely banned although two previous acts of Congress directed to this end had been declared unconstitutional and a proposed amendment to the Constitution for the elimination of this evil had failed to obtain the ratification of a sufficient number of states. By federal authority agencies were set up for the enforcement of industrial and labor agreements, the investigation of all causes of complaint, and the mediation of disputes that might arise.

Officials of the National Recovery Administration went so far in their efforts to discourage strikes as to arouse fear at one time on the part of organized labor that compulsory arbitration might be the ultimate result. Under the anti-trust laws in the past, employers have been denied the right of combination for the purpose of fixing prices and limiting output in restraint of competition, but under the N.R.A. codes wider privileges in these respects were granted and the anti-trust laws were held in abeyance so that employers might be encouraged to co-operate through code agreements and trade associations for the regulation and revival of business.

Formerly even state laws have been declared unconstitutional when they limited hours of work or established minimum wages for men, but the federal government assumed the power to introduce such regulations when they seemed desirable as means of reducing unemployment and increasing purchasing power. Previously unions were left to their own devices in their attempts to force collective bargaining upon employers, but under the New Deal labor was given the right to demand that employers meet labor's representatives in reaching agreements and it was further declared that workers had the right to join unions of their own choice. These are a few of the instances of the extension of federal authority over matters formerly either left to the jurisdiction of the states or not regulated by law at all. Whatever the ultimate effect of the New Deal may be, the national government has established precedents for dealing with labor problems on a national scale that would have been considered impossible only a few years ago.

The United States and the International Labor Organization

Further evidence of a new interest on the part of the federal government in the affairs of labor is the fact that in 1933 the United States sent official delegates for the first time to a meeting of the International Labor Organization. The occasion of this meeting was the Seventeenth Session of the International Labor Conference. These delegates recommended that the United States become a member of this Organization. An American delegation also attended the Session of the Conference in 1934, and, in June of this year, President Roosevelt was granted authority to accept membership in the International Labor Organization on behalf of the United States by a Joint Resolution which received the unanimous approval of the Senate and more than a two-thirds majority in the House of Representatives. On August 20, 1934, the President exercised this authority by which the United States accepted membership in the International Labor Organization. This action involves fuller participation and more direct co-operation on the part of the United States in the international labor movement.

CHAPTER VI.

The Movement in Perspective

In the first important stage of the movement for international labor legislation between 1880 and 1890, greatest unanimity of opinion obtained in support of five propositions often repeated in the various resolutions of the period. These propositions called for the establishment by international agreement of:

(1) *Fourteen years as the minimum age for the admission of children into industry.*—This principle was incorporated in a draft convention approved at the First Session of the International Labor Conference in Washington in 1919 and subsequently ratified by twenty-six countries by 1934. The Second Session in 1920 adopted a convention fixing fourteen as the minimum age for the admission of children to employment at sea and twenty-eight states have ratified this. The Third Session in 1921 submitted a convention applying this principle (with the exception of work outside school hours) to children employed in agriculture, which has been adopted by seventeen countries. Another convention approved at the same session declared that young persons under the age of eighteen shall not be employed on vessels as trimmers or stokers and this has been ratified by twenty-eight countries. A convention adopted by the Sixteenth Session in 1932 fixed fourteen as the minimum age for the admission of children to non-industrial employment. This convention is in process of being ratified by members of the International Labor Organization.

(2) *A maximum workday.*—Between 1880 and 1890 opinion was about equally divided as to whether this should be an eight-hour day or a ten-hour day. The eight-hour day has been fixed as the standard workday by draft conventions of the International Labor Organization, of which, one, adopted in 1919, applied to industrial undertakings and by 1934 received the ratification of sixteen countries and the conditional ratification of four others.

Another convention of this group applied to hours of work in commerce and offices. It was drafted in 1930 and had been ratified unconditionally by five states and conditionally by one by the fall of 1934. In 1931 a draft convention limited hours of work in coal mines to seven hours and forty-five minutes in the day, and in 1934 a convention applying to automatic sheet-glass works limited hours to an average of forty-two per week and a spell of work to eight hours.

(3) *Weekly rest.*—At the Third Session in 1921 this principle was made the subject of a convention applying to industrial establishments. It provided that the working staff should enjoy in every seven days a period of rest comprising at least twenty-four consecutive hours. Twenty-four countries have registered their ratifications.

(4) *Prohibition of the night-work of women and young persons.*—The Bern Convention of 1906 forbidding the employment of women in industry at night had been ratified by twelve governments and eleven colonies before the outbreak of the World War. A new convention was drafted at Washington in 1919 and was ratified by thirty states. A revision of this convention occurred at the Eighteenth Session of the International Labor Conference in 1934. In 1925 night-work in bakeries was forbidden by a convention applying to both sexes and to proprietors as well as workers. Ten states have ratified it. Prohibition of the night-work of young persons employed in industry was the subject of a draft convention approved at Washington in 1919. It has been ratified by thirty states.

(5) *Protection of the worker against the dangers of his occupation.*—Between 1880 and 1890 occupational hazards were referred to in general terms. They were analyzed and more specifically attacked in the proposals of the next period (1890-1920).

In the period extending from 1890 to 1920, ten other principles became prominent topics for consideration by the advocates of international labor legislation:

(1) *International exchange of facts relating to labor legisla-*

tion and the administration of labor laws.—It has become a well established practise for governments to exchange data of this nature. The International Labor Office is a clearing house for the collection and distribution of information. Each member of the International Labor Organization agrees to make an annual report to this Office concerning the measures that it has taken in order to make effective the conventions which have been ratified. At least once in ten years (sometimes once in five years) the Governing Body presents to the General Conference a report on the working of each convention. The conventions often specify the information which is to be submitted to the International Labor Office.

(2) *Protection against phosphorus poisoning.*—The Bern Convention of 1906 prohibited the use of white phosphorus in the manufacture of matches. At the First Session in Washington, the General Conference of the International Labor Organization recommended that each member adhere to this Bern Convention. By the spring of 1934 thirty-one members had ratified it. A revised draft convention concerning workmen's compensation for occupational diseases, adopted at the Eighteenth Session in 1934, specified phosphorus poisoning as a disease for which compensation shall be paid to incapacitated workmen.

(3) *Protection against lead poisoning.*—A draft convention for the protection of workers against the dangers of white lead in painting was adopted by the General Conference at its Third Session in 1921. This has been ratified by twenty-two states and conditionally ratified by one other country. The Seventh Session in 1925 adopted a convention providing compensation for workmen incapacitated by occupational diseases which included lead poisoning.

(4) *Protection against other occupational poisons and diseases.* —The convention last referred to also applied to cases of mercury poisoning and anthrax infection. It was ratified by twenty-eight countries. At the Eighteenth Session this convention was revised so as to include other occupational poisons and diseases.

(5) *Establishment of the principle of the equal treatment of foreigners and citizens with respect to the social insurance (par-*

ticularly accident insurance) laws of each country.—This principle was applied in a series of bipartite treaties on accident insurance between European countries prior to the war, and it formed the subject of the draft convention of 1925 on equality of treatment for national and foreign workers as regards workmen's compensation for accidents. This convention has been ratified by thirty-three states. The principle was also stated in the draft convention of 1919 on unemployment in a clause concerning unemployment insurance, and again in the draft convention on unemployment allowances adopted at the Eighteenth Session in 1934. Subject to certain conditions, it was further applied in the six draft conventions on invalidity, old-age, and orphans' and widows' insurance for industrial and agricultural workers adopted at the Seventeenth Session of the General Conference in 1933.

(6) *Systematic inspection and regulation of home work.*— This is a field which involves many difficulties from the standpoint of international control. No convention on this specific problem has as yet been adopted. Some phases of home work have received incidental regulation in certain conventions such as those fixing the minimum age for the admission of children into employment and providing that such work as is permitted shall not prejudice their attendance at school. In the convention of 1928 concerning the creation of minimum wage fixing machinery, it was stipulated that each ratifying member should undertake to establish or maintain such machinery for workers in certain trades, and in particular in home working trades, where wages are low and conditions of work are not effectively regulated by collective agreement.

(7) *Limitation of day-work of women and young persons.*— A draft convention adopted at Bern in 1913 provided a maximum ten-hour workday for young persons under sixteen and women without distinction of age employed in industry. The war prevented its ratification. New industrial standards and subsequent conventions concerning the maximum workday and the age for the admission of children into industry have rendered the revival of this type of convention unnecessary.

(8) *Problem of unemployment.*—At its first meeting in Wash-

ington the General Conference approved a draft convention outlining measures for the prevention and decrease of unemployment. This has been ratified by thirty states. At the next session a draft convention was drawn up to provide unemployment indemnity for seamen in case of shipwreck. This has been ratified by twenty-one countries. Another convention, the purpose of which was to provide facilities for finding employment for seamen, has been ratified by twenty-three states. At its Seventeenth Session the Conference adopted a convention providing for the eventual abolition of private or fee-charging employment agencies and at the following session it approved a convention ensuring benefit or allowances to the involuntarily unemployed.

(9) *Employment of women before and after childbirth.*—This was the subject of a draft convention approved at the Washington Conference in 1919. It has been ratified by sixteen members of the International Labor Organization.

(10) *Protection for seamen.*—Special sessions have been held by the International Labor Conference to deal exclusively with the problems relating to seamen. At the Conference of Genoa in 1920 three draft conventions were approved dealing respectively with: (1) the minimum age for the admission of children to employment at sea (2) unemployment indemnity in case of shipwreck (3) employment for seamen. These conventions have been mentioned above in the sections relating to minimum age and unemployment. Although the Third Session in 1921 was not one of the special conferences devoted to maritime matters, it approved a convention requiring medical examination of children and young persons employed at sea. Twenty-six countries have ratified this convention. The Ninth Session in 1926 was a conference on maritime problems. It formulated two conventions on the respective subjects of seamen's articles of agreement and repatriation of seamen. By 1934 the one convention had been ratified by eighteen countries and the other by sixteen. At the Twelfth Session in 1929 measures that were adopted for the prevention of industrial accidents included a draft convention requiring the marking of the weight on heavy packages transported by vessels and a convention for the protection of workers employed in loading and unloading

ships. The former has been ratified by twenty-five states and conditionally by two others; the latter was ratified by only four states, but at the Sixteenth Session in 1932, this convention was revised, and, by the fall of 1934, it had been accepted in its new form by four states.

Since 1920 the draft conventions of the International Labor Organization have covered the following subjects in addition to those already mentioned:

(1) *Rights of association for agricultural workers.*—The convention on this subject, adopted at the Third Session in 1921, undertook to secure for these workers the same rights of association and combination as are enjoyed by industrial workers. Twenty-seven states have ratified this.

(2) *Prohibition of night-work in bakeries.*—A convention on this subject was drafted at the Seventh Session in 1925. It has been ratified by ten countries.

(3) *Inspection of immigrants on board ship.*—A convention aiming to simplify and make uniform this procedure for the better protection of immigrants was adopted at the Eighth Session in 1926. It has been ratified by sixteen states and conditionally ratified by three other states.

(4) *Means for fixing minimum wages.*—The Eleventh Session in 1928 dealt with this problem in a draft convention providing for the creation and maintenance of machinery whereby minimum rates of wages can be fixed for workers in trades paying exceptionally low wages and having no arrangements for the effective regulation of wages. This has been ratified by sixteen countries.

(5) *Protection of forced or compulsory labor.*—A convention, adopted at the Fourteenth Session in 1930, undertook to furnish protection for workers of this category and to bring about the suppression of this kind of labor within the shortest possible period. Sixteen states ratified this convention by 1934.

(6) *Social insurance.*—Conventions of the International Labor Organization now cover workmen's compensation for accidents and diseases, sickness insurance, invalidity insurance, old-age pensions, widows' and orphans' insurance, and unemployment insur-

ance. At the Third Session in 1921 a draft convention was approved which specified that each ratifying state should undertake "to extend to all agricultural wage-earners its laws and regulations which provide for the compensation of workers for personal injury by accident." This has been ratified by nineteen countries. At the Seventh Session in 1925 a draft convention was approved to secure compensation for workmen who suffered injury due to an industrial accident. This has been ratified by sixteen states. At the same session the draft convention on equality of treatment for national and foreign workers who are victims of such accidents was approved and also a draft convention providing compensation for workers incapacitated by industrial diseases. The latter was ratified by twenty-eight countries. It was revised at the Eighteenth Session. At the Tenth Session in 1927 there were prepared two conventions providing compulsory sickness insurance for workers in industry and agriculture respectively. These have been ratified by sixteen states in the one instance and eleven in the other. At the Seventeeth Session in 1933 there were drawn up three conventions providing respectively invalidity, old-age, and orphans' and widows' insurance for industrial and commercial workers and three other conventions providing corresponding kinds of insurance for agricultural workers. These six conventions included the principle, subject to certain conditions, of equality of treatment of nationals and foreigners with respect to the insurance benefits. Unemployment benefit was the subject of a draft convention submitted by the Eighteenth Session in 1934. It also stipulated: "Foreigners shall be entitled to benefit and allowances upon the same conditions as nationals—provided that any Member may withhold from the nationals of any Member or State not bound by this Convention equality of treatment with its own nationals in respect of payments from funds to which the claimant has not contributed."

Three steps essential to the bringing of international labor law into successful operation are:

(1) Collection and tabulation of statistics and information prerequisite to the drafting of scientific labor laws;

(2) Comparative study of the theory and practise of national law in order to derive therefrom suitable international laws;

(3) Effective organization in order to secure the drafting, adoption and enforcement of international labor law.

In 1869 Massachusetts organized the first official labor bureau in the world for the systematic study of labor conditions and the compilation of statistics for presentation to a legislative body. Similar bureaus were established by other states and among their functions was included that of factory inspection and general supervision of the enforcement of labor law.

In 1884 the United States Bureau of Labor was established under the Department of Commerce. This was the first permanent bureau of labor statistics created by a national government.* Later (1888) an independent department known as the Department of Labor was organized with a commissioner as chief and therefore not of a rank that would entitle him to a place in the Cabinet. In 1903 the Department of Labor was transformed into the Bureau of Labor under the newly created Department of Commerce and Labor. For ten years the interests of workers and employers were represented by the same executive department, until, by Act of Congress, in 1913, a separate Department of Labor was established with representation in the President's Cabinet.

An English office for labor statistics was created in 1886, but the official British Bureau of Labor was not organized until 1893.

In 1896 Belgium established a labor bureau as the outgrowth of an office which was originally under the Department of Agriculture and Industry, and later under the separate Department of Labor.

A bureau of labor statistics was established in Austria in 1908, in Italy and Sweden in 1902, in Norway in 1903. In Spain the Department of the Interior included a labor bureau (1894). In 1903 the Institute of Social Reform set up (1) a Section of

*Bulletin of the Bureau of Labor. No. 54, Sept. 1904, Washington, pp. 1023-1086.
First Annual Report of the Secretary of Labor, 1913, Washington, pp. 8-9.

Statistics (2) a Section of Publications (3) a Section of Inspection.

The French Superior Council of Commerce and Industry was formed in 1881, having consultative power, and, after 1894, it collaborated with a permanent Consultative Commission. The French Labor Office was established in 1891. It had two separate departments, the one for field service and the other for making written inquiries and tabulating all statistics of the Office. In 1900 this was transformed into the Department of Labor with three bureaus; viz., (1) Bureau of Labor and General Statistics (2) Inspection of Labor (3) Trades Organizations and Councils of *Prudhommes*.

Denmark formed a general statistical bureau in 1895, and Holland, in 1899. Other offices partaking of the nature of labor bureaus were organized in New South Wales (1892), New Zealand (1891), Canada (1900), and Ontario (1900).

The countries of Europe have furnished the most instructive examples for the study of national labor legislation. After Germany's introduction of compulsory social insurance in the 80's, the question of state insurance became one of general interest to European nations, and in order to make possible an exchange of views and experimental knowledge on the subject the First International Congress on Accidents to Labor and Workmen's Insurance was convened at Paris in 1889 at the time of the Paris Exposition. A series of biennial congresses followed under the auspices of a permanent committee which was formed at that time and out of which developed the International Association on Social Insurance (Permanent Committee on Social Insurance) having its principal office at Paris. Its quarterly bulletins and the reports of its proceedings covered this field of social reform in a most thorough manner.

In 1912 England put into operation the first national system of compulsory insurance against unemployment. For a number of years previous to this, Norway and Denmark had national laws regulating voluntary insurance of this type, while voluntary unemployment insurance by workmen's societies with public subsidy but without public regulation existed by 1914 in Luxemburg,

France, Holland, Belgium, Switzerland, and Italy. Switzerland had public voluntary unemployment funds. In Germany there were systems of communal unemployment insurance with subsidies for industrial societies and social organizations. The relative merits of compulsory and voluntary unemployment insurance were disputed; the voluntary method was represented by the system in vogue in Ghent and commonly known as the "Ghent System," which operated upon the principle of the subsidization by public bodies of the unemployment insurance funds of industrial unions.

The international labor movement has built upon the information furnished by national agencies and the study of national labor legislation. It has also evolved an effective organization for securing the drafting and adoption of international labor laws. There remains the question of a sanction, or that which is to induce the international observance of such laws. International law has been popularly conceived as possessing but an inchoate sanction at best. The solution of this problem, which has been deemed a principal difficulty in most international movements, has constituted one of the most interesting and hopeful features of the international labor movement. The social reformers and public-spirited men who were leaders in this movement recognized two principles:

(1) Public opinion is the fundamental sanction of international agreements;

(2) That sanction can be made effective only by an efficient organization through which the public will can express itself.

Although socialists and trade-unionists at their international meetings frequently declared themselves in favor of international labor legislation, they did not furnish any organization through which the public actually secured the adoption of such legislation. The agitation of socialists for international action to achieve the political aims of socialism and the efforts of unionists to obtain legislation favorable to themselves among different nations supplied what may be termed the background of the movement to protect labor by international laws. A few governments, notably that of Switzerland, exerted a great influence in favor of such legislation; but the organization which proved to be the most effective channel for the expression of public opinion and the most efficient agent in obtaining the official adoption of international labor laws before the war was the private association known as the International Association for Labor Legislation. The means by which it brought about the adoption and enforcement of international labor legislation included the activities of its International Labor Office functioning continuously in the endeavor to keep men of affairs and the appropriate institutions in every part of the world in touch with important statutes, opinions and events, which had any direct bearing upon the aims of the international labor movement. Action with reference to these events and aims was secured through the national sections of the Association in various countries and through international meetings. The Association gained its ends largely by bringing pressure to bear upon public officials and governments. Although the national sections worked for improved conditions in the various countries, the Association recognized that the protection of labor through international laws was the ultimate goal of its efforts.

The International Association for Labor Legislation, like all human institutions, had its defects, and critics did not fail to point them out. For example, Mr. L. S. Woolf in his work *International Government* published by the Fabian Society said:

. . . . . It would not be unfair to say that within the Association the impetus comes mainly from peoples who can be discribed as "social reformers" and secondly from Labour. The capitalist and employing interest is hardly represented at all. This can best be shown by a consideration of the membership of the British Section. It will be found that the individual members are almost all social reformers, while the affiliated societies consist of nearly thirty labour organizations, nearly ten societies of which the object is some kind of social reform, and only one association of employers. The result is that at a general meeting of the International Committee you do not find the great captains of industry present or the national federations of capitalists and employers represented, and the conferences are composed of the delegates of Governments, social reformers, representatives of organized labour, and a very few of the more enlightened employers.

We shall see that this criticism concerning the representation of employers does not apply to the new International Labor Organization created by the Peace Treaty, in which capital has equal representation with labor.

The war interrupted the activities of the International Association for Labor Legislation and caused the suspension of national and international labor laws, demonstrating that protective labor institutions cannot function properly except in times of peace. The movements for the maintenance of peace and for the international protection of labor are so interdependent that any league for the peaceful control of international activities would be foredoomed to failure if it alienated a large proportion of the working classes of the earth by omitting an adequate program for the international conservation of proper labor standards.

Therefore it is not strange that one of the principal subjects covered by the Peace Treaty of 1919 is the international regulation of industrial conditions and the international protection of labor for the avowed purpose of maintaining universal peace, because, as stated in the preamble to the labor section of the Treaty, "such a peace can be established only if it is based upon social justice." The Peace Treaty consists of fifteen parts. Part I is the Covenant of the League of Nations. In Article 23 of this Covenant is a clause stating that the members of the League "will endeavor to secure and maintain fair and humane conditions of labor for men, women and children, both in their own countries and in all countries to which their commercial and industrial relations extend, and for that purpose will establish and maintain the necessary international organizations." Part XIII* of the Peace Treaty fulfills this pledge by creating a permanent official International Labor Organization. This Labor Organization consists of:

(1) A General Conference of representatives of the countries which are members:

(2) An International Labor Office controlled by a Governing Body and located at Geneva.

Thus the Treaty of Peace established instruments similar to those which the International Association for Labor Legislation had proved to be most effective for international labor regulation. The private International Labor Office has been superseded by the official International Labor Office, and the meetings called

---

*For Part XIII of the Peace Treaty, see the Supplement, p. 401. The benefits of existing social insurance are guaranteed to workers in ceded German territories by Article 312 which is not in Part XIII of the Treaty.

through the initiative of the Association have been superseded in their task of drawing up draft conventions by the official Sessions of the General Conference of the International Labor Organization.

This General Conference meets at least once every year. Every member of the Labor Organization is authorized to appoint four delegates, two of whom represent the government, while the other two represent respectively employers and employees. Thus, if each member appoints its full quota, capital and labor together have the same voting strength as the government, for each delegate votes individually. In the past, however, some members frequently have failed to appoint representatives of employers or employees. The representatives of these two groups are to be chosen by the government in agreement with the industrial organizations "which are most representative of employers or workpeoples" (Art. 389). Delegates may be accompanied by advisers who "shall not speak except on a request made by the delegate whom they accompany and by the special authorization of the President of the Conference, and may not vote" (Art. 389). Advisers are allowed to speak and vote when they act as deputies of their delegates. Decisions in the General Conference are reached by majority vote of the delegates save for five special exceptions in which a two-thirds vote is required (Articles 389, 391, 402, 405, 422).

The International Labor Office is controlled by a Governing Body consisting of thirty-two persons, eight of whom represent the governments of the nations of chief industrial importance. In case of any dispute as to which nations are of chief industrial importance, the Council of the League of Nations decides. The nations designated at the Eighteenth Session of the General Conference in June, 1934, as belonging to this class were: Belgium, France, Great Britain, Italy, Japan, Germany, Canada, and India.‡ The government delegates of the states not included among the eight governments of chief industrial importance appoint eight

‡ At the Session of the Governing Body in January, 1935, the list of eight nations of chief industrial importance was revised. The United States and Soviet Russia replaced Belgium and Canada. The United States and Russia thus acquired permanent seats on the Governing Body.

representatives to the Governing Body. The persons thus selected in June, 1934, represented Spain, China, Poland, Finland, Argentine Republic, Czechoslovakia, Brazil, and Mexico. Of the sixteen members representing governments, at least six must be representatives of non-European states. Of the remaining sixteen members of the Governing Body, eight are chosen by the delegates to the General Conference who represent employers, and eight by the delegates who represent labor. At least two delegates of each of these two groups must represent non-European states. The term of office of each member of the Governing Body is three years.* The Governing Body chooses one of its own members to act as chairman, regulates its own procedure, and determines its own times of meeting. Special meetings are held upon the written request of at least twelve of its members. The Governing Body also appoints the Director of the International Labor Office. The Director chooses the staff which must include women appointees. He acts as secretary of the Conference. Besides the collection and distribution of information, the duties of the Labor Office include preparing the agenda for meetings of the general Conference (with a view to the conclusion of international conventions), editing and publishing in French and English a periodical paper, executing the measures prescribed for the settlement of international disputes, and such other tasks as the Conference may assign. Correspondence between the government of any member and the Director is carried on through the government representative on the Governing Body, or through officials nominated by the government for this purpose. The Labor Office is "entitled to the assistance of the Secretary-General of the League of Nations in any matter in which it can be given." (Art. 398).

The General Conference may prepare draft conventions to be submitted for ratification to the members of the International Labor Organization, and it may draw up recommendations for consideration with a view to their adoption by the national legis-

*In accordance with the Standing Orders of the Governing Body each government represented on the Governing Body is entitled to appoint a deputy member of a different nationality. Also, of the employers' and workers' groups, each is entitled to eight deputy members.

latures of the members. Each member agrees, within one year if possible, and at least within eighteen months from the closing of the Conference, to submit the recommendations or draft conventions to the competent national authorities for legislative enactment or for other action. If after its best endeavors, a member fails to obtain the legislative or administrative action necessary for its adoption of a recommendation or for its adherence to a proposed convention, its obligation ceases. Moreover, in the case of a federal state, the power of which to enter into an international agreement is limited because of its constitutional system, special exception is made by which a draft convention may be treated as a recommendation only. This is of special significance to the United States which has joined the International Labor Organization with the express reservation that it assumes no obligations under the League of Nations.

If any organization of employers or workers files a complaint with the International Labor Office that any member is failing in the proper enforcement of a convention which it has ratified, the Governing Body may request the accused government to state its view of the case. If no satisfactory statement or explanation is received within a reasonable time, the Governing Body may publish the charge and such statements or replies, if any, that were made with reference to it. If the complaint is made by a member or if it originates with the Governing Body itself, the procedure just described may be followed, or the Governing Body may apply to the Secretary-General of the League for the appointment of a Commission of Enquiry. Each member agrees to nominate "three persons of industrial experience, of whom one shall be a representative of employers, one a representative of workers, and one a person of independent standing, who shall together form a panel from which the members of the Commission of Enquiry shall be drawn." The Governing Body may reject any of the nominees by a two-thirds vote. "Upon the application of the Governing Body, the Secretary-General of the League of Nations shall nominate three persons, one from each section of this panel, to constitute the Commission of Enquiry, and shall designate one of them as the President of the Commission. None of these three persons shall be a person nominated to the panel by any member directly concerned in the complaint." (Art. 412).

It is the task of the Commission of Enquiry to investigate the question at issue between the parties, to prepare a report containing its findings and recommendations, and to indicate "the measures, if any, of an economic character against a defaulting government which it considers to be appropriate, and which it considers other governments would be justified in adopting." (Art. 414). In case the recommendations of the Commission of Enquiry are not acceptable to any of the governments concerned in the complaint, the matter may be referred to the Permanent Court of International Justice, the decision of which is final. Moreover if any member fails to take proper action with reference to recommendations or draft conventions, any other member has the right to refer the matter to this Court.

"In the event of any member failing to carry out within the time specified the recommendations, if any, contained in the report of the Commission of Enquiry, or in the decision of the Permanent Court of International Justice, as the case may be, any other member may take against that member the measures of an economic character indicated in the report of the Commission or in the decision of the Court as appropriate to the case." (Art. 419).

By these provisions of the Treaty of Peace international labor legislation was accorded an official sanction. The labor section of the Treaty has been popularly called the "Labor Charter" and the "Magna Charta of Labor."*

*For a discussion of the proceedings of the International Labor Organization, see the Introduction, pp. xxxvii—

PART II

Early International Labor Legislation

CHAPTER I.

CONVENTIONS SIGNED AT BERN*

Conference of Bern. May 8-17, 1905.

IN the spring of 1905, fifteen European States assembled their representatives behind closed doors at the Conference of Bern with the object of outlining international conventions to prohibit the use of white phosphorus in the manufacture of matches and also to interdict the night-work of women. The sessions were secret, in deference to the earnest solicitation of British delegates,** and not because of any fear in this instance lest the diplomats might have in mind the perpetration of acts of which to be ashamed. It was optional with the conferees to conclude conventions on the spot, reserving of course the exchange of ratifications to their governments; or to draft, under the scrutiny and approval of technical experts, tentative agreements, leaving it to the governments to transform the same into conventions by direct negotiations; or merely to draw up non-obligatory resolutions.[1] The second of these three courses of possible action was that unanimously adopted. It is interesting to note that even Belgium, whose representative at the Conference of Berlin (1890) had protested against the aim of giving practical effect to the resolutions there formulated, emphatically acceded to the action now proposed. Although the outlines of the agreements in view were prepared with the prospect of their probable revision, it was nevertheless understood that by their signatures the delegates pledged their governments to a decision on the matter of adhesion or non-adhesion, with the presumption in favor of their adhesion to, and international execution of, the principles sub-

---

*For copies of the Conventions, see Appendices.
**Sir Malcolm Delevingne in *The Origins of the International Labor Organization,* Vol. I, p. 36, says: "the report that this was done at the request of the British Delegation was incorrect, though it was given currency in some quarters at the time..."
[1] G. B. Bd. IV, (1905) S. I.

scribed. This presumption gained additional force from the fact that many governments had deputed to the Conference officials or parliamentarians of high rank and recognized predilection for the project of regulating labor by means of treaties. Therefore in the deliberations of this body there was something more at stake than the mere discussion of the "whys and wherefores" of the international regulation of labor, or the passage of a laudable *voeu* as a grand finale of the session; it was to make the original drafts [2] of labor conventions destined not only to become law in a majority of the nations of Europe as well as in many of their colonial possessions, but also the first international conventions ever executed [3] by a number of parties, for the avowed and sole purpose of internationally protecting labor.

The Conference divided into two committees for the tasks in hand. Considerable difficulty arose with regard to the abolition of white (yellow) phosphorus from industry, due to the competing interests of the different States. Neither of the two late belligerents in the Far East, Japan and Russia, being present, the participation of either of them in the proposed measures was entirely problematical, while at the same time it was recognized that any restriction of the employment of white phosphorus, exclusive of Japan, would cause serious prejudice to the trade of England, Hungary, and Norway. An agreement, however, was finally reached, by the articles of which it would become unlawful, after Dec. 31, 1910, to import (*introduire*), manufacture, or offer for sale matches containing white or, as the Germans termed it, yellow phosphorus; provided all the countries represented at the meeting, and also Japan, should adhere and deposit their record of ratification by Dec. 31, 1907, thereby agreeing to put the Convention into actual operation three years after that date, *viz.*, on Jan. 1, 1911. But in this connection the spokesman of the committee took pains to intimate that failure in the immediate fulfillment of certain of these conditions would not necessarily preclude the Convention's ultimate realization.

The States which refused to sign the phosphorus pact were

[2] *G. B.* Bd. IV, pp. 1-2.
[3] In this volume the terms "execute" and "execution" in reference to treaties are not used to connote the act of "signing," but rather of "bringing into force."

Denmark, which observed the failure of such an attempt in certain of its possessions, and Norway, Sweden, and Great Britain. The States adhering were: Germany, Austria, Hungary, France, Spain, Belgium, Holland, Luxemburg, Italy, Portugal, and Switzerland.[4]

The agreement relative to the night-work of women did not yield to as concise and brief a statement as its contemporary. The first Article placed a sweeping interdiction upon industrial night-work for all women, debarring exceptions subjoined. The adoption of this measure presaged the advent of radical reform in legislation among many of the countries. Spain prohibited the night-work of females under the age of fourteen only; Luxemburg and Hungary, under sixteen; Denmark, Norway and Sweden under eighteen; Portugal and Belgium under twenty-one. Article I further designated as subject to this prohibition all industrial enterprises employing more than ten laborers, excluding such as engaged only members of the occupier's own immediate family. The quest for a satisfactory basis by which to delimit the application of the law was fraught with no little difficulty since great dissimilarity prevailed among the standards employed by different countries in reference to the work of women. Great Britain, France, and Holland prohibited the night-work of the sex in large and small industries; in Belgium, generally speaking, the statutes forbade it to the young, which was likewise the basis of prohibition in Spain and Luxemburg; in Denmark, Italy, and Portugal, prohibitory law confined itself to establishments employing over five workers or using power-driven machinery; in Switzerland it applied to manufactories having more than five workers with power-driven machinery or with employees under eighteen years of age, or having more than ten workers without power-driven machinery; in Austria and Hungary, it involved establishments with more than twenty laborers, power-driven machinery, or with labor shifts, *etc.*; while in Germany, Norway, and Sweden, still other regulations obtained less definite but pertaining to enterprises possessed of the char-

[4] The following States had previously passed laws prohibiting or restricting the use of white phosphorus in the match industry: Germany (1903, but to take effect in 1907), France (1898), Holland (1901), Switzerland (1898), Denmark (1874).

acteristics of large-scale industry. The committee, after reviewing this diversity in legislation, excluded from the scope of the agreement industries employing not more than ten laborers, on the grounds that such supplied the local market only, were not of international concern, and employed but a minor percentage of the feminine working population anyway. The use of power-driven machinery was found to offer no satisfactory basis of demarcation since the use of small motors and electrical devices had become so universal that the smallest industries and home shops would thereby become included in international regulation, while the number of female employees thereby protected would be negligible. Regulation of such small concerns was held to belong to the domain of the individual states. Having thus determined the size of the industrial enterprises comprehended, Article I next indicated the general categories of business contemplated by the term, "industrial enterprise," specifying as included therein, mines, quarries, and manufacturing establishments, to the exclusion of purely agricultural or commercial undertakings. The spokesman of the committee explained that the manufacture of raw sugar from beets would be classified as an industrial enterprise, while the hotel business on the other hand would be without the meaning of the regulation. The precise delimitation, however, of these categories is left to the legislation of each State.

Article II stipulated that the legal international night of rest for women was to be of eleven hours' duration, including in all cases the hours between 10 p.m. and 5 a.m. Switzerland had proposed an invariable period of rest extending from 8 p.m. to 6 a.m.; but fortunately the above device was hit upon for both rigidity and elasticity of regulation at one and the same time; the clause adopted leaves it to each nation to arrange certain of the hours of the international night to suit the convenience of its industry, while other hours, *viz.*, from 10 p.m. to 5 a.m., essential to the rest of the worker, are made determinate and obligatory in all countries irrespective of their industrial peculiarities. Thus concomitant and consistent with its rigidity and uniformity of regulation, the instrument leaves to each nation the option of fixing the international night between eight or more differing periods of time, namely, 6 p.m.-5 a.m.; 6½-5½; 7-6; 7½-6½; 8-7; 8½-7½; 9-8; 10-9. Moreover, eleven hours constitute merely the legal minimum; it is optional with each State to extend the period of rest if desired. This elasticity was designed to render the agreement applicable to all countries, whether of frigid or equatorial temperature; and when later at the Diplomatic Conference in 1906 it was transformed into a Convention, there were added provisions that made for its still greater adaptableness in this respect. It should be noted that these observations with reference to the outlines apply with equal force to this Convention, of which they were but the precursor and which subsequently became law between the nations.

The method just described of defining the international night was without precedent. In all the legislation of the States, such periods of uninterrupted rest had been established by stipulating the time from a definite evening hour to a definite morning hour; *e.g.*, two States had chosen the hour from 7 p.m. to 5 a.m.; six States, 8-6; one, 8½-5½; one, 8-5; four, 9-5; and one, 9-6.

The exceptions to the prohibition of women's night-work were provided for in Section 2 of Article II and in Articles III-V. For the sake of signatories having no law covering the night-work of adult females, the length of the night's rest could be limited to ten hours for a transitional period of three years, which would obviously be reckoned from the time of the Convention's execution, Jan. 1, 1911, and would consequently extend to Jan. 1, 1914.[5] Exemptions from the prohibition's operation might also be made in cases of extreme necessity, or when required to avert the otherwise inevitable loss of materials susceptible of rapid deterioration, while for industries subject to the influence of the seasons as well as for any industry under unusual circumstances, the length of nocturnal rest might be reduced to ten hours during sixty days in the year. Moreover. in providing for the deposition of ratifications not later than Dec. 31, 1907,[5] three years subsequent to which the Convention would come into force (Jan. 1, 1911),[5] it was stated that in so far as its terms applied to manufactories of raw beet sugar, wool combing and weaving establishments, or open works of mining operations suspended at least four months in the year on account of climatic conditions,

[5] These dates were later changed.

the three-year interim between the deposition of ratifications and subsequent execution might be extended to ten years.

The signers of this draft convention were: Denmark, Austria, Hungary, Belgium, Germany, Italy, France, Spain, Luxemburg, Norway, Holland, Portugal, Switzerland. The representatives of Great Britain declared their lack of authority to sign but maintained that the British Government shared the sentiments which animated the Conference. Sweden's delegates similarly voiced the hope that the principles advocated by the Conference would succeed to adoption by their country, perhaps before the expiration of the time provided by the instrument. The United States was not represented in these deliberations.

Intervening Events.

In a Circular Note [6] of June 26, 1905, the Swiss Federal Council proposed to the powers the convocation of a diplomatic conference to enact the preceding tentative agreements into real Conventions. Under date of June 14, 1906,[7] another Circular Letter recorded the results of the proposal to the effect that favorable replies had been received from Germany, Austria, Hungary, France, Belgium, Denmark, Italy, Luxemburg, Switzerland and the Netherlands. Portugal and Sweden were ready to accede to the agreement that related to the work of women; Norway sympathizd with the movement, but was not ready to participate; the United Kingdom was ready to adhere to the prohibition of the night-work of women under certain conditions. In her conditions, England stipulated that all the States engaged in international competition should adhere; that the adhesion of other States, in which certain industries might develop, should be made possible; and that there should be a sufficient guarantee that the provisions of the Convention would be executed. Furthermore, the British Government asked that some conclusion be arrived at both with respect to the period during which the Convention should apply and the feasibility of instituting a standing commission to investigate alleged contraventions of the same

[6] *E. B.* I, (7-8) p. XXXII.
[7] *Ibid.*, pp. XXXII—XXXIII.

as well as to propose whatever amendments chemical or mechanical inventions might make necessary from time to time. With reference to the interdiction of the use of white phosphorus the Government refused to express an opinion.

On June 12, 1906, Mr. Sarrien of the French Cabinet known by his name referred to the Bern Conventions in the following language: [8]

"The conflicts between capital and labor are becoming daily more frequent and more acute, they run the risk of affecting adversely the prosperity of commerce and industry, and we believe that it is time to study seriously the means of preventing their return. . . .

". . . Economic problems are playing every day a more important rôle in the equilibrium of the world, and certain social questions cannot be completely solved by international legislation without an international agreement.

". . . An initial step is being taken in this direction on the initiative of the Committee of the International Association for the Legal Protection of Labor. A Convention has been drafted with a view to insuring the prohibition of the industrial nightwork of women, as well as the prohibition of the use of white phosphorus in the manufacture of matches. The 5th of last April we made known that the Republic would give its definite and unreserved adhesion to that Convention.

"We shall seek to extend by degrees the sphere of these international agreements on labor questions. Thus, in the social and economic sphere as in the domain of politics properly so-called, we shall hope to serve at the same time the cause of the internal peace of the Republic and that of universal peace."

The Swiss Note of June 14 fixed the date of the impending Conference for Sept. 17, and the place at Bern. Another Note, sent Sept. 4, announced that the Japanese Government would not participate. The Note also laid before the governments the proposal [9] of the British Secretary of Foreign Affairs for the

[8] L. Chatelain—*La Protection internationale ouvrière*, pp. 5-6.
[9] *E. B.* I, (7-8) pp. XXXIII; XXXV.

establishment of a permanent International Commission whose task it should be to superintend the execution of International Labor Conventions in conjunction with such duties as the following:

1. To give opinions on disputed points and complaints;
2. To investigate and report facts in the case;
3. As a last resort in cases of dissension, to promote arbitral proceedings at the request of one of the High Contracting Parties;
4. To consider programs for conferences on industrial questions.

International Diplomatic Conference of Bern. Sept. 17-26, 1906.

The above proposal was unacceptable to Germany, Austria, Hungary, and Belgium, it being asserted that although representatives of particular countries would have expert knowledge of the systems peculiar to their country, nevertheless the other members of the commission could outvote them at pleasure in the adoption of measures of vital import to those systems and affecting them adversely; and that, besides, the proper method of settling disputed points would be to call further conferences.

Two Conventions [10] were signed on Sept. 26, 1906, by the plenipotentiaries of the contracting States, reserving ratification to their respective governments. The States signatory to the Convention for the Prohibition of the Night-Work of Women were: France, Spain, Germany, Austria, Hungary, the United Kingdom, Italy, Luxemburg, the Netherlands, Portugal, Denmark, Sweden, Switzerland, and Belgium. Denmark was to be allowed to postpone the deposit of her ratifications until the Danish Factory Act of April 11, 1901 should be revised during the autumn of 1910.[11] That Great Britain and Sweden were of the number is to be specially noted as they did not sign the draft agreement in the former Conference in 1905; while Norway, a signer of the agreement of 1905, was not among the signatories in 1906.

Nothing contemplated by the agreement of the previous year was excluded from the Convention; the latter did, however, am-

[10] *E. B.* I, (4-8), pp. 273-276.
[11] *E. B.* I, (7-8) p. xxxiv.

plify, add to, and make more precise the terms of its model. The first four articles of the two documents were practically identical. Article V was a departure; it evinced unwonted pains on the part of the envoys to emphasize the obligations inherent in the Convention, declaring that it was incumbent upon each of the contracting parties to take the administrative measures necessary to insure on its territory the strict execution of the provisions. In addition to this, it stipulated a procedure that might be said to partake slightly of the nature of a sanction: the governments were to communicate to one another all laws and regulations upon the subject, then or thereafter in force, and to make periodic transfer of reports concerning their application. Thereby dereliction in the enforcement of the Convention could be readily apprehended by sister States whose joint diplomatic effort might avail to restore the delinquent to the path of rectitude.

Still further did the Convention outdo its archetype, when it came to specify the potential scope of its operations; for by Article VI, colonies, possessions, and protectorates could adhere when notification to that effect should be tendered the Swiss Federal Council by their metropolitan government. Also, sovereign powers outside of Europe were contemplated specifically in the provisions of Articles VII and IX. The aforesaid Articles endeavored to lend sufficient elasticity to the Convention to make it adaptable to peculiar circumstances and conditions that might otherwise preclude its application. For example, upon notifying the adhesion of colonies, possessions, or protectorates, the home government could except from the operation of the law such native works as did not admit of inspection; or, if conditions of climate or native population in dependencies, or States outside of Europe, were such as to make the international night untenable, the period of unbroken rest could be reduced below the established minimum of eleven hours on condition that compensatory rest should be accorded during the day.

The date for closing the *procès-verbal* of the deposit of ratifications was extended from Dec. 31, 1907, to the same date in 1908, leaving an interval of two years instead of three before the time (Jan. 1, 1911) set for the Convention's execution. Non-signatory States could declare their adhesion by an act addressed to the Swiss Federal Council, in which case, as also in case of a colony, possession, or protectorate, the interval before execution would be reckoned from the date of adhesion. No party to the Convention could lawfully denounce it within twelve years of the closing of its record of ratification, thus guaranteeing it a fair trial. Thereafter, it might be denounced from year to year, the revocation to take effect one year after it had been notified to the Swiss Federal Council by the proper authority.

The powers signing the second Convention respecting the prohibition of the importation, manufacture, or sale of matches containing white (yellow) phosphorus were: Switzerland, Denmark, France, Italy, Luxemburg, the Netherlands, and the German Empire. Italy in particular had much at stake in this move as she was one of the most important producers of matches. Five States which signed the agreement of 1905 failed to sign the Convention. These States were Austria and Hungary, excusing themselves because of the non-adhesion of Japan; Portugal, because in 1895 it had granted a match monopoly to last for thirty years; and Belgium, and Spain. Denmark had not signed the outlines, but now adhered to the Convention. Norway, Sweden, and the United Kingdom did not sign on either occasion, although the British delegates signified willingness to adhere if all the others did likewise. By the agreement of the year preceding, the execution of the phosphorus law had been made conditional upon the concurrence therein of all the States represented and Japan, but this condition was not attached to the Convention of 1906.

The same stipulation that found place in the other Convention in emphasis of the obligation rigidly to enforce the law enjoined thereby and mutually to report all official action germane to the matter, were added to this Convention by Article II; while, in further similarity to the first Convention, its sphere of application was so extended as to render possible the adhesion of colonies, possessions, or protectorates, and States not then signatory. The ratifications of the co-signatory nations were to be deposited by Dec. 31, 1908, and the Convention was to come into force three years from that date (Jan. 1, 1912), while for non-signatory States and dependencies, a period of five years was to intervene between the time of notifying their adhesion and making good its execution. Also, the provisions for denunciation paralleled those of the first Convention, with the one exception that five years instead of twelve constituted the period within which it could not lawfully be abrogated by any one of the parties to it.

Into the Conference's deliberations relative to the first Convention, there had been injected a discussion of vital import to both, as well as to all such conventions that may ever be framed; it seemed to provoke no slight difference of opinion at the time and perturbed the Conference not a little. This concerned the institution of a sanction. English delegates advocated the adoption of the following most clearly defined sanction up to that time proposed for labor conventions signed by several governments.

"The High Contracting Parties agree upon the creation of a commmission charged with superintending the execution of the provisions of the present convention. That commission should be composed of delegates of the different contracting States. . . . The commission shall have the function of expressing opinion on litigious questions and complaints which shall be submitted to it. It shall have only the function of authentication and examination. It shall make on all the questions which shall be submitted to it, a report which shall be communicated to the States concerned. In the last resort, a question in litigation shall, on demand of one of the High Contracting Parties, be submitted to arbitration. In case the High Contracting Parties should be disposed to call conferences on the subject of the condition of laborers, the commission shall be charged with the discussion of the program and shall serve as an organ for the exchange of preliminary views." [12]

But this seemed to some to risk the subversion of law and administrative powers of the State and to constitute an attack upon the principle of their sovereignty. Indeed, infinite wisdom and due diligence would certainly need to be exercised by a commission appointed to the stupendous task of ascertaining and investigating on an international scale the various industries in which women might be found to be employed at night in contravention

[12] L. Chatelain, *op. cit.*, pp. 118-119.

of the law. This question of a proper sanction constitutes one of the most difficult and vital problems of the whole movement; for unless the uniform and effective enforcement of international law on labor can be realized, it is self-evident that it is foredoomed to failure. An attenuated *voeu* was finally signed by representatives of ten States for the institution of a commission of purely consultative character to which questions or disputed points might be referred and whose duty it would be to give opinions as to equivalent conditions pursuant to which there might be accepted the adhesions of states outside of Europe, as well as of possessions, colonies, protectorates, where the climate or condition of the natives would demand modifications of detail in the Convention. Such a commission might also serve as a medium for convening conferences. Nevertheless, the contracting States would have the right to submit questions to arbitration in conformity to Article 16 of The Hague Convention, even if the matter had previously been the object of an expression of opinion by the commission.

Results of the Bern Convention on Night-Work.

One month (Oct. 23, 1906) after the foregoing events, the Swiss Federal Government sent to the various powers duplicates of the Conventions signed at Bern, and called attention to the fact that the time allowed for depositing ratifications expired Dec. 31, 1908,[13] and requested the governments to express their pleasure with reference to the establishment of the permanent international commission of supervisory powers that had been proposed over the signatures of ten States. The States however did not create such a commission.

The Government of Luxemburg was empowered to ratify and enforce the Bern Convention.[14] Hitherto employment in mines, open mining and quarries had been forbidden entirely to women, while girls under sixteen were not allowed employment at night in any industrial establishment at all; otherwise the night-work of women had not been prohibited; but now by adhesion to the Convention, the prohibition of night-work was extended to all

[13] *E. B.* I, (9-12) p. lv.
[14] *Ibid.* II, (1) p. V.
Act of August 3, 1907.

women and the minimum night's rest which had been eight hours long was increased to eleven hours; thus, the ratification and enforcement of the Convention in Luxemburg marked a distinct advance in the protective legislation of that country, and serves to illustrate the character of reforms wrought among the signatory powers in general.

Although Great Britain had refused to sign either the agreement (1905) or the Convention (1906) on the subject of woman's work, she adhered within the prescribed time limit (Dec. 31, 1908), accompanied by a most gratifying brood of dependencies. By an Act under date of August 9, 1907, the English Parliament repealed sections of the Factory and Workshop Act and of the Coal Mines Regulation Act of 1887, conflicting with the Bern Convention on night-work. Denmark, Spain, Italy and Sweden, not having deposited their ratifications before Dec. 31, 1908, entered into an agreement with the remaining signatory States by which these four nations gained the privilege, equally with those States that did not sign the Convention (see Article IX), to notify their adhesion at a subsequent date. Although for Denmark special exception had previously been made, she did not give notice of adherence. Also Spain did not ratify the Convention; but by an Act of July 11, 1912, she prohibited the night-work of married women and widows having children, in shops and factories after date of Jan. 14, 1914. As regards unmarried women and childless widows, the number of such employees is to be gradually reduced by 6% every year until Jan. 14, 1920; from this date the night-work of women is to be entirely prohibited. Under the special provision, Italy adhered by an Act addressed to the Swiss Federal Council Dec. 29, 1909, and Sweden similarly under date of Jan. 14, 1910. The Bill relating to Sweden's participation had been rejected by both Chambers of the Government in 1908, and again it was reported unfavorably by the Committee in 1909; but this time it was passed by both Chambers in spite of the Committee's adverse report.[15] The Acts of Sweden illustrate the manner in which exceptions legally may be taken to the Convention.[16] Two procla-

[15] *E. B.* V, (2) p. xvii.

mations (June 9, and Aug. 11, 1911) allow exemptions in the preparation of preserved fruit and vegetables and in salting of herring, in pursuance of the Act (Nov. 20, 1909) prohibiting the night-work of women, which in conformity to the terms of the international Convention on the subject, empowers the government to make exceptions to such prohibition in the preparation of materials subject to rapid deterioration.

In a Circular Note [17] of March 19, 1909, the Swiss Federal Council put forward the proposal that the period of time provided for compliance with the terms of the Convention should be computed from Jan. 1, 1909 in the case of States which deposited their ratifications within the limit prescribed. This was to interfere in no way with the later adhesion of other parties; the proposition involved considerable correspondence [18] and not meeting with the unanimous consent of the States, failed. The Belgian and French Governments suggested that the period of two years, at the immediate close of which the Convention was to be brought into force, should be reckoned from Jan. 14, 1910. On this date had occurred the adhesion of Sweden, the last of twelve States to ratify the instrument. The Federal Council interpreted the proposal as meaning also that the period of ten years reserved for sugar beet factories, woolen mills, *etc.* (See Art. VIII) should extend from the same date, which would thus determine a uniform time for the Convention's execution by every one of the States that had ratified, in spite of previous irregularity in their adhesions. To this proposition, the Federal Council gave its assent (Note of April 9, 1910) [19] with the hope that it would be found acceptable by the States which were to be interviewed on the matter; *i.e.*, Germany, Austria, Hungary, Belgium, Denmark, Spain, France, the United Kingdom, Italy, Luxemburg, the Netherlands, Portugal, and Sweden. All except Spain and Denmark expressed approval, and thus it was decided that the Convention should go into operation Jan. 14, 1912 in the case of the dozen States which had adhered on or before Jan. 14, 1910.[20]

[16] *E. B.* VI, (4) p. xlvii.
[17] *Ibid.*, V, (2) p. xi.
[18] *Ibid.*, V, (2) pp. xi.-xvii.
[19] *Ibid.*, V, (2) pp. xiv-xvii.
[20] *Ibid.*, V, (3) pp. l-li.

This Convention prohibiting night-work to women was adhered to by the following countries and colonies:

Country	Date of Adhesion	Date of Coming into Force
	Within prescribed time	
Germany	limit Dec. 31, 1908.	14th Jan. 1912
Austria	"	"
Hungary	"	"
Belgium	"	"
France	"	"
The United Kingdom	"	"
Luxemburg	"	"
The Netherlands	"	"
Portugal	"	"
Switzerland	"	"

French Colonies

| Algeria | 26th Mar. 1909 | 14th Jan. 1912 |
| Tunis | 15th Jan. 1910 | 15th Jan. 1912 |

British Colonies

Ceylon	21st Feb. 1908	14th Jan. 1912
Fiji Islands	"	"
Gibraltar	"	"
Gold Coast	"	"
Leeward Islands	"	"
New Zealand	"	"
Northern Nigeria	"	"
Trinidad	"	"
Uganda Protectorate	"	"
Italy	29th Dec. 1909	"
Sweden	14th Jan. 1910	"

Spain did not notify her adhesion to the Convention, but she nevertheless prohibited the night-work of women. Greece passed a law by which the prohibition of the night-work of women was decreed on 24th Jan./16th Feb., 1912, satisfying in all respects the conditions of the Bern Convention, although Greece is not a party to it. Night-work was forbidden to women in Japan and India in 1911, but in the former State the regulation applies only to establishments with more than fifteen workers and the night's rest need be only of six hours' duration, while in India the law does not in general apply to establishments which do not employ more than forty-nine persons at any time of the year.

In 1905 the prohibition or lack of prohibition of the night-work of women stood as follows.[21]

1. States without prohibition: Japan. (Estimated number of unprotected female employees: 250,000.)

2. Night-work allowed on a basis similar to the regulations governing day-work: South Australia, California, Illinois, Louisiana, Maine, Maryland, Michigan, Minnesota, New Hampshire, North Dakota, Oklahoma, Pennsylvania, Rhode Island, South Carolina, Virginia. (Unprotected females over sixteen years of age in the United States: 227,000.)

3. Limitation of the day-work of women to eleven hours and the night-work of girls between fourteen and sixteen to eight hours: Spain.

4. Prohibition of night-work to young persons only: Belgium, Portugal, Denmark, Sweden, Finland, Norway, New South Wales, Hungary, Luxemburg, Ohio, Georgia, Wisconsin. (Estimated number of unprotected female employees in the above States: 350,000.)

5. Night-work of women prohibited in certain kinds of occupations: (a) Mines and textile industries: Russia; (b) Factories, mines, blast furnaces: Austria (countries represented in Reichsrat), East Indies (for establishments employing over 50), Luxemburg, Finland, Sweden; (c) Factories, mines, blast furnaces and shops with motor power: Germany, Switzerland (for establishments employing over five workers).

6. Prohibition of night-work of females in establishments without motor power but which employ over:
5 laborers: Denmark, Portugal, Ontario.

[21] *Publications de l'Association internationale pour la protection légale des travailleurs.* No. 4. p. 6 et suiv.

4 laborers: Victoria.
3 laborers: Canton Bale-Ville.
2 laborers: Queensland, New Zealand, Cantons of St. Gall and Glarus.
1 laborer: Cantons of Zurich, Bern, Lucerne, Soleure, Argovie, Neuchatel.

7. Prohibition of the night-work of women in principle, subject to exceptions: Great Britain, Switzerland, Germany, France, Holland, Austria, Russia, Italy (beginning with 1907), Manitoba, Quebec, Nova-Scotia, Queensland, Victoria, New Zealand, East Indies, New York, New Jersey, India, Massachusetts, Nebraska.

8. Extension of the principle of the prohibition of the night-work of women to home industry: Holland.

The following were among the non-signatory countries in respect of the Bern Convention on woman's work: [22]

1. Europe: Denmark, Greece, Lichtenstein, Monaco, Norway Roumania, Russia, Finland, and all the Balkan States.
2. Africa: Abyssinia, Congo, Egypt, The South African Union, Rhodesia, Bechuanaland, Swaziland, Zanzibar, Liberia, the German and Portuguese Colonies, Madagascar, Morocco, Reunion, Senegal.
3. Asia: All States and Colonies with the exception of Ceylon.
4. America: All States excepting Trinidad and the Leeward Islands.
5. Australia and Polynesia: All States excepting New Zealand and Fiji.

Results of the Convention Prohibiting the Use of White Phosphorus.

For the six States which deposited their ratifications within the prescribed term and without reservation the time fixed for the execution of the Convention was Jan. 1, 1912. Italy alone of the seven signatories failed in this respect but she was allowed to adhere later. Although Great Britain had not signed the Convention at Bern, she gave notice of adhesion Dec. 28, 1908, and so completed atonement for seeming obstinacy with reference to the agreements and Conventions signed by other powers at Bern

[22] *Publications of International Labor Office.* No. 8, p. 85.

in preceding years. We may forgive England; but what about the States who said: "I go" and "went not"?

The following subscribed to the Convention which prohibited the use of white (yellow) phosphorus in the manufacture of matches:

Country	Date of Adhesion	Date of Coming into Force
	Within prescribed time	
Germany	limit Dec. 31, 1908	1st Jan. 1912
Denmark including Faroe Islands and Danish Antilles	"	"
France	"	"
Luxemburg	limit Dec. 31, 1908.	14th Jan. 1912
The Netherlands	"	"
Switzerland	"	"
French Colonies		
Somali Coast	26 Nov. 1909	26 Nov. 1914
Réunion	"	"
Madagascar & Dependencies	"	"
French West Africa	"	"
Settlements in Oceania	"	"
New Caledonia	"	"
Tunis	15 Jan. 1910	15 Jan. 1915
Great Britain and Ireland	28 Dec. 1908	28 Dec. 1913
British Colonies		
Orange River Colony	3 May, 1909	3 May, 1914
Cyprus	4 Jan. 1910	4 Jan. 1915
East Africa Protectorate	"	"
Gibraltar	"	"
Malta	"	"
Mauritius	"	"
Seychelles	"	"
Southern Nigeria	"	"
Uganda Protectorate	"	"
The United Kingdom	"	"
Northern Nigeria	24 Feb. 1910	24 Feb. 1915

Leeward Islands	26 Mar. 1910	26 Mar. 1915
Virgin Islands		
St. Christopher & Niero		
Montserrat		
Dominica		
Antigua		
Fiji Islands	20 June 1910	20 June 1915
Gambia	22 Oct. 1910	22 Oct. 1915
Gold Coast	"	"
Sierra Leone	"	"

	From 3 May 1909	
Union of South Africa	retroactively	3 May 1914
Canada	20 Sept. 1914	20 Sept. 1919
Bermuda	19 Dec. 1910	19 Dec. 1915
Southern Rodesia	20 Feb. 1911	20 Feb. 1916
New Zealand	27 Nov. 1911	27 Nov. 1916
Italy	6 July 1910	6 July 1915
Dutch Indies	7 Mar. 1910	7 Mar. 1915
Spain	29 Oct. 1909	29 Oct. 1914
Norway	10 July 1914	10 July 1919

The manufacture and sale of white phosphorus matches was prohibited in Victoria, Western Australia, Tasmania and New South Wales. The United States also placed a prohibitive tax on such matches and prohibited their importation and exportation.

The following are countries that permitted the manufacture of phosphorus matches: [23]

1. Free manufacture (a) in Europe: Belgium, Russia (subject to a different tax on white phosphorus), Sweden (prohibition of their sale in Sweden), Turkey; (b) outside Europe: all Asiatic States (with the exception of Cyprus and the Dutch and East Indies), America (with the exception of the United States, Canada, the Danish and British Antilles, and Mexico), Abyssinia, Egypt, Zanzibar.

2. Countries with State monopoly: Bulgaria, Greece, Portugal,

[23] *Publication of the Internaticnal Labor Office.* No. 8, p. 87.

Roumania, (State monopoly, but with use of sesquisulphide), Servia.

Of the above only Japan and Sweden are of importance as exporting countries.

In answer to a Swiss Circular Letter (July 17, 1911) asking whether the importation of sample matches made with white phosphorus should be forbidden the replies were as follows: [24]

Affimative.
Great Britain
Italy
Denmark
France
Spain

Negative.
Germany
The Netherlands
Luxemburg

This appears to be a quibble hardly worthy, in the light of the terms of the Convention, of the three powers negatively inclined. But it is a fair example of those differences of opinion which make the questions of interpretation and sanction such intricate and vital problems in international law. Is the word *introduction* in the French version of the Convention merely to be interpreted as "introduction" for industrial purposes rather than in the strict sense of "importation," and consequently is the importation of sample phosphorus matches to be condemned? It would be interesting to understand the object of importing sample cases of phosphorus matches whose "introduction," "manufacture" and "sale" within the realm is forbidden.

Bern Conference. Sept. 15-25, 1913.

Delegates to the sixth biennial meeting of the International Association for Labor Legislation, held at Lugano, Switzerland, in 1910, undertook measures to prepare the way for a second series of international conferences to draft international conven-

[24] *E. B.* VII, (1-2) p. 1-4.

tions prohibiting the night-work of young persons entirely, and also the day-work of women and of young persons in excess of ten hours. This led to the preparation by the Bureau of a program to serve in case a conference should be called to outline such agreements; and by a Swiss Circular Letter of Jan. 31, 1913,[25] this program was submitted to the States invited to support the project; *viz.*, Germany, Austria, Hungary, Belgium, Bulgaria, Denmark, Spain, France, Great Britain, Greece, Italy, Luxemburg, Norway, the Netherlands, Portugal, Roumania, Russia, Servia, Sweden. In consequence, delegates from the above States, with the exception of Servia, Roumania, Luxemburg, Greece, and Bulgaria, assembled with the representatives of Switzerland at Bern, Sept. 15, 1913.

The tentative agreements intended to be later transformed into conventions by an international Diplomatic Conference, in conformity to the precedent set by the Bern Conventions of 1906, followed in general the program worked out by the Bureau; but varied from it in a number of respects by reason of both additions and subtractions. The first agreement prohibiting night-work to young persons, received the signatures of delegates from Switzerland, Sweden, Portugal, Holland, Norway, Italy, the United Kingdom, Germany, France, Spain, Belgium, Hungary, and Austria. According to the principles that were adopted and made applicable to all concerns where more than ten persons were employed, the prohibition was to be general for employees under sixteen years of age, and absolute for all under fourteen. Industrial undertakings were defined in the same sense as industrial enterprises in the Bern Convention respecting the work of women, and the night of rest prescribed for young workers was also to be the same as the international night of eleven hours fixed by that Convention. Certain exceptions to this last rule, however, were allowed for coal and lignite mines and bakeries, also, for colonies, possessions, protectorates, or extra-European countries, where climate or conditions of native population might require a different regulation; but in all such cases the shortening of the night was to be compensated by rest in the daytime. Moreover, work during the night by individuals over fourteen years of age might

[25] *E. B.* VIII, (3-4) 1913 pp. 103-106.

be allowed when public interest demanded it, or in case of *force majeure* where there occurs an interruption in business impossible to foresee and non-periodic in character. In so far as this agreement might be found to afford better protection to girls under sixteen, it was to supercede the Convention of 1906 on night-work. Two years after the closing of the record of deposit, the proposed convention was to come into force, with the exception that its execution might be delayed for ten years in respect of employees over fourteen years of age in specified processes in glass works, rolling mills, and forges; in the meantime, however, life or limb of the young in these processes was not to be exposed to any special risk or danger.

These provisions were not the exact counterpart of recommendations made by the Bureau of the International Association in the program submitted by it. It had proposed to prohibit the work in question to young persons under eighteen instead of under sixteen; by way of special exceptions for States in which similar regulations had not previously existed, it had contemplated a period of transition in which night-rest for young people between sixteen and eighteen could be legally limited to ten hours instead of extended to the required length of eleven hours; among the exceptions pertaining to workers over fourteen, provision had been made for the prohibition's suspension in case of the manufacture of raw materials susceptible of rapid deterioration or otherwise unavoidable injury; and for seasonal industries, a way was to be left open whereby the period of uninterrupted night-rest could be reduced to ten hours sixty times a year under extraordinary circumstances. The period for bringing the agreement into force in glass and steel industries was fixed at five years for workers over sixteen instead of at ten years for workers over fourteen. None of these proposals found their way into the draft sanctioned at Bern.

The second of the draft conventions concerned the determination of a working day for workers under sixteen and women; and, with the exception of Norway, it was signed by the same countries as signed the former agreement. As regards the program that the Bureau had submitted, the age limit for young workers was changed by the Conference from eighteen to sixteen, while the principles in general were amplified and made much more specific in detail. The prospective convention stood for a ten-hour day, but at the same time allowed the period of work to be otherwise limited through the device of fixing a maximum of sixty hours of work per week with the length of no single workday to exceed ten and one-half hours. The definition of industrial undertakings and the size necessary to include the same within the purview of the proposed convention were identical with the determinations on these points in the other agreement. Hours of work were to be interrupted by one or more rest periods, one of which, at least, was to occur immediately after the first six hours of work; in cases where work was not of more than six hours' duration, no break would be necessary. Extension of the prescribed workday was to be permitted when public interests demanded it, and also under the following circumstances: in cases of *force majeure* involving an interruption of manufacture impossible to foresee and not of periodic nature, in cases where raw materials might otherwise be subjected to rapid deterioration or loss; and in seasonal industries as well as in any industry under exceptional circumstances. Total work including overtime, even in case of the above exceptions outside of "public interest" and *"force majeure,"* was not to exceed twelve hours a day save in fish, vegetable, and fruit establishments; and overtime was not to exceed 140 hours per year except in the industries first mentioned together with manufactories of brick, tiles, clothing, feather articles, articles of fashion, and artificial flowers, all of which might if necessary extend overtime to not over 180 hours per calendar year. Nevertheless in no case, not even in any of the above exceptions outside of "public interest" and *"force majeure,"* was the working day to be extended for young workers under sixteen.

The agreement would come into force two years after closing the record of the deposition of ratifications; however, for manufactories of raw sugar from beets, of machine-made embroidery, and in textile mills for spinning and weaving, the interval might be extended from two to seven years, while in States where it was the custom to require eleven hours of work of women and children, the postponement of the agreement's execution might be equally prolonged under certain conditions specified.

These draft conventions having been approved by the Conference, were submitted to the governments interested by a Swiss communication of Sept. 29, 1913.[26] Several weeks later another Letter (Dec. 30, 1913)[27] to the same parties including Luxemburg, whose delegate had been unavoidably detained from the Conference, conveyed the protocol of the meeting. The same Letter proposed Sept. 3, 1914 as the date for holding an international Diplomatic Conference to turn the outlines into real conventions. A later Note (July 14, 1914)[28] stated that the Conference could be considered as assured in view of the favorable replies anticipated and already received, although Russia had intimated dissatisfaction with the agreements, declaring them unsuitable to her conditions of industry, and therefore not of a character to make it desirable for her to participate. Norway also had announced a disinclination to take part, asserting that her own legislation conferred more extensive protection than that offered by the conventions proposed, and that a Bill then pending promised a further extension of her protective law. In conclusion, the Swiss Note recommended that the method of procedure at the Diplomatic Conference of Bern in 1906 be followed in the impending meeting; also that certain sections of the Convention of 1906 pertaining to woman's work be included in the agreement on night-work under consideration; and that editorial improvements be made in the wording of the texts of the proposed conventions.

A Circular Letter of Aug. 7, 1914 contained the following:[29]

"In our Circular Letters of 30th December, 1913, and 14th July, 1914, we had the honor of sending to your Excellency certain communications with respect to an International Diplomatic Conference relating to labor regulation and to submit proposals to your Excellency. The Conference was to have met in Bern on 3rd September, but the present political events do not seem to

[26] *E. B.* VIII, (9-10) 1913, p. 363-366.
[27] *E. B.* IX, (1914) (3) p. 62.
[28] *E. B.* (IX) (7) (1914) p. 287-288.
[29] *E. B.* **IX, (11-12)** (1914), p. lxxiii.

permit this. We feel sure that you will agree with our decision that the Conference be postponed to some future date."

In Austria a Decree of the Ministry of Commerce under date of Sept. 11, 1915 [30] granted exceptional permission for the nightwork of women and young persons in view of the extraordinary circumstances created by the war. The fact that prohibitions on the subject had been adhered to by Austria, without official modification, throughout the first year of the conflict, (one of the avowed reasons for such adherence being that some of the prohibitions had an international basis) portends much for the enforcement of such law in times of peace. Moreover, even then, the permission was not granted indiscriminately, but rather only on condition that the merits of each case should be carefully tested by the industrial inspector and passed upon by provincial authorities, or in case of disagreement, by the Ministry of Commerce.

[30] *E. B.* **XI**, (1-2) (1916) p. 31-32.

CHAPTER II

PROTECTIVE LABOR TREATIES*

At the second meeting of the International Association for Labor Legislation at Cologne (Sept. 26-27, 1902), representatives of the French and Italian Governments entered into informal negotiations with reference to the conclusion of a labor treaty. The matter, which had been broached even previous to this occasion, did not become the subject of immediate action; for a year and over it dragged along with the prospects of its realization growing constantly brighter, until at last, the preliminaries being completed, it became, April 15, 1904,[1] the first of a new order of treaties reciprocally insuring the protection of workmen. By its terms Italians working in France received, in effect, the promise that some day they would enjoy benefits of French labor legislation heretofore denied to foreigners, while Italy agreed to superimpose upon the economic framework of her country certain of the perfections of labor control applied by her neighbor. The advantages reciprocally derived were not identical, a fact which becomes important when the *pro's* and *con's* of international regulation are debated. France benefited in that a competitor became subject to certain restrictions upon industry and Italy profited by the increased protection to be accorded to her laboring classes, in the first instance, by herself. It forms an interesting puzzle to inquire whose was the greater gain. This is not however a complete statement of the situation.

By its preamble the two general purposes of the Treaty[2] were presented as follows:

(1) To grant to nationals of either country laboring in territory of the other reciprocal banking accommodations and advantages of social insurance;

* For copies of the treaties, see Appendix I.
[1] *G. B.* Bd. 3. S. x.
F. B.—Bulletin de l'Office International du Travail, t. III. (1-3) p. I-VI.
[2] A.D. 1904, t. 92, p. 1269-1274.

(2) To guarantee the mutual maintenance of protective labor measures, and co-operation in the advancement of labor legislation.

As regards reciprocal privileges in the use of banks, precise and effective rules were laid down; in the matter of labor inspection, Italy undertook an important obligation; with reference to the rest, mere principles were announced upon which to negotiate understandings of the future.

The Treaty privileged the nationals of either country to transfer deposits without charge from the State Savings Bank of France to the Postal Savings Bank of Italy, or *vice versa;* and funds thus transferred became subject to the rules applied by the receiving bank to the deposits of its country's citizens. This was the only outstanding provision whose terms of reciprocity were identical and that was made executory by the terms of the Treaty. The one other Article whose application was not left wholly contingent upon future circumstances was Article IV. In this Italy promised to complete throughout her whole kingdom a system of labor inspection offering, for the application of the law, guarantees analagous to those of the French system, and organized with respect to the objects of its special care; *i.e.,* women and children, along four general lines:

(1) Prohibition of night-work;
(2) Age for admission to work;
(3) Length of the workday;
(4) Obligation of weekly rest.

Italy's engagement was its own admission of the inadequacy of labor inspection within her territory. In the matter of regulating the night-work of women, she had been very far behind France in the enactment of prohibitory law, and her legislation had remained likewise much inferior in respect of the age limits fixed for the classes to whom such work was forbidden. Similarly deficient or tardy had been Italian legislation concerning the age limits determined for the admission of children into factories. Differences also prevailed in the law respecting the workday; Italy permitted a longer day of work for women and children than did France. But conditions were more on a par as regarded weekly rest. The former decreed such rest for all children under fifteen; the latter, for children under eighteen; and both, for all women. The Italian Government agreed by Article IV of the Treaty to study the means of reducing the daily work of women, and each Government promised to publish an annual and detailed report on the application of statutes and regulations governing child and female labor. By comparison and improvement of legislation, it was anticipated that glaring dissimilarities in the labor laws of the two countries would gradually disappear, and so prepare the way for the conclusion of future agreements.

The rest and major content of the Treaty belonged to what might be termed the realm of speculation; in other words, it outlined what other treaties might enact. In Article I on the subject of bank transfers, provision was made whereby by future agreement the private banks of one country might transfer funds to those of the other, if not gratuitously, at least, at reduced rates. The private banks contemplated were those of industrial centers and frontier towns. It was desired that investments by nationals of one country in savings institutions of the other should receive especially favorable treatment at the hands of the contracting Governments.

With reference to workmen's insurance or pensions, the principle was laid down that the part of the benefit due as a result of premiums paid or deposits made, was to be surrendered to the laborer upon his withdrawal from the undertaking in which he was insured; otherwise, although an enterprise in France could demand equal insurance premiums from French and Italian laborers, it might refuse to make any return in the event of the foreigner's withdrawal as a consideration for the protection relinquished and the payments already made.

Three elements may enter into workmen's insurance:

(1) The contribution of the laborer, for which the Treaty provided as above noted;

(2) That of the employer, regarding which it merely stipulated that there should be reciprocity of regulation between the countries;

(3) State subventions, the benefits of which were to be enjoyed only by the State's own citizens. A country could subsidize

a citizen's pension acquired from an institution of the other country if it chose to do so.

Pensions acquired in one State were to be made payable in the other through the medium of insurance institutions and postal service. For employees laboring alternately in France and Italy and thus prevented from fulfilling the requisite conditions for insurance in either country, there was to be devised a special system under which pensions could be made to accrue to such workmen.

In case accident befell a laborer of either country, working in the territory of the other, he or his assigns were to be entitled to accident benefits on equal terms with the subjects of the land in which the accident occurred. This was the principle so earnestly debated and advocated throughout the Delegates' Meetings of the International Association and destined to be incorporated into a noteworthy series of treaties on accident insurance. Certain laws of France involved the direct derogation of this principle. By her municipal law of April 9, 1898, a foreign laborer, the victim of an accident, upon ceasing to reside in French territory, was obliged to accept a sum compounded to three times the amount of his annuity in lieu of all further pension; and by Act of March 31, 1905, the same principle was retained, with the provision that a foreign insuree's assigns might receive compensation even if they ceased to reside on French territory. If, however, the assigns were not resident in France at the time of the accident, they forfeited all right to compensation. Fortunately the law of 1905 allowed for the modification of these provisions in pursuance of reciprocity treaties on accident insurance, and so safeguarded the possibility of the realization of this principle as advocated by the Treaty of April 15, 1904.

In case of the advent of insurance against unemployment in both countries, an agreement was contemplated by which Frenchmen and Italians working in the territory of either contracting party might share the privileges of such insurance.

In cases where these agreements provided for by Article I should become established, they were to be binding for a period of five years only; thereafter, they might be abandoned upon one year's notice, or otherwise be allowed to renew themselves from year to year by tacit consent. Unforeseen circumstances were to be able to work either abrogation or the more perfect adaptation of the measures if time rendered their original forms undesirable. Of such character were the possibilities contemplated by this Article.

A signal abuse which for some time had attracted the serious attention of governmental authorities was the traffic in Italian children furnished with work certificates falsifying their age so as to admit them to French industry prior to their attainment of the legal age. There was a class of recruiting officers or middlemen who made a business of this traffic. To set on foot measures to stop the evil and preclude its recrudescence, Article II of the Treaty forecast an agreement that would necessitate governmental certification of the documents involved and a rigid inspectorate, protecting reciprocally young workers of either country when employed in the other. There was also suggested the plan of forming protective Committees including in their membership as many compatriots of the young foreigners as possible, and functioning in districts where large numbers of them were employed. Because of the small number of French children employed in Italy, this provision became of benefit principally to the much larger number of young Italian laborers in French territory.

On the occasion of an international labor conference in which one of the contracting parties took part, the other was to feel duty bound similarly to participate according to the engagement of Article III of the Treaty.

By Article V, each party reserved the right to denounce the compact at any time by making known its intention one year in advance. Occasion for denunciation would be found in failure to enforce the systems of inspection prescribed or to respect the obligations assumed in reference to protective law for women and children (see Art. 4, S 2), or in any gross violation of the spirit of the instrument, as for example, the curtailment of protective law covering the subjects treated. A protocol [8] was attached, which specified by name the laws of each country whose proper execution was made compulsory by the terms of the in-

[3] *G. B.* Bd. 3, (1904). S. 154.

strument, and named the bodies in each country competent to interpret the same in its relation to the laws and to judge as to whether occasion for its annulment had been given by the other party. However much detractors may have laughed at France and Italy over the theoretical parts of their Convention of April 15, France and Italy laughed last, as time revealed.

Swiss-Italian Treaty. July 13, 1904.

On 13th July of the same year, Italy signed with Switzerland a commercial Treaty [4] containing an Article whose provisions were to be made effective by a separate act independent of the execution of the rest of the Treaty. This Article (No. 17) authorized the mutual investigation on the part of the contracting powers of the question of workmen's insurance with the object of according in so far as possible to the citizens of each working in the territory of the other equal or equivalent advantages. It is clear that this looked forward to some such arrangement as that contemplated by the Franco-Italian Treaty on the subject, although that Treaty announced the principle of the equality of treatment of foreigners and citizens, while this merely specified reciprocity in the treatment of foreigners.

German-Italian Treaty, Dec. 3, 1904.

It is very evident that Italy did a full year's work in 1904 with respect to labor agreements; just before the year closed, she concluded with Germany a commercial Treaty[5] identical in its terms with Article 17 of the Swiss-Italian Treaty. The action would seem to presuppose an intention upon the part of Italy to work radical improvement in her insurance system; for were Germany to accord to Italian workmen within her realm insurance advantages equal to those enjoyed by her own subjects and then to demand that Italy give German subjects on Italian soil equally favorable privileges, a much heavier burden in the way of reform would be imposed upon Italy than upon Germany.

Compulsory insurance against disease had been established in

[4] 2. Chatelain, *op. cit.*, p. 193.
[5] *Ibid.*, p. 194.

Germany as early as 1883; employees met two-thirds of the expenses of the system, and employers, one-third. Compulsory accident insurance had been introduced by a law of 1884; under it employers became members of insurance associations and were obliged to defray the cost of all indemnities. In 1889 there had been organized an insurance system against sickness and old age, to which all salaried persons over sixteen years old and not having an annual income in excess of 1000 marks were compelled to subscribe, thereby receiving invalidity benefits in case of need, and a regular pension at the age of seventy if payments had been made for a period of thirty years. The funds were derived partly from contributions of employees classified into five groups paying different premium rates; partly, from employers who duplicated the premiums of the employees; and the rest, from the State which made an annual donation of fifty marks for each pension. By way of comparison, we may note that in 1910 France prescribed for laborers receiving less than three thousand francs a system of insurance which, not unlike Germany's, derived its support from contributions of employees, employers, and the State, but which made sixty-five instead of seventy the pensionable age. Sickness insurance is prescribed for certain classes. The French system has both compulsory and voluntary features. In both France and England, as well as in Germany, the incidence of compensation for accidents falls entirely upon the shoulders of employers.[6]

Italy's systems of insurance were very inadequate, being non-compulsory in character in so far as related to invalidity and old age, although she had obligatory accident insurance. A state system largely voluntary in character could hardly possess much stability and certainly could not accord to German workmen in Italy the same guarantees that could be granted to Italian laborers in Germany. The self-imposed task that Italy contemplated was not a small one.

Treaty Between Germany and Austria-Hungary, Jan. 19, 1905.

In a commercial Treaty between Germany and Austria-Hungary of Jan. 19, 1905, an article of practically the same nature

[6] Carlton, *History and Problems of Organized Labor.* p. 310 *et seq.*

as that of the two preceding Treaties was included.[7] In addition to specifying the need of reciprocity in the matter of insurance, it propounded the broader subject of reciprocity "in protection of labor." For Austria and Hungary, as for Italy, the thought of contracting a labor treaty with Germany prognosticated general improvement in their protective labor régimes. Austria possessed compulsory accident insurance supported by laborers and employers, and had also compulsory sickness insurance. Hungary did not have general regulations covering accident insurance; but had a special system for agricultural workers which was obligatory in respect of accidents and voluntary in respect of invalidity, paying benefits in case of death, old age, or incapacity.

Accident Insurance Treaty Between Luxemburg and Belgium. April 15, 1905.

But destiny had reserved for the Kingdom of Belgium and the Grand-Duchy of Luxemburg the honor of devising the first insurance Treaty [8] to specify, in addition to general aims, a *modus operandi* for their realization; in other words, instead of cogitating upon possible law, it laid down the law, and thereby gave to a long mooted principle its first practical international application. As between the signatory countries, it established that subjects of one State injured through an industrial accident within the territory of the other should be entitled to the same compensations and guarantees as subjects of the State within which the injury was received, exception being made in case of laborers injured when employed temporarily; *i.e.*, for not more than six months, by a business concern whose headquarters were located in the State that was not the scene of the accident. In such cases the insurance law applicable would be that of this latter State. By a supplementary agreement of May 22, 1906, the terms of this exception were specified as being applicable to persons employed by transport lines and working intermittently, but habitually, in the country other than the home of the enterprise.[9] Outside of these exceptions, persons were to be eligible to receive insurance bene-

[7] L. Chatelain, *op. cit.*, p. 198.
[8] *G. B.* Bd. IV. S. 305-506.
[9] *E. B.* I, (9-12) pp. 373-374.

fits in the foreign State, who would have been eligible to such had the accident occurred in their native State. As pertained to documents, stamps, records, *etc.*, advantages and exceptions incident to the insurance administration of one State were to be equally applicable to the administration within its confines of the law of the other State, while the magistrates of the two High Contracting Parties were pledged to lend reciprocal assistance in execution of the law. Ratifications were to be exchanged as soon as possible in Brussels, and the Treaty was to go into effect ten days after its official publication and to be terminated one year after the day of its denunciation by either party. By an Act of May 12, 1905,[10] the Government of Luxemburg was empowered to modify laws of the realm when necessary in order to put into operation an international agreement that aimed at reciprocity in insurance administration. The ratfications of the Treaty were exchanged in the following autumn, Oct. 25, 1905.

German-Luxemburg Accident Insurance Treaty. Sept. 2, 1905.

The next Treaty on accident insurance,[11] signed by the German Empire and the Grand-Duchy of Luxemburg during the same fall, confined itself to an affirmative statement of that which constituted the exception in the Belgian-Luxemburg agreement. Employees of an enterprise extending its operations from one country into the other for a period of not over six months at most, remained subject to the accident insurance legislation of the State in which the enterprise was domiciled, even if the accident occurred in the other State. Forestry and agricultural pursuits were excluded from the purview of this arrangement. Railroad employees were specifically included. If dispute arose as to what laws were applicable, the decision rested with the authorities of the State in which the headquarters of the business firm involved in the accident were located; *i. e.*, in Germany, with the Imperial Insurance Office, and in Luxemburg, with the Government. A decision by either authority was final and binding upon underwriters of the other country. To guard the party entitled against injustices of delay arising from uncertainty as to what statutes

[10] *E. B.* Vol. I, (1906) (9-12) p. 372.
[11] *G. B.* Bd. IV, S. 306-308.

applied in a given case, the insurers first invoked were to take care of the injured party, until it should be determined upon whom the burden of indemnity was ultimately to fall. Other points of minor interest were covered including rules that were to govern in case an establishment so changed its place of operation as to pass from the accident insurance laws of one country to those of the other.

Franco-Italian Pact. Jan. 20, 1906.

As the year 1906 opened, the Franco-Italian Treaty of 1904 began to bear fruit. It had introduced reciprocity in the transfer of funds without charge between the national banks of the two countries, and had proposed a similar arrangement between the private banks of the two countries located in industrial centers or frontier towns. To give effect to this latter possibility, an agreement[12] was now completed whereby deposits to the amount of 1500 francs could be transferred without expense between the private banking institutions of these countries. The monies transmitted were to become subject in such matters as interest to the regulations of the receiving bank, while orders on the International Post Office (*mandats d'office*) were to constitute the medium of transfer and to be exempt from tax. Ratifications were exchanged at Paris Dec. 11, 1906.

Franco-Belgian Accident Insurance Treaty. Feb. 12, 1906.

The Franco-Belgian Treaty[13] was practically the same as the Belgian-Luxemburg Treaty: Subjects of one of the contracting parties meeting with an industrial accident in the territory of the other were to have the same guarantees and compensations as were provided for the citizens of the State in which the accident occurred. The same principle of the equality of treatment of foreigners and citizens held for assigns of the injured parties and so wrought an exception to the French law of 1905, denying to dependents of foreigners equal rights with those of Frenchmen. Also as in the other Treaty, exception was made for temporary

[12] *A. d.* 1906, t 97, p. 147.
[13] *E. B.* I, (4-6), pp. 153-154.

employment of not over six months' duration, attention being called to the fact that this exception included persons engaged in transportation enterprises and employed intermittently, whether regularly or not, in the country other than that where the undertaking held its domicile. In case of accident under these circumstances, the law of the undertaking's domicile applied. The Treaty was to take effect one month after its official publication. Ratifications were exchanged June 7, 1906.

A Note of March 12, 1910 [14] enlarged upon Article 4, which had merely authorized the authorities of France and Belgium to lend mutual aid in reciprocal execution of the engagement. This Note, which was not to come into operation within three months after it was signed, obligated the signatory States, upon the termination of an inquiry in respect of an accident, to give notice to the proper consular authority in order that he might take cognizance thereof in behalf of the interested parties.

National Accident Insurance Acts.[15] *1901-1906.*

Notifications of the German Federal Council, under dates of 1901, 1905 and 1906, advert to another phase of the international regulation of accident insurance. The Notification of June 29, 1901 set aside in favor of Italian and Austro-Hungarian subjects provisions of Section 21 of the German Accident Insurance Act and of Section 9 of the Building Accidents Insurance Act, which had debarred foreign assigns not domiciled in Germany at the time of the accident from claiming compensation or indemnities; likewise the Notification revoked in so far as concerned the same nationalities, provisions of Section 94 (2) of the German Accident Insurance Act and Section 37 (1) of the Building Accidents Insurance Act, which had suspended the right of German indemnity to foreign insurees as long as they were not residents of the country. Similar exceptions were made on May 9, 1905 in favor of the Grand-Duchy of Luxemburg, and on Feb. 22, 1906 in favor of Belgian subjects laboring in Germany. By an Act of Dec. 24, 1903, Belgium had erased distinctions between natives and for-

[14] *E. B.* VI, (1), p. 6.
[15] *E. B.* II, (I) p. 1; *E. B.* I, (1-3), pp. V, I. See also the work of E. Mahaim: *Le Droit international ouvrier* (1913).

eigners before the accident insurance laws of her land; thus having accorded to her Teutonic neighbors for two years and over advantages which the action of the German Federal Council now reciprocated. These Acts illustrate what can be accomplished in the cause of the international protection of labor by applying the principle of reciprocity in national labor legislation.

Franco-Italian Accident Insurance Pact. June 9, 1906.

In an agreement [16] of June 9, 1906, France and Italy adopted definite measures by which to realize in practise the recommendations of the Treaty of 1904 on the subject of reparation for injuries caused by accidents. The principle which had now become common to such treaties was adopted; *viz.*: citizens of either country injured while at work in the territory of the other acceded to the same insurance privileges as were accorded to citizens of the country where the accident happened. To assigns also, whether resident or not in the country of the accident at the time of the accident, or whether having subsequently ceased to reside there, the same principle of the equality of treatment of foreigners and citizens applied. Thus the French law's derogation of the principle was now superseded in so far as concerned Italian as well as Belgian workmen.

The Treaty provided that French employers could engage an Italian institution to insure Italian assigns not resident in France, conformably to a table of provisional rates annexed to the agreement and subject to revision thereafter. If an *entrepreneur* or insurer vested in the French National Old Age Pensions Fund his liabilities toward Italian laborers, the function of paying the pension might, on demand of an Italian insuree, be turned over to the Italian National Workmen's Disablement and Old Age Provident Fund, the French institution paying quarterly to the latter the monies due. In case of benefits having a fixed rate, the French Fund might make the payment in a lump sum and thereby avoid the nuisance of quarterly payments. Similar stipulations operated for the accommodation of French workmen acquiring indemnities in Italy. Direct remittances from the Italian

[16] *E. B.* II, (1), pp. 2-4.

Fund to French entitled parties were to be made by postal money orders. (*mandats d'office.*)

Should a special inquiry be concluded with reference to an accident, intelligence of the same was to be immediately given to the consular authority of the district within which the injured workman lived when the casualty took place. Fiscal advantages or exemptions granted by one State to documents prerequisite to the acquisition of insurance monies were to apply equally in the other State. If an Italian pensioner not resident in France should fail to receive payments due and appeal to the Guarantee Fund established by French law, competence to deal with the difficulty would not reside in the municipal authorities as under customary procedure, but would rest in the Italian consular authorities at Paris. The conditions governing the exercise of consular power in such cases were to be determined by the authorities concerned in the two countries. Necessity might work the suspension of the stipulations of the Treaty wholly or in part. If one of the powers gave notice of intention to terminate the agreement in accordance with the regulations specifically prescribed for such action, the force of the arrangement was not to be impaired in so far as it concerned redress due for accidents occurring up to the time of its expiration. The prerogatives and obligations vested in national Funds and consular authorities by the terms of the Treaty were to become of no effect upon its expiration, with necessary exceptions, however, for the regulation of accounts then running and the payment of pensions for which the capital *in toto* had been previously received by a Fund.

Franco-Luxemburg Accident Insurance Treaty. June 27, 1906.

In the same month that France signed the preceding agreement, she signed with Luxemburg an accident insurance Treaty[17] of the same nature as the other Treaties already discussed. The principles covering the Treaty that France signed with Belgium (Feb. 21, 1906) may be repeated almost verbatim in an analysis of this act. It was concluded for an indefinite lapse of time, reserving the right of denunciation to each party under condition of a year's notice.

[17] *E. B.* II, (1), pp. 4-5.

Franco-German Understanding With Reference to Letters Rogatory.

Before the close of the year 1906, a commendable precedent had been established by the harmonious action of French and German authorities with reference to the status of letters rogatory pertaining to labor accidents and functioning between the two countries.[18] It seems that the German Secretary of State for Foreign Affairs had received from the French Ambassador a letter rogatory emanating from a French justice and requesting the adduction on German soil of evidence relating to a certain industrial accident. The German authorities graciously deferred to the request, whereupon the Government of France vouchsafed its readiness to reciprocate the favor whenever a similar contingency should lead Germany to solicit it. A common basis for the treatment of such letters was thus established in a manner highly creditable to the national administrators concerned. This spirit of accommodation is efficacious for the removal of mountains in international relations.

German-Netherlands Accident Insurance Treaty. Aug. 27, 1907.

The German-Netherlands Treaty [19] like the German-Luxemburg Treaty stipulated that persons employed temporarily (not over six months) in one State by an enterprise domiciled in the other should be subject to the compulsory accident insurance laws of the undertaking's headquarters. It differed from some of the other Treaties in its pains to specify that it was compulsory insurance law that was contemplated, and also in the fact that the traveling staff of transportation lines was to be subject to the insurance law of their line's domicile irrespective of the length of their employment on foreign soil or the foreign situs of any accident. But these topics which constituted the gist of the German-Luxemburg Treaty, were made to appear the exceptions in the present Treaty, whose principal and affirmative declaration was that, subject to the exceptions noted, those enterprises belonging to categories of undertakings covered by the insurance laws of both

[18] Chatelain—*La Protection internationale ouvriére.* p. 227.
[19] E. B. II, (3), pp. 350-351.

States and having headquarters in one State but operating in the territory of the other, should be governed by the accident insurance law of the country of operation. Thus it did not specify the equality of treatment of foreigners and subjects; but in so far as law in either country did not discriminate against foreigners, one might infer that equality of treatment would result from its terms.

Provision was made whereby in case of litigation authorities of one country could obtain the sworn depositions of witnesses resident in the other, while exemptions in respect of stamp duties and fees in the administration of the law of one Government were to apply equally to the administration within its borders of the accident insurance law of the other contracting Government. Also, premium rates were not to be varied by one State so as to be prejudicial to employers whose business houses had headquarters in the other. The basis of ascertaining in the currency of one country the equivalent of wages paid in the other was to be determined in a manner specified, whenever the administration of the law necessitated such calculations. Upon the conclusion of the year following the notice of its denunciation by either party, the agreement would become null and void.

A supplementary Treaty [20] of May 30, 1914 decreed that persons were to become subject to the operation of this agreement even though their domicile should not be that of the institution that carried their risk. This addition may be interpreted as indicating that, in so far as accident insurance law did not positively discriminate against foreigners, it was desired that its privileges should be shared equally by both native and foreign operatives; and so would indicate that the Treaty favored more than an optional or supererogatory application of the principle of the equality of citizens and foreigners before the insurance laws of either country.

Franco-British Accident Insurance Treaty. July 3, 1909.

The span of two years intervened before another accident insurance Treaty was signed. This time it was between France

[20] E. B. X, (7-8), p. 197.

and the United Kingdom.[21] With the pronunciamento that was its chief principle, we are quite familiar; *viz.*, that of the reciprocal accord of accident insurance to foreign laborers and assigns on the same terms as to citizens. The customary exception for employment of less than six months' duration on soil other than that of the undertaking's domicile was inserted including specifically the intermittent employment common to transportation service. Ratifications were exchanged Oct. 13, 1910, and the Decrees notifying the Convention's promulgation were published in France Oct. 28, 1910. In giving effect to this Treaty a British Order in Council stated that questions as to English liability for compensation to French citizens, or amounts of such indemnity, *etc.*, were to be adjudicated by the County Court. Certain conditions were prescribed by which the responsibility for the payment of insurance to French pensioners who had returned to France, was transferred from English to French authorities, that is from the jurisdiction of the County Court to the *Caisse nationale Francaise des Retraites pour la Vieillesse*. An arrangement subsequent, and giving effect, to the Treaty, between the British Secretary of State for the Home Department and the French Minister of Labor, provided that in case of periodic payments to a pensioner who went back to France to live, remittance by the County Court to such an insuree should be made every three months, the recipient providing each time a certificate from the Mayor of the Commune in which he lived, testifying that he was alive. The recipient was also to obtain, as often as the County Court required, a medical certificate specifying whether or not he still remained incapacitated. Such certificates were to be authenticated by a *visé* of the prefectoral administration which would attest the status of both the Mayor and the doctor concerned.

Hungarian-Italian Accident Insurance Treaty. Sept. 19, 1909.

The fundamental principle in the Hungarian-Italian accident insurance Treaty[22] of 1909 was the same as in the preceding Treaty. But a feature new to this class of treaties was the declaration that workmen, who coincident with employment outside of

[21] E. B. IV, (3), pp. 163-164.
[22] E. B. V, (1), pp. 1-3.

territory of either of the contracting countries suffered injury in the service of a business concern domiciled in one of them, were to be entitled to compensation under the compulsory insurance law of the concern's domicile, unless the insurance legislation of the country where the accident happened was found to cover the case. Dependents of injured parties were to receive compensation irrespective of their place of residence at the time of or after the accident. In case subjects resided in one country and drew pension from an institution of the other, means were provided, as in some former treaties, whereby the insurance company in question might transfer its obligation to the institution of the country where the pensioner resided. Moreover, documents exempt from fees when used in drawing pension in one State were to be favored similarly when used for the same purpose within the territory of the other.

Another distinctive feature, also new to treaties of this class, had to do with the creation of a Court of Arbitration in case the pact gave rise to litigious differences. Such a Court was to be instituted upon demand of one of the parties, each State choosing as arbitrators two subjects of its own who would select a presiding officer from some third power. The State in which to convene the Court in the first instance would be determined by agreement and thereafter automatically by the principle of alternation. The precise spot for court proceedings would be designated and made ready by the State selected. These provisions could be varied if the States agreed to carry on the proceedings in writing. Upon application of the Court to the Government, recourse might be had to the authorities of either State for the serving of summons or letters of request in accordance with the customs of Civil Court proceedings. Seven years were to elapse before the Treaty could be denounced, and thereafter withdrawal could in no case be effected until Dec. 31st of the year following that in which warning was given. Certain other provisos were also included to the end that defeasance should not work injustice to those who had become pensioners when the Treaty was in force.

Franco-Italian Pact. June 10, 1910.

We have seen that in consequence of the Franco-Italian Treaty of April 15, 1904, which established a system of monetary transfer to operate between the French National Savings Bank and the Post Office Savings Bank of Italy, various other agreements in execution of principles therein stated were subsequently entered upon; *viz.*, the agreement of Jan. 20, 1906 governing the transference of deposits between ordinary French and Italian savings banks; that of June 9, 1906 regulating compensation for industrial accidents; and now that of June 10, 1910 in protection of young workers of either country employed within the other.[23] Thus despite the critic's animadversion of its hypothesizing tendencies, the Franco-Italian Convention of 1904 has demonstrated that the spinning of theories even on the part of treaties may after all constitute a road to their actual realization in law.

Shortly after the conclusion of the Treaty in 1904, France had proposed a basis upon which to formulate measures protecting in the manner suggested the young workers of both countries; and Italy, considerably disturbed about the employment of young Italians in French glass works, agreed to dispatch a representative to enter into negotiations with reference to the French proposals. The negotiations extended over the years 1905-1909 and finally culminated in the agreement of 1910, by which young Italians desiring to work in France and young Frenchmen desiring to work in Italy were obliged to obtain the necessary employment book through compliance with regulations which were in general as follows: The young person in question accompanied by a parent or guardian produced before a consul of his government the employment book issued by his own country. If he was under fifteen years of age, the consent of his legal protector had to be conveyed in a duly legalized document and deposited at the consulate. When the consular certificate duly certified and bearing the applicant's photograph had thus been procured, he could obtain the requisite employment book from the Mayor or proper communal authority of the foreign State wherein he desired to labor. Where children between the ages of twelve and thirteen were concerned, additional certificates were required, particularly, the French elementary school certificate or the Italian certificate prescribed by Act of July 15, 1877. (No. 3961.)

At the very beginning of the negotiations over the agreement

[23] *E. B. V*, (4), pp. 329-332.

five years previous, Italy had requested that Italian children under fifteen be denied employment books by French authorities; but inasmuch as French children were admitted to work at the ages of twelve and thirteen, the authorities could not see their way clear to make special exceptions in favor of Italian children. Moreover such action would be extraneous to what was contemplated by the Treaty of 1904, which had merely stated that the nature of the documents and forms of the certificates required for presentation to consular and mayoral offices should be determined and properly inspected, and that committees of protection should be organized. The French authorities promised, however, to introduce into the Treaty such measures as would adequately protect young Italian employees, especially those in unhealthy occupations such as the manufacture of glass. Some of its protective measures relating to children under fifteen have been mentioned. The following clauses of the Treaty in further extension of the protective principle are worthy of complete citation: "Employment in unhealthy and dangerous trades shall be regulated by the law in force in the country where the work is performed. In the case of glass and crystal works, dangerous and unhealthy operations which, at the date of the signing of this agreement, may not lawfully be performed by young persons in Italy, shall not be lawfully performed by young persons in France, and reciprocally.

"In view of the fact that the age of protected persons is not identical under the French Act of 2nd November, 1892, and the Italian Act of 10th November, 1907, the Decrees issued in both countries in pursuance of their respective Acts shall specify the age of persons whom it shall not be lawful to employ in the operations in question.

"The two Governments shall use their best endeavors to introduce uniformity in the age of protected persons by means of internal regulations. With this object they shall, if necessary, promise an international Agreement within the meaning of S 3 of the Convention of April 15, 1904."

Various documents and certificates that might be issued from time to time in pursuance of the Treaty were to be exempt from fees in conformity to the law of both countries and their preparation by consular authorities was to be without charge to the young persons concerned. A strict inspectorate with confiscation of all employment books or certificates irregularly issued was also required, together with the record of all such confiscations. Finally in fulfillment of that contemplated by the Treaty of 1904, protective committees were to be organized in large industrial centers, including in their membership as many of the young workers' fellow countrymen as possible and giving gratuitous service. The enforcement of the law in general and of Acts particularly specified, the detection of its violation or any malfeasance in respect thereto, and the reporting of the same to proper authorities were to be within the province of the committees' supervision. The Treaty was to remain in force five years, and if not denounced six months previous to the conclusion of that period, it would continue to be binding for another five-year period, and so on. This is an important feature and is certainly conducive to much greater stability and certainty in international relations than in the cases where treaties may be denounced from year to year.

Franco-Italian Arrangement, August 9, 1910.

Within a short time Italy and France concluded another agreement growing out of the Treaty of 1904. This arrangement[24] prescribed conditions under which the beneficiaries of persons, whether Italians or Frenchmen, could draw their pensions from institutions of the country in which they lived, although the pension had been originally acquired from an institution of the other country.

German-Swedish Treaty Contemplating Workmen's Insurance. May 2, 1911.

A Treaty of Commerce and Navigation[25] between Germany and Sweden imitated the example of the Swiss-Italian and German-Italian Treaties of 1904, wherein workmen's insurance became an object of contemplation for the parties concerned, in relation to the question of according equal advantages to the sub-

[24] Mahaim—*Le Droit international ouvrier*, Annexe V, p. 328.
[25] E. B. VII, (11-12) p. cv.

jects of either party laboring within the boundaries of the other. While seeming to contemplate a broader field than accident insurance only, the praiseworthy ends presented by these Treaties had not up to this time (1911) been realized between any of the parties to them, even in the wellbeaten path of accident insurance understandings.

Franco-Danish Treaty. Aug. 9, 1911.

An entirely new type of Treaty made its appearance in the series we are considering, Aug. 9, 1911, called the Franco-Danish Treaty of Arbitration.[26] It provided that differences of a judicial character arising out of the interpretation of treaties were, in default of settlement by diplomatic channels, to be submitted to arbitration at The Hague, except in cases that affected the independence, honor, or vital interest of either of the contracting States, or the interest of third powers; which means, as we pointed out with reference to the proposal of the Portuguese Delegation at The Hague, that either party can reserve from adjudication at The Hague anything it pleases.

But the Franco-Danish Treaty contains the earnest of an advance to higher ground in these particulars. Four classes of questions are by it entirely excluded from any appeal to the reservation above remarked; in other words, the contracting States agreed that under all circumstances certain questions should, as a last resort, automatically become subject to arbitration at The Hague. Of these classes thus made the subjects of compulsory arbitration, the last two are of particular interest to us:

"(3) Interpretation and application of the stipulations of the Convention relating to trade and navigation.

"(4) Interpretation and application of the stipulations of the Convention relating to the matters hereunder indicated:

"Industrial property, literary and artistic property, international private right as regulated by the Hague Conventions, international protection of workers, posts and telegraphs, weights and measures, sanitary questions, submarine cables, fisheries, measurement of ships, white slave trade."

[26] 2E. B. VI, (3), pp. 229-230.

The disagreements relating to No. 4 and subject to judicial authority under territorial law, were to await the decision of national jurisdiction before they were referred to arbitration, and awards of the arbitration tribunal were not to affect previous judicial decisions; but the contracting parties agreed to take measures on occasion to bring about the adoption of the arbitrator's interpretation by the State tribunals. Thus while the Arbitral Tribunal was precluded from annulling the decisions of national tribunals, its decisions were to be looked up to as a standard by which to unify diverse principles of judicial interpretation obtaining within the judicatures of the two countries. Should the parties disagree as to whether a difference belonged to the category of disputes to be submitted to compulsory arbitration, the Treaty invested the Arbitral Tribunal with authority to decide; or, should the parties be unable to reach a compromise, after a year's notification by one of them authority would vest in the Permanent Court to establish such a compromise. The Convention would renew itself for five-year periods under tacit consent.

Swedish-Danish Sick Funds Compact.

Another novel international arrangement [27] was that entered into in the same year (1911) between *Sveriges Allmänna Sjukkasseforbund* ("Swedish General Association of Sick Funds") and *De samverkande danske centralforeningar af Sjukkasson* ("United Central Associations of Sick Funds of Denmark"), terminable after one year's notice by either party. This agreement, entirely unofficial, made it possible for a member of Sick Funds in one Association, changing his residence to the country of the other, to become immediately a member of the Sick Funds there, wholly unhampered by any requirement of entrance fee, age, state of health, period of waiting, *etc.* After Dec. 31, 1911, persons who joined Sick Funds after their fortieth birthday, would not become entitled to this privilege of transfer. The Association with which a constituent cancelled his conection was relieved of all liabilities of the case, and the withdrawer became subject to any special conditions governing the Sick Funds to which he

[27] *E. B.* VII, (11-12) p. cv.

transferred his membership. Annual reports were to be exchanged between the Associations, specifying all Sick Funds, belonging to either organization, that were parties to the agreement. Any serious differences arising between such Sick Funds of the two countries were to be resolved by the chief organizations of each, or as a last appeal, by the Sick Funds Inspector of the country to which membership had been transferred. Jan. 1, 1912 was set as the date for the agreement to take effect.

Draft for Spitzenbergen Convention. Jan. 26, 1912.

A draft [28] under date of Jan. 26, 1912 for an international Convention in respect of labor at Spitzenbergen laid down rules under which employers were to enter into a written contract with each workman; and, in case of sickness, accord to the laborer proper attendance free of charge. In case of accident the employer, beside complying with the foregoing requirement was to pay an indemnity. Another equally salutary stipulation, unusual to drafts for international conventions, and evidently based on the principle that an ounce of prevention is worth a pound of cure, was the prohibition of the sale of alcoholic beverages to the worker by or on behalf of the employer.

German-Belgian Accident Insurance Treaty. July 6, 1912.

Approximately six months after the date of this proposal,[29] Belgium and Germany entered into an accident insurance Treaty[30] that complemented insurance legislation of the two States in 1903 and 1906 respectively. Except for State or transportation undertakings, enterprises domiciled within one country and extending their sphere of operation into the other were to become subject to the accident insurance laws of the country where operations were carried on, provided compulsory accident insurance obtained for the category of establishments in question

---

[28] *Bulletin of the International Labor Office.* IX, (8-10) p. 319.

[29] For another Convention of something of this character signed (Oct. 20, 1906) by England and France concerning the recruitment of native laborers in the New Hebrides, see *E. B.* II, (3) pp. 345-350.

[30] *E. B.* VIII, (2), pp 47-49.

in both States. We recognize that this agrement is of the same type as the German-Netherlands Treaty. With slight variations, the general exception met with in most of these treaties held good for this; that is, for the first six months of operation in territory of the foreign State, undertakings would be subject to the insurance legislation of the home State in so far as concerned employees who had been previously attached to the works when functioning in the home State. In calculating the period of operation outside the country of domicile with reference to a series of works carried on concurrently or successively, the time would be reckoned from the beginning of the first to the termination of the last of such works; but should an interval of over thirty days elapse between the completion of one operation and the commencement of the next, a new period of six months would begin for the operation in question.

Certain State undertakings were to be subject in all cases to the accident insurance regulations of the home State, while, as provided in the German-Netherlands Treaty, the staff of the traveling portions of transportation enterprises were to be protected in all cases by the insurance laws of the home State. Actions for civil liability connected with accidents were to occur under the law of the country whose legislation on compensation applied in the case. The agreement contained the usual stipulations relative to engaging the mutual assistance of authorities in execution of the laws of one State within the other, including exemptions from stamp duties, the intermediacy of consular agencies, the establishment of a standard by which to express value in different systems of coinage, *etc.* Notice of its discontinuance might be given at any time; at the end of the year following such notice, the Treaty would be terminated. The documents ratifying the Treaty were exchanged on 10th January, 1913.

German-Italian Accident Insurance Treaty. July 31, 1912.

Less than a month after the conclusion of the German-Belgian Treaty, the most comprehensive insurance Treaty[31] yet drawn up was signed by the representatives of Germany and Italy. Thus

[31] *E. B.* VIII, (3-4), pp. 99-103.

the suggestions of the German-Italian Treaty of 1904 at last materialized, and on an unprecedented scale; for the departments of this Treaty were distinct and four in number, including:
  I. Accident Insurance.
  II. Invalidity, Old Age and Survivors' Insurance.
  III. General Provisions.
  IV. Final Provisions (in part, contemplating future conventions).

The part devoted to accident insurance was another repetition of the principle of the equality of foreigners and citizens before the law of the country in which they labored. The agreement held good for Italian Accident Insurance of agricultural laborers only in case they were insured according to the Italian Act of Jan. 31, 1904. A person might vacate his right to pension by accepting a lump sum equal to three times the amount of his annuity; if the insurers preferred to make over to a pensioner a capital sum equivalent to the value of, and in lieu of, his periodic pension, the insuree was obliged to accept.

The provisions of Part II dealing with invalidity, old age and survivors' insurance were more complicated. It should be remembered in this connection that contributions for the purchase of insurance in German institutions were derived in part from employers as well as from employees, and that not only was insurance compulsory, but it extended its benefits under certain conditions even to Germans working outside their State; *e.g.,* in Italy. Contributions for and in behalf of Italian subjects to the German Invalidity and Survivors' Insurance were to be equal to payments for German subjects, even if the Italians were enrolled at the same time in an institution of their own land; *viz., Cassa Nazionale di Previdenza per la invalidita e per la vecchiaia degli operai,* or *Cassa Invalidi della Marena Mercantile.* An Italian thus doubly enrolled might demand that half of the money used to purchase his insurance in the German institution be paid, in his behalf, by the German insurer to the Italian Fund; in which case the Italian subject or his assigns could claim insurance from the Italian institution only. For claims arising previous to the application for transfer, the German institution would stand liable. Italians might also transfer to their own national institutions additional voluntary insurance bought under German law. Military duty in Italy was to be reckoned as the equivalent of such duty in Germany under the insurance law of the latter. Differences in the insurance legislation of the two States rendered many stipulations of the Treaty applicable to only one of the parties to it.

The subjects of Germany in Italy were privileged to enroll as members of the Italian National Provident Fund upon an equal footing with Italian subjects save for certain exceptions specified. Such a German insuree could require the refund by the Italian institution of all payments made to it in his behalf, should he leave Italy before the contingency of insurance arose. Italian employers paying premiums to the Fund for workmen of their own nationality were obligated to do the same for German workers. The fundamental principle governing the insurance of Germans in the Mercantile Marine Invalidity Fund of Italy was the same as for the other Fund. If a German drawing pension from either Fund voluntarily situated his home beyond Italian territory, his policy lapsed upon his receipt of a payment triple the amount of his annuity. Should the German leave the country upon the order of Italian authorities, his pension would not suffer suspension, although it might be terminated by the process of triplication; but if his departure were in consequence of conviction for crime, his pension would be forfeited.

Part III of the Treaty, declarative of general provisions after the order of treaties already studied, enjoined that mutual assistance be accorded by the authorities of each body politic in all matters concerned with the execution of the law; that exemptions from stamp duties and fees, decreed by one country for its own administration, were to be extended to the administration within its confines of the insurance laws of the other; and that the proper consular authorities were always to be notified of the conclusion of an inquiry into an accident relevant to insurance proceedings. Also for the purpose of taking evidence or serving legal papers in foreign jurisdiction, arrangements were contemplated whereby the assistance of the consular authorities of either country might be invoked.

There were also stipulations heretofore unknown to this class of treaties. For the administration of German insurance within

Italy, the latter was to send to the German Government a list of the names of Italian doctors, hospitals, *etc.* suitable for medical treatment of injured Germans, besides also seeing to it that expenses in connection with these individuals and institutions should not become excessive.

Part IV, entitled "Final Provisions," was of the order of resolutions that looked toward future agreements, which we have discovered to be sometimes condemned and frequently made light of as insufficiently practical; but in view of the offspring which they now can boast, we are justified in lending them for a few moments at least our careful and respectful attention. The signatories considered a future convention enlarging the scope of this agreement so as to include agricultural insurance, when such a system should be introduced in Italy as might be deemed equivalent to German Agricultural Accident Insurance. Likewise they looked forward to the conclusion of a convention placing their respective subjects upon the same footing with respect to invalidity, old-age, and survivors' insurance, when Italy in this phase of insurance had evolved an organization equal to that of Germany.

The date for the Treaty's coming into force was April 1, 1913; it could be denounced at any time and would cease to be valid at the end of the year following such notice. Ratifications were exchanged at Berlin March 25, 1913, and six days later there appeared in Germany official notifications with reference to special measures to be pursued in execution of certain of its articles and paragraphs.

German-Spanish Accident Agreement Respecting Sailors.

An accident contract[32] respecting sailors was concluded between Germany and Spain by an exchange of Diplomatic Notes on Nov. 30, 1912 and Feb. 12, 1913. By this agreement, if a Spanish sailor on board a German ship met with an accident in a German port, or was brought to a German port after the accident, German officials were to notify the competent Spanish consul; similar procedure was obligatory if the port was non-Ger-

[32] E. B. VIII, (6-7), p. 247.

man; and if the port was Spanish and at the same time a chief town of a province the civil Government or else the Alcade was to be notified. In case the accident occurred on the high seas, it was incumbent upon the German Consul to notify, if possible, the proper authorities within twenty-four hours from the moment the ship entered a Spanish port. By interchanging the words "Spanish" and "German" reciprocal action was specified for a German injured in the employ of a Spanish ship, except that in the clause last referred to in the agreement, the last two words; *viz.*, "Spanish port" seem to have been retained in the reciprocal rephrasing of the clause instead of inserting the naturally expected words "German port."

Treaty Between Italy and the United States. Feb. 25, 1913.

By reason of the fact that the prerogatives of labor legislation have inhered principally in the individual commonwealths of the American Republic rather than in congressional legislation, and because constitutional tradition upholding the theory of the partibility of soverignty has been very jealous of what is known as "state's rights" in contradistinction to national centralization of authority, the liberty that the United States might otherwise have felt free to exercise in matters pertaining to international agreements in protection of labor has been greatly lessened. An example of about the best we have done thus far in the way of a protective labor Treaty is the agreement signed between Italy and the United States under date of Feb. 25, 1913 in amendment of an old Treaty of Commerce and Navigation of Feb. 26, 1871. The principle clause of the late agreement [38] is as follows:

"The citizens of each of the High Contracting Parties shall receive in the States and Territories of the other the most constant security and protection of their persons and property and for their rights, including that form of protection granted by any State or national law which establishes a civil responsibility for injuries or for death caused by negligence or fault, and gives to relatives or heirs of the injured party a right of action which shall not be restricted on account of the nationality of said relatives or heirs; and shall enjoy in this respect the same rights and privi-

---

[38] *E. B.* VIII, (9-10), p. 363.

leges as are or shall be granted to nationals, provided that they submit themselves to the conditions imposed on the latter."

There is comparatively little federal law in America, other than that covering federal employees or employees engaged in interstate commerce, that may be termed distinctively protective labor law. As an example of such law we may note that the use of white phosphorus in the manufacture of matches has been effectively prevented through a statute prohibiting the importation or exportation of matches containing the substance, and levying a prohibitive tax upon such matches.[34] At the same time state laws are very diverse and in many instances very deficient, which is a situation that cannot continue indefinitely if we are to maintain a place in the sphere of industrial legislation compatible and comparable with the dignity of our social and political position in the world.

Franco-Swiss Insurance Agreement. Oct. 13, 1913.

In the same year (1913) France and Switzerland entered into an understanding [35] to prevent Frenchmen or foreigners working on French soil and regularly employed by the Swiss Federal Railroads from becoming subject to the old-age insurance systems of both France and Switzerland. The legislation of the two countries was dissimilar, but the agreement dissipated the difficulties which had arisen by stipulating that such employees on French soil might be insured in the Swiss system in place of the French; but if not insured in either, they were obliged to take out protection according to the terms of French law.

As a side light upon the compulsory old-age insurance of railroad employees obtaining in both France and Switzerland, it is worthy of note that by an Act of July 21, 1909,[36] France compelled the great railway lines to insure all employees in a retiring pension scheme, to which contributions were made by the railway companies and by means of deductions from the salaries of the employees. The scope of old-age pension in France was extended

---

[34] *United States Statutes at Large* (1911-1913), Vol. 37, Part I, p. 81. Chap. 75.—An Act to provide for a tax upon white phosphorus matches, and for other purposes.

[35] *E. B.* IX, (3), p. 61.

[36] *E. B.* IV, (4) pp. 302-305.

by an Act of April 5, 1910,[37] entitling to its benefits employees of both sexes in industry, agriculture, commerce, and the liberal professions, servants, state employees not insured in civil or military systems, and employees of Departments and communes. It was in general a compulsory system with support derived from state subsidies, contributions of employers, and either compulsory or voluntary contributions of insured parties according as the case might require. Foreign laborers came within the terms of its requirements without benefit of employers' contributions or budgetary subventions except as reciprocity treaties with other countries might provide for such privileges.

Italian-German War Arrangement. May 12-21, 1915.

The following clause explains an agreement[38] between Italy and Germany after the outbreak of the World War; and just before Italy's Declaration of War upon Austria-Hungary (May 23, 1915). "The subjects of either of the two States shall continue to enjoy the benefits provided in the laws in force in the other country in the matter of social insurance. The power to take advantage of the rights in question shall not be resticted in any manner."

* * *

There are certain principles which in general are common to these international agreements covering insurance, particularly accident insurance. In brief they stipulate for:

(1) Equality of treatment of foreigners and citizens working in the same country, before the insurance law of that country.

(2) An exception for the first six months of an establishment's operation on foreign soil, during which the insurance laws of the State of its domicile apply.

(3) Inclusion of transportation lines in the above exception.

(4) Mutual aid in the administration of the laws of one country within the territory of the other.

(5) Reciprocal grant of special exemptions in the administration of the insurance law of one State within the territory of the other (usually, to the effect that special advantages and exceptions incident to the insurance legislation of one State shall apply

[37] E. B. V, (4) pp. 361-375.
[38] E. B. XI, (6-7), p. 181.

to the administration within its territory of the insurance law of the other).

(6) Denunciation of the Treaty to take effect one year after notice; (or, as sometimes stated, at the expiration of the year following the denunciation).

(7) Notification of the inquiry into an accident to the proper consular authority, (frequently, under the condition that such notification be tendered immediately, upon the conclusion of the inquiry, to the consul in the district where the injured party resided at the time of the accident.)

(8) Facilities by which insurance acquired by individuals in a foreign country may be paid to them through institutions of their own country.

(9) A forecast of possible treaties of the future.

The foregoing treaties on accident insurance may be roughly classified in groups according to the above principles. Treaties completely characterized by principle No. 9 in so far as relates to workmen's insurance are the Swiss-Italian (1904), the German-Italian (1904), the German-Austro-Hungarian (1905), and the German-Swedish (1911). The same is true of the Franco-Italian Treaty (1904) in so far as it relates to accident insurance.

A group of agreements providing in general that firms operating in the territory of the other country less than six months are to be subject to the accident insurance law of the country of operation, are the German-Luxemburg Treaty (1905) to which principles 2-3-4-5 apply, the German-Netherlands Treaty (1907) to which principles 2-4-5-6 are applicable, and the German-Belgian Treaty (1912) to which apply the same principles 2-4-5-6.

The category to which belong the largest number of treaties, is distinguished by a precise declaration of the principle that, in respect of compensation for accidents, subjects of either party working in the territory of the other are to enjoy equal privileges with the citizens of the land in which they labor. This group in which are all of the following treaties, may be further subdivided. To the Belgian-Luxemburg Treaty (1905), the Franco-Luxemburg Treaty (1906), and the Franco-Belgian Treaty (1906), principles 1-6 inclusive apply, covering also principle 7 in the case of the last-named Treaty; by the Franco-Italian agreement (1906), the Hungarian-Italian agreement (1909), and the German-Italian agreement (1912), principles 1-4-5-6-7-8 are clearly stated, including No. 9 in the instance of the German-Italian Treaty. The Franco-British Treaty (1909) contains principles 1-2-3-4-6-8.

Much however that is not stated in a treaty in so many words may be enacted in pursuance of its interpretation by a protocol or by administrative authorities. Moreover, the existence of other law may make unnecessary a statement of principle that would otherwise occur. Therefore, if an insurance treaty does not formally specify that subjects of both countries are to be treated equally in respect of the insurance law of either, it is patent that the omission of itself constitutes no proof that the principle is not applied by the parties in question. Thus we find Germany by virtue of her national legislation applying various phases of this principle in her treatment of laborers of Belgium and Luxemburg within her territory, although her accident insurance Treaties with these countries do not make any statement specifically to this effect,

APPENDIX I.

Labor Law Internationally Adopted.

CONTENTS

APPENDIX I.

Labor Law Internationally Enacted

Exhibit. Page.
1. Draft of an International Convention Respecting the Prohibition of the use of White (Yellow) Phosphorus in the Manufacture of Matches (1905) 174
2. Draft of an International Convention Respecting the Prohibition of Night-Work for Women in Industrial Employment (1905).... 174
3. International Convention Respecting the Prohibition of Night-Work for Women in Industrial Employment (September 26, 1906) 175
4. International Convention Respecting the Prohibition of the use of White (Yellow) Phosphorus in the Manufacture of Matches (September 26, 1906) 178
5. Convention Between France and Italy (April 15, 1904)........ 180
6. Agreement, Concluded on the 9th June, 1906, Between France and Italy, Relating to Compensation for Injuries Resulting from Industrial Accidents 184
7. Agreement, Concluded on 10th June, 1910, Between France and Italy, Relating to the Protection of Young Persons of French Nationality Employed in Italy and *Vice Versa* 189
8. Treaty of Commerce Between Switzerland and Italy (July 13, 1904) Extract 194
9. Treaty of Commerce Between the German Empire and Italy, (December 3rd, 1904) Extract 195
10. Treaty of Commerce Between the German Empire and Austria-Hungary, (Jan. 19, 1905) Extract.............................. 195
11. Treaty on Accident Insurance Between the Grand-Duchy of Luxumburg and Belgium, (April 15, 1905) 195
11a. Supplementary Convention Between Luxumburg and Belgium, (May 22, 1906) 197
12. Treaty on Insurance Between Germany and Luxumburg, (Sept. 2, 1905) 197
13. Franco-Belgian Treaty Relating to Compensation for Injuries Resulting from Industrial Accidents, (Feb. 21, 1906)............ 200

CONTENTS (Continued)

Exhibit   Page

13a. Note, Dated 12th March, 1910, in Pursuance of the Convention Respecting Compensation for Injuries Resulting from Industrial Accidents, Concluded at Paris on the 21st February, 1906 Between France and Belgium 201

14. (German Empire) Notification to Repeal Provision of the Accident Insurance Acts in Favor of the Grand-Duchy of Luxumburg, (May 9, 1905) 202

15. Convention Between France and Luxumburg Relating to Compensation for Injuries Resulting from Industrial Accidents, (June 27, 1906) 203

16. Treaty Between the German Empire and the Netherlands Relating to Accident Insurance, (August 27, 1907) 205

16a. Supplementary Treaty Between the German Empire and the Netherlands, (May 30, 1914) 208

17. Convention Signed at Paris the 3rd day of July, 1909, Between France and the United Kingdom 208

18. Agreement Between Hungary and Italy Respecting Accident Insurance, (Sept. 19, 1909) 210

19. Treaty of Commerce and Navigation Between the German Empire and Sweden, (May 2, 1911) Extract......................... 215

20. Franco-Danish Treaty of Arbitration, (Aug. 9, 1911)........... 215

21. Convention Between the German Empire and Belgium in Regard to Insurance Against Industrial Accidents, (July 6, 1912) 217

22. Convention Between the German Empire and the Kingdom of Italy with Respect to Workmen's Insurance, (July 31, 1912)..... 221

23. Agreement Between the German Empire and Spain Concerning the Reciprocal Communication of Accidents to Spanish Sailors on German Ships and of German Sailors on Spanish Ships (Concluded by Exchange of Diplomatic Notes on 30th of Nov., 1912, 12 February, 1913) 227

24. Treaty Between Italy and the United States, Amending the Treaty of Commerce and Navigation Concluded 26th February, 1871 (Feb. 25, 1913) 228

25. Agreement Between France and Switzerland Relating to Pensions to be Granted to Members of the Staff of the Swiss Federal Railroads Employed on French Territory (Oct. 13, 1913)...... 229

EXHIBITS

EXHIBIT I.

Draft of an International Convention Respecting the Prohibition of the Use of White (Yellow) Phosphorus in the Manufacture of Matches (1905)

Article 1.—Beginning with January 1, 1911, the importation, manufacture, or sale of matches containing white (yellow) phosphorus shall be prohibited.

Art. 2.—The records of ratification shall be deposited not later than December 31, 1907.

Art. 3.—The Government of Japan shall be invited to declare its adhesion to the present Convention before December 31, 1907.

Art. 4.—The Convention shall take effect on condition of the adhesion of all the States represented at the conference and of Japan.

(Translation: *G. B.—Bulletin des Internationalen Arbeitsamtes*, Bd. IV, p. 1.)

EXHIBIT 2.

Draft of an International Convention Respecting the Prohibition of Night-Work for Women in Industrial Employment (1905).

Article 1.—The industrial night-work of all women shall be prohibited, save for the exceptions hereafter stated:

The Convention shall apply to all industrial enterprises which employ more than ten men and women workers; it shall not apply in any case to undertakings in which only members of the family are engaged.

It shall be incumbent upon each of the contracting parties to define just what is meant by the term "industrial enterprises." In any case the same shall include mines and quarries, as well as manufacturing industries; the line of demarcation between industry on the one hand and agriculture and commerce on the other shall be specified by the legislation of each State.

Art. 2.—The night-rest contemplated in the preceding article shall be of at least eleven consecutive hours' duration. In these eleven hours must be included in every State the interval from 10 p. m. to 5 a. m.

However, in the States in which the industrial night-work of adult female employees is not now regulated, the duration of uninterrupted rest may, by way of transition and for a period of not more than three years, be limited to ten hours.

Art. 3.—The interdiction of night-work may be suspended:

1. In cases where there occurs in an enterprise an interruption of work, impossible to foresee and nonperiodic in character caused by natural forces;

2. In cases where the occupation involves materials susceptible of very rapid deterioration, when night-work shall be required in order to save such materials from inevitable destruction.

Art. 4.—In the industries subject to the influence of the seasons, and in every industry in case of exceptional circumstances, the period of unbroken night-rest may be reduced to ten hours on sixty days in the year.

Art. 5.—The records of the ratification of the Convention must be deposited by December 31, 1907, at the latest.

The Convention shall come into force three years from the date of the deposition of the ratifications.

That interim shall be ten years:

1. For manufactories of raw beet sugar;
2. For wool combing and weaving;
3. For open mining operations suspended at least four months in the year because of climatic conditions.

(Signed at Bern on 16th May, 1905.)

(Translation: *Ibid.*, pp. 1-2.)

EXHIBIT 3.

International Convention Respecting the Prohibition of Night-Work for Women in Industrial Employment
(Sept. 26, 1906).

Article 1.—Night-work in industrial employment shall be prohibited for all women without distinction of age, with the exceptions hereinafter provided for.

The present Convention shall apply to all industrial undertakings in which more than ten men or women are employed: it shall not in any case apply to undertakings in which only the members of the family are employed.

It is incumbent upon each contracting state to define the term "industrial undertakings." The definition shall in every case include mines and quarries and also industries in which articles are manufactured and materials transformed: as regards the latter, the laws of each individual country shall define the line of division which separates industry from agriculture and commerce.

Art. 2.—The night rest provided for in the preceding article shall be a period of at least 11 consecutive hours; within these 11 hours shall be comprised the interval between 10 in the evening and 5 in the morning.

In those states, however, where the night-work of adult women employed in industrial occupations is not as yet regulated, the period of uninterrupted rest may provisionally, and for a maximum period of three years, be limited to 10 hours.

Art. 3.—The prohibition of night-work may be suspended—

(1) In the cases of *force majeure,* when in any undertaking there occurs an interruption of work which it was impossible to foresee and which is not of a periodic character.

(2) In cases where the work has to do with raw materials or materials in course of treatment which are subject to rapid deterioration, when such night-work is necessary to preserve the said materials from certain loss.

Art. 4.—In those industries which are influenced by the seasons, and in all undertakings in the case of exceptional circumstances, the period of the uninterrupted night rest may be reduced to 10 hours on sixty days of the year.

Art. 5.—It is incumbent upon each of the contracting states to take the administrative measures necessary to ensure the strict execution of the terms of the present Convention within their respective territories.

Each Government shall communicate to the others through the diplomatic channel the laws and regulations which exist or shall hereafter come into force in their country with regard to the subject matter of the present Convention, as well as the periodical reports on the manner in which the said laws and regulations are applied.

Art. 6.—The present Convention shall only apply to a colony, possession or protectorate when a notice to this effect shall have been given on its behalf by the Government of the Mother Country to the Swiss Federal Council.

Such Government when notifying the adhesion of a colony, possession or protectorate shall have the power to declare that the Convention shall not apply to such categories of native labour as it would be impossible to supervise.

Art. 7.—In extra-European states, as well as in colonies, possessions or protectorates, when the climate, or the condition of the native population shall require it, the period of the uninterrupted night rest may be shorter than the minima laid down in the present Convention provided that compensatory rests are accorded during the day.

Art. 8.—The present Convention shall be ratified and the ratifications deposited with the Swiss Federal Council by December 31, 1908, at the latest.

A record of this deposit shall be drawn up of which one certified copy shall be transmitted to each of the contracting states through the diplomatic channel.

The present Convention shall come into force two years after the date on which the record of deposit is closed.

The time limit for the coming into operation of the present Convention is extended from two to ten years in the case of—

1. Manufactories of raw sugar from beet.
2. Wool combing and weaving.
3. Open mining operations, when climatic conditions stop operations for at least four months every year.

Art. 9.—The states non-signatories to the present Convention shall be allowed to declare their adhesion to it by an act addressed to the Swiss Federal Council, who will bring it to the notice of each of the other contracting states.

Art. 10.—The time limits laid down in Article 8 for the coming into force of the present Convention shall be calculated in the case of non-signatory states as well as of colonies, possessions or protectorates, from the date of their adhesion.

Art. 11.—It shall not be possible for the signatory states, or the states, colonies, possessions or protectorates who may subsequently adhere, to denounce the present Convention before the expiration of twelve years from the date on which the record of the deposit of ratification is closed.

Thenceforward the Convention may be denounced from year to year.

The denunciation will only take effect after the lapse of one year from the time when written notice has been given to the Swiss Federal Council by the Government concerned, or, in the case of a colony, possession or protectorate, by the Government of the mother country. The Federal Council shall communicate the denunciation immediately to the Governments of each of the other contracting states.

The denunciation shall only be operative as regards the state, colony, possession or protectorate, on whose behalf it has been notified.

In witness whereof the plenipotentiaries have signed the present Convention.

Done at Berne this twenty-sixth day of September, nineteen hundred and six, in a single copy, which shall be kept in the archives of the Swiss Confederation, and one copy of which, duly certified, shall be delivered to each of the contracting states through the diplomatic channel.

(E. B.—*English Bulletin of the International Labor Office*, Vol. I, (4-8), pp. 273-275).

EXHIBIT 4.

International Convention Respecting the Prohibition of the Use of White (Yellow) Phosphorus in the Manufacture of Matches (Sept. 26, 1906).

(1) The High Contracting Parties bind themselves to prohibit in their respective territories the manufacture, importation, and sale of matches which contain white (yellow) phosphorus.

(2) It is incumbent upon each of the contracting states to take the administrative measures necessary to ensure the strict

LABOR LAW INTERNATIONALLY ADOPTED

execution of the terms of the present Convention within their respective territories.

Each Government shall communicate to the other through the diplomatic channel the laws and regulations which exist or shall hereafter come into force in their country with regard to the subject matter of the present Convention, as well as the reports on the manner in which the said laws and regulations are applied.

(3) The present Convention shall only apply to a colony, possession or protectorate when a notice to this effect shall have been given on its behalf by the Government of the mother country to the Swiss Federal Council.

(4) The present Convention shall be ratified, and the ratifications deposited with the Swiss Federal Council by December 31, 1908, at the latest.

A record of the deposit shall be drawn up, of which one certified copy shall be transmitted to each of the contracting states through the diplomatic channel.

The present Convention shall come into force three years after the date on which the record of the deposit is closed.

(5) The states non-signatories to the present Convention shall be allowed to declare their adhesion by an act addressed to the Swiss Federal Council, who will bring it to the notice of each of the other contracting states.

The time limit laid down in Article 4 for the coming into force of the present Convention is extended in the case of the non-signatory states, as well as of their colonies, possessions or protectorates, to five years, counting from the date of the notification of their adhesion.

(6) It shall not be possible for the signatory states, or the states colonies, possessions or protectorates who may subsequently adhere, to denounce the present Convention before the expiration of five years from the date on which the record of the deposit of ratification is closed.

Thenceforward the Convention may be denounced from year to year.

The denunciation will only take effect after the lapse of one year from the time when written notice has been given to the

Swiss Federal Council by the Government concerned, or, in the case of a colony, possession or protectorate, by the Government of the mother country; the Federal Council shall communicate the denunciation immediately to the Governments of each of the contracting states.

The denunciation shall only be operative as regards the state, colony, possession or protectorate on whose behalf it has been notified.

In witness whereof the Plenipotentiaries have signed the present Convention.

Done at Berne this twenty-sixth day of September, Nineteen hundred and six, in a single copy which shall be kept in the archives of the Swiss Federation, and one copy of which duly certified shall be delivered to each of the contracting powers through the diplomatic channel.

(*Ibid*, pp. 275-276.)

EXHIBIT 5.

Convention Between France and Italy (April 15, 1904).

The President of the French Republic and His Majesty the King of Italy desiring by international agreement to insure to workers reciprocal guarantees analagous to those which treaties of commerce have provided for the products of labor and particularly;

(1) To secure to their subjects working in the foreign country, the enjoyment of their savings and to procure for them the benefit of social insurance, and

(2) To guarantee to workers the maintenance of protective measures and to co-operate for the advancement of labor legislation, have resolved to conclude a convention to that effect and have named for their plenipotentiaries, *etc.* . . . .

Article 1.—Negotiations shall be entered into at Paris after the ratification of the present Convention for the conclusion of arrangements based on the principles hereafter stated and designed to regulate the detail of their application, exception being made for the Arrangement relative to the State Savings Bank of France and the Postal Savings Bank of Italy contemplated in paragraph (a) below, which shall be annexed to the Convention.

(a) The funds deposited as savings, either in the State Savings Bank of France or the Postal Savings Bank of Italy, can, on demand of the interested parties, be transferred without charge from the one to the other bank, each of the banks applying to the deposits thus transferred the general rules which it applies to deposits made in it by its own nationals.

A law of transfer, on a corresponding basis may be established between the different private savings banks of France and Italy, having their domicile in large industrial centers or in frontier towns. Without requiring absolute gratuity of transfer, this law shall stipulate for the co-operation of the Post Office either gratuitously or at reduced rates.

(b) The two governments shall facilitate, through the medium both of the Post Office and the National Funds, the payment of insurance premiums of Italians resident in France to the National Provident Fund of Italy, and of Frenchmen residing in Italy to the National Pension Fund of France. They shall facilitate, likewise, the payment in France of pensions acquired, either by Italians, or by Frenchmen, to the National Fund of Italy, and reciprocally.

(c) The admission of manual workers and other employees of Italian nationality to old-age and perhaps invalidity insurance, in the general system of labor pensions now under consideration of the French Parliament, as well as the participation of laborers and employees of French nationality in the system of workingmen's pensions in Italy, shall be regulated immediately after the passage of legislative provisions in the contracting countries.

The part of the pension corresponding to the deposits of the worker or employee or to deductions from his wage shall accrue to him in full.

As to the part of the pension corresponding to the contribution of the employer an arrangement shall be made upon the principle of reciprocity.

The part of the pension which will be eventually derived from State subsidies shall be left to the estimate of each State and paid from its funds to its nationals having acquired a pension in the other country.

The two contracting States shall facilitate through the medium both of the Post Office and their insurance Funds the payment in Italy of pensions acquired in France, and reciprocally.

The two governments shall study a special system for the acquisition of pensions by workers and employees who have worked successively in the two countries during minimum periods to be determined without fulfilling in either of the two the conditions required for workingmen's pensions.

(d) The workers and employees of Italian nationality injured in France by reason or at the instance of their labor, and also their representatives resident in France, shall be entitled to the same indemnities as Frenchmen, and reciprocally.

The Italian beneficiaries of annuities ceasing to reside in France as well as dependants of the injured parties who were not resident in France at the time of the accident, shall be entitled to pensions to be determined. The capital sums equivalent to the actuarial value of the benefits in accordance with a scale annexed to the Arrangement, shall be deposited in the National Provident Fund of Italy to be applied by it as a guarantee of the payment of the annuity. The Italian National Accident Insurance Fund shall likewise insure French employers according to a conventional scale, against their liabilities to representatives not being resident in France, of injured Italian workmen, if such employers desire to be relieved from the obligation of making inquiries and all other similar proceedings. Equivalent advantages shall be reciprocally guaranteed to French workmen injured in Italy.

(e) The admission of Italian workmen and employees in France to insurance institutions or relief funds against unemployment subsidized by the State, and the admission of French laborers and employees in Italy into similar institutions shall, in case of the passage of legal provisions relative to these institutions in both countries, be thereafter regulated.

(f) The arrangements provided for in the present article shall be concluded for a period of five years. The contracting parties must give notice one year in advance, if it is their intention to terminate the agreement upon the expiration of that period. In the absence of such notice, the arrangement shall be extended from year to year, for a period of one year, by tacit renewal.

Art. 2. (a)—In order to avoid errors or false declarations the two governments shall define the character of the documents to be presented to Italian Consulates by young Italians engaged to work in France, as well as the form of the certificates to be furnished by the said Consulates to the Mayoral offices before delivering to children the employment books prescribed by child-labor legislation. The labor inspectors shall require the presentation of the certificates upon each visit and shall confiscate employment books wrongfully possessed.

(b) The French government shall organize Protection Committees including among their members as many Italians as possible in industrial regions where a large number of young Italians not living with their families are employed through middlemen.

(c) The same measures shall be adopted for the protection of young French workers in Italy.

Art. 3.—In case the initiative shall be taken by one of the two contracting States, or by one of the States with whom they maintain diplomatic relations, to convoke an international conference of various governments with the object of bringing about uniformity by means of conventions in certain provisions of protective labor laws, the adhesion of one of the two Governments to the proposal of the Conference shall entail upon the other Government a response favorable in principle.

Art. 4.—At the moment of signing this Agreement the Italian Government engages to complete the organization throughout the whole kingdom, and more particularly in those regions where industry is developed, a factory inspection system operating under the authority of the State, and affording, for the application of the laws, guarantees analagous to those which the factory inspection system of France presents.

The inspectors shall enforce the observance of the laws in force on the work of women and children, and especially the provisions which relate to—

1. The prohibition of night-work;
2. The age of admission to work in industrial shops;
3. The length of the workday;
4. The obligation of weekly rest.

The Italian Government engages to publish an annual detailed report on the application of the laws and regulations relative to the work of women and children. The French Government assumes the same obligation.

The Italian Government furthermore declares that it intends to apply itself to the study and gradual realization of the progressive reduction of the length of the workday of women in industry.

Art. 5.—Each of the two contracting parties reserves to itself the option of denouncing at any time the present Convention and the Arrangements provided by Article 1, by giving notice one year in advance, if there is evidence that the legislation relative to work of women and children has not been respected by the other party, in the matters specified in Article 4 paragraph 2, in default of adequate inspection, or by reason of sufferances contrary to the spirit of the law, or in case the legislature shall diminish the protection decreed in favor of labor in respect of the same points.

Art. 6.—The present Convention shall be ratified and the ratifications shall be exchanged at Rome as soon as possible.

In witness whereof, the plenipotentiaries have signed the present Convention and affixed their seals thereto.

Drawn up in duplicate at Rome, April 15, 1904.

(Translation: *Archives diplomatiques*, 1904, t. 92, p. 1269-1274.)

N. B. Part II of this Convention relates to the transfer of funds deposited in the Savings Banks of the two countries.

EXHIBIT 6.

Agreement, Concluded on the 9th June, 1906, Between France and Italy, Relating to Compensation for Injuries Resulting From Industrial Accidents.

(1) Italian workmen or employees who meet with accidents arising out of or in the course of their employment on French

territory, or their representatives, shall have the same rights to compensation as French workmen or employees, or their representatives, and *vice versa*.

(2) The same rule shall apply, subject to the conditions contained in the following articles, to claimants who were not residing within the territory of the country where the accident happened at the time when it occurred, or who subsequently ceased to reside therein.

(3) If an accident is followed by an inquiry, notice of the conclusion of the inquiry shall be given immediately to the consular authority of the district within which the injured workman was living at the time when the accident occurred, in order that the said authority may take note of the inquiry in the interests of the claimants.

(4) Employers and insurers in either country shall have the right to pay installments of benefit or compensation due through the agency of the consular authority, contemplated in the preceding article, of the other country. The said authority shall produce the papers of identity and life certificates, and also make provision for forwarding instalments of benefit or compensation to subjects of his country residing within his district at the time of the accident.

(5) The Italian National Accident Insurance Fund shall insure French employers, on the model scale appended to this agreement, against their liabilities to representatives, not being resident in France, of injured Italian workmen, if such employers desire to be relieved from the obligation of making inquiries and other proceedings.

The proper authorities of the two countries shall revise this provisional scale as soon as possible in the light of statistical data to be collected hereafter.

(6) If an employer or insurer has made provision with the French National Old Age Pensions Fund for pensions to Italian workmen or their representatives, payment of such pensions shall, at their request, be made to them through the Italian National Workmen's Disablement and Old Age Provident Fund. In this case the French National Fund shall settle with the Italian

Fund by forwarding every quarter the amount of the pension claims which would have been payable in France.

In the case of benefits, the rate of which is definitely fixed, the French National Fund may settle with the Italian National Fund by depositing a capital sum equivalent to the actuarial value of the benefit in accordance with the scale on which the same has been acquired; this deposit shall be devoted to the purchase of an annuity in accordance with the scale in force for the Italian National Fund at the time.

(7) If an employer or insurer has deposited with the Italian National Provident Fund compensation due to French workmen, the Fund shall, on application, forward to them by money order (*mandat postal*) the amount which would have been payable in Italy.

In the case of benefits the rate of which is definitely fixed, the Fund may discharge its liabilities by depositing with the French National Pension Fund a capital sum equivalent to the actuarial value of the benefit in accordance with the scale on which the same has been acquired; this deposit shall be devoted to the purchase of an annuity in accordance with the scale in force for the French National Fund at the time.

Compensation falling due for fatal accidents incurred by French workmen in Italy may be deposited in the form of a lump sum with the French Deposit Fund (*Caisse des dépots et consignations*), which shall hold the amount at the disposal of the interested parties on their claim being proved.

(8) The money orders contemplated in the first paragraph of Article 7, and sums forwarded by the National Pension Fund to the Italian National Provident Fund, or reciprocally, shall take the form of office orders (*mandats d'office*) under the conditions set forth in Article 5 of the agreement relating to the transfer of deposits between the ordinary savings banks of the two countries.

(9) The two national funds shall always reserve the right to amend their respective scales in the future.

(10) Exemption from taxes and any financial advantages granted by French law to documents which have to be presented

in order to obtain compensation, shall apply equally in cases where the documents in question are required for the payment of compensation under Italian law, and *vice versa.*

(11) If an Italian workman, not resident in France, fails to receive the compensation to which he is entitled, and if he applies to the Guarantee Fund established by French law, the duties devolving, in connection with such applications, upon the municipal authorities, shall be fulfilled, on his behalf, by the Italian consular authorities in Paris, under conditions to be determined by the authorities concerned in the two countries.

(12) Each of the two contracting parties reserves the right, in the case of *force majeure,* or of urgent circumstances, to suspend the terms of this agreement, wholly or in part, in so far as it concerns the respective functions of the national funds of the two countries. Notice of suspension shall be given, through diplomatic channels, to the proper authorities of the other State.

The notice shall fix the date after which the regulations relating to the said functions shall cease to have effect.

(13) The proper authorities of the two countries shall agree together upon the proofs to be furnished in the cases contemplated in Articles 4, 5, 6, 7, and the conditions under which the said articles shall apply to injured workmen or their dependants not residing either in France or Italy.

They shall at the same time draw up detailed rules and regulations necessary for the execution of this agreement.

(14) This agreement shall come into force on a day to be agreed upon by the two States after its promulgation in accordance with their respective laws.

Except in the case contemplated in the Convention of 15th April, 1904, this agreement shall remain in force for five years. The two contracting parties shall be mutually bound to give one year's notice of their intention to terminate the agreement at the conclusion of this period. In the absence of such notice, the agreement shall be renewed from year to year, for the term of one year, by tacit consent.

(15) If one of the two contracting parties shall have announced its intention of withdrawing from the agreement, the

agreement shall continue to have full force, as far as concerns the rights of injured persons or their representatives, against their employers in respect of all accidents occurring before the expiration of the agreement. Notwithstanding, it shall cease to have effect on its expiration as far as concerns the duties devolving upon the consular authorities and the obligations or functions of the National Funds of the two countries, except as regards the settlement of accounts then current, and the distribution of annuities, the capital value of which they may have received previously.

SCHEDULE.

	Annual Premiums of Insurance payable in respect of each 1,000 frs. paid in Wages.
Industrial Undertakings in general	4.98
Mines	12.36
Quarries	10.02
Brick Works	4.62
Iron and Steel Works	3.50
Metal works (other than iron and steel), Scientific instruments, musical instruments	1.14
Metal works (other than iron and steel)	0.96
Scientific instruments	1.38
Chemical industries	4.26
Gas and water	3.30
Building operations	6.96
Special for chimney-sweeping	5.82
State railways	7.72
Private railways	6.54
Street railways (An economic and legal classification peculiar to Germany, corresponding to the ordinary division of industries into great, medium and small)	4.20
Freight, warehousing, cartage	9.84
Cartage	14.46
Inland navigation	18.30

(*E. B.* 11, (I), pp. 2-4).

EXHIBIT 7.

Agreement Concluded on 10th June, 1910, Between France and Italy Relating to the Protection of Young Persons of French Nationality Employed in Italy and Vice Versa.

(1) The provisions of the Agreement are concerned with the provisions of the French Act of 2nd November, 1892, on the one hand, and with the provisions of the Italian Act of 10th November, 1907 (Codified Text), Text E. B., II, p. 578, on the other hand, and their object is to better secure the protection of young people of Italian nationality in France and of young people of French nationality in Italy.

Except in so far as concerns the alternative elementary school certificate contemplated in Sect. 4, and regardless of the special penalties hereinafter provided, all the provisions of the aforesaid French Act and, in particular, the provisions relating to age and penalties shall apply to young persons of Italian nationality employed in France. Reciprocally, the provisions of the aforesaid Italian Act shall apply to young persons of French nationality employed in Italy.

(2) In order to obtain an employment book contemplated in the Acts of 2nd November, 1892, and 10th November, 1907, or in any subsequent enactments regulating the granting of employment books in either country, young persons of Italian nationality in France and young persons of French nationality in Italy must produce to the Communal Authority a certificate conformable to the prescribed model (Schedule A) issued by the Consul concerned. Notwithstanding, such certificate shall not be required in the case of young persons of Italian nationality whose birth is registered in the French civil registers, nor in the case of young persons of French nationality whose birth is registered in the Italian civil registers.

Both in France and Italy it shall be unlawful for a Mayor to issue an employment book, unless the Consul's certificate is produced to him, bearing a photograph of the owner of the certificate stamped on the certificate itself by the Consul, or signed by the owner of the certificate in the presence of the Consul. The Mayor shall attest the certificate, seal it with the Communal

Seal, and attach it to the employment book as an integral part of the same.

Every Consul shall keep a register of the Consular certificates issued by him, showing the forenames, surname, sex, age and place of birth, of each young person concerned, and the date when and the grounds on which the certificate was issued. Every Consul shall, at the end of each year, send in to the French Ambassador at Rome or the Italian Ambassador at Paris, as the case may be, statistics of, and a report on, the certificates entered in the register. The Ambassadors shall forward the documents in question to the Authorities concerned in their respective countries.

Every Mayor shall keep a register of the employment books issued by him, showing the forenames, surname, sex and age, of each young person concerned, the date of the Consular certificate and the date when the employment book was issued.

(3) In order to obtain a Consular certificate, a young person must come before the Consul, accompanied by his father, mother or guardian, and must produce his employment book obtained in his country of origin.

He may also be accompanied by any other relative of full age or by the person who desires to employ him. Notwithstanding, in either case if he has not yet completed the fifteenth year of his age, he must produce a document, duly legalised, giving the consent of the person who possesses legal authority over him. The document in question shall be deposited at the Consulate.

In the event of the young person being unable to produce an employment book issued to him in his country of origin he may instead produce his birth certificate or a certificate of birth conformable to the prescribed model (Schedule B) and a certificate of identity attested by two of his compatriots known to the Consul. Nothing in this paragraph shall affect any written consent contemplated in the foregoing paragraph.

(4) With regard to the employment in France of children between twelve and thirteen years of age, the certificate prescribed in the Italian Act of 15th July, 1877 (No. 3961), may be produced in lieu of the elementary school certificate prescribed in the French Act of 28th March, 1882. Similarly in the case of

French children between twelve and thirteen years of age employed in Italy, the certificate prescribed in the French Act may be produced in lieu of the certificate prescribed in the Italian Act. Such certificates shall not be required in the case of young persons of Italian nationality in France or young persons of French nationality in Italy who have completed the thirteenth year of their age.

In order to make use in France of an Italian school certificate a young person must produce it to the Italian Consul, in addition to the documents specified above in Sect. 3, and a note to that effect shall be entered in the Consular certificate (Model A). Reciprocally, the same formalities shall be complied with in Italy when it is desired to make use of a French certificate.

(5) The documents in pursuance of which the Consular certificate is granted, and which are returnable to the persons concerned, shall be stamped by the Consul with a special stamp (ink stamp), stating that they have been used to obtain a certificate authorising their owner to commence work.

(6) Consular certificates (Model A), certificates of birth (Model B), and the documents giving the consent of the parents, shall be exempt from all duties and fees, conformably to the provisions of the law of both countries respecting employment books and the documents required in order to obtain the same.

The preparation of documents and all official transactions, correspondence or legalisation of documents, incumbent upon the Consular Authorities, in pursuance of this Agreement, shall be undertaken without any charge to the young persons of Italian or French nationality concerned.

(7) The employer shall preserve the employment book during the whole continuance of the employment of the young person in question, and it shall be returnable on the termination of his employment.

The Labour Inspectors and the representatives of the Judicial Police shall, when visiting industrial establishments, examine all employment books and Consular certificates, and shall confiscate any which are found to have been issued in an irregular manner, or to be in the possession of any young person other than the persons in respect of whom they were issued.

Notice of confiscation conformable to Model C shall be sent

within three days to the Prefect, who, within the same term, shall forward the notice to the Consul in whose jurisdiction the commune in which the employment book was confiscated is situate. The Consul shall send a copy of this notice, together with a letter conformable to Model D, to all his Italian colleagues in France or his French colleagues in Italy, in order that they may be kept informed, in case of need, of the confiscation of employment books and certificates. Every Consul or Consular agent shall keep a register of confiscated employment books and certificates.

Persons found to have falsified, altered, transferred or unlawfully made use of an employment book shall be dealt with by the the Judicial Authorities.

(8) Employment in unhealthy and dangerous trades shall be regulated by the law in force in the country where the work is performed. In the case of glass and crystal works, dangerous and unhealthy operations which, at the date of the signing of this Agreement, may not lawfully be performed by young persons in Italy, shall not be lawfully performed by young persons in France, and reciprocally.

In view of the fact that the age of protected persons is not identical under the French Act of 2nd November, 1892, and the Italian Act of 10th November, 1907, the Decrees issued in both countries in pursuance of their respective Acts shall specify the age of persons whom it shall not be lawful to employ in the operations in question.

The two Governments shall use their best endeavours to introduce uniformity in the age of protected persons by means of internal regulation. With this object they shall, if necessary, promote an international Agreement within the meaning of Sect. 3 of the Convention of 15th April, 1904.

(9) The two Governments shall organise in the large industrial centres Protection Committees, whose services shall be gratuitous, and which shall, as far as possible, be composed of compatriots of the young persons in question. The Sub-Prefect, or a Prefectorial Councillor, the Mayor of the commune where the Committee acts, and the Labour Inspector of the commune

on the one hand, and the Consul on the other, shall be *ex-officio* members of the Committee.

Within six months after the ratification of this Agreement at least one Committee shall be constituted in every French district (*Arrondissement*) where more than fifty young persons of Italian nationality are employed.

These Committees shall supervise:

(1) The strict enforcement of the Laws and Orders relating to the employment of young persons of Italian or French nationality. For this purpose they shall inform the Labour Inspectors of all contraventions of which they become aware, and, in particular, of cases where young persons are employed in work beyond their strength;

(2) The strict observance: in France, of the requirements respecting the granting of certificates of fitness contemplated in Sect. 2, paragraphs 3, 4, and 5 of the Act of 2nd November, 1892; in Italy, of the requirements respecting medical certificates contemplated in Sect. 2 of the Act of 10th November, 1907, and respecting the conditions for the recognition of fitness prescribed by Order in pursuance of the said Act;

(3) The application to children of Italian nationality and their relations of the provisions of the French Act of 28th March, 1882, respecting compulsory elementary education, and the application to children of French nationality and their relations of the provisions of the Italian Act of 15th July, 1877.

The Committees, with the assistance of the Authority concerned, and subject to the requirements of the law of the country in question, shall also see that young persons lodged elsewhere than with their families, are properly and humanely treated, and that all hygienic and moral requirements are observed in their case. In cases where the conditions of feeding, clothing or housing are found to be defective, and in case of rough or bad treatment, the Committees shall put the matter before the local Authorities, who shall act according to the circumstances of the case.

Finally, these committees may, when necessary, extend their protection to all Italian workmen in France and to all French workmen in Italy, irrespective of age.

(10) The Authorities concerned in both countries shall issue simultaneously the Orders and Regulations which they may consider necessary for the execution of this Agreement.

(11) It is understood that the Consular agents may undertake all the operations entrusted to Consuls in pursuance of this Agreement.

(12) This Agreement shall in both countries be submitted to Parliament for approval. It shall be ratified and come into operation one month after the exchange of ratifications, which shall take place at Paris. It shall remain in force for five years, and if it is not denounced six months before the conclusion of this period, it shall be renewed for another period of five years, and so on thereafter.

(Schedules: Models A, B, C and D.)
(*E. B.* V, (4) pp. 329-332.)

EXHIBIT 8.

Treaty of Commerce Between Switzerland and Italy
(July 13, 1904).

(Extract)

Article 17.—The contracting parties engage to examine by common and amicable consent the treatment of Italian laborers in Switzerland and of Swiss laborers in Italy in regard to Workmen's Insurance, with the aim of securing by suitable arrangements to the workmen of each nation respectively, working in the territory of the other, a treatment which shall accord to them as far as possible equivalent advantages.

These arrangements shall be sanctioned by a separate act independent of the coming into force of the present treaty.

(Translation: L. Chatelain, *La protection internationale ouvrière*, p. 193.)

EXHIBIT 9.

Treaty of Commerce Between the German Empire and Italy (December 3, 1904).

(Extract)

Art. 4.—The contracting parties engage to examine by common and amicable consent the treatment of Italian laborers in Germany and of German laborers in Italy in regard to Workmen's Insurance, with the aim of securing by suitable arrangements to the workmen of each nation respectively, working in the territory of the other, a treatment which shall accord to them as far as possible equivalent advantages.

These arrangements shall be sanctioned by a separate act independent of the coming into force of the present treaty.

(Translation: *Ibid.,*:p. 194.)

EXHIBIT 10.

Treaty of Commerce Between the German Empire and Austria-Hungary (January 19, 1905).

(Extract)

Art. 6.—The contracting parties engage to examine by amicable agreement the treatment of the workmen of each party, working in the territory of the other, in respect of the protection of labor and Workmen's Insurance, with the object of insuring reciprocally to these workers by suitable arrangements, a treatment which shall accord to them as far as possible equivalent advantages.

These arrangements shall be sanctioned by a separate act independent of the coming into force of the present treaty.

(Translation: *Ibid.,* p. 198.)

EXHIBIT II.

Treaty on Accident Insurance Between Grand-Duchy of Luxemburg and Belgium (April 15, 1905).

Article 1.—Luxemburg workers meeting with industrial accident in Belgium, and likewise their dependents, shall enjoy the same compensation and the same guarantee of compensation as Belgian subjects.

Reciprocally, Belgian workers meeting with industrial accident in the Grand-Duchy of Luxemburg, and likewise their dependants, shall enjoy the same compensation and guarantees as Luxemburg subjects.

Art. 2.—An exception to the foregoing rule shall be made in case of persons without distinction of nationality, who are working temporarily, that is not over six months, on the territory of that one of the two contracting States in which the accident occurred, but for an undertaking domiciled within the territory of the other State. In such case only the legislation of the latter State shall apply.

Art. 3.—The stipulations of Art. 48, No. 2, and of Art. 49, paragraph 4, of the Luxemburg law of April 5, 1902 are suspended in favor of subjects of Belgian nationality.

Art. 4.—The stipulations of Art. 1, 2 and 3 of this Treaty shall apply to those persons who are considered equivalent to workers by the laws on industrial accident insurance of the two contracting States.

Art. 5.—The exemptions allowed as regards stamp and court fees, and the gratuitous delivery stipulated for by the legislation of Luxemburg relating to industrial accidents, are herewith extended to proofs, certificates and documents contemplated by this legislation which have to be drawn up or delivered in execution of the Belgian law.

Reciprocally, the exemptions allowed by the Belgian legislation are hereby extended to proofs, certificates and documents contemplated by this legislation which have to be drawn up and delivered in execution of the Luxemburg law.

Art. 6.—The authorities of Luxemburg and Belgium shall lend each other mutual assistance with a view to facilitating reciprocally the execution of the law relating to industrial accidents.

Art. 7.—This Treaty shall be ratified and the ratifications exchanged at Brussels as soon as possible.

It shall come into force ten days after it has been published in the two countries in accordance with the forms prescribed by their respective laws; and it shall remain in force until the expiration of one year from the day of its denunciation by one of the two contracting parties.

In witness whereof the plenipotentiaries of both parties have signed the present Treaty and affixed their seals thereto.

Drawn up in duplicate at Brussels, April 15, 1905.

(Translation: *Bulletin des Internationalen Arbeitsamtes.* Bd. IV, S. 305-306.)

EXHIBIT IIA.
Supplementary Convention Between Luxemburg and Belgium (May 22, 1906).

(1) The provisions following shall be added as a second paragraph to No. 2 of the Convention of April 15, 1905:

"The above shall hold good for persons engaged in transport undertakings and occupied intermittently, but habitually, in countries other than that in which the principal establishment of the undertaking is domiciled."

(2) This additional Convention shall have the same force and hold good for the same period as the Convention of April 15, 1905.

It shall be duly ratified, and these ratifications shall be exchanged at Brussels as soon as possible. It shall come into force ten days after its publication in the forms prescribed by the laws of the two countries.

In witness thereof the Plenipotentiaries have signed this additional Convention, and have affixed their seals thereto.

Made and duplicated at Brussels, May 22, 1906.

(*E. B.* I., (9-12), pp. 373-374.)

EXHIBIT 12.
Treaty on Industrial Accident Insurance Between Germany and Luxemburg (September 2, 1905).

Article 1.—Undertakings to which the compulsory accident insurance laws of the two States apply, with the exception of agricultural and forest works, and which are domiciled within the territory of one State and carry on operations temporarily within the territory of the other, shall, in the absence of other agreements between the competent insurance carriers of the two countries approved by the German Chancellor and the Grand-Ducal Government of Luxemburg, be subject, in respect of persons employed in their temporary branches in the territory of the other State to the accident insurance legislation of the State where the undertaking's main office is situated. In the meaning of this agreement a temporary branch within the territory of the other State is one whose presumable duration will not exceed six months. For each separate branch within the territory of the other State the period of time shall be reckoned separately.

Persons thus temporarily employed include the traveling staff of transport lines who cross the borders on through trains and also persons who without change of their business domicile are deputied in urgent circumstance to serve as substitutes on railroads within the territory of the other State, for not over six months.

Art. 2.—In case of doubt as to whether according to the provisions of Article 1, the accident insurance laws of the one or the other State are applicable, and if the insurance carriers of the two countries cannot come to an agreement between themselves and with the managers of the undertaking, and in case of compensation proceedings with the party entitled to indemnity, the authorities of the State in which the undertaking in question carries on operations shall have exclusive and final authority to decide—that is to say in Germany, the Imperial Insurance Office, and in Luxemburg, the Government.

The decision rendered conformably to paragraph 1 is binding upon the insurers in the other State and serves as the rule, without retroactive effect, to be followed, particularly in matters pertaining to contributions and indemnities, and for the question as to whether the officials in the one or the other State are responsible for the final treatment of the case. Before the decision by one of the two parties designated in paragraph 1, a hearing is to be given to the insurance carriers concerned and to the employer, and in case compensation proceedings are involved, also to the claimant; the decision rendered is to be communicated to the parties concerned.

Art. 3.—If an accident occurs furnishing without doubt occasion for indemnity, and yet there is doubt as to whether the payment is to be made by the insurance carriers of the one or the other State, the underwriter first involved in the case conformably to the legal proceedings valid for him shall, in the meanwhile, take care of the entitled parties.

The final incidence of indemnity shall fall upon that underwriter who shall thereafter be designated as the party obligated to pay compensation.

Art. 4.—If in accordance with the principles of this agreement, single undertakings or branches of undertakings pass from the accident insurance jurisdiction of one country to that of the other, the change shall be effected at the end of the current year only. By agreement of the insurer of the two countries, the transfer with legal effect for all parties concerned can be reckoned from the time of the coming into force of the present agreement.

Obligations resulting from accidents before the time of transfer, must be met by that insurer by whom the undertaking responsible for the accident was insured before the time of the transfer.

Art. 5.—In the execution of the accident insurance laws, especially in the ascertaining of such industrial accidents as come under the accident insurance laws of the home State but occur in the territory of the other State, the competent officials and authorities shall lend mutual legal aid irrespective of their duty to investigate these accidents officially as soon as possible.

Art. 6.—The foregoing terms shall apply by analogy to official employees of the German Empire, of a German Federated State, or of a German province or district, who are employed in undertakings in which insurance is compulsory which are designated by Article 1 but who in place of being insured under the German system of accident insurance are entitled to accident benefit within the meaning of Sect. 7 of the German industrial accident insurance law.

In that case the authorities competent to make decisions conformable to Article 2, differ from those designated by that Article in that for imperial employees the Imperial Insurance Office is replaced by the Chancellor; and for the employees of the States, provinces and districts, by the central authorities of the particular States.

In cases when the German laws on accident relief apply, the provisions of these laws on the compensation of other accident claims under the German law, shall also apply to compensation claims made in pursuance of the laws of Luxemburg in respect of an accident occurring in Luxemburg.

Art. 7.—This Treaty shall come into force one month after its conclusion and it can be denounced by either party on January 1 of each year, with the same to take effect the first day of January of the year next following.

In witness whereof the plenipotentiaries of both parties have signed the present Treaty and affixed their seals thereto.

Drawn up in duplicate in Luxemburg, Sept. 2, 1905.

(Translation: *Bulletin des Internationalen Arbeitsamtes*, Bd. IV, S. 306-308.)

EXHIBIT 13.

Franco-Belgian Treaty Relating to Compensation for Injuries Resulting From Industrial Accidents (Feb. 21, 1906).

(1) Belgian subjects meeting with industrial accidents in France, and likewise their dependants, shall enjoy the compensation and guarantees granted to French citizens by the legislation in force relating to compensation for industrial accidents.

Reciprocally, French subjects meeting with industrial accidents in Belgium, and likewise their dependants, shall enjoy the compensation and guarantees granted to Belgian citizens by the legislation in force relating to compensation for industrial accidents.

(2) Notwithstanding an exception to the rule shall be made if the persons in question were sent out of their own country temporarily, and occupied for less than the last six months on the territory of that one of the two contracting States where the accident occurred, but were taking part in an undertaking established within the territory of the other. In such case the persons interested shall have a right only to the compensation and guarantees provided by the legislation of the latter State.

The same rule shall apply to persons attached to transport undertakings, and employed intermittently, whether regularly or not, in the country other than that where the undertaking is domiciled.

(3) The exemptions allowed as regards stamps, records and registration, and the free delivery stipulated for by the Belgian legislation relating to industrial accidents, are hereby extended to proofs, certificates and documents contemplated by the legislation in question which have to be drawn up or delivered in pursuance of the French law.

Reciprocally, the exemptions allowed and free delivery stipulated for by the French legislation are hereby extended to proofs, certificates and documents contemplated by the legislation in question which have to be drawn up or delivered in pursuance of the Belgian law.

(4) The French and Belgian authorities shall lend each other mutual assistance with a view to facilitating reciprocally the execution of the laws relating to industrial accidents.

(5) The present Treaty shall be ratified and the ratifications exchanged at Paris as soon as possible.

The Treaty shall come into force in France and Belgium one month after it has been published in the two countries in accordance with the forms prescribed by their respective laws.

It shall remain in force until the expiration of one year from the day after it shall have been denounced by one or other of the contracting parties. In testimony whereof the respective plenipotentiaries have signed the present Treaty and affixed their seals thereto.

(*E. B. I.*, (4-6), pp. 153-154.)

EXHIBIT 13A.

Note, Dated 12th March, 1910, in Pursuance of the Convention Respecting Compensation for Injuries Resulting From Industrial Accidents, Concluded at Paris on the 21st February, 1906, Between France and Belgium.

In the application of Article 4 of the said convention, the two signatory States agree that in case of an accident giving occasion for an inquiry, notice of the termination of the said inquiry shall be given immediately to the consular authority of the district where the victim was residing at the time of the accident, in order that the authority in question may take note of the said inquiry in the interests of the interested parties.

This agreement shall not come into operation for three months after it is signed.

(*E. B.* VI, (1) p, 6.)

EXHIBIT 14.

(*German Empire*) Notification to Repeal Provisions of the Accident Insurance Acts in Favor of the Grand-Duchy of Luxemburg (*May 9, 1905*).

The Federal Council, at the sitting of the 4th of May, 1905, resolved as follows:

(1) The provisions of No. 94 (2) of the Industrial Accidents Insurance Act, and of No. 37, paragraph 1, of the Building Accidents Insurance Act, relating to the suspension of annuities in the case of foreigners whose usual residence is not in the interior, shall not apply to subjects of the Grand-Duchy of Luxemburg, even in cases when the annuitants do not usually reside within those districts of the Grand-Duchy of Luxemburg recognised by the resolution of the Federal Council adopted on the 13th October, 1900, as frontier districts within the meaning of the said provisions. (Cf. the Notification of the 16th October, 1900. *Zentralblatt für das Deutsche Reich*, p. 540.)

Notwithstanding, so long as an annuitant resides neither within the territory of the German Empire nor in the Grand-Duchy of Luxemburg, the right to draw an annuity shall depend upon his observing the past or future regulations issued for German subjects by the Imperial Insurance Office, in pursuance of No. 94 (3) of the Industrial Accidents Insurance Act. In respect of such annuities, the date of the coming into force of the regulations of the Imperial Insurance Office, dated the 5th July, 1901, shall be held to be the day when this resolution comes into force.

(2) The territory of the Grand-Duchy of Luxemburg shall be held to be a frontier district, so that the provisions of No.

21 of the Industrial Accidents Insurance Act, No. 22 of the Accident Insurance Act for Agriculture and Forestry, No. 9 of the Building Accidents Insurance Act, and No. 27 of the Marine Accidents Insurance Act, relating to the exclusion of claims for dependants' annuities in the case of dependants of foreigners not having their usual residence in the interior at the time of the accident, shall not apply to such dependants, if their usual residence is within the territory of the Grand-Duchy.

(3) The provisions of No. 21 of the Industrial Accidents Insurance Act and No. 9 of the Building Accidents Insurance Act, relating to the exclusion of claims for dependants' annuities, shall not apply to subjects of the Grand-Duchy of Luxemburg, even though their usual residence at the time of the accident was not within the territory of the Grand-Duchy of Luxemburg. (See No. 2 above.)

(4) The preceding provisions shall apply retrospectively from the 15th April, 1903, as far as concerns claims not legally settled at the time when the resolution comes into force.

(5) This resolution shall come into force on the 15th May, 1905.

(*E. B.* II, (1) pp. 1-2. See also *E. B.* I, (1-3) pp. V. I.)

EXHIBIT 15.

Convention Between France and Luxemburg Relating to Compensation for Injuries Resulting From Industrial Accidents (June 27, 1906).

(1) Subjects of the Grand-Duchy of Luxemburg meeting with industrial accidents in France and likewise their dependants, shall enjoy the compensations and guarantees granted to French subjects by the legislation in force relating to compensation for industrial accidents.

Reciprocally, French subjects meeting with industrial accidents in Luxemburg, and likewise their dependants, shall enjoy the compensation and guarantees granted to subjects of the Grand Duchy of Luxemburg by the legislation in force relating to compensation for industrial accidents.

(2) Notwithstanding, an exception to this rule shall be made if the persons in question were sent out of their own country temporarily, and occupied for less than the six months last past on the territory of that one of the two contracting States where the accident occurred, but were taking part in an undertaking established within the territory of the other. In such case the persons interested shall have a right only to the compensation and guarantees provided by the legislation of the latter State.

The same rule shall apply to persons attached to transport undertakings, and employed intermittently, whether regularly or not, in the country other than that where the undertaking is domiciled.

(3) The exemptions allowed as regards stamps, records and registration, and the free delivery stipulated for by the legislation of the Grand-Duchy relating to industrial accidents, are hereby extended to proofs, certificates and documents contemplated by the legislation in question which have to be drawn up and delivered in pursuance of the French law.

Reciprocally, the exemptions allowed and free delivery stipulated for by the French legislation are hereby extended to proofs, certificates and documents contemplated by the legislation in question which have to be drawn up and delivered in pursuance of the law of the Grand-Duchy of Luxemburg.

(4) The French authorities and the authorities of the Grand-Duchy of Luxemburg shall lend each other mutual assistance with a view to facilitating reciprocally the execution of the law relating to industrial accidents.

(5) The present Treaty shall be ratified and the ratifications exchanged at Paris as soon as possible.

The Treaty shall come into force in France and in the Grand Duchy of Luxemburg one month after it has been published in the two countries in accordance with the forms prescribed by their respective laws.

It shall remain in force until the expiration of one year from the day after it shall have been denounced by one or other of the contracting parties. In testimony whereof the respective plenipotentiaries have signed the present Treaty and affixed their seals thereto. Drawn up in duplicate at Paris, 27th June, 1906.

(*E. B.* 11, (1) pp .4-5).

EXHIBIT 16.

Treaty Between the German Empire and the Netherlands Relating to Accident Insurance (Aug. 27 1907).

(1) Undertakings to which the accident insurance laws of the two Contracting States apply and which are domiciled within the territory of one State and carry on business also within the territory of the other, shall, subject to the exceptions contemplated in Articles 2 and 3, be subject, in respect of business carried on within the territory of either State, exclusively to the accident insurance laws of that State.

Where, in accordance with the preceding paragraph, an undertaking carrying on business outside the territory of one State is subject to the insurance laws of the other, such undertaking shall be held to be an undertaking within the meaning of the said laws. Further regulations for the enforcement of the Treaty shall be drawn up independently by each State according to the needs of their respective systems of accident insurance.

In Germany the said regulations shall be drawn up by the Imperial Chancellor or an authority designated by him, and in the Netherlands by the department having authority for the time being. The regulations so drawn up shall be communicated to the two Governments.

(2) In the case of transport undertakings carrying on operations across the frontier, the accident insurance laws of the country where the undertaking is domiciled shall alone apply in respect of the travelling staff, regardless of the extent of the the operations carried on in the two respective countries. The travelling staff shall remain subject to the said insurance laws also in respect of other classes of employment carried on on behalf of such transport undertakings outside their country of domicile.

(3) Persons employed in a department of any kind of undertaking where insurance is compulsory under the laws of their own country, shall, on being transferred to work in the other country, remain in respect of all branches of their employment in the said country, for the first six months of such employment,

subject exclusively to the accident insurance laws of the country where the firm is domiciled, provided that the rules contained in Article 2 shall not be affected hereby. If the employment in the said country is interrupted for a period not exceeding 30 days, such period shall be included in the six months' limit. If the period during which the employment is interrupted exceeds 30 days, the course of the six months shall be held to be broken off, and, on the resumption of employment in the said country, a new term of six months shall be held to begin. In applying the preceding rules, account shall not be taken of any period before this Treaty comes into force.

(4) Where the accident insurance laws of one country are applicable, the rules contained in such laws for proving claims thereunder in respect of accidents occurring outside the realm, shall apply, by analogy, to compensation claims made in pursuance of the laws of the other country in respect of an accident occurring in such country.

(5) In administering the accident insurance laws the proper authorities shall give each other mutual assistance in determining the facts of any case.

Where, in dealing with an accident insurance case, the authorities of one country deem it necessary to procure the sworn depositions of witnesses and experts in the other country, a request to this effect duly submitted through diplomatic channels shall be acceded to. The authorities instructed by the Government of the said country or having jurisdiction without such instructions shall summon the witnesses or experts by official action and, if necessary, use such means of compulsion as are prescribed in the case of similar proceedings in their own country.

(6) Rules in force in one country relating to exemptions from stamp duties and fees in the case of accident insurance business, shall apply by analogy in respect of the administration in such country of the accident insurance laws of the other.

(7) Manufacturers shall not be required to pay higher contributions or premiums in respect of the accident insurance of one country for the reason that their undertakings are domiciled in the other.

(8) The provisions of Articles 4-7 shall apply to undertakings subject to the accident insurance laws of one of the two countries, even in cases where the conditions set forth in Article I, do not obtain.

(9) The terms of this Treaty shall apply by analogy to those officials of the German Empire, of a German Federated State, or of a German group of parishes (Kommunalverband) who are employed in undertakings in which insurance is compulsory, but who are, notwithstanding, entitled to accident benefit within the meaning of German legislation, instead of being insured under the German system of accident insurance.

(10) Where, in administering the accident insurance laws of one country, it is necessary to calculate the value of wages expressed in terms of the currency of the other country ,such conversion shall be affected by taking as a general basis an average rate of exchange, which shall be determined by each of the two Governments for the purposes of the administration of the law in their respective countries and which shall be communicated by each Government to the other.

(11) This Treaty shall be ratified and the ratifications exchanged as soon as possible. The Treaty shall come into force one month after the first day of the month following the exchange of ratifications.

Notice of withdrawal from the Treaty may be given by either party at any time, and the Treaty shall expire on the conclusion of the calender year next following such notice.

Liabilities in respect of accidents occurring before this Treaty comes into force, shall continue thereafter to be fulfilled by the insurance institution wherein the branch in question of the undertaking was formerly insured. Similarly, on the expiration of this Treaty, liabilities in respect of accidents which occurred while the Treaty was in force, shall continue to be fulfilled by the previous insurance institution.

In witness whereof the plenipotentiaries have signed this Treaty in duplicate and set their seals thereto.

(*E. B.* II, (3) pp. 350-351.)

EXHIBIT 16A.

Supplementary Treaty Between the German Empire and the Netherlands (May 30, 1914).

(I) The following new Section shall be inserted between No. 3 and 4 in the Treaty of 27th August, 1907, respecting accident insurance, concluded between the German Empire and the Netherlands:

3a. Where, in pursuance of No. 1 to 3, the undertakings there designated are subject to the accident insurance of one of the parties to the Treaty, the persons employed in the undertakings shall be subject to the insurance even if they do not reside in the territory of the said party.

(II) The rule contained in the new No. 3a, contemplated in No. I, shall apply to accidents which happened before the coming into force of the present Treaty, provided that no decision having the force of law has been issued in respect of such accidents either before or on the day when the Treaty comes into force.

(III) This Treaty shall be ratified by His Majesty the German Emperor and Her Majesty the Queen of the Netherlands, and the ratifications shall be exchanged as soon as possible.

The Treaty shall come into force on the fourteenth day after the exchange of ratifications.

(*E. B.* X, (7-8) p. 197.)

EXHIBIT 17.

Convention Signed at Paris the 3rd Day of July, 1909, Between France and the United Kingdom.

(1)—British subjects who meet with accidents arising out of their employment as workmen in France, and persons entitled to claim through or having rights derivable from them, shall enjoy the benefits of the compensation and guarantees secured to French citizens by the legislation in force in France in regard to the liability in respect of such accidents.

Reciprocally, French citizens who meet with accidents arising out of their employment as workmen in the United Kingdom of Great Britain and Ireland, and persons entitled to claim through or having rights derivable from them, shall enjoy the benefits of the compensation and guarantees secured to British subjects by the legislation in force in the United Kingdom of Great Britain and Ireland in regard to compensation for such accidents, supplemented as specified in Article 5.

(2) Nevertheless, the present Convention shall not apply to the case of a person engaged in a business having its headquarters in one of the two Contracting States, but temporarily detached for employment in the other Contracting State, and meeting with an accident in the course of that employment, if at the time of the accident the said employment has lasted less than six months. In this case the persons interested shall only be entitled to the compensation and guarantees provided by the law of the former State.

The same rule shall apply in the case of persons engaged in transport services and employed at intervals, whether regular or not, in the country other than that in which the headquarters of the business are established.

(3) The British and French authorities will reciprocally lend their good offices to facilitate the administration of their respective laws as aforesaid.

(4) The present Convention shall be ratified, and the ratifications shall be exchanged at Paris, as soon as possible.

It shall be applicable in France and in the United Kingdom of Great Britain and Ireland to all accidents happening after one month from the time of its publication in the two countries in the manner prescribed by their respective laws, and it shall remain binding until the expiration of one year from the date on which it shall have been denounced by one or other of the two Contracting Parties.

(5) Nevertheless, the ratification mentioned in the preceding article shall not take place till the legislation at present in force in the United Kingdom of Great Britain and Ireland in regard to workmen's compensation has been supplemented, so far as concerns accidents to French citizens arising out of their employment as workmen, by arrangements to the following effect:

(a) That the compensation payable shall in every case be fixed by an award of the County Court.

(b) That in any case of redemption of weekly payments the total sum payable shall, provided it exceeds a sum equivalent to the capital value of an annuity of £4 (100 fr.), be paid into Court, to be employed in the purchase of an annuity for the benefit of the person entitled thereto.

(c) That in those cases in which a lump sum representing the compensation payable shall have been paid by the employer into the County Court, if the injured workman returns to reside in France, or if the dependents resided in France at the time of his death or subsequently return to reside in France, the total sum due to the injured workman or to his dependants shall be paid over through the County Court to the *Caisse Nationale Francaise des Retraites pour la Viaillesse,* who shall employ it in the purchase of an annuity according to its tariff at the time of the payment; and further, that in the case in which a lump sum shall not have been paid into Court, and the injured workman returns to reside in France, the compensation shall be remitted to him through the County Court at such intervals and in such way as may be agreed upon by the competent authorities of the two countries.

(d) That in respect of all the acts done by the County Court in pursuance of the legislation in regard to workmen's compensation, as well as in the execution of the present Convention, French citizens shall be exempt from all expenses and fees.

(e) That at the beginning of each year His Majesty's principal Secretary of State for the Home Department will send to the *Department du Travail et de la pre Prevoyance sociale* a record of all judicial decisions given in the course of the preceding year under the legislation in regard to workmen's compensation in the case of French citizens injured by accident in the United Kingdom of Great Britain and Ireland.

(*E. B.* IV, (3) pp. 163-164. See also *E. B.* VI, (1) pp. 5-6; (2) p. 169; (4) pp. CXX-CXXI; *E. B.* VII, (7) pp. 298-299.)

EXHIBIT 18.

Agreement Between Hungary and Italy Respecting Accident Insurance (Sept. 19, 1909).

(1) Workmen and employees, being Hungarian subjects, who

meet with accidents in occupations for which insurance is compulsory under the Italian Act, No. 51, dated 31st January, 1904 (codified text), and any later Acts amending the same, together with their dependants entitled to compensation, shall have a claim to the same treatment and compensation as Italian subjects under the said Italian Act (codified text) and any later Acts amending the same. On the other hand workmen and employees, being Italian subjects, who meet with accidents in occupations for which insurance is compulsory under the Hungarian Act No. XIX., of 1907, and any later Acts amending the same together with their dependants entitled to compensation, shall have a claim to the same treatment and compensation as that granted to Hungarian subjects for industrial accidents by the Hungarian Act No. XIX., of 1907, and any later Acts amending the same.

The mutual right contemplated in the preceding paragraph shall extend also to workmen and employees employed in occupations for which insurance is compulsory, by firms being domiciled or having permanent representation within the territory of one of the two States, who meet with industrial accidents when working outside the territory of both, unless the industrial accidents legislation in force in the State where the accident occurs applies to such workmen or employees.

Similarly, dependants of any such persons having met with an industrial accident shall have a claim to compensation even if at the time of the accident they were not within the territory of that one of the two States where the accident occurred.

In addition, compensation shall be paid to workmen or employees having met with industrial accidents who after the said accident return and live permanently in their own country.

The dependants of a workman or employee having met with an industrial accident shall receive compensation even if they have never resided within the territory of the State where the accident occurred, or if after residing there they betake themselves permanently to a foreign country.

(2) The proper authorities of one of the two States having in hand the investigation of an industrial accident sustained by a workman or employee belonging to the other State, shall forward a copy of the report on the investigation within eight days of the issue of the same, to the proper consular authorities of the place where the accident occurred.

(3) At the request of the Italian consular authorities the proper Hungarian authorities shall lend their assistance in determining whether in the case of a person residing in Hungary the conditions attached to the receipt of an annuity are satisfied, or whether any changes have been introduced likely to affect the amount of the compensation payable. The same shall apply on the other hand to Italian authorities in the event of a similar request on the part of the Austro-Hungarian consular authorities.

(4) Hungarian subjects awarded compensation in pursuance of sect. 1 of this agreement shall, if they are not resident in Italy, be bound to observe the regulations for such cases issued by the Italian institution concerned, and *vice versa*.

(5) An Hungarian institution which, in pursuance of Hungarian law is required to pay an annuity to an Italian subject resident in Italy may relieve itself of its obligation by paying to the proper Italian institution the captal corresponding to the annuity in question in accordance with the tariff of the latter in force at the time the payment is made. In such case the said Italian institution shall take over the payment of the annuity subject to such conditions and regulations as may be adopted in agreement with the Hungarian institution concerned.

On the other hand, an Italian institution which, in pursuance of the Italian Act, is required to pay an annuity to a Hungarian subject resident in Hungary, may relieve itself of its obligations by paying to the Hungarian institution concerned the capital corresponding to the annuity in question in accordance with the tariff of the latter institution in force at the time when the payment is made. In such case the said Hungarian institution shall take over the payment of the annuity subject to such conditions and regulations as may be adopted in agreement with the Italian institutions concerned.

The Hungarian institution concerned may, in addition, charge the proper Italian institution to pay out in its stead, to Italian subjects resident in Italy, annuities payable under the Hungarian Act, and *vice versa*. Such payments shall be made subject to such conditions and regulations as may be mutually agreed upon by the two institutions.

Agreements may also be come to by the Hungarian and Italian institutions concerned in reference to financial transactions carried on by post in connection with the payment of compensation.

(6) The Hungarian and Italian institutions concerned shall have power to vary the rules contained in sect. 4. They may also vary the tariffs contemplated in Sect. 5 of the Agreement, provided only that equality in the treatment of the subjects of the two States shall be maintained.

(7) In the preceding articles the Hungarian institution concerned shall mean the National Institution for the Maintenance of Invalid Workmen and for Insurance against Accident (*Országos Munkásbetegsegélyzö és Balesetbiztositó Pénztár*) of Budapest or of Zagabria, according as the injured person belongs to the one or the other, and the Italian institution concerned shall mean the Italian National Workmen's Invalidity and Old Age Insurance Institution (*Cassa Nazionale italiana di previdenza per la invalidità a per la vecchiaia degli operai*).

(8) Any exemptions from taxes and fees and any other fiscal exemptions allowed by the laws of either of the two States in the case of documents relating to the drawing of compensation shall apply equally in cases where such documents are used in the other State for the drawing of compensation in pursuance of the laws there in force.

(9) Disputes which arise between the two States respecting the interpretation and application of this Agreement shall be referred to arbitration on the demand of one of the two States.

For every such dispute a Court of Arbitration shall be instituted as follows:—Each of the two States shall name two suitable persons, being its own subjects, as arbitrators; these shall agree amongst themselves as to the choice of a President belonging to a third friendly State. The two States reserve to themselves the right of nominating in advance and for a definite term the person who shall act as President in the end of any dispute.

The Court of Arbitration shall sit on the first occasion within the territory of the State chosen by agreement for the purpose; on the second occasion within the territory of the other, and so on, alternately in one or the other State. The State where the Court is to sit shall determine the place where the sitting shall be held, and shall make arrangements for the rooms, employees and attendants necessary in connection with the work of the Court. The President shall preside in the Court. Resolutions shall be adopted by a majority. The two States shall agree in each separate case or once for all upon the procedure to be observed by the Court. In the absence of any such agreement the Court shall adopt its own procedure. The proceedings may, if neither of the two States object, be carried on in writing. In this case the provisions of the preceding paragraph may be varied.

As regards the serving of the summonses to appear before the Court of Arbitration and letters of request, the authorities of either State shall, on the application in that behalf of the Court to the Government concerned, lend their assistance in the same manner as they are in the habit of doing on the application of the Civil Courts of the country.

(10) This Agreement shall come into force thirty days after the exchange of ratifications and shall remain in force for at least seven years. On the conclusion of the term the Agreement may be set aside after notice at any time; notwithstanding, it shall remain in force after such notice until 31st December of the year following that when the notice was given.

Even after the said notice has been given this Agreement shall continue to apply without limitation to the claims of injured persons and their dependants to whom compensation is due from the institutions named in this Agreement in respect of industrial accidents occurring not later than 31st December in the year following that on which notice was given.

On the said date the power given to consular authorities and the rights and duties of the institutions in their mutual relations under this Agreement shall cease, except as regards the settlement of accounts outstanding between the institutions at the time and the payment of all those annuities for which they have been paid the capital value in advance.

(11) The provisions of sections 1 to 8 of this Agreement shall apply retrospectively back to 1st July, 1908.

(12) This Agreement shall be ratified and the ratifications shall be exchanged at Rome as soon as possible.

(*E. B.* V, (1) pp. 1-3.)

EXHIBIT 19.

Treaty of Commerce and Navigation Between German Empire and Sweden (May 2, 1911).

(Extract)

"The contracting parties undertake to examine by amicable arrangement the question of the treatment of Swedish workers in Germany and German workers in Sweden in respect of Workmen's Insurance, with the object of securing to the workmen of either country, in the other, by means of agreements adapted to that end, treatment which gives them as far as possible equal advantages.

Such arrangements shall be made by special agreement, and quite apart from the coming into force of the present treaty."

(E. B. VII, (11-12) p. cv.)

EXHIBIT 20.

Franco-Danish Treaty of Arbitration (Aug. 9, 1911).

(1) Differences of a judicial character, and especially those relating to the interpretation of the Treaties existing between the two contracting parties which might hereafter arise between them, and which it had been found impossible to arrange by diplomatic methods, shall be submitted to arbitration under the terms of the Convention for the pacific settlement of international disputes, signed at The Hague on the 18th of October, 1907, subject in all cases to the condition that they do not affect the vital interests, the independence, or the honour of either the contracting States, and that they do not touch the interests of other Powers.

(2) Differences relating to the following questions shall be submitted to arbitration without the power to appeal to the reservations mentioned in Article I.

(a) Pecuniary claims under the head of damages, where the question of indemnity is recognized by both parties.

(b) Debts arising from contracts claimed from the Government of either of the parties by the Government of the other party as being due to the subjects of the respective State.

(c) Interpretation and application of the stipulations of the Convention relating to trade and navigation.

(d) Interpretation and application of the stipulations of the Convention relating to the matters hereunder indicated:

Industrial property, literary and artistic property, international private right as regulated by The Hague Conventions, international protection of workers, posts and telegraphs, weights and measures, sanitary questions, submarine cables, fisheries, measurement of ships, white slave trade.

In differences relating to the matters contemplated under No 4 of the present Article, and with regard to which, according to the territorial law, the judicial authority would be competent, the contracting parties shall be under the obligation of not submitting the question in dispute to arbitration until after the national jurisdiction shall have definitely pronounced.

Arbitration judgments given in the cases contemplated in the preceding paragraph shall have no effect on previous judicial decisions.

The contracting parties engage to take, or, if occasion requires, to propose to the legislative power the necessary measures in order that the interpretation given in the arbitration judgment in the cases above contemplated may be adopted thereafter by their tribunals.

(3) In each particular case the High Contracting Parties shall sign a special engagement stating clearly the subject of the dispute, the scope of the power of the arbitrators, the procedure, and the delays to be observed as regards the operations of the arbitration tribunal.

The Contracting Parties shall agree to invest the Arbitration Tribunal contemplated in the present Convention with the power of deciding in the event of disagreement between them, as to whether a dispute which has arisen between them shall come under the heading of disputes to be submitted to compulsory arbitration, in conformity with Articles 1 and 2 of the present Convention.

(4) If, within the year following the notification by that

party most desirous for a compromise, the High Contracting Parties should not succeed in coming to an understanding on the measures to be taken, the Permanent Court shall be competent to establish the compromise. It may take cognizance of the matter by request of a single one of the parties.

The compromise shall be decided in conformity with the provisions of Articles 54 and 55 of The Hague Convention for the pacific regulation of international disputes, dated 18th October, 1907.

(5) The present Convention shall continue for a term of five years, with power of tacit continuance for successive terms of five years, from the time of exchanging the ratifications.

(6) The present Convention shall be ratified as soon as possible, and the ratification shall be exchanged at Copenhagen.

(*E. B.* VI, (3) pp. 229-230.)

EXHIBIT 21.

Convention Between Germany and Belgium in Regard to Insurance Against Industrial Accidents (July 6, 1912).

I.—*Regulations in regard to undertakings whose sphere of operations extend over the territory of both countries.*

1. In regard to undertakings which have their headquarters within the territory of one of the contracting parties and whose sphere of operations extends over the territory of the other party, whenever these are subjected on both sides to the regulations of compulsory compensation for injuries resulting from industrial accidents (insurance against industrial accidents) saving those exceptions mentioned in Articles 2and 4, the legislation of the country in which they are carried out shall be exclusively applied, as far as the said operations are concerned.

This rule shall apply, regardless of the place at which the staff was engaged, provided that the matter deals with work to be carried out either in Germany or in Belgium.

2. As regards any undertakings which are financed, either by the German Empire, a Federated German State, a German Commune, or an Association of German Communes, or an Association of Belgian Communes or Provinces, the legislation of the

country in which the undertaking has its headquarters shall be exclusively applicable, even to operations undertaken on the territory of the other country by a public representative in the employ of the said undertaking.

3. In transport undertakings, as far as the moving (travelling) portions of the undertaking are concerned, which extend from one territory to another, whatever may be the relative importance of the operations carried out on either side, that legislation shall be exclusively applied which is in force in the country in which the undertaking has its headquarters. The staff of the travelling part shall remain subject to this legislation, even should they be engaged on work connected with other departments of the undertaking and which are carried out on the territory of the other country.

4. Without prejudice to the regulations of Articles 2 and 3, in undertakings of all kinds, the legislation of that country in which the undertaking has its headquarters shall continue to apply exclusively for the first six months during which the undertaking carries out operations on the territory of the other country, as far as concerns these persons who, until they were occupied in this latter country, were attached to a portion of the undertaking subjected to the said legislation.

5. For the purpose of calculating the time limit during which the undertaking carries out operations outside the country in which its headquarters are found (Article 4) several operations undertaken concurrently must be considered as forming only one and the same work, which extends from the commencement of the first of these portions until the completion of the last.

The same rule shall apply should it be a question of works undertaken successively, one after the other, and which are not separated by an interval of more than 30 days. Should the interval be over 30 days, a fresh time limit of six months shall commence from the resumption of operations.

The time previous to the coming into force of the present Convention shall be included in the time limit.

6. If, in pursuance of Articles 1 and 4, an undertaking whose headquarters are in one of the countries should be subjected to the legislation of the other country, as far as the business carried

out on the territory of the latter is concerned, the work included in this business shall be considered as an undertaking in the sense of the said legislation.

7. Whenever, in one of the countries, grants have been allowed by way of legal indemnity, relative to an accident, the consequences of which, in virtue of the present Convention, must be compensated for according to the legislation of the other country, the party liable shall be bound to reimburse the said grants, setting it off against the indemnity which is due from him.

8. Whenever an accident which has taken place on the territory of one of the countries comes under the application of the legislation relative to compensation for injuries resulting from industrial accidents, of the other country, that legislation shall apply likewise as far as actions for civil liability are concerned, to which the accident may give rise, according to the legislation of the first country.

This rule shall apply even when an undertaking is only subjected in one of the two countries to the laws of compulsory compensation for injuries resulting from industrial accidents.

II.—*Regulations in regard to reciprocal relations in the matter of Compensation for Injuries resulting from industrial Accidents in general.*

9. In order to facilitate on either side the carrying out of the legislation relative to industrial accidents, the competent administrative and judicial authorities shall give each other mutual assistance and shall lend each other judicial assistance according to the regulations in force in civil and commercial matters. In urgent cases the authorities shall even give, officially the necessary means of information as if it were a question of carrying out their national law.

10. The provisions in force in one of the countries according to which exemptions from stamp and other fiscal duties or advantages of another class may be accorded in regard to industrial accidents, shall apply whenever it is a case of carrying out in the said country the legislation of the other country.

11. Whenever the party to whom the indemnity is due does not reside in the country of the party who is liable to pay the indemnity, but comes from the other country, the party liable may

legally make payments to the Consular Authority of the country of the creditor, in the district in which the said debtor lives or where the headquarters of his business are situated.

The Consular Authority must act as intermediary for the communication of the necessary certificates (life certificate, widowhood certificate, *etc.*).

12. As far as the questions mentioned in Article II are concerned the territorial spheres and districts of the Consular Authorities shall be fixed by an arrangement to be concluded between the two Governments.

13. In the application of legislation in regard to industrial accidents of one of the countries, whenever it may be necessary to express the value of remuneration for work in coinage of the other country, the conversion shall take place on a basis of a mean value determined by each of the two Governments for the application of its legislation, which information it shall cause to be transmitted to the other Government.

14. The system of insurance adopted for the German officials, instead of insurance against accidents, shall be assimilated to the said insurance as far as the present Convention is concerned.

III.—*Temporary Regulations and Final Regulations.*

15. The obligations resulting from accidents which took place previous to the coming into force of the present Convention shall remain, even in the future, at the charge of the person previously liable.

16. The regulations relative to the carrying out of the present Convention shall be decreed by each of the contracting parties, in their respective autonomy, as far as it may be necessary in regard to their jurisdiction, namely, in Germany by the Chancellor of the Empire or by the authority which he shall appoint, in Belgium, by the competent authority according to the circumstances. The two Governments shall communicate to each other the regulations thus made.

17. The present Convention shall be ratified by H. M. The German Emperor and by H. M. the King of the Belgians, and the ratifications shall be interchanged as soon as possible.

The Convention shall come into force on 1st February, 1913. It may be denounced at any time by the two parties, and it shall cease at the expiration of the year following the denunciation.

In the event of the denouncing of the present Convention the obligations resulting from accidents which have taken place whilst the Convention was still in force shall continue to be carried out by the parties previously liable.

(*E. B.* VIII, (2) pp. 47-49.)

EXHIBIT 22.

Convention Between the German Empire and the Kingdom of Italy With Respect to Workmen's Insurance
(July 31, 1912).

PART I.—Accident Insurance.

(1) The two contracting parties place the subjects of their respective countries and their survivors on an equal footing with the subjects of the other country and their survivors with respect to benefits derived from the German Industrial Accident Insurance and the German Seamen's Accident Insurance on the one hand and from the Italian Accident Insurance on the other hand.

This condition shall hold good for the Italian Accident Insurance of agricultural labourers, only if the latter are subject to the accident insurance according to the Italian Act dated 31st January, 1904, now in force.

(2) The principle of equality of rights (sect. 1) shall not exclude a payment being made, in the place of an annuity, of three times the amount of the annuity, with the consent of the person entitled thereto, or of a capital sum corresponding to the value of the annuity, without the consent of the person entitled thereto.

In the German Accident Insurance the general regulations issued by the Federal Council shall apply for the calculation of the corresponding capital value.

In the Italian Accident Insurance the general regulations which hold good for the conversion of the capital amount of compensation into an annuity, shall apply.

PART II.—Invalidity, Old Age, and Survivors' Insurance.

(3) The same contributions to the German Invalidity and Survivors' Insurance shall be paid for Italian subjects as for German subjects, even if the former are enrolled as members of the National Workmen's Provident Fund for Invalidity and old age (*Cassa Nazionale di Previdenza per la invalidità e per la vecchiaia degli operai*), or of the Mercantile Marine Invalidity Fund (*Cassa Invalidi della Marina Mercantile*).

If an Italian subject is enrolled as member of one of the said funds, the insurer of the German Invalidity and Survivors' Insurance shall, upon request of the former, pay over to the National Provident Fund half the amounts, which are used for him after the application has been made, as contributions of the Italian subject to the fund in which he is enrolled. All particulars, especially with respect to the issue of corresponding receipt cards, shall be determined by the Imperial Chancellor; the latter shall previously secure the consent of the Italian Government, in so far as the National Provident Fund is concerned.

In the case of paragraph 2 an insured Italian subject and his survivors shall not be entitled to claim the benefits of the German Invalidity and Survivor's Insurance unless such benefits must be granted for an insurance case arising previously to the making of the application. Contributions, of which half are to be paid over to the National Provident Fund in accordance with paragraph 2, shall not be taken into consideration with respect to the claim to such benefits.

(4) Article 3, paragraphs two and three, shall hold good also for Italian subjects who make use of the voluntary additional insurance, according to the German law. The German insurers shall pay over the full amount of the additional stamps.

(5) With respect to maintaining the rights to claim the benefits of the German invalidity and Survivor's Insurance, the fulfillment of the obligation of active military service in Italy is placed on a par with the fulfillment of the obligation of German subjects to serve under the colours.

(6) German subjects residing in Italy shall be entitled to be enrolled as members of the Italian National Provident Fund, under the same conditions and with the same effects as Italian

subjects, in so far as Articles 7, 8, 10, and 11 do not contain any contrary stipulations.

(7) German subjects shall be insured with the National Provident Fund under the condition of repayment of the contributions (tariff of reserved capital). Upon application of the insured person, the contributions, including the amounts paid by others on behalf of the person enrolled, shall be refunded, should the insured person die or leave Italian territory before the contingency of insurance arises; in the latter case they shall be paid to the insured person.

If employers in Italy pay contributions to the National Provident Fund for their national workers or for certain classes of the same, they shall be bound to pay such contributions to the said fund also in a corresponding manner for their German workers.

(8) The transfer from the Workmen's Insurance to the National Insurance, which takes place according to Italian legislation when the conditions for inscription in the register of Workmen's Insurance with the National Provident Fund do not apply, shall entail for a German insured person the loss of the right to claim repayment of contributions only if he expressly agrees with the transfer.

(9) German subjects belonging to the crew of an Italian sea-going ship shall be placed on the same footing as Italian subjects with respect to insurance with the Mercantile Marine Invalidity Fund, in so far as nothing to the contrary is hereinafter stipulated. For such German subjects the inscription in the Italian register of seamen shall be a condition of the insurance.

If a German subject insured in this manner leaves Italian territory previous to the contingency of the insurance arising, without belonging to the crew of an Italian sea-going vessel, the contributions paid for him shall be refunded upon his request.

(10) As long as a German subject who is entitled to an annuity from one of the said Italian funds, voluntarily has his ordinary abode outside the territory of the Italian State, his annuity shall remain suspended; in such a case his claim shall be compounded by the payment of triple the amount of his annuity.

So long as a German subject has been exiled from Italian territory, in consequence of a criminal conviction, his annuity shall remain in suspense.

If a German subject has left Italian territory in virtue of an order of an Italian authority, his annuity shall not remain in suspense, except in the cases referred to in paragraph 2. The Italian fund, however, may compound his claim with his consent, by the payment of triple the amount of his annuity.

(11) Disputes with respect to the compounding of claims shall be decided by such proceedings as are prescribed for annuity claims in the Italian Invalidity and Old Age Insurance Act.

(12) Should the Italian Invalidity, Old Age, and Survivors' Insurance be extended to a larger circle of persons, the above conditions shall be correspondingly applied.

PART III.—General Provisions.

(13) With respect to the administration of the Accident Insurance as well as of the Invalidity, Old Age, and Survivors' Insurance of one country in the other, mutual support and legal assistance shall be given by the competent authorities. Legal assistance shall be given, in so far as no contrary provisions are contained in the following articles, in accordance with the provisions in force for civil and commercial matters.

(14) The Italian Government shall communicate to the German Government a list of medical men, clinical establishments and hospitals, which, in the administration of the German Workmen's Insurance in Italy, are specially suitable for medical treatment and advice. It shall also take care that the expenses for treatment, examination and advice by the medical men named in the list and for maintenance in the institutions therein mentioned are kept within reasonable limits.

(15) The regulations of one country, according to which there exist exemptions from stamp duty and fees or other privileges with respect to the Accident Insurance and the Invalidity, Old Age, and Survivors' Insurance shall be correspondingly applied, in so far as it may be necessary to administer in such country the respective workmen's insurance of the other country.

(16) In the case of an accident happening to an Italian subject, the German Department concerned shall immediately give notice to the Italian Consular Authority, which is competent for

the district in question, of the termination of the inquiry into the accident.

The Italian Consular Authority may claim to follow the proceedings in connection with the inquiry and any subsequent proceedings to the same extent as the parties directly concerned.

The provisions of paragraph 2 shall be applied in a corresponding manner to the German Invalidity and Survivors' Insurance.

(17) Should it be necessary to obtain evidence in Italy for establishing the claim of an Italian subject arising out of the German Accident Insurance, or of the German Invalidity and Survivors' Insurance, the German insurers and the German Insurance Authorities may avail themselves of the intermediary of the competent Italian Consular Authority for their district. The inquiries made in this manner shall be free of cost, with the exception of the medical evidence.

(18) If, for the purpose of the administration of the German Accident Insurance and of the German Invalidity and Survivors' Insurance, it should be necessary to serve documents, fixing certain periods, upon Italian subjects, who are not residing within the territory of the German Empire and whose abode is not known, the Department having to effect the service shall claim the intermediary of the Italian Consular Authority in the district of which the Department is situate.

The Consular Authority shall send to the Department having to effect the service, within one week after receipt of the document, the certificate of the Post Office as to the delivery of the document. Should the Department demand it, the Consular Authority shall cause inquiries to be made as to the whereabouts and delivery of the document and communicate to the Department in question the information which it may receive in the matter from the Post Office. If the document is returned by the Post Office to the Consular Authority as undelivered, the Consular Authority shall transmit it immediately, with the annotations of the Post Office, to the Department having to effect the service.

If the Consular Authority is not in a position to effect delivery of the document, the same shall be returned without delay, at latest before the expiration of one week from receipt, to the Department having to effect the service.

If the intermediary of the Consular Authority for effecting the service has been made use of without result, the Department having to effect the service shall be at liberty to effect such service by other means.

The intermediary of the Italian Consular Authority may also be claimed for the service of documents which do not fix time limits.

(19) The Italian Government shall introduce a procedure corresponding to that referred to in sections 16-18, when administering the Italian Workmen's Insurance in connection with German subjects, as soon as the German Government places at its disposal the intermediary of its Consuls.

(20) The contracting parties reserve to themselves the right to come to an arrangement by way of exchange of notes, as to the manner in which payments arising out of the Workmen's Insurance of the one country, to persons entitled to the same who are staying in the other country, shall be affected.

(21) In matters which are regulated by this Part, the local competence and the districts of the Consular Authority shall be determined according to an arrangement to be come to between the two Governments.

PART IV.—Final Provisions.

(22) The two contracting parties reserve to themselves the right, by an additional convention, to arrange that the subjects of the two countries shall be placed on the same footing, with respect to agricultural accident insurance on a larger scale, as soon as a system of accident insurance is introduced in Italy which may be equivalent to the German Agricultural Accident Insurance.

(23) In the same way the two contracting parties reserve to themselves the right, by an additional convention, to arrange that the subjects of the two countries shall be placed on the same footing, with respect to Invalidity, Old Age, and Survivors' Insurance as soon as a system of Invalidity, Old Age, and Survivors' Insurance is introduced in Italy which can be considered as equivalent to the German Invalidity and Survivors' Insurance.

(24) This convention must be ratified by His Majesty the German Emperor and His Majesty the King of Italy, and the deeds of ratification shall be exchanged as soon as possible.

(25) The convention shall come into force on 1st April, 1913.

Notice of discontinuance of the convention may be given at any time by either party, and it shall cease to be in force on the expiration of the year following that in which notice was given.

(*E. B.* VIII, (3-4) pp. 99-103).

EXHIBIT 23.

Agreement Between the German Empire and Spain Concerning the Reciprocal Communication of Accidents to Spanish Sailors on German Ships and of German Sailors on Spanish Ships. (Concluded by Exchange of Diplomatic Notes on 30th November, 1912 —12 February, 1913.)

(1) Should a Spanish sailor, employed on a German ship, meet with an accident during the execution of his work, and the ship be in a German port, or, after the accident, anchor in a German port, the German authorities, to whom the skipper has given notice in pursuance of the Regulations, shall notify the competent Spanish Consul; if the ship is in a non-German port, the German Consul to whom the skipper has given notice in pursuance of the Regulations, must communicate with the competent Spanish Consul. If the port is Spanish and at the same time the chief town of a province, the Civil Government or else the Alcade shall be notified. Should the accident take place on the high seas, the German Consul is bound, if possible, to notify the accident to the proper authorities within 24 hours from the moment the ship enters a Spanish port.

(2) Should a German sailor, employed on a Spanish ship, meet with an accident during the execution of his duties, and the ship be in a Spanish port, or after the accident, anchor in a Spanish port, the Spanish authorities, to whom the skipper has given notice in pursuance of the Regulations, shall notify the

competent German Consul; should the port not be Spanish, the Spanish Consul to whom the skipper has given notice in pursuance of the Regulations shall notify the competent German Consul, and, should the port be German, the Harbour Police. Should the accident take place on the high seas the Spanish Consul shall be bound, if possible, to notify the accident to the proper authorities within 24 hours from the moment the ship enters a Spanish port.

(*E. B.* VIII, (6-7) p. 247.)

EXHIBIT 24.

Treaty Between Italy and the United States, Amending the Treaty of Commerce and Navigation Concluded 26 February, 1871 (Feb. 25, 1913).

(1) It is agreed between the High Contracting Parties that the first paragraph of Article III of the Treaty of Commerce and Navigation, 26th February, 1871, between Italy and the United States, shall be replaced by the following provision:

The citizens of each of the High Contracting Parties shall receive in the States and Territories of the other the most constant security and protection of their property and for their rights, including that form of protection granted by any State or national law which establishes a civil responsibility for injuries or for death caused by negligence or fault, and gives to relatives or heirs of the injured party a right of action, which right shall not be restricted on account of the nationality of said relatives or heirs; and shall enjoy in this respect the same rights and privileges as are or shall be granted to nationals, provided that they submit themselves to the conditions imposed on the later.

(11) The present Treaty shall be ratified by His Majesty the King of Italy, in accordance with the constitutional forms of that kingdom, and by the President of the United States, by and with the advice and consent of the Senate thereof, and shall go into operation upon the exchange of the ratifications thereof, which shall be effected at Washington as soon as practicable.

(*E. B.* VII.-VIII. (9-10) p. 363.)

EXHIBIT 25.

Agreement Between France and Switzerland Relative to Pensions to Be Granted to Members of the Staff of the Swiss Federal Railroads Employed on French Territory (Oct. 13, 1913).

The Swiss Federal Council and the Government of the French Republic, in an endeavour to prevent the French or foreign members of the staff employed on French soil by the General Administration of the Swiss Federal Railroads from coming under the regulations concerning old age pensions of both countries, by the application of the Swiss and the French Acts, have agreed on the following provisions:

(1) The members of the staff permanently employed within French territory by the General Administration of the Swiss Federal Railroads who benefit in Switzerland by old age insurance corresponding to the provisions of the French Act dated 21st July, 1909, shall be exempt from the application of the French Act relative to old age insurance for workers.

(2) The members of the staff employed by the General Administration of the Swiss Federal Railroads who do not belong to any Old Age Pension Fund, more especially those who are only temporarily employed by the said General Administration, shall remain subject to the provisions of No. 1 of the above-mentioned French Act concerning old age insurance for workers.

(3) The present Agreement shall be ratified, and the ratification documents exchanged, at the earliest possible moment. The Agreement shall come into operation on the date on which the ratification documents are exchanged, and shall remain in force until one year after the date on which notice of termination of the Agreement shall be given.

(*E. B.* IX, (3) p. 61.)

In taking a calm retrospect of my life, from the earliest remembered period of it to the present hour, there appears to me to have been a succession of extraordinary or out-of-the-usual-way events, forming connected links of a chain, to compel me to proceed onward to complete a mission of which I have been an impelled agent, without merit or demerit of any kind on my part.
—ROBERT OWEN, Sevenoaks Park, Sevenoaks, September, 1857.

APPENDIX II.
Labor Resolutions Internationally Subscribed

CONTENTS

APPENDIX II.

Labor Resolutions Internationally Subscribed.

Exhibit Page
1. Proposals of the Congress at Roubaix (1884) 239
2. Law Proposition Before French Chamber, (1885).............. 239
3. Proposition Before the Reichstag, (1886) 240
4. Proposals of the Swiss Federal Council, (1889) 240
5. Program of the Swiss Federal Council, (1889).................. 241
6. Resolutions Prepared at The Hague, (1889) 243
7. Resolutions of the Conference at Berlin, (1890)............... 244
8. Recommendations Discussed at Zurich, (1897) Extract........ 247
9. Program of the Congress of Brussels, (September 27-30, 1897).. 248
10. Statutes of the International Association for the Legal Protection of Labor, (1900)...................................... 249
11. Resolutions of the First Delegates' Meeting (Basel, Sept. 27-28, 1901) 252
    A. L'Annuaire de législation du travail 253
    B. Publication of Bulletin 253
    C. Night-Work of Woman 253
    D. Accident Statistics 253
    E. Unhealthful Industries using Lead and White Phosphorus.. 253
    F. Accident and Sickness Insurance of Aliens................ 254
12. Resolutions of the Second Delegates' Meeting (Cologne, Sept. 23-24, 1902) 254
    A. Night-Work of Women 254
    B. Use of Lead and White Phosphorus 255
13. Resolutions of the Committee Meeting at Basel (Sept. 11, 1903).. 255
    A. White Phosphorus 255
    B. Lead and Lead Compounds 256
    C. Night-Work of Women 257
14. Resolutions of the Third Delegates' Meeting, (Basel Sept. 26-28, 1904) 258
    I. International Protection of Laborers 258
    II. Organization of the Association 258
    III. Finances and International Labour Office 259

CONTENTS (Continued)

Exhibit   Page

    IV. The Struggle Against the Dangers of Occupational Poisoning 260
        A. Lead and Lead Compounds 260
        B. Industrial Poisons 260
        C. Prizes Offered to the Association 262
    V. Night-Work of Young Persons 262
    VI. Home-Work 263
    VII. Legal Limitation of the Workday...................... 263
    VIII. Social Insurance 264

15. Resolutions of the Fourth Delegates' Meeting (Geneva, Sept. 27-29, 1906) 264
    I. International Conventions 264
    II. Finances, International Labour Office, Statutes of New Sections, Standing Orders 264
    III. Administration of Labour Laws 264
    IV. Employment of Children 265
    V. Night-Work of Young Persons 265
    VI. Legal Maximum Working Day 266
    VII. Home-Work 266
    VIII. Industrial Poisons 267
    IX. Workmen's Insurance 268

16. Resolutions of the Fifth Delegates' Meeting (Lucerne Sept. 28-30, 1908) 269
    I. International Conventions 269
    II. Finances, Bulletin, Staff Regulations, Library, etc........ 269
    III. Administration of Labour Laws 271
    IV. Employment of Children 271
    V. Night-Work of Young Persons 271
    VI. Maximum Working Day 273
    VII. Home-Work 274
    VIII. Industrial Poisons 276
        A. White Phosphorus 276
        B. Lead 276
            1. Painting and Decorating 276
            2. Ceramic Industry 277
            3. Polygraphic Industry 278
        C. List of Industrial Poisons 279
    IX. Working in Caissons 279
    X. Workmen's Insurance; Treatment of Foreigners in case of Accident 279

17. Resolutions of the Sixth Delegates' Meeting, (Lugano Sept. 26-28, 1910) 281

CONTENTS (*Continued*)

Exhibit	Page
I. International Labour Conventions of Berne, (1906)	282
II. New Sections, Finances, Co-operation with other International Associations, Exhibition of Hygiene, etc.	282
III. Administration of Labour Laws	283
IV. Child Labour	284
V. Night-Work of Young Persons	284
VI. Maximum Working Day	285
A. Ten-hour Workday for Women	285
B. Ten-hour Workday for Young Persons	286
C. Ten-hour Workday for Men in Textile Industries	286
D. Workday in Continuous Processes	286
E. Eight-hour Shift in Mines	287
F. Hours in Specially Dangerous Industry	287
VII. Workmen's Holidays	288
VIII. Home-Work	288
A. General	288
B. Machine-made Embroidery	290
IX. Industrial Poisons	290
A. White Phosphorus	290
B. Lead	290
b. Geramic Industry	291
b. Germanic Industry	291
c. Polygraphic Industry	294
C. Protection of Homeworkers from Industrial Poisons	297
D. List of Industrial Poisons	297
X. Work in Compressed Air	297
A. Work in Caissons	297
B. Divers	299
XI. The Protection of Railway Servants and Prevention of Accidents. Automatic Coupling	299
XII. Workmen's Insurance	299
18. Resolutions of the Seventh Delegates' Meeting (Zurich, Sept. 10-12, 1912)	300
1. Publication of Reports	300
2. Finances	300
3. Bulletin of the International Labour Office	301
4. New National Sections	301
5. Co-operation with Other International Associations	301
6. Next Delegates' Meeting	302
7. International Conventions	302
8. The Administration of International Labour Treaties	303
9. Child Labour	303
10. Saturday Half-Holiday	304
11. Hours of Labour in Continuous Industries	304

CONTENTS (Continued)

Exhibit	Page
12. **Protection of** Railroad Employees	305
13. Protection of Dock Workers	306
14. Hygienic Working Day	306
15. Workmen's Holidays	306
16. Legal Relations Between Employers and Employed	307
17. The Truck System and deductions from Wages	307
18. Home Work	308
19. Machine-Made Swiss Embroidery	310
20. List of Industrial Poisons	311
21. Lead	311
22. Handling of Ferrosilicon	312
23. Principles for the Protection of Persons Employed in Mining, the Construction of Tunnels, Stone Quarries, etc., on an International Basis	313
24. The International Prevention of Anthrax Among Industrial Workers and of Mercurial Poisoning in Fur-cutting and Hat-making	314
25. Work in Caissons	314
26. Diving Operations	314
27. Mortality Among Working Classes	314
28. Treatment of Foreign Workmen Under Insurance Legislation	315
19. *Voeu*	316
20. Draft for an International Convention Respecting the Prohibition of Night-Work for Young Persons Employed in Industrial Occupations, (Sept. 25, 1913)	318
21. Draft for an Internatioal Convention to Fix the Working day for Women and Young Persons Employed in Industrial Occupations, (Sept. 25, 1913)	320
22. Constitution of the American Section of the International Association on Unemployment. Extract	322
23. Constitution of the American Association for Labour Legislation	323
24. Justification of the Principle of the Prohibition of Night-Work of Women	325
25. Report of the United States Section of the International High Commission	326

EXHIBIT I.

Proposals of the Congress at Roubaix (1884)

International legislation relating to:

A.—The prohibition of the work of children under fourteen years of age;

B.—The limitation of the work of men and women;

C.—The prohibition of night-work, excepting, however, certain cases determined by the exigencies of modern mechanical production;

D.—The prohibition of certain branches of industry and of certain modes of manufacture detrimental to the health of the workers.

E.—The establishment of an international minimum wage and workday of eight hours.

(Translation: L. Chatelain, *La protection internationale ouvrière*, p. 61.)

EXHIBIT 2.

Bill Before French Chamber (1885).

The following proposition was laid before the French Chamber:

"Article 1.—The French Government will reply favorably to the proposals of the Swiss Government concerning international labor legislation.

"Article 2.—The French Government will assume the initiative concurrently with the Swiss Government in entering as soon as possible into the necessary negotiations with foreign governments with a view to international labor legislation.

"Article 3.—This international law shall have as its object:

"1. The prohibition of industrial work of children under fourteen years of age;

"2. The limitation of the work of women and those minors, who are especially protected by law;

"3. Measures of hygiene, health and safety in the shops, with the purpose of safeguarding the health, the moral and physical development and the life of the workers;

"4. Protection and insurance against accidents;

"5. Inspection of mills, factories, shops and yards (*chantiers*) by inspectors one-half of whose number are to be appointed by the Minister of Public Works and one-half chosen by the workers;

"6. The establishment for adults of a normal, or at least a maximum, workday;

"7. Establishment of a weekly day of rest;

"8. The institution of an international bureau of labor and industrial statistics, charged with studying and proposing the means of furthering and codifying international labor legislation.

"Article 4.—A committee of eleven members shall be appointed to present a detailed plan of international labor legislation, after having taken the opinion of the different labor organizations of France."

(Translation: *Ibid.*, p. 19.)

EXHIBIT 3.

Proposition Before the Reichstag (1886).

Proposal made with the object of having "the Reichstag take the resolution:

"To call upon the Chancellor of the Empire to convoke a conference of the principal industrial States for the purpose of formulating the uniform basis of an international agreement concerning protective labor legislation, an agreement that would establish for all the States convened;

1. A workday not exceeding ten hours, whatever the kind of establishment;

2. The prohibition of night-work in every kind of establishment with certain exceptions;

3. The prohibition of the work of children under fourteen years of age."

(Translation: *Ibid.*, p. 44.)

EXHIBIT 4.

Proposals of the Swiss Federal Council (1889).

1. Prohibition of Sunday work;

2. Establishment of a minimum age for admission of children to factories;

3. Establishment of a maximum workday for young workers;
4. Prohibition of the employment of young people and women in operations particularly injurious to health and dangerous;
5. Limitation of night-work for young persons and women;
6. Mode of executing the conventions that may be concluded.

(Translation: *Archives diplomatiques,* 1889, t. XXX, p. 78.

EXHIBIT 5.

Program Proposed by the Swiss Federal Council (1889).

I. Prohibition of Sunday Work.

1. In what measure is there reason for *restricting of Sunday work?*
2. What are the establishments or processes for which, by their very nature, the interruption or suspension of work is inadmissible and Sunday work should consequently be *permitted?*
3. Can some measures be taken in these establishments or processes for the purpose of giving Sunday rest to individual workers?

II. Determination of a Minimum Age for Admission of Children into Factories.

1. Is there occasion for the determination of a minimum age for admitting children into factories?
2. Should the minimum age be the same in all countries, or on the other hand should it be determined in relation to the more or less early physical development of the child according to the climatic conditions of the different countries?
3. What should be the minimum age determined in either of these two cases?
4. Can exceptions to the minimum age once determined, be allowed if the number of workdays is reduced or the workday shortened?

III. Determination of the Maximum Workday for Young Workers.

1. Is it expedient to determine a maximum workday for young workers?
Ought the hours of compulsory school instruction be included?
2. Ought this maximum workday to be graded according to the different age groups?

3. Of how many hours of work (with or without actual rest periods) ought the maximum workday to consist in the one or the other case. (See 1 and 2)?

4. Between what hours of the day ought the time of work to be distributed?

IV. Prohibition of Employment of Young People and Women in Operations Particularly Injurious to Health or Dangerous.

1. Is it necessary to restrict the employment of young people and women in establishments particularly injurious to health or dangerous?

2. Ought the persons of these two categories to be excluded from these establishments?

Entirely (young people up to what age?), or partly (young people up to a certain age? Women at certain times?).

Or indeed ought the workday of young persons and women in these operations to be reduced?

What is the minimum of the requirements to be adopted in the last two cases?

3. What are the operations injurious to health or dangerous, to which the above provisions ought to be applied (See 1 and 2)?

V. Limitation of Night-Work for Young Persons and Women.

1. Ought young persons to be excluded entirely or partially from night-work?

To what age should that exclusion extend? Under what conditions can they be partially admitted?

2. Ought women without distinction of age to be excluded from night-work?

In case of admission is it advisable to enact certain restrictions by law?

3. What are the hours included within the term, night-work, or in other words when does night-work commence and end?

VI. Enforcement of the Provisions Adopted.

1. To what kinds of establishments (mines, factories, shops, *etc.*, are the provisions adopted to be applicable?

2. Should a term be appointed for compliance with the provisions adopted?

3. What are the measures to be taken for the enforcement of the provisions adopted?

4. Ought regularly recurring conferences of delegates from the participating States to be provided for?

5. What tasks ought to be assigned to these conferences? (Translation: *Ibid.*, 1890 t. XXXIII, p. 372-373.)

EXHIBIT 6.

Resolutions Prepared at The Hague (1889).

1. It is expedient for labor organizations and socialist parties both of the Old World and the New to strive for international labor legislation and to support the Swiss Republic in the intergovernmental conference called at Bern for this purpose;

2. This international legislation, in order to protect the existence and liberty of labor, in order to reduce unemployment, and to make the crises of overproduction of rare occurence, must, first of all, take up the following points:

A. Prohibition of child labor under fourteen years of age, and the reduction of the workday to six hours for young people between fourteen and eighteen years of age;

B. Limitation of the workday of adults to eight hours;

C. Compulsory weekly rest or prohibition of the employment of labor more than six days in seven;

D. Prohibition of night-work, except in certain cases to be determined in accordance with the necessities of modern mechanical production;

E. Prohibition of certain kinds of industry and of certain methods of manufacture prejudicial to the health of the workers;

F. Establishment of an international minimum wage equal for the workers of both sexes;

3. For the enforcement of the above provisions, there shall be appointed national and international inspectors chosen by the workers and remunerated by the State;

The election of the international inspectors shall be notified through diplomatic channels and within the space of a month to the different contracting powers.

These inspectors, to the number of ——— per country and appointed for ——— years, shall have authority to enter at all times every shop, mill, factory, yard (*chantier*), *etc.*, to ascertain violations, make official report, and bring to justice offenders.

This control shall be extended to home manufacturing for the same reason of social hygiene for which the right of inspection has been given to the committees on unhealthy dwellings.

(Translation: Chatelain, *La protection internationale ouvr.ére,* p. 21.)

EXHIBIT 7.

Resolutions of Conference of Berlin (*1890*).

1. Regulation of Work in Mines.

It is desirable: 1. That the lower age limit at which children can be admitted to underground works in mines shall be progressively raised, in proportion as circumstances will allow it, to the age of fourteen; for meridian (Southern) countries that limit shall be fixed at twelve.

Underground work is forbidden to persons of the feminine sex.

2. In case the character of the mine does not permit the removal of all dangers to health, arising from conditions natural or incidental to the operation of certain mines or of certain works connected with them, the length of the working day must be limited.

To each nation is left the task of attaining this object by legislative or administrative measures, or by agreement between the operators and workers, or in any other way in accordance with the principles and practice of each nation.

3. A. That the safety of the workers and the salubrity of the work shall be assured by every means at the disposal of science, and placed under state supervision.

B. That the engineers charged with the direction of the operations, shall be exclusively men of experience and duly attested technical competence.

C. That the relations between the mine workers and the mining engineers shall be as direct as possible so as to possess the character of mutual confidence and respect.

D. That mutual benefit societies shall be organized conformably to the usages of each country, designed to insure the mine laborer and his family against disease, accidents, old age and death; that institutions which can better the lot of the miner and attach him to his profession, shall be developed more and more.

E. That efforts toward the prevention of strikes may be made with the object of guaranteeing the continuity of coal production.

Experience tends to prove that the best preventive measure is that by which employers and miners agree to arbitrate, in every case where differences could not be settled by a direct agreement.

II. Regulation of Sunday-Work.

It is desirable, subject to necessary exceptions and delays in each country that a weekly day of rest be assured to persons to whom this protective legislation applies; that a day of rest be assured to all industrial workers; that this day of rest shall fall on Sunday for persons to whom the protective legislation applies.

Exceptions may be allowed for establishments which require continuity of production for technical reasons, or which furnish to the public objects of prime necessity, which must be manufactures daily, also to establishments which, by nature, can function only in fixed seasons, or which depend upon the irregular action of natural forces.

It is desirable that, even in the establishments of this class, each laborer shall have one free Sunday in two.

In order that the exceptions may be determined from similar points of view, it is desirable that the different governments agree on the manner of regulation.

III. Regulation of Child Labor.

It is desirable that children of both sexes, under a certain age, shall be excluded from work in industrial establishments; that this limit shall be fixed at twelve years, except for meridian (Southern) countries where the limit may be ten years; that these limits shall be the same for all industrial establishments without discrimination; that the children shall have first satisfied requirements of elementary instruction; that children under fourteen shall work neither at night nor on Sunday; that their actual work shall not exceed six hours per day and shall be broken by a rest of at least one-half hour; that children shall be excluded from unhealthy or dangerous occupations, or else be admitted only under certain protective conditions.

IV. Regulation of the Work of Young Persons.

It is desirable that young workers of both sexes between fourteen and sixteen years of age shall not work either at night or on Sunday; that their actual work shall not exceed ten hours per day and shall be broken by a rest of at least one and one-half hours' duration; that exceptions shall be permitted for certain industries.

That restrictions shall be provided for operations particularly unhealthful or dangerous.

That protection shall be assured to young boys between sixteen and eighteen years of age in that which concerns the maximum workday, night-work, Sunday work, employment in occupations particularly unhealthful or dangerous.

V. Regulation of Women's Work.

It is desirable that girls and women shall not work at night.

That their actual work shall not exceed eleven hours during the day and shall be interrupted by a rest of at least one and one-half hours' duration.

That exceptions shall be permitted in certain industries and that restrictions shall be provided for occupations particularly unhealthful or dangerous.

That lying-in women shall not be admitted to work within four weeks after their delivery.

VI. Enforcement of the Provisions Adopted by the Conference.

In cases where the governments wish to give effect to the acts of the Conference, the following provisions are recommended:

That the enforcement of the measures undertaken in each State shall be supervised by a sufficient number of specially qualified officials appointed by the government and independent of the employers and also workers.

The annual reports of these officials, published by the governments of the different countries, shall be communicated to the other governments. Each State shall publish periodically, in so far as possible in similar form, statistical abstracts.

As to the questions discussed at the Conference, the participating States shall exchange between themselves the statistical abstracts, bearing on those questions as well as the text of the regulations decreed by legislative or administrative action, and having reference to the questions discussed at the Conference.

It is desirable that another Conference of the States shall take place in the future, and that the States shall then communicate to each other the experience gained as a result of the present Conference in order to be able to make any changes or improvements.

The undersigned submit these resolutions to their respective governments, subject to the reservations and with the observations made in the sessions of the 27th and 28th of March and recorded in the minutes of those sessions.

Berlin, March 29, 1890.

Translation: *Archiv. dipl.*, 1890, t. XXXV, p. 175-178.)

EXHIBIT 8.

Recommendations Discussed at the Congress of Zurich (1897.)

(Extract)

I. Inspection inclusive of large and small industrial establishments, mines, transportation, business, home work and agricultural establishments which employ machinery, by independant officials selected, more than in the past, from experts. These inspectors shall have workers as their assistants and be numerous enough to be able to inspect each establishment every six months. Special inspectors must be provided for agriculture.

The enforcement of the regulations relating to woman's work shall be exercised by women inspectors paid by the State and chosen in part from the working women.

II. Absolute right of organization for all manual workers and other kinds of employees of the two sexes, especially official recognition of all the offices and committees, established by the workers for the control of labor protection. Likewise recognition of trade unions and law of control.

Violation of the right of organization is punishable.

III. Introduction of universal suffrage, equal, direct and secret, for election to all representative bodies, in order to insure a more genuine influence of the labor class upon all Parliaments.

IV. Active propaganda by trade unions and political organizations by means of lectures, pamphlets, meetings, journals, and above all, parliamentary action.

V. Organization of periodical international Congresses; presentation of similar bills at the same time to different legislatures.

(Translation: Chatelain, *La proteition internationale ouvriére,* p. 80-81.)

EXHIBIT 9.

Program of the Congress of Brussels (Sept. 27-30, 1897).

The program submitted to the deliberations of the Congress (Brussels 1897) contains many questions: 1. Question: Evolution of labor legislation in the different countries since the Conference of Berlin.

"What modifications has protective labor legislation undergone in each country since the Conference of Berlin?

"What is the respective situation of the different industrial States in regard to the resolutions taken by the Conference on child labor, work of young persons, work of women and work in mines?"

2. Question: Regulation of work of Adults.

"Ought male workers and adults to be subjected to a protective régime? Especially, ought the law to limit in a general manner the length of their work?

3. Question: International Protection.

"Is international protection of laborers possible and desirable? In what measure and under what form?"

4. Question: Home Work.

"Is it feasible to regulate labor conditions in small industry and in home work? If so, what should be the practical measures to be recommended?"

5. Question: Dangerous Industries.

"Is it expedient and desirable that special regulations which are imposed in many countries upon dangerous industries should be put into operation concurrently in all industrial states?"

6. Question: Labor Inspection.

"What are the proper means of insuring the best enforcement of protective labor laws, in particular what ought to be the rights and duties of factory inspectors?"

7. Question: International Labor Statistics.

"Is it desirable that international reports be instituted between the labor offices and that international labor statistics be compiled?"

(Translation: *Ibid.*, p. 83-84.)

EXHIBIT 10.

Statutes of the International Association for the Legal Protection of Labor.

(1) There is hereby organized an international association for the legal protection of labor. The seat of the association is in Switzerland.

(2) This association has for its object:

1. The bringing together of those who in the different industrial countries consider protective legislation of working people as necessary.

2. The organization of an international labor office which will have for its mission the publication, in French, German, and English, of a periodical collection of the labor legislation in all countries, or to lend its coöperation to such a publication.

This collection will comprise:

(a) The text of a résumé of all laws, regulations, and decrees in force relating to the protection of the working people in general, particularly woman and child labor, the limitation of the hours of labor of male workers and adults, Sunday rest, periodical repose, dangerous industries;

(b) An historical summary of these laws and regulations;

(c) A résumé of official reports and documents concerning the interpretation and execution of these laws and decrees.

3. To facilitate the study of labor legislation in the various countries, and especially to furnish to members of the association information regarding the legislation in force and its application in the several States.

4. To further, by the preparation of memoirs and otherwise, the study of the question of the concordance of the various protective labor laws, as well as that of international statistics of labor.

5. To convoke the international congresses on labor legislation.

(3) The association is composed of all persons and societies (other than the national sections) who adhere to the object of the association, as indicated in articles 1 and 2, and who remit to the treasurer an annual contribution of 10 francs ($1.93.).

(4) Any member who by the end of one year has neglected or refused to pay his dues will be considered as having resigned.

(5) The members have a right to the publications to be issued by the association.

They also have the right to receive gratuitously from the bureau the results of inquiries that may have been instituted, and conformably to special regulations, such information as may come within the competence of this bureau.

(6) The association is under the direction of a committee composed of members belonging to the various States admitted to representation thereon.

(7) Each State will be represented on the committee by six members, as soon as 50 of its citizens will have joined the association.

After that, each new group of fifty members will be entitled to one additional seat, the total number of members of the committee from any State not to exceed ten.

The governments will be invited to designate one delegate each, who will have the same rights in the committee as the other members.

(8) The duration of the terms of members of the committee is not limited, and the committee is recruited by cooptation.

The election of new members of the committee to replace those who have died or resigned will take place upon the nomination of the members belonging, respectively, to the States having a right to the representation.

The vote is by secret ballot, at a meeting of the committee, the notice of which will contain an indication of the candidates presented. The members who do not attend this meeting may send their votes to the president in a sealed envelope.

(9) The committee is competent to pass any resolutions needful for the accomplishment of the object of the association. It

shall meet in a general assembly at least once every two years. It may be convoked by the bureau, whenever the latter judges it necessary or when at least fifteen members of the committee request it.

The choice of the meeting place will be made by the consultation in writing of all the members of the committee, by the secretary-general, within a time fixed by the bureau.

(10) The committee elects from among its members a bureau composed of a president, a vice-president, and a secretary-general; The committee also appoints the treasurer of the association.

(11) The mission of the bureau is to take the steps necessary for the execution of the resolutions of the committee. It manages the funds of the association. It makes each year a report to the committee of the administration of its affairs. It appoints the clerks and other persons necessary for the work of the association. It places itself in communication, in all industrial States, with specialists and other competent persons disposed to furnish information regarding the labor laws and their application. These persons receive the title of correspondents of the association.

(12) The secretary-general has charge of the correspondence of the association, of the committee, and of the bureau, as well as of the publications and of the information service.

(13) The treasurer receives the dues and has charge of the funds. He makes no payments without the visa of the president.

(14) A national section of the association may be formed in a country, on condition that it has at least 50 members and pays into the treasury of the association an annual contribution of at least 1,000 francs ($193). The statutes of such a section must be aproved by the committee.

Such a section has the right to provide for the vacancies which occur on the committee from among the representatives of its country.

The members of a national section have the same rights as those of the association, with the reservation that the publications to be furnished them by the association, as well as the representation on the committee, will be proportionate to its annual contributions.

(15) The present statutes can not be revised, either wholly or in part, except at a meeting of the committee, and then only by a two-thirds majority of the members present, and when the proposition of revision has been inserted in the notice of meeting.

(*Bulletin of the Bureau of Labor.* No. 54 Sept. 1904. Washington, pp. 1081-1082.)

EXHIBIT 11.

Resolutions of the First Delegates' Meeting (Basel, Sept. 27-28, 1901).

A.

I. a. The statutes of all the sections have been approved and the sections recognized by the Association.

b. Note has been made of the Constitution of the Italian section which conforms to the Constitution (Statutes) of the International Association.

II. The Bureau of the International Association has been asked to investigate the manner in which Articles 7 and 14 of the Statutes of the Association could be revised.

III. The Bureau of the International Association has been asked to take up with the Committee the question of determining the treatment to be accorded a proposition of Mr. Caroll Wright requesting that each labor bureau of the United States be represented by a delegate with consultative authority on the International Committee.

B.

I. The President has been invited to express in the form that seems to him appropriate, to the Governments of the Swiss Confederation, the French Republic, the Kingdoms of Italy and Holland, and the Canton of Basle the thanks of the Association; by granting subventions, by delegating official representatives, by furnishing quarters, these Governments have aided very notably in the creation of the International Labor Office. The Constituent Assembly desires also to extend its thanks to all persons who have aided in its work, as well as to the press which has been favorable to it.

II. The Assembly deems the report of Professor Bauer, Director of the International Office, upon the purpose of that Office, very interesting as an expression of his personal opinions. It congratulates Mr. Bauer, but it calls attention expressly to the fact that, according to the Statutes of the Association, the activities of the International Labor Office should be confined to investigatoins of a purely scientific order. This being granted, the Assembly proposes to determine acordingly the nature of the more immediate activities of the International Office, activities that must be undertaken gradually to the extent that the resources of the Office will permit.

A. Negotiations with Belgium for the publication and distribution of the *L'Annuaire de legislation du travail*.

B. Publication of a Bulletin containing:

1. In one of the first numbers the titles and purposes of protective labor laws in each country, indicating the sources where the complete text can be found.

2. A table of parliamentary action relating to protective labor legislation in the different countries.

3. The resolutions of congresses, and especially associational congresses, national and international, relative to the protection of labor.

4. As far as available, the texts and analyses of new laws and regulations promulgated for the protection of labor.

5. A bibliography of official publications and of private publications of a documentary nature, relating to the legal protection of labor and to labor statistics, indicating the title, contents, size, price, and publisher.

C. Investigations as to the actual condition and effect of night-work of women in the different countries, as well as the results obtained in the industries where night-work has been suppressed. The report shall distinguish the differences existing in the definition of night hours in the different countries and the consequences which ensue.

D. Establishment of a uniform form for industrial accident statistics in the different countries.

E. Investigations as to the degree of unhealthfulness and the actual legislation pertaining to unhealthful industries, and especially as to: 1. those which manufacture or use lead colors; 2. those which manufacture or use white phosphorus.

F. Comparative investigations of the legislation of different countries concerning accident insurance and sickness insurance and civil responsibility with reference to persons who work in a country other than that which is the home of their family.

III. In general, information concerning the protection of labor shall be furnished gratuitously to Governments; it shall be given gratuitously to private individuals only when the latter shall belong to one of the national sections or to the International Association.

IV. The Assembly recommends that the sections encourage and facilitate in every way relations between the Labor Office and workingmen's and employers' Associations. To this end, the most effective means will be to furnish the Labor Office the addresses of these Associations. The sections can also address circulars to them inviting them to send their printed documents to the International Office.

V. The Assembly also proposes that the investigations indicated under headings C D E and if possible, F, serve as the basis for the deliberations and conclusions of the next meeting of the International Association, which will take place at Cologne in September, 1902.

(Translation: *Publications de l'Association internationale pour la protectional légale des travailleurs.* No. 1. p. 131 and 133.)

EXHIBIT 12.
Resolutions of the Second Delegates' Meeting (Cologne, Sept. 23-24, 1902.)

The resolutions were as follows:

1. "The condition of legislation on the night-work of women in the majority of the large industrial States, and, as proved by the reports published by the sections, the influence of that legislation on the state of industry in general and on that of different enterprises and laborers in particular, justify the absolute prohibition in principle of the night-work of women. The international Committee instructs a Commision to investigate the means of introducing that general prohibition and of examining how the ex-

ceptions that exist may be gradually suppressed. This commission shall make its report within two years. Each national section has the right to appoint two delegates on the Commission. The Commission shall call into consultation competent persons selected from among workmen and employers. The governments shall be notified in sufficient time of the meetings of the Commission in order that they may be represented.

II. "The dangers that the handling and use of white phosphorus and lead present to the health of the workers being particularly serious there is urgent need for the institution of a commission charged with the investigation of the ways and means adapted to the elimination of those dangers and of bringing about by international agreement the general prohibition of white phosphorus and the suppression in as far as possible of the use of white lead.

"This task shall devolve upon the commission charged to report upon the first proposition.

"The international Committee will immediately start proceedings through the agency of its bureau with governments and communal authorities to the end that the use of ceruse may be prohibited in the works of the State, the cities and townships."

(Translation: *Ibid.*, No. 2, p. 45.)

EXHIBIT 13

Resolutions of the Commission Meeting at Basel (Sept. 11, 1903).

A. Prohibition of the Use of White Phosphorus in the Match Industry.

I. In execution of the tasks delivered to it at Cologne by the International Association for the Legal Protection of Labor, the Commission calls upon the Bureau to request of the Federal Council of the Swiss Confederation its good offices in initiating an international Conference having for its aim the prohibition by means of an international Convention of the use of white phosphorus in the match industry.

II. The Bureau in co-operation with a subcommittee shall, before March 1, 1904, send to the different governments an explanatory memorandum of the question of white phosphorus; it shall send that memorandum to the governments represented upon the Committee through the agency of their respective delegates. The memorandum shall be addressed directly to the other governments by the Bureau.

B. Lead and Lead Colors.

1. The Commission thinks that it is not necessary to resort to international agreements in the matter of the use of ceruse in the painting trade.

It is of opinion that this question does not raise any serious difficulty with reference to international competition and that the more general regulation relative to lead and its compounds would be more profitably the object of an international conference.

II. The Commission is of the opinion that it is advisable for the Bureau and the national sections to pursue energetically in each country the prohibition of the use of white lead in public and private painting works. The national sections are invited to send to the Bureau before March 1, 1904, a report on the measures they have taken for the purpose of bringing about the suppression of the use of white lead in painting. The Bureau shall give an account at the next meeting of the Committee of the measures that have been taken up with the governments.

III. The Commission charges the Bureau of the International Association to invite the sections to take up measures with their governments as soon as possible by setting forth the facts as to the number of establishments in which cases of lead poisoning have been discovered and presenting the data collected in the different countries by the International Labor Office, in order that:

(1) The necessary investigations may be made in order to ascertain completely the present condition of affairs. (2) If in spite of scientific research for the discovery of innocuous substitutes, the prohibition of the use of lead seems impossible, the dangers which threaten the health of the workers may be eliminated or at least diminished in so far as possible by the rigorous application of the special regulations already existent or by the promulgation of new protective regulations for each of the different categories of industry that manufacture or use lead or its compounds.

The question of lead in its entirety must be placed upon the program of the next meeting of the Committee in order that the ways and means may be considered to introduce the improvements which have been recognized to be possible.

C. Prohibition of the Night-Work of Women Employed Outside of Their Home.

I. In compliance with order given to it at Cologne by the International Association for the Legal Protection of Labor, the Commission calls upon the Bureau to request of the Federal Council of the Swiss Confederation its good offices in initiating an international conference having for its aim the prohibition by means of an international convention of night-work of women in industry.

II. The Bureau in co-operation with a subcommission shall, before March 1, 1904, send to the different Governments a memorandum on the question of night-work of women; it shall send that memorandum to the government represented on the Committee through their respective delegates. The memorandum shall be addressed directly to the other governments by the Bureau.

That memorandum shall definitely state that the prohibition of night-work of women ought to insure to all working women employed in an industrial establishment, that is outside of their home, a rest of twelve consecutive hours between evening and morning. In case the immediate introduction of night-rest of twelve hours' duration presents difficulties, the period of night-rest may be fixed at ten hours for a period of transition. The memorandum shall explain the different resolutions adopted by the Commission.

1. Exceptions may be provided in case of imminent or actual accident.

2. Women assigned to work upon materials subjected to very rapid deterioration, as, for example, in fish and certain fruit industries, may be allowed to work at night on each occasion when it is necessary in order to save the materials from otherwise unavoidable loss.

3. Seasonal industries and those whose needs are similar shall find, in the transitional provision prescribing a night's rest of ten hours, the additional hours for work of which they may be in need in their present state of organization.

4. Periods of time may be set within which to bring about the realization of these reforms.

(Translation: *Ibid.*, No. 3. p. 6-8.)

EXHIBIT 14

Resolutions of the Third Delegates' Meeting (Basel, Sept. 26-28, 1904).

I. International Protection of Laborers.

1. The Committee of the International Association notes with satisfaction the work of the special Commission and approves the acts inspired by it and executed by the Bureau.

2. The Bureau of the International Association is instructed to express to the High Swiss Federal Council its profound appreciation of the Council's intention to comply with its request and convoke an international conference for the legal protection of workers.

3. The Bureau of the International Association is instructed to express the gratitude of the Association to the High Governments of the French Republic and the Kingdom of Italy which, by the conclusion of a protective labor Treaty, have taken an initiative that will promote the international protection of labor.

These letters shall be signed also by the Presidents of the sections.

II. Organization of the Association.

1. The statutes of the Swiss section are approved in their present form.

2. Each of the sections of the International Association for the Legal Protection of Labor shall appoint one of its members, or a special Committee, instructed to work, either with the Bureau of the International Association, or independently of it, for the foundation of sections in sympathy with the principles of the International Association in the countries that are not yet represented in the Association, and for the carrying on of propaganda through the press.

The sections shall notify the Bureau of the International Association of the persons designated, or the appointments made in pursuance of the preceding paragraph.

The sections shall present to each of the general Assemblies a report on their activities in the matter of propaganda.

3. The Bureau of the International Association is instructed to consult with the sections and governments in due time for the purpose of determining the place and exact date of the next General Assembly of the Committee.

III. Finances and International Labor Office.

1. After having verified the accounts of the year 1902-1903, the General Assembly discharges the Bureau of the International Association of its obligations for these two years.

2. Beginning with the year 1905, a single budget shall be made out for each year: that of the International Association; in this the budget of the International Office shall constitute a separate chapter. The proposed budget shall be submitted each year for the approval of the Presidents of the Sections before becoming final.

3. (a) The Sections assume the obligation of printing at their own expense the reports which they present to the general assemblies and of furnishing gratuitously 115 copies to the Bureau of the Association.

(b) The Sections of the countries whose governments do not yet grant any subvention to the Association or at least the subvention designated in the budget, are under obligation to take proceedings before their respective governments in order to induce the latter to grant to the International Association the annual subventions designated in their budget.

(c) The Sections pledge themselves to make all possible effort to insure a wider sale of the Bulletin, and in particular to institute proceedings with their governments and communal authorities in order that the latter may recommend to public administrations subscription to the Bulletin.

4. In spite of the measures to be taken by the sections, (see 3a to c) the present financial situation of the Association is such as to seriously endanger the regular functioning of the International Labor Office in as much as the receipts are out of all proportion to the high expenses resulting from the activities in the preparation of international labor protection. In view of these facts, the Assembly calls upon the governmental representatives

present to inform their respective governments of the present financial situation, with or without preliminary agreement, in order that they may increase their regular subventions.

5. The General Assembly approves the proposed budget for the year, 1905, as modified by the Committee.

6. The Association notes with satisfaction the report of the International Labor Office. It thanks the officials of that office for their devoted and zealous services.

IV. The Struggle Against the Dangers of Occupational Poisoning.

A. Lead and Lead Compounds.

1. The question of lead ought to be studied separately for each group of industries of certain importance manufacturing or using lead, such as: Shops manufacturing lead and zinc, manufactories of lead colors, ceramic and painting industries, manufactories of electric accumulators, polygraphic industries, plumbing, file cutting and cutting of precious stones, dyeing, *etc., etc.* New investigations should be made if there is need in order that there may be prescribed for each of these industries the special protective regulations necessary, or that certain uses of lead or of its compounds may even be prohibited.

A committee shall be instructed to study separately the different groups of dangerous industries, to draw up the practical conclusions of its studies, and then to frame standard regulations. It shall submit to the Bureau the results of its work as soon as completed for each group of industry.

2. As regards the use of white lead in the painting industry, the Association supports without modification the recommendation already adopted in favor of the suppression of the use of this material in all works where other substances can be used in its place. It furthermore thinks that strict regulations must, of necessity, be enacted where its suppression has not yet been obtained.

3. The Association decrees that the Bureau shall distribute to the Sections as soon as possible the report by which Mr. de Vooys undertakes to show that the use of lead glazes can be dispensed with in the ceramic industry.

B. Industrial Poisons.

LABOR RESOLUTIONS INTERNATIONALLY SUBSCRIBED

(a) The Bureau is instructed to secure, in the most suitable way, the adoption of the following fundamental principles for combatting in a systematic manner the dangers of industrial poisoning.

1. It shall be the duty of the medical practitioners and hospital administrations to bring to the attention of the competent authorities the cases of industrial poisoning designated by administrative regulations.

The physicians shall be remunerated for the service rendered.

2. In cases where the law will require the attendance of physicians upon an establishment, it is important that the physician of these establishments which manufacture or use industrial poisons shall be absolutely independent of the employers of these establishments.

3. The establishments manufacturing or employing industrial poisons must be declared as such by the heads of the establishment. That declaration must contain an enumeration of the poisons manufactured or handled in the establishment.

4. Sick funds and mutual relief societies ought in their own interest to give very special attention to those of their members who work in establishments manufacturing or using poisons; they ought to make special morbidity investigations and to communicate the results of the same to labor inspectors in order to enable them to combat effectively the causes of poisoning.

5. It is advisable to promote in medical schools the study of industrial poisoning; the attention of young doctors must be directed by special courses to the importance of labor hygiene and the prophylaxis of occupational diseases.

6. In order to insure a really efficient supervision of establishments which produce or use industrial poisons, it is expedient, besides the medical practitioners already mentioned, to place in charge medical inspectors having a thorough and special knowledge of industrial hygiene.

7. (a) It is advisable to regulate the length of the workday in each dangerous industry by taking account of the degree of toxicity of the industrial poisons handled.

(b) The Bureau is invited to instruct a committee of experts to draw up and make public a list of substances which should be considered as industrial poisons, and to classify these poisons according to the seriousness of the disease caused by each.

The Bureau shall insure wide publicity to this list.

C. Prizes offered to the Association.

The Association accepts with thanks, on conditions reported by the Bureau, the prizes that have been offered it for combatting the dangers which the use of lead presents to workers.

It instructs the Bureau to convey to the generous donors an expression of its profound gratitude.

The Bureau must designate the experts left to the selection of the Association from among the candidates presented by the national sections.

V. Night-Work of Young Persons.

The Association without prejudice to the program of the International Conference and considering the urgency of the suppression of night-work of young persons, invites the Bureau to lay before the sections this question and to place it upon the program of the next meeting of the Association.

The Bureau is authorized to entrust its study to a Committee and to invite the sections to appoint their delegates to it.

Proposed *Questionnaire* for the Sections.

1. What is the number of children and young persons employed in your country (actual number and percentage of the whole number of workers)?

What is the number of those employed at night:

(a) By age?
(b) By industry?

2. How many are there who fall under the head of exceptions, in what industries and under what form.

3. What are the effects of the exceptions, how do they justify themselves, what exceptions could be done away with, what would be the result of such action, both from the technical and economic point of view? (Obtain this information chiefly from factory inspection reports.)

4. What difficulties would oppose themselves in your country to making eighteen the age limit for the protection of young workers?

5. What is the legal length of night-rest; what is the length of

night-work allowed in exceptional cases, for what reasons? (Inquiries should be made of the teaching force, medical force, *etc.*)

6. In what industries have violations of the prohibition of night-work been discovered; what were the reasons?

7. Give the same information relative to employees other than manual workers.

VI. Home Work.

1. The national sections are invited by the Bureau of the International Association to start under conditions which they shall determine and in accordance with a program the details of which are left to their own free discretion, an investigation on the two following points:

(a) What has been the influence of protective labor legislation on the development of home work in that which concerns specially women and young workers?

(b) What are the principal abuses resulting either from the absence or insufficiency of regulation of this kind of labor both from the point of view of the duration of the work of these classes of workers and from that of the hygienic conditions and security of the place of work?

2. The sections must apply in as far as possible, the monographic method, that is to say, they must carry on their investigation not upon the whole of the industries of the country, but on certain industries chosen by them for the purpose.

3. The scope of the inquiry includes:

(a) Home work properly so-called, that is to say work done in the home by the worker with or without the assistance of one or more helpers, for the account of an entrepreneur. It is advisable to include in this category certain home workers whose independence is only apparent and who are really very dependent upon manufacturers or big retail stores.

(b) The work done in shops free wholly or in part from legal regulation either because they are family shops, or by reason of the small number of workers regularly employed, or by reason of the nature of the industry, or for any other cause.

VII. Legal Limitation of the Workday.

The International Association for the legal protection of workers invites the sections to make a study of the question of legal limitation of the workday of manual workers and all other employees in commercial and industrial establishments.

And it requests the sections to prepare for the next general meeting reports on the status of the question in the different countries.

VIII. Social Insurance.

1. As regards the rights guaranteed to the workers and his dependents by legislation on insurance and professional responsibility, there is no occasion for discriminating between beneficiaries because of their nationality, their domicile, or their residence. The law of the domicile of the enterprise for which the laborer works is applicable.

2. The national sections shall, before the next general assembly, furnish the Bureau of the Association with a report on the ways and means of applying this principle within each country and in international relations from the twofold point of view of civil responsibility and insurance organization.

(Translation: *Ibid.*, No. 3, p. 171-176.)

EXHIBIT 15.
Resolutions of the Fourth Delegates' Meeting, Geneva, (September 27-29, 1906).

I. International Conventions.

The Board of the International Association for Labour Legislation is instructed to convey the thanks of the Association to those Governments which have become parties to the Labour Conventions signed at Berne on September 26, 1906, and to congratulate the High Swiss Federal Council on the success of its efforts.

II. Finances, International Labour Office, Statutes of New Sections, Standing Orders.

The Board of the International Association is instructed to convey the thanks of the Association to those Governments which, by increasing their State subsidies, have substantially helped towards the improvement in the financial condition of the Association, and thereby enabled the International Labour Office to maintain its efficiency.

III. Administration of Labour Laws.

The Sections are requested to report to the Board on the measures taken, in accordance with legal enactment or special order in their respective countries, to secure the observance of Labour Laws. To this end, a list of questions will be submitted to the Sections by the Board. On receiving the replies to these questions, the Board shall draw up a comparative report on the steps taken to secure the effective Administration of the Labour Laws in the various countries.

IV. Employment of Children.

The Board is instructed to invite the Sections to report on the conditions and extent of the employment of children and the existing legal provisions for the protection of children employed, and to lay before the next Delegates' Meeting a report compiled from the reports so obtained.

V. Night Work of Young Persons.

1. Night-Work shall be in general forbidden for young persons under 18 years of age.

2. This prohibition is absolute for young persons under 14 years of age.

3. For young persons 14 years of age and upwards exceptions are allowed:

(a) In cases of *force majeure*, or exceptional circumstances.

(b) In industries the materials of which are of a highly perishable nature, in order to prevent serious damage.

4. Night-Work is absolutely forbidden in all places where goods are exposed for sale, hotels and public-houses, as well as in counting-houses attached to commercial and industrial establishments where Night-Work is forbidden.

5. The night's rest shall last at least 11 hours, and shall in all cases include the period from 10 p. m. to 5 a. m.

6. Provision may be made for periods of transition.

7. The International Association expresses its hope that inspection will be efficiently carried out.

8. The meeting instructs a Commission to ascertain by what methods practical effect can be given to the above resolutions. This Commission shall present a report within two years. Each Section has the right to nominate two delegates to this Commission and to name experts from amongst employers and workmen to assist at the deliberations of the Commission.

The Governments will have timely notice of all impending sittings of the Commission in order that they may be able to send representatives.

VI. Legal Maximum Working Day.

The International Association is of opinion:

1. That the determination by law of a maximum period of daily work is of the highest importance for the maintenance and promotion of the physical and intellectual welfare of workmen and employees.

2. That, over and above limitations of hours of work brought about by the efforts of Trade Unions, the intervention of the legislature is necessary in order to set a limit to daily hours of work in general.

3. That, to enable the Association to judge as to the expediency of international agreements on this subject, it is desirable that the International Labour Office should lay before the next Delegates' Meeting a report concerning—

(a) The actual hours of work of adult workmen and employees.

(b) The effects, especially on the productive capacity of workmen and technical improvements, of those limitations which have been already brought about either by law, special order, or the initiative of employers or trade unions.

The International Labour Office is authorized to limit this investigation to particular branches of industry if a general investigation should be found disproportionately beset with difficulties.

VII. Home Work.

The Association is of the opinion that the bad conditions shown to exist in home industries necessitate State intervention.

The sections are requested:

A. (a) To urge upon their respective Governments the enactment of legal provisions requiring employers (undertakers or sub-contractors):

(1) To keep a register of all workers employed by them outside their premises, and to hold it at all times at the disposal of the public authorities.

(2) To provide each person, when the work is given out, with exact written particulars of the piecework rates and the cost of materials, and to post the rates of pay current in the business on a notice affixed in all pay offices.

(b) To consider the means of procuring a wide publicity for

the information concerning wages obtained by legal provisions as recommended above.

B. To promote the extension to out-workers of legal provisions relating to inspection of workplaces, as well as of systems of workmen's insurance.

C. To demand, in the interests both of the public and of the workers, the most stringent enforcement of existing sanitary laws and bye-laws in unhealthy workrooms where home work is carried on, and to promote such regulations where they do not yet exist.

D. To initiate and encourage the formation and active work of trade unions among home workers, buyers' leagues, *etc.*, with a view to promoting private initiative.

E. The Board is instructed to indicate, with the co-operation of a sub-committee:

a) The branches of domestic industry in each country, the products of which compete in the world's markets with those of other countries; the field of such competition; and the conditions of work and organization in the industries in which such competition is found.

(b) Those home industries in which the absence of sick insurance, long hours of work (especially of women and children), inadequacy of wages, periodic slackness of work, call most urgently for measures of protection for the workers.

VIII. Industrial Poisons.

1. With the object of carrying out Resolution IV, A. I, passed at the Delegates' Meeting, 1904, the Association requests the Board to invite the Sections to nominate as soon as possible experts to institute investigations in their respective countries, and to report before January 1, 1908, at latest, on the best methods of combating the dangers attendant on the manufacture and use of lead paints and colours, especially in the ceramic and the polygraphic industries.

These reports shall be sent to the International Labour Office, which shall proceed to appoint three experts of three different nationalities. These experts shall draw up a final report based upon those presented.

The Board is requested to place at the disposal of the Commission of three any of the essays entered for the prize competition which it considers might be of service to them.

2. The several Sections are requested by the Board to submit reports on the prohibition of the use of lead paints and colours before March 1, 1908, at latest. These reports should state whether such prohibition is enacted by law or by special order, and whether it applies to public or private works only or to both; they should contain information as to the effects of the prohibition, and as to experiments which might with advantage be made with leadless colours.

3. With a view to carrying out Resolution B (b) passed by the Delegates' Meeting, 1904, the Commission recommends the appointment of three experts of three different nationalities, whose duty shall be to draw up a final statement, based on the lists provided by the Sections, of the most important industrial poisons arranged in order of the degree of danger attending their use.

4. The Delegates' Meeting of the International Association for Labour Legislation expresses the hope that the Governments which have not signed the convention concerning the prohibition of the use of white phosphorus will, in the near future, adhere to this measure for securing the health of the workers. The Association urges the Sections in these countries to undertake the necessary inquiries, and to exert themselves to the utmost to promote the introduction of the aforesaid prohibition.

IX. Workmen's Insurance.

The International Association for Labour Legislation concludes from the reports of the various Sections that it is possible to establish the principle of the equality of foreigners and natives as regards insurance by means of an International Convention.

The Sections are therefore requested:

(1) To present to the next Delegates' Meeting a Draft of an International Convention, concerning, in the first place, accident insurance, which would establish this principle both as regards the amount of the indemnity and the conditions of procuring the same.

(2) To continue to work by means of National Legislation or International Treaties, towards the realisation of this princi-

ple, until it is fully recognized by an International Convention.

(3) To report to the next Delegates' Meeting what degree of modification or addition by further enactments would be re-required to bring the laws of their respective countries into correspondence with the principle laid down.

(E. B. *English Bulletin of the International Labor Office* 1, (4-8) pp. 318,322).

EXHIBIT 16.

Resolutions of the Fifth Delegates' Meeting (Lucerne, Sept. 28-30, 1908).

I. *International Conventions.*

The Board of the International Association is requested to convey, after December 31st, 1908, the thanks of the Association to the Governments of those States which shall then have ratified the labour conventions signed at Berne on September 26th, 1906.

The Board is requested to transmit to the Government of Sweden a memorandum expressing the thanks of the Association for the efforts made in the matter of the ratification of the Berne Convention relating to the night work of women; regretting that these efforts were not successful; and expressing the hope that when further steps are taken, the desired result will be attained.

II. *Finances, Bulletin, Staff Regulations, Library, etc.*

A. Finances.

1. The Fifth Delegates' Meeting adopts with pleasure the reports of the Board, the Treasurer and the International Labour Office, and expresses its thanks for their work.

2. The Treasurer's financial statements, being duly audited, are adopted.

3. The Budget for 1909 and 1910 is adopted, subject to the following modifications:

The item for printing ("Bulletin") shall be increased to 18,000 francs, out of which 4,000 francs shall be devoted annually towards the expenses of the English edition. A further sum, not to exceed 2,000 francs annually shall be granted, if necessary, to meet any deficit in respect of the English edition. A sum not exceeding 2,0000 francs shall also be granted to meet any deficit in respect of the English edition during 1908.

B. Bulletin of the International Labour Office.

1. Until the financial position of the Association shows a further improvement, the Board is requested to refrain from enlarging the "Bulletin."

2. The Board is recommended to take all possible steps to secure the prompt and regular publication of the "Bulletin," and to reduce the expenses as far as possible.

C. Pension Insurance of the Employees in the International Labour Office.

The Fifth Delegates' Meeting approves the regulations for the insurance of the employees, with the following amendments:

1. The first sentence of clause 1 shall read as follows: "The International Association for Labour Legislation shall be the insuring party through the Board."

2. Clause 5 shall read as follows: "In the event of a contract of employment being ended either on the part of the Labour Office or on that of an employee, the policy of the employee who thus leaves the service of the Association shall under all circumstances be handed over to the employee as his own property."

3. Clause 6 shall be omitted.

D. Salaries of the Employees of the International Labour Office.

The meeting approves the scheme relating to salaries with the following amendments:

1. Clause 3 par. 2, shall be omitted.

2. Clause 6 shall read as follows: "In exceptional cases the Board may grant special payment, if an employee works overtime at the request of the director for four or more weeks, arising out of stress of work or other causes."

3. Clause 7 shall be omitted.

E. Catalogue of the Library of the International Labour Office.

The Labour Office is requested to do its utmost to expedite the compilation of the subject catalogue of the library, and, on request, to allow copies of any sections of this catalogue to be made at the expense of persons desiring the same.

F. Place and Time of the Next Meeting.

The Delegates' Meeting resolves the next (Sixth) Delegates' Meeting of the International Association shall be held in the autumn of 1910 at Lugano.

III. Administration of Labour Laws.

In pursuance of the resolutions of the Fourth Delegates' Meeting relating to the Administration of Labour Laws, the Meeting resolves as follows:

1. The International Labour Office is requested to complete the preliminary report on the administration of labour laws, and to submit the same for criticism to the Governments and Sections concerned.

2. The International Labour Office shall draw the attention of the Governments to the report when completed. Suitable steps shall be taken to make the report as widely known as possible among the general public.

3. The International Labour Office is requested to report from time to time to the Delegates' Meetings on any changes introduced affecting the administration of labour laws.

IV. *Employment of Children.*

The Sections are requested to seek means to secure, as far as possible, the complete prohibition of child labour, and, in so doing, to be guided by the following principles:

1. The employment of children to be subject to regulation in all occupations carried on for purposes of gain.

2. Such regulations to apply to all children employed; in agriculture, a distinction to be made between children working for their parents and for strangers respectively.

3. Children not to be employed for purposes of gain during school age; in so far as school attendance is not compulsory, employment to be permitted on the conclusion of the fourteenth year of age, or, in agriculture, of the thirteenth year.

V. Night Work of Young Persons.

The Delegates' Meeting leaves it to the Board of the Association to choose the occasion for proposing to the Governments the conclusion of an international agreement relating to the prohibition of the night work of young persons, but hereby adopts the following definite proposals which, in the opinion of the meeting, could be introduced in the present state of affairs.

The Meeting resolves, at the same time, to leave the Special Commission appointed in pursuance of Resolution V (8), of the Fourth Delegates' Meeting, constituted as at present, with the duty of continuing the collection and compilation of data bearing on the possibility of prohibiting the night work of young persons, until the time is ripe for approaching the Governments on the matter. It shall be, in addition, the duty of the Commission to inquire whether the technical development of any branches of industry has, in the meantime, advanced sufficiently to admit of the further extension of the proposed prohibition of the night work of young persons. The Board is requested to issue jointly with a sub-committee to be elected from amongst the members of the Special Commission, a publication setting forth the actual conditions under which the night work of young persons is carried on in the various countries, and the possibility of doing away with such night work (as was done as regards the prohibition of the night work of women).

The definite recommendations of the Delegates' Meeting on this subject are as follows:

1. The night work of young persons to be, in general, prohibited in the industrial occupations until the conclusion of the eighteenth year of their age.

2. The prohibition to be absolute until the conclusion of the fourteenth year of their age, and until they are exempt from school attendance.

3. Night work may be permitted for young persons over fourteen:

(a) In cases of *force majeure* when the manufacturing process is subjected to an interruption impossible to foresee, and not of a periodical character;

(b) In industries where the materials used, whether as raw materials or in any manufacturing process, are of a highly perishable nature, where necessary, in order to prevent damage to the materials in question.

(c) In the glass industry, in the case of young persons employed in "gathering" the liquid glass from the furnaces, provided that:

1. The period of their employment at night shall be limited by law, and

2. The number of young persons so employed is limited to that required for the purpose of training the necessary number of skilled workmen.

This exception to be allowed only as a temporary measure;

(d) In iron works, for young persons employed in rolling, provided that they are over sixteen years of age.

4. The Delegates' Meeting expresses no opinion on the resolution adopted at Geneva, in 1906, recommending that night work should be absolutely forbidden "in all places where goods are exposed for sale, hotels and public houses, as well as in counting houses, *etc.*" and refers the same back to the Special Commission for consideration.

5. The night's rest shall last at least eleven hours, and shall, in all cases, include the period from 10 p. m. to 5 a. m.

6. Provision may be made for periods of transition.

7. The Delegates' Meeting expresses the hope that inspection will be efficiently carried out.

8. The Delegates' Meeting maintains that the regular night work of young persons is always to be regarded as an abuse, which, in principle, should not be tolerated in any circumstances. Until it is possible to abolish such night work entirely by means of an international agreement, the Meeting invites all the national Sections to work actively to secure the removal or diminution of this abuse.

VI. *Maximum Working Day.*

In pursuance of the principles adopted by resolution of the Fourth Delegates' Meeting, held at Geneva, respecting the maximum working day, namely:

"1. The determination by law of a maximum period of daily work is of the highest importance for the maintenance and promotion of the physical and intellectual welfare of workmen and employees.

"2. Over and above limitations of hours of work brought about by the efforts of Trade Unions, the intervention of the legislature is necessary in order to set a limit to daily hours of work in general."

The Delegates' Meeting resolves:

1. As regards the employment of women:

The period of employment for all women subject to the provisions of the Berne Convention on the Night Work of Women, to be limited by international agreement to ten hours. This legal maximum period of employment to be introduced by degrees.

2. As regards male workers in the textile industry:

The same maximum of ten hours to be introduced by degrees for men employed in the textile industry.

3. As regards persons employed in coal mines:

(a) A maximum eight hours day to be introduced for all workmen employed below ground.

(b) The Board is requested to appoint a Commission to determine what shall be the technical definition of an "eight hours shift."

4. As regards the period of employment in smelting works, rolling mills, and glass works:

(a) In view of the fact that the information compiled is still incomplete, the Labour Office is requested to continue the study of this question.

(b) The Governments should be urged to institute inquiries into the period of employment in these industries.

(c) The Sections are requested to procure in their respective countries expressions of opinion from technical experts in the branches of industry concerned on the best methods of regulating hours of work.

VII. Home Work.

A. General.

1. The Delegates' Meeting draws further attention to, and reaffirms the measures recommended at Geneva in 1906 (Compulsory registration, publication of wage lists, extension of inspection, social insurance, sanitary regulations, promotion of trade organizations consumers' leagues *etc.*).

2. The Delegates' Meeting is of the opinion that in introducing the above measures and those recommended below, consideration must always be given to the special characteristics of the various domestic industries.

3. The Delegates' Meeting considers that bad conditions in home work are due primarily to inadequacy of wages, and that, consequently, it is of the first importance to find means of raising wages.

To this end the Delegates' Meeting—

(a) Urges the formation of trade organizations amongst home workers, the conclusion of collective agreements, and the legal recognition of such agreements in countries where the law fails at present to recognize the same;

(b) Requests the Sections to make inquiries as to how far it would be practicable to introduce in their respective countries a law giving the Courts power to annul agreements for starvation wages and wage agreements of an usurious nature, and to punish employers who conclude such agreements;

(c) Requests the Sections—

(1) To study the question of the organization of wages boards;

(2) In cases where trade organization has proved unworkable, and where conditions permit, to invite their Governments to try the introduction of minimum wages by appointing joint wages boards to determine rates of wages; for this purpose use could be made, if desired, of the provisions of the English bill on the subject. Any such experiment should be made first in those domestic industries where it could apparently be most easily enforced, and where the work in question is the main occupation of the majority of the persons concerned;

(3) To report to the Association on the results attained; the British Section is, in particular, requested to report regularly on experience gained in the United Kingdom.

4. In view of the wide scope of the home work problem, the Delegates' Meeting is of opinion that it is not at present practicable to consider all the other measures proposed, especially the extension of labour laws to home work. The consideration of these questions is, therefore, postponed to a future meeting.

5. The Delegates' Meeting invites the National Sections to study means whereby it may be rendered possible in practice to subject home workers to factory legislation (normal periods of employment, hygiene and security in workplaces). For this purpose existing legislation and legislative proposals should be taken into consideration.

B. Machine-Made Swiss Embroidery (*Schifflistickerei*).

The Delegates' Meeting requests the German, Austrian, American, French, and Swiss Sections to investigate the question whether the regulations relating to conditions of work in the embroidery trade proposed in the memorial drafted by the Board, could be made the basis of international negotiations between the countries concerned. The Sections in question are requested to report to the Board, who will then decide whether a special commission should be convened to consider the matter.

VIII. Industrial Poisons.

A. White Phosphorus.

The Delegates' Meeting thanks the Austrian and British Sections for their scientific work, their efforts to arouse public opinion, and their Parliamentary activities, as a result of which the adhesion of their Governments to the convention prohibiting the use of white phosphorus is expected. The Meeting also thanks the Spanish and Hungarian Sections, which, with a like end in view, have instituted inquiries and presented petitions. The Board is instructed to express the thanks of the Association to the Governments in questions, as soon as the prohibition in question is introduced, and to thank the British Government without delay for introducing a Bill to prohibit the manufacture and importation of white phosphorus matches, and also the Austrian House of Representatives for the resolutions it has adopted in this sense, and the Austrian Government for their sympathetic attitude.

The Board is requested to continue its efforts in those countries which have not yet joined in the Berne Convention, especially in Belgium and Sweden.

The dangers to the consumer attached to the use of white phosphorus matches make it desirable for countries where such matches are not produced, but only imported (*e. g., Australia*), to prohibit their importation. Such prohibition would incidentally facilitate the introduction of the prohibition in countries which have, as yet, refused to adhere to the Berne Convention merely out of consideration for their export trade.

B. Lead.

1. Painting and Decorating.

The Delegates' Meeting repeats the wish, expressed at previous meetings, that the use of lead paints and colours should be prohibited. In particular, the Meeting is decidedly of opinion that, according to present-day experience, the use of white lead can be dispensed with for internal painting and decoration, and could, therefore, be prohibited. As regards the use of lead paints and colours for all other classes of painting, in particular the use of white lead for external painting and of red lead for other classes of work, the Meeting considers that it would be advisable for the Governments to institute experiments respecting the possibility of prohibiting its use. The Meeting draws further attention to the Geneva resolution inviting the Sections to report to every Delegates' Meeting on the state of affairs in their respective countries.

Until a general prohibition of lead paints and colours is introduced, all vessels and cases in which substances containing lead are distributed for purposes of trade or use, should be marked in an unmistakable manner, so as to show that their contents contain lead and are poisonous. Workmen employed in preparing or manipulating paints and colours containing lead should always have their attention drawn to the danger of poisoning.

All workmen so exposed to danger, even those employed in small workshops and those who do not work in a definite establishment, should be medically examined at regular intervals.

2. Ceramic Industry.

The Delegates' Meeting resolves that an International Commission, consisting of three experts, be appointed, with the duty of compiling regulations for the prevention of lead poisoning in the ceramic industry. The results arrived at by this Commission shall be submitted to the national Sections for consideration at least one year before the convocation of the next Delegates' Meeting. The criticisms of the Sections shall be forwarded within six months to the Commission, who shall hand in their final draft to the Board within the following three months.

The following principles shall be taken as the basis of the deliberations of the Commissions:

1. The use of lead glazes to be restricted as far as possible. To this end the Governments should encourage and promote the introduction of leadless glazes by official researches undertaken

in collaboration with the interested parties, and, in general, promote technical and hygienic improvements in the ceramic industry through the medium of technical schools and lectures.

2. In so far as lead glazes necessarily continue in use, soluble lead constituents should be replaced by well fritted and, as far as possible, insoluble compounds.

3. The preparation of lead fritts and glazes should be effected as far as possible in special glaze factories, or in perfectly adapted glaze departments of large firms.

4. In small potteries with low temperature furnaces, either well fritted glazes or galena (not red lead or litharge) should be used, according to technical requirements. Further, in the very smallest undertakings (domestic industry) workrooms should be separated from dwelling-rooms.

5. Even where carried on as a domestic industry, the ceramic industry should be subject to industrial inspection.

3. Polygraphic Industry.

The Delegates' Meeting resolves to appoint another International Commission, consisting of three experts, to prepare regulations for the prevention of lead-poisoning in the polygraphic industry. As in the case of the Commission on the ceramic industry, this Commission shall report on the polygraphic industry to the national Sections one year before the next Delegates' Meeting. The criticisms of the Sections shall be forwarded to the Commission within six months, and the Commission shall hand in its final report to the Board within the following three months.

The principles laid down in the prize essays and those purchased, and in the reports presented by the Sections, and the recommendations set out below, shall be taken as the basis of the deliberations of the Commission as far as concerns the typographical industry.

Experience has shown the excellent working of the general hygienic provisions regulating conditions of work in the letterpress printing trade contained in the German Order. But these provisions would need to be extended and supplemented in order to be applicable under present conditions in all countries. In particular, the questions of cleanliness and ventilation, and of temperature in rooms where lead is melted for type-setting machines, stereotyping, or type-founding need to be regulated in detail. Further, it would seem desirable to prohibit eating and smoking in workrooms, to prohibit the employment of women in typefounding, and to introduce provisions requiring type cases to be cleaned by suction. Provisions regulating the use of lead colours, similar to those proposed for painting and decorating, should be introduced also in the polygraphic industry. Lead and bronze dust generated in processes regularly carried out, should be drawn off by an apparatus from which the dust cannot escape. As a general rule, the different branches of work in the polygraphic industry should be carried on in separate rooms.

C. List of Industrial Poisons.

The Delegates' Meeting resolves that the list of poisons drawn up by Professor Sommerfeld be referred to the Sections for consideration.

IX. Working in Caissons.

The Delegates' Meeting resolves to entrust, at an early date, the compilation of a comprehensive report on work in caissons to a small Special Commission of experts. This Commission shall present its report to the Board for the use of the Sections within one year at latest.

X. Workmen's Insurance: Treatment of Foreigners in Case of Accident.

1. In pursuance of Resolution IX adopted at Geneva, the Delegates' Meeting expresses the wish, that, either by national legislation, by treaties between two States, or by a general International Convention brought about by the initiative of the Government of one such State; the principle of equal rights for foreigners and subjects of a State should be brought into force, not only as regards the amount of compensation payable, but also as regards the conditions for receiving the same.

To this end the Meeting recommends adoption of the following principles already embodied in certain treaties now in force:

Cf. Treaty between France and Italy dated April 15, 1904
Cf. Treaty between Belgium and Luxemburg dated April 15, 1905
Cf. Treaty between Germany and Luxemburg dated Sept. 2, 1905
Cf. Treaty between France and Belgium dated Feb. 21, 1906
Cf. Treaty between Belgium and Luxemburg dated May 22, 1906
Cf. Treaty between France and Italy dated June 9, 1906
Cf. Treaty between France and Luxemburg dated June 27, 1906
Cf. Treaty between Germany and Holland dated Aug. 27, 1907

(a) Foreigners meeting with industrial accidents and their dependants to be placed in the same position as subjects of a State, in respect of compensation for injuries resulting from such accidents, both as regards the amount and the conditions under which it is payable.

(b) In the case of transport undertakings extending over two countries, the law of the country where the undertaking has its domicile shall apply in respect of the travelling staff, regardless of the relative extent of the business done in the two countries respectively.

The travelling staff remain under the said law, even though occasionally employed in work which is attached to some other department of the undertaking.

(c) Similarly in the case of undertakings carried on in both countries, the law of the country where the undertaking is domiciled shall continue to apply in the case of workmen and employees who are only temporarily employed, and that for less than six months, outside the country where the undertaking is domiciled.

(d) If an industrial accident occurs for which compensation is undoubtedly payable, but a doubt arises as to who is liable to pay the compensation or as to which legislation should apply, the insurer who is first concerned with the case shall pay compensation provisionally to the person entitled to receive the same, until the incidence of the liability is finally determined.

Provisional compensation so paid shall be reimbursed by the person found liable to pay the compensation.

(e) In enforcing the laws in question, the official bodies concerned shall render each other mutual assistance.

They shall be bound to make the necessary inquiries for the determination of the facts of any case.

The procedure for dealing with cases of accidents to foreigners should be made as simple and expeditious as possible.

(f) Documents, certificates, *etc.*, drawn up and delivered by one State to another in administering laws relating to industrial accidents, shall not be subject to any fees or taxes beyond those which would have been imposed, under the circumstances, in the country of origin.

LABOR RESOLUTIONS INTERNATIONALLY SUBSCRIBED

2. The Delegates' Meeting requests the Sections of those countries which are backward in the matter of treaties respecting the insurance of foreign workmen, to promote the conclusion of such treaties as soon as possible, and, in order to facilitate their work, to enter, if possible, into communication with the Sections of the Association in the other countries concerned.

(*Publications of the International Association for Labor Legislation:* No. 6. pp. 111-121.)

EXHIBIT 17

Resolutions of the Sixth Delegates' Meeting at Lugano (Sept. 26-28, 1910.)

SUMMARY.

I. International Labour Conventions of Berne, 1906.
II. New Sections and Constitutions of Sections, Finances and "Bulletin," Co-operation with other International Associations, Exhibitions of Hygiene at Dresden and Rome, Place and Date of the next Meeting.
III. Administration of Labour Laws.
VI. Child labour.
V. Maximum working day.
   A. Ten hour maximum working day for women in establishments employing ten or more workers.
   B. Ten hour maximum working day for young persons.
   C. Ten hour working day for men in textile industries.
   D. Working day in continuous processes.
   E. Eight-hour shift in mines.
   F. Hours of work in specially dangerous industries.
VII. Workmen's holidays.
VIII. Homework.
   A. General.
   B. Machine-made Swiss embroidery.
IX Industrial poisons.
   A. White phosphorus.
   B. Lead.
     (a) Painting and decorating.
     (b) Ceramic industry.
     (c) Polygraphic industry
   C. Protection of homeworkers from industrial poisons.
X. Work in compressed air.
   A. Work in caissons.
   B. Divers.
XI. The protection of railway servants and prevention of accidents. Automatic coupling.
XII. Workmen's insurance.

NB. Subjects newly introduced in the programme of the Association are marked #. Items of the Lugano programme are marked ##.

I. INTERNATIONAL LABOUR CONVENTIONS OF BERNE, 1906.

(1) The Bureau is instructed to petition the Danish and Spanish Governments to ratify at an early date the Berne Convention of September 26th, 1906, respecting the night work of women.

The Bureau is instructed to take appropriate measures to secure the accession of Norway, Russia and Finland, Turkey, East India, the Australian and Canadian Colonies, and South Africa, to this Convention.

(2) The Delegates' Meeting expresses its most cordial thanks to the French, British and Dutch Governments for the adhesion of their colonies and protectorates to the Berne Convention of September 26th, 1906, respecting the prohibition of the use of white (yellow) phosphorus in the match industry, to the Australian Commonwealth for prohibiting the use of white phosphorus, to the American Section for its efforts in this direction in the United States, and to the Hungarian Minister of Commerce who has announced that the prohibition of white phosphorus will most probably be introduced in Hungary at an early date.

The Bureau is instructed to persevere in its efforts to procure the adhesion of countries which have not yet joined the Convention and, especially Belgium, Norway, Sweden, India, South Africa and Japan.

II. NEW SECTIONS AND CONSTITUTIONS OF SECTIONS. FINANCES AND "BULLETIN." CO-OPERATION WITH OTHER INTERNATIONAL ASSOCIATIONS. EXHIBITIONS OF HYGIENE AT DRESDEN AND ROME. PLACE AND DATE OF THE NEXT MEETING.

A. New Sections and Constitutions of Sections.

The constitutions of the Norwegian and Swedish Sections are approved.

B. Finances and "Bulletin."

(1) The Delegates' Meeting acknowledges with satisfaction the reports of the Bureau, the Treasurer, and the International Labour Office, and thanks them heartily for their activity.

(2) The treasurer's accounts, vouchers and cash have been audited and found correct.

(3) The Budget for 1910 and 1911 is approved. The Meeting

approves the advance payment of 3000 frs., requested and made in consequence of the issue of the English edition of the "Bulletin" having been expedited. In renewing contracts for the publication of the "Bulletin" every effort shall be made to reduce the cost of printing.

(4) The Delegates' Meeting expresses to the Government of the United States its hearty thanks for the increase in its appropriation.

(5) The Delegates' Meeting instructs the Bureau to express to the British Government its hearty thanks for sending official representatives, and, at the same time, to convey to it, by these delegates, a request that the British Government may make a contribution towards the expenses of the International Labour Office, as is done by the Governments of all the industrial States of Europe and by the United States of America. This request shall emphasize the fact that such a contribution will be mainly applied to meeting the expenses of the English edition of the "Bulletin," which is translated and printed in England. In case the Government of Great Britain should make an appropriation for the International Labour Office, the Bureau is authorized, in its discretion, to contribute towards the expenses of translating the "Bulletin" into English a sum not exceeding in any year the sum actually received from the British Government.

C. Co-operation with other International Associations.

The Bureau is authorized to enter into communication with other Associations whose aims are similar to those of the International Association for Labour Legislation, in order to come to an understanding regarding any financial or economic questions in which they may have a common interest.

D. International Exhibitions at Dresden and Rome.

The Delegates' Meeting leaves the Bureau free to exhibit at the Exhibitions of Hygiene at Dresden and Rome any statistical tables or publications relating to industrial hygiene.

E. Place and Date of the Next Meeting.

The Delegates' Meeting resolves that the next (VIIth) Delegates' Meeting of the International Association shall take place in the autumn of 1912 in Zurich.

III. Administration of Labour Laws.

(1) The Delegates' Meeting takes note of the proof of the first comparative report drawn up by the International Labour Office on the measures adopted in European countries to enforce labour laws. This proof shall be submitted to the Sections with a view to its being amended and supplemented.

(2) The Bureau is instructed to request the Governments, with a view to making the administration of labour laws in the different countries comparable, to supply data at least on the following points:

1. The nature and number of the establishments subject to inspection and of workers affected:
2. The number of establishments actually inspected and of workers affected;
3. The number of visits of inspection paid by inspectors, distinguishing visits paid at night;
4. The number of cases where persons were cautioned or where penalties were imposed for infringements of the law;
5. The nature and results of arrangements for securing the co-operation of the workers in the enforcement of the law:

   (a) By including workers in the staff of inspection;
   (b) By the institution of regular relations between the inspecting staff and organized and unorganized workers;
   (c) By giving workmen's trade unions the right to take legal proceedings.

The data desired under 1 to 3 above should be classified according to industries.

The headings of the tables in inspectors' reports should be given in one of the three principal languages.

IV. CHILD LABOUR.

A special Commission is appointed with instructions to examine the execution, in the several countries, of the laws for the protection of child labour, and to prepare a comprehensive compilation of the results of the investigations undertaken by the Sections in pursuance of the Lucerne resolutions.

V. NIGHT WORK OF YOUNG PERSONS.

Being convinced that the Lucerne resolutions form an adequate basis for the international regulation of the night work of young persons, the Delegates' Meeting instructs the Bureau to request the Swiss Federal Council to invite the Governments to an international Conference on the subject.

The Meeting instructs the Sub-Commissions to continue its work in pursuance of the Lucerne resolutions and to inquire whether the exceptions to the prohibition of the night work of young persons declared by the Lucerne resolutions to be permissible could not be further limited in the case of young persons employed in glass works and rolling mills. These investigations shall be continued until such time as the request for the international regulation of the question shall be presented to the Swiss Federal Council.

Being convinced that it is reasonable to determine a definite period for the application of transitory provisions, the Delegates' Meeting resolves that Resolution V, 6, of the Lucerne resolutions shall read as follows:

"Any transitory provisions applicable to rolling mills and glass works, contained in an international convention for the regulation of the night work of young persons, should apply only for a definite period, which it is suggested should be fixed at five years."

The Meeting is of opinion, that, in the absence of sufficient information, it would not be expedient to include in an international convention the question of the night work of young persons in hotels, restaurants and public houses, shops and *offices*. Notwithstanding, the Meeting wishes to draw the attention of the various National Sections to the interest which every country has in the legal limitation of the night work of young persons of both sexes in these occupations.

VI. MAXIMUM WORKING DAY.

##A. Ten Hour Maximum Working Day for Women in Establishments Employing Ten or More Workers.

The Delegates' Meeting confirms the resolutions of the Fifth Delegates' Meeting, and, in view of the fact that several States have by national legislation introduced the ten hour working day for women, believes that the time has come to extend this ten hour working day to all States by international treaty, at least in the case of establishments employing ten or more workers.

The Bureau is authorized to take such steps as may be necessary to bring about such a treaty, and to draw up a memorandum on the subject.

The Sections shall for this purpose report to the Bureau by 1st February, 1911, on the present state of legislation and legal decisions on the hours of work of women in their countries. The Memorandum of the Bureau shall be laid as soon as possible before a Special Commission of five members.

B. Ten hour Maximum Working Day for Young Persons.

In view of the fact that several States have by national legislation introduced the ten hour maximum working day for young persons, the Delegates' Meeting believes that the time has come to extend the same by international treaty to all States.

The Bureau is authorized to take the steps necessary to bring about such a treaty and to prepare for this purpose a Memorandum which will take into consideration the special circumstances in individual States and define exactly any exceptions which may be necessary.

The Sections shall for this purpose report to the Bureau by 1st February, 1911, on the present state of legislation and legal decisions on the hours of work of young persons in their countries.

The Bureau's Memorandum shall be laid as soon as possible before the Special Commission on the maximum working day for women.

C. Ten Hour Working Day for Men in Textile Industries.

The Commission considers it unnecessary to consider again the question of limiting the working day of men in the textile industries, since it is of opinion that the limitation of the working day of women necessarily involves the limitation of the working day of men.

It reserves the right, however, to take up the Lucerne resolution again, at a later date, if experience should show that this is necessary.

#D. Working Day in Continuous Processes.

The Delegates' Meeting considers the twelve hour day, which is still the general custom in continuous processes, to be injurious to health. In particular, working periods of 18, 24 and even 36 hours (in changing shifts) are to be condemned.

The Bureau is instructed to appoint a Special Commission as

soon as possible and to present to it the material which is now available as well as any further material which may be secured through the aid of the National Sections.

This Commission shall report in particular on the following points:

1. On the best methods of arranging shifts;
2. On the possibility of prohibiting the night work of adults in certain continuous processes or of regulating such work where for technical reasons work must be carried on at night;
3. On the necessity for the international regulation of this matter.

The Delegates' Meeting expects this Commission to prepare its report and proposals for reform as soon as possible, and at any rate in time for the next Meeting. A Sub-Commission may be appointed if necessary to investigate the conditions of certain industries, such as the iron and glass trades.

E. Eight-hour Shift in Mines.

In pursuance of the resolutions of the Fifth Delegates' Meeting of the International Association for Labour Legislation with regard to the definition of the eight-hour shift for workmen employed below ground in coal mines, the Sixth Delegates' Meeting is of opinion that the length of a shift should be reckoned as the period between the time when the first man of such shift to descend leaves the surface until the time when the first man of the shift to return completes his ascent to the surface.

The Bureau is requested to recommend to the various States to take this definition as the basis of their legislation regulating the duration of shifts.

In applying the above definition, the Sixth Delegates' Meeting re-affiirms the Lucerne resolution of 1908 recommending the introduction by law of a maximum eight-hour shift for all underground workers in coal mines.

F. Hours of Work in Specially Dangerous or Unhealthy Industries.

The Delegates' Meeting re-affiirms the resolution of 1906 and at the same time declares that it is desirable for the proper authorities to have legal power to regulate the daily period of employment of adult men in processes and trades especially dangerous to health.

Accordingly the Delegates' Meeting expresses the desire that the Bureau will place this subject upon the agenda of the next meeting.

VII. WORKMEN'S HOLIDAYS.

The question of holidays for workmen and employees shall be placed upon the agenda of the Next Delegates' Meeting.

The Bureau is instructed to prepare a summary of existing laws on this subject in the various countries and to draw up statistical tables showing the number of establishments in which holidays are allowed, and the numbers of workmen and employees affected.

VIII. HOMEWORK.

A. General.

(1) The Delegates' Meeting re-affirms the declaration of the Delegates' Meeting at Lucerne that the miserable position of the home worker is due primarily to inadequate payment and that consequently it is of the first importance to find means of raising wages.

Having this end in view:

1. The Delegates' Meeting recommends afresh the organization of homeworkers in trade unions and the conclusion of collective wage-agreements. The Meeting regards the unfettered right of combination as th enecessary basis of such collective agreements. In countries where collective agreements are not yet legally recognized under existing law, recognition should be secured in such a manner as to ensure their legal validity and their extension when required to homeworkers in the same occupations who were not originally concerned in the conclusion of the agreements. The Delegates' Meeting urges the National Sections to get into touch with existing organizations of workers with a view to promoting the conclusion of collective agreements with employers' federations.

II. The Delegates' Meeting recommends the adoption by legislation of the principle that wage agreements for insufficient amounts or of an usurious nature should be null and void, and that the conclusion of such agreements should be subject to penalties. The Meeting regards this principle as essential, but at the same time it recognises that the difficulties of its application are such as to prevent its adoption from being in any degree a practical solution of the problem.

III. The Delegates' Meeting is of the opinion that at the present time there is no really effective remedy for the evils of home work but the establishment of wages boards such as those provided for in the British Act. The Meeting is of the opinion that in setting up these wages boards the following principles should be observed:—

(a) The boards should have power to fix minimum rates of wages for home workers in certain industries and certain districts.

(b) The average daily earnings of persons employed in workshops in the manufacture of the same articles should not fall below those of home workers paid under the conditions contemplated above.

(c) The Delegates' Meeting is of the opinion that no legislation for fixing minimum rates of wages for home workers can be effective unless it provides for the imposition of penalties upon employers who fail to pay the prescribed rates of wages.

(d) The Delegates' Meeting is of the opinion that Inspectors should be appointed to enforce the payment of the prescribed rates of wages.

(e) Trade associations of employers and workers should have power to take legal proceedings arising out of the legislation contemplated above.

(2) The Meeting reiterates and re-affirms the measures recommended at Geneva and Lucerne (Compulsory registration, publication of wages lists, extension of inspection, social insurance and sanitary regulations, promotion of trade unions, consumers' leagues, etc.).

(3) The Sections shall report to the Bureau every year on June 1st on the organisation of wages boards, the methods of determining rates of wages and the consequent results, as well as on the realisation of the resolutions of the Delegates' Meetings at Basle, Geneva and Lucerne. The Bureau shall then compile a comparative report and incorporate the same with future editions of the Comparative Report on the Administration of Labour Laws.

(4) The Delegates' Meeting congratulates the British Government and Parliament on their successful initiative in the matter of the protection of home workers. In addition the Bureau

is instructed to express to the British Board of Trade the warmest thanks of the Association for the Memorandum on the Trade Boards Act presented to the Meeting.

B. Machine-made Swiss Embroidery.

The Delegates' Meeting considers that it is desirable for hours of work in the Machine-made Swiss embroidery trade where carried on as a home industry, to be uniformly regulated in all the countries concerned.

The Board is instructed to approach the interested parties through the medium of the Sections, and to convene, if possible within a year, a meeting of a Special Commission (consisting in the first place of representatives of Germany, Austria, Italy, France and Switzerland) appointed to report to the next Delegates' Meeting on appropriate measures to be adopted on this matter, including transitory provisions.

The Sections concerned are requested, within their respective spheres, to take such steps as may seem good to them to secure the adoption of a uniform system of regulation and to promote at the same time measures for the protection of the home industry in question, and, in particular, the institution or encouragement of so-called crisis funds, which could be secured for instance by an agreement between Switzerland and the district of the Vorarlberg where the industry is carried on.

Should the Special Commission agree in the meantime upon such uniform regulations, the Bureau shall have authority, in its discretion, to submit the same to the Governments concerned.

IX. INDUSTRIAL POISONS.

A. White Phosphorus.

(See I International Labour Conventions of Berne 1906, 2.)

B. Lead.

(a) Painting and Decorating. The Delegates' Meeting is of the opinion that the time has come to prohibit the use of lead paints and colours for interior work and to require that all receptacles containing such colours shall be clearly marked to that effect. The Bureau is instructed to approach the National Sections on the matter, being guided by the principles set forth in the petition submitted to the Meeting. The Sections are requested to give the petition their active support on its presentation to their Governments.

(b) Ceramic Industry. The Delegates' Meeting resolves to recommend to the Governments, by means of a petition presented by the Bureau, the following principles for the regulation of hygienic conditions in the ceramic industry.

Principles for the Regulation of Hygienic Conditions in the Ceramic Industry.

I. The Governments should take steps towards the abolition of the use of lead in the ceramic industry.

To this end the following measures should be adopted:

1. In the manufacture of china and earthenware fired at a high temperature the use of lead glaze should be prohibited.

2. As regards the manufacture of earthenware fired at a low temperature a provisional list of articles should be drawn up which can at the present time, be manufactured without lead. This list, which would be subject to extension, should contain articles of common use such as pots, washing basins, dishes, mugs, bowls, *etc.*, electrical insulators, *etc.*

3. As regards the manufacture of common pottery and plain stove tiles fired at a low temperature, such as are manufactured on the Continent both in small workshops and in the workers' homes, litharge and red lead should be replaced by galena or any other less dangerous glaze. The preparation and use of unfritted glazes and the fritting process should be prohibited in such works.

The following measures would tend to encourage the gradual adoption of leadless glazes in the ceramic industry:

(a) The instruction and assistance of all occupiers in the industry wishing to make a practical trial of the use of leadless glazes.

(b) The strict enforcement of hygienic regulations in works using lead glazes.

II. Existing regulations for factories and workshops should alone apply to establishments where leadless glazes are exclusively and permanently used.#

Factory Inspectors should have power to take, for purposes of analysis at any stage and at any time, samples of glaze and of the substances used in the preparation of the same.

III. The following regulations should be adopted in the case of works using lead glazes:

1. The proper authorities shall have power to require, where necessary, the glazes used to be modified in order to prevent injury to the health of workmen employed in contact with the same.

2. The mixing, grinding and transportation of lead glazes as well as the lead used in their preparation, shall be effected either in a thoroughly damp state or in apparatus which permits no dust to escape.

3. Frit-kilns must be so arranged that the molten frit can flow off into water, and frits must always be drawn off in such a manner.

4. Calcining shall be effected in a place separated from all the other workplaces, and exhaust ventilation in good working order shall be placed over the openings of the furnace.

5. Effective exhaust ventilation shall be applied in a suitable manner at all points where dust is generated, such as the openings of grinding and mixing apparatus, of transport apparatus, and of frit-kilns, and benches where glazes are applied in a dry state, where glazes or colours are applied by dusting, or where ware-cleaning is carried on.

All places where lead glazes or the lead used in their preparation are handled must be at least 3.5 metres in height and 15 cubic metres of air-space shall be allowed for each workman.

The floor must be impervious and washable, and the walls covered to a height of two metres, with a smooth and washable coating or paint.

6. No glazes shall be manufactured or used in living or sleeping rooms, and no lead glazes or lead used in their preparation, or pottery covered with unfired glaze shall be brought into or stored in such rooms.

Where more than five persons are employed full time in an

\# Within the meaning of these provisions leadless non-poisonous glazes shall mean all compositions or frits used for glazing in the ceramic industry which contain not more than 1% of lead. Compositions containing no lead compound other than galena shall be held to be leadless. All other glazes shall be held to contain lead within the meaning of these provisions.

undertaking the said processes shall not be carried on in living or sleeping rooms or in rooms where other work is carried on, nor shall glazes, the lead used in their preparation, or pottery covered with unfired glaze be brought into or stored in such places.

7. On the conclusion of a suitable period or transition no female person shall in any circumstances be employed in any kind of work whatsoever which would bring her into contact with unfired lead glazes or compounds or with the lead used in their preparation. No male young persons under eighteen years of age shall be employed in such work except in so far as may be necessary for the purposes of learning the trade.

No young persons under eighteen or women shall be employed in any circumstances in the calcining process or in cleaning places where the above-mentioned substances or objects covered with unfired glaze have been manipulated or stored.

8. Hours of work shall be reduced for all persons employed in the processes mentioned in the preceding paragraphs in proportion to the dangers attendant upon the respective processes, and especially in the case of workmen in the calcining process, who shall not be so employed continuously.

9. All workpeople employed in the manufacture of glazes containing lead, as well as those who come into contact with raw glazes or the lead used in their preparation, shall wear special working clothes.

10. The employer shall supply without charge a sufficient quantity of suitable working clothes, drinking and washing water, glasses, soap and towels. The employer shall provide for the washing of the said working clothes and towels.

11. No person shall eat, drink or smoke in, or bring any food, drink or tobacco into places where lead glazes or the lead used in their preparation are handled, or which are used for storing these substances or pottery covered with unfired lead glazes.

12. The workpeople in question shall be examined every three months by a medical practitioner, appointed by the State Authorities. The result of the examinations shall be entered in a register kept for the purpose which shall be open to inspection by the inspecting authority.

13. No workman who is suffering from lead-poisoning, or who has been found by the medical practitioner named in Section 12 to be unfit on medical grounds for work in contact with lead, shall be employed in the above mentioned branches of the trade, or in rooms where such work is carried on, during such period as may be fixed by the medical practitioner, but the employer shall employ him elsewhere.

14. Two cloak-rooms shall be provided, one for working and one for outdoor clothes, with a suitable lavatory and bath-room between the two. A messroom shall also be provided.

In small undertakings there shall be provided at least dust-proof cupboards where the workers' outdoor and working clothes shall be kept separately, and lavatory accommodation.

15. Employers shall give all workpeople contemplated in paragraph 9 on their entering the employment printed instructions as to the dangers of lead poisoning and its prevention, and shall affix such instructions in the workplaces.

16. In the case of establishments using lead glazes so composed that the consequent risk to health is small, temporary exemptions from the preceding provisions may be allowed by the authorities in exceptional circumstances.

(c) *Polygraphic Industry.* The Delegates' Meeting resolves to recommend to the Governments by means of a petition presented by the Bureau, the following principles for the regulation of hygienic conditions in the polygraphic industry.

Principles for the Regulation of Hygienic Conditions in Printing Works and Type Foundries.

(1) All places in which employees come into contact with lead or its alloys or compounds shall be well lighted and easily heated and ventilated. There must be an allowance of at least 15 cubic metres of air space and three square metres of floor space for each person employed. Workrooms in new premises shall be at least 3 metres in height.

(2) Work contemplated in Section 1 which causes any considerable amount of dust or an appreciable rise of temperature (such as the melting of lead or type-metal, the use of more than one monotype or linotype machine, stereotyping, finishing and dressing type, and bronzing with powdered bronze) shall be car-

ried out in separate workrooms which must not be in a basement, except where the work is carried on only in exceptional circumstances. In large establishments the composing rooms must be separate from other work-rooms.

(3) Rooms must be well lighted with both natural and artificial light, so as to protect adequately the eyesight of the persons employed, consideration being paid to the nature of the work.

(4) The floors of all places mentioned in Section 1 shall be without cracks and washable or covered with a substance for preventing dust. The walls must be covered to a height of two metres with a smooth washable coating or paint of light colour. No shelves or other appliances where dust can accumulate shall be fitted up, except such as are necessary for the work.

(5) In larger establishments suitable lavatories and cloakrooms separated from the workrooms shall be provided. In small establishments arrangements shall be made for employers to keep their outdoor and working clothes in separate cupboards, and lavatory accommodation with sufficient water laid on, together with a plentiful supply of drinking water shall be provided. In type foundries, large printing works and works where night work is the rule, mess rooms shall be provided.

(6) Women and young persons under eighteen years of age shall not be employed in the occupations contemplated in Section 1, provided that apprentices may be employed in any occupations for the purposes of learning the trade, but shall in no circumstances clean the workrooms or cases. The question of whether women should be admitted or excluded from the occupations of composing and operating type-setting machines, shall be definitely decided after thorough investigations have been made (see last paragraph) into the degree of danger attending these occupations.

(7) The floors of all workplaces, cloakrooms and lavatories, shall be cleaned every day. Once a week all rooms shall be thoroughly cleaned, and after working hours as far as workrooms are concerned. A *sufficient* number of spittoons shall be provided. The workrooms shall be thoroughly aired several times a day.

(8) Compositors' tables and shelves must be fixed close to the floor, or else arranged in such a way that there is a distance of at least 25 centimetres between the floor and the lowest shelf. Cases in regular use must be cleaned when necssary and not less often than once in three months; other cases must be cleaned before use. The cleaning of the cases shall be effected by suction, or where necessary in the open air provided that suitable precautions are taken to protect the workers from dust.

(9) Melting pots and crucibles shall be fitted with sufficiently large pipes for drawing off their contents, and the crucibles and pipes shall be covered so as to be heat proof.

The temperature of workplaces where founding, stereotyping or typesetting by machinery is carried on shall not exceed 25° centigrade, unless the outdoor temperature exceeds 18°C in the shade, in which case the difference shall not exceed 7°C.

(10) Colouring matter containing lead shall be prepared by mechanical means only.

(11) Bronzing with bronze powder shall be effected only by machines allowing no dust to escape and provided with exhaust ventilation. Bronzing with bronze powder shall not be effected by hand, except where the work is undertaken only in exceptional circumstances and rarely, in which case respirators covering mouth and nose shall be worn.

(12) All workmen employed in occupations contemplated in Section 1 shall wear washable working clothes.

(13) No unpurified and injurious substances shall be used to clean rollers or type, *etc.*

(14) No persons shall eat, drink or smoke in the workplace, or bring any food, drink or tobacco into them.

Workmen shall wash their faces, mouths and hands before every break in work, and before leaving work. The employer shall provide without charge towels and soap and for each workman a separate glass for rinsing the mouth.

(15) Workmen employed in composing, in melting and casting type, in linotyping, in stereotyping and in finishing and dressing type, shall be medically examined every three months by a medical practitioner, approved by the State authorities for the purpose.

Persons whom the medical practitioner shall declare unfit shall not be employed in the occupations contemplated in Section 1 during such period as may be prescribed by him. The employer shall be bound to employ such persons in some other manner.

All apprentices shall be medically examined before beginning their apprenticeship.

#In view of the inadequate and inexact nature of the documentary information available on the extent to which compositors and the operators of type-setting machines are exposed to the danger of poisoning, a fresh investigation shall be undertaken, the results of which shall be laid before the Delegates' Meeting at Zurich in 1912. (See paragraph 6.)

C. Protection of Homeworkers from Industrial Poisons.

The question of the protection of homeworkers from industrial poisons shall be placed upon the Agenda of the next Delegates' Meeting.

D. List of Industrial Poisons.

The Delegates' Meeting takes note of the admirable list of industrial poisons drafted by Prof. Sommerfeld and amended by Dr. Fischer and the Commission in the light of practical experience, and expresses its sincere thanks to these two authors.

At the same time the Meeting recognises the absolute impossibility of drawing up a complete list corresponding to industrial conditions for the time being in all countries, without the cooperation of the National Sections. The Bureau is requested to transmit to the Sections and to the Permanent Council of Hygiene the list, which is now in course of preparation by a Sub-Commission. The sections shall thereupon, with the assistance of their respective Governments, revise and supplement the list by April 1st, 1911. The Bureau shall then arrange, in agreement with the Permanent Council of Hygiene, for the publication of the list.

X. WORK IN COMPRESSED AIR.

A. Work in Caissons.

Since the protection of workers in caissons cannot be regarded as directly affected by international competition, it is not a subject for international agreement. But at the same time it is expedient for the International Association for Labour Legislation to urge the various Governments to introduce legislation for the protection of Caisson workers as has been done in France and Holland. The principles here following should form the basis of such regulations.

Principals for the Regulation of Work in Caissons.

1. The danger to life and health to which persons working in caissons under a high air-pressure (from about 1.5 atmospheres in excess of atmospheric pressure) are in general exposed, must be regarded as appallingly great.

2. The danger can be reduced to a very considerable extent by the adoption of suitable prophylactic and therapeutic measures. The introduction of such measures consequently forms an important branch of labour legislation.

3. Protective measures cannot be expected to succeed unless they are designed on the right lines and strictly carried out. Consequently it is necessary for such regulations to be introduced by State legislation, and enforced by administrative authorities, and for contraventions to be punishable.

4. Regulations for the protection of Caisson workers should contain provisions:

(a) Requiring the admission of persons to work in caissons to be dependent upon the result of a strict medical examination.

(b) Requiring the organisation of a regular system of medical supervision on the works and wherever possible a permanent staff of medical officers.

(c) Fixing exactly the periods of employment and the manner of locking-in and unlocking, according to the depth of the works and the pressure.

d) Prescribing suitable hygienic regulations respecting the air-supply in the caisson and air-locks, variations of temperature, accommodation for workmen on the works, the conduct of workmen, *etc.*

(e) Prescribing all arrangements necessary for the safety of the workmen.

(f) Ensuring that suitable appliances for treating persons taken ill—especially a properly fitted up recompression lock—and the necessary staff for attending them shall be available.

(g) Requiring a register to be kept on the works containing:

the name and forename of every person subject to medical examination, particulars of the result of each examination, and particulars of all cases where medical treatment was given on the works and the results of the same.

#B. Divers.

Since divers, especially those employed in salvage operations, are liable to be called upon to work in foreign waters or on ships of a different nationality, it seems advisable that their occupation should be regulated by international agreement.

The members of the Permanent Council of Hygiene shall collect from every country the regulations and official and private instructions respecting diving operations.

The International Labour Office shall thereupon transmit copies of these regulations, etc., to the members of the Special Commission, which shall prepare a report of the subject for the next Delegates' Meeting.

#XI. THE PROTECTION OF RAILWAY SERVANTS AND PREVENTION OF ACCIDENTS: AUTOMATIC COUPLING.

The Bureau is instructed to make a further report to the next Delegates' Meeting regarding the international prevention of accidents and the protection of those employed on railroads and in the carrying trade. The Sections are requested to petition their Governments for the introduction of automatic couplers.

XII. WORKMEN'S INSURANCE. EQUAL TREATMENT OF FOREIGN WORKMEN.

(1) The Association requests the American Section to continue its efforts to secure the passage in the several States of the Union of suitable laws for insurance against sickness and accident, which shall not discriminate against alien workers and thus carry out Resolution IX adopted at Geneva, and Resolution X adopted at Lucerne, and it thanks this Section for the initiative which it has taken in this queston of the protection of immigrants.

##(2) A Special Commission is appointed with instructions to seek ways and means by which the equal treatment of native and foreign workmen may be guaranteed, not only in respect of insurance against industrial accidents, but also in other departments of social insurance, and to report to the next Delegates' Meeting.

(Report of the Sixth General Meeting, *Ibid.*, No. 7, pp. 160-174.)

Exhibit 18.

Resolutions of the Seventh Delegates' Meeting at Zurich (Sept. 10-12, 1912.)

SURVEY

1. Publication of Reports.
2. Finances.
3. Bulletin of the International Labor Office.
4. New National Section.
5. Co-operation with other International Associations.
6. Next Delegates' Meeting.
7. International Conventions.
8. The Administration of International Labor Treaties.
9. Child Labor.
10. Saturday Half-holiday.
11. Hours of labor in Continuous Industries.
12. Protection of Railroad Employees.
13. Protection of Dock Workers.
14. Hygienic Working Day.
15. Workmen's Holidays.
16. Legal Relations between Employers and Employed.
17. The Truck System and Deductions from Wages.
18. Home Work.
19. Machine-made Swiss Embroidery.
20. List of Industrial Poisons.
21. Lead.
22. Handling of Ferrosilicon.
23. Principles for the Protection of Persons employed in Mining, the Construction of Tunnels, Stone Quarries *etc.*, on an International Basis.
24. The International Prevention of Anthrax amongst Industrial Workers and of Mercurial Poisoning in Fur-cutting and Hat-making.
25. Work in Caisons.
26. Diving Operations.
27. International Statistics of Morbidity and Mortality amongst the Working Classes.
28. Treatment of Foreign Workmen under Insurance Legislation.

1. Publication of Reports.

The Bureau is requested to communicate with the national sections in order to seek means of simplifying and expediting the publication of the reports presented to the Delegates' Meeting.

2. Finances.

I. The Delegates' Meeting acknowledges with satisfaction the reports of the Bureau, the Treasurer, and the International Labour Office and thanks them heartily for their activity.

II. The Treasurer's accounts, vouchers, and cash have been audited and found correct.

The Delegates' Meeting wishes to express to the retiring Treasurer, Mr. Councillor Wullschleger, cordial appreciation of his past services.

III. The Budget for 1912 and 1913 is approved.

3. Bulletin of the International Labour Office.

The Delegates' Meeting thanks the British Government most cordially for the subvention granted to the International Labour Office, which has enabled the Office to bring out the English Bulletin in the same form as the French and German Bulletins, and to cover the expenses out of the grants from countries using the English Edition.

In view of the fact that under present circumstances the English Edition must, in the interests of efficiency, be translated and printed in an English-speaking country, the Delegates' Meeting approves the arrangements made by the Bureau in this respect.

The Delegates' Meeting, nevertheless, hopes to procure considerable increases in the contributions of English-speaking countries towards the International Association and the International Labour Office, by the foundation of new Sections, by the support of further Governments, and by increases in existing Government subventions.

4. New National Section.

The Delegates' Meeting welcomes the foundation of a Section in Finland and approves its statutes.

5. Cooperation with other International Associations.

I. The Delegates' Meeting instructs the Bureau to discuss with the Presidents of the International Associations on Unemployment and on Social Insurance, steps to promote social reform, tending to facilitate the work of the three Associations serving its ends. The Delegates' Meeting requests the Bureau, in this connection, to see that the autonomy of the International Association for Labour Legislation and the liberty to choose its branches of work and the manner of carrying them out, shall be guaranteed, and that the relations of the national Sections with the International Association shall not be interfered with in any respect. The Bureau is requested to report to the next Delegates' Meeting on the result of the negotiations in order that resolutions may be adopted on the matter. But the Bureau is authorised to co-operate at once, subject to the above conditions, with the two other Associations.

II. The Bureau is authorised to enter into relations with the Bureau of the International Home Work Congress with a view to co-ordinating the efforts of the two organisations.

6. Next Delegates' Meeting.

The Delegates' Meeting resolves that the VIIIth Delegates' Meeting shall be held at Berne in 1914.

7. International Conventions.

I. The Delegates' Meeting ratifies the steps taken by the Bureau.

II. The Bureau of the International Association is instructed to thank the Swiss Department of Industry very cordially for the intention they have expressed of recommending to the Swiss Federal Council to convoke, at the request of the Association, a second international conference on labour legislation.

III. The Bureau of the International Association is instructed to express to the Spanish Government the thanks of the Association for having introduced the legal prohibition of the night work of women.

IV. The Delegates' Meeting expresses most cordial thanks to the Government of New Zealand and the Union of South Africa for their adhesion to the international convention of Berne respecting the prohibition of the use of white (yellow) phosphorus in the match industry; to the Hungarian Government for the prohibition of white phosphorus in the manufacture of matches; to the Federal Government of the United States for the prohibition of the importation and exportation of poisonous phosphorus matches and the imposition of a prohibitive tax; and to the Government of the Mexican Republic for introducing the prohibition likewise. The Association wishes on this occasion to thank the American Section again for their zealous work in promoting this legislation.

V. The Bureau is instructed to continue their exertions in those countries which have not yet signed the two Berne Conventions.

VI. The Delegates' Meeting requests the Bureau to draw the attention of the national Sections to the interpretation given in different countries to the Berne Conventions. The Bureau is recommended to insert in the quarterly reports particulars of information received from the national Sections on this matter.

8. The Administration of International Labour Treaties and of Labour Laws.

I. The Delegates Meeting invites the national Sections which have not yet done so, to submit the petition on the reform of official statistics to their Governments.

II. Since Art. 5 of the International Convention of September 26th, 1906, respecting the prohibition of the night work of women in industrial occupations, provides that the Governments should exchange through diplomatic channels their periodical reports on the administration of laws and orders concerned with the subject of the Convention, it is desirable that these reports should be published by the Signatory States in a form such as to make it possible for each of the Governments concerned to compare the standard of administration to the labour treaties in the other Signatory States.

III. In view of the fact that it is not possible to give a reply at present to some of the questions contained in paragraphs II and III of the proposals of the Bureau, the Delegates' Meeting requests the Bureau to enter into an agreement directly with the Governments on the subject of the elaboration of uniform statistics which will enable it to publish every four years the comparative report on the administration of labour laws.

With this object the Governments shall be invited to appoint an international commission of statistical experts and inspectors of labour.

IV. The Delegates' Meeting requests the national Sections to endeavor to persuade the Governments to appoint a large number of women inspectors, and to arrange that at least one woman inspector shall be stationed in each centre of industry where the employment of women or children is general.

9. Child Labour.

The Sections are requested to establish special Child Labour Committees with the duty of:

(a) Supplying the information desired in the International Labour Office's *questionnaire,* and

(b) Reporting, on the basis of this information, to the next

Delegates' Meeting on ways and means of carrying out and extending the existing laws for the protection of children.

The Bureau shall prepare a comparative survey of these reports, and present it to the International Special Commission on Child Labour. This Commission shall submit definite proposals to the next Delegates' Meeting.

10. Saturday Half-holiday.

In view of the fact: That a free Saturday afternoon is necessary in order to give working women a real rest on Sundays;

That this institution alone is able to insure to the workers in every week a full day of family life;

That this Saturday half-holiday is already introduced wholly or partially for children, young persons and women, and even for adult workmen in the legislation of the German Empire, the United Kingdom, Greece, the Netherlands and Switzerland;

That the initiative of the employers' and workmen's associations is endeavoring to promote the extension of the Saturday half-holiday in all industrial countries;

The Delegates' Meeting desires that the Saturday half-holiday for women workers and young persons should be made the subject of an international convention; and instructs the sub-commission on the maximum 10 hours working day to draw up, in conjunction with the Bureau, a report to be laid before the next Delegates' Meeting.

11. Hours of Labour in Continuous Industries.

I. In view of the resolutions of the Lugano meeting and of the facts presented to the special Commission in London, the Delegates' Meeting is of the opinion that the eight hour shift in continuous industries (industries working night and day) is the best shift system for such work and should be strongly recommended both from the point of view of the physical and moral welfare of the workers and in the social and economic interest of society generally.

II. The Delegates' Meeting is of the opinion that the reports presented by the different national Sections have shown that in the iron and steel industries (blast furnaces, iron and steel works, rolling mills) the eight hour day is very necessary and is practicable for the shift workers.

The Delegates' Meeting instructs the Bureau to request the

Swiss Federal Council to address to the Governments as soon as possible the request to arrange a conference of the interested States with a view to arriving at an international agreement as to the introduction of the eight hour day for those workers.

III. The Delegates' Meeting is of the opinion that as regards glass works, the investigations are sufficiently advanced for the conclusion at any rate of an international convention on the basis of a working week of 56 hours on the average with an uninterrupted weekly rest of 24 hours. The Bureau is requested to choose the most favorable time for taking steps to this end.

IV. The Delegates' Meeting is of the opinion that as regards other continuous industries the national Sections should by investigations prepare the way for the introduction of the eight hour day or of a corresponding maximum week.

(a) In continuous industries, where the working day (*i. e.*, hours during which the workmen are required to be present at the works) exceeds ten hours in 24, or where each set of men works more than six shifts per week.

(b) And in those industries (*e. g.* paper and pulp mills, chemical industries) where conditions seem to be ripe for the introduction of the three shift system in many countries.

12. Protection of Railway Employees.

I. The Bureau is instructed to approach the railway administrations of all countries and request them to complete the tables respecting time on duty, hours of work, night's rest, leave, days of rest.

II. These tables shall then be submitted, together with any other results from inquiries now in progress, to a special Commission consisting of seven members. This Commission shall report before the next Delegates' Meeting assembles on:

(a) The diversity in the number of accidents among employees of the same class in different countries and if possible on the causes of this diversity.

(b) The differences in the organisation of the service (time on duty, hours of work, overtime, periods of rest, length of the day of rest, days of leave) and on the causes of these differences as far as they can be ascertained.

(c) Institutions for the settlement of disputes, respecting hours of work and wages in the railway service, and their success.

(d) The basis of statistics of sickness in the railway service.

III. The special Commission shall have authority to institute analogous investigations respecting the conditions of labour of telegraphists (including radio-telegraphists) and telephonists.

13. Protection of Dock Workers.

The Bureau is instructed to request the national Sections of countries having seaports to make an investigation into the labour conditions of dock workers with special reference to the number of hours worked, and to report before the next Delegates' Meeting.

When instituting investigations into the hours of work of dock labourers the national Sections shall likewise have the duty of considering the question of maximum loads for dock labourers.

14. Hygienic Working Day.

I. The Bureau is instructed to express the thanks of the Association to the Governments which have instituted special inquiries into the hours of labour in particularly unhealthy trades, and requests them and other Governments to extend their inquiries to other unhealthy industries which are not mentioned in the list of May, 1912. The supplementary list shall be drawn up by the Bureau after consultation with the Permanent Council of Hygiene.

II. A special Commission shall be appointed by the Bureau in agreement with the national Sections and the Permanent Council of Hygiene, with the duty of drawing up a memorial containing particulars of existing legislation, of the hours of labour actually prevailing, and of the accident, sickness and mortality rates in all trades considered to be dangerous and unhealthy, and also proposals respecting the prohibition of the employment of children, young persons and women, and the limitation of their hours of labour, and also of those of adult men. This memorial shall be submitted in proof to the next Delegates' Meeting.

15. Workmen's Holidays.

The national Sections are requested to approach their Governments with a petition that they will complete the inquiries into workmen's holidays.

16. Legal Relations between Employers and Employed.

The Delegates' Meeting requests the Bureau to ask the Sections whether and how far they are disposed to draw up a statement of the existing legal prescriptions and customs in their countries which regulate the individual and collective relations between employers and employed both in the course of and outside employment, and to communicate the results to the International Labour Office.

17. The Truck System and Deductions from Wages.

I. In view of the abuses which have arisen, in a great number of industries, in respect of the use of disciplinary fines and deductions for damages, as well as of the numerous varieties in the truck system (payment in kind, or by means of bonds and tickets to be drawn on the establishment of the employer), of which the general result is to reduce the wages of unskilled workers and women, the Delegates' Meeting requests the national Sections to submit to their respective Governments, in accordance with the spirit of protective legislation already in force, legislative proposals as follows:

(a) In all industries, whether carried on in the factory or the home, the payment of wages in kind or by means of bonds payable in the form of goods on sale in establishments conducted by the employers shall be prohibited in principle.

(b) The whole system of fines and deductions for damage (the case of wilful and malicious damage only excepted) shall be abolished. Provided that, even in the case of malicious damage, the employer shall not be authorised to impose any penalty without the order of the Court. Where the complete suppression of deductions does not appear to be immediately possible, such deductions shall neither be established nor exacted except by agreement either with the workpeople concerned, or with their organizations where any such organization exists.

(c) Materials (used in the process of manufacture) must be furnished gratuitously by the employer to the factory worker and the home worker alike. In the case of tools supplied to the worker by the employer any charge made by the employer shall be for the cost price only.

The Sections are requested to forward by every means in their power the drafting and discussion of Bills embodying the desire expressed by the Delegates' Meeting.

II. In certain countries there exist Pension and Thrift funds to which workmen and employees are compelled to subscribe. In case of annulment of their engagements for any cause, they lose the rights which they have acquired by the payment of these subscriptions. The Delegates' Meeting recommends the passing of laws securing to workmen compelled to pay these subscriptions the repayment of all sums contributed by them, should they be dismissed before they have acquired a right to pension.

III. The Delegates' Meeting requests, in addition, that legislative steps should be taken to remove the abuses which have arisen in connection with the building of working men's dwellings erected in order to deprive the workman of the exercise of rights with which legislation has invested him for the protection of his interests.

18. Home Work.

The Delegates' Meeting declares again most emphatically, in view of the fresh studies and experimental inquiries made during the two years last past, that the miserable conditions of a large proportion of the home workers is caused especially by their absolutely insufficient wages, and that no improvement can be hoped for so long as means are not found to raise wages.

To this end the Delegates' Meeting recommends again:

I. The organisation of home workers in trade unions and the conclusion of collective wage agreements. The meeting regards the unfettered right of combination as the necessary basis of such collective agreements. In countries where collective agreements are not yet legally recognised under existing law, recognition should be secured in such a manner as to ensure their legal validity and their extension when required to home workers in the same occupations who were not originally concerned in the conclusion of the agreement. The Delegates' Meeting urges the national Sections to get into touch with the existing organisations of workers with a view to promoting the conclusion of the collective agreements with employers and employers' federations.

II. The adoption by legislation of the principle that wage

agreements for insufficient amounts or of an usurious nature should be null and void, and that the conclusion of such agreements should be subject to penalties. The meeting regards this principle as essential, but at the same time, it recognises that the difficulties of its application are such as to prevent its adoption from being in any degree a practical solution of the problem.

III. The Delegates' Meeting believes that any legislation in favour of home workers will be ineffective so long as it is not founded on minimum rates fixed by wages boards constituted according to the following principles.

(1) The board shall be composed of an equal number of employers and employees, chosen generally by the parties or, if this is impossible, by bodies acting on their behalf or failing these, by the Government.

The President shall not be an employer or an employee and shall be elected by the board. The Government shall appoint him in case of disagreement. He shall have the casting-vote;

(2) The minimum wage shall be fixed so that a home worker of ordinary capacity may earn as time wage a sum approximately equal to fair wages paid in factories and workshops where similar trades are carried on in the town or district. The wage must be at least high enough to ensure to the worker under normal living conditions sufficient food and healthy housing;

(3) The board shall fix officially the minimum wage and publish it at once;

(4) If possible the board shall establish a scale of minimum wages rates for all the different operations of the trade;

(5) To the amount of wages must be added the cost of tools and materials furnished by the worker, the value of time wasted, etc.;

(6) The minimum wage must be paid to the worker net without any deduction in favour of employer or middleman;

(7) If collective agreements exist in a trade, the minimum wage board must endeavour to extend the benefits of such collective agreements to all home workers also;

(8) For operations not included in the scale named under (4) the employer must prove in each particular case coming before the board that the conditions allow the average worker to earn at least the minimum time wage.

Disputes shall be settled by the wages boards;

(9) The board shall establish likewise scales of payment, and if possible minimum wages, for the apprentices in the trade, even where the apprentices are employed in workshops;

(10) Every violation of the law shall constitute a penal offence in each case and in respect of each worker concerned;

(11) Every trade organisation and any person interested in the trade and every society qualified for the purpose may inform the board that wages paid are below the minimum wage fixed for the trade. All such persons or organisations may take legal action;

(12) The minimum wages fixed by the local boards may be reviewed by a central commission of revision acting officially and without delay. This commission may modify and co-ordinate local decisions. The Governments shall select the members of such commission in equal numbers from the employers and employees composing the local boards.

IV. The Delegates' Meeting invites the Members of Parliament belonging to the International Association to introduce, or cause to be introduced, bills corresponding to the accepted resolution.

The national Sections are requested to engage in an energetic campaign in order to convince the public of the necessity of fixing minimum wages for home industries.

19. Machine-made Swiss Embroidery.

The Delegates' Meeting still considers it desirable, under the provisions of the Lugano resolutions of 1910, to make uniform regulations for hours of work in the Swiss Embroidery Home-industry, and so far as possible to prohibit night work. But in view of the fact that since the Meeting of Lugano progress has been made in the introduction of automatic embroidery-machines in factories, and that similar machines will probably be introduced in the next few years to an increasing extent, the Delegates' Meeting considers it desirable that when regulations are made concerning hours of labour in small establishments, regulations should be made at the same time respecting hours of labour in factories using automatic machines. Such regulation is necessary because automatic machines, since attended by adult men only, may be run unlimited hours, both day and night, although there is no technical reason for such continuous labour; while the other machines tended by women also, are subject to certain legal limitations as to hours of labour.

The Bureau of the International Association for Labour Legislation is instructed (1) to draw the attention of the countries concerned (Germany, Switzerland, Austria, France, the United States, Italy, Russia) to the danger which threatens the entire embroidery industry as a result of overtime, and even more of the continuous operation of the automatic embroidery machines, and (2) to request the Governments to take steps as soon as possible by means of international agreements, to establish such uniform regulations as shall protect the interests of the embroidery industry.

The Bureau is instructed to inform the Sections of the different countries, within three months, of the steps it has taken in approaching the Governments with a view to the realisation of this object.

20. List of Industrial Poisons.

I. The Delegates' Meeting expresses its thanks to the authors of the list of industrial poisons, Dr. Sommerfeld and Dr. Fischer, to the Institute of Industrial Hygiene at Frankfurt-on-Main, and to the member of the Permanent Council of Hygiene who reported on the matter, Dr. Teleky.

II. The Delegates' Meeting notes with pleasure that the list of industrial poisons has been translated into English, French, Italian and Finnish and hopes that the other national Sections will follow this example.

III. The Permanent Council of Hygiene is requested to undertake a revision of the list of industrial poisons every four years.

21. Lead.

I. *Painters and Decorators.* The Delegates' Meeting, noting with satisfaction that the use of colours containing lead in the painting of the interior of buildings has been prohibited in several countries, requests the national Sections to present reports on investigations which have been undertaken in their countries, and in particular on inquiries and experience relating to the use of colours not containing lead in the painting of metal in engineering workshops and similar works.

II. *Polygraphic Industry.* In view of the inadequacy of the information available respecting the danger of poisoning to which women are exposed when employed in type-setting, whether by hand or by linotypes, the inquiry should be continued.

The French and British Sections are requested to undertake inquiries from the hygienic and medical point of view and to present the results to the next Delegates' Meeting.

III. *Ceramic Industry.* The national Sections are requested to report on the application in their countries of the regulations already presented to the Governments respecting hygienic conditions in the ceramic industry, with a view to the conclusion of an International Convention on the restriction of the use of lead in the ceramic industry.

22. Handling of Ferrosilicon.

I. The Bureau is instructed to present the following principles to the Governments:

Principles for the prevention of risks involved in the conveyance of ferrosilicon.

(1) Ferrosilicon—especially when prepared by the electrical method—gives rise to dangerous gases, in particular phosphuretted hydrogen and arseniuretted hydrogen, merely by the action of dampness in the air. This causes the risk of poisoning and explosion.

(2) In order to avoid poisoning and explosions, ferrosilicon should be secured against wet and dampness both in storing and transport. The ferrosilicon itself, the packing cases and packing materials must be dry, that is to say, free from water and also from ice.

(3) Packing cases ought to be water-tight and so durably constructed that they cannot be damaged in transport. Unpacked ferrosilicon should only be kept in places secure against wet.

(4) The rooms in which ferrosilicon is stored or transported should be so constructed that they can be thoroughly ventilated and they should always be kept ventilated. In this connection care should be taken to see that the gases given off cannot penetrate to living rooms. Such rooms ought consequently to have no connection whatever with rooms in which there is any ferrosilicon, packed or unpacked.

(5) Occupiers or persons who store or transport ferrosilicon

should be required not only to adopt the necessary precautionary measures in a suitable manner, but also to instruct persons coming into contact with ferrosilicon as to its dangers.

II. Further inquiries ought to be made into the question of whether ferrosilicon containing less than 30 per cent. or more than 70 per cent. of silicon involves a risk of poisoning or not, and into the possibility of prohibiting the manufacture of ferrosilicon containing from 30 to 70 per cent. of silicon.

23. Principles for the Protection of Persons Employed in Mining, the Construction of Tunnels, Stone Quarries, etc., on an International Basis.

I. *Ankylostomiasis.* In view of the serious danger caused by ankylostomiasis not only to miners and tunnel workers, but also to the whole working population of certain districts, and of the excellent results obtained by suitable supervision and treatment of the workers, it appears expedient that ankylostomiasis should be checked as soon as possible by means of an international agreement.

The Bureau is requested to appoint a sub-commission to draw up detailed provisions on the basis of the following principles, and to seek ways and means for bringing about an international agreement on this matter. The principles to be observed are:

(1) Shipping companies conveying emigrant workers from infected countries should be required to undertake the examination of such workers and the treatment of persons affected with the disease.

(2) Persons emigrated from affected areas should undergo medical examination with a view to the detection of ankylostomiasis, before being engaged to work in mines, the construction of tunnels, stone quarries, or brick works.

(3) In mines, tunnelling operations, stone quarries and brick works, a series of measures are necessary: as, for example, the collection and removal in a manner not open to objection, of human refuse (regular and clean sanitary conveniences), the exercise of special cleanliness, dry workplaces, medical examination, and the provision of medical treatment and suitable remedies.

(4) It is necessary for the medical men entrusted with the

examinations and supervision in question to be suitably trained.

II. *Protection of workers in mines, tunnelling operations and stone quarries.* The Bureau is requested to undertake, in consultation with technical experts in mining in the different countries, a comparative study of legislation for the protection of miners on the basis of the principles drafted by Dr. Fischer, and to submit a memorial on the subject to the next Delegates' Meeting.

Provisions respecting the protection of workers in tunnelling operations and stone quarries should be prepared in a similar manner, but drawn up separately.

24. The International Prevention of Anthrax amongst Industrial Workers and of Mercurial Poisoning in Fur-cutting and Hat-making.

The question of anthrax is referred to a sub-commission, which shall submit detailed proposals to the next Delegates' Meeting. In addition, a sub-commission shall submit to the next Delegates' Meeting detailed proposals respecting the prevention of mercurial poisoning in fur-cutting and hat-making.

25. Work in Caissons.

The Delegates' Meeting requests the Bureau to arrange for the Permanent Council of Hygiene to draw up, with the co-operation of experts, a memorial respecting the results of experience as regards work in caissons and showing how use may be made of such experience in practice.

This memorial shall be submitted to the next Delegates' Meeting and afterwards presented to the Governments

25. Diving Operations.

The Delegates' Meeting requests the Bureau to arrange for the Permanent Council of Hygiene to draw up, with the co-operation of experts, a report on the possibility and desirability of establishing international regulations for diving operations.

27. International Statistics of Morbidity and Mortality amongst the Working Classes.

I. The Bureau is requested to present to the next Delegates' Meeting, with the co-operation of the national Sections and of the Permanent Council of Hygiene, a report on the essential differences in the morbidity and mortality statistics relating to the working classes in the different trades and in the different countries, and to make proposals on the question of how these divergencies can be removed.

II. In addition, the national Sections are requested to report not later than July 1st, 1913, for the next Delegates' Meeting, on the methods of compiling, and the present position as regards, morbidity and mortality statistics relating to the working classes.

III. The Delegates' Meeting recommends that the aim of these reports should be especially the establishment of a uniform classification of the causes of death in the different occupations, in order that the Governments may adopt it as the basis of uniform statistics of mortality by trades.

28. Treatment of Foreign Workmen under Insurance Legislation.

I. In connection with the resolutions adopted by the Delegates' Meeting at Basel (1901 and 1904), Geneva (1906), Lucerne (1908) and Lugano (1910) respecting the treatment of foreign workers under Insurance Legislation, the Delegates' Meeting expresses thanks in the first place to the States and Governments which have given effect as far as possible in their national legislation and in international treaties to the principles recommended by the International Association.

The Delegates' Meeting again requests the American Section to continue its efforts to secure the passage in the several States of the Union of suitable laws for insurance against sickness and accident, which shall not discriminate against alien workers and thus carry out Resolution IX adopted at Geneva, and Resolution X adopted at Lucerne, and it thanks this Section for its activity in this matter.

II. The Governments represented at the meetings of the Association and the national Sections are again urgently recommended to see that these principles are developed and extended in sickness, accident, old age and invalidity insurance legislation.

The Delegates' Meeting draws the attention of the national Sections and the Governments concerned also to the various systems of maternity insurance. These systems should, as far as possible, fix a uniform period of benefit of 8 weeks, and also approximately equal maintenance benefits, in order that, in cases of difference of domicile and country of insurance, it may be easier to effect a transfer or make over the insurance in pursuance of international agreements.

III. As regards the execution of the wishes expressed under II, the Delegates' Meeting draws attention especially to the following points:

(1) As regards the benefits paid by insurance institutions to foreigners, no difference should be made between the subjects of a State and Foreign workmen in all countries and branches of insurance in which the State does not directly supplement either the premiums or the benefits.

(2) But where the grants are made out of public money, the benefits paid to insured foreigners and their dependents may be reduced in comparison to those paid to subjects of the State at most by an amount corresponding approximately to such grants.

(3) The Governments should take the necessary measures by means of international agreements to render the provisions of No. 2 unnecessary.

(4) It should be made possible by international agreements to settle the claims of insured persons and their dependents living outside the country of insurance by a sum down or by paying the capital value of the benefit to a corresponding insurance institution in their place of residence abroad, or in any other appropriate manner.

IV. Failure to insure foreign workmen in the case of only temporary sojourn and employment in a country, is injurious both to the workmen concerned and also to their country of origin, and involves at the same time a disadvantage to the workers of the country in question on the labour market. The benefits of insurance should therefore be extended to such workmen.

(*E. B.,* VII, (8-10) *Supplement.*)

Exhibit 19.

VOEU

At the moment of proceeding to the signature of the Convention on the Night-Work of Women the Delegates of Denmark, Spain, France, Great Britain, Italy, Luxemburg. the Netherlands, Portugal, Sweden, and Switzerland, convinced of the utility of assuring the greatest possible unity to the regulations which will be issued in conformity with the present Convention, express the desire that the various questions connected with the said Convention which may have been left doubtful by the same, may be, by one or several of the contracting parties, submitted to the consideration of a Commission on which each cosignatory State would be represented by a delegate or by a delegate and assistant-delegates.

This Commission would have a purely consultative character. In no circumstances would it be able to undertake any inquiry into or to interfere in any way in the administrative or other acts of the States.

The Commission would make a report which would be communicated to the contracting States on the questions submitted to it.

The Commission could further be called upon:

1. To give its opinion as to the equivalent provisions, on condition of which the adhesion of extra-European States, as well as possessions, colonies, protectorates, might be accepted in cases where the climate or the condition of the natives may necessitate modifications in the details of the Convention.

2. Without prejudice to the initiative of each contracting State, to serve as an instrument for a preliminary exchange of views, in cases where the High Contracting Parties are in agreement, as to the utility of convening new conferences on the subject of the condition of the working classes.

The Commission would meet at the demand of one of the contracting States, but not more than once a year, except in the case of an agreement between the contracting States for a supplementary meeting owing to exceptional circumstances. It would meet in each of the capitals of the European contracting States successively and in alphabetical order.

It would be understood that the contracting States would reserve to themselves the right of submitting to arbitration, in conformity with Article 16 of the Convention of The Hague, the questions which may be raised by the Convention of to-day's date, even if they had been the subject of an expression of opinion by the Commission.

The Delegates mentioned above request the Swiss Government (who agree) to be good enough, until the closing of the record of deposit of ratifications of the Convention to continue the negotiations for the adhesion to the present *Voeu* of the States whose delegates have not signed it.

This *Voeu* will be converted into a Convention by the contracting states, through the agency of the Swiss Government, as soon as it shall have received the concurrence of all the states signatories to the Convention.

Berne, September 26, 1906.

(*E. B.* I, (7-8) p. 277.)

Exhibit 20.

Draft for an International Convention Respecting the Prohibition of Night-Work for Young Persons Employed in Industrial Occupations (Sept. 25, 1913).

(1) Night-work in industrial occupations shall be prohibited for young persons under the age of 16 years.

The prohibition shall be absolute in all cases up to the age of 14 years.

The present Convention shall apply to all industrial undertakings where more than 10 persons are employed; it shall not apply in any case to undertakings where only members of the family are employed.

It shall be the duty of each of the contracting States to define the meaning of "industrial undertakings." Mines and quarries and industries for the manufacture and transformation of materials shall, in all cases, be included in this definition; as regards the latter point, the limit between industry on the one hand, and agriculture and commerce on the other, shall be defined by national legislation.

(2) The night's rest contemplated in Article 1 shall have a duration of at least 11 consecutive hours. In all the contracting States these 11 hours must include the period between 10 p. m. and 5 a. m.

In coal and lignite mines it shall be permissible to vary the hours of rest contemplated in the first paragraph, provided that the interval between two periods of work habitually lasts 15 hours, and in all cases 13 hours at least.

The period from 10 p. m. to 5 a. m. contemplated in the first paragraph may, in the case of the bakery industry, be replaced by the period from 9 p. m. to 4 a. m. in those States where night-work is prohibited by national legislation for all workers engaged in this industry.

(3) The prohibition of night-work may be suspended for young workers over 14 years of age:

(a) If the interest of the State or any other public interest absolutely demands it.

(b) In case of "force majeure" where there occurs in an undertaking an interruption of manufacture which it was impossible to foresee and not being of a periodical character.

(4) The provisions of this Convention shall apply to girls under 16 years of age wherever these provisions afford more extensive protection than those of the Convention of September 26th, 1906.

(5) In extra-European States, as well as in Colonies, Possessions, or Protectorates, when the climate or the condition of the native population shall require it, the period of the uninterrupted night's rest may be shorter than the minimum of 11 hours laid down in the present Convention, provided that compensatory rests are accorded during the day.

(6) The present Convention shall come into force two years after the date on which the record of deposit is closed.

The time limit for bringing into force the prohibition of the night-work of young persons over 14 years of age in industrial occupations shall be increased to 10 years:

(a) In glass works, for persons employed before the melting, annealing and re-heating furnaces.

(b) In rolling mills and forges where iron and steel are worked up with continuous furnaces, for the workers engaged in occupations directly connected with the furnaces, in both cases, however, on condition that the night employment shall only be permitted in work of a kind to promote the industrial development of the young workers and which presents no particular danger to their life or health.

(*E. B.* VIII, (9-10) pp. 364-365.)

Exhibit 21.

Draft for an International Convention to Fix the Working Day for Women and Young Persons Employed in Industrial Occupations (Sept. 25, 1913.)

(1) The maximum period of employment in industrial occupations of women without distinction of age and of young persons up to the age of 16 years shall, subject to the exceptions hereafter mentioned, be 10 hours a day.

The working day may also be limited by fixing a maximum of 60 hours per working week, with a daily maximum of 10½ hours.

The present convention shall apply to all industrial undertakings where more than 10 persons are employed; it shall not apply in any case to undertakings where only members of the family are employed.

It shall be the duty of each of the contracting States to define the meaning of "industrial undertakings." Mines and quarries and industries for the manufacture and transformation of materials shall in all cases be included in this definition; as regards the latter point, the limit between industry, on the one hand, and agriculture and commerce on the other, shall be defined by national legislation.

(2) The hours of work shall be interrupted by one or more breaks, the regulations of which shall be left to national legislation, subject to two conditions, namely:

Where the daily period of employment does not exceed six hours, no break shall be compulsory.

Where the daily period of employment exceeds this limit, a break of at least half an hour shall be prescribed during or immediately after the first six hours' work.

(3) Subject to the reservations specified in Article 4, the maximum period of employment may be extended by overtime:

(a) If the interest of the State or any other public interest absolutely demands it.

(b) In case of "force majeure" where there occurs in an undertaking an interruption of manufacture which it was impossible to foresee and not being of a periodical character.

(c) In cases where the work is concerned either with raw materials or materials in course of treatment which are susceptible to very rapid deterioration, when such overtime is necessary to preserve these materials from certain loss.

(d) In industries subject to seasonal influences.

(e) In exceptional circumstances, for all undertakings.

(4) The total hours of work, including overtime, shall not exceed 12 hours a day, except in factories for the preserving of fish, vegetables, and fruit.

Overtime shall not exceed a total of 140 hours per calendar year. It may extend to 180 hours in the manufacture of bricks, tiles, men's, women's and children's clothing, articles of fashion, feather articles, and artificial flowers, and in factories for the preserving of fish, vegetables and fruit.

It shall not be permissible, in any case, to extend the working day for young workers of either sex under 16 years of age.

This Article shall not apply in the cases contemplated in (a) and (b) of Article 3.

(5) This Convention shall come into force two years after the date on which the record of deposit is closed.

The time limit for bringing it into force shall be extended:

(a) From two to seven years in the manufacture of raw sugar from beetroot, and of machine-made embroidery, and in the spinning and weaving of textile materials.

(b) From two to seven years in States where the legal duration of the working day for women without distinction of age and for young persons employed in industrial occupations still amounts to 11 hours, provided that, except as regards the exemptions contemplated in preceding Articles, period of employment shall not exceed 11 hours a day and 63 hours a week.

Drawn up at Berne on September 25th, 1913, in one copy, which shall be deposited in the Swiss Federal Archives and a certified copy of which shall be presented through the diplomatic channel to each of the Governments represented at the Conference.

(*Ibid.*, pp. 365-366.)

Exhibit 22
Constitution of the American Section of the International Association on Unemployment.

(Extract)

The purpose as expressed in the by-laws of the Association on Unemployment is:

"(A) To assist the International Association in the accomplishment of its task (Section 1, ss. 3 and 4, of the Statutes of the International Association):

The aim of the Association is to co-ordinate all the efforts made in different countries to combat unemployment.

Among the methods the Association proposes to adopt in order to realize its object the following may be specially noticed:

(a) The organization of a permanent international office to centralize, classify and hold at the disposition of those interested, the documents relating to the various aspects of the struggle against unemployment in different countries.

(b) The organization of periodical international meetings, either public or private.

(c) The organization of special studies on certain aspects of the problem of unemployment and the answering of inquiries on these matters.

(d) The publication of essays and a journal of unemployment.

(e) Negotiations with private institutions, or the public authorities of each country, with the object of advancing legislation on unemployment, and obtaining comparable statistics or information and possibly agreements or treaties concerning the question of unemployment.

(b) To co-ordinate the efforts made in America to combat unemployment and its consequences, to organize studies, to give information to the public, and to take the initiative in shaping improved legislation and administration, and practical action in times of urgent need."

(*Bulletin trimestriel de l'association internationale pour la lutte contre le chômage, Quatriéme Annee*, No. 2. Avril-Juin 1914, p. 339.)

Exhibit 23.

Constitution of the American Association for Labor Legislation.
Adopted Feb. 15, 1906

Amended Dec. 30, 1907; Dec. 30, 1908; Dec. 29, 1909; Dec. 29, 1910.

Article I. Name.

This Society shall be known as the American Association for Labor Legislation.

Article II. Objects.

The objects of this Association shall be:

1. To serve as the American branch of the International Association for Labor Legislation, the aims of which are stated in the appended Article of its Statutes.

2. To promote uniformity of labor legislation in the United States.

3. To encourage the study of labor conditions in the United States with a view to promoting desirable labor legislation.

Article III. Membership.

Members of the Association shall be elected by the Executive Committee. Eligible to membership are individuals, societies and institutions that adhere to its objects and pay the necessary subscriptions. The minimum annual fees for individuals shall be three dollars, or five dollars if the member wishes to receive the Bulletin of the International Association. In states in which there is a State Association $1 of the dues shall be paid over to the State Association. The minimum annual fee for societies and institutions shall be five dollars, and they shall receive one copy of the Bulletin, and for each two-dollar subscription an additional copy.

Article IV. Officers.

The officers of the Association shall be a president, ten vice-presidents, a secretary and a treasurer. There shall also be a General Administrative Council consisting of the officers and not less than twenty-five or more than one hundred persons. The General Administrative Council shall have power to fill vacancies in its own ranks and in the list of officers; to appoint an Executive Committee from among its own members, and such other committees as it shall deem wise; to frame by-laws not inconsistent with this constitution; to choose the delegates of the Association to the Committee of the International Association; to conduct the business and direct the expenditures of the Association. It shall meet at least twice a year. Eight members shall constitute a quorum.

Article V. Meetings.

The annual meeting and other general meetings of members shall be called by the General Administrative Council and notice thereof shall be sent to members at least three weeks in advance. Societies and institutions shall be represented by two delegates each. The annual meeting shall elect the officers and other members of the General Administrative Council.

Meetings of the General Administrative Council shall be called by the Executive Committee. Notice of such meetings shall be sent to members of the Council at least three weeks in advance.

Amendments to the constitution, after receiving the approval of the General Administrative Council, may be adopted at any general meeting. Fifteen members shall constitute a quorum.

Article II of the Statutes of the International Association Defining the Aims of the Association.

(See Constitution of the International Association, Exhibit 10.)

BY-LAWS.

1. *Committees.* The Council shall elect an Executive Committee, as well as committees on Finance, Legislation, and Publicity, and such other committees as occasion may require.

2. *Powers of the Executive Committee.* The Executive Committee shall exercise, subject to the General Administrative Council, the powers of the Council in the intervals between its sessions.

3. *International Obligations.* The Executive Committee shall choose the members of Committees and Commissions and the reporters required by votes of the International Association.

(*Am. Labor Leg. Rev.* VII, (I) pp. 196-197.)

Exhibit 24.

Justification of the Principle of the Prohibition of Night-Work of Women.

The effects of the prohibition of night-work of women, in the countries where it embraces workwomen of every age have been as follows:

1. The number of women employed, especially of those above twenty-one years of age, has in general increased. It is true that the improvements in the processes of technical production, which have permitted the use of cheap, and unskilled labor, have been a factor in this increase. With regard to women workers as a whole ,there is not evident in Great Britain, Germany, Austria, France, Holland or in the United States any general decrease in opportunities for work. In many places, on the other hand, woman's labor has replaced child labor, and as a result of the enlargement of a certain number of establishments, a more intensive workday has been substituted, in the case of women, for night-work.

2. In consequence of this increase of demand, women have not in general suffered a loss in wages, and on the contrary, the wage has been increased in many cases by reason of greater rapidity and better quality of work.

3. It has been observed that coincident with the prohibition of night-work of women in the States in which it has been put into force, there has been a decrease in the death rate both of women and children. The rate of mortality among women has decreased in Great Britain and in Germany, more rapidly than the rate of mortality among men.

4. The greater powers of resistance and the better health evidenced among women in the States where night-work has been suppressed, and where the length of work has been decreased and rest increased, have permitted housewives to better perform their domestic duties; the preparation of food, bringing up and care of children, the keeping of the linen in repair and the home in order, *etc., etc.*

5. It has been established also that neither the prohibition of night-work of women nor the limitation of their day work have

exercised any appreciable influence on exportation especially in that which concerns manufactured textile products.

Accordingly then, the prohibition of night-work of women is in the first place a measure of public hygiene. It is also necessary, to secure, from the States which belong to the first category of the preceding chapter, such as Japan, Spain and some of the States of the Union, the adhesion in principle to the system of prohibiting the night-work of women.

As regards the principal States of the second category of the preceding chapter (States where the prohibition applies only to young workers), it has been established that the night-work of women has almost always been actually practised in certain definite industries, and during periods of full operation on the part of the industries, in a word, that it is not at all the rule. These States should not find any difficulty then, it would seem, in establishing the principle of the prohibition of the night-work of all women, subject to necessary exceptions which will be treated later.

Finally, in States where night-work has been limited to certain kinds of industry, it should be of interest to obtain, as a transitional provision in the countries which have not yet adopted this measure, the extension of the prohibition of night-work to all shops, even if not provided with motor power. The exceptions permitting night-work of women in small establishments without motor power, are very harmful to the health of the women workers. Remembering the difficulties in the way of applying this measure to women working at home, it is necessary to obtain from the various States legal protection at least for all women working in shops.

Only after the prohibition of night-work of women in the small shops has been obtained, can the work be continued and a similar prohibition be obtained for home work.

(Translation: *Publications de L'Association internationale pour la protection légale des travailleurs*, No. 4(p. 9-10.)

Exhibit 25.

Report of the United States Section of the International High Commission.

"Sir: By the First Pan American Financial Conference, which

was held at Washington in May, 1915, with a view to bring about closer financial and commercial relations between the American Republics and to that end to foster uniformity of law and procedure in such matters, it was recommended that, in order to carry out these great objects, there should be created an International High Commission, a section of which should be established in each country. This recommendation was promptly carried into effect in the countries concerned; and by the act of Congress of February 7, 1916, the United States section was endowed with a legal status. Each section consists of nine members, and is composed of jurists, financiers, and technical administrators.

"During the past quarter of a century a great good has been accomplished by means of conferences between the independent countries of America, such as the four international American conferences (Washington, 1889-90; Mexico, 1901-2; Rio de Janeiro, 1906; Buenos Aires, 1910), the Conference on the Coffee Trade (New York, 1902), the Customs Congress (New York, 1903), and the series of sanitary conferences, the fifth of which was held in Washington in 1905. But in spite of all that had been attained there was a general sense of the need of direct, continuous, sustained effort to improve the financial and economic relations between the Americas and to remove the obstacles which existed in their satisfactory development. To meet this want is the prime object of the International High Commission and its respective national sections.

"Students of the history of international co-operation agree that there are three fundamental factors in a successful international union—(1) periodical conferences, (2) an international organ or bureau, (3) an effective means of carrying out the measures adopted. In the relations of the American Republics during the last 25 years the first two elements have not been lacking. The American Governments have repeatedly manifested their willingness to enter into the discussion of their common problems; and in the Pan American Union they have an organ which has, under the wise guidance of the diplomatic representatives of American Republics at Washington, contributed and will continue richly to contribute to the harmony and prosperity of the American nations.

"What has been wanting is a persistent and organized effort to carry out the recommendations of the conferences. In contrast with the readiness to sign conventions on technical matters there has been at time some reluctance to ratify them. The United States has occasionally been remiss in this regard, and the members of the United States section of the International High Commission consider it important to urge prompt fulfillment of this duty.

"* * * An early meeting of the commission was decided upon for the purpose of determining its modus operandi and of giving the necessary stimulus to useful study. Tentatively, November 1, 1915, was fixed as the date and Buenos Aires as the place, but it was later found necessary to allow more time, and the date was changed to April 3, 1916."

* * *

Topic VIII. Report of the Sixth Committee.

"The topics considered by this committee were proposed by the Uruguayan and Argentine Governments, respectively. With reference to labor legislation, His Excellency, Pedro Cosio, the Minister of Finance of Uruguay, pointed out the difficulty in improving the conditions under which productive labor is carried on and urged the need of insuring general knowledge of the principles of labor legislation. In order that America may be the "land of promise" he insisted that it must defend the laborer from excessive hours, unfair wage conditions, and dangerous occupations. The workman and workwoman must be assured, too, that society will not abandon them if they fall sick from overwork nor permit them to be reduced to starving or begging if they arrive at old age in poor circumstances, and, that, finally, society will find sure means of educating them and of aiding and encouraging them in their just and legitimate aspirations.

"The commission was impressed by the general desire to cooperate more effectively in protecting and strengthening the laboring population of the Americas. As, however, an international labor convention is not practicable now, the commission could only recommend that each Government enact progressive labor and social welfare legislation and provide for systematic exchange of technical and statistical literature.

LABOR RESOLUTIONS INTERNATIONALLY SUBSCRIBED

"The Department of Labor of the United States and similar departments in Latin America might easily exchange all their publications; and the system could be extended so as to include all civic bodies interested. The publication of the Pan American Union will possibly serve to make better known the work accomplished in this field in the United States and in Europe; and legislative and executive commissions, as well as organizations of the character of the American Society for Labor Legislation, will wish to co-operate with the Pan American Union. Thus those countries whose economic and industrial conditions give sufficient promise of sustained public interest in this subject, may soon avail themselves of the excellent procedure devised by the International Labor Association for the conclusion of international labor agreements."

(International High Commission, United States Section. Reports. 64th Congress. 2nd Session. House of Representatives, Document No. 1788, pp. 5-6, 23-24.)

Short Bibliography

Lowe: *International Aspects of the Labor Problem,* W. D. Gray, New York, 1918.

Bauer: *International Labor Legislation and the Society of Nations,* Bulletin of the United States Bureau of Labor Statistics, No. 254, Government Printing Office, Washington, D. C., 1919.

Ayusawa: *International Labor Legislation,* Longmans, Green & Co., New York, 1920.

Lowe and Magnusson: *Historical Survey of International Action Affecting Labor,* Bulletin of the United States Bureau of Labor Statistics, No. 268, Miscellaneous Series, Government Printing Office, Washington, D. C., 1920.

Hetherington: *International Labour Legislation,* Methuen and Company, London, 1920.

Solano, editor: *Labour as an International Problem,* MacMillan and Company, London, 1920.

Miller: *International Relations of Labor.* Alfred A. Knopf, New York, 1921.

National Industrial Conference Board: *The International Labor Organization of the League of Nations,* The Century Co., New York, 1922. *The Work of the International Labor Organization,* New York, 1928.

Johnston: *International Social Progress,* The Macmillan Company, New York, 1924.

Behrens: *The International Labour Office,* L. Parsons, London, 1924.

Chisholm: *Labour's Magna Charta,* Longmans, Green & Co., London, 1925.

Barnes: *History of the International Labour Office,* Williams and Norgate, London, 1926.

Périgord: *The International Labor Organization,* D. Appleton and Company, New York, 1926.

Stewart: *Canadian Labor Laws and the Treaty,* Columbia University Press, 1926.

Lorwin: *Labor and Internationalism,* The Macmillan Company, New York, 1929.

Hubbard: "The Co-operation of the United States with the League of Nations and with the International Labour Organisation," *International Conciliation,* No. 274, November 1931.

The Annals of the American Academy of Political and Social Science, "The International Labor Organization," Vol. 166, March 1933.

Shotwell, editor: *The Origins of the International Labor Organization,* 2 vols. (Published by the Carnegie Endowment for International Peace in the Series—*The Paris Peace Conference, History and Documents*—under the General Editorship of James Brown Scott), Columbia University Press, New York, 1934.

Wilson: *Labor in the League System,* Stanford University Press, 1934.

Publications of the International Labor Office, Geneva, Switzerland. Branch Office, International Labor Office, Jackson Place, Washington, D. C.
World Peace Foundation, 40 Mount Vernon Street, Boston, Massachusettes.

BIBLIOGRAPHY

(showing the early development of the International Labor Movement up to the beginning of the World War)

BIBLIOGRAPHY.

Contents.

Key to Periodicals...	334
Publications in German...	339
1904	340
International Labor Congresses.............................	340
International Labor Organizations...........................	341
1905	342
International Labor Congresses.............................	342
International Labor Organizations...........................	343
1906	344
International Labor Conferences............................	344
International Labor Legislation.............................	345
International Labor Organizations...........................	346
1907	346
International Labor Conferences............................	346
International Labor Legislations............................	348
International Labor Organizations...........................	349
1908	349
International Labor Legislation.............................	352
International Labor Congresses.............................	352
International Labor Organizations...........................	353
1910	353
International Labor Congresses.............................	353
International Labor Legislation.............................	355
International Labor Organizations...........................	355
1911	356
International Labor Congresses.............................	356
International Labor Legislation.............................	357
International Labor Organizations...........................	358
1912	358
International Labor Congresses.............................	358
International Labor Legislation.............................	359
Interantional Labor Organizations...........................	359
1913	359
International Labor Congresses.............................	359
International Labor Legislation.............................	362
International Labor Organizations...........................	362
1914	363
International Labor Congresses.............................	363
International Labor Legislation.............................	363
International Labor Organizations...........................	364

1915 364
   International Labor Legislation............................... 364
   International Labor Organizations............................ 364
Publications in French.. 364
   1904 368
      International Labor Conferences............................ 368
   1905 369
      International Labor Conferences............................ 369
   1906 370
      International Labor Conferences............................ 370
      International Labor Legislation............................ 370
   1907 371
      International Labor Conferences............................ 371
      International Labor Legislation............................ 371
      International Labor Organizations.......................... 371
   1908 372
      International Labor Legislation............................ 372
      International Labor Organizations.......................... 372
      International Labor Congresses............................. 372
   1909 373
      International Labor Legislation............................ 373
      International Labor Congresses............................. 373
      International Labor Organizations.......................... 373
   1910 373
      International Labor Congresses............................. 374
   1911 374
      International Labor Conferences............................ 375
   1912 375
      International Labor Congresses............................. 375
   1913 376
      International Labor Congresses............................. 376
   1914 377
      International Labor Congresses............................. 377
      International Labor Legislation............................ 377
Publications in English... 378
   1904-1915 378
Publications in Italian... 382
   1904-1914 382
Publications in Spanish 385
Publications in Roumania 386
Publications in Sweden 386
Publications in Hungary 386
Publications in Denmark 387
Publications in Holland 387
Publications in Finland 387

PERIODICALS.

A.Cath.—Association catholique, Paris.
Acc. et Ass.—Congrès international des Accidents du travail et des Assurances sociales, Bulletin du Comité permanent, Paris.
A.d.—Archives diplomatiques.
A.D.G.Z.—Allgemeine Deutsche Gärtner-Zeitung, Berlin.
A.F.—American Federationist, Washington.
A.Fr.—Arbeiterfreund, Berlin.
A.G.—Arbeitgeber, Berlin.
A.Gen.—Arbeitergenossenschaft, Wien.
Ai.Z.—Arbeiterinnenzeitung, Wien.
A.M.—Arbeitsmarkt, Berlin.
Am.—Ameise, Charlottenburg.
A.N.M.I.—Amtliche Nachrichten des Ministeriums des Innern, Wien.
A.O.—Association ouvrière, Paris
Ar.—Akademie revue socialistiká, Prag.
A.R.—Allgemeine Rundschau, Leizig.
A.S.—Arbeiterschutz, Wien.
A.S.G.—Annalen für Sozialpolitik und Gesetzgebung, Berlin.
Ask.—Arbetarsskyddet, Stockholm.
A.S.S.—Archiv für Sozialwissenschaft und Sozialoplitik, Tübingen.
Ass.—L'Assicurazione.
A.St.—Arbeiterstimme, Bern.
A.T.Fin.—Afbetsstatistik Tidskrift utgiven af industristyrelsen i Finland, Helsingfors.
A.V.—Arbeiter-Versorgung, Grunewald-Berlin.
B.—Blätter für Armenwesen, Graz.
B.A.L.C.—Bulletin de l'Association internationale pour pour la lutte contre le chômage, Paris.
B.Arb.—Bergarbeiter, Oberhausen (Rheinland).
B.Arg.—Boletin de la Union industrial argentina, Buenos Aires.
B.A.S.—Bulletin des assurances sociales, Paris.
B.C.T.—Bulletin du Comité central du Hravail industriél, Bruxelles.
B.D.T.—Boletin del Departamento Nacional del Trabajo, Buenos Aires.
B.F.N.—Bulletin de la Fédération nationale du bâtiment et des travaux publics, Paris.
B.G.—Blätter für Genossenschaftswesen, Berlin.
Bhd.—Der Ban handwerker, Magdeburg.
B.Intl.—Bulletin der internationalen Union der Holzarbeiter, Berlin.
B.L.S.A.—Bulletin des Ligues sociales d'acheteurs.
B.M.I.E.S.—Bulletin mensuel des institutions économiques et sociales (Institut international d'agriculture), Rome.
B.M.T.—Bulletin du Ministère du Travail, Paris.
Bol.M.S.—Boletin del Museo Social, Barcelona.
B.O.T.—Bulletin de l'office du travail, Paris.

BIBLIOGRAPHY

B.R.S.—Boletin del Instituto de Reformas Sociales, Madrid.
B.R.V.—Blätter für vergleichende Rechtswissenschaft und Volkswirtschaftslehre, Berlin.
B.S.t.R.—Buletinul Statistic al României, Bucarest.
B.S.V.—Blätter für selbstverwaltung, Brünn.
B.U.L.—Bollettino dell'Ufficio del lavoro, Roma.
B.U.L.(N.S.)—Bollettino dell 'Ufficio del lavoro (Nuova Serie) Roma.
B.Z.—Bildhauer-Zeitung, Berlin.
C.—Concordia, Berlin.
C.G.D.—Correspondenzblatt der Generalkommission der Gewerkschaften Deutschlands, Berlin.
C.F.L.—Confederazione del lavoro, Milano.
Conf.L.—Confederazione del lavoro, Milano.
Co.—Der Coiffeur, Bern. (Coiffeurgehilfen-Zeitung)
Cr.—Courier, Publikationsorgan des Deutschen Transportarbeiter-Verbandes, Berlin.
Cr.s.—Critica sociale, Milano.
D.B.K.Z.—Deutsche Bäcker-und Konditoren-zeitung, Hamburg.
D.C.—Dominion of Canada, Labour Gazette (Dominion du Canada, Gazette du Travail), Ottawa.
Dev.—Devoir, Paris.
E.B.—English Bulletin of the International Labor Office.
Ec.Fr.—Economiste francais, Paris.
Eis.—Eisenbahner, Wien.
E.J.—Economic Journal, London.
E.S.—Espana Social, Madrid.
E.Z.—Oesterreichische Eisenbahnzeitung, Wien.
F.B.—French Bulletin of the International Labor Office.
Fr.—Frauenbewegung, Berlin.
Frk.Z.—Frankfurter Zeitung, Frankfurt.
G.—Gewerkverein, Berlin.
G.B.—German Bulletin of the International Labor Office.
Gen.—Genossenschaft, Wien.
Gew.—Gewerkschaft, Berlin.
G.Ing.—Gesundheits-Ingenieur, München.
Gl.—Gleichheit, Stuttgart.
G.P.—Graphische Presse, Berlin (formerly Leipzig).
G.R.—Gesetz und Recht, Breslau.
Gr.—Grundstein, Hamburg.
G.Sch (or Gsch.)—Gewerkschaft, Wien.
H.—Handelsstand, Hamburg.
H.A.—Heimarbeiterin, Berlin.
H.G.Z.—Handlungsgehülfenzeitung, Berlin-Hamburg.
H.M.—Handelsmuseum, Wien.
Ho.A.—Holzarbeiter, Köln.

Ho.—Der Hoteldiener.
H.T.—Helvetische Typographia, Basel.
H.Z.—Holzarbeiterzeitung, Berlin (formerly Stuttgart).
I.—Industrie, Wien.
I.G.—Internationales Genossenschafts-Bulletin, Zürich.
I.:M.:R:.—Internationale Metallarbeiter-Rundschau, Stuttgart.
J.—Jugendfürsorge Berlin.
J.A.—Jugendliche Arbeiter, Wien.
J.L.—Justice, London.
J.L.N.Z.—Journal of Department of Labour, New Zealand, Wellington.
J.St.S.—Journal of the Royal Statistical Society, London.
K.—Kampf, Wien.
K.Bl.—Korrespondenzblatt d. Verbandes der Tapezierer und verwandter Berufsarten Berlin.
K.R.—Konsumgenossenschaftliche Rundschau, Hamburg.
Ku.—Kupferschmied.
L.A.—Ledararbeiter, Berlin.
L.G.—Labor Gazette, London (Board of Trade).
L.Gen.—Oesterreichische landswirtschaftliche Genossenschaftspresse, Wien.
L.L.—Labor Leader, London.
M.—Mutualidad, Madrid.
M.A.S.—Medicina delle assicurazione sociali.
M.C.B.S.—Maandschrift van het Centraal Bureau voor de Statistiek, 'sGravenhage
Medd.—Sociala Meddelanden från k. Kommerskollegii Afdeling for Arbetsstatistik, Stockholm.
M.R.—Medizinische Reform, Berlin.
M.R.V.K.—Mitteilungen des Rheinischen Vereins für Kleinwohnungswesen, Düsseldorf.
M.S.(Ann.)—Musée Social (Annales), Paris.
M.soc.—Mouvement social, Paris.
N.F.—Nordisk T. for Faengselsvaesen.
N.T.—Nationalokonomisk Tidsskrift, Kjobenhavn.
N.Y.—New York Department of Labor Bulletin, Albany.
N.Z.—Neue Zeit, Stuttgart.
O.e.M.—Oesterreichischer Matallarbeiter, Wien.
Oe.Zop.V.—Oesterreich, Zeitschrift für offentliche und private Versicherung, Wien.
P.—Proletareier, Hannover.
P.O.—Parlement et Opinion, Paris.
Q.J.—Quarterly Journal of Economics, Boston.
Q.P.—Questions pratiques de législation ouvrière et d'économie sociale, Paris.
R.A.—Reichsarbeitsblatt, Berlin.
Ram.—Ramazzini, Firenze. (Giornole italiano di medicina sociale).
R.D.I.P.—Revue de droit international privé.

BIBLIOGRAPHY

Ref.Soc.—Reforme Sociale, Paris.
Rev.C.—Revista catolica de las questiones sociales, Madrid.
Rev.ec.int.—Revue économique internationale, Paris.
Rev. Tr.—Revue due travail, Bruxelles.
R. I. C.—Revue internationale du chômage, Paris.
Rif.Soc.—Riforma sociale Torino-Roma.
R.P.P.—Revue politique et parlementaire, Paris.
R.S.A.T.—Revue suisse des accidents du travail, Genève.
R.S.C.—Revue socialiste catholique, Louvain.
S.—Lo spettatore, rivista politica, Roma.
S.B.—Staats-Bürger, Leipzig und Berlin.
S.B.H.I.—Schweizerische Blätter für Handel und Industrie (Bulletin commercial et industriel suisse), Genf.
Sch.—Schuhmacherfachblatt, Gotha.
Schm.Z.—Schmiede-zeitung, Hamburg.
S.C.V.—Schweizer Konsumverein, Basel.
S.E.—Szakszervezeti Ertesito, Budapest.
S.K.—Soziale Kultur, M.—Gladbach.
S.K.V.—Schweizer Konsumverein, Basel.
S.M.—Sozialistische Monatshefte, Berlin.
S.P.—Soziale Praxis, Berlin.
S.R.—Soziale Rundschau, Wien.
S.R.V.—Soziale Rundschau (Wachenbeilage zum "Vaterland.") Wien.
S.T.—Sozial-Technik, Berlin.
S.W.S.—Schweizerische Blätter für Wirtschafts—und Sozialpolitik, Bern.
S.Z.—Sattler Zeitung, Berlin.
Tab.—Tabakarbeiter, Leipzig.
T.A.—Tidskrift for Arbejderforsikring, Kjøbenhavn.
T.—Times, London.
T.B.—Textilarbeiter, Bern.
Tex.—Textilarbeiter, Berlin.
Tex.W.—Textilarbeiter, Wien.
T.I.—Tidskrift for Industria.
T.M.E.—Társadalmi Museum Ertesitöje, Budapest.
T.N.—Travail national, Paris.
Tö.—Töpfer, Berlin.
T.Z.—Textilarbeiter-Zeitung, Düsseldorf.
Um.—Umanitaria, Milano.
V.—Vorwärts.
V.Bl.—Volkswirtschaftliche Blätter, Berlin.
V.I.N.—Vie internationale, Bruxelles.
V.M.U.—Volkswirtschaftliche Mitteilungen aus Ungarn, Budapest.
W.A.Z.—Westdeutsche Arbeiterzeitung, M.—Gladbach.
W.I.N.—Women's Industrial News, London.
W.L.L.—World's Labour Laws, London.
W.N.O.—Wochenschrift des niederösterreichischen Gewerbvereine.

W.S.M.—Wochenschrift für soziale Medizin, Berlin.
W.T.U.—Women's Trade Union Review, London.
W.Y.T.—Women's Trade Union Review, London.
Y.R.—Yale Review New Haven.
Z.—Zimmerer, Hamburg.
Z.C.G.D.—Zentrallblatt der christlichen Gewerkschaften Deutschlands, Koln. (M Gladbach)
Z.G.H.—Zeitschrift für Gewerbehygiene, Unfallverhütung und Arbeiterwohlfahrtseinrichtungen, Wein.
Z.G.St.—Zeitschrift für die gesamte Staatswissenschaft, Tübingen.
Z.K.J.—Zeitschrift für Kinderschutz und Jugendfürsorge, Wien.
Z.R.(orZrd).—Zeitrad, Wien.
Z.Vers.—Zeitschfirt für die gesamte Versicherungswissenschaft, Berlin.
Z.V.S.V.—Zeitschrift für Volkswirtschaft, Sozialpolitik und Verwaltung, Wien, Leipzig.

BIBLIOGRAPHY

PUBLICATIONS IN GERMAN

1. Adler, Georg.—Die Frage des internationalen Arbeiterschutzes. (1888).
2. Bulletin des Internationalen Arbeitsamtes.
3. Dochow, F.—Zeitschrift für internationales Privat—und öffentliches Recht, Liepzig, 1906.
4. Francke, E.—Der Internat. Arbeiterschutz, Dresden, 1903.
5. Schriften der internationalen Vereinigung für gesetzlichen Arbeitsschutz, Jena, 1901-1906.
6. Schriften der internation. Vereinigung für gesetzlichen Arbeiterschutz. Berichte und Verhandlungen der Konstituierenden Versammlung, abgehalten zu Basel, am 27. und 28. September 1901. Herausgegeben vom Bureau der internationalen Vereinigung für gesetzlichen Arbeiterschutz. Jena, G. Fischer; Bern, Schmid & Francke, 1901.
7. Jahresbericht des internationalen Buchdruckersekretariats pro 1901. (Rapport annuel du secrétariat typographique international pour 1901) Basel, Buchdruckerei des Schweizerischen Tyrographenbundes, 1902.
8. Apostol, Dr. P. N.—Der V. internationale Arbeiterversicherungskongress in Paris. *Promischlennost i Sdorówje* 1902. 1.
9. VI. internationaler Arbeiterversicherungskongress (Düsseldorf, 17.-24. Juni 1902). Bericht des schweiz. Delegierten an den Vorsteher des schweiz. Industriedepartements. S. W. S. X. 19.
10. XI. internationaler Kongress für Hygiene und Demographie Brüssel. *Oesterreichisches Sanitätswesen*. XIV. 47., Wien.
11. Feigenwinter, Dr. E.—Internationale Vereinigung für gesetzlichen Arbeiterschutz. *Monatsschrift für christliche Sozialreform,* XXIV. 10. Basel.
12. Müller, Dr. H.—Internationaler Arbeiterschutz. *Zeit.* XXXIII. 421. Wien.
13. Fuchs, Dr.—Die Verhandlungen der internationalen Vereinigung für gesetzlichen Arbeiterschutz in Basel am 9., 10., u. 11. Sept. 1903. S. P. XII. 52.
14. Protokoll der internationalen Buchdruckerkonferenz. Abgehalten am 14. und 15. April 1903 im Rathaussaale zu Strassburg. Basel 1903.
15. Internationales Regierungskongress für Arbeiterschutz. S. P. XIII. 30.
16. Internationaler Genossenschaftskongress in Budapest. L. Gen. 1. 4.
17. Kongress der Internationalen Genossenschafts-Allianz. A. Gen. II. 4.
18. Verhandder Steinsetzer, Pflasterer und Berufsgenossen Deutschlands.
19. Denschrift der erste international Strassenkongress zu Paris und die Arbeiterschaft des Steinsetzer—(Pflaster-) Gewerbes.
20. Hue, O. Internationale Bergarbeiterkongresse N. Z. 1901. 39.
21. Die internationale Vereinigung für gesetzlichen Arbeiterschutz. H. M. 1901 XVI. 43.

22. Internationaler Kongress de socialistischen Transportarbeiter in Paris. S. R. II. 2.
23. Gugax, Dr. P.—Der internationale Textilarbeiterkongress in Zurich (1-6 Juni). S. W. S. X. 12.
24. Baudert, A.—Der fünfte internationale Textilarbeiterkongress. N. Z. XX. 2, 13.
25. Internationaler Textilarbeiter kongress C. G. D. XII. 26.
26. Francke, Prof. Dr. C.—Der Internationale Arbeiterversicherungskongress in Düsseldorf. S. P. XI. 38.
27. Der VI. internationale Arbeiterversicherungskongress in Düsseldorf. S. P. XI. 40.
28. VI internationaler Arbeiterverischerungs kongress. (Düsseldorf. 17-24. Juni 1902) S. W. S. X. 19.
29. Zum VI internationalen Wohnungskongress in Düsseldorf. S. P. XI. 37, 39.
30. Der VI. internationale Wohnungskongress 1902. S. R. III. 7.
31. Der internationale Bergarbeiterkongress. S. P. XI. 36.
32. Der fünfte internationale Genossenschaftskongress. S. P. XI. 45.
33. Der fünfte internationale Textilarbeiterkongress. S. P. XI. 37.

1904.

1. Jahresbericht des Internationalen Buchdruckersekretariats pro 1903. Basel, Schweiz. Typographenbund, 1904.
2. Hertz, Dr. Jak. Internationaler Arbeiterschutz. S. M. 1904. XXX. 8.
3. Die französisch-italienische Arbeiterschutzkonvention. A. A. 1904. II. 4.
4. Internationaler Arbeitsmarkt (Belgien, Deutsches Reich, England, Frankreich, April 1904) S. R. 1904. V. 6, 7, 8.
5. Internationaler Arbeitsmarkt (Belgien, Deutsches Reich, England, Frankreich vom Juli 1904 bis März 1905.) S. R. 1904. No. 9. 10. 11. 12; 1905. No. 1. 2. 3. 4. 5.
6. Internationale Streikstatistik. (Der Arbeitsmarkt (Jastrow) 1904. VIII. No. 1.
7. Ein internationales Gesundheitsamt. B. S. V. 1904. XV. No. 21; Die Humanität, 1904. XVII. 12., Reichenberg; B. S. V. 1904. XV. 17.
8. Erster internationaler Bericht über die Gewerkschaftsbewegung 1903. Herausgeg. von dem Internationalen sekretär der gewerkschaftlichen Landeszentralen. Verlag der Generalkommission der Gewrkschaften Deutschlands. Berlin 1904.

International Labor Congresses.

1. Schmid, F.—Der XI. internationale Kongress für Hygiene und Demographie in Brüssel 1903. Bericht zu Handen des h. schweiz. Bundesrates erstattet. Bern, Scheitlin Spring & Cie., 1904.
2. Internationales Informationsbureau der Metallarbeiter. Bericht der

englischen Sektion 1904. Zur Benutzung für den internationalen Metallarbeiterkongress in Amsterdam. Herausgegeben in Auftrage des vorbereitenden Ausschusses. 1904.
3. Generalversammlung (III.) der internat. Vereinigung für gesetzlichen Arbeiterschutz. S. P. XIV. 1904 1.
5. Generalversammlung der internationalen Arbeiterschutzvereinigung in Basel. C. G. D. 1904. XIV. 40.
6. Internationale Berufskongresse. C. G. D. 1904. XIV. 29.
7. Böhmert, Prof. Dr. V.—Der III. internationale Frauenkongress in seinen Beziehung zur Arbeiterfrage. A. Fr. 1904. XLII. 2.
8. Die interessen der Arbeiterinnen und der internationale Frauenkongress. C. G. D. 1904. XIV. 26.
9. Der VI. Kongress der Internat. Genossenschafts—Allianz. *Nachrichten des Verbandes landswirtschaftlicher Genossenschaften in Schlesien.* 1904. IX. 14. Bielitz; Gen. 1904. XXXIII. 32.
10. Der VI. internationale Genossenschaftskongress in Budapest. *Blätter für Genossenschaftswesen,* 1904. 27.
11. Die internationale Arbeiterschutzkonferenz. I. 1904. IX. No. 43.
12. Vom internationalen Sozialisten Kongresse in Amsterdam. I. 1904. IX. No. 37.
13. Kautsky, K.—Den Kongress zu Amsterdam. N. Z. 1904. XXII. 2. Bd. No. 48.
14. Wolff, H. W.—Der internationale Genossenschaftskongress zu Budapest. B. G. 1904. No. 48; A. Fr. 1904. XLII.
15. Der internationale Genossenschaftskongress in Budapest. L. Gen. 1904. I. No. 14; A. Gen 1904. II. 11; Gen. 1904. XXXIII. No. 45. 41. 42; S. C. V. 1904. IV. No. 49-51, 53. IV. No. 46. 47. 48.
16. Der internationale Genossenschaftskongress in Budapest und die *Konsumgenossenschaftliche Bundschau.* Gen. 1904. XXXIII. No. 46.
17. Zum VI. internationalen Genossenschaftskongress in Budapest. S. C. V. 1904. IV. No. 36. 37. 38; B. G. 1904. No. 45.
18. Internationale Gewerkschaftskongress. Gsch. 1904. n. f. VI. No. 17.
19. Tabakarbeiterkongress, ein internationaler. Ai. Z. 1904. XIII. No. 20.
20. Transportarbeiterkongress, der internationale. Zrd. 1904. I. No. 5.
21. III. Generalversammlung der Internat. Vereinigung für gesetzlichen Arbeiterschutz. S. R. 1904. 10.

International Labor Organizations.

1. Schweizerische Vereinigung zur Förderung des internationalen Arbeiterschutzes. Heft 9. I. Statuten der schweizerischen Vereinigung vom 17. Dezember 1903. II. Bericht des Vorstandes über die Tätigkeit des Vereins in 2. Halbjahre 1903. Bern 1904.
2. Internationale Vereinigung für gesetzlichen Arbeiterschutz. B. S. V. 1904. XV. No. 22.
3. Gesellschaft für soziale Reform, Internationale Vereinigung für

gesetzlichen Arbeiterschutz. A. S. 1904. XV. No. 20.
1905.
1. Verhandlungsbericht der 3. Gen. Vers. des Komitees der internat. Vereinig. für gesetzl. Arbeiterschutz, nebst Jahresberichten der internat. Vereinig, und des internat. Arbeitsamtes. Herausgeg. vom Bureau. Jena, G. Fischer, 1905.
2. Die internationale Regelung des Arbeiterschutzes. Die Phosphorfrage *Die Arbeit.* 1905. XII. No. 16. Wien.
3. Jahresbericht des internat. Buchdruckersekretariats für 1904. Basel, Schweiz. Typogr. Bund, 1905.
4. Der Jahresbericht der internationalen Genossenschafts—Allianz. Gen. 1905. XXXIV. No. 32.
5. Internat. Arbeitsmarkt. S. R. 1905. VI. No. 6-9; R.A. 1905. III. No. 5-10.

International Labor Congresses.

1. Der internationale Frauenkongress in Berlin 1904. Bericht mit ausgewählten Referaten. Herausgeg. im Auftrage des Vorstandes des Bundes deutscher Frauenvereine von Marie Stritt. Berlin, C. Habel, 1905.
2. Böhmert, Prof. V.—Die internationalen Bestrebung für Arbeiterschutz und Volkerfrieden. (Ein Kernpunkt der Arbeiterfrage) A. Fr. 1905. XLIII. 2.
3. Frey, E.—Die internat. Arbeiterschutzkonferenz in Bern. S. W. S. 1905. XIII. 17.
4. Zinner, D.—Die internationale Arbeiterschutzkonferenz in Bern. C. G. D. 1905 XV. No. 23.
5. Die internationale Regelung des Arbeiterschutzes. (Zu den letzten Beschlüssen der Berner Konferenz) *Die Arbeit.* 1905. XII. No. 841. Wien.
6. Die Berner Regierungskonferenz für internat. Arbeiterschutz und das Weissphosphorverbot. A. S. 1905. XVI. No. 11.
7. Zur internationalen Arbeiterschutzkonferenz in Bern. A. S. 1905. No. 12.
8. Die internationale Arzeiterschutzkonferenz. Z. G. H. 1905. XIV. No. 16.
9. Internationale Konferenz für Arbeiterschutz in Bern vom 8.-17. Mai 1905. R. A. 1905. III. No. 7.
10. Internat. Arbeiterschutzkonferenz in Bern. S. R. 1905. VI. No. 6.
11. Baudert, A.—Der VI internationale Textilarbeiterkongress in Mailand. N. Z. 1905. XXIII. II. No. 44.
12. Kongress, III. internat. der christl. Textilarbeiterorganisationen in Lüttich vom 2. bis 1. August, 1905. R .A. 1905. III. No. 11; S. P. 1905. XIV. No. 45.
13. Internationaler Textilarbeiterkongress, III. *Der christliche Gewerkschafter,* 1905. II. No. 16. Wien.

14. Der internationale Textilarbeiterkongress in Mailand. *Oesterreichische Wollen-und Leinenindustrie,* 1905. XXV. No. 14. Richenberg.
15. Internationaler Kongress, II. der gegenseitigen Hilfsund Krankenkassen in Lüttich. A. S. 1905. XVI. No. 17. 18.
19. Der VI internat. Textilarbeiterkongress. S. P. 1905. XIV. No. 42.
20. Internat. Tuberkulosekongress III. S. P. 1905. XV. 5.
21. Die internat. Konferenz der Sekretäre der Gewerkschaftlichen Landeszentralen. Gsch. 1905. n. f. VII. No. 13.
22. Nachlänge von der internationalen Gewerkschaftskonferenz. Gsch. 1905. n. f. VII. No. 14.
23. Brod. J.—Internationaler Kongress der gegenseitigen Hilfsund Krankvereine in Lttich. *Volkstümliche zeitschrift für praktische Arbeiterversicherung.* 1905. XI. No. 18. Magdeburg.
24. Der VII. internat. Arbeiterversicherungskongress. I. 1905. X. No. 38; S, R. 1905. VI. No. 9; Z. G. H. 1905. XIV. No. 17.
25. Wagner, Dr. M.—Der internat. Arbeiterversicherungskongress. S. K. 1905. XXV. 11.
26. Internat. Wohnungskongress, VII. in Lüttich. *Zeitscrift für Wohnungswesen.* 1905. III. No. 22. Berlin.
27. Fuchs, Prof. Dr. K. F.—Der VII. internationale Wohnungskongress in Lüttich. S. P. 1905. XV. (I. II.) No. 50. 51.
28. Der VII. internat. Wohnungskongress. *Beamtenbauzeitung,* 1905. III. No. 9. Wien.
29. Berlepsch. Die Regierungskonferenz für internationalen Arbeiterschutz in Bern. S. P. 1905. XIV. No. 31.
30. Die amtliche Einladung zur internationalen Regierungskonferenz für Arbeiterschutz. S. P. 1905. XIV. No. 16.
31. Internationale Regierungskonferenz für Arbeiterschutz in Bern. R. A. 1905. III. No. 2.
32. Die Ergebnisse der internationalen Regierungskonferenz für Arbeiterschutz in Bern. S. P. 1905. XIV. No. 34.
33. Von der Berner internationalen Arbeiterschutzkonferenz. S. P. 1905. XIV. No. 35; S. R. 1905..1.
34. Der VII. internationale Arbeiterversicherungskongress, *Der christiche gewerkschafter,* Wien, 1905. 19.
35. Stier-Somlo.—Die erste internationale Arbeiterschutzkonvention, 1905. B. R. V. Juli.
36. Internat. Tuberkulosekongress zu Paris; 1905. S. R. 1905. VI. 10.

International Labor Organizations.

1. Reichesberg, N.—Bestrebungen und Erfolge der internationalen Vereinigung für gesetzlichen Arbeiterschutz und des internationalen Arbeitsamtes. S. W. S. 1905. XIII. No. 3. 4. 5,
2. Ein Jahrbuch der internationalen Gewerkschaftsbewegung. (1) Gsch. 1905; N. F. VII. No. 6. 7.
3. Gründung eines internationalen Gesundheitsamtes. G. Ing. 1905. **XXVIII. No. 3.**

1906.

1. Internationale Regelung der Arbeitzeit in der Baumwollindustrie. I. 1906. XI. 13.
2. Kleeis, Fr.—Eine internationale Gesellschaft für Arbeiterversicherung. *Volkstümliche Zeitschrift für praktische Arbeiterversicherung,* Magdeburg, 1906. XII. 2.
3. Internationale Arbeiterversicherung. Deutsche Wirtschaftszeitung, Berlin, 1906. II. 2.
4. Internat. Jahresbericht des internat. Buchdrucker-Sekretariats, 1905. Rapport annual, die Sekretariat Typogr. International. Basel, Schweiz. Typogr.—Bund, 1906.
5. Erster Bericht des internat. Steinhauersekretariats pro 1904 und 1905. Bern, Unionsdrucherer, 1906.
6. Dochow, F.—Zeitschrift für Internationales Privat-und öffentliches Recht, Liepzig, 1906.

International Labor Conferences.

1. Die internationale diplomatische Arbeiterschutzkonferenz in Bern. Z. G. H. 1906. XIII. 17.
2. Internationaler diplomatischer Arbeiterschutz. Gsch. 1906. VIII. 19.
3. Der Genfer Kongress der Internationalen Arbeiterassoziation und die Gewerkschaftsfrage. C. G. D. 1906. XVI. 41.
4. Delegiertenversammlung der internationalen Vereinigung für gesetzlichen Arbeiterschutz von 27-29 September 1906 zu Genf. A. S. 1906. XVII. 20.
5. Die internationale Regierungskonferenz für Arbeiterschutz. S. P. 1906. XVI. 1.
6. Zur internationalen Regierungskonferenz für Arbeiterschutz in Bern. A. S. 1906. XVII. 20.
7. Die internationalen Arbeiterschutz-Staats-verträge. R. A. 1906. IV. 10; S. P. 1906. XVI. 3.
8. Inter. diplomatische Arbeiterschutzkonferenz Bern 19.-26. Sept.; Internat. Vereingung für gesetzlichen Arbeiterschutz. M. R. 1906. XIV. 43.
9. Internationales Uebereinkommen über die Verwendung weissen (gelben) Phosphors in der zundhölzscheninduśtrie. S. R. 1906. VII. 11.
10. Internationales Uebereinkommen über die industrielle Nachtarbeit der Frauen. S. R. 1906. VII. 10.
11. IV. Generalversammlung der international Vereinigung für gesetzlichen Arbeiterschutz. S. R. 1906. VII. 10.
12. Das internationale Uebereinkommen betreffend das Verbot der Verwendung weissen (gelben) Phosphor in der Streichholzindustrie. A. S. 1906. XVII. 21.
13. Die Phosphornekrose. Aus den Schriften der internationalen Vereinigugng für gesetzlichen Arbeiterschutz. A. S. 1906. XVII. 17.

14. Zur Frage des Phosphorverbotes auf der internationalen Arbeiterschutzkonferenz in Bern. A. S. 1906. XVII. 19.
15. I. Internationaler Kongress gegen Arbeitslosigkeit. S. R. 1906. VII. 11.
16. Erster internationaler Kongress für gewerbliche Berufskrankheiten. S. R. 1906. VII. 7.
17. Interationaler Hutarbeiterkongress, C. G. D. 1906. XVI, 34.
18. Francke Prof. Dr. E.—Die 4 .Generalversammlung der Internationalen Vereinigung für gesetzlichen Arbeiterschutz. S. P. 1906. XVI. 1.
19. Hue. O.—Vom internationalen Bergarbeiterkongress. Gew. 1906. X. 25.
20. Frey, E.—Verhandlungen der diplomatischen Konferenz für internationalen Arbeiterschutz. Bern, 17-26. September, 1906. S. W. S. XIV. 18.
21. Kahn, O.—Der I. internationale Kongress zu bekämpfung Arbeitslosigkeit. S. P. 1906. XVI. 6.
22. Kögler, K.—Der VII. Arbeiterversicherungskongress. Z. V. S. V. XIV. 6.
23. Pieper, Dr.—Internationale Vereinigung für Gesetzlichen Arbeiterschutz S. K. 1906. XXVI. 11.
24. Rambousek, Dr.—Der erste internationale Kongress für Arbeiterkrankheiten in Mailand. Z. G. H. 1906. XVIII. 12, 13, 14.
25. Hahn, M.—Internationale Kongress für Gewerbekrankheiten in Mailand. G. 1906. 20 U 21. Juli.
Mailand. G. 1906. 20 U 21, Juli.
26. Reichesberg, N.—Die IV. Delegiertenversammlung der Internationalen Vereingung für gesetzlichen Arbeiterschutz. (Genf. vom 27.-29. September 1906) S. W. S. 1906. XIV. 17.
27. IV. Delegiertversammlung der Internat. Vereinig. für gesetzl. Arbeiterschutz. S. P. 1906. XV. 41.
28. Der Internat. Transportarbeiterkongress. S. P. 1906. XV. 43.
29. Weingartz, B.—Internat. Kongress der Bergarbeiter. C. G. D. 1906. XVI. 25.
30. XVII. internationaler Bergarbeiterkongress in London, S. R. 1906. VII. 6.
31. Internat. Konferenz der Handlungs-und Ladengehilfen. C. G. D. 1906. XVI. 27.
32. Ein internat. Kongress für Arbeiterkrankheiten. S. P. 1906. XV. 40.
33. Manes A. Eindruck vom Wiener Arbeitsversicherungs—Kongresse. Z. Vers. 1906. Jan.
34. Internat. Verband der Grubenarbeiter. Der 17. internat. Kongress im Westminster Palace Hotel. Victoria Street, London, Dienstag, den S. June 1906 und an den folgenden Tagen. Manchester, T. Ashton, 1906.

International Labor Legislation.

1. Internationaler Arbeiterschutz. H. M. 1906. XXI. 43.
2. Schippel, M.—Die Konkurrenz der fremden Arbeitskräfte zur Tage-

sordnung des Stuttgarter Internationalen Kongresses, S. M. 1906. X. (XII.) 11. 9.
3. Kaff, S.—Internationaler Arbeiterschutz. C. G. D. 1906. XVI. 5.
4. Internationale Arbeiterschutzverträge. S. P. 1906. XV. 42.

International Labor Organizations.

1. Die internationale Gewerkschaftsbewegung. S. P. 1906. XV. 48.
2. Das Jahrbuch über die internationale Gewerkschaftsbewegung. Gsch. 1906. II. Mai.
3. Springer, R.—Nationalismus und Internationalismus in der Gewerkschaftsbewegung. Gsch. 1906. VIII. 3. 4.
4. Die Internationale über die Gewerkschaften. N. Z. 1906. 22 Sept.
5. Jannson, W.—Internationales aus der Gewerkschaftsbewegung. N. Z. 1906. XXIV. II. 33.
6. Der 2 internat. Bericht über die Gewerkschaftsbewegung im Jahre 1904. C. G. D. 1906. XVI. 15. 16.
7 Die internat. Gewerkschaftsbewegung im Jahre 1904. R. A. 1906. IV. 6.

1907.

International Labor Conferences.

1. Internationale Arbeiterkongresse. H. T. 1907. L. 35.
2. Vom internationalen Arbeiterkongress. Gew. 1907. 36. S. 721-725.
3. Der internationale Arbeiterkongress. Gew. 1907. 33, S. 665-668.
4. Die erste internationale Gemeindearbeiter-Konfrenz. Gew. 1907. 34, S. 681-686.
5. Vom internationalen Sozialistenkongress. G. 1907. 68, S. 269.
6. Vom XVIII. internationalen Bergarbeiterkongress. G. 1907. 76, S. 302-303.
7. Der internationale Sozialistenkongress. 1907. E. Z. 1907. 21, S. 1.
8. Internationale Transportarbeiterkonferenz. E. Z. 1907. 25, S. 6.
9. Der internationale Kongress in Stuttgart. A. St. 1907. 17, S. 133-135.
10. Kautsky, K.—Der Stuttgarterkongress. N. Z. 1907. XXV. 48.
11. Michels, R.—Der erste internationale Kongress zur Kekämpfung der Arbeitslosigkeit. N. Z. 1907. XXV. 14.
12. Reichesberg, J.—Der internationale Sozialistenkongress in Stuttgart. S. W. S. 1907. 12.
13. Die Gewerkschaftsfrage auf dem internationalen Sozialistenkongress in Stuttgart. Z. C. G. D. 1907. VII. 20.
14. Internationaler Kongress für Sonntagsgruhe. Z. C. G. D. 1907. VII. 23.
15. Internationaler Bergarbeiterkongress. Z .C. G. D 1907. VII. 20.
16. IV. internationaler Kongress christlicher Textilarbeiterorganisationen. Z. C. G. D.. 1907. VII. 18.
17. Zum internationalen sozialistischen Arbeiter-und Gewerkschaftskongress in Stuttgart. C. G. D. 1907. 33, S. 513-515.
18. 5. Internationale Konferenz der Sekretäre der gewerkschaftlichen Landeszentralen. C. G. D. 1907. 39, S. 617-620.

19. Sechster internationaler Kongress der Lithographen Steindrucker verw. Berufe. C. G. D. 1907. 41, S. 653.
20. Der vierzehnte internationale Kongress für Hygiene und Demographei. C. G. D. 1907. 41, S. 656.
21. Internationale Berufskonferenz. C. G. D. 1907. 35, 36, 37, 38, 39, S. 554-555, 569-571, 589-590, 600-602, 620-623.
22. Internationale Berufskongress und Konferenzen. C. G. D. 1907. 22, S. 344-345.
23. Achtzehnter internationaler Bergarbeiterkongress in Salzburg; C. G. D. 1907. 41. S. 653-655.
24. Vom internationalen sozialistischen und Gewerkschaftskongress in Stuttgart. C. G. D. 1907. 35, S. 550-554.
25. Internationaler Buchdruckerkongress. C. G. D. 1907. 32, S. 505.
26. Kloth, E.—Internationale Konferenz der Vertreter der Buchbinder-Verbände. C. G. D. 1907. 31, S. 494-496.
27. Internationale Steinsetzerkonferenz. C. G. D. 1907. 9, S. 140-141.
28. Internationale Gewerkschaftskongresse. S. P. 1907. XVI. 49.
29. Der 14, internationale Kongress für Hygiene und Demographie. S. P. 1907. XVII. 3.
30. Der 18. internationale Bergarbeiterkongress in Salzburg. S. P. 1907. 1.
31. Die internationale Zimmererkonferenz. S. P. 1907. XVI. 31.
32. Internationale Gewerkschaftskongresse. G. P. 1907. XX. 38.
33. Internationale Gewerkschaftskongresse. Gsch. 1907. 17. 18. 19, S. 345-348, 369-371, 380-383.
34. Fünfte internationale Konferenz der Sekretäre der gewerkschaftlichen Landeszentralen in Christiania. Gsch. 1907. 18, S. 358-365.
35. Internationale Fachkongresse. Gsch. 1907. 16, S. 331-334.
36. Sechster internationaler Lithographenkongress. Gsch. 1907. 19, S. 379-380.
37. Worner, Z.—Ergebnisse des internationalen Kongresses für Versicherungswissenschaft. Z. G. St. 1907. 2.
38. Internationaler Kongress der Bäcker, Konditoren und Verwandter Berufsgenossen. V. 1907. 29, VIII.
39. XVIII. internationaler Bergarbeiterkongress in Salzburg. B. Arb. 1907. X. 39, 40, 41.
40. 18. Internationaler Bergarbeiterkongress. W. A. Z. 1907. IX. 40.
41. Der 18. internationale Bergarbeiterkongress in Salzburg. A. S. XVIII. 20, S. 322-323.
42. VIII. internationaler Wohnungskongress in London. W. S. M. 1907. 33, S. 391-393; M. R. 1907. 15 Aug.
43. Katscher, L.—Vom achten internationalen Volkswohnungskongress. Gen. 1907. 37, 38.
44. Internationaler Kongress für Hygiene und Demographie. J. 1907. 9. XIV.
45. Mitteilung, betr. die Veranstaltung eines **internationalen Kinderschutzkongresses in Berlin**. B. 1907. 7. 8.

46. Die internationale Jugendkonferenz in Stuttgart. J. A. 1907. 10, S. 3.
47. Erster Internationaler Kongress der Bächer, Konditoren und verwandter Berufsgenossen, abgehalten zu Stuttgart am 24, und 25. August 1907. Hamburg, Allmann, 1907.
48. Sechster internationaler Kongress der Lithographen und Steindrucker, 1907. Abgehalten am 19. bis 21. September 1907 in Kopenhagen, Berlin, O. Sillier, 1907.
49. Internationaler Arbeiterversicherungs-Kongress. 7. Tagung, Wien, 17.-23. Sept. 1905. Wien, F. Deutsche, 1907.
50. Stradal, A. G.-Der 8. internationale Wohnungskongress in London, vom. 3.-10. August 1907. (S.-A. aus: Oesterr. Wochenschrift für den öffentlichen Baudienst, 1907. 43, 44.) Wien, Selbstverlag, 1907.
51. Schweiz. Vereinigung zur Förderung des internationalen Arbeiterschutzes, Die Diplomatenkonferenz für Arbeiterschutz. (Bern, 17.-26. September 1906.) Bericht von alt Bundesrat E. Frey, Bern, Die IV. Delegiertenversammlung der Internationalen Vereinigung für gesetzlichen Arbeiterschutz. (Genf. 27.-29. September 1906.) Bericht von Professor Dr. N. Reichesberg, Bern. 21 p. Bern, Schertlin, Spring & Cie, 1907.
52. Internationale Vereinigung für gesetzlichen Arbeiterschutz. Verhandlungsbericht der vierten Generalversammlung des Komitees der Internationalen Vereinigung für gesetzlichen Arbeiterschutz, abgehalten zu Genf vom 26.-29. September 1906, nebst Jahresberichten der I. V. und des Int. Arbeitsamtes und synoptischen Uebersichten. XVI.-157 p. Jena, Gustav Fischer, 1907.
53. Eckhardt, F.—Der internationale Bergarbeiterkongress. A. R. 1907. 41. p. 571-572.
54. I. internationale Friseurgehilfen Konferenz. Co. 1907. X. 17.
55. V. internationaler Buchdruckerkongress in Paris. H. T. 1907.
56. Der internationale Holzarbeiterkongress. H. Z. 1907. XVI. 34.
57. I. Internationale Friseurgehülfen-Konferenz: Protokoll der Verhandlungen am 26. und 27. August im Gewerkschaftshause zu Stuttgart. Hamburg, Etzkorn, 1907.
58. Internationaler Genossenschaftsbund. Protokoll der Verhandlungen des VII. Kongresses in Cremona am 22. bis. 25. IX. 1907. VIII 238 p. Berlin und London.
59. Internationale Union der Holzarbeiter 1907. Protokolle der internationalen Holzarbeiterkongresse zu Amsterdam 1904 und Stuttgart 1907.

International Labor Legislation.

1. Die Arbeiterschutzgesetzbung des Auslandes im Jahre 1906. A. S. XVIII. 19, S. 303-306.
2. Internationales Abkommen über die Nachtarbeit der in der industrie beschäftigten Frauen in Luxemburg. S. P. 1907. XVI. 49.
3. Das internationale Abkommen über die Nachtarbeit der in der Industrie beschäftigten Frauen in Frankreich. S. P. 1907. XVI. 39.

4. Internationale Unfallversicherungsabkommen. W. N. O. 1907. 49. Gsch. 1907. 22.
5. Dochow, F.—Vereinheitlichung des Arbeiterschutzrechtes durch Staatsverträge. Ein Beitrag zum internationalen Verwaltungsrecht. VII-III p. Berlin, C. Heymann, 1907.
6. Reichesberg, Prof. Dr. N.—Die IV. Delegiertenversammlung der Internationalen Vereinigung für gesetzlichen Arbeiterschutz (Genf. September, 1906). Veröffentlichungen der Scweiz Vereinigung zur Förderung des internationalen Arbeiterschutzes, Heft. 18:21. S. Bern. Scheitlin, Spring & Cie, 1907.

International Labor Organizations.

1. Der dritte internationale Bericht über die Gewerkschaftsbewegung 1905. C. G. D. 8 u. 9; G. P. 1907. XX. 15, 16, 19, 20, A. St. 1907. 5.
2. Eine internationale Statistik der Stärke der Gewerkschaften. C. G. D. 1907. 48, S. 759.
3. Die internationale Gewerkschaftsbewegung im Jahre 1905. R. A. 1907. V. 3; S. R. 1907. VIII. 5.
4. Das Jahrbuch über die internationale Gewerkschaftsbewegung. Gsch. 1907. 6.
5. Janson, W.—Der internationale Gewerkschaftsbericht für 1905. N. Z. 1907. XXV. 30.
6. Internationale Gewerkschaften. H. Z. 1907. XVI. 33.
7. Internationale Gewerkschaftsorganisation. E. Z. 1907. 16, S. 3-4.
8. Jahresbericht 1906. Rapport Annuel. Basel, Schweizer. Typographenbund, 1907.
9. Internationales Sekretariat der im Strassenbau beschäftigten Arbeiter. Zweite internationale Konferenz der im Strassenbau beschäftigten Arbeiter, abgehalten am 17. Februar 1907 im Volkshaus zu Leipzig. Berlin, Selbstverlag.
10. Internationale Gewerkschaftsorganisation. Eis. 1907. XV. 16.
11. Die internationale Buchdruckerorganisation im Jahre 1906. H. T. 1907 L. 34.
12. Eine internationale Buchdruckerstatistik. A. St. 1907. 17, S. 135-136.
13. Internationaler Buchdrucker-Sekretariat: Die Gehilfenorganzationen im Buchdruckergewerbe. II. Serie: Der Strand am 1. Januar 1905. Basel, Schweizer. Typographenbund, 1907.
14. Die internationale Buchdruckerorganisation. C. G. D. 1907. 31.

1908.

International Labor Legislation.

1. Internationaler Arbeiterschutz A. S. 1908. XIX. 3.
2. Die Arbeiterschutzgesetzgebung des Auslandes im Jahre 1906. Oe. M. 1908. XVIII. 10. (Jahre 1908. A. S. 1909. XX. 12).

3. Dove, H. Ansätze zur internationalen Regelung des Arbeiterschutzes. B. R. V. 1908. IV. 32.
4. Internationaler Arbeiterschutz. G. 1908. XL. 77.
5. Verhandlungen über internationalen, Arbeiterschutz in der Britischen Vereinigung für Arbeitsgesetzgebung. S. P. 1908. XVII. 37.
6. Schweden und die Berner Konvention betr. die Nachtarbeit der Frauen. C. G. D. 1908. XVIII. 22.
7. Internationaler Arbeiterschutz. *Bhd.* 1908. IX. 22.
8. Die ausländische Arbeitsgesetzgebung im Jahre 1908. L. Z. 1908. XVI. 34.

International Labor Congresses.

1. Der Internationale Sozialistische und Gewerkeschaftskongress in Stuttgart (im August 1907) R. A. 1908. VI. 2.
2. Internationale Konferenz der Hotel-Restaurant-und Café-Angestellten zu Berlin. Ho. 1908. XI. 11.
3. Internationaler Verein für Sonntags feier. Verhandlungen des XII. Internationalen Kongress für Sonntagfeier gehalten den 27. bis 29. Sept. 1907 in Frankfurta. M. Reden und Berichte. 224 p. Leipsig, J. C. Hinrichs, 1908. M. 250.
4. V. Delegier tenversammlung des Internationalen Vereinegung für gesetzlichen Arbeiterschutz. P. 1908. XVII. 42; *Ref.* A. V. 1908. IV. 20;—S. R. 1908. IX.⅞;—W. A. Z. 1908. X. 41.
5. Erste internationale Konfernz christl. Gewerkschaftsfuhrer. B. K. 1908. XIII. 33, 35;—W. A. Z. 1908. X. 33; TZ. 1908. X. 33.
6. XIX. Internationaler Bergarbeiter-Kongress in Paris. B. Arb. 1908. XI. 25, 26, 27;—B. K. 1908. XIII. 25, 26;—Tex. 1908. XX. 27;—Z. C. G. D. 1908. VIII. 13.
7. Der internationale Textilarbeiterkongress Gsch. 1908. X. 12.
8. Der 7. internationale Textilarbeiterkongress C. G. D. 1908. XVIII. 23.
9. Siebenter internationale Textilarbeiterkongress in Wien. Tex. 1908. XX. 23.
10. Baudert. Der siebente internationale Textilarbeiterkongress in Wien. N. Z. 1908. 38.
11. VIII. Internationaler Kongress für Arbeiterversicherung. S. P. 1908. IX.⅞.
12. Internationales Buchdrucker Secretariat. Protokoll des V. internationalen Buchdruckerkongresses in Paris. Vom 9. bis 13. Juli 1907. 166p. Basil, Schweiz, Typographenbund, 1908.
13. Verband deutcher Gastwertsgehülfen. I. Internationale Konferenz der Hotel-Restaurant-und Café-Angestellen. Berlin, 17.-20. Mai 1908. 41p. Berlin, Selbstverlag, 1908.
14. Ein internationaler Arbeiterschutzkongress. *Sch.* 1908. XXII. 42.
15. Die internationale Vereinigung für gesetzlichen Arbeiterschutz an ithrer Generalversammlung in Luzern. B. K. 1908. XIII. 44, 45;—H.

BIBLIOGRAPHY

A. 1908. VIII. 11;—M. R. 1908. XVI. 41;—S. R. 1908. IX. 10;—S. W. S. 1908. XVI. 15/16;—Z. C. G. D. 1908. VIII. 21.
16. Francke, Prof. Dr. E. Die 5. Generalversammlung der Internationaler Vereinigung für gesetzlichen Arbeiterschutz. S. P. 1908. XVIII. 2.
17. Katcher, L. Internationale Vereinigung für gesetzlichen Arbeiterschutz (Delegiertenkonferenz.) S. T. 1908. VII. 34.
18. Der 8. internationale Arbeitervericherungskongress in Rom. G. 1908. XL. 82;—M. R. 1908. XVI. 43-46;—*Ref.* A. V. 1908. XV. 21;—S. R. 1909. X. 1.—Z Vers 1908. VIII. p. 391.
19. Fürst, Dr. M. Der VIII. Internationale Kongress für Arbeiterversicherung in Rom und die Aerzte. *Ref.* A. V. 1908. IV. 21.
20. Maner, Prof. Dr., Der III. Internationale Kongress für Arbeiterversicherungskongress. C. 1908.
21. Stier—Somlo, Prof. Dr. Die materiellen Ergebnisse desarbeiterversicherungskongress in Rom, vom 10, bis 16. Oktober 1908. *Ref.* A. V. 1908. IV. 1, 23.
22. Zacher, Dr. Der 8. Internationale Arbeiterversicherungskongress. (Rom 12.—16. Oktober 1908) S. P. 1908 XVIII. 7.
23. V. Sauter, Dr., II. Internationaler Mittelstandskongress in Wien, Oktober, 1908. S. P. 1908. XVIII. 7.
24. Protokoll über den internationalen Glasarbeiterkongress zu Paris. Abgeh. vom 28. Aug. bisl. Sept. 1908. 51 p. Dresden, P. Kluge, 1908.
25. Protokoll über die Verhandlungen der internationalen Schneiderkonferenz; abgehalten am 24. Aug. 1908 Zu Frankfurt A.M. 66 p. Berlin, H. Stühmer.
26. Bericht über die I. internationale Konferenz christlicher gewerkschaftsführer im Zürich, 1908. (Deutsch, Französisch, Holländisch) 84 Köln, Christl gewerkschaftsverlag.

International Labor Organizations.

1. Der Vierte internationale Bericht über die Gewerkschaftsbewung 1906. A. St. 1908. XXVIII. 6.
2. Internationaler Sekretär der gewerkschaftlichen Landeszentralen. Vierter internationaler Bericht über die Gewerkschaftsbewegung 1906. Berlin, Generalkommission der gewerkschaften Deutschlands, 1908.
3. Internationales Steinhaversekretariat. Zweiter Bericht pro 1906 and 1907, 21 p. Bern, Unionsdruckerei, 1908.
4. Die gewerkschaftliche Internationale. D. B. K. Z. 1908. XIV. 26.
5. Die internationale Gewerkschaftsbewegung im Jahre 1906. R. A. 1908. VI. 5;—S. R. 1908 IX. 5;—S. Z. 1908. XXII. 12; Z. C. G. D. VIII. 13.
6. Der vierte internationale Bericht über die Gewerkschaftsbewegung 1906. C. G. D. 1908. XVIII. 21, 23.
7. Fortschrift der internationalen Gewerkschaftsbewegung. v. *Anz.* 1908. XXII. 21.

8. Die internationale Starke der Christlichen Gewerkschaften. S. R. V. 1908. 11. 22.
9. Internationale Bergarbeiterbewegung. C. G. D. 1908. XVIII. 19.
10. Die Arbeiterorganisationen der Kulturstaaten. G. 1908. XL. 79.
11. Bericht über die I. internationale Konferenz christlicher Gewerkschaftsführer im Zürich, 1908. (Deutsch, Französisch, Holländisch, 84 Köln, Christl, Gewerkschaftsverlag.

1909.

International Labor Legislation.

1. Bauer, Prof. Dr. St.—Die neuere der kinderschutzgesetzgebung im Deutschland un dim Grossbritannien. (Separatabdruck aus den Arch iv für Sozialwissenschaft und Gozialpolitik). Tübingen und Leipzig, J. C. B. Mohr.
2. Die internationale Schumacherbewegung, Sch. 1909. XXIII. 47.
3. Internationaler Genossenschaftsbund. I. G. 1909. II. 7, 8, 9.
4. Lüders, E. Internationale Frauenbewegung und internationaler Arbeiterinnenschutz. *Fr.* 1909. XV. 7(
5. Liefmann, Prof. Dr. R. Die Kartellund Trustgesetzgebunz des Auslandes. S. P. 1909 XVIII. 15.

International Labor Congresses.

1. 6. Internationale Gewerkschaftskonferenz. A. D. G. Z. 1909. XIX. 37; Gew. 1909. XIII. 37; G. P. 1909. XXII. 37; F. 1909. XVIII. 37. Tö. 1909. XVIII. 37.
2. Sechste internationale Konferenz der Gewerkschaftlichen Landeszentralen. C. G. D. 1901. XIX. 37; Z. C. G. D. 1909. IX. 22.
3. Sechste internationale konferenz der Vertreter der Gewerkschaftlichen Landeszentralen. Tex. 1909. XXI. 38, 39.
4. Babron, J.—Bericht über die 6. internationale Gewerkschaftskonferenz in Paris. Sch. 1909. XXIII. 38.
5. Eine internationale konferenz über Arbeitslosigkeit. S. R. 1909. X. 7.
6. Internationaler Kongress für Bergbau, Hüttenwesen, angewandte Mechabik und praktische Geologie, Dusseldorf 1910; S. T. 1909. VIII. 23.
7. Siebenter internationaler Hutarbeiterkongress. C. G. D. 1909. XIX. 38.
8. Internationale Konferenz der Tabakarbeiter. Tab. 1909. 46.
9. Moldenhauer, Prof. Dr. jur—Ergebnisse des VI Internationalen Kongresses für Versicherungswessenschaft in Wien. Z. Vers. 1909. IX. 4.
10. Internationaler Steinarbeiterverband, .Protokoll über die Verhandlungen des III. Internationale Kongresses, abgehalten in Kassel am 11. u. 12. April 1908. 23 p. Bern, Genossenschaft Unionsdruckerei, 1909.
11. Bureau der Internationalen Vereinigunz für gesetzlichen Arbeiterschutz. Schriften no. 6. Verhandlungsbericht der fünften Generalversamsmlung des Konitees, abgehalten zu Luzern vom 28.—30. Septem-

ber 1908 nebst Jahresberichten der Internationalen Vereinigung und des Internationalen Arbeitsamets. 227 p. Jena, Gust. Fischer, 1909.
12. Manes, Prof. Dr. Eindrücke com VIII. internationalen Arbeiterversicherungskongress in Rom. Z. *Vers.* 1909. IX. I.
13. Eine internationale Konferenz uber Arbeitslosigkeit. S. P. 1909 XVIII. 38.
14. Zum XX. internationalen Bergarbeiterkongress. B. *Arb* 1909. XII. 24-26;—B. K. 1909. XIV. 24-26;—Ho. 1909. XII. 12.
15. Der 11. internationale Aerztekongress für gewerbliche Unfälle in Rom. M. R. 1909. XVII. 6;— Z. G. H. 1909. XVI. 12.
16. Internationale Transportarbeiter Federation. Protokoll über die Verhandlungen des sechsten internationalen Transportarbeiter-Kongress sowie der Konferenzen der Eisenbahner und Seeleute. Abgehalten in Wien vom 24. bis 29. Aug. 1908. Bericht des Zentralrates für 1906, 1907, 1908. VI. 159 p. Hamburg, H. Jochade, 1909.
17. Protokoll über den internationalen Glasarbeiterkongress zu Paris. Abgeh. com 28. bis 1. Sept. 19.

International Labor Organizations.

1. Internationales Buchdrucker-Sekretariat Jahresbericht 1909. Deutsch und Französisch, Stuttgart, Selbstverleg.
2. Die internationale Gewerkschaftsbewegung. B. Z. 1909. XIX. 34, 36.
3. Die internationale Gewerkschaftsbewegung im Jahre 1907. S. R. 1909. X. 9; Z. C. G. D. 1909. IX. 18.
4. Der fünfte internationale Bericht über die Gewerkschaftsbewegung 1907. C. G. D. 1909. XIX. 28, 29.
5. Die Gewerkschaftsbewegung diesseits und jenseits des Ozeans. C. G. D. 1909. XIX. 32; L. Z. 1909. XVII. 27.
6. Internationales Jahrbuch der Gewerkschaften. *Gsch.* 1909. XI. 10.
7. 5. internationaler Bericht über die Gewerkschaftsbewegung P. 1909. XVIII. 25.
8. Internationale Gewekschaftsbewegung. A. D. G. Z. 1909. XIX. 21;— Eis. 1909. XVII. 15;—*Sch.* XVII. 15;—*Sch.* 1909 XXIII. 25.
9. Internationale Maurerbewegung. *Gr.* 1909 XXII. 19.

1910

International Labor Congresses.

1. Internationaler Sozialistenkongress zu Kopenhagen 1910. (Protokoll) Berlin, Buchhandlung Vorwärts.
2. 21. Internationaler Bergarbeiterkongress in Brüssel 1910. (Deutsche Ausgabe).
3. Internationaler Metallarbeiter Bund. Berichte der aneschlossenen Landesverbände an den VI. Internationalen Metallarbeiter-Kongress in Birmingham 1910. Stuttgart, Alex. Schlicke & Cie, 1910.

4. Bericht des österreicheischen Metallarbeiterververbandes an den 6. Kongress des Internationalen Metallarbeiterverbandes in Birmingham 1910. Wien. Selbstverlag des Verbandes.
5. Internationale Kongresse im Jahre 1909. R. A. 1910. 5.
6. Internationale Sozialisten-oder internationale Gewerkschaftskongresse. Schm. Z. 1910. XXIV. 19, 20.
7. Der 9. internationale Wohnungskongresse. S. P. 1910. XIX. 36.
8. Internationale Konferenzen für Sozialversicherung. A. N. M. I. 1910. XXII. 4.
9. Fünfter Kongress der Internationalen Vereinigung christlicher Textilarbeiterorganisationen; Mailand 1910. T. Z. XII. 14, 15.
10. Zum VIII. Internationalen Genossenschaftskongress in Hamburg. I. G. 1910. III. 9, 10.
11. Der VIII. Internationale Genossenschaftskongress im Spiegel der genossenschaftlichen Presse. I. G. 1910. III. 11, 12.
12. Internationale Konferenz für Sozialversicherung. C. G. D. 1910. XX. 42; A. S. 1910. XXI. 19, 20,—(Düttmann) A. V. 1910. 27.
13. Internationaler Bergarbeiter-Kongress. B. Arb. 1910. XIII. 34, 35.
14. 6. Internationaler Mettallarbeiterkongress, Birmingham 31. Oktober bis 2. November 1910. C. G. D. 1910. XX. 46.
15. Der Weltbund der Diamantarbeiter. (Kongress com 20.—24. Juni 1910.) C. G. D. 1910. XX. 30.
16. Der Internationale Holzarbeiterkongress in Kopenhagen. H. Z. 1910. XVIII. 38.
17. Der VII. Internationale Transportarbeiterkongress in Kopenhagen. Eis. 1910. XVIII. 25.
18. Internationale Vereinigung für gesetzlichen Arbeiterschutz. Verhandlungsbericht der VI. Generalversammlung, abgehalten zu Lugano am 26.-28. IX. 1910 nebst Jahresberichten der Internationalen Vereinigung und des Internationalen Arbeitsamtes. Jena, Gustav Fischer, 1910.
19. Protokoll der II. internationalen Buchbinderkonferenz zu Erfurt. Berlin, Selbstverlag, 1910.
20. Internationaler Bäckerkongress in Kopenhagen. Hamburg, O. Altmann, 1910.
21. Internationales Sekretariat der Arbeiter öffentlicher Betriebe. Protokoll der zweiten Internationalen Konferenz der Arbeiter öffentlicher Betriebe. Berlin, Selbstverlag, 1910.
22. Hanauer. J.—Internationaler Heimarbeitskongress. C. G. D. 1910. XX. 40.
23. Zum IX. Internationalen Wohnungskongress. A. S. 1910. XXI. 12, 18; C. 1910. XVII. 19.
24. Vom Internationalen Kongress in Kopenhagen. C. G. D. 1910. XX. 34, 36.
25. Der Internationale Sozialistenkongress und die Konsumvereine. I. G. 1910. III. 10.

26. Marott, Emil.—Zum Internationalen sozialistischen Kongress in Kopenhagen. S. M. 1910. XIV. 16-18.
27. Internationale Gewerkschaftskonferenzen in Kopenhagen. C. G. D. 1910. XX. 38, 39.
28. Die zweite Internationale Konferenz sozialistischer Frauen zu Kopenhagen. Gl. 1910. XX. 25.
29. Internationaler Kongress zur Bekämpfung der Arbeitslosigkeit, 19.-21. September in Paris (Sorbonne). C. G. D. 1910. XX. 41.
30. Der internationale Genossenschaftskongress in Hamburg vom 5.-7. September 1910. S. K. V. X. 38; K. R. VII. 37, 40, 41.
31. XI. Internationaler Kongress zur Bekämpfung der Gewerbekrankheiten. A. S. 1910. XXI. 21.

International Labor Legislation.

1. Francke, Prof. Dr. Ernst.—VI. Generalversammlung der Internationalen Vereinigung für gesetzlichen Arbeiterschutz. Lugano 25-28 September 1910. S. P. 1910. XX. 1.
2. VI. Generalversammlung der Internationalen Vereinigung für gesetzlichen Arbeiterschutz. Lugano 25.-28. September 1910. C. 1910. XVII. 22; C. G. D. 1910. XX. 43; A. O. 1911. XVIII. 476.
3. Francke, Prof. Dr. E.—Internationale Arbeiterschutzverträge. S. B. 1910. I. 13.
4. Zwei Jahrzehnte internationaler Arbeiterschutz. Ho. A. 1910. XI. 41.
5. Die Inkraftsetzung der internationalen Konventionen betreffend die Verbote der industriellen Nachtarbeit der Frauen und der Verwendung des giftigen Phosphors. C. G. D. 1910. XX. 34.
6. Die Arbeiterschutzgesetzgebung des Auslandes im Jahre 1909. A. S. 1910. XXI. 8.
7. Die ausländische Arbeitsgesetzgebung im Jahre 1909. L. A. 1910. XVIII. 13.
8. Krüger, G. Der Arbeiterinnenschutz in der Gesetzgebung der Kulturstaaten. S. M. 1910. XIV. (XVI.) 14.
9. Die Entwicklung der Invaliden—und Altersversorgung im Ausland. S. Z. 1910. XXIV. 2.
10. Pieraccini, Prof. (Vortrag) Berufskrankheiten der Keramiker und die internationale Arbeitergesetzgebung. Am. 1910. XXXVII. 20.
11. Reichesberg, N.—Arbeiterschutzverträge. Handwörterbuch der Schweizerischen Volkswirtschaft, 1910. 3.

International Labor Organizations.

1. Die Arbeitersekretariate im Deutschen Reich in Jahre 1909. (Statistik) C. G. D. 1910. XX. 31.
2. Ein internationaler Verband der Seeschiffahrtsunternehmer. S. K. 1910. April.
3. Die Entwicklung des Internationalen Genossenschaftsbundes seit dem Kongress in Budapest 1904. J. B. D.

4. Die Revision der statuten des Internationalen Genossenschaftsbundes. K. R. 1910. 12.
5. Internationaler Heimarbeiterschutz. H. A. 1910. X. 11.
6. Die internationale Gewerkschafts bewegung in Jahre 1908. D. B. K. Z. 1910. XVI. 26.
7. Legien, Carl.—Die Gewerkschaftliche Internationale. S. M. XIV. (XVI.) 1910. 7.
8. Internationale Transportarbeiter. Bericht des generalrates der Internationalen Federation für 1908 und 1909. Berichte der Organisationen. Berichte der Hafeninspektion. Bericht über die Lohn—und Arbeitsverhältnisse der Chauffeurs, Deutsche Ausgebe, Berlin, H. Jochade.
9. Die Revision der Statuten des I. G. B. I. G. 1910. III. 4, 5, 6.
10. Cornelissen C.—Ueber dem internationale Syndikalismus. A. S. S. 1910. Jan.
11. Huggler, August.—Internationalität der Gewerkschaften in der Schweiz. K. 1910. 8.
12. Der Stand der internationalen Töpferbewegung. Tö. 1910. XIX. 21.
13. Die christlichen Textilarbeiterorganisationen unserer internationalen Vereinigung. T. Z. 1910. XII. 13.
14. Internationales Buchdruckersekretariat (Sécrétariat International Topographique). Jahresbericht 1909. Stuttgart. Schwäbische Tagwacht, 1910.
15. Internationaler Wettbewerb um Unfallverhütungseinrichtungen. S. T. 1910. IX. 11.
16. Oesterreichisches Komitee für internationale Sozialversicherung. S. R. 1910. XI. 4.

1911.

1. Müller, Dr. Hans.—Die Entwicklung der Grosseinkaufsgenossenschaften im Jahre 1910. K. R. 1911. VIII. 17.
2. Internationale Preisausschreiben für Schutzvorrichtungen und Systeme zur Verhütung von Unglucksfällen bei der Arbeit auf der Internationalen Weltausstellung in Turin. S. T. 1911. X. 4.
3. Braun, Adolf.—Internationale Gewerksgenossenschaften. K. IV. 3.
4. Die internationale Grosseinkaufsgesellschaft. I. G. 1911. IV. 2.
5. Was lehrt uns die Entwicklung der internationalen Genossenschaftsbewegung? I. G. 1911. IV. 4, 5, 6.
6. Internationale Konsumvereinsstatistik pro 1909. I. G. 1911. IV. 2.
7. Die Internationale Hygieneausstellung und die Gewerkschaften. D. B. K. Z. 1911. XVII. 7, 8.
8. Andor, A.—Die Reziprozität auf dem Gebiete der Arbeiterversicherung zwischen Ungar und Oesterreich. V. M. U. 1911. 1.
9. Die Arbeitersekretariate im Deutschen Reich im Jahre 1910. Gew. 1911. XV. 27.

International Labor Congresses.

1. Internationaler Kongress für Wohnungshygiene. S. P. 1911. XXI. 3.
2. Die 2. Internationale Konferenz für Sozialversicherung, Dresden, 15.-

16. September 1911. S. P. 1911. XX. 52; M. R. 1911. XIX. 20, 21; A. S. 1911. XXII. 19.
3. Die 7. internationale Gewerkschaftskonferenz. S. P. 1911. XX. 48.
4. Der 23. Internationale Bergarbeiterkongress, London, 24.-28. Juli 1911. S. P. 1911. XX. 45.
5. Internationaler Glasarbeiterkongress. C. G. D. 1911. XXI. 41.
6. Verhandlung der Budapester Konferenz betreffs Organisation des Arbeitsmarktes 7. und 8. X. 1910. Leipzig, A. Deichert, 1911.
7. Centralrat der internationalen Transportarbeiter—Föderation. Protokoll des 7. Internationalen Transportarbeiterkongresses und der Konferenzen der Hafenarbeiter und Seeleute in Kopenhagen vom 23.-27. August 1910. Berlin, H. Jochade, 1911.
8. Internationaler Holzarbeiterverband. Protokoll des 5. Internationalen Holzarbeiterkongresses in Kopenhagen 1910. Berlin, Selbstverlag, 1911.
9. Internationaler Verband der Lithographen und Steindrucker. VII. Internationaler Kongress in Amsterdam 1910. Berlin, O. Lillier, 1911.
10. Internationaler Verband der Schuhmacher. Bericht des Internationalen Sekretariats und der Landesorganisationen an den IV. Internationalen Kongress und Protokoll des IV. Internationalen Kongresses zu Kopenhagen 1910. Nürnberg, J. Simon, 1911.
11. II. Internationale Friseurgehilfenkonferenz. Protokoll der Verhandlungen am. 22, 23, und 24. August 1911 in Zürich. Berlin, Selbstverlag, 1911.
12. Nachklänge zum Internationalen Genossenschafts-Kongress in Hamburg. I. G. 1911. IV. 1.
13. Protokolle des 8. Internationalen Textilearbeiterkongresses zu Amsterdam 1911. Berlin, Vorstand des deutschen Verbandes, 1911.

International Labor Legislation.

1. Die internationale Arbeiterschutzgesetzgebung für Transportarbeiter. Cr. 1911. XV. 2.
2. Internationales Arbeitsamt. Erster vergleichender Bericht über die zur Durchführung der Arbeiterschutzgesetze getroffenen Massnehmen. Die Gewerbeaufsicht in Europa. Jena, Gustav Fischer, 1911.
3. Teleky, Dr. L.—II. Internationaler Kongress für Berufskrankheiten, Brüssel, 10.-14. September 1910. (Separatabdruck aus der österreichischen Vierteljahresschrift für Gesundheitspflege) Wien, Moritz Perles, 1911.
4. Srbik, Fritz V.—Die wichtigsten europäischen Auswanderungsgesetze mit Berückeichtigung der beiden österreichischen Entwürfe. Wien. Staatsdruckerei, 1911.
5. Internationaler Arbeiterschutz. H. G. Z. 1911. XV, G. R. 1912. IV. 3.

International Labor Organizations.

1. Generalkommission der Gewerkschaften Deutschlands. Achter Internationaler Bericht über die Gewerkschaftsbewegung 1910. Berlin, Selbstverlag, 1911.
2. Der 7. Internationale Bericht über die Gewerkschaftsbewegung vom Jahre 1909. Tex. 1911. XXIII. 47, 49; C. G. D. 1911. XXI. 31, 32; Gew. 1911. XV. 27.
3. Leipart.—Die internationale Union der Holzarbeiter. B. Intl. 1911. 45.
4. Von der Internationalen Vereinigung der Textilarbeter. A. G. 1911. 12.
5. Der achte internationale Bericht über die gewerkschaftsbewegung im Jahre 1910. 1911. XXII. 3, 4, 6. C. G. D.

1912.

International Labor Congresses.

1. Internationaler Kongress für Hygiene und Demographie, Washington 23.-30. September 1912. M. R. 1912. XX. 23.
2. III. Internationaler medizinischer Unfallkongress in Düsseldorf. M. R. 1912. XX. 17, 18.
3. XXIII. internationaler Bergarbeiterkongress. B. Arb. 1912. XV. 29-32; C. G. D. 1912. XXII. 31.
4. Der VI. internationale Buchdruckerkongress vom 12.-15. August 1912 in Stuttgart. C. G. D. 1912. XXII. 35.
5. Der VI. internationale Kongress christlicher Textilarbeiterorganisationen. T. Z. 1912. XIV. 32, 33.
6. Internationaler Kongress der Krankenpflegerinnen. M. R. 1912. XX. 21; Fr, 1912. XVIII.
7. Internationales Kürschner-Sekretariat. Protokoll der Verhandlungen der V. Internationalen Kürschner-Konferenz; abgehalten in Wien am 30.-31. Juli und 1. August 1912. Berlin, A. Regge, 1912.
8. Zimmerman, W.—Die Internationale Konferenz über die Arbeitszeit in industrien mit ununterbrochenem Betriebe S. P. 1912. XXI. 38.
9. Der I. Internatonale Technische Kongress für Unfallverhütung und industrielle Hygiene in Mailand 27.-31. Mai. 1912. Z. G. H. 1912. XIX. 8-10.
10. Zimmerman, W.—Die VII. Delegiertversammlung der Internationalen Vereinigung für gesetzlichen Arbeiterschutz in Zürich. S. P. 1912. XXI. 51.
11. Internationale Vereinigung für gesetzlichen Arbeiterschutz. Z. C. G. D. 1912. XII. 20; W. A. Z. 1912. XIV. 40.
12. Freund, R.—Internationale Soziale Woch. S. P. 1912. XXI. 45.
13. Die soziale Woche in Zürich 2.-12. September 1912. A. S. 1912. XXIII. 20; Sch. 1912. XXVI. 38, 39.
14. II. Internationaler Heimarbeiterkongress, Zürich 8. September 1912. M. R. 1912. XX. 20.

BIBLIOGRAPHY

International Labor Legislation.

1. Jastrow, J.—Arbeiterschutz (Textbücher zu Studien über Wirtschaft und Staat) Berlin, G. Reimer, 1912.
2. Die Schutzgesetzgebung für Frauenarbeit in den verschiedenen Ländern (La legislation du travail des femmes dans les différents pays). La Hague Correspondence internationale, 1912.
3. Deutschland und der internationale Arbeiterschutz. Sch. 1912. XXVI. 14.
4. Internationler Arbeiterschutz. H .G. Z. 1911. XV; G. R. 1912. IV. 3.
5. Vom internationlen Arbeiterschutz. Z. C. G. D. 1912. XII. 14; W. A. Z. 1912. XIV. 27; Tex. 1912. XXIV. 49.
6. Der gesetzliche Arbeiterschutz auf der VII. Delegiertenversammlung der internationalen Vereinigung in Zürich. K. Bl. 1912. XVI. 39.

International Labor Organizations.

1. Generalkommission der Gewerkschaften über die Gewerkschaftsbewegung 1911. Berlin, Selbstverlag, 1912.
2. Internationales Jahrbuch für Politik und Arbeiterbewegung. Jahrgang 1912. Berlin, Vorwärts, 1912.
3. Die Gewerkschaftsinternationale 1910. S. P. 1912. XXI. 21, 32.
4. Die Stärke und Leistungsfähigkeit der internationalen Gewerkschaften Oesterreichs im Jahre 1911. Gsch. 1912. XIV. 1.
5. Jochade, H.—Die internationale Transport—arbeiter—Föderation, Berlin, Selbstverlag, 1912.

1913.

1. Die internationale Entwicklung der Arbeiterversicherung. P. 1913. XXII. 2-5.
2. Das Abkommen zwischen Deutschland und Italien über Arbeiterversicherung. S. P. 1912-1913. XXII. 27.
3. Das Weltparlament. Der IX. internationale Genossenschaftskongress in Glasgow im August 1913. I. G. 1913. VI. 8.
4. Moldenhauer, P.—Internationale Fortschritte der Sozialversicherung, Hannover, Helwing, 1913.

International Labor Congresses.

1. Die zweite internationale Arbeiterschutzkonferenz in Bern vom 15. bis 23. September 1913. Frk. z. 1913. VIII. 275. Erstes Morgenblatt.
2. Eine internationale Arbeiterschutzkonferenz. Gsch. 1913. XV. 9.
3. Eine neue internationale Arbeiterschutzkonferenz. C. G. D. 1913. XXIII. 8.
4. Der VIII. internationale Hutarbeiterkongress in Mailand 15.-19. September 1912. C. G. D. 1913. XXIII. 2.
5. III. Internationale Konferenz der Sattler und Portefeuiller. C. G. D. 1913. XXIII. 22.

6. Die zweite Internationale Arbeiterschutzkonferenz der Industriestaaten Europas. S. P. 1912/1913. XXII. 52. 1913/1914. XXIII. 1; Z. G. H. 1913. XX. 17, 18; C. G. D. 1913. XXII. 41; A. S. 1913. XX. 20
7. Die Internationale Berner Konferenz über den Jugendlichenschutz und die österreichischen Industriellen. S. P. 1913/1914. XXIII. 3.
8. Die Rolle Oesterreichs auf der internationalen Arbeiterschutzkonferenz in Bern. O.e.M. 1913. XXIII. 41.
9. III. Internationaler Kongress für Gewerbekrankheiten im September 1913 in Wien. A. S. 1913. XXIV. 14, Z. G. H. 1913. XX. 13-14.
10. Bayer.—Zum II. Internationalen Kongresse für Rettungswesen und Unfallverhütung in Wien. Z. G. H. 1913. XX. 21-22.
11. II. Internationler Kongress für Rettungswesen und Unfallverhütung in Wien, 9. bis 13. September 1913. Z. G. H. 1913. XX. 15-18; O.e.M. 1913. XXIII. 39.
12. Bureau der Internationalen Vereinigung für gesetzlichen Arbeiterscutz. Schriften. M. 8. Verhandlungsbericht der siebenten Generalversammlung des Komitees, abgehalten zu Zürich vom 10.-12. September 1912, nebst Jahresberichten der Internationalen Vereinigung und des Internationalen Arbeitsamtes und dem Berichte der Spezialkommission über Arbeitszeit in ununterbrochenen Betrieben. Jena, G. Fischer, 1913.
13. Der X. Internationale Wohnungskongress. S. P. 1913/1914. XXIII. 3; M. R. V. K. 1913. IX. 9.
14. Erste Generalversammlung der Internationalen Vereinigung zur Bekämpfung der Arbeitslosigkeit vom 5.-9. September 1913 in Gen. S. P. 1912/1913. XXII. 51.
15. Bloch, W.—Der internationale Jugendschutzkongress in Brüssel 23.-26. Juli 1913; C. 1913. XX. 22; S. P. 1912/1913. XXII. 49.
16. Lederer, M.—Zum internationalen Jugendfürsorgekongress in Brüssel; Z. K. J. 1913. V. 7-9.
17. VIII. Internationale Konferenz der Vertreter der Gewerkschaftlichen Landeszentralen und Konferenz der internationalen Berufssekretäre am 16, 17. und 18. September 1913 in Zürich. G. R. S. 1913. V. 9. Ku. 1913. XXVIII. 29; C. G. D. 1913. XXIII. 40.
18. Die Kommissionssitzungen der Internationalen Vereinigung für gesetzlichen Arbeiterschutz in Basel, (Kinderarbeit und Bleifrage in der keramischen Industrie.) S. P. 1912/1913. XXII. 51.
19. XXIV. internationaler Bergarbeiterkongress. B. Arb. 1913. XVI. 31-33.
20. Kummer, F.—Zum internationalen Metallarbeiterkongress vom 6. August und folgende Tage in Berlin. Ku. 1913. XXVIII. 22, 25.
21. VII. Internationaler Metallarbeiterkongress. C. G. D. 1913. XXIII. 34; O.e.M. 1913, XXIII. 29-31, 33.
22. Internationaler Kongress der Diamantarbeiter. C. G. D. 1913. XXIII. 47.

23. Ein internationaler Steinarbeiterkongress. C. G. D. 1913. XXIII. 46, Sten. 1913. VII. 4.
24. Internationaler Holzarbeiterkongress in Wien 1914 (4 sprachig). B. Intl. 1913. September-Oktober.
25. Internationale Konferenz der Buchbinderverbände. C. G. D. 1913. XXIII. 32.
26. III. Internationale Konferenz der Zimmerer am 15. und 16. Dezember 1913 zu Hamburg. Z. 1913. XXV. 52.
27. Der IX. internationale Baumwollkongress in Scheveningen. Tex. 1913. XXV. 28.
28. VI. Internationale Schneiderkonferenz. C. G. D. 1913. XXIII. 32.
29. VIII. Internationaler Transportarbeiterkongress, abgehalten zu London am 26. August 1913 und den folgenden Tagen. Cr. 1913. XVII. 36, 37; G. R. S. 1913. V. 9; C. G. D. 1913. XXIII. 40.
30. Zur III. internationalen Konferenz der Arbeiter öffentlicher Betriebe in Zürich vom 23. bis 25. September 1913. Gew. 1913. XVII. 33, 40, 41.
31. Protokolle der internationalen Konferenz für Arbeiterschutz. Bern 15.-25. September 1913. Bern, Stampfli, 1913.
32. Internationales Sekretariat der Arbeiter öffentlicher Betriebe. Protokoll der III. Internationalen Konferenz der Arbeiter öffentlicher Betriebe; abgehalten vom 23. bis 25. September 1913 in Zürich. Berlin, Selbstverlag, 1913.
33. Protokoll über die Verhandlungen des IV. Steinarbeiterkongresses abgehalten am 12. und 13. Oktober 1913 in Brüssel. Zürich, Genossenschaftsdruckerei, 1913.
34. Hopf, F. E.—Bericht über den III. Internationalen Kongress für Wohnungshygiene in Dresden vom 2.-7. Oktober 1911. Dresden, Buchdruckerei der Dr. Güntz'schen Stiftung, 1913.
35. Internationaler Metallarbeiterbund. Berichte der angeschlossenen Landesverbände an den VII. internationalen Metallarbeiterkongress in Berlin 1913. Stuttgart, A. Schlicke, 1913.
36. III. internationale Konferenz der Sattler, Taschner, Riemer und ortfeuiller, abgehalten in Wien 9. und 10. Mai 1913. Berlin, Joh, Sassenbach, 1913.
37. Internationales Buchbindersekretariat. Protokoll der III. internationalen Konferenz von Vertretern der Buchbinderverbände, abgehalten in Brüssel 23.-26. Juni 1913. (4 sprachig) Berlin, Selbstverlag, 1913.
38. Schuler, H.—Internationale Konferenz für Arbeiterschutz 1913. Zürich, Berichthaus, 1913.
39. Sekretariat des Internationalen Metallarbeiterfundes. Der VII. internationale Metallarbeiterkongress am 6. und 7. August 1913 im gewerkschaftshaus in Berlin. Offizieler Bericht. (Deutsch, französisch, und englisch) Stuttgart, Schlicke, 1913.
40. Internationales Buchdrucker-Sekretariat in Stuttgart; Protokoll des VI. internationalen Buchdrucker-Kongresses in Stuttgart 12.-15, August 1912, Stuttgart, Selbstverlag, 1913.

THE INTERNATIONAL PROTECTION OF LABOR

International Labor Legislation.

1. Reichesberg, N.—Der internationale Arbeiterschutz in den letzten 12 Jahren. Bern, M. Drechsel, 1913.
2. Internationaler Arbeiterschutz. G. 1913. XIV. 16.
3. Bauer, St.—Fortgang und Tragweite der internationalen Arbeiterschutzverträge. A. S. G. 1913. III. 1-2.
4. Schaeffer, A.—Die Stickereiindustrie und internationaler Arbeiterschutz. S. B. H. I. 1913. XX. 9.
5. Der internationale Arbeiterschutz in den letzten 12 Jahren. Am. 1913. XL. 37.
6. Die Arbeiterschutzgesetzgebung des europäischen Auslandes im Jahre 1912. A. S. 1913. XXIV. 1913.

International Labor Organizations.

1. Internationale Tansportarbeiter-Föderation: Die sozial-ökonomischen rechtlichen und organisatorischen Verhältnisse sowie Streiks und Lohnbewegungen der Eisenbahner Strassenbahner, Seeleute, Hafen— und Transportarbeiter etc. aller Länder währnd 1908 und 1909. Bericht über die Hafen-Inspektion in verschiedenen Ländern. Bericht über die Lohn-und Arbeitsverhältnisse der Chauffeure. Berlin, H. Jochade.
2. Der neunte internationale Bericht über die Gewerkschaftsbewegung vom Jahre 1911. C. G. D. 1912. XXIII. 9-11.
3. Die internationale Gewerkschaftsbewegung im Jahre 1911. Gsch. 1913. XV. 4.
4. Brod, J.—Eine internationale Statistik der Betriebsunfälle. A. S. 1913. XXIV. 7.
5. Die Gewerkschaftsbewegung in Deutschland und Oesterreich, die Arbeitersozialpolitik und die Kämpfe zwischen Unternehmern und Arbeitern im Jahre 1912. (Separatabdruck aus Band 36, Heft 2. 1913 des Archivs für Sozialwissenschaft und Sozialpolitik). Tübingen, J. C. B. Mohr, 1913.
6. Laderer, E.—Jahrbuch der sozialen Bewegung in Deutschland und Oesterreich 1912. VIII. +227. Tübingen, J. C. B. Mohr, 1913.
7. Internationales aus der Gewerkschaftsbewegung. S. P. 1913/1914. XXIII. 5, 6.
8. Die internationalen Beziehung der deutschen Arbeitgeber-, Angestellten- und Arbeiterverbände. R. A. 1913. XI. 12.
9. Heyde, L.—Die Berufsvereine des Auslandes. S. P. 1913/1914. XXIII. 13.
10. Die Internationale Union der Holzarbeiter im Jahre 1913. B. Intl. 1913. Dezember.
11. Internationaler Metallarbeiter-Bund. Bericht des Sekretärs an den VII. internationalen Metallarbeiterkongress zu Berlin (3 sprachig). 24 p. Stuttgart, A. Schlicke, 1913.

BIBLIOGRAPHY

12. Statut der Internationalen Buchbinderföderation und des Internationalen Buchbindersekretariats nebst Gegenseitigkeitsvertrag=Statuts de la Fédération Internationale des Relieurs et du Secretariat International des Relieurs avec Contrat de Réciprocité—Rules of the International Bookbinders' Union and of the International Bookbinders' Secretariat with Reciprocal Agreement. Berlin, Selbstverlag, 1913.
13. Internationale Transportarbeiter-Föderation. Berichte der Organisationen über die sozial-ökonomischen, rechtlichen und organisatorischen Verhältnisse der Eisenbahner, Strassenbahner, Seeleute, Hafen- und Transportarbeiter etc. aller Länder während 1910, 1911 und 1912. Berlin, H. Jochade, 1913.
14. Bericht des Zentralrats der Internationalen Transportarbeiter-Föderation an den Internationalen Kongress, abgehalten vom 26. bis 30 August 1913 in London. Berlin, H. Jochade, 1913.
15. Generalkommission der Gewerkschaften Deutschlands. X. Internationaler Bericht über die Gewerkschaftsbewegung, 1912. Berlin, Selbstverlag, 1913.

1914.

International Labor Congresses.

1. Bütow.—43. Versammlung des Internationalen Verbandes der Dampfkessel-Ueberwachungsvereine in Moskau 1913. S. T. 1914. XIII. 8.
2. Internationaler Textilarbeiter-Kongress in Blackpool (England) vom 8. bis 13. Juni 1914; T. B. 1914. XIII. 26; Tex. W. 1914. XV. 25, 26.
3. Unser Kongress in Wien. (Internationale Holzarbeiter-Union). B Intl. (4 sprachig) 1914. XI. 2-6.
4. III. Internationale Konferenz der Zimmerer. Zo. 1914. X. 1, 2.
5. Verhandlungen des III. internationalen medizinischen Unfallkongresses zu Düsseldorf 1912. Düsseldorf, Schwann.
6. Internationaler genossenschaftsbund. Protokoll der Verhandlungen des IX. Kongresses des F. G. B. Glasgow, 25-28. August 1913, London, Selbstverlag, 1914.

International Labor Legislation.

1. Bauer, St.—Fortgang und Tragweite der internationalen Arbeiterschutzverträge. A. S. G. 1914. III.
2. Francke, E.—Die internationalen Arbeiterschutzverträge. S. P. 1914. XXIII. 37.
3. Stojentin, V.—Zur Frage der internationalen Vereinbarungen für gesetzlichen Arbeiterschutz. A. G. 1914. 10.
4. Die Arbeitsgesetzgebung des Auslands im Jahre 1913. A. S. 1914. XXV. 9.
5. Internationale Vereinigung für gesetzlichen Arbeiterschutz. 2 Denkschriften zur Vorbereitung der II. internationalen Arbeiterschutzkonferenz von Bern 1913. Jena, Fscher, 1914.

International Labor Organizations.

1. Legien, C.—Die gewerkschaftliche Internationale 1910 bis 1913. S. M. 1914. XX. I. Band. 1. Heft.
2. Die internationale Gewerkschaftsbewegung im Jahre 1912. Gsch. 1914. XVI. 12-14.
3. Braun, A.—Die internationalen Beziehungen der gewerkschaften. N. Z. 1914. XXXIII. 1. 3. 4.
4. Internationaler Bericht über die Gewerkschaftsbewegung vom Jahre 1912. C. G. D. 1914. XXIV. 16-18.
5. III. Bericht über die internationale Organisation der Fabrikarbeiter. P. 1914. XXIII. 3, 5, 6.
6. Heiss, Cl.—Die Berufsvereine des Auslandes. V. Bl. 1914. XIII. 1-4.
7. Berichte der angeschlossen Verbände an den Internationalen Kongress der Holzarbeiter. (viersprachig). B. Intl. 1914. XI. 7, 9.
8. Die Internationale Union der Holzarbeiter im Jahre 1913. (viersprachig) B. Intl. 1914. XI. 10.
9. Oesterreichisches Komitee für internationale Sozialversicherung. Veröffentlichungen aus Anlass der für September 1914 in Paris anberaumten internationalen Sozialversicherungskonferenz. Referate von Schmitt, Kaan, Eldersch, Kienböch, Kögler, Widholz, Schnitzler, Blaschke, Oe. Zop. V. 1914. V. 1-2.

1915.

International Labor Legislation.

1. Kampffmeyer, P.—Internationale Vereinbarungen und Arbeiterklasse. S. M. 1915. XXI. 12.
2. Arbeiterschutzgesetzgebung des Auslandes im Jahre 1914. A. S. 1915. XXVI. 7.

International Labor Organizations.

1. Braun, A.—Internationale Verbindung der Gewerkschaften, A. S. S. 1915. XXXIX. 3.
2. Kampffmeyer, P.—Die internationalen Verbindungen der Gewerkschaften. S. M. 1915. XXI. iii. Oktober-Dezember.
3. Winnig, A.—Der Krieg und die gewerkschaftliche Internationale. S. M. 1915. XXI. 1.
4. Die europäischen Gewerkschaften während der Kriegzeit. Gr. 1915. XXVIII. 11.
5. Die Stärke und Leistungsfähigkeit der internationalen Gewerkschaften Oesterreichs im Jahre 1914. Gsch. 1915. XVII. 28.
6. Die Metallarbeiter der Vereinigten Staaten und der Internationale Metallarbeiter-Bund (Dreisprachig). I. M. R. 1915. X. 10.
7. Reid, W. H.—Aus der Geschichte der "International Union of Timberworkers" in America. (4 sprachig) B. Intl. 1915. XII. 4.

PUBLICATIONS IN FRENCH.

1. Boilley.—Législation internationale du travail.
2. Malon.—Précis de socialisme. p. 242 et suiv.

BIBLIOGRAPHY

3. Gauwes.—Traité d'Economie politique, t. III.
4. Traité de Législation industrielle, p. 172 et suiv. 544 et suiv. (Paul Pic).
5. Bulletin de l'office internationall du travail.
6. Bulletin trimestriel de l'association internationale pour la lutte contre le chômage.
7. Bulletin des Assurances Sociales.
8. Bulletin de la commission internationale permanente pour l'etude des maladies professionelles.
9. Crick, D.—La législation internationale du travail. *Revue de Droit international*, annee 1905. p. 432 et 543.
10. Armand-Hahn, J. P.—Annales des sciences politiques. Vol. XX. p. 156.
11. Brants.—(V.)—Législation du travail comparée et internationale, 1903.
12. Massé, Daniel.—Législation du travail et lois ouvrières.
13. Richard, Albert.—L'Association internationale des travailleurs.
14. Cheysson, F.—La réglementation internationale du travail. L'internationalisme dans la question sociale, *Réforme sociale*, No. 98-99, 16 janv. et 1 février 1890.
15. Curti, Th. (député).—Un office international pour la protection du travail, *Revue politique et parlement*. mai. 1896.
16. Dekurtins, Dr.—Mémoire sur la question de la protection ouvrière, Berne 1889.
La législation internationale des travailleurs, 1891.
17. Numa Droz.—La législation internationale du travail, *Revue suisse*, février 1889.
18. Jacquemins, Rolin.—Article de la *Revue de droit international*, 1890, t. XXII. p. 21 et suiv.
19. Leroy-Beaulieu, Paul.—La conférence internationale de Berne. *Economiste francais*, 4 mai 1889.
20. Journal, *Le Temps*.—Numéros des 2, 8, 11 février, 14, 20 mars, 1 avril 1890.
21. Mahaim.—La question de la protection internationale des travailleurs, *Revue d'Economie polit*. 1888.
22. Politis, Dr. E. Nicholas.—La Conférence de Berlin, *Revue internationale de sociologie*, juil.—aout 1894.
23. Rescrits de Guillaume II.—*Revue de Droit international*, 1890 tome 1. —*Revue des Deux-Mondes*, 1 Mars 1890.—*Revue socialiste*, 1890, tome I.
24. Lohmann|—Législation industrielle des Etats du continent européen.
25. Serwy.—Le mouvement ouvrier socialiste international, *l' Avenr social*, février 1902.
26. Jamais Emile.—Article de la *Revue bleue*, 15 Mars 1890.
27. Réforme Sociale.—Numéros de janv. à juin 1889, p. 81 et 82, 92 et 93, 16 janvier 1890, p. 94.

28. **Congrès de Zurich 1897.**—*Revue socialiste,* octobre 1897. *Revue d'Economie politique,* art. d'Albert Dufourg, p. 598.—*Revue du Droit public,* 198, p. 73 et suiv.
29. Pic, Paul.—Article sur le Congrès de Bruxelles, 1897.
    Revue d'Economie politique, 1897, p. 1053 en collaboration avec M. Brouilhet.
    Revue de Droit public et de la science politique, 1897, p. 559.
    Annales de Droit commercial 1898, p. 253.
    Annuaire de la société d'économie politique de Lyon, années 1897-1898.
30. Guyot, Yves.—*Revue politique et parlementaire,* décembre 1897.
31. Dejace.—*Réforme sociale,* novembre 1897. *Journal des Economistes.*—Numéro de décembre 1897. Article sur le Congrès d'Anvers 1898, numéro d'octobre 1898.
32. Rapin, Oscar.—*Revue socialiste,* octobre 1897.
33. Tabacovici (Georges) . . . De la Législation internationale du travail, 1896.
34. Descamps, Chevalier.—Les offices internationaux et leur avenir, *Bulletin de l'Académie royale de Belgique,* année 1894.
35. Pic, Paul.—Article sur le Congrès international pour la protection légale des travailleurs de Paris, juillet 1900, *Questions pratiques de législation ouvrière et d'Economie sociale,* 1900, p. 250 et suiv.
36. Godart, J.—Article sur le Congrès international de Bâle, 1901, *Questions pratiques,* 1901, p. 316 et suiv.
37. Pic, Paul.—*Revue d'Economie politique,* 1901, p. 689, le Congrès de Paris 1900.
38. Lévy, G.—Congrès de Cologne 1902, *Questions pratiques,* 1902, p. 363 et suiv.
39. Pic, Paul.—Rapport au Congrès de Cologne sur l'interdiction du travail de nuit des femmes, *Questions pratiques,* 1902, p. 299 et suiv.
40. Millerand, A.—Les traités de travail, la réunion de Bâle 1903. *Revue politique et parlementaire,* 10 octobre 1903.
41. Lichtenberger.—La législation ouvrière et le mouvement industrial moderne, conféfence faite à Nancy, 1903, Imprimerie Pierron.
42. Jacquemins, Rolin.—La Conférence de Berlin, *Economiste francais,* 1 mars 1891.
43. Morisseaux (directeur de l'office du travail de Belgique).—La législation du travail.
44. Valleroux, Hubert.—La législation internationale du travail, *Economiste francais,* 1897, 2 semestre, p. 627 et 725.
45. Michel, Georges.—Compte-rendu de la séance de la société d'économie politique de Paris du 6 décembre 1897, *Economiste francais,* 1897, 2 semestre p. 765.
46. Descamps, Chevalier.—Essai sur l'organisation de l'arbitrage international, *Revue de droit international et législation comparée,* 1896, t. XXVIII, p. 1.

BIBLIOGRAPHY

47. Simon, Jules.—Rapport sur la conférence de Berlin 1890.
48. Archives diplomatiques, tome, XXXIII. 1890, p. 179.
49. Compte rendu du Congrès international du patronage de la jeunesse ouvrière tenu à Paris du 10 au 13 juin 1900.
50. Congrès international du patronage de la jeunesse ouvrière, tenu à Paris du 10 au 13 juin 1900. Procèsverbaux sommaires, par P. Griffaton (secrétaire général du congrès) 27 S. Paris, 1901.
51. Congrès international des accidents de travail et des assurances sociales, 5. session tenue à Paris du 23 au. 30 juin 1900. Tome 1. Rapports présentés. Paris, 1901.
52. Publications de l'Association internationale pour la protection légale des travailleurs. No. 1. L'Association internationale pour la protection légale des travailleurs. Assemblée constitutive tenue à Bâle les 27 et 28 septembre 1901. Rapports et compte-rendu des séances publiés par le Bureau de l'Association internationale pour la protection légale des travailleurs. Paris, H. Le Soudier; Jena, G. Fischer; Berne, Schmid & Francke, 1901.
53. Courcelle, B.—Traité de la législation ouvrière. Paris, 1901.
54. Congrès international des accidents du travail et des assurances sociales, tenu à Paris du 23 au 30 juin 1900. Paris, Béranger.
55. Brants, Prof. Victor.—Législation du travail comparée et internationale. Essai d'introduction. Louvain, Ch. Peeters; Paris, V. Lecoffre, 1902.
56. L'Association internationale pour la protection légale des travailleurs: le Congrès de Cologne. M. S. VII. Octobre.
57. Le XIII. Congrès international des mineurs et les projets de secrétariat permanent. M. S. VII. Oct.
58. L'Association internationale pour la protection légale des travailleurs. B. O. T. IX. 12.
59. Brants, V.—Législation du travail comparée et internationale. Paris, Lecoffre et Louvain, 1903.
60. Moucy, R. de—Traité sur les accidents du travail. Exposé de la législation et de la jurisprudence. Paris. P. Dupont, 1902.
61. Réunion de la Commission de l'Association internationale pour la protection légale des travailleurs. B. O. T. X. 9.
62. Le XI. congrès international d'hygiène et de démographie. B. O. T. X. 9.
63. Les revendication des mineurs et le congrès international de Londres. M. S. 1901. VI. 8.
64. Procès-verbal de la conférence typographique internationale tenue les 14 et 15 avril 1903 à l'hôtel de ville de Strasbourg (Alsace). Bâle 1903.
65. Réunion de la Commission de l'Association internationale pour la protection légale des travailleurs. B. O. T. X. 9.
66. Lemire.—Congrès international des Jardins ouvriers, 24-25 oct. 1903. Paris, Chevalier et Rivière. Compte-rendu.

67. Fédération internationale des employés. Congrès international, tenu à Bruxelles en 1903. Compte-rendu stenographique, Liège, L. Mercenier.
68. La mise en vigeur de la convention de travail franco-italienne du 15 avril 1904. B. O. T. XI. 10.
69. Compte-rendu du congrès international des accidents du travail et des assurances sociales à Paris, 23-30 juin 1900.
70. Brants, Victor.—Ou en est la législation internationale du travail? *Revue sociale catholique,* janvier 1900.
71. Mahaim, E.—Etudes sur l'association professionelle. Liège, Imp. Vaillant-Carmanne, 1890, I Vol. in 8.
72. Renaudel, Pierre.—Pour la socialisme, broch. de 128 pages, Paris, 1903.
73. Brisson, Pierre.—Histoire du travail et des travailleurs, p. 481 et suiv.
74. Chatelain, L.—La protection internatonale ouvrière.
75. Archives diplomatiques (2 Serie) 1890. t. XXXIII. p. 325-328, p. 373-374; t. XXXIV. p. 269-276; t. XXXV. p. 18-74, 137-185; t. XXXVI. p. 15-78; (3 Serie) 1904. t. 92. p. 1269-1274.

1904

1. Association international pour la protection légale des travailleurs. Discussions de la Section nationale francaise. Paris, Alcan, 1904.
2. Jay, R.—La protection légale des travailleurs, Paris ,1904.
3. Mahaim.—Protection internationale du travail, *Revue économique internationale,* octobre 1904.
4. Barrault, Henry Emile.—La convention franco-italienne du 15 avril 1904, *Bulletin de la Société de protection des apprentis,* juillet-aout-septembre, 1904.
5. Alfassa, Maurice.—L'Association internationale pour la protection légale des travailleurs, *Revue politique et parlementaire,* 10 novembre 1904, p. 330.
6. Brants, Victor.—La protection internationale du travail, Louvain, *Institut sup. de philosophie,* année 1904.
7. Rapport annuel du Secretariat typographique international pro 1903. Bâle, Schweig. Typographenbund. 1904.

International Labor Conferences.

1. L'Association internationale pour la protection légale des travailleurs: le congres de Bâlè (septembre 1904) B. O. T. 1904. XI. No. 11.
2. Le congrès socialiste international d'Amsterdam. M. S. 1904. Annales No. 10.
3. Pic, Paul.—Une étape decisive, le traité de travail franco-italien, *Questions pratiques,* année 1904, p. 120.

Le Congrès de Bâle, 1904, *Questions pratiques,* année 1904, p. 413 et suiv. et année 1905, p. 4 et suiv.

La convention franco-italienne du 15 avril 1904 et le Droit internationale, *Revue generale de Droit international public,* t. XI. 1904, p. 515.

4. Brants, V.—L'entente internationale pour la protection du travail à l'assemblee de Bâle. (Sept. 1904) Réf. Soc. XXIV. 22.
5. Congrès international des Accidents du Travail et des Assurances Sociales. Bulletin du Comité permanent. Quinzièmé année, 1904. No. 2. Mai-Juni. Paris.
6. Mahaim, Ernest.—L'Association internationale pour la protection légale des travailleurs. Son histoire—son—but—son oeuvre. Extrait de la Revue économique internationale. Oktobre 1904. Bruxelles, J. Goemare.

1905.

1. Rapport annuel du Secrétariat typographique international pour 1904. Bâle, Schweiz. Typographenbund. 1905.
2. La Législation internationale de la mutualité. Dev. 1905. t. 29 Sept.
3. Association internationale pour la protection légale des travailleurs. Deux mémoires présentés aux gouvernements des Etats industriels en vue de la convocation d'une conférence internationale de protection ouvrière. Paris. Levrault & Co., 1905.
4. Archives diplomatiques, 1905, Vol. III. p. 271.
5. Revue de Droit international, 1905, p. 432. (D. Crick).
6. Pic, Paul.—Revue de Droit international privé, 1905, p. 259.

International Labor Conferences.

1. La conférence internationale pour la protection des ouvriers. Dev. 1905. t. 29. Février.
2. La conférence internationale pour la protection des travailleurs. M. S. X. 1905. Annales. No. 2.
3. Pic, Paul.—La quatrième Congrès de l'association internationale pour la protection légale des travailleurs, Bâle, septembre 1904 Q. P. 1905. No. 2.
4. Le VI. Congrès de l'alliance cooperative internationale M. S. 1904. Annales, No. 11 Dev. (t. 29.) janvier 1905.
5. Union typographique internationale Convention annuelle, Dominion of Canada. L. G. 1905. VI. 3.
6. Pic, P..—Le Congrès de Berne 1905, Q. P. 1905. p. 94 et suiv., 159 et suiv.
Rapport présenté au Congrès international de Droit comparé.
La condition juridique des travailleurs étrangers, *Journal de Droit international privé*. 1905. p. 273 et suiv, et 860 et suiv.
7. Congrés international de la tuberculose à Paris du 2 au 7 octobre 1905. *Revue d'Hygiene et de Police sanitaire.* 1905. XXVII. No. 4, Paris.
8. Compte-rendu officiel du sixième Congrès de l'alliance coopérative internationale. Paris, Guillaumin & Co., 1905.
9. Brants, V.—La conférence internationale de Berne pour la protection du travail. Réf. Soc. 1905. XXV. No. 17.
10. Pic, P.—Le quatrième congrès de l'Association internationale pour la protection légale des travailleurs. Bâle. sept. 1904. Q. P. 1905. No. 6.

11. Hahn, A.—L'Association internationale pour la protection légale des travailleurs. *Annales des Sciences Politiques,* 1905. Mars. Paris.
12. Mahaim, E.—La conférence de Berne concernant la protection ouvrère. Rev. ec. i. 1905. II. 3.
13. La conférence internationale de Berne pour la protection ouvrière. Rev. Tr. 1905. No. 6; B. O. T. 1905. XII. No. 6.
14. Congrès international de la tuberculose à Paris du 2 au 4 octobre 1905. *Revue d'Hygiene et de Police sanitaire,* 1905. XXVII. No. 4. Paris.
15. Rollin, A.—Au congrès international de la mutualité. *Solidarité sociale.* 1905. 15.
16. Millerand, A.—La conférence officielle de Berne, 1905, Paris, 1905.

1906.

1. Raynaud, B.—Droit international ouvrier, Paris, 1906.
2. Mahaim.—Rev. écon. internat., novembre 1906.
3. Martin Saint-Leon.—La protection légale des travailleurs, Musée social, octobre 1906.
4. Brants.—L'Association pour la protection légale des travailleurs, *Revue sociale catholique,* décembre 1906.

International Labor Conferences.

1. Conventions internationales de Berne sur l'interdiction du travail de nuit des femmes et sur l'interdiction de l'emploi du prosphors blanc dans l'industrie des allumettes. B. O. T. 1906. XIII. 11.
2. La 4 assemblée générale de l'Association internationale pour la protection légale des travailleurs. B. O. T. 1906. XIII. 13.
3. L'Association international pour la protection légale des travailleurs. A. cath. 1906. XXXI. t. LXII. 6.
4. 5 congrès international de la science de l'assurance, Acc. et Ass. 1906. XVII. 3.
5. XVII congres international des mincurs. M. S. 1906.
6. Les conventions internationales de Berne. A. cath. 1906. XXXI. t. LXII. 5.
7. Mahaim, E.—Protection ouvrière internationale. Les conventions de Berne et l'Assemblée de Genève. Rev. éc. int. 1906. November.
8. Brants, V.—L'Association pour la protection légale du travail. 1 session de Genève (26-29 septembre 1906) R. S. C. 1906. Dec.
9. Chaptal, L.—Le congrès international du tuberculose. Ref. Soc. 1906. XXVI. 2.
10. Congrès international de sans emploi. Dominion of Canada. L. G. 1906. VI. 11.
11. Premier congrès international contre le chômage. Dec. 1906. XXX. Mai.
12. Mahaim.—La protection ouvrière internationale, la convention de Genève et l'Assemblée de Genève, Revue économique internationale, novembre, 1906.

International Labor Legislation.

1. Office du Travail de Belgique, Annuaire de la législation du travail, année 1905. Bruxelles. 1906.

1907.

1. Wodon, M. L.—Project de Convention Internationale relative aux Accidents du travail. Nr. VII. des publications du Comité Belge pour le progrès de la législation du travail. 11 p. Liège, Aug. Bénard.
2. Les conventions diplomatiques pour les accidents du travail. T. N. 1907. 18. Aug.
3. Pic.—Revue générale de droit international, 1907, p. 495.

International Labor Conferences.

1. David, E.—La conférence syndicale internationale de Christiania. M. Soc. 1907. Nov. p. 420-423.
2. 8Congrès international des Assurances sociales, Rome. 12-16 octobre, 1908. Acc. et Ass. 1907. 3.
3. Amieux, A.—Quatrième Assemblée générale de l'Association internationale pour la protection légale des travailleurs, Q. P. janvier-février, 1907.
4. Pic, P.—La seconde Conférence internationale de Berne et l'Assemblée de Genève, *Revue générale de Droit international public*, mai-sout, 1907, p. 495.
5. Septième congrès d'alliance cooperative internationale tenu a Crémone en 1907. Paris. frs. 3, 50.
6. Union internationale des ouvriers du bois. 1907. Procèsverbaux des congrès internationaux des ouvriers du bois tenus a Amsterdam en 1904 et à Stuttgart en 1907.
7. Secrétariat international des ouvriers employés à la construction de routes (Paveurs). Compte-rendue de la 2e conférence internationale tenue a Leipzig, le 19 février 1907. 24 p. Berlin, A. Knoll. fr.—, 60.

International Labor Legislation.

1. De Saint-Albin, L. Etat actuel de la réglementation international du travail. (Thèse) 181 p. Paris, Giard & Brière, 1907.

International Labor Organizations.

1. Secrétaire International des Centres Nationaux des Syndicats (C. Legien) Troisième Rapport International sur le Mouvement Syndical, Berlin, C. Legien, 1907.
2. Fédération internationale des mineurs. Compte-rendu des travaux du seizième congrès international des mineurs tenu à Liège du 7 au du 7 au 11 aout 1907. Manchester, T. Ashton fils.
3. Secrétariat international des ouvriers employés à la construction de routes (Paveurs). Compte-rendu de la II. Conférence Internationale tenue à Leipzig, le 19 février 1907. Berlin, Secrétariat international. Secrétaire: A. Knoll.
4. Dumas, E.—L'organisation internationale des ouvriers métallurgiques. M. Soc. 1907. 2. p. 149-160.

5. Secrétariat du Bureau socialiste international. L'internationale ouvrière et socialiste. Rapports soumis au Congrès socialiste international de Stuttgare par les organisations socialistes d'Europe, d'Australia et d'Amérique sur leur activité pendant les années 1904-1907. Préface d'Emile Vandervelde. Bruxelles, 1907.

1908.

International Labor Legislation.

1. Bauer, Prof. Dr. Etienne La protection légalé des travailleurs et l'office international du travail 14 p. Lousanne, Payat & Cie, 1908.
2. Chatelain, L.-La protection internationale ouvrière. Thèse X. et 244. Paris, A. Rousseau, frs. 5,—
3. Metin, A. Les traités ouvrièrs. Accords internationaux de prevoyance et de travail. (Textes officielles, commentaire et historique.) 272 p. Paris, A. Colen, 1908. frs. 3, 50.
4. Boissard, A. La réalisation de l'égalité entre nationaux et étrangers, au point de vue de l'indemnisation des accidents du travail, par voie de convention, internationale. Rapport présenté à l'Association Internationale pour la protection légalé des travailleurs. Paris, F. Alcan & Guillaumin; L. Larose & L. Tenin, 1908.
5. Metin, A.—Les traités ouvriers, Paris, 1908.
6. Chatelain, L.—La protection international ouvrière.

International Labor Organizations.

I. Secrétariat International des travailleurs de la pierre. Deuxième rapport pour les années 1906 et 1907. 21 p. Berne. Impr. de l'Union (Co-opérative), 1908.

International Labor Congresses.

1. Le congrès international des mineurs. B. C. T. 1908. XIV. 12.
2. Le conférence internationale des ligues sociales d'acheteurs. Genève. 1908. 662 p. Fribourg (Suisse), Fragnière frères.
3. Secrétariat typographique internationale. Procès-verbal du Ve congrès typographique international à Paris die 9 au 13 juillet 1907. D'après le relevé sténographique. 173 p. Berne, Imprimerie coopérative, 1908.
4. Assemblée générale le l'Association internationale pour la protection légale des travailleurs. A. cath. 1908. XXXIII. 4;—B. O. T. 1908. XV. 11.
5. Mahaim, E.—L'Association internationale pour la protection légale des travailleurs à Lucern. Rev. éc. int. 1908. 15.—20. Nov.
6. Première conférence internationale des ligues sociales d'acheteurs. B. O. T. 1908. XV. 10.
7. Association internationale pour la protection légale des travailleurs. Publication No. 6. Compte-rendu de la cinquième assemblée générale du Comte de l'association internationale pour la protection légale des

travailleurs, tenue à Lucerne, les 28, 29, et 30 septembre 1908, suivi des rapports annuels de l'association internationale et de l'Office internationale du travail et de tableux synoptiques. 216 p. Paris, Berger-Levrault Cie. frs. 5, —.

1909.

International Labor Legislation.

1. Pic, P. La protection légal des travailleurs et le droit international ouvrier. 172 p. Paris, Alcan, 1909.

International Labor Congresses.

1. Fédération internationale des Travailleurs de la pierre. Procèsverbal des délibérations du IIIme Congrès international tenu à Cassel les llet 12 Avril 1908. 24 p. Berne ,Imprimerie de l'Union (Coopérative,) 1909.
2. Federation internationale des ouvriers de transport Procésvarbal du sixième congrès international des ouvriers de transport et des conférenses des travailleurs des chemins de fer et des marins. Tenus à Vienne du 24 au 29 aout 1908. Rapport du Conseil Central pour 1906, 1907, 1908, VI+ 158 p. Hambourg, H. Jochade, 1909.
3. Le projet de conférence internationale contre le chômage. B. A. S. 1909. XX. 3.
4. Bellom, M.—La conférence internationale du chômage. E. Fr. 1909. 34. p. 272-273.
5. Le deurième congrès international medical des accidents du travail. B. A. S. 1909. XX. 3.

International Labor Organizations.

1. Duplessix, E. L'organisation internationale. I. Vol., 151 p. Paris, Larose, 1909. frs. 3, —.
2. Maire, Henry.—L'organisation et la représentation des interêts professionels en Belgique, en Hollande, en Allemagne, aux Etats-Unis et en France. Paris, Jouve, 1909.

1910.

1. Office Internationale du travail. Premier rapport comparée su l'application des lois ouvrières. L'Inspection du Travail en Europe. Paris, Berger-Levrault, 1910.
2. Capitant, H.—Les conventions internationales sur les accidents du travail. R. D. I. P. 1910. Juin.
3. Le travail legislatiff en Belgique et dans les Parlements étrangers. (Décember 1909) Rev. Tr. 1910. XV. 2 (Jan.-Avr. 1910) Rev. Tr. 1910. XV. 4, 6, 8, 10.
4. Secretariat international den Travailleurs de 1 Pierre. Troisième rapport, comprenant les annés 1908-1909. Wallisellen, Zürich. F. Lienendinger & Cie.

6. Mahaim, E.—Les abonnements d'ouvriers sur les lignes de chemino de fer belge et leurs effets sociaux .(Memoires de l'Institut de sociologie Solvay, No. 11) Bruxelles, Misch et Thron, 1910, 1 Vol.
7. Annuaire du Mouvement Co-opératif Internationale. 1910.

International Labor Congresses.

1. Congrés mondial des associations internationales Bruxelles, 9-11 mai 1910. Rapport No. 17. Rapport sur l'organisation des congrés internationaux par M. C. M. Gariel Bruxelles. Secretariat du congrès, 1910.
2. Conférence internationale des Assurances Sociales. La Haya, 6-8 Septembre 1910. B. A. S. 1910. XXI.
3. Varin.—II. Congrès international des Maladies professionelles. Bruxelles 10-14 Septembre 1910. R. S. A. T. 1910. IV. 5.
4. Fédération Internationale des Ouvriers sur Métaux. Rapports des Unions affiliées des differents pays au VI. Congrès International des Ouvriers sur Métaux à Birmingham, 1910. Stuttgart, Alex Schlicke & Cie., 1910.
5. Congrès des Accidents du Travail. Bulletin des Assurances Sociales: Conférence Internationale de la Haye 6-8 Septembre 1910. Rapports et Compte-Rendu. Paris, Musée social, 1910.
6. Conférences internationales sur les réformes industrielles et sociales. D. C. 1910. XI. 5.
7. Perlstein, Max.—Les Débats du Congrès de Copenhague. M. soc. 1910. Octobre.
8. Levy, G.—Le congrès de Copenhague. Les forces de l'Internationale. *Grand Rev.* 1910. Novembre.
9. Louis, Paul.—Le congrès socialiste international de Copenhague. M. S. (Ann.) 1910. Octobre.
10. Association internationale pour la protection légale des travailleurs. Publication No. 7: Compte-rendu de la sixième assemblée générale du comité de l'Association internationale pour la protecton légale des travailleurs, Lugano 26-28 Septembre 1910, suivi de rapports annuels de l'Association internationale et de l'Office international du travail. Paris, Berger-Levrault & Cie., 1910.
11. Fédération internationale des Employés Congrès tenu à Genève les 20, 21 et 22. aout 1909. Compte-rendu analytique. Liège, Imprimerie Coopérative, 1910.
12. Picard, R.—La question du travail à domicile et le Congrès international de Bruxelles (15-17 septembre 1910) *grande Rev.* 1910. Oct.

1911

1. Le travail lélislatif dans les Parlements étrangers. Rev. Tr. 1911. XVI. 14, 18, 22, 24.
2. Combes de Lestrades: Les lois sur l'industrie en Austriche et en Allemagne. M. S. (Ann.) 1911. XVIII. 11. Supplement.

3. Mahaim, E.—Le protection légale des travailleurs. Lecture faite en la séance publique de la Classe des lettres et des sciences morales et politiques de l'Académie Royale de Belgique, le 3 mai 1917. Bruxelles, Hayez, 1911.
4. Les assurances sociales en Europe. Etude sur la législation internationale et statistique des résultats. B. S. t. R. 1911.
5. Office Central des Institutions Internationales, Bruxelles. Son Organization, ses Service, ses Travaux. Bruxelles, 1911.

International Labor Conferences.

1. Fédération Internationale des Postes, Télégraphes et Téléphones. Compte-rendu de la conférence de Paris, 6 et 7 Juin 1911. Paris, Imprimerie Veuve Denis, 1911.
2. Congrès international de Rome, Réunion der Bureau du jeudi 8 juin 1911; la grève considerée comme cas de force majeure. B. F. N. 1911. VI. 65.
3. Le Congrès international des travailleurs du bois. R. I. C. 1911. I. 1.
4. Compte-rendu de la Conférence internationale du chômage, Paris 18-21 septembre 1910. Tome 1-3. Prais. M. Rivière & Cie., 1911.
5. Mahaim, Ernest.—La session de Lugano de l'Association internationale pour la protection légale des travailleurs. Rev. éc. int. 1911. Janvier.
6. Bellom, M.—Les assurances sociales devant la Conférence de la Haye. R. P. P. 1910. Nov.; et Ass. 1911. XXII. 1.

1912.

1. Les Assurances sociales en Europe. VI. Les accords internationaux. B. O. T. 1912. XIX. 6.
2. Le travail lélislatif dans les parlements étrangers. Rev. Tr. 1912. XVII. 16.
3. Bry, G.—Cours élémentaire de législation industrielle. Paris, Société du Recueil Sirey, 1912.

International Labor Congresses.

1. Bureau de l'Association Internationale pour la Protection legale des Travailleurs. Publication No. 8. Compte-rendu de la 7 assemblée générale du comité tenue à Zurich les 10, 11, et 12 Septembre, 1912 suivi de rapports annuels de l'Association Internationale et de l'Office International du Travail. Paris, Berger-Levrault, 1912.
2. La semaine sociale de Zurich. B. O. T. 1912. XIX. 10.
3. Le congrès international du travail à domicile a Zurich les 8 et 9 septembre 1912. A. O. 1912. XIX. 539.
4. Exposition Internationale et Universelle de Bruxelles 1910. Exposition du travail à domicile. I. Congrès international du travail à domicile réuni à Bruxelles en septembre 1910. Compte-rendu des séances. Bruxelles, Misch et Thron, 1912.

1913

1. Fédération internationale des ouvriers du transport. Extrait du *Neuvième rapport international sur le mouvement syndical de* 1911. Berlin, H. Jochade, 1913.
2. Noaro, G. C.—Le convention Italo-Allemande 31 juillet 1912, 25 mars 1913. Les conditions fondamentales d'un nouveau droit international pour la prévoyance sociale. B. M. I. E. S. 1913. IV. 12.
3. Fédération Internationale des Ouvriers du Transport. Rapports des organisations sur les conditions sociales, économiques, légales et sur les conditions d'organisation du personnel des chemins de fer et des tramways, des marnes, des ouvriers des ports et du transport, etc. de tous les pays pendant les années 1910, 1911 et 1912. Berlin, H. Jochade, 1913.
4. Rapport due Conseit Central de la Fédération Internationale des Ouvriers de Transport au Congrès International tenu du 26 à 30 Aout 1913 é Londres. Berlin. H. Jochade, 1913.
5. Pic, P.—Les assurances sociales en France et à l'estranger. Paris, Alcan, 1913.
6. Office central des associations internationales. Organisation ouvrière internationale. Syndicalisme et internationalisme. Les fédérations internationales de métiers. Le secrétariat international des fédérations syndicales nationales. Bruxelles, Lamberty, 1913.
7. Mahaim, Ernest.—Le droit international ouvrier Librairie de la Societe du Recueil Sirey, 22 Rue Soufflet, Paris.

International Labor Congresses.

1. III. Conférence internationale des assurances sociales Zurich 10-11 septembre, 1912. B. A. S. 1913. XXIV. 1.
2. III. Conférence internationale des assurances sociales XI. réunion du comité permanent international des assurances sociales à Zurich 10-11 septembre 1912. (Compte-rendu preparé par les soins de P. Logoz et Ed. Fuster.) Paris, Musée social, 1913.
3. Secrétariat typographique international: Procès-verbal lu VI. congrès typographique international à Stuttgart du 12 au 15 aout 1912. Stuttgart, édition privée, 1913.
4. Pic, P.—La semains sociale de Zurich. Q. P. 1913. XIV. 1-3, 6.
5. Blondel, G.—Note sur le congrès du travail à domicile.
6. Fagnot, F. La conférence internationale de législation ouvrière. P. O. 1913. III. 21.
7. Les resolutions de la conférenz internationale de législation ouvrière. A. O. 1913. XX. 577; P. O. 1913. III. 22.
8. La conférence internationale de Berne, 15-25 septembre 1913. B. O. T. 1913. XX. 10; A. O. 1913. XX. 573.
9. La I. assemblée de l'association internationale pour la lutte contre le chômage. Gand. 5 et 6 septembre 1913. B. M. T. 1913. XX. 11; B. A. L. C. 1913. III. 3, 4.

10. Conférence internationale des Ligues sociales d'Acheteurs à Anvers 26-28 septembre 1913. Compte-rendu. B. L. S. A. 1913. IX. 4; B. M. T. 1913. XX. 12.
11. Actes de la conférence pour la protection ouvrière; réunie à Berne du 15 au 25 septembre 1913. Berne, Stampfli.
12. Congrès de l'alliance co-opérative internationale a Glasgow. A. O. 1913. XX. 572.
13. Damau, P.—IV. congrès international d'assainissement et de salubrité de l'habitation. Anvers 31 aout—7 septembre 1913. I. Section: Hygiène le l'émigrant. Logement à terre. Anvers, 1913.
14. Premier congrès international de la protection de l'enfance Bruxelles 1913. Bruxelles, Moniteur Belge, 1913.
15. Second congrès international du travail à domicile. Zurich, 8-9, septembre 1912. Rapports et comptes-rendus des séances. Bruxelles, Misch et Thron, 1913.
16. X. congrés international d'agriculture, Gand 1913. Bruxelles, 1913.
17. Rapports du X. congrès international des habitations à bon marché, La Haye-Schéveningen, Septembre, Rotterdam, Nijghen van Ditmar, 1913.

1914.

International Labor Congresses.

1. Protocole du IV. congrès des travailleurs de la pierre tenu à Bruxelles les 12 et 13 Octobre 1913. La Chaux-de-Fonds, Imprimerie Co-opérative, 1914.
2. Huitième assemblée des délégués de l'Association internationale pour la protection légale des travailleurs. V. I. N. 1914. V. 3.
3. Association pour la lutte contre le chômage. Assemblée générale de Gand 5-6 septembre 1913. Procès-verbaux des réunions et documents annexes. B. A. L. C. 1914. IV. 2.
4. Conférence internationale des déléés et membres des ligues sociales d'acheteurs tenue à Anvers les 26, 27 et 28 septembre 1913. Compte-rendu. B. L. S. A. 1914. 1.
5. Congrès des assurances sociales, Washington, 1915. B. A. S. 1914. XXX. I.

International Labor Legislation.

1. Le mouvement syndical international en 1912. V. I. N. 1914. V. 5.
2. Bourgeois,L.—L'organisation internationale de la prévoyance sociale. B. A. S. 1914. XXV. 1.
3. Le développeent de la législation sociale en Europe et aux Etats-Unis en 1913. B. M. T. 1914. XXI. 2.
4. Législation du travail en Belgique et dans les parlements étrangers. Rev. Tr. 1914. XIX. 2, 4.
5. Protection légale des travailleurs. V. I. N. 1914. V. 1-2.
6. Année sociale internationale 1913-1914, Paris, Gabalda, 1914.

PUBLICATIONS IN ENGLISH.

1. Bulletin of the International Labor Office.
2. Conference of Delegates from the General Federations of Trade Unions of the Allied Countries. Historical Survey of the Efforts to Co-ordinate and Internationalize Labor Legislation. Issued by the Central Federation of Trade Unions, London.
3. Reinsch.—Public International Unions.
4. Bauer.—International Labor Office, *Economic Journal*, 1903.
5. American Labor Legislation Review.
6. Report of the Proceedings of the Third International Congress for the Welfare and Protection of Children. Held at London, 15-18 July, 1902. P. S. King & Son, 1902.
7. Bauer, Prof. Dr. St.—The International Labour Office in Basle. E. J. XIII. 51.
8. Annual Convention of the International Association of Factory Inspectors. D. C. IX. 3.
9. Documentary History of American Industrial Society by Commons and Andrews, Vol. IX. pp. 43-46, 333-378.
10. Fairies, John Culbert.—The Rise of Internationism, pp. 52, 89-90.
11. Bulletin fo the Bureau of Labor, No. 54, Sept. 1904, Washington, pp. 1023-1986.
12. Publications of the International Association for the Legal Protection of Labor. No. 5, 6, 7, 8.
13. Supplementary Appendix to Vol. I. of the Life of Robert Owen. pp. X-XII, 209-222.
14. Carlton.—History and Problems of Organized Labor, p. 310.
15. Woolf, L. S.—International government. (See 1916.)

1904.

1. International Labor Statistics. N. Y. 1904. 22.

1905.

1. Cockburn, J.—Report on the International Workmen's Congress in Vienna, 1905, together with an account of the system of Workmen's Insurance, including Old Age Pensions, in Germany. Melbourne, J. Kemp.
2. Fehlinger, H.—Trades unionism in Europe. A. F. 1905. XII. No. 2.
3. International Labor Legislation. Y. R. 1905. XIV. 3.
4. The Tuberculosis Congress. T. 1905. October 10.
5. The Labour Market. T. 1905. 16 May, 15 July, 16 Aug.-Nov.

1906.

1. International Typographical Union. Fifty-second session, Colorado Springs, Colo., August 13-18, 1906. Colorado Springs. See also Reports of Committee on Laws, and Report of Eight Hour Committee.

BIBLIOGRAPHY

2. International Spinners' Union. Convention Report. Held in Boston, Mass., Sept. 13, 14, 15, 1906.
3. The Berne Conference. The Geneva Convention. Should our Constitution be Amended? Y. R. 1906. XV. 3.
4. Taussig, F. W.—Wages and Prices in Relation to International Trade. Q. J. 1906. XX. 4.
5. International Society of Sculpotors, Painters, and Gravers. Times, London, 1906. Jan. 11.
6. International Federation of Textile Workers' Associations. Periodical Reports, No. 1. Contains statistics of wages and hours in Germany, England, Austria, Holland, Denmark, and Belgium. (In English, French and German) Manchester, "Cotton Factory Times" Office, 1906.

1907.

1. International Strikes in Europe. Am. Monthly Cons. Rep. No. 319. Washington, Gov. Print. Office, 1907.
2. International Conference on Labor Regulation at Berne, September, 1906. Memorandum with the Text of the Documents signed at the Conference. London, King & Son.
3. The International Socialist and Labor Congresses. L. L. 1907. 23, 30. Aug.; J. L. 1907. 24, 31. Aug.
4. Executive Committee of the International Co-operative Alliance. International Co-operative Bibliography. London, King & Son.
5. International Labor Legislation. Dispatches on the Subject from the Colonial Office referred to the minister of Labor, D. C. 1907, 1 p. 78-81.
6. International Association of Factory Inspectors. Twenty-first annual convention held at Hartford, Connecticut, June 4th, 5th and 6th, 1907, 122 p.
7. International Union of Wood-Workers. Proceedings of the international Wood-Workers' Congress in Amsterdam 1904 and Stuttgart 1907. 63+62+61 p. Stuttgart, 1907.
8. The international secretariate of workers employed in road making. Second International Conference of workers employed in road making held on February 17, 1907 in Leipzig. 14 p. Berlin, A. Knoll. M. —, 30.

1908.

1. International Federation of Textile Workers' Associations. Report No. 5 December 1907, Ashton-under-Lyne, Andrew, 1908.
2. First International Congress of Consumers' Leagues. T. I. 1908. 11. 7.

1909.

1. Master Cotton Spinners' and Manufacturers' Associations. Report of sirth international Congress of delegated representatives held at Milan, May, 1909. London, P. S. King & Son.

2. "British Section." The Lucerne Conference. W. T. U. 1909. 72.
3. International Transportworkers' Federation. Proceedings of the VI International Convention of transportworker's railwaymen's and seamen's conferences. Held in Vienna from August 24th to 29th incl. 1908. Report of the Central Council for 1906, 1907, 1908. VI 155 p. Hamburg, H. Jochade, 1909.
4. International Association for Labour Legislation. Publication No. 6. Report of the fifth general meeting of the committee of the International Association for Labour Legislation held at Lucerne, September 28th to 30th, 1908. Together with the annual reports of the Internation Labour Office and appendices. Issued by the Board of the International Association for Labour Legislation. 121 p. Woolwich, Labour legislation. Labour representation newspaper printing and publishing Co. Ltd. 1909.
5. Authorities of the Trades' Union Congress and parliamentary committee, report of proceedings at the forty-second annual Trades Union Congress, London, September 6th-11th, 1909 206 p. London, Co-operative Printing Society Ltd., 1909.
6. Co-operation in Europe. (Arena, U. S. A.) J. L. N. Z. 1909. XVII. 194.

1910.

1. President Gompers in Europe. A General View of European Working Class Conditions. A. F. 1910. 17. 1.
2. Potter, D.—International Labor Legislation. E. J. 1910. September.
3. Linotype and Monotype and the International Typographical Union. A. F. 1910. XVII. 11.
4. International Metalworkers' Federation. Reports of the affiliated National Organizations to the VI. International Metalworkers Congress at Birmingham 1910. Stuttgart, Alex Schlicke & Cie., 1910.
5. Proceedings of the Sixth International Convention of Transport Workers of the Railwaymen's and Seamen's Conferences, held in Vienna from August 24-29, 1908. International Transportworkers Federation, 1909. Hamburg, Besenbinderhof, H. Jochade.
6. The International Conference on Unemployment. J. St. S. 1910. Dec.

1911.

1. Lubin, David.—International Institute of Agriculture and its Bearings on Labor. A. F. 1911. XVIII. 6.
2. International Trade Union Statistics. N. Y. 1911. 48.
3. International Unemployment Conference. Charity Organis. Dev. 1911. 10.
4. International Association for Labor Legislation. Publication No. 7: Report of the Sixth General Meeting of the Committee of the International Association for Labor Legislation, Lugano, Sept. 26-28, 1910. Annual Reports of the International Association and of the International Labor Office and Appendices. London, King & Son. 1911.

BIBLIOGRAPHY

5. Sanger, Sophy.—Industrial Laws and International Agreement. W. T. U. 1911. 1.
6. Women and International Labor Legislation: The Lugano Conference. W. I. N. 1911. 1.
7. International Labor Office. First comparative report on the administration of labor laws. Inspection in Europe. London, King & Son, 1911.
8. Sanger, Sophy.—The International Conference on Unemployment. W. I. N. 1911. January.

1912.

1. Bureau of the International Association for Labor Legislation. Publication No. 8: Report of the Seventh General Meeting of the Committee held at Zurich, September 1012, 1912. Annua-l Reports of the International Labor Office and Appendices. London, P .S. King & Son, 1912.
2. International Association of Bureaus of Labor. Proceedings. Factory Inspection and Industrial Commissioners. (Twenty-eighth Annual Convention). Washington, 1912.
3. International Trade Union Statistics. N. Y. 1912. XIV. 52.

1913.

1. International Federation of Trade Unions (auch Deutsch und französisch). I. M. R. 1913. VII. 10.
2. Deibler, F. S.—The Amalgamated Wood Workers' International Union of America; a Historical Study of Trade Unionism in its Relation to the Development of an Industry. Madison, University of Wisconsin, 1913.
3. International Transport Workers' Federation. Reports of the Organizations concerning the Social-economic Conditions, State of Organizations and Rights enjoyed by the Tramwaymen, Seamen, Dock and Transport Workers, etc. in all Countries for the Years 1910, 1911, 1912. Berlin, H. Jochade, 1913.
4. Report of the Central-Council of the International Transport Workers' Federation submitted to the International Congress to be held August 26-30, 1913 in London. Berlin, H. Jochade, 1913.

1914.

1. International Conference for the Protection of Workpeople. D.C. 1914. XIV. 9.
2. More about the Berne Conference. W. L. L. 1914. III. 4.

1915.

1. International Legislation for the Protection of Workers. (3 sprachig). I. M. R. 1915. X. 2, 4-6.

1916.

1. Woolf, L. S.—International Government (Fabian Bookshop, 25 Tothill Street, Westminster; and George Allen and Unum, Limited, 40, Museum Street, London, W. C.) pp. 180-192, 211-216.

PUBLICATIONS IN ITALIAN.

- **XI.** Congresso internazionale d'igiene e demografia. Rivista della beneficenza publica, delle instituzioni di previdenza e di igiene sociale. Sept. 1903.
2. Congresso (Primo) internazionale per l'infanzia (tenuto in) Firenze, ottobre 1896: memorie, discussioni e processi verbali pubblicati sotto la direzione del presidente dall'ing. Enrico Bianciardi, segretario del congresso, coadiuvato dall'avv Giacomo Ceroni e dall'avv. Lamberto Lamberti. Vol. II. Milano, stab. tip. Enrico Reggiani, 1902. 8.
3. Convenzione fra l'Italia e la Francia per regolare la protezione degli operai. B. U. L. I. 3.
4. Valentini-Fersini, G. Protezione e legislazione internazionale del lavoro; prod romi di un diritto internazionale operaio. XV+288 p. Torino. L. 4, —.

1904.

1. Congresso internazionale del partito socialista. B. U. L. 1904. No. 2.
2. A. Nicolo.—Il lavoro nelle risaie. Osservazioni sul reante progetto di legge compilato dal Consiglio del lavoro. Pisa, 1914.
3. Assemblea de comitato dell'associazione internazionale per la protezione legale dei lavoratori. B. U. L. 1904. II. No. 3.

1905.

1. Il Congresso internazionale per il risanamento e l'igiene delle abitazione in Parigi. B. U. L. 1905. III. No. 1.
2. Conferenza internazionale per la protezione oprai in Berna. B. U. L. 1905. III. No. 5.
3. Manfredi, V.—La condizione dello strancero nelle leggi sulle assicurazioni contro gl'infortuni e sulla responsibilità professionale. Estratto della Rivista Internazionale di scienze sociali e discipline ansilarie. Roma, 1905.
4. Congresso internazionale medico per gli infortuni sul lavoro, tenuto in Liegi dal 28 maggio al 3 Giugno 1905. B. U. L. 1905. IV. 3.

1906.

1. IV. Assemblea del Comitato dell'Associazione internazionale per la protezione legislativa dei lavoratori. B. U. L. 1906. VI. 4.
2. Il Conbresso internazionale di Vienna per la assicurazioni operaie. Cr. s. 1906. XVI. 2.6.
3. II. Congresso contro la disoccupazione. Um. 1906. II. 15. 22.
4. Primo Congresso internazionale per la lotta contro la disoccupazione. B. U. L. 1906. VI. 4.

5. Pagliari, rof. F.—Il Congresso della resistenza e il Congresso internazionale per la lotta contro la disoccupazione. Cr. s. 1906. XVI. 19.
6. Michels, R.—Il primo Congresso internazionale per la lotta contro la disoccupazione, Ref. Soc. 1906. Dec.
7. Pagliari, Prof. F.—Il primo Congresso internazionale contro la disoccupazione. Cr. s. 1906. XVI. 21.
8. Convenzioni internazionale per la protezione dei lavoratori stipulate nella Conferenza tenuta a Berna il 26 settembre 1906. B. U. L. 1906. Oct.
9. Congresso internazionale pro riposa settimanale. B. U. L. 1906. Nov.
10. Michels, R.—I. Sindacati Tedeschi e la lotta contro la Disoccupazione. Atti del I, Congresso Internazionale per la lotta contro la Disoccupazione. Milano, Societá Umanitariá, 1906.

1907.

1. V. Assemblea internazionale dei delegati dei segretariati nazionali, B. U. L. 1907. VIII. 4.
2. VII. Congresso socialista internazionale. B. U. L. 1907. VIII. 3.
3. XII. Congresso internazionale sul riposo festivo. B. U. L. 1907. VIII. 4.
4. XIV. Congresso internazionale d'igiene e di demografia. B. U. L. 1907. VIII. 6.
5. I. Congresso internazionale dei lavoranti panattieri e pasticceri. B. U. L. 1907. VIII. 4.
6. Congresso internazionale dei muratori. B. U. L. 1907. VIII. 3.
7. Pagliari, F.—Il movimento operaio internazionale. Cr. s. 1907. XVII. 9.
8. Atti del III. Congresso risicolo internazionale: Pavia, 27, 28, 39, ottobre, 1906. Milano, Abbiate, 1907.
9. Resoconto del III. Congresso internazionale della mutualità, Milano, 21-23 settembre, 1906. Milano, Strazza, 1907.

1908.

1. Seconda relazione intorno al movimento internazionale dei lavoratori della petra degli anni 1906 e 1907. 18 p. Lugano, Cooperativa Tipografica Sociale, 1908.
2. Vassembles generale dell' Associazione internazionale per la protezione legislativa dei lavoratori. B. U. L. 1908 X. 4.
3. II Congresso internazionale delle associazioni agrarie cooperative. B. U. L. 1908. X. 4.
4. VIII. Congresso internazionale delle assicurazioni sociali. B. U. L. 1908. X. 4.

5. Cattaneas, M. Il congresso internazionale di Londra per le case popolari. *Ref. Soc.* 1908. XIX. 3.
6. Atti del IV. congresso internazionale D'assistenza publica at privata. Vol. IV. 280 p. Milano.
7. Ottavo congresso internazionale. *Assn.* 1908. 584.

1909

1. Merloni ,Prof. G.—L'isolamento del Sindacalismo alla Conferenza internazionale operaia. Cr. s. 1909. XIX. 18.
2. Federazione internazionale dei lavoratori delle pietra. Verbale dei deliberati del III. congresso internazionale tenutosi a Kassel nei giorni 11, 12 aprile 1908, Berne, Tipagr. dell'Unione (Cooperatina), 1909.

1910

1. La VI. Assemblea dell'Associazione internazionale per la protezione legale dei lavoratori (Lugano 1910). Publicazioni della Sezione italiana. Nuova Serie. Roma, Officina poligrafica.

1911

1. Monti, A.—Il Congresso internazionale di Bruxelles per lo studio delle Malattie del lavoro. Ram. 1911. V. 3.
2. Il segretariato internazionale delle organizzazioni operaie nel 1909 B. U. L. 1911. XVI. 3.
3. Locatelli, A. F.—Le leggi sul lavoro e il diritto internazionale operaio, con prefazione del Prof. E. Catellani, Padova, Fratelli Drucker, 1911.

1912

1. L'organizzazione operaia internazionale nel 1910. C. F. L. 1912. VI. 249.
2. VII. Assemblea generale dell'Associazione internazionale per la protezione legale dei lavoratori. B. U. L. 1912. XVIII. 10.
3. III. Congresso medico internazionale per gli infortuni del lavoro. M. A. S. 1912. V. 8-9.

1913

1. Conferenza internazionale di Berna per la disciplina del lavoro delle donne e degli adolescenti. B. U. L. (N. S.) 1913. 17.
2. III. Congresso internazionale per le malattie del lavoro. B. U. L. 1913. 11.
3. Congresso dell'associazione internazionale per la lotta contro la disoccupazione. C. F. L. 1913. VII. 291. B. U. L. 1913. 16.
4. Ottava Conferenza internazionale dei sindacati. C. F. L. 1913. VII. 287.
5. Lo sviluppo della legislazione sociale in Europa nel 1912. C. F. L. 1913. VII. 287.

BIBLIOGRAPHY

1914.

1. Legislazione sul lavoro in Italia e all'estero. B. U. L. 1914. XXI. 1-3.
2. Il movimento internazionale dei sindacati nel 1912. B. U. L. 1914. XXI. 2-3; B. U. L. (N. S.) 1914. 11. 7; Conf. L. 1914. VIII. 301.
3. Resoconto del IV. Congresso internazionale dei lavoranti in pietra, Bruxelles 12-13, ottobre 1913. Lugano, Sanvito, 1914.

PUBLICATIONS IN SPANISH.

1. VI. Congreso de la alianza cooperativa internacional. B. R. S. 1904. I. No. VI.
2. IV. Congreso internacional de beneficencia publica y privada. B. R. S. 1906. III. 25.
3. I. Congreso internacional de enfermedades profesionales. B. R. S. 1906. III. 25.
4. XI. Congreso internacional de descanso semanal. B. R. S. 1906. III. 30.
5. Congreso internacional de obreros de transportes terrestres y marítimos. B. R. S. 1906. III. 27.
6. XVII. Congreso internacional de mineros. B. R. S. 1906. III. 26.
7. I. Congreso internacional para la lucha contra el paro. B. R. S. 1906. III. 30.
8. Movimento social internacional; convenciones internacionales sobre la prohibición del trabajo nocturno de las mujeres y sobre la prohibición del empleo del fosforo blanco. B. Arg. 1907. 458. p. 20-22.
9. Movimento obrero internacional en 1905. B. R. S. 1907. XXXV. p. 964-967.
10. La asociacion internacional para la proteccion legal de los trabajadores. "El Mercurio." 1907. 21. July.
11. Montolíu, C.—VIII. Congreso cooperativo internacional celebrado en Hamburgo. Bol. M. S. 1910. I. 5.
12. Convención internacional sobre la prohibición del trabajo nocturno de las mujeres empleades en la industria. Bol. M. S. 1910. I. 6.
13. Congresos internacionales y legislación social durante el año 1908. B. D. T. 1910. Marzo.
14. Congreso Cooperativo Internacional. B. D. T. 1911. 17.
15. IX. Congreso internacional de Agricultura. (Madrid 1-6 de Majo inclusivo) E. S. 1911. II. 7.
16. Eza. Conferencia internacional sobre la falta de trabajo, en Gante. E. S. 1911. II. 11.
17. Maluquer y Salvador, J.—Notas sobre el seguro obrero internacional. E. S. 1911. II. 10.
18. El Congrés internacional de l'habitació barata a Schéveningue. Bol. M. S. 1913. IV. Octobre.
19. La primera assamblea internacional contra'l paro forcós. Bol. M. S. 1913. IV. Octobre.

20. VIII. Conferencia internacional de centrales sindicales. B. R. S. 1913. X. Diciembre.
21. López Nuñez, A., Figueras, M., Madariaga, R., Tallada, J. Los congresos sociales de Zurich en Septiembre de 1912. La VII. assamblea de la Asociacón internacional para la protección legal de los trabajodores, Madrid, Minuesa de los Rios, 1913, p. 1.
22. Conferencia internacional de Sendicatos cristianos en Zurich. Rev. c. 1908. XIV. (Agosto).
23. Biblioteca social de mutualidad La Va asamblea general de la Asociación internacional para la protección legal de los tratajadores (Lucerna, 28.—30 Septiembre 1908) Cuenta rendia a la sección española de la asociacion par su delegado José Manuel de Bayo y Gonzalez Elipe. 23 p. Madrid, Est. Tip de la Viuda e Hijos de M. Tello, 1908.
24. Conventio entre Francia e Italia sobre el Trabaja. B. R. S. I. 1.
25. El III. congrés internacional de les malatties professionals a Viena. Bol. M. S. 1914. V. 25.
26. Asamblea de la Asociación internacional para la Protección legal de los Trabajadores. B. R. S. 1909. VI. 55.

PUBLISHED IN ROUMANIA.

1. Les assurances sociales en Europe. Etude sur la législation internationale et statistique des résultats. B. S. t. R. 1911.

PUBLISHED IN SWEDEN.

1. Sjunde internationella berättelsen öfver fackföreningsrorelsen. Medd. 1911. 7.
2. Tionde internationella berättelsen öfver fackföreningsrorelsen (1912). Medd. 1914. V. 4.
3. Fürst, Th.—Den internationella arbetarskyddslagstiftningen. Konferensen i Bern 1913. Ask. 1913. 10-12.
4. Arbetslöshetskongressen i Gent. Medd. 1913. IV. 10.
5. VIII. internationale fagforeningskonferense i Zurich. Medd. 1913. VIII. 10.
6. Internationell arbetarskyddstutällning i New York. Ask. 1913. 9.

PUBLISHED IN AUSTRIA-HUNGARY.

1. Gáal, J.—Jelentés a nemzetközi törvényes munkásvedelmi egyesületnek 1906. évi szeptember 26-29ik napjain Genfben tartott nagygyulesérol. Budapest, Révai, 1907.
2. Nemzetközi jelentés a szakszervezeti mozgalomról. S. E. 1907. III. p. 17.

BIBLIOGRAPHY

3. Tayerle, R.—Mezinárodní hnutí odborové v Evrope. Ar. 1907. XI. 12.
4. Máday, A.—A törvényes munkásvédelem nemzetközi szabályozása. Különlenyomat. Budapest, Politzer, 1910.
5. Gáal, J—Jelentés az 1912 évi szeptember hó 6-12 én Zürich ben Aartott szociálpolitikai nemzetközi tanácskozásokról. Budapest, Kilián, 1912.
6. Marschan, Géza.—A szociálpolitikai törvenyhozás, 1913—ban. Európa és Amerikai Egyesült-Allamok. T. M. E. 1914. VI. 2.

PUBLISHED IN DENMARK.

1. Jensen, A.—Den internationale Arbejderbeskyttelses Konference i Bern, N. T. 1905. Sept. Oct.
2. Den ottende internationale Arbejderforsikringskongres i Rom. T. A. 1909. V. 4, 5.
3. Den 8 de internationale arbejderforsikringskongress i Rom. N. T. 1909. 2.
4. Trap. Cordt. Den internationale Arbejderforsikringskonference i Scheveningen, 1910. T. A. 1911. VII. 2.
5. International Kongres til Forebyggelse af Ulykkestilfaelde under Arbejdet. T. A. 1912. VIII. 2.
6. Trap. C.—Den 7 internationale Arbejderforsikringskonference i Wien. N. T. 1905. Nov.-Dec.

PUBLISHED IN HOLLAND.

1. Erste algemeen vergadering van de Internationale Vereeniging ter bestrijding der Werkloosheid. M. C. B. S. 1913. VIII. 10.
2. Vooys, J. P. de.—De internationale vereeningung voor wettelijke bescherming der arbeiders aan het werk. Overgedrukt uit *Vragen der Tijds*. Haarlem, H. D. Tjeenk Willink & Zoon, 1904.

PUBLISHED IN FINLAND.

1. Snellman, G. R.—Ofversikt af Lagstiftningen angaende arbetareskydd i Europa färnmästa Stater samt i Australien, Helsingfors, 1906.
2. Redogörelse för de socialpolitiska Kongresserna i Haag, Paris och Lugano. A. T. Fin. 1911. V. 1.
3. Den sociala veckan i Zürich. A. T. Fin. 1912. 4.
4. Andra internationella arbetarskyddskonferensen i Bern. Medd. 1913. IV. 10; A. T. Fin. 1913. VII. 6.
5. Suomen Työväensuojelus-ja sosialivakuutusyhdistys. Gent'in työttömyyskongressi (Einar Böok). Helsinki, Helsingin usi Kirjapaino-Osakeyhtiö, 1914.

INDEX

INDEX

(*See also Tables of Contents of Bibliography, p. 332, of Appendix I, p. 171 and of Appendix II, p. 235*).

Accident Insurance—See Insurance, Social Insurance, and Treaties.
Accident reports—81, 88.
Accidents—lviii—lx, 80, 99, 100.
Adler, Georg—xxv, 23.
Agricultural enterprises—xlv, xlvi, lvi, lxvi, 35, 115.
Aix-la-Chapelle (1818)—11.
Aliens—xl, 4, 42, 51, 59, 62, 63, 97, 98, 151, 165-68.
See Assigns.
American Association for Labor Legislation—
See Sections, and United States.
American Emigrant Company—16.
American Federation of Labor—xxiii, xxiv, 89.
American Labor Legislation Review—87.
Anarchists—16.
Andrews, J. B.—59, 87.
Ankylostomiasis—63.
Anthrax—xli, 63-64, 97.
Appendices I and II—169, 233.
Arbitration—32, 56-57, 153, 157-158.
Arkwright—7.
Army—55.
Assigns under social insurance—l, lxvi, lxvii, 62, 140, 146, 148, 149, 152, 161, 162, 167, 168.
Assumption of risk—84.
Audiganne—xxv.
Bakeries—xlii, l, lii, 100.
Bank transfers—138, 139, 140, 146.
Beet sugar—115, 116, 125, 134.
Berlepsch—29, 31, 37, 40.
Bern Conference (1905)—xxxiv, 44, 46, 112-117, 174, 175.

Bern Conference (1906)—xxxiv, 47, 69, 119-130, 135, 175-180.
Bern Conference (1913)—xxxiv, 59, 61, 64, 76, 131-136, 318-321.
Bern Conventions—26, 51, 52, 58, 68, 72-73, 112-132, 174-180.
On day-work (tentative)—3, 33, 58, 59, 98, 133-136, 320.
On night-work of women (tentative)—114-117, 119, 174.
On night-work of young persons (tentative)—3, 33, 58, 59, 76-78, 132-135, 318.
On use of phosphorus (tentative) 113-114, 118, 174.
Bern Conventions—
Adherents—126-131.
On night-work of women—3, 33, 72, 75, 96, 114-117, 118, 119-121, 123-128, 133-136, 175.
On use of phosphorus—3, 51, 61, 69, 73, 75, 118, 121-122, 129-131, 178.
Bibliography—331.
Bismarck—xxxiii, 17, 23, 28, 31.
Blanqui—xxv, 12.
Bluntschli—xxv, 14.
Bouches-du-Rhone, Council of—27.
Braber—xxv, 14.
Brentano—xxv, 14, 24.
Bryce—92.
Bulletin de l'Office International du Travail—40.
Bulletin des Internationalen Arbeitsamtes—40.
Bulletin of the International Labor Office—40, 48, 58.
Bureaus—See Labor Bureaus.
Burma—12.

INDEX

Caissons—58, 59, 60.
Cameron, A. C.—16.
Canada—58, 130.
Cartwright—7.
Cauwés—xxxvi, 40.
Ceramic industry—58, 59, 60, 62.
Chamberlain—89.
Chatelain—11.
Child Labor—xli-xliii, lxiv, lxv, 13, 21, 22, 23, 26, 27, 31, 32, 33, 35, 47, 48, 58, 59, 62, 90, 92, 95, 96, 98, 131-136, 138, 141, 154-156. See Italian child laborers, and night-work of young people.
Childbirth—xl, xlv, 99.
China—12.
Circular Note—See Federal Council, Swiss.
Climate—67, 72, 120, 132.
Coal Mines—lxiii, lxiv, 96.
Cohn, Gustave—18, 20.
Columbia University—88.
Commercial Treaty—See Treaties.
Commercial Treaty Concessions—24.
Commission Plan—See Wisconsin—89.
Committee Meeting (Basel, 1903)—See Delegates' Meetings.
Commons, John R.—87, 89.
Compensation Laws—See Workmen's Compensation, and Insurance.
Conference of Berlin (1890)—xxxiii, 30, 34, 35, 112, 244.
Conference of London (1912)—60.
Conference on Weekly Day of Rest—54-56.
See Weekly rest.
Congress on Accidents to Labor and Workmen's Insurance—xxxiii, 103.
Congress on Cultivation of Rice—56.
Congress on Home Work—xxx, xxxi, 61.

Congress on Unemployment—xxx, 53, 54, 322.
Congresses of
Amsterdam (1904)—16.
Basel (1869)—16.
(1912)—xvii, 16.
Berlin (1890)—xxxiii, 28-30, 31-34, 35, 112, 244.
Bern (1876)—16.
(1917)—xxiv.
(1919)—xix.
See Bern Conference.
Brussels (1856)—14.
(1868)—16.
(1874)—16.
(1891)—xvii, 16, 34.
(1897)—xxv, 36, 37, 248.
Chur (1881)—16.
Copenhagen (1910)—16.
(1915)—xviii.
Dresden (1871)—16.
Frankfort (1857)—14.
Frankfurt-on-Main (1882)—20.
Geneva (1866)—15.
(1873)—16.
(1920)—xx.
Ghent (1877)—16.
Industrial Christian Manufacturers (1879)—18.
Kienthal (1916)—xviii.
Laredo (1918)—xxiv.
Lausanne (1867)—16.
Leeds (1916)—xxiii, xxiv.
London (1864)—15.
(1871)—16.
(1888)—xvi, xxi, 16.
(1896)—16, 34.
(1915-1918)—xviii.
Lyons (1877)—18.
Mexico City (1921)—xxiv.
Montlucon (1887)—25.
Moscow (1919-1920)—xx.
Paris (1883)—xvi, xxi, 16, 21.
(1886)—xvi, xxi, 16, 24.
(1889)—xvii, 16, 27.

INDEX

(1900)—xxvi, 38—41.
(1900)—16.
Roubaix (1884)—21, 239.
San Salvador (1911)—xxiv.
St. Imier (1872)—16.
Stockholm (1917)—xix.
Stuttgart (1907)—xxii, 16.
Switzerland (1883)—21.
The Hague (1872)—16.
(1889)—27, 243.
Verviers (1877)—16.
Vienna (1915)—xviii.
Zimmerwald (1915)—xviii.
Zurich (1893)—xvii, 16, 34.
(1897)—35, 247.
See Delegates' Meetings.
Constituent Assembly of the International Association for the Legal Protection of Labor—See Delegates' Meetings.
Constitution of the United States—86, 96, 110.
Continuous industries—60, 63.
Contributory negligence—85.
Cotton Gin—7.
Crompton—7.
Customs Service—55.
Day Work.—See Bern Conventions, and Workday.
Delegates' Meetings of the International Association for Labor Legislation.
First Meeting (Basel, 1901)—41-42, 252.
Second Meeting (Cologne, 1902)—42, 43, 137, 254.
Committee Meeting (Basel, 1903)—43, 45, 255.
Third Meeting (Basel, 1904)—44-46, 258.
Fourth Meeting (Geneva, 1906)—47-52, 264.
Fifth Meeting (Lucerne, 1908)—57, 58, 269.

Sixth Meeting (Lugano, 1910)—58, 59-61, 131, 132, 281.
Seventh Meeting (Zurich, 1912)—60, 61-64, 300.
Diseases, occupational—xxix, xxx, l, li, lxviii, 60, 80, 82-84 88, 97, 142, 143.
Divers—60.
Dock workers—See Merchant service.
Domestic system—8.
Double discussion or reading—See Second discussion or reading.
Dumas, J. B.—xxv, 17.
Educational requirements—13, 23, 32, 154-155.
Efficiency, doctrine of—5-7.
Embroidery—34, 58, 59, 63, 134.
Employers' liability—42, 84, 85.
Employment bureaus—See Labor Bureaus.
Esche-Hughes Bill—89, 90, 164, 165.
Farnam, Henry W.—59.
Federal Council, German—51, 147.
Federal Council, Swiss—
Notes of 1881—19, 66.
1887-1889—25-27, 240, 241.
1890—27.
1892—34.
1896—34.
1904—44.
1905-1906—117, 118, 119, 123.
1909—125.
1910—125.
1911—60, 61, 131.
1913—135.
1914—135.
Program of 1889—26, 240, 241.
Fellow servant doctrine—84.
Ferrosilicon—63.
Fitch, John—60.
Forced Labor—lxi, lxii, 100.
Franck, Dr.—20, 66.

392

INDEX

Franco-Belgian Treaty (1906)—51, 146, 147, 200.
  (1910)—147, 201.
Franco-British Convention concerning recruitment of native laborers in the New Hebrides—159, note.
Franco-British Treaty—151, 152, 208.
Franco-Danish Treaty—157, 215.
Franco-Italian Treaty (1904)—43, 44, 137-142, 153, 154, 180-184.
  (Jan. 20, 1906)—146.
  (June 9, 1906)—51, 148, 149, 184-188.
  (June 10, 1910)—153-156, 189.
  (Aug. 9, 1910)—156.
Franco-Luxemburg Treaty—51, 149, 203.
Franco-Swiss Treaty—165, 166, 229.
Frankel, L. K.—59.
Frey, Colonel—17, 18, 19.
Fur-cutting—64.
General Conference — xxxvii-lxix, 106-110.
German-Austro-Hungarian Treaty —143, 144, 195.
German-Belgian Treaty—159, 160, 217.
German Catholic Party—21.
German-Italian Treaty (1904)—142, 143, 195.
  (1912)—160-163, 221.
German-Luxemburg Treaty — 145, 146, 150, 197.
German-Netherlands Treaty (1907) —150, 151, 160, 205.
  (1914))—151, 208.
German-Spanish Sailors' Accident Agreement—163, 164, 227.
German-Swedish Treaty—156, 157, 215.
"Ghent system"—104.
Gilbert, Prentiss B.—lxx, lxxi.
Glarus, Commission of—13, 14.

Glass Factories—lxviii, 63, 96, 133, 154, 155.
Gompers, Samuel—xxxvii, xxxviii, 89.
Governing Body—xlviii, lxxi, lxxii, 106—110.
Greece—126, 127.
Hague Conventions—56, 57, 123.
Hague Tribunal—74, 106.
Hahn—xxv, 14.
Hargreaves—7.
Hatch, Leonard—83.
Hat-making—64.
Heavy packages—lviii, lix, 99, 100.
Henrotte—37.
Hertling—xxxiii.
Holidays, labor—60, 62, 63.
Home work—xxx, xxxi, xlvi, lvii, 36, 45, 49, 58, 59 61, 63, 98, 100.
Hotel business—49, 115.
Hungarian-Italian Treaty—152, 153, 210.
Illumination, factory—79.
India—xlii, lxxi, 127, 128.
Industrial Revolution—8.
Industry, national—5, 6, 21.
Inspection—See Labor Inspection.
Insurance—li, lxv-lxviii, 4, 9, 10, 22, 32, 44, 45, 46, 51, 59, 60, 62, 63, 80, 90, 100, 101, 139, 140, 142.
Insurance—(See Treaties, and Social Insurance)
  Accident—l, 10, 23, 32, 42, 59, 97, 98, 100, 101, 140, 149, 159. (See Treaties and National Accident Insurance Acts).
  Invalidity — lxvi-lxviii, 100, 101, 142-144.
  Old Age—lxvi-lxviii, 32, 47, 89, 101, 143, 144, 161, 162, 164, 165. (See Treaties, and Social Insurance).
  Sickness—lv-lvii, 10, 32, 47, 63, 100, 101, 142-144, 158, 161, 162.

393

INDEX

(See Treaties, Social Insurance, and Diseases).
Survivors'—lxvi-lxviii, 100, 101. (See Assigns).
Unemployment—xxxix, lxviii-lxix, 98-101, 140.
International — See International Workingmen's Association.
International, The First—xvi, 14-16.
The Second—xvii, xx, 16.
The Third—xx.
International Association for the Legal Protection of Labor—See International Association for Labor Legislation.
International Association for Labor Legislation—xxvi, xxvii, 37-41, 74, 87-90, 105-107, 249.
American Section—See Sections.
Bulletins—See Bulletin.
Bureau—40.
Committee—40.
Constitution—40, 41, 249.
Meetings—See Delegates' Meetings.
Office—40, 41, 42, 44.
Permanent Council of Social Hygiene—40.
Sections—See Sections.
Subventions—40, 48.
International Association on Social Insurance — xxviii, xxix, 60, 61, 103.
International Association on Unemployment—xxx, 53, 60, 61.
American section—322.
Other sections—xxx.
International congresses—See Conferences, and Congresses.
International Employment Bureau—See Labor Bureaus.
International High Commission—64, note, 326-329.
International Home Work Congress—xxx, xxxi, 61.

International Labor Bureau — See Labor Bureaus.
International Labor Law—See Law.
International Labor Organization—xxxvii-lxxiii, 93, 94, 106-110, 399-
Members—lxxiii.
International Night—115, 116, 120, 132.
See Bern Conventions.
International Seafarers' Federation—xliv.
International Workingmen's Association—xvi, 14-16.
Interstate Compacts—86, 91.
Invalidity—See Insurance.
Iron Works—63, 133.
Italian-American Treaty—164, 165.
Italian child laborers—42, 141, 154-156.
Italian-German War Arrangement—166-168.
Japan—xlii, lxxi, 12, 127, 131.
Jay—xxvi.
Kay—7.
King, Hon. W. L. Mackenzie—59.
Labor Bureaus—
Employment bureaus—xxxix, xl, lxv, lxvi, 99.
International Employment Bureau—54.
International Labor Bureau—22, 34, 35, 37, 38, 40.
International Labor Office—106-110.
National Labor Bureaus—
Austria—102.
Belgium—102.
Canada—103.
Denmark—103.
France—103.
Great Britain—102.
Holland—103.
Italy—102.
Massachusetts—102.
New South Wales—103.

INDEX

New Zealand—103.
Norway—102.
Ontario—103.
Spain—102.
Sweden—102.
United States—102.
Labor congresses—See Congresses.
Labor inspection—xli, xlix, lv, 27, 32, 33, 35, 39, 47, 138.
In United States—81, 83, 84.
Laissez faire—9, 86.
L'Annuaire de la Législation du travail—37.
Lavoisier—7.
Law, International—3, 4, 104.
Law, Labor—82-84.
Law proposition, French (1885)—22.
Law proposition, German (1885)—23.
Lead—xli, xlvi, 37, 42, 43, 45, 50-51, 52-53, 58, 60, 61, 62, 79, 80, 97.
League of Nations—xxxvii, 106, 109.
Legislative Drafting Research Fund of Columbia University—88.
Legrand, Daniel—xxv, 12.
Leisure time—See Spare time.
Leroy-Beaulieu—22.
Letters rogatory—150.
Lighting, factory—79, 80.
List of industrial poisons—45, 51. 58, 61.
Lohman—18.
Loom—7.
Luzzatti—38.
Luxemburg-Belgian Treaty (1905)—51, 144, 145, 195.
(1906)—144, 197.
Mahaim—xxvi, 40.
Manufacturers—4, 13, 115.
Massachusetts Labor Bureau—102.
Matches—See Phosphorus, and Bern Conventions, and Sample phosphorus matches.

Maybach—29.
Mercantilists—9.
Merchant service—lix, lx, lxiv, 55, 63, 98, 100.
Mercurial poisoning—li, 63, 64, 97.
Mexico—xxiv, 61.
Millerand—38.
Mine fatalities—79.
Miners' XVII International Congress—46.
Minimum wage—lvii, 21, 27, 47, 98, 100.
Mining—lxiii, lxiv, 4, 31, 32, 58, 63, 96, 115, 116, 123, 124, 133.
Moore, J. B.—57, note.
Morbidity and mortality—63, 83.
Mortality—See morbidity.
Mothers' pensions—89.
Mun, Count Albert de—xxxiii, 21.
National Accident Insurance Acts—51, 147, 148.
See Social Insurance
National Labor Bureaus—See Labor Bureaus.
Navy—55.
Necrosis—See "phossy jaw."
Neill, Charles P.—59.
New Deal—92, 93.
New Hebrides—159, note.
Newspaper employees—54.
Night-rest — See International Night, and Night-work.
Night-work—13, 15, 21, 23, 25, 26, 39, 96. (See Bern Conventions.)
Of women—xl, xli, xlv, xlviii, 3, 13, 15, 25, 26, 33, 42-44, 47, 61, 80, 96, 114-117, 119-121, 123-128, 136, 138, 325.
Of young persons—xlii, xlv, 3, 13, 26, 33, 45, 49, 58, 80, 96, 127, 132, 133, 136, 138, 139, 318-320.
See Bakeries.
Nyssens—37.
Occupational diseases—See Diseases.

395

INDEX

Old-Age pensions—See Insurance.
Oliver, Thomas—82.
Orphans—See Insurance, Survivors'
Owen, Robert—11, 12.
Painting—See Lead.
Parliament, French—21, 22.
Peace—52, 77, 106, 118, 136.
Peace Conference at The Hague (1907)—56, 57.
Peace Conference of Paris, 1919—xxxvii, 90, 91, 105, 106, 401-412.
Permanent Committee on Social Insurance—See International Association on Social Insurance.
Permanent Council of Social Hygiene—See International Association for Labor Legislation.
Phillippovich—40.
Phosphorus, white—3, 37, 42-44, 51, 61, 89, 90, 97, 113, 114, 118, 121, 122, 128-131, 164, 165.
 See Bern Conventions, and Poisons, industrial.
 In United States—89, 90, 165.
"Phossy jaw"—74, 75, 77, 79.
Physiocrats—9.
Poisons, industrial—37, 42-45, 48, 50, 51, 52, 53, 59, 60, 61, 62, 63, 64, 89, 90, 97.
 See Bern Conventions, and Lead and Phosphorus.
Polygraphic trades—52, 53, 58, 59, 60, 62. See Lead.
Pope Leo XIII.—31.
Portuguese Delegation—56.
Post-office employees—54, 55.
Prize Contest—45, 52, 53.
Protection, doctrine of—6.
Protective Committees—See Italian Child Laborers.
Quarrying—4, 63, 123.
Railroad employees—55, 60, 63, 165, 166.
Refund of insurance premiums—63, 161, 162.

Reichstag—23, 240.
Rescripts of William II.—28-30, 31.
Rice—56.
Roebuck—7.
Roosevelt, Franklin D.—93, 94.
Roosevelt, Theodore—87.
Russia—lxxi, lxxii, 108.
Sailors—4.
Sample phosphorus matches—69, 130, 131.
Sanction—51, 74, 104-110, 120, 122-124.
Sarrien—77, 118.
Scherrer—40.
Schoenberg—xxv.
Seamen—xliii, xliv, xlvii, liii-lv, lviii-lx, 99, 100.
Sections of International Association for Labor Legislation—41, 42, 47.
 Austria—41.
 Belgium—41.
 Denmark—47.
 England—47.
 Finland—61.
 France—41.
 Germany—41.
 Holland—41.
 Hungary—41.
 Italy—41.
 Norway—59.
 Spain—47.
 Sweden—59.
 Switzerland—41.
 United States—xxvii, 47, 59, 62, 63, 87-90, 323.
Sessions of the General Conference, 1st-18th (1919-1934) — xxxviii-lxix.
Shuttle drop box—7.
Sickness, cost of—80.
Sickness Insurance—See Insurance
Smith, Adam—9.

INDEX

Social Insurance—(See Insurance).
  In Austria—144.
  England—143.
  France—143.
  Germany—142, 143, 161.
  Hungary—144.
  Italy—143.
  United States—88, 89, 91.
Social Democratic Party — xvi, xxxiii, 18, 23.
Socialist Labor Party, Christian—14.
Socialists—xvi-xxi, 14, 16, 18, 35, 104.
"Social Week"—61.
Spare time—xlix.
Spinner, mule—7.
Spinner, roller—7.
Spinners—14.
Spinning jenny—7.
Spitzenbergen Convention—159.
Standard Labor Law—88.
"States rights"—86.
Steam engine—7.
Stein, Lorenz von—18, 20.
Stokers—xlvii, 95.
Strikes—5, 20, 28, 32, 77, 118.
Sumner, Helen—59.
Sunday rest — See weekly rest — xxviii, 13, 14, 54.
Sunday work—13, 80, 81.
Swedish-Danish Sick Funds—158, 159.
Swiss-Italian Treaty—142, 194.
Switzerland—20, 30, 34, 61.
  See Federal Council.
Telegraph service—55.
Telephone service—55.
Tentative Agreements of Bern— See Bern Conventions (tentative).
Thiersch—xxv.
Toniolo—40.
Trade Unions—xxi-xxv, 9, 21, 35, 104.
Treaties — Accident Insurance — xxxv, xxxvi, 166-168.

Franco-Belgian (1906)—51, 146, 147, 200.
Franco-British (1909)—151, 152, 208.
Franco-Italian (9 June, 1906)— 51, 148, 149, 184-188.
  (1904)—43, 44, 137-142, 153, 154, 180-184.
Franco-Luxemburg (1906) — 51, 149, 203.
German-Belgium (1912) — 159, 160, 217.
German-Italian (1912)—160, 221.
German-Luxemburg (1905)—145, 146, 150, 197.
German-Netherlands (1907) — 150, 151, 160, 205.
  (1914)—151, 208.
Hungarian-Italian (1909) — 152, 153, 210.
Luxemburg-Belgian (1905) — 51, 144, 145, 195.
  (1906)—144, 197.
Treaties, Arbitration—157, 158, 215. See Hague Conventions.
Treaties, Commercial—
  German - Austro - Hungarian (1905)—143, 144, 195.
  German-Italian (1904)—142, 143, 195.
  German-Swedish (1911) — 156, 157, 215.
  Swiss-Italian (1904)—142, 194.
Treaties, Old-age and Invalidity Insurance — 160-163, 165, 166, 221, 229.
Treaties, Workmen's Insurance — 156, 157, 215.
  Franco-Belgian (1906)—51, 146, 147, 200.
  (1910)—147, 201.
  Franco-British (1909)—151, 152, 208.

INDEX

Franco-Italian (1904) — 43, 44, 137-142, 153, 154, 180-184.
   (9, June, 1906)—51, 148, 149, 184-188.
Franco-Luxemburg (1906) — 51, 149, 203.
Franco-Swiss (1913) — 165, 166, 229.
German - Austro - Hungarian (1905)—143, 144, 195.
German-Belgian (1912)—159, 160, 217.
German-Italian (1904)—142, 143, 195.
   (1912)—160-163, 221.
German-Luxemburg (1905)—145, 146, 150, 197.
German-Netherlands (1907) — 150, 151, 160, 205.
   (1914)—151, 208.
German-Swedish (1911) — 156, 157, 215.
Hungarian-Italian (1909) — 152, 153, 210.
Luxemburg-Belgian (1905) — 51, 144, 145, 195.
   (1906)—144, 197.
Swiss-Italian (1904)—142, 194.
Treaty between Italy and the United States—164, 165, 228.
Treaty, Sailors' Accident—163, 164, 227.
Treaty; War Arrangement — 166-168.
Trimmers—xlvii, 95.
"Trucking"—63.
Unemployment—xxxix, xl, xliii-xlv, 23, 53, 54, 61, 98, 99.
   See Insurance, unemployment, and International Association on Unemployment.

United States—16, 35, 59, 61, 62, 63, 68, 73, 75, 79-94, 102, 108, 109, 164, 165.
   Entrance into the International Labor Organization—lxix-lxxi, 93, 94.
Vaillant—21, 22.
Villermé—xxv, 12.
Ventilation, factory—80.
Wages boards—63.
Wagner, Adolph—xxv, 14.
War—4, 70, 74, 82, 87, 136.
Watt—7.
"Wealth of Nations"—9.
Weaving—7, 116.
Weber, Adna F.—87.
Weekly rest—xxviii, xlvii, 13, 14, 22, 24, 25, 26, 27, 31, 32, 33, 35, 54-56, 96.
Weyl, Theodore—82.
Whitney—7.
Widows—See Insurance, Survivors'
William II. of Germany—28, 31.
Wilson, Wm. B.—xxxviii.
Wilson, Woodrow—xxxviii, 87.
Wisconsin Commission Plan—89.
Wolowski, Louis—xxv, 17.
Woman's work—22, 23, 24, 31, 32, 33, 35, 47, 58, 59, 62, 96, 98, 99, 114-117, 133-136, 138, 139.
   See night-work, and Bern Conventions.
Wool-combing—116, 125.
Woolf, L. S.—105.
Workday, length of—xxxviii, xxxix, xliv, lxii, lxiii, lxviii, 21, 22, 23, 24, 26, 27, 32, 35, 39, 47, 49, 50, 58, 59, 62, 72, 95, 96, 98.
   See Bern Convention (tentative) on day-work.
Workmen's Compensation Laws—xlvi, 1, 80, 89, 91, 97, 98, 100, 101.

SUPPLEMENT
The International Labor Organization

CONTENTS
Page

The Constitution of the International Labor Organization........ 401

Draft Conventions

1. Hours of work in industry (1st Session, 1919).................. 412
2. Unemployment 418
3. Childbirth 420
4. Night-work of women... 423
5. Minimum age in industry..................................... 427
6. Night-work of young persons in industry...................... 429
7. Minimum age at sea (2nd Session, 1920)....................... 434
8. Unemployment indemnity in case of shipwreck................. 436
9. Employment for seamen....................................... 437
10. Minimum age in agriculture (3rd Session, 1921)................ 441
11. Rights of combination in agriculture........................... 444
12. Workmen's compensation in agriculture........................ 444
13. Use of white lead in painting.................................. 445
14. Weekly rest in industry.. 446
15. Minimum age for trimmers or stokers......................... 448
16. Medical examination for young persons at sea.................. 449
17. Workmen's compensation for accidents (7th Session, 1925)...... 459
18. Workmen's compensation for diseases.......................... 463
19. Equality of treatment for nationals and foreigners (accidents).... 465
20. Night-work in bakeries.. 466
21. Inspection of emigrants on board ship (8th Session, 1926)........ 468
22. Seamen's articles of agreement (9th Session, 1926)............... 471
23. Repatriation of seamen.. 474
24. Sickness insurance in industry and commerce (10th Session, 1927).. 480
25. Sickness insurance for agricultural workers..................... 483
26. Minimum wage fixing machinery (11th Session, 1928)............ 488
27. Weight of heavy packages transported by vessels (12th Session, 1929) 498
28. Protection of dockers against accidents......................... 500
29. Forced or compulsory labor (14th Session, 1930)................ 507
30. Hours of work in commerce and offices......................... 516
31. Hours of work in coal mines (15th Session, 1931)................ 521
32. Protection of dockers against accidents (revised) (16th Session, 1932) 526
33. Minimum age in non-industrial employment..................... 534
34. Fee-charging employment agencies (17th Session, 1933)........... 540
35. Old-age insurance in industry, commerce, etc..................... 543
36. Old-age insurance in agriculture................................ 548
37. Invalidity insurance in industry, commerce, etc.................. 553
38. Invalidity insurance in agriculture.............................. 558
39. Widows' and orphans' insurance in industry, commerce, etc........ 564
40. Widows' and orphans' insurance in agriculture................... 570

CONTENTS (Continued)

	Page
41. Night-work of women (revised) (18th Session, 1934)	582
42. Workmen's compensation for diseases (revised)	584
43. Hours of work in automatic sheet-glass works	587
44. Unemployment benefit or allowances	588

RECOMMENDATIONS

1. Unemployment (1st Session, 1919) 420
2. Reciprocity of treatment of foreign workers 420
3. Prevention of anthrax 425
4. Protection of women and children against lead poisoning 426
5. Establishment of Government health services 426
6. Application of the Berne Convention concerning white phosphorus. 427
7. Limitation of hours of work in the fishing industry (2nd Session, 1920) 432
8. Limitation of hours of work in inland navigation 433
9. Establishment of national seamen's codes 434
10. Unemployment insurance for seamen 435
11. Prevention of unemployment is agriculture (3rd Session, 1921) .. 440
12. Childbirth (agriculture) 441
13. Night work of women in agriculture 441
14. Night work of children and young persons in agriculture 443
15. Development of technical agricultural education 443
16. Living-in conditions of agricultural workers 443
17. Social insurance in agriculture 444
18. Weekly rest in commercial establishments 447
19. Migration statistics (4th Session, 1922) 449
20. Organization of systems of inspection (5th Session, 1923) 450
21. Utilization of workers' spare time (6th Session, 1924) 456
22. Minimum scale of workmen's compensation (7th Session, 1925) ... 461
23. Jurisdiction in disputes on workmen's compensation 463
24. Workmen's compensation for occupational diseases 465
25. Equality of treatment (accident compensation) 466
26. Protection of female emigrants at sea (8th Session, 1926) 470
27. Repatriation of masters and apprentices (9th Session, 1926) ... 475
28. Inspection of the conditions of work for seamen 476
29. General principles of sickness insurance (10th Session, 1927) . 485
30. Application of minimum wage fixing machinery (11th Session, 1928) 490
31. Prevention of industrial accidents (12th Session, 1929) 493
32. Responsibility for the protection of power-driven machinery ... 499
33. Reciprocity as regards the protection against accidents of dockers .. 507
34. Consultation of organizations for the safety of dockers 507
35. Indirect compulsion to labor (14th Session, 1930) 515
36. Regulation of forced or compulsory labor 516
37. Regulation of hours of work in hotels, restaurants, etc. 520
38. Regulation of hours of work in theatres, etc. 520
39. Regulation of hours of work in hospitals, etc. 521
40. Reciprocity for the safety of dockers (16th Session, 1932) 534
41. Age for admission of children to non-industrial employment 538
42. Employment agencies (17th Session, 1933) 542
43. Invalidity, old-age and survivors' insurance 577
44. Unemployment insurance and relief (18th Session, 1934) 592

LABOR
in the
PEACE TREATY

Complete Official Text of Part XIII. of the Treaty of Peace With Germany and the Covenant of the League of Nations, Laying Down General Principles of Labor Protection, Establishing a Permanent International Organization for Promoting World-Wide Adoption of Protective Standards, and Arranging for the First Official Annual International Labor Conference at Washington, in October, 1919.

PART XIII.

Labor

SECTION I.

Organization of Labor.

Whereas the League of Nations has for its object the establishment of universal peace, and such a peace can be established only if it is based upon social justice;

And whereas conditions of labor exist involving such injustice, hardship and privation to large numbers of people as to produce unrest so great that the peace and harmony of the world are imperilled; and an improvement of those conditions is urgently required; as, for example, by the regulation of the hours of work, including the establishment of a maximum working day and week, the regulation of the labor supply, the prevention of unemployment, the provision of an adequate living wage, the protection of the worker against sickness, disease and injury arising out of his employment, the protection of children, young persons and women, provision for old age and injury, protection of the interests of workers when employed in countries other than their own, recognition of the principle of freedom of association, the organization of vocational and technical education and other measures;

Whereas also the failure of any nation to adopt humane conditions of labor is an obstacle in the way of other nations which desire to improve the conditions in their own countries;

The **High Contracting Parties,** moved by sentiments of justice and humanity as well as by the desire to secure the permanent peace of the world, agree to the following:

CHAPTER I.

Organization.

ARTICLE 387.

A permanent organization is hereby established for the promotion of the objects set forth in the Preamble.

The original Members of the League of Nations shall be the original Members of this organization, and hereafter membership of the League of Nations shall carry with it membership of the said organization.

ARTICLE 388.

The permanent organization shall consist of:
(1) A General Conference of Representatives of the Members, and,
(2) An International Labor Office controlled by the Governing Body described in Article 393.

ARTICLE 389.

The meetings of the General Conference of Representatives of the Members shall be held from time to time as occasion may require, and at least once in every year. It shall be composed of four Representatves of each of the Members of whom two shall be Government Delegates and the two others shall be Delegates representing respectively the employers and the workpeople of each of the Members..

Each Delegate may be accompanied by advisers, who shall not exceed two in number for each item on the agenda of the meeting. When questions specially affecting women are to be considered by the Conference, at least one of the advisers should be a woman.

The Members undertake to nominate non-Government Delegates and advisers chosen in agreement with the industrial organizations, if such organizations exist, which are most representative of employers or workpeople, as the case may be, in their respective countries.

Advisers shall not speak except on a request made by the Delegate whom they accompany and by the special authorization of the President of the Conference, and may not vote.

A Delegate may by notice in writing addressed to the President appoint one of his advisers to act as his deputy, and the adviser, while so acting, shall be allowed to speak and vote.

The names of the Delegates and their advisers will be communicated to the International Labor Office by the Government of each of the Members.

The credentials of Delegates and their advisers shall be subject to scrutiny by the Conference, which may, by two-thirds of the votes cast by the Delegates present, refuse to admit any Delegate or adviser whom it deems not to have been nominated in accordance with this Article.

INTERNATIONAL LABOR ORGANIZATION

Article 390.

Every Delegate shall be entitled to vote individually on all matters which are taken into consideration by the Conference.

If one of the Members fails to nominate one of the non-Government Delegates whom it is entitled to nominate, the other non-Government Delegate shall be allowed to sit and speak at the Conference, but not to vote.

If in accordance with Article 389 the Conference refuses admission to a Delegate of one of the Members, the provisions of the present Article shall apply as if that Delegate had not been nominated.

Article 391.

The meetings of the Conference shall be held at the seat of the League of Nations, or at such other place as may be decided by the Conference at a previous meeting by two-thirds of the votes cast by the Delegates present.

Article 392.

The International Labor Office shall be established at the seat of the League of Nations as part of the organization of the League.

Article 393.
(As Amended in 1934)

The International Labor Office shall be under the control of a Governing Body consisting of thirty-two persons:

Sixteen representing Governments, Eight representing the Employers, and Eight representing the Workers.

Of the sixteen persons representing Governments, eight shall be appointed by the Members of chief industrial importance, and eight shall be appointed by the Members selected for that purpose by the Government Delegates to the Conference excluding the Delegates of the eight Members mentioned above. Of the sixteen Members represented six shall be non-European States.

Any question as to which are the Members of chief industrial importance shall be decided by the Council of the League of Nations.

The persons representing the Employers and the persons representing the Workers shall be elected respectively by the Employers' Delegates and the Workers' Delegates to the Conference. Two Employers' representatives and two Workers' representatives shall belong to non-European States.

The period of office of the Governing Body shall be three years.

The method of filling vacancies and of appointing substitutes, and other similar questions, may be decided by the Governing Body subject to the approval of the Conference.

The Governing Body shall, from time to time, elect one of its number to act as its Chairman, shall regulate its own procedure, and shall fix its own times of meeting. A special meeting shall be held if a written request to that effect is made by at least twelve of the representatives on the Governing Body.

Article 394.

There shall be a Director of the International Labor Office, who shall be appointed by the Governing Body, and, subject to the instructions of the Governing Gody, shall be responsible for the efficient conduct of the International Labor Office and for such other duties as may be assigned to him.

The Director or his deputy shall attend all meetings of the Governing Body.

Article 395.

The staff of the International Labor Office shall be appointed by the Director, who shall, so far as is possible with due regard to the efficiency of the work of the Office, select persons of different nationalities. A certain number of these persons shall be women.

Article 396.

The functions of the International Labor Office shall include the collection and distribution of information on all subjects relating to the international adjustment of conditions of industrial life and labor, and particularly the examination of subjects which it is proposed to bring before the Conference with a view to the conclusion of international conventions, and the conduct of such special investigations as may be ordered by the Conference.

It will prepare the agenda for the meetings of the Conference.

It will carry out the duties required of it by the provisions of this Part of the present Treaty in connection with international disputes.

It will edit and publish in French and English, and in such other languages as the Governing Body may think desirable, a periodical paper dealing with problems of industry and employment of international interest.

Generally, in addition to the functions set out in this Article, it shall have such other powers and duties as may be assigned to it by the Conference.

Article 397.

The Government Departments of any of the Members which deal with questions of industry and employment may communicate directly with the Director through the Representative of their Government on the Governing Body of the International Labor Office, or failing any such Representative, through such other qualified official as the Government may nominate for the purpose.

Article 398.

The International Labor Office shall be entitled to the assistance of the Secretary-General of the League of Nations in any matter in which it can be given.

Article 399.

Each of the Members will pay the travelling and subsistence expenses of its Delegates and their advisers and of its Representatives attending the meetings of the Conference or Governing Body, as the case may be.

All the other expenses of the International Labor Office and of the meetings of the Conference or Governing Body shall be paid to the Director by the Secretary-General of the League of Nations out of the general funds of the League.

The Director shall be responsible to the Secretary-General of the League for the proper expenditure of all moneys paid to him in pursuance of this Article.

INTERNATIONAL LABOR ORGANIZATION

CHAPTER II.

Procedure.

ARTICLE 400.

The agenda for all meetings of the Conference will be settled by the Governing Body, who shall consider any suggestion as to the agenda that may be made by the Government of any of the Members or by any representative organisation recognized for the purpose of Article 389.

ARTICLE 401.

The Director shall act as the Secretary of the Conference, and shall transmit the agenda so as to reach the Members four months before the meeting of the Conference, and, through them, the non-Government Delegates when appointed.

ARTICLE 402.

Any of the Governments of the Members may formally object to the inclusion of any item or items in the agenda. The grounds for such objection shall be set forth in a reasoned statement addressed to the Director, who shall circulate it to all the Members of the Permanent Organisation.

Items to which such objection has been made shall not, however, be excluded from the agenda, if at the Conference a majority of two-thirds of the votes cast by the Delegates present is in favour of considering them.

If the Conference decides (otherwise than under the preceding paragraph) by two-thirds of the votes cast by the Delegates present that any subject shall be considered by the Conference, that subject shall be included in the agenda for the following meeting.

ARTICLE 403.

The Conference shall regulate its own procedure, shall elect its own President, and may appoint committees to consider and report on any matter.

Except as otherwise expressly provided in this Part of the present Treaty, all matters shall be decided by a simple majority of the votes cast by the Delegates present.

The voting is void unless the total number of votes cast is equal to half the number of the Delegates attending the Conference.

ARTICLE 404.

The Conference may add to any committees which it appoints technical experts, who shall be assessors without power to vote.

ARTICLE 405.

When the Conference has decided on the adoption of proposals with regard to an item in the agenda, it will rest with the Conference to determine whether these proposals should take the form (a) of a recommendation to be submitted to the Members for consideration with a view to effect being given to it by national legislation or otherwise, or (b) of a draft international convention for ratification by the Members.

In either case a majority of two-thirds of the votes cast by the Delegates present shall be necessary on the final vote for the adoption of the recommendation or draft convention, as the case may be, by the Conference.

In framing any recommendation or draft convention of general application the Conference shall have due regard to those countries in which climatic conditions, the imperfect development of industrial organisation or other special circumstances makes the industrial conditions substantially different and shall suggest the modifications, if any, which it considers may be required to meet the case of such countries.

A copy of the recommendation or draft convention shall be authenticated by the signature of the President of the Conference and of the Director and shall be deposited with the Secretary-General of the League of Nations. The Secretary-General will communicate a certified copy of the recommendation or draft convention to each of the Members.

Each of the Members undertakes that it will, within the period of one year at most from the closing of the session of the Conference, or if it is impossible owing to exceptional circumstances to do so within the period of one year, then at the earliest practicable moment and in no case later than eighteen months from the closing of the session of the Conference, bring the recommendation or draft convention before the authority or authorities within whose competence the matter lies, for the enactment of legislation or other action.

In the case of a recommendation, the Members will inform the Secretary-General of the action taken.

In the case of a draft convention, the Member will, if it obtains the consent of the authority or authorities within whose competence the matter lies, communicate the formal ratification of the convention to the Secretary-General and will take such action as may be necessary to make effective the provisions of such convention.

If on a recommendation no legislative or other action is taken to make a recommendation effective, or if the draft convention fails to obtain the consent of the authority or authorities within whose competence the matter lies, no further obligation shall rest upon the Member.

In the case of a federal State, the power of which to enter into conventions on labor matters is subject to limitations, it shall be in the discretion of that Government to treat a draft convention to which such limitations apply as a recommendation only, and the provisions of this Article with respect to recommendations shall apply in such case.

The above Article shall be interpreted in accordance with the following principle:

In no case shall any Member be asked or required, as a result of the adoption of any recommendation or draft convention by the Conference, to lessen the protection afforded by its existing legislation to the workers concerned.

ARTICLE 406.

Any convention so ratified shall be registered by the Secretary-General of the League of Nations, but shall only be binding upon the Members which ratify it.

INTERNATIONAL LABOR ORGANIZATION

Article 407.

If any convention coming before the Conference for final consideration fails to secure the support of two-thirds of the votes cast by the Delegates present, it shall nevertheless be within the right of any of the Members of the Permanent Organisation to agree to such convention among themselves.

Any convention so agreed to shall be communicated by the Governments concerned to the Secretary-General of the League of Nations, who shall register it.

Article 408.

Each of the Members agrees to make an annual report to the International Labor Office on the measures which it has taken to give effect to the provisions of conventions to which it is a party. These reports shall be made in such form and shall contain such particulars as the Governing Body may request. The Director shall lay a summary of these reports before the next meeting of the Conference.

Article 409.

In the event of any representation being made to the International Labor Office by an industrial association of employers or of workers that any of the Members has failed to secure in any respect the effective observance within its jurisdiction of any convention to which it is a party, the Governing Body may communicate this representation to the Government against which it is made and may invite that Government to make such statement on the subject as it may think fit.

Article 410.

If no statement is received within a reasonable time from the Government in question, or if the statement when received is not deemed to be satisfactory by the Governing Body, the latter shall have the right to publish the representation and the statement, if any, made in reply to it.

Article 411.

Any of the Members shall have the right to file a complaint with the International Labor Office if it is not satisfied that any other Member is securing the effective observance of any convention which both have ratified in accordance with the foregoing Articles.

The Governing Body may, if it thinks fit, before referring such a complaint to a Commission of Enquiry, as hereinafter provided for, communicate with the Government in question in the manner described in Article 409.

If the Governing Body does not think it necessary to communicate the complaint to the Government in question, or if, when they have made such communication, no statement in reply has been received within a reasonable time which the Governing Body considers to be satisfactory, the Governing Body may apply for the appointment of a Commission of Enquiry to consider the complaint and to report thereon.

The Governing Body may adopt the same procedure either of its own motion or on receipt of a complaint from a Delegate to the Conference.

When any matter arising out of Articles 410 or 411 is being considered by the Governing Body, the Government in question shall, if not already represented thereon, be entitled to send a representative to take part in the proceedings of the Governing Body while the matter is under consideration. Adequate notice of the date on which the matter will be considered shall be given to the Government in question.

Article 412.

The Commission of Enquiry shall be constituted in accordance with the following provisions:

Each of the Members agrees to nominate within six months of the date on which the present Treaty comes into force three persons of industrial experience, of whom one shall be a representative of employers, one a representative of workers, and one a person of independent standing, who shall together form a panel from which the Members of the Commission of Enquiry shall be drawn.

The qualifications of the persons so nominated shall be subject to scrutiny by the Governing Body, which may by two-thirds of the votes cast by the representatives present refuse to accept the nomination of any person whose qualifications do not in its opinion comply with the requirements of the present Article.

Upon the application of the Governing Body, the Secretary-General of the League of Nations shall nominate three persons, one from each section of this panel, to constitute the Commission of Enquiry, and shall designate one of them as the President of the Commission. None of these three persons shall be a person nominated to the panel by any Member directly concerned in the complaint.

Article 413.

The Members agree that, in the event of the reference of a complaint to a Commission of Enquiry under Article 411, they will each, whether directly concerned in the complaint or not, place at the disposal of the Commission all the information in their possession which bears upon the subject-matter of the complaint.

Article 414.

When the Commission of Enquiry has fully considered the complaint, it shall prepare a report embodying its findings on all questions of fact relevant to determining the issue between the parties and containing such recommendations as it may think proper as to the steps which should be taken to meet the complaint and the time within which they should be taken.

It shall also indicate in this report the measures, if any, of an economic character against a defaulting Government which it considers to be appropriate, and which it considers other Governments would be justified in adopting.

Article 415.

The Secretary-General of the League of Nations shall communicate the report of the Commission of Enquiry to each of the Governments concerned in the complaint, and shall cause it to be published.

Each of these Governments shall within one month inform the Secretary-General of the League of Nations whether or not it accepts the recommendations contained in the report of the Commis-

INTERNATIONAL LABOR ORGANIZATION

sion; and if not, whether it proposes to refer the complaint to the Permanent Court of International Justice of the League of Nations.

Article 416.

In the event of any Member failing to take the action required by Article 405, with regard to a recommendation or draft Convention, any other Member shall be entitled to refer the matter to the Permanent Court of International Justice.

Article 417.

The decision of the Permanent Court of International Justice in regard to a complaint or matter which has been referred to it in pursuance of Article 415 or Article 416 shall be final.

Article 418.

The Permanent Court of International Justice may affirm, vary or reverse any of the findings or recommendations of the Commission of Enquiry, if any, and shall in its decision indicate the measures, if any, of an economic character which it considers to be appropriate, and which other Governments would be justified in adopting against a defaulting Government.

Article 419.

In the event of any Member failing to carry out within the time specified the recommendations, if any, contained in the report of the Commission of Enquiry, or in the decision of the Permanent Court of International Justice, as the case may be, any other Member may take against that Member the measures of an economic character indicated in the report of the Commission or in the decision of the Court as appropriate to the case.

Article 420.

The defaulting Government may at any time inform the Governing Body that it has taken the steps necessary to comply with the recommendations of the Commission of Enquiry or with those in the decision of the Permanent Court of International Justice, as the case may be, and may request it to apply to the Secretary-General of the League to constitute a Commission of Enquiry to verify its contention. In this case the provisions of Articles 412, 413, 414, 415, 417 and 418 shall apply, and if the report of the Commission of Enquiry or the decision of the Permanent Court of International Justice is in favour of the defaulting Government, the other Governments shall forthwith discontinue the measures of an economic character that they have taken against the defaulting Government.

CHAPTER III.

General.

Article 421.

The Members engage to apply conventions which they have ratified in accordance with the provisions of this Part of the present Treaty to their colonies, protectorates and possessions which are not fully self-governing.

(1) Except where owing to the local conditions the convention is inapplicable, or

(2) Subject to such modifications as may be necessary to adapt the convention to local conditions.

And each of the Members shall notify to the International Labor Office the action taken in respect of each of its colonies, protectorates and possessions which are not fully self-governing.

Article 422.

Amendments to this Part of the present Treaty which are adopted by the Conference by a majority of two-thirds of the votes cast by the Delegates present shall take effect when ratified by the States whose representatives compose the Council of the League of Nations and by three-fourths of the Members.

Article 423.

Any questions or dispute relating to the interpretation of this Part of the present Treaty or of any subsequent convention concluded by the Members in pursuance of the provisions of this Part of the present Treaty shall be referred for decision to the Permanent Court of International Justice.

CHAPTER IV.

Transitory Provisions.

Article 424.

The first meeting of the Conference shall take place in October, 1919. The place and agenda for this meeting shall be as specified in the Annex hereto.

Arrangements for the convening and the organisation of the first meeting of the Conference will be made by the Government designated for the purpose in the said Annex. That Government shall be assisted in the preparation of the documents for submission to the Conference by an International Committee constituted as provided in the said Annex.

The expenses of the first meeting and of all subsequent meetings held before the League of Nations has been able to establish a general fund, other than the expenses of Delegates and their advisers, will be borne by the Members in accordance with the apportionment of the expenses of the International Bureau of the Universal Postal Union.

Article 425.

Until the League of Nations has been constituted all communications which under the provisions of the foregoing Articles should be addressed to the Secretary-General of the League will be preserved by the Director of the International Labor Office, who will transmit them to the Secretary-General of the League.

Article 426.

Pending the creation of a Permanent Court of International Justice disputes which in accordance with this Part of the Present Treaty would be submitted to it for decision will be referred to a tribunal of three persons appointed by the Council of the League of Nations.

INTERNATIONAL LABOR ORGANIZATION

ANNEX.

First Meeting of Annual Labor Conference, 1919.

The place of meeting will be Washington.

The Government of the United States of America is requested to convene the Conference.

The International Organising Committee will consist of seven Members, appointed by the United States of America, Great Britain, France, Italy, Japan, Belgium and Switzerland. The Committee may, if it thinks necessary, invite other Members to appoint representatives.

Agenda:

(1) Application of principle of the 8-hours day or of the 48-hours week.

(2) Question of preventing or providing against unemployment.

(3) Women's employment:
   (a) Before and after child-birth, including the question of maternity benefit;
   (b) During the night;
   (c) In unhealthy processes.

(4) Employment of children:
   (a) Minimum age of employment;
   (b) During the night;
   (c) In unhealthy processes.

(5) Extension and application of the International Conventions adopted at Berne in 1906 on the prohibition of night work for women employed in industry and the prohibition of the use of white phosphorus in the manufacture of matches.

SECTION II.

General Principles.

Article 427.

The High Contracting Parties, recognising that the well-being, physical, moral and intellectual, of industrial wage-earners is of supreme international importance, have framed, in order to further this great end, the permanent machinery provided for in Section I and associated with that of the League of Nations.

They recognise that differences of climate, habits and customs, of economic opportunity and industrial tradition, make strict uniformity in the conditions of labor difficult of immediate attainment. But holding as they do, that labor should not be regarded merely as an article of commerce, they think that there are methods and principles for regulating labor conditions which all industrial communities should endeavour to apply, so far as their special circumstances will permit.

Among these methods and principles, the following seem to the High Contracting Parties to be of special and urgent importance:

> First.—The guiding principle above enunciated that labor should not be regarded merely as a commodity or article of commerce.
> Second.—The right of association for all lawful purposes by the employed as well as by the employers.
> Third.—The payment to the employed of a wage adequate to maintain a reasonable standard of life as this is understood in their time and country.

Fourth.—The adoption of an eight-hours day or a forty-eight-hours week as the standard to be aimed at where it has not already been attained.

Fifth.—The adoption of a weekly rest of at least twenty-four hours, which should include Sunday wherever practicable.

Sixth.—The abolition of child labor and the imposition of such limitations on the labor of young persons as shall permit the continuation of their education and assure their proper physical development.

Seventh.—The principle that men and women should receive equal remuneration for work of equal value.

Eighth.—The standard set by law in each country with respect to the conditions of labor should have due regard to the equitable economic treatment of all workers lawfully resident therein.

Ninth.—Each State should make provision for a system of inspection in which women should take part, in order to insure the enforcement of the laws and regulations for the protection of the employed.

Without claiming that these methods and principles are either complete or final, the High Contracting Parties are of opinion that they are well fitted to guide the policy of the League of Nations; and that, if adopted by the industrial communities who are members of the League, and safeguarded in practice by an adequate system of such inspection, they will confer lasting benefits upon the wage-earners of the world.

Draft Conventions and Recommendations
Adopted by

THE INTERNATIONAL LABOR CONFERENCE OF THE LEAGUE OF NATIONS

Washington, D. C., October 29-November 29, 1919.

I.

Draft Convention Limiting the Hours of Work in Industrial Undertakings to Eight in the Day and Forty-eight in the Week.

The General Conference of the International Labor Organization of the League of Nations,

Having been convened at Washington by the Government of the United States of America, on the 29th day of October, 1919, and

Having decided upon the adoption of certain proposals with regard to the "application of principle of the 8-hours day or the 48-hours week," which is the first item in the agenda for the Washington meeting of the Conference, and

Having determined that these proposals shall take the form of a draft international convention,

Adopts the following Draft Convention for ratification by the Members of the International Labor Organisation, in accordance with the Labor Part of the Treaty of Versailles of 28 June, 1919, and of the Treaty of St. Germain of 10 September, 1919:

ARTICLE 1.

For the purpose of this Convention, the term "industrial undertaking" includes particularly:

(a) Mines, quarries, and other works for the extraction of minerals from the earth.

(b) Industries in which articles are manufactured, altered, cleaned, repaired, ornamented, finished, adapted for sale, broken up or demolished, or in which materials are transformed; including shipbuilding and the generation, transformation, and transmission of electricity or motive power of any kind.

(c) Construction, reconstruction, maintenance, repair, alteration, or demolition of any building, railway, tramway, harbor, dock, pier, canal, inland waterway, road, tunnel, bridge, viaduct, sewer, drain, well, telegraphic or telephonic installation, electrical undertaking, gas work, waterwork or other work of construction, as well as the preparation for or laying the foundations of any such work or structure.

(d) Transport of passengers, or goods, by road, rail, sea or inland waterway, including the handling of goods at docks, quays, wharves or warehouses, but excluding transport by hand.

The provisions relative to transport by sea and on inland waterways shall be determined by a special conference dealing with employment at sea and on inland waterways.

The competent authority in each country shall define the line of division which separates industry from commerce and agriculture.

Article 2.

The working hours of persons employed in any public or private industrial undertaking or in any branch thereof, other than an undertaking in which only members of the same family are employed, shall not exceed eight (8) in the day and forty-eight (48) in the week, with the exceptions hereinafter provided for.

(a) The provisions of this Convention shall not apply to persons holding positions of supervision or management nor to persons employed in a confidential capacity.

(b) Where by law, custom, or agreement between employers' and workers' organizations, or where no such organizations exist between employers' and workers' representatives, the hours of work on one or more days of the week are less than eight (8), the limit of eight (8) hours may be exceeded on the remaining days of the week by the sanction of the competent public authority, or by agreement between such organizations or representatives; provided, however, that in no case under the provisions of this paragraph shall the daily limit of eight (8) hours be exceeded by more than one hour.

(c) Where persons are employed in shifts it shall be permissible to employ persons in excess of eight (8) hours in any one day and forty-eight (48) hours in any one week, if the average number of hours over a period of three weeks or less does not exceed eight (8) per day and forty-eight (48) per week.

Article 3.

The limit of hours of work prescribed in Article 2 may be exceeded in case of accident, actual or threatened, or in case of urgent work to be done to machinery or plant, or in case of "force majeure," but only so far as may be necessary to avoid serious interference with the ordinary working of the undertaking.

Article 4.

The limit of hours of work prescribed in Article 2 may also be exceeded in those processes which are required by reason of the nature of the process to be carried on continuously by a succession of shifts, subject to the condition that the working hours shall not exceed fifty-six in the week on the average. Such regulation of the hours of work shall in no case affect any rest days which may be secured by the national law to the workers in such processes in compensation for the weekly rest day.

ARTICLE 5.

In exceptional cases where it is recognized that the provisions of Article 2 can not be applied, but only in such cases, agreements between workers' and employers' organizations concerning the daily limit of work over a longer period of time, may be given the force of regulations, if the Government, to which these agreements shall be submitted, so decides. The average number of hours worked per week, over the number of weeks covered by any such agreement, shall not exceed forty-eight.

ARTICLE 6.

Regulations made by public authority shall determine for industrial undertakings:

(a) The permanent exceptions that may be allowed in preparatory or complementary work which must necessarily be carried on outside the limits laid down for the general working of an establishment, or for certain classes of workers whose work is essentially intermittent.

(b) The temporary exceptions that may be allowed, so that establishments may deal with exceptional cases of pressure of work.

These regulations shall be made only after consultation with the organizations of employers and workers concerned, if any such organizations exist. These regulations shall fix the maximum of additional hours in each instance, and the rate of pay for overtime shall not be less than one and one-quarter times the regular rate.

ARTICLE 7.

Each Government shall communicate to the International Labor Office:

(a) A list of the processes which are classed as being necessarily continuous in character under Article 4;

(b) Full information as to working of the agreements mentioned in Article 5, and

(c) Full information concerning the regulations made under Article 6 and their application.

The International Labor Office shall make an annual report thereon to the General Conference of the International Labor Organization.

ARTICLE 8.

In order to facilitate the enforcement of the provisions of this Convention, every employer shall be required:

(a) To notify by means of the posting of notices in conspicuous places in the works or other suitable place, or by such other method as may be approved by the Government, the hours at which work begins and ends, and where work is carried on by shifts the hours at which each shift begins and ends. These hours shall be so fixed that the duration of the work shall not exceed the limits prescribed by this Convention, and when so notified they shall not be changed except with such notice and in such manner as may be approved by the Government.

(b) To notify in the same way such rest intervals accorded during the period of work as are not reckoned as part of the working hours.

(c) To keep a record in the form prescribed by law or regulation in each country of all additional hours worked in pursuance of Articles 3 and 6 of this Convention.

It shall be made an offense against the law to employ any person outside the hours fixed in accordance with paragraph (a), or during the intervals fixed in accordance with paragraph (b).

ARTICLE 9.

In the application of this Convention to Japan the following modifications and conditions shall obtain:

(a) The term "industrial undertaking" includes particularly—

The undertakings enumerated in paragraph (a) of Article 1;

The undertakings enumerated in paragraph (b) of Article 1, provided there are at least ten workers employed;

The undertakings enumerated in paragraph (c) of Article 1, in so far as these undertakings shall be defined as "factories" by the competent authority;

The undertakings enumerated in paragraph (d) of Article 1, except transport of passengers or goods by road, handling of goods at docks, quays, wharves, and warehouses, and transport by hand, and,

Regardless of the number of persons employed, such of the undertakings enumerated in paragraphs (b) and (c) of Article 1 as may be declared by the competent authority either to be highly dangerous or to involve unhealthy processes.

(b) The actual working hours of persons of fifteen years of age or over in any public or private industrial undertaking, or in any branch thereof, shall not exceed fifty-seven in the week, except that in the raw-silk industry the limit may be sixty hours in the week.

(c) The actual working hours of persons under fifteen years of age in any public or private industrial undertaking, or in any branch thereof, and of all miners of whatever age engaged in underground work in the mines, shall in no case exceed forty-eight in the week.

(d) The limit of hours of work may be modified under the conditions provided for in Articles 2, 3, 4 and 5 of this Convention, but in no case shall the length of such modification bear to the length of the basic week a proportion greater than that which obtains in those Articles.

(e) A weekly rest period of twenty-four consecutive hours shall be allowed to all classes of workers.

(f) The provision in Japanese factory legislation limiting its application to places employing fifteen or more persons shall be amended so that such legislation shall apply to places employing ten or more persons.

(g) The provisions of the above paragraphs of this Article shall be brought into operation not later than 1 July, 1922, except that the provisions of Article 4 as modified by paragraph (d) of this Article shall be brought into operation not later than 1 July, 1923.

(h) The age of fifteen prescribed in paragraph (c) of this Article shall be raised, not later than 1 July, 1925, to sixteen.

ARTICLE 10.

In British India the principle of a sixty-hour week shall be adopted for all workers in the industries at present covered by the factory acts administered by the Government of India, in mines, and in such branches of railway work as shall be specified for this purpose by the competent authority. Any modification of this limitation made by the competent authority shall be subject to the provisions of Articles 6 and 7 of this Convention. In other respects the provisions of this Convention shall not apply to India, but further provisions limiting the hours of work in India shall be considered at a future meeting of the General Conference.

ARTICLE 11.

The provisions of this Convention shall not apply to China, Persia, and Siam, but provisions limiting the hours of work in these countries shall be considered at a future meeting of the General Conference.

ARTICLE 12.

In the application of this Convention to Greece, the date at which its provisions shall be brought into operation in accordance with Article 19 may be extended to not later than 1 July, 1923, in the case of the following industrial undertakings:

(1) Carbon-bisulphide works,
(2) Acids works,
(3) Tanneries,
(4) Paper mills,
(5) Printing works,
(6) Sawmills,
(7) Warehouses for the handling and preparation of tobacco,
(8) Surface mining,
(9) Foundries,
(10) Lime works,
(11) Dye works,
(12) Glassworks (blowers),
(13) Gas works (firemen),
(14) Loading and unloading merchandise;

and to not later than 1 July, 1924, in the case of the following industrial undertakings:

(1) Mechanical industries: Machine shops for engines, safes, scales, beds, tacks, shells (sporting), iron foundries, bronze foundries, tin shops, plating shops, manufactories of hydraulic apparatus;

(2) Constructional industries: Lime-kilns, cement works, plasterers' shops, tile yards, manufactories of bricks and pavements, potteries, marble yards, excavating and building work;

(3) Textile industries: Spinning and weaving mills of all kinds, except dye works;

(4) Food industries: Flour and grist-mills, bakeries, macaroni factories, manufactories of wines, alcohol, and drinks, oil works, breweries, manufactories of ice and carbonated drinks, manufactories of confectioners' products and chocolate, manufactories of sausages and preserves, slaughterhouses, and butcher shops;

(5) Chemical industries: Manufactories of synthetic colors, glassworks (except the blowers), manufactories of essence of turpentine and tartar, manufactories of oxygen and pharmaceutical products, manufactories of flaxseed oil, manufactories of glycerine, manufactories of calcium carbide, gas works (except the firemen);

(6) Leather industries: Shoe factories, manufactories of leather goods;

(7) Paper and printing industries: Manufactories of envelopes, record books, boxes, bags, bookbinding, lithographing, and zinc-engraving shops;

(8) Clothing industries: Clothing shops, underwear and trimmings, workshops for pressing, workshops for bed coverings, artificial flowers, feathers, and trimmings, hat and umbrella factories;

(9) Woodworking industries: Joiners' shops, coopers' sheds, wagon factories, manufactories of furniture and chairs, picture-framing establishments, brush and broom factories;

(10) Electrical industries: Power houses, shops for electrical installations;

(11) Transportation by land: Employees on railroads and street cars, firemen, drivers, and carters.

ARTICLE 13.

In the application of this Convention to Roumania the date at which its provisions shall be brought into operation in accordance with Article 19 may be extended to not later than 1 July, 1924.

ARTICLE 14.

The operation of the provisions of this Convention may be suspended in any country by the Government in the event of war or other emergency endangering the national safety.

ARTICLE 15.

The formal ratifications of this Convention, under the conditions set forth in Part XIII of the Treaty of Versailles of 28 June, 1919, and of the Treaty of St. Germain of 10 September, 1919, shall be communicated to the Secretary General of the League of Nations for registration.

ARTICLE 16.

Each Member which ratifies this Convention engages to apply it to its colonies, protectorates and possessions which are not fully self-governing:

(a) Except where owing to the local conditions its provisions are inapplicable; or

(b) Subject to such modifications as may be necessary to adapt its provisions to local conditions.

Each Member shall notify to the International Labor Office the action taken in respect of each of its colonies, protectorates, and possessions which are not fully self-governing.

ARTICLE 17.

As soon as the ratifications of two Members of the International Labor Organization have been registered with the Secretariat, the Secretary General of the League of Nations shall so notify all the Members of the International Labor Organization.

ARTICLE 18.

This Convention shall come into force at the date on which such notification is issued by the Secretary General of the League of Nations, and it shall then be binding only upon those Members which have registered their ratification with the Secretariat. Thereafter this Convention will come into force for any other Member, at the date on which its ratification is registered with the Secretariat.

ARTICLE 19.

Each Member which ratifies this Convention agrees to bring its provisions into operation not later than 1 July, 1921, and to take such action as may be necessary to make these provisions effective.

ARTICLE 20.

A Member which has ratified this Convention may denounce it after the expiration of ten years from the date on which the Convention first comes into force, by an act communicated to the Secretary General of the League of Nations for registration. Such denunciation shall not take effect until one year after the date on which it is registered with the Secretariat.

ARTICLE 21.

At least once in ten years the Governing Body of the International Labor Office shall present to the General Conference a report on the working of this Convention, and shall consider the desirability of placing on the agenda of the Conference the question of its revision or modification.

ARTICLE 22.

The French and English texts of this Convention shall both be authentic.

II.
DRAFT CONVENTION CONCERNING UNEMPLOYMENT.

ARTICLE 1.

Each Member which ratifies this Convention shall communicate to the International Labor Office, at intervals as short as possible and not exceeding three months, all available information, statistical or otherwise, concerning unemployment, including reports on measures taken or contemplated to combat unemployment. Whenever practicable, the information shall be made available for such communication not later than three months after the end of the period to which it relates.

ARTICLE 2.

Each Member which ratifies this Convention shall establish a system of free public employment agencies under the control of a central authority. Committees, which shall include representatives of employers and of workers, shall be appointed to advise on matters concerning the carrying on of these agencies.

Where both public and private free employment agencies exist, steps shall be taken to co-ordinate the operations of such agencies on a national scale.

The operations of the various national systems shall be co-ordinated by the International Labor Office in agreement with the countries concerned.

ARTICLE 3.

The Members of the International Labor Organization which ratify this Convention and which have established systems of insurance against unemployment shall, upon terms being agreed between the Members concerned, make arrangements whereby workers belonging to one Member and working in the territory of another shall be admitted to the same rates of benefit of such insurance as those which obtain for the workers belonging to the latter.

ARTICLE 4.

The formal ratifications of this Convention, under the conditions set forth in Part XIII of the Treaty of Versailles of 28 June, 119, and of the Treaty of St. Germain of 10 September, 1919, shall be communicated to the Secretary General of the League of Nations for registration.

ARTICLE 5.

Each Member which ratifies this Convention engages to apply it to its colonies, protectorates and possessions which are not fully self-governing:

(a) Except where owing to the local conditions its provisions are inapplicable; or

(b) Subject to such modifications as may be necessary to adapt its provisions to local conditions.

Each Member shall notify to the International Labor Office the action taken in respect of each of its colonies, protectorates and possessions which are not fully self-governing.

ARTICLE 6.

As soon as the ratifications of three Members of the International Labor Organization have been registered with the Secretariat, the Secretary General of the League of Nations shall so notify all the Members of the International Labor Organization.

ARTICLE 7.

This Convention shall come into force at the date on which such notification is issued by the Secretary General of the League of Nations, but it shall then be binding only upon those Members which have registered their ratifications with the Secretariat. Thereafter this Convention will come into force for any other Member at the date on which its ratification is registered with the Secretariat.

ARTICLE 8.

Each Member which ratifies this Convention agrees to bring its provisions into operation not later than 1 July, 1921, and to take such action as may be necessary to make these provisions effective.

ARTICLE 9.

A Member which has ratified this Convention may denounce it after the expiration of ten years from the date on which the Convention first comes into force, by an act communicated to the Secretary General of the League of Nations for registration. Such denunciation shall not take effect until one year after the date on which it is registered with the Secretariat.

ARTICLE 10.

At least once in ten years the Governing Body of the International Labor Office shall present to the General Conference a report on the working of this Convention, and shall consider the desirability of placing on the agenda of the Conference the question of its revision or modification.

ARTICLE 11.

The French and English texts of this Convention shall both be authentic.

III.
RECOMMENDATION CONCERNING UNEMPLOYMENT.

ARTICLE 1.

The General Conference recommends that each Member of the International Labor Organization take measures to prohibit the establishment of employment agencies which charge fees or which carry on their business for profit. Where such agencies already exist, it is further recommended that they be permitted to operate only under Government licenses, and that all practicable measures be taken to abolish such agencies as soon as possible.

ARTICLE 2.

The General Conference recommends to the Members of the International Labor Organization that the recruiting of bodies of workers in one country with a view to their employment in another country should be permitted only by mutual agreement between the countries concerned and after consultation with employers and workers in each country in the industries concerned.

ARTICLE 3.

The General Conference recommends that each Member of the International Labor Organization establish an effective system of unemployment insurance, either through a Government system or through a system of Government subventions to associations whose rules provide for the payment of benefits to their unemployed members.

ARTICLE 4.

The General Conference recommends that each Member of the International Labor Organization co-ordinate the execution of all work undertaken under public authority, with a view to reserving such work as far as practicable for periods of unemployment and for districts most affected by it.

IV.
RECOMMENDATION CONCERNING RECIPROCITY OF TREATMENT OF FOREIGN WORKERS.

The General Conference recommends that each Member of the International Labor Organization shall, on condition of reciprocity and upon terms to be agreed between the countries concerned, admit the foreign workers (together with their families) employed within its territory, to the benefit of its laws and regulations for the protection of its own workers, as well as to the right of lawful organization as enjoyed by its own workers.

V.
DRAFT CONVENTION CONCERNING EMPLOYMENT OF WOMEN BEFORE AND AFTER CHILDBIRTH.

The General Conference of the International Labor Organization of the League of Nations,

INTERNATIONAL LABOR ORGANIZATION

Having been convened at Washington by the Government of the United States of America on the 29th day of October, 1919, and

Having decided upon the adoption of certain proposals with regard to "women's employment, before and after childbirth, including the question of maternity benefit," which is part of the third item in the agenda for the Washington meeting of the Conference, and

Having determined that these proposals shall take the form of a draft international convention,

Adopts the following Draft Convention for ratification by the Members of the International Labor Organization, in accordance with the Labor Part of the Treaty of Versailles of 28 June, 1919, and of the Treaty of St. Germain of 10 September, 1919:

ARTICLE 1.

For the purpose of this Convention, the term "industrial undertaking" includes particularly:

(a) Mines, quarries, and other works for the extraction of minerals from the earth.

(b) Industries in which articles are manufactured, altered, cleaned, repaired, ornamented, finished, adapted for sale, broken up or demolished, or in which materials are transformed; including shipbuilding, and the generation, transformation, and transmission of electricity or motive power of any kind.

(c) Construction, reconstruction, maintenance, repair, alteration, or demolition of any building, railway, tramway, harbor, dock, pier, canal, inland waterway, road, tunnel, bridge, viaduct, sewer, drain, well, telegraphic or telephonic installation, electrical undertaking, gas work, water work, or other work of construction, as well as the preparation for or laying the foundation of any such work or structure.

(d) Transport of passengers or goods by road, rail, sea, or inland waterway, including the handling of goods at docks, quays, wharves, and warehouses, but excluding transport by hand.

For the purpose of this Convention, the term "commercial undertaking" includes any place where articles are sold or where commerce is carried on.

The competent authority in each country shall define the line of division which separates industry and commerce from agriculture.

ARTICLE 2.

For the purpose of this Convention the term "woman" signifies any female person, irrespective of age or nationality, whether married or unmarried, and the term "child" signifies any child whether legitimate or illegitimate.

ARTICLE 3.

In any public or private industrial or commercial undertaking, or in any branch thereof, other than an undertaking in which only members of the same family are employed, a woman—

(a) Shall not be permitted to work during the six weeks following her confinement.

(b) Shall have the right to leave her work if she produces a medical certificate stating that her confinement will probably take place within six weeks.

(c) Shall, while she is absent from her work in pursuance of paragraphs (a) and (b) be paid benefits sufficient for the full and healthy maintenance of herself and her child provided either out of public funds or by means of a system of insurance, the exact amount of which shall be determined by the competent authority in each country, and as an additional benefit shall be entitled to free attendance by a doctor or certified midwife. No mistake of the medical adviser in estimating the date of confinement shall preclude a woman from receiving these benefits from the date of the medical certificate up to the date on which the confinement actually takes place.

(d) Shall in any case, if she is nursing her child, be allowed half an hour twice a day during her working hours for this purpose.

Article 4.

Where a woman is absent from her work in accordance with paragraphs (a) or (b) of Article 3 of this Convention, or remains absent from her work for a longer period as a result of illness medically certified to arise out of pregnancy or confinement and rendering her unfit for work, it shall not be lawful, until her absence shall have exceeded a maximum period to be fixed by the competent authority in each country, for her employer to give her notice of dismissal during such absence, nor to give her notice of dismissal at such a time that the notice would expire during such absence.

Article 5.

The formal ratifications of this Convention, under the conditions set forth in Part XIII of the treaty of Versailles of 28 June, 1919, and of the Treaty of St. Germain of 10 September, 1919, shall be communicated to the Secretary General of the League of Nations for registration.

Article 6.

Each Member which ratifies this Convention engages to apply it to its colonies, protectorates, and possessions which are not fully self-governing:

(a) Except where, owing to the local conditions, its provisions are inapplicable; or

(b) Subject to such modifications as may be necessary to adapt its provisions to local conditions.

Each Member shall notify to the International Labor Office the action taken in respect of each of its colonies, protectorates, and possessions which are not fully self-governing.

Article 7.

As soon as the ratifications of two Members of the International Labor Organization have been registered with the Secretariat, the Secretary General of the League of Nations shall so notify all the Members of the International Labor Organization.

Article 8.

This Convention shall come into force at the date on which such notification is issued by the Secretary General of the League of Nations, but it shall then be binding only upon those Members which have registered their ratifications with the Secretariat. Thereafter this Convention will come into force for any other Member at the date on which its ratification is registered with the Secretariat.

Article 9.

Each Member which ratifies this Convention agrees to bring its provisions into operation not later than 1 July, 1922, and to take such action as may be necessary to make these provisions effective.

ARTICLE 10.

A Member which has ratified this Convention may denounce it after the expiration of ten years from the date on which the Convention first comes into force, by an act communicated to the Secretary General of the League of Nations for registration. Such denunciation shall not take effect until one year after the date on which it is registered with the Secretariat.

ARTICLE 11.

At least once in 10 years the Governing Body of the International Labor Office shall present to the General Conference a report on the working of this Convention, and shall consider the desirability of placing on the agenda of the Conference the question of its revision or modification.

ARTICLE 12.

The French and English texts of this Convention shall both be authentic.

VI.
DRAFT CONVENTION CONCERNING EMPLOYMENT OF WOMEN DURING THE NIGHT.

The General Conference of the International Labor Organization of the League of Nations,
 Having been convened at Washington by the Government of the United States of America, on the 29th day of October, 1919, and Having decided upon the adoption of certain proposals with regard to "women's employment: during the night," which is part of the third item in the agenda for the Washington meeting of the Conference, and
 Having determined that these proposals shall take the form of a draft international convention,
Adopts the following Draft Convention for ratification by the Members of the International Labor Organization, in accordance with the Labor Part of the Treaty of Versailles of 28 June, 1919, and of the Treaty of St. Germain of 10 September, 1919:

ARTICLE 1.

For the purpose of this Convention, the term "industrial undertaking" includes particularly:
 (a) Mines, quarries, and other works for the extraction of minerals from the earth;
 (b) Industries in which articles are manufactured, altered, cleaned, repaired, ornamented, finished, adapted for sale, broken up or demolished, or in which materials are transformed; including shipbuilding, and the generation, transformation, and transmission of electricity or motive power of any kind;
 (c) Construction, reconstruction, maintenance, repair, alteration, or demolition of any building, railway, tramway, harbor, dock, pier, canal, inland waterway, road, tunnel, bridge, viaduct, sewer, drain, well, telegraphic or telephonic installation, electrical undertaking, gas work, waterwork, or other work of construction, as well as the preparation for or laying the foundations of any such work or structure.

The competent authority in each country shall define the line of division which separates industry from commerce and agriculture.

ARTICLE 2.

For the purpose of this Convention, the term "night" signifies a period of at least eleven consecutive hours, including the interval between ten o'clock in the evening and five o'clock in the morning.

In those countries where no Government regulation as yet applies to the employment of women in industrial undertakings during the night, the term "night" may provisionally, and for a maximum period of three years, be declared by the Government to signify a period of only ten hours, including the interval between ten o'clock in the evening and five o'clock in the morning.

ARTICLE 3.

Women without distinction of age shall not be employed during the night in any public or private industrial undertaking, or in any branch thereof, other than an undertaking in which only members of the same family are employed.

ARTICLE 4.

Article 3 shall not apply:

(a) In cases of force majeure, when in any undertaking there comes an interruption of work which it was impossible to foresee, and which is not of a recurring character.

(b) In cases where the work has to do with raw materials or materials in course of treatment which are subject to rapid deterioration, when such night work is necessary to preserve the said materials from certain loss.

ARTICLE 5.

In India and Siam, the application of Article 3 of this Convention may be suspended by the Government in respect to any industrial undertaking, except factories as defined by the national law. Notice of every such suspension shall be filed with the International Labor Office.

ARTICLE 6.

In industrial undertakings which are influenced by the seasons and in all cases where exceptional circumstances demand it, the night period may be reduced to ten hours on sixty days of the year.

ARTICLE 7.

In countries where the climate renders work by day particularly trying to the health, the night period may be shorter than prescribed in the above articles, provided that compensatory rest is accorded during the day.

ARTICLE 8.

The formal ratifications of this Convention, under the conditions set forth in Part XIII of the Treaty of Versailles of 28 June, 1919, and of the Treaty of St. Germain of 10 September, 1919, shall be communicated to the Secretary General of the League of Nations for registration.

ARTICLE 9.

Each Member which ratifies this Convention engages to apply it to its colonies, protectorates and possessions which are not fully self-governing:
  (a) Except where owing to the local conditions its provisions are inapplicable; or
  (b) Subject to such modifications as may be necessary to adapt its provisions to local conditions.

Each Member shall notify to the International Labor Office the action taken in respect of each of its colonies, protectorates and possessions which are not fully self-governing.

ARTICLE 10.

As soon as the ratifications of two Members of the International Labor Organization have been registered with the Secretariat, the Secretary General of the League of Nations shall so notify all the Members of the International Labor Organization.

ARTICLE 11.

This Convention shall come into force at the date on which such notification is issued by the Secretary General of the League of Nations, but it shall then be binding only upon those Members which have registered their ratifications with the Secretariat. Thereafter this Convention will come into force for any other Member at the date on which its ratification is registered with the Secretariat.

ARTICLE 12.

Each Member which ratifies this Convention agrees to bring its provisions into operation not later than 1 July, 1922, and to take such action as may be necessary to make these provisions effective.

ARTICLE 13.

A Member which has ratified this Convention may denounce it after the expiration of ten years from the date on which the Convention first comes into force, by an act communicated to the Secretary General of the League of Nations for registration. Such denunciation shall not take effect until one year after the date on which it is registered with the Secretariat.

ARTICLE 14.

At least once in ten years, the Governing Body of the International Labor Office shall present to the General Conference a report on the working of this Convention, and shall consider the desirability of placing on the agenda of the Conference the question of its revision or modification.

ARTICLE 15.

The French and English texts of this Convention shall both be authentic.

VII.
RECOMMENDATION CONCERNING THE PREVENTION OF ANTHRAX.

The General Conference recommends to the Members of the International Labor Organization that arrangements should be made for the disinfection of wool infected with anthrax spores, either in the country exporting such wool or, if that is not practicable, at the port of entry in the country importing such wool.

VIII.
RECOMMENDATION CONCERNING THE PROTECTION OF WOMEN AND CHILDREN AGAINST LEAD POISONING.

The General Conference recommends to the Members of the International Labor Organization that in view of the danger involved to the function of maternity and to the physical development of children, women and young persons under the age of eighteen years be excluded from employment in the following processes:

(a) In furnace work in the reduction of zinc or lead ores.

(b) In the manipulation, treatment, or reduction of ashes containing lead, and in the de-silverizing of lead.

(c) In melting lead or old zinc on a large scale.

(d) In the manufacture of solder or alloys containing more than ten per cent. of lead.

(e) In the manufacture of litharge, massicot, red lead, white lead, orange lead, or sulphate, chromate or silicate (frit) of lead.

(f) In mixing and pasting in the manufacture or repair of electric accumulators.

(g) In the cleaning of workrooms where the above processes are carried on.

It is further recommended that the employment of women and young persons under the age of eighteen years in processes involving the use of lead compounds be permitted only subject to the following conditions:

(a) Locally applied exhaust ventilation, so as to remove dust and fumes at the point of origin.

(b) Cleanliness of tools and workrooms.

(c) Notification to Government authorities of all cases of lead poisoning, and compensation therefor.

(d) Periodic medical examination of the persons employed in such processes.

(e) Provision of sufficient and suitable cloak-room, washing, and mess-room accommodation, and of special protective clothing.

(f) Prohibition of bringing food or drink into work rooms.

It is further recommended that in industries where soluble lead compounds can be replaced by non-toxic substances, the use of soluble lead compounds should be strictly regulated.

For the purpose of this Recommendation, a lead compound should be considered as soluble if it contains more than five per cent. of its weight (estimated as metallic lead) soluble in a quarter of one per cent. solution of hydrochloric acid.

IX.
RECOMMENDATION CONCERNING THE ESTABLISHMENT OF GOVERNMENT HEALTH SERVICES.

The General Conference recommends that each Member of the International Labor Organization which has not already done so should establish as soon as possible, not only a system of efficient factory inspection, but also in addition thereto a Government service especially charged with the duty of safeguarding the health of the workers, which will keep in touch with the International Labor Office.

X.
RECOMMENDATION CONCERNING THE APPLICATION OF THE BERNE CONVENTION OF 1906, ON THE PROHIBITION OF THE USE OF WHITE PHOSPHORUS IN THE MANUFACTURE OF MATCHES.

The General Conference recommends that each Member of the International Labor Organization, which has not already done so, should adhere to the International Convention adopted at Berne in 1906 on the prohibition of the use of white phosphorus in the manufacture of matches.

XI.
DRAFT CONVENTION FIXING THE MINIMUM AGE FOR ADMISSION OF CHILDREN TO INDUSTRIAL EMPLOYMENT.

The General Conference of the International Labor Organization of the League of Nations,

Having been convened by the Government of the United States of America at Washington, on the 29th day of October, 1919, and

Having decided upon the adoption of certain proposals with regard to the "employment of children: minimum age of employment," which is part of the fourth item in the agenda for the Washington meeting of the Conference, and

Having determined that these proposals shall take the form of a draft international convention,

Adopts the following Draft Convention for ratification by the Members of the International Labor Organization, in accordance with the Labor Part of the Treaty of Versailles of 28 June, 1919, and of the Treaty of St. Germain of 10 September, 1919:

ARTICLE 1.

For the purpose of this Convention, the term "industrial undertaking" includes particularly:

(a) Mines, quarries and other works for the extraction of minerals from the earth.

(b) Industries in which articles are manufactured, altered, cleaned, repaired, ornamented, finished, adapted for sale, broken up or demolished, or in which materials are transformed; including shipbuilding, and the generation, transformation, and transmission of electricity and motive power of any kind.

(c) Construction, reconstruction, maintenance, repair, alteration, or demolition of any building, railway, tramway, harbor, dock, pier, canal, inland waterway, road, tunnel, bridge, viaduct, sewer, drain, well, telegraphic or telephonic installation, electrical undertaking, gas work, water work, or other work of construction, as well as the preparation for or laying the foundations of any such work or structure.

(d) Transport of passengers or goods by road or rail or inland waterway, including the handling of goods at docks, quays, wharves, and warehouses, but excluding transport by hand.

The competent authority in each country shall define the line of division which separates industry from commerce and agriculture.

ARTICLE 2..

Children under the age of fourteen years shall not be employed or work in any public or private industrial undertaking, or in any branch thereof, other than an undertaking in which only members of the same family are employed.

ARTICLE 3.

The provisions of article 2 shall not apply to work done by children in technical schools, provided that such work is approved and supervised by public authority.

ARTICLE 4.

In order to facilitate the enforcement of the provisions of this Convention, every employer in an industrial undertaking shall be required to keep a register of all persons under the age of sixteen years employed by him, and of the dates of their births.

ARTICLE 5.

In connection with the application of this Convention to Japan, the following modifications of article 2 may be made:

(a) Children over twelve years of age may be admitted into employment if they have finished the course in the elementary school;

(b) As regards children between the ages of twelve and fourteen already employed, transitional regulations may be made.

The provision in the present Japanese law admitting children under the age of twelve years to certain light and easy employments shall be repealed.

ARTICLE 6.

The provisions of article 2 shall not apply to India, but in India children under twelve years of age shall not be employed.

(a) In manufactories working with power and employing more than ten persons;

(b) In mines, quarries, and other works for the extraction of minerals from the earth;

(c) In the transport of passengers or goods, or mails, by rail, or in the handling of goods at docks, quays, and wharves, but excluding transport by hand.

ARTICLE 7.

The formal ratifications of this Convention, under the conditions set forth in Part XIII of the Treaty of Versailles of 28 June, 1919, and of the Treaty of St. Germain of 10 September, 1919, shall be communicated to the Secretary General of the League of Nations for registration.

ARTICLE 8.

Each Member which ratifies this Convention engages to apply it to its colonies, protectorates, and possessions which are not fully self-governing:

(a) Except where owing to the local conditions its provisions are inapplicable; or

(b) Subject to such modifications as may be necsssary to adapt its provisions to local conditions.

INTERNATIONAL LABOR ORGANIZATION

Each Member shall notify to the International Labor Office the action taken in respect to each of its colonies, protectorates, and possessions which are not fully self-governing.

Article 9.

As soon as the ratifications of two Members of the International Labor Organization have been registered with the Secretariat, the Secretary General of the League of Nations shall so notify all the members of the International Labor Organization.

Article 10.

This Convention shall come into force at the date on which such notification is issued by the Secretary General of the League of Nations, but it shall then be binding only upon those Members which have registered their ratifications with the Secretariat. Thereafter this Convention will come into force for any other Member at the date on which its ratification is registered with the Secretariat.

Article 11.

Each Member which ratifies this Convention agrees to bring its provisions into operation not later than 1 July, 1922, and to take such action as may be necessary to make these provisions effective.

Article 12.

A Member which has ratified this Convention may denounce it after the expiration of ten years from the date on which the Convention first comes into force, by an act communicated to the Secretary General of the League of Nations for registration. Such denunciation shall not take effect until one year after the date on which it is registered with the Secretariat.

Article 13.

At least once in ten years, the Governing Body of the International Labor Office shall present to the General Conference a report on the working of this Convention, and shall consider the desirability of placing on the agenda of the Conference the question of its revision or modification.

Article 14.

The French and English texts of this Convention shall both be authentic.

XII.

DRAFT CONVENTION CONCERNING THE NIGHT WORK OF YOUNG PERSONS EMPLOYED IN INDUSTRY

The General Conference of the International Labor Organization of the League of Nations,

Having been convened by the Government of the United States of America at Washington, on the 29th day of October, 1919, and

Having decided upon the adoption of certain proposals with regard to the "employment of children: during the night," which is part of the fourth item in the agenda for the Washington meeting of the Conference, and

Having determined that these proposals shall take the form of a draft international convention,

Adopts the following Draft Convention for ratification by the Members of the International Labor Organization, in accordance with the Labor Part of the Treaty of Versailles of 28 June, 1919, and of the Treaty of St. Germain of 10 September, 1919:

Article 1.

For the purpose of this Convention, the term "industrial undertaking" includes particularly:

(a) Mines, quarries and other works for the extraction of minerals from the earth.

(b) Industries in which articles are manufactured, altered, cleaned, repaired, ornamented, finished, adapted for sale, broken up or demolished, or in which materials are transformed; including shipbuilding, and the generation, transformation, and transmission of electricity or motive power of any kind.

(c) Construction, reconstruction, maintenance, repair, alteration, or demolition of any building, railway, tramway, harbor, dock, pier, canal, inland waterway, road, tunnel, bridge, viaduct, sewer, drain, well, telegraphic or telephonic installation, electrical undertaking, gas work, water work, or other work of construction, as well as the preparation for or laying the foundations of any such work or structure.

(d) Transport of passengers or goods by road or rail, including the handling of goods at docks, quays, wharves, and warehouses, but excluding transport by hand.

The competent authority in each country shall define the line of division which separates industry from commerce and agriculture.

Article 2.

Young persons under eighteen years of age shall not be employed during the night in any public or private industrial undertaking, or in any branch thereof, other than an undertaking in which only members of the same family are employed, except as hereinafter provided for.

Young persons over the age of sixteen may be employed during the night in the following industrial undertakings on work which by reason of the nature of the process is required to be carried on continuously day and night:

(a) Manufacture of iron and steel; processes in which reverberatory or regenerative furnaces are used, and galvanizing of sheet metal or wire (except the pickling process);

(b) Glass works;
(c) Manufacture of paper;
(d) Manufacture of raw sugar;
(e) Gold mining reduction work.

Article 3.

For the purpose of this Convention, the term "night" signifies a period of at least eleven consecutive hours, including the interval between ten o'clock in the evening and five o'clock in the morning.

In coal and lignite mines work may be carried on in the interval between ten o'clock in the evening and five o'clock in the morning, if an interval of ordinarily fifteen hours, and in no case of less than thirteen hours, separates two periods of work.

Where night work in the baking industry is prohibited for all workers, the interval between nine o'clock in the evening and four o'clock in the morning may be substituted in the baking industry for the interval between ten o'clock in the evening and five o'clock in the morning.

In those tropical countries in which work is suspended during the middle of the day, the night period may be shorter than eleven hours if compensatory rest is accorded during the day.

ARTICLE 4.

The provisions of articles 2 and 3 shall not apply to the night work of young persons between the ages of sixteen and eighteen years in cases of emergencies which could not have been controlled or foreseen, which are not of a periodical character, and which interfere with the normal working of the industrial undertaking.

ARTICLE 5.

In the application of this Convention to Japan, until 1 July, 1925, Article 2 shall apply only to young persons under fifteen years of age and thereafter it shall apply only to young persons under sixteen years of age.

ARTICLE 6.

In the application of this Convention to India, the term "industrial undertakings" shall include only "factories" as defined in the Indian Factory Act, and article 2 shall not apply to male young persons over fourteen years of age.

ARTICLE 7.

The prohibition of night work may be suspended by the Government, for young persons between the ages of sixteen and eighteen years, when in case of serious emergency the public interest demands it.

ARTICLE 8.

The formal ratifications of this Convention, under the conditions set forth in Part XIII of the Treaty of Versailles of 28 June, 1919, and of the Treaty of St. Germain of 10 September, 1919, shall be communicated to the Secretary General of the League of Nations for registration.

ARTICLE 9.

Each Member which ratifies this Convention engages to apply it to its colonies, protectorates and possessions which are not fully self-governing:

(a) Except where owing to the local conditions its provisions are inapplicable; or

(b) Subject to such modifications as may be necessary to adapt its provisions to local conditions.

Each Member shall notify to the International Labor Office the action taken in respect of each of its colonies, protectorates and possessions which are not fully self-governing.

ARTICLE 10.

As soon as the ratifications of two Members of the International Labor Organization have been registered with the Secretariat the Secretary General of the League of Nations shall so notify all the Members of the International Labor Organization.

ARTICLE 11.

This Convention shall come into force at the date on which such notification is issued by the Secretary General of the League of

Nations, and it shall then be binding only upon those Members which have registered their ratifications with the Secretariat. Thereafter this Convention will come into force for any other Member at the date on which its ratification is registered with the Secretariat.

ARTICLE 12.

Each Member which ratifies this Convention agrees to bring its provisions into operation not later than 1 July, 1922, and to take such action as may be necessary to make these provisions effective.

ARTICLE 13.

A Member which has ratified this Convention may denounce it after the expiration of ten years from the date on which the Convention first comes into force, by an act communicated to the Secretary General of the League of Nations for registration. Such denunciation shall not take effect until one year after the date on which it is registered with the Secretariat.

ARTICLE 14.

At least once in ten years the Governing Body of the International Labor Office shall present to the General Conference a report on the working of this Convention, and shall consider the desirability of placing on the agenda of the Conference the question of its revision or modification.

ARTICLE 15.

The French and English texts of this Convention shall both be authentic.

PROTECTION FOR SEAMEN.

Draft Conventions and Recommendations
Adopted by
THE INTERNATIONAL LABOR CONFERENCE OF THE LEAGUE OF NATIONS.
(Second Meeting.)
Genoa, June 15-July 10, 1920.

RECOMMENDATION CONCERNING THE LIMITATION OF HOURS OF WORK IN THE FISHING INDUSTRY.

The General Conference of the International Labor Organization of the League of Nations,

Having been convened at Genoa by the Governing Body of the International Labor Office, on the 15th day of June, 1920, and

Having decided upon the adoption of certain proposals with regard to the "Application to seamen of the Convention drafted at Washington, last November, limiting the hours of work in all industrial undertakings, including transport by sea and, under conditions to be determined, transport by inland waterways, to 8 hours in the day and 48 in the week. Consequential effects as regards manning and the regulations relating to accommodation and health on board ship," which is the first item in the addenda for the Genoa meeting of the Conference, and

    Having determined that these proposals shall take the form of a recommendation,

Adopts the following Recommendation, to be submitted to the Members of the International Labor Organization for consideration with a view to effect being given to it by national legislation or otherwise, in accordance with the Labor Part of the Treaty of Versailles of 28 June, 1919, of the Treaty of St. Germain of 10 September, 1919, of the Treaty of Neuilly of 27 November, 1919, and of the Treaty of the Grand Trianon of 4 June, 1920:

    In view of the declaration in the Treaties of Peace that all industrial communities should endeavor to adopt, so far as their special circumstances will permit, "an eight-hours' day or a forty-eight hours' week as the standard to be aimed at where it has not already been attained," the International Labor Conference recommends that each Member of the International Labor Organization enact legislation limiting in this direction the hours of work of all workers employed in the fishing industry, with such special provisions as may be necessary to meet the conditions peculiar to the fishing industry in each country; and that in framing such legislation each Government consult with the organizations of employers and the organizations of workers concerned.

RECOMMENDATION CONCERNING THE LIMITATION OF HOURS OF WORK IN INLAND NAVIGATION.

I.

    That each Member of the International Labor Organization should, if it has not already done so, enact legislation limiting in the direction of the above declaration in the Treaties of Peace [that all industrial communities should endeavor to adopt, so far as their special circumstances will permit, "an eight hours' day or a forty-eight hours' week as the standard to be aimed at where it has not already been attained"] the hours of work of workers employed in inland navigation, with such special provisions as may be necessary to meet the climatic and industrial conditions peculiar to inland navigation in each country, and after consultation with the organizations of employers and the organizations of workers concerned.

II.

    That those Members of the International Labor Organization whose territories are riparian to waterways which are used in common by their boats should enter into agreements for limiting in the direction of the aforesaid declaration, the hours of work of persons employed in inland navigation on such waterways, after consultation with the organizations of employers and the organizations of workers concerned.

III.

    That such national legislation and such agreements between riparian countries should follow as far as possible the general lines of the Draft Convention concerning hours of work adopted by the International Labor Conference at Washington, with such exceptions as may be necessary for meeting the climatic or other special conditions of the countries concerned.

IV.

That in the application of this Recommendation, each Member of the International Labor Organization should determine for itself, after consultation with the organizations of employers and the organizations of workers concerned, what is inland navigation as distinguished from maritime navigation, and should communicate its determination to the International Labor Office.

V

That each Member of the International Labor Organization should report to the International Labor Office, within two years after the adjournment of the Genoa Conference, the progress which it has made in the direction of this Recommendation.

RECOMMENDATION CONCERNING THE ESTABLISHMENT OF NATIONAL SEAMEN'S CODES.

In order that, as a result of the clear and systematic codification of the national law in each country, the seamen of the world, whether engaged on ships of their own or foreign countries, may have a better comprehension of their rights and obligations, and in order that the task of establishing an International Seamen's Code may be advanced and facilitated, the International Labor Conference recommends that each Member of the International Labor Organization undertake the embodiment in a seamen's code of all its laws and regulations relating to seamen in their activities as such.

DRAFT CONVENTION FIXING THE MINIMUM AGE FOR ADMISSION OF CHILDREN TO EMPLOYMENT AT SEA.

Article 1.

For the purpose of this Convention, the term "vessel" includes all ships and boats, of any nature whatsoever, engaged in maritime navigation, whether publicly or privately owned; it excludes ships of war.

Article 2.

Children under the age of fourteen years shall not be employed or work on vessels, other than vessels upon which only members of the same family are employed.

Article 3.

The provisions of Article 2 shall not apply to work done by children on school-ships or training ships, provided that such work is approved and supervised by public authority.

Article 4.

In order to facilitate the enforcement of the provisions of this Convention, every shipmaster shall be required to keep a register of all persons under the age of sixteen years employed on board his vessel, or a list of them in the articles of agreement, and of the dates of their births.

Article 5.

Each Member of the International Labor Organization which ratifies this Convention engages to apply it to its colonies, protectorates, and possessions which are not fully self-governing:

(a) Except where owing to the local conditions its provisions are inapplicable; or

(b) Subject to such modifications as may be necessary to adapt its provisions to local conditions.

Article 6.

The formal ratifications of this Convention under the conditions set forth in Part XIII of the Treaty of Versailles of 28 June, 1919, of the Treaty of St. Germain of 10 September, 1919, of the Treaty of Neuilly of 27 November, 1919, and of the Treaty of the Grand Trianon of 4 June, 1920, shall be communicated to the Secretary-General of the League of Nations for registration.

Article 7.

As soon as the ratifications of two Members of the International Labor Organization have been registered with the Secretariat, the Secretary General of the League of Nations shall so notify all the Members of the International Labor Organization.

Article 8.

This Convention shall come into force at the date on which such notification is issued by the Secretary General of the League of Nations, but it shall then be binding only upon those Members which have registered their ratifications with the Secretariat. Thereafter this Convention will come into force for any other Member at the date on which its ratification is registered with the Secretariat.

Article 9.

Subject to the provisions of Article 8, each Member which ratifies this Convention agrees to bring its provisions into operation not later than 1 July, 1922, and to take such action as may be necessary to make these provisions effective.

Article 10.

A Member which has ratified this Convention may denounce it after the expiration of ten years from the date on which the Convention first comes into force, by an act communicated to the Secretary General of the League of Nations for registration. Such denunciation shall not take effect until one year after the date on which it is registered with the Secretariat.

Article 11.

At least once in ten years, the Governing Body of the International Labor Office shall present to the General Conference a report on the working of this Convention, and shall consider the desirability of placing on the agenda of the Conference the question of its revision or modification.

RECOMMENDATION CONCERNING UNEMPLOYMENT INSURANCE FOR SEAMEN.

The General Conference, with a view to securing the application to seamen of Part III of the Recommendation concerning Unemployment adopted at Washington on 28 November, 1919, recommends that each Member of the International Labor Organization should establish for seamen an effective system of insurance against unemployment arising out of shipwreck or any other cause, either by means of Government insurance or by means of Government subventions to industrial organizations whose rules provide for the payment of benefits to their unemployed members.

DRAFT CONVENTION CONCERNING UNEMPLOYMENT INDEMNITY IN CASE OF LOSS OR FOUNDERING OF THE SHIP.

Article 1.

For the purpose of this Convention, the term "seamen" includes all persons employed on any vessel engaged in maritime navigation.

For the purpose of this Convention, the term "vessel" includes all ships and boats, of any nature whatsoever, engaged in maritime navigation, whether publicly or privately owned; it excludes ships of war.

Article 2.

In every case of loss or foundering of any vessel, the owner or person with whom the seaman has contracted for service on board the vessel shall pay to each seaman employed thereon an indemnity against unemployment resulting from such loss or foundering.

This indemnity shall be paid for the days during which the seaman remains in fact unemployed at the same rate as the wages payable under the contract, but the total indemnity payable under this Convention to any one seaman may be limited to two months' wages.

Article 3.

Seamen shall have the same remedies for recovering such indemnities as they have for recovering arrears of wages earned during the service.

Article 4.

Each Member of the International Labor Organization which ratifies this Convention engages to apply it to its colonies, protectorates and possessions which are not fully self-governing:

(a) Except where owing to the local conditions its provisions are inapplicable; or

(b) Subject to such modifications as may be necessary to adapt its provisions to local conditions.

Each Member shall notify to the International Labor Office the action taken in respect of each of its colonies, protectorates and possessions which are not fully self-governing.

Article 5.

The formal ratifications of this Convention under the conditions set forth in Part XIII of the Treaty of Versailles of 28 June, 1919, of the Treaty of St. Germain of 10 September, 1919, of the Treaty of Neuilly of 27 November, 1919, and of the Teaty of the Grand Trianon of 4 June, 1920, shall be communicated to the Secretary General of the League of Nations for registration.

Article 6.

As soon as the ratifications of two Members of the International Labor Organization have been registered with the Secretariat, the Secretary General of the League of Nations shall so notify all the Members of the International Labor Organization.

Article 7.

This Convention shall come into force at the date on which such notification is issued by the Secretary General of the League of Nations, and it shall then be binding only upon those Members which have registered their ratifications with the Secretariat. Thereafter this Convention will come into force for any other Member at the date on which its ratification is registered with the Secretariat.

Article 8.

Subject to the provisions of Article 7, each Member which ratifies this Convention agrees to bring its provisions into operation not later than 1 July, 1922, and to take such action as may be necessary to make these provisions effective.

Article 9.

A Member which has ratified this Convention may denounce it after the expiration of ten years from the date on which the Convention first comes into force, by an act communicated to the Secretary-General of the League of Nations for registration. Such denunciation shall not take effect until one year after the date on which it is registered with the Secretariat.

Article 10.

At least once in ten years, the Governing Body of the International Labor Office shall present to the General Conference a report on the working of this Convention, and shall consider the desirability of placing on the agenda of the Conference the question of its revision or modification.

DRAFT CONVENTION FOR ESTABLISHING FACILITIES FOR FINDING EMPLOYMENT FOR SEAMEN.

Article 1.

For the purpose of this Convention, the term "seamen" includes all persons, except officers, employed as members of the crew on vessels engaged in maritime navigation.

Article 2.

The business of finding employment for seamen shall not be carried on by any person, company, or other agency, as a commerical enterprise for pecuniary gain; nor shall any fees be charged directly or indirectly by any person, company or other agency, for finding employment for seamen on any ship.

The law of each country shall provide punishment for any violation of the provisions of this Article.

Article 3.

Notwithstanding the provisions of Article 2, any person, company or agency, which has been carrying on the work of finding employment for seamen as a commercial enterprise for pecuniary gain, may be permitted to continue temporarily under Government license, provided that such work is carried on under Government inspection and supervision so as to safeguard the rights of all concerned.

Each Member which ratifies this Convention agrees to take all practicable measures to abolish the practice of finding employment for seamen as a commercial enterprise for pecuniary gain as soon as possible.

Article 4.

Each Member which ratifies this Convention agrees that there shall be organized and maintained an efficient and adequate system of public employment offices for finding employment for seamen without charge. Such system may be organized and maintained, either:

(1) By representative associations of shipowners and seamen jointly under the control of a central authority, or,

(2) In the absence of such joint action, by the State itself.

The work of all such employment offices shall be administered by persons having practical maritime experience.

Where such employment offices of different types exist, steps shall be taken to co-ordinate them on a national basis.

Article 5.

Committees consisting of an equal number of representatives of shipowners and seamen shall be constituted to advise on matters concerning the carrying on of these offices; the Government in each country may make provision for further defining the powers of these committees, particularly with reference to the committees' selection of their chairmen from outside their own membership, to the degree of State supervision, and to the assistance which such committees shall have from persons interested in the welfare of seamen.

Article 6.

In connection with the employment of seamen, freedom of choice of ship shall be assured to seamen and freedom of choice of crew shall be assured to shipowners.

Article 7.

The necessary guarantees for protecting all parties concerned shall be included in the contract of engagement or articles of agreeemnt, and proper facilities shall be assured to seamen for examining such contract or articles before and after signing.

Article 8.

Each Member which ratifies this Convention will take steps to see that the facilities for employment of seamen provided for in this Convention shall, if necessary, by means of public offices, be available for the seamen of all countries which ratify this Convention, and where the industrial conditions are generally the same.

Article 9.

Each country shall decide for itself whether provisions similar to those in this Convention shall be put in force for deck-officers and engineer-officers.

Article 10.

Each Member which ratifies this Convention shall communicate to the International Labor Office all available information, statistical or otherwise, concerning unemployment among seamen and concerning the work of its seamen's employment agencies.

The International Labor Office shall take steps to secure the co-ordination of the various national agencies for finding employment for seamen, in agreement with the Governments or organizations concerned in each country.

INTERNATIONAL LABOR ORGANIZATION

Article 11.

Each Member of the International Labor Organization which ratifies this Convention engages to apply it to its colonies, protectorates and possessions which are not fully self-governing:

(a) Except where owing to the local conditions its provisions are inapplicable; or

(b) Subject to such modifications as may be necessary to adapt its provisions to local conditions.

Each Member shall notify to the International Labor Office the action taken in respect of each of its colonies, protectorates and possessions which are not fully self-governing.

Article 12.

The formal ratifications of this Convention under the conditions set forth in Part XIII of the Treaty of Versailles of 28 June, 1919, of the Treaty of St. Germain of 10 September, 1919, of the Treaty of Neuilly of 27 November, 1919, and of the Treaty of the Grand Trianon of 4 June, 1920, shall be communicated to the Secretary-General of the League of Nations for registration.

Article 13.

As soon as the ratifications of two Members of the International Labor Organization have been registered with the Secretariat, the Secretary-General of the League of Nations shall so notify all the Members of the International Labor Organization.

Article 14.

This Convention shall come into force at the date on which such notification is issued by the Secretary General of the League of Nations, and it shall then be binding only upon those Members which have registered their ratifications with the Secretariat. Thereafter this Convention will come into force for any other Member at the date on which its ratification is registered with the Secretariat.

Article 15.

Subject to the provisions of Article 14, each Member which ratifies this Convention agrees to bring its provisions into operation not later than 1 July, 1922, and to take such action as may be necessary to make these provisions effective.

Article 16.

A Member which has ratified this Convention may denounce it after the expiration of ten years from the date on which the Convention first comes into force, by an act communicated to the Secretary-General of the League of Nations for registration. Such denunciation shall not take effect until one year after the date on which it is registered with the Secretariat.

Article 17.

At least once in ten years, the Governing Body of the International Labor Office shall present to the General Conference a report on the working of this Convention, and shall consider the desirability of placing on the agenda of the Conference the question of its revision or modification.

THE INTERNATIONAL PROTECTION OF LABOR

THIRD SESSION*
(Geneva, 24 October - 19 November 1921).
Recommendation [No. 11] concerning the prevention of unemployment in agriculture.

The General Conference of the International Labour Organisation of the League of Nations,

Having been convened at Geneva by the Governing Body of the International Labour Office, and having met in its Third Session on 25 October 1921, and

Having decided upon the adoption of certain proposals with regard to the prevention of unemployment in agriculture, which is included in the third item of the agenda of the Session, and

Having decided that these proposals shall take the form of a recommendation,

adopts the following Recommendation to be submitted to the Members of the International Labour Organisation for consideration with a view to effect being given to it by national legislation or otherwise, in accordance with the provisions of Part XIII of the Treaty of Versailles and of the corresponding Parts of the other Treaties of Peace:

I.

The General Conference of the International Labour Organisation,

Considering that the Draft Convention and Recommendations concerning unemployment adopted at Washington are in principle applicable to agricultural workers, and recognising the special character of unemployment in agriculture,

Recommends that each Member of the International Labour Organisation should consider measures for the prevention of or providing against unemployment amongst agricultural workers suitable to the economic and agricultural conditions of its country, and that it should examine particularly from this point of view the advisability:—

(1) of adopting modern technical methods to bring into cultivation land which is at present not worked or only partially developed, but which could by such means be made to yield an adequate return;

(2) of encouraging the adoption of improved systems of cultivation and the more intensive use of the land;

(3) of providing facilities for settlement on the land;

(4) of taking steps to render work of a temporary nature accessible to unemployed agricultural workers by means of the provision of transport facilities;

(5) of developing industries and supplementary forms of employment which would provide occupation for agricultural workers who suffer from seasonal unemployment, provided that steps be taken to ensure that such work is carried on under equitable conditions;

(6) of taking steps to encourage the creation of agricultural workers' co-operative societies for the working and purchase or renting of land; and

---

*The first Recommendation and Draft Convention, adopted at this Session, are given in full; the others are reprinted without the Preambles and the Standard Articles of the conventions. For the complete official texts of the draft conventions and recommendations, adopted at this Session and all other Sessions of the General Conference, see the publications of the International Labor Office, from which the parts of the texts on this page and the following pages are reprinted.

INTERNATIONAL LABOR ORGANIZATION

of taking steps to this end to increase agricultural credit especially in favour of co-operative agricultural associations of land workers established for the purpose of agricultural production.

II.

The General Conference recommends that each Member of the International Labour Organisation furnish the International Labour Office with a periodical report dealing with the steps taken to give effect to the above Recommendation.

Recommendation [No. 12] concerning the protection, before and after childbirth, of women wage-earners in agriculture.

The General Conference of the International Labour Organisation recommends:

That each Member of the International Labour Organisation take measures to ensure to women wage-earners employed in agricultural undertakings protection before and after childbirth similar to that provided by the Draft Labour Convention adopted by the International Labour Conference at Washington for women employed in industry and commerce, and that such measures should include the right to a period of absence from work before and after childbirth and to a grant of benefit during the said period, provided either out of public funds or by means of a system of insurance.

Recommendation [No. 13] concerning night work of women in agriculture.

The General Conference of the International Labour Organisation recommends:

That each Member of the International Labour Organisation take steps to regulate the employment of women wage-earners in agricultural undertakings during the night in such a way as to ensure to them a period of rest compatible with their physical necessities and consisting of not less than nine hours, which shall, when possible, be consecutive.

Draft Convention [No. 10] concerning the age for admission of children to employment in agriculture.

The General Conference of the International Labour Organisation of the League of Nations,

Having been convened at Geneva by the Governing Body of the International Labour Office, and having met in its Third Session on 25 October 1921, and

Having decided upon the adoption of certain proposals with regard to the employment of children in agriculture during compulsory school hours, which is included in the third item of the agenda of the Session, and

Having determined that these proposals shall take the form of a draft international convention,

adopts the following Draft Convention for ratification by the Members of the International Labour Organisation, in accordance with the provisions of Part XIII of the Treaty of Versailles and of the corresponding Parts of the other Treaties of Peace:

ARTICLE 1.

Children under the age of fourteen years may not be employed or work in any public or private agricultural undertaking, or in any branch thereof, save outside the hours fixed for school attendance. If they are employed outside the hours of school attendance, the employment shall not be such as to prejudice their attendance at school.

ARTICLE 2.

For purposes of practical vocational instruction the periods and the hours of school attendance may be so arranged as to permit the employment of children on light agricultural work and in particular on light work connected with the harvest, provided that such employment shall not reduce the total annual period of school attendance to less than eight months.

ARTICLE 3.

The provisions of Article 1 shall not apply to work done by children in technical schools, provided that such work is approved and supervised by public authority.

ARTICLE 4.

The formal ratifications of this Convention under the conditions set forth in Part XIII of the Treaty of Versailles and of the corresponding Parts of the other Treaties of Peace, shall be communicated to the Secretary-General of the League of Nations for registration.

ARTICLE 5.

This Convention shall come into force at the date on which the ratifications of two Members of the International Labour Organisation have been registered by the Secretary-General.

It shall be binding only upon those Members whose ratifications have been registered with the Secretariat.

Thereafter, the Convention shall come into force for any Member at the date on which its ratification has been registered with the Secretariat.

ARTICLE 6.

As soon as the ratifications of two Members of the International Labour Organisation have been registered with the Secretariat, the Secretary-General of the League of Nations shall so notify all the Members of the International Labour Organisation. He shall likewise notify them of the registration of ratifications which may be communicated subsequently by other Members of the Organisation.

ARTICLE 7.

Subject to the provisions of Article 5, each Member which ratifies this Convention agrees to bring the provisions of Articles 1, 2 and 3 into operation not later than 1 January 1924 and to take such action as may be necessary to make these provisions effective.

ARTICLE 8.

Each Member of the International Labour Organisation which ratifies this Convention engages to apply it to its colonies, possessions and protectorates, in accordance with the provisions of Article 421 of the Treaty of Versailles and of the corresponding Articles of the other Treaties of Peace.

ARTICLE 9.

A Member which has ratified this Convention may denounce it after the expiration of ten years from the date on which the Convention first comes into force, by an act communicated to the Secretary-General of the League of Nations for registration. Such denunciation shall not take effect until one year after the date on which it is registered with the Secretariat.

INTERNATIONAL LABOR ORGANIZATION

Article 10.

At least once in ten years, the Governing Body of the International Labour Office shall present to the General Conference a report on the working of this Convention and shall consider the desirability of placing on the agenda of the Conference the question of its revision or modification.

Article 11.

The French and English texts of this Convention shall both be authentic.

Recommendation [No. 14] concerning night work of children and young persons in agriculture.

The General Conference of the International Labour Organisation recommends:

I.

That each Member of the International Labour Organisation take steps to regulate the employment of children under the age of fourteen years in agricultural undertakings during the night, in such a way as to ensure to them a period of rest compatible with their physical necessities and consisting of not less than ten consecutive hours.

II.

That each Member of the International Labour Organisation take steps to regulate the employment of young persons between the ages of fourteen and eighteen years in agricultural undertakings during the night, in such a way as to ensure to them a period of rest compatible with their physical necessities and consisting of not less than nine consecutive hours.

Recommendation [No. 15] concerning the development of technical agricultural education.

The General Conference of the International Labour Organisation recommends:

That each Member of the International Labour Organisation endeavour to develop vocational agricultural education and in particular to make such education available to agricultural wage-earners on the same conditions as to other persons engaged in agriculture.

That each Member of the International Labour Organisation send a report to the International Labour Office at regular intervals containing as full information as possible as to the administration of the laws, the sums expended, and the measures taken in order to develop vocational agricultural education.

Recommendation [No. 16] concerning living-in conditions of agricultural workers.

The General Conference of the International Labour Organisation recommends:

I.

That each Member of the International Labour Organisation, which has not already done so, take statutory or other measures to regulate the living-in conditions of agricultural workers with due regard to the special climatic or other conditions affecting agricultural work in its country, and after consultation with the employers' and workers' organisations concerned, if such organisations exist.

II.

That such measures shall apply to all accommodation provided by employers for housing their workers either individually, or in groups, or with their families, whether the accommodation is provided in the houses of such employers or in buildings placed by them at the workers' disposal.

III.

That such measures shall contain the following provisions:

(a) Unless climatic conditions render heating superfluous, the accommodation intended for workers' families, groups of workers, or individual workers, should contain rooms which can be heated.

(b) Accommodation intended for groups of workers shall provide a separate bed for each worker, shall afford facilities for ensuring personal cleanliness, and shall provide for the separation of the sexes. In the case of families, adequate provision shall be made for the children.

(c) Stables, cowhouses and open sheds should not be used for sleeping quarters.

IV.

That each Member of the International Labour Organisation take steps to ensure the observance of such measures.

Draft Convention [No. 11] concerning the rights of association and combination of agricultural workers.

ARTICLE 1.

Each Member of the International Labour Organisation which ratifies this Convention undertakes to secure to all those engaged in agriculture the same rights of association and combination as to industrial workers, and to repeal any statutory or other provisions restricting such rights in the case of those engaged in agriculture.

(For the Standard Articles, see Draft Convention, No. 10)

Draft Convention [No. 12] concerning workmen's compensation in agriculture.

ARTICLE 1.

Each Member of the International Labour Organisation which ratifies this Convention undertakes to extend to all agricultural wage-earners its laws and regulations which provide for the compensation of workers for personal injury by accident arising out of or in the course of their employment.

(For the Standard Articles, see Draft Convention, No. 10)

Recommendation [No. 17] concerning social insurance in agriculture.

The General Conference of the International Labour Organisation recommends:

That each Member of the International Labour Organisation extend its laws and regulations establishing systems of insurance against sickness, invalidity, old age and other similar social risks to agricultural wage-earners on conditions equivalent to those prevailing in the case of workers in industrial and commercial occupations.

INTERNATIONAL LABOR ORGANIZATION

Draft Convention [No. 13] concerning the use of white lead in painting.

Article 1.

Each Member of the International Labour Organisation ratifying the present Convention undertakes to prohibit, with the exceptions provided for in Article 2, the use of white lead and sulphate of lead and of all products containing these pigments, in the internal painting of buildings, except where the use of white lead or sulphate of lead or products containing these pigments is considered necessary for railway stations or industrial establishments by the competent authority after consultation with the employers' and workers' organisations concerned.

It shall nevertheless be permissible to use white pigments containing a maximum of 2 per cent. of lead expressed in terms of metallic lead.

Article 2.

The provisions of Article I shall not apply to artistic painting or fine lining.

The Governments shall define the limits of such forms of painting, and shall regulate the use of white lead, sulphate of lead, and all products containing these pigments, for these purposes in conformity with the provisions of Articles 5, 6 and 7 of the present Convention.

Article 3.

The employment of males under eighteen years of age and of all females shall be prohibited in any painting work of an industrial character involving the use of white lead or sulphate of lead or other products containing these pigments.

The competent authorities shall have power, after consulting the employers' and workers' organisations concerned, to permit the employment of painters' apprentices in the work prohibited by the preceding paragraph, with a view to their education in their trade.

Article 4.

The prohibitions prescribed in Articles 1 and 3 shall come into force six years from the date of the closure of the Third Session of the International Labour Conference.

Article 5.

Each Member of the International Labour Organisation ratifying the present Convention undertakes to regulate the use of white lead, sulphate of lead and of all products containing these pigments, in operations for which their use is not prohibited, on the following principles:

I. *(a)* White lead, sulphate of lead, or products containing these pigments shall not be used in painting operations except in the form of paste or of paint ready for use.

   (b) Measures shall be taken in order to prevent danger arising from the application of paint in the form of spray.

   (c) Measures shall be taken, wherever practicable, to prevent danger arising from dust caused by dry rubbing down and scraping.

II. *(a)* Adequate facilities shall be provided to enable working painters to wash during and on cessation of work.

   (b) Overalls shall be worn by working painters during the whole of the working period.

   (c) Suitable arrangements shall be made to prevent clothing put off during working hours being soiled by painting material.

III. *(a)* Cases of lead poisoning and of suspected lead poisoning shall be notified, and shall be subsequently verified by a medical man appointed by the competent authority.
(b) The competent authority may require, when necessary, a medical examination of workers.

IV. Instructions with regard to the special hygienic precautions to be taken in the painting trade shall be distributed to working painters.

ARTICLE 6.

The competent authority shall take such steps as it considers necessary to ensure the observance of the regulations prescribed by virtue of the foregoing Articles, after consultation with the employers' and workers' organisations concerned.

ARTICLE 7.

Statistics with regard to lead poisoning among working painters shall be obtained:
(a) As to morbidity—by notification and certification of all cases of lead poisoning.
(b) As to mortality—by a method approved by the official statistical authority in each country.

(*For the Standard Articles, see Draft Convention, No. 10*)

Draft Convention [No. 14] concerning the application of the weekly rest in industrial undertakings.

ARTICLE 1.

For the purpose of this Convention, the term "industrial undertakings" includes:

(a) Mines, quarries, and other works for the extraction of minerals from the earth.

(b) Industries in which articles are manufactured, altered, cleaned, repaired, ornamented, finished, adapted for sale, broken up or demolished, or in which materials are transformed; including shipbuilding and the generation, transformation and transmission of electricity or motive power of any kind.

(c) Construction, reconstruction, maintenance, repair, alteration, or demolition of any building, railway, tramway, harbour, dock, pier, canal, inland waterway, road, tunnel, bridge, viaduct, sewer, drain, well, telegraphic or telephonic installation, electrical undertaking, gas work, waterwork, or other work of construction, as well as the preparation for or laying the foundations of any such work or structure.

(d) Transport of passengers or goods by road, rail, or inland waterway, including the handling of goods at docks, quays, wharves or warehouses, but excluding transport by hand.

This definition shall be subject to the special national exceptions contained in the Washington Convention limiting the hours of work in industrial undertakings to eight in the day and forty-eight in the week, so far as such exceptions are applicable to the present Convention.

Where necessary, in addition to the above enumeration, each Member may define the line of division which separates industry from commerce and agriculture.

ARTICLE 2.

The whole of the staff employed in any industrial undertaking, public or private, or in any branch thereof shall, except as otherwise provided for by the following Articles, enjoy in every period of seven days a period of rest comprising at least twenty-four consecutive hours.

This period of rest shall, wherever possible, be granted simultaneously to the whole of the staff of each undertaking.

It shall, wherever possible, be fixed so as to coincide with the traditions or customs of the country or district.

ARTICLE 3.

Each Member may except from the application of the provisions of Article 2 persons employed in industrial undertakings in which only the members of one single family are employed.

ARTICLE 4.

Each Member may authorise total or partial exceptions (including suspensions or diminutions) from the provisions of Article 2, special regard being had to all proper humanitarian and economic considerations and after consultation with responsible associations of employers and workers, wherever such exist.

Such consultation shall not be necessary in the case of exceptions which have already been made under existing legislation.

ARTICLE 5.

Each Member shall make, as far as possible, provision for compensatory periods of rest for the suspensions or diminutions made in virtue of Article 4, except in cases where agreements or customs already provide for such periods.

ARTICLE 6.

Each Member will draw up a list of the exceptions made under Articles 3 and 4 of this Convention and will communicate it to the International Labour Office, and thereafter in every second year any modifications of this list which shall have been made.

The International Labour Office will present a report on this subject to the General Conference of the International Labour Organisation.

ARTICLE 7.

In order to facilitate the application of the provisions of this Convention, each employer, director, or manager, shall be obliged:

(a) Where the weekly rest is given to the whole of the staff collectively, to make known such days and hours of collective rest by means of notices posted conspicuously in the establishment or any other convenient place, or in any other manner approved by the Government.

(b) Where the rest period is not granted to the whole of the staff collectively, to make known, by means of a roster drawn up in accordance with the method approved by the legislation of the country, or by a regulation of the competent authority, the workers or employees subject to a special system of rest, and to indicate that system.

(For the Standard Articles, see Draft Convention, No. 10)

Recommendation [No. 18] concerning the application of the weekly rest in commercial establishments.

The General Conference recommends:

I.

That each Member of the International Labour Organisation take measures to provide that the whole of the staff employed in any commercial establishment, public or private, or in any branch thereof, except as otherwise provided for by the following paragraphs, should enjoy in every period of seven days a period of rest comprising at least twenty-four consecutive hours.

It is further recommended that this period of rest should, wherever possible, be granted simultaneously to the whole of the staff of each establishment, and that it should, wherever possible, be fixed so as to coincide with the days already established by the traditions or customs of the country or district.

II.

That each Member take the steps necessary to secure the application of this Recommendation and to define any exceptions which the Member may consider to be necessary.

If exceptions are found necessary, it is recommended that the Member should draw up a list of such exceptions.

III.

That each Member should communicate to the International Labour Office the list of the exceptions made in pursuance of paragraph II, and thereafter every two years any modifications of this list which it shall have made, in order that the International Labour Office may present a report thereon to the International Labour Conference.

Draft Convention [No. 15]
fixing the minimum age for the admission of young persons to employment as trimmers or stokers.

ARTICLE 1.

For the purpose of this Convention, the term "vessel" includes all ships and boats, of any nature whatsoever, engaged in maritime navigation, whether publicly or privately owned; it excludes ships of war.

ARTICLE 2.

Young persons under the age of eighteen years shall not be employed or work on vessels as trimmers or stokers.

ARTICLE 3.

The provisions of Article 2 shall not apply:

(a) to work done by young persons on school-ships or training-ships, provided that such work is approved and supervised by public authority;

(b) to the employment of young persons on vessels mainly propelled by other means than steam;

(c) to young persons of not less than sixteen years of age, who, if found physically fit after medical examination, may be employed as trimmers or stokers on vessels exclusively engaged in the coastal trade of India and of Japan, subject to regulations made after consultation with the most representative organisations of employers and workers in those countries.

ARTICLE 4.

When a trimmer or stoker is required in a port where young persons of less than eighteen years of age only are available, such young persons may be employed and in that case it shall be necessary to engage two young persons in place of the trimmer or stoker required. Such young persons shall be at least sixteen years of age.

ARTICLE 5.

In order to facilitate the enforcement of the provisions of this Convention, every shipmaster shall be required to keep a register of all persons under the age of eighteen years employed on board his vessel, or a list of them in the articles of agreement, and of the dates of their births.

ARTICLE 6.

Articles of agreement shall contain a brief summary of the provisions of this Convention.

(*For the Standard Articles, see Draft Convention, No. 10*)

Draft Convention [No. 16]
concerning the compulsory medical examination of children and young persons employed at sea.

ARTICLE 1.

For the purpose of this Convention, the term "vessel" includes all ships and boats, of any nature whatsoever, engaged in maritime navigation, whether publicly or privately owned; it excludes ships of war.

ARTICLE 2.

The employment of any child or young person under eighteen years of age on any vessel, other than vessels upon which only members of the same family are employed, shall be conditional on the production of a medical certificate attesting fitness for such work, signed by a doctor who shall be approved by the competent authority.

ARTICLE 3.

The continued employment at sea of any such child or young person shall be subject to the repetition of such medical examination at intervals of not more than one year, and the production, after each such examination, of a further medical certificate attesting fitness for such work. Should a medical certificate expire in the course of a voyage, it shall remain in force until the end of the said voyage.

ARTICLE 4.

In urgent cases, the competent authority may allow a young person below the age of eighteen years to embark without having undergone the examination provided for in Articles 2 and 3 of this Convention, always provided that such an examination shall be undergone at the first port at which the vessel calls.

(*For the Standard Articles, see Draft Convention, No. 10*)

FOURTH SESSION
Geneva, 18 October - 3 November 1922)

Recommendation [No. 19] concerning communication to the International Labour Office of statistical and other information regarding emigration, immigration and the repatriation and transit of emigrants.

I.

The General Conference recommends that each Member of the International Labour Organisation should communicate to the International Labour Office all information available concerning emigration, immigration, repatriation, transit of emigrants on outward and return journeys and the measures taken or contemplated in connection with these questions.

This information should be communicated so far as possible every three months and within three months of the end of the period to which it refers.

II.

The General Conference recommends that each Member of the International Labour Organisation should make every effort to communicate to the International Labour Office, within six months of the end of the year to which they refer, and so far as information is available, the total figures of emigrants and immigrants, showing separately nationals and aliens and specifying particularly, for nationals, and, as far as possible, for aliens:

(1) Sex.
(2) Age.
(3) Occupation.
(4) Nationality.
(5) Country of last residence.
(6) Country of proposed residence.

III.

The General Conference recommends that each Member of the International Labour Organisation should, if possible, make agreements with other Members providing for:

(a) The adoption of a uniform definition of the term "emigrant."
(b) The determination of uniform particulars to be entered on the identity papers issued to emigrants and immigrants by the competent authorities of Members who are parties to such agreements.
(c) The use of a uniform method of recording statistical information regarding emigration and immigration.

FIFTH SESSION

(Geneva, 22 - 29 October 1923).

Recommendation [No. 20] concerning the general principles for the organisation of systems of inspection to secure the enforcement of the laws and regulations for the protection of the workers.

The General Conference of the International Labour Organisation of the League of Nations,

Having been convened at Geneva by the Governing Body of the International Labour Office, and having met in its Fifth Session on 22 October 1923, and

Having decided upon the adoption of certain proposals with regard to the general principles for the organisation of factory inspection, the question forming the agenda of the Session, and

Having determined that these proposals should take the form of a recommendation,

adopts, this twenty-ninth day of October of the year one thousand nine hundred and twenty-three, the following Recommendation, to be submitted to the Members of the International Labour Organisation for consideration with a view to effect being given to it by national legislation or otherwise, in accordance with the provisions of Part XIII of the Treaty of Versailles and of the corresponding Parts of the other Treaties of Peace:

Whereas the Treaty of Versailles and the other Treaties of Peace include among the methods and principles of special and urgent importance for the physical, moral and intellectual welfare of the workers the principle that each State should make provision for a system of inspection in which women should take part, in order to ensure the enforcement of the laws and regulations for the protection of the workers;

Whereas the resolutions adopted at the First Session of the International Labour Conference concerning certain countries where special conditions prevail involve the creation by these countries of an inspection system if they do not already possess such a system;

Whereas the necessity of organising a system of inspection becomes specially urgent when Conventions adopted at Sessions of the Conference are being ratified by Members of the Organisation and put into force;

Whereas while the institution of an inspection system is undoubtedly to be recommended as one of the most effective means of ensuring the enforcement of Conventions and other engagements for the regulation of labour conditions, each Member is solely responsible for the execution of Conventions to which it is a party in the territory under its sovereignty or its authority and must accordingly itself determine in accordance with local conditions what measures of supervision may enable it to assume such a responsibility;

Whereas, in order to put the experience already gained at the disposal of the Members with a view to assisting them in the institution or reorganisation of their inspection system, it is desirable to indicate the general principles which practice shows to be the best calculated to ensure uniform, thorough and effective enforcement of Conventions and more generally of all measures for the protection of the workers; and

Having decided to leave to each country the determination of how far these general principles should be applied to certain spheres of activity;

And taking as a guide the long experience already acquired in factory inspection;

The General Conference recommends that each Member of the International Labour Organisation should take the following principles and rules into consideration:

I. SPHERE OF INSPECTION.

1. That it should be the principal function of the system of inspection which should be instituted by each Member in accordance with the ninth principle of Article 427 of the Treaty of Versailles to secure the enforcement of the laws and regulations relating to the conditions of work and the protection of the workers while engaged in their work (hours of work and rest; night work; prohibition of the employment of certain persons on dangerous, unhealthy or physically unsuitable work; health and safety, etc.).

2. That, in so far as it may be considered possible and desirable, either for reasons of convenience in the matter of supervision or by reason of the experience which they gain in carrying out their principal duties, to assign to inspectors additional duties which may vary according to the conceptions, traditions and customs prevailing in the different countries, such duties may be assigned, provided:

(a) that they do not in any way interfere with the inspectors' principal duties;

(b) that in themselves they are closely related to the primary object of ensuring the protection of the health and safety of the workers;

(c) that they shall not prejudice in any way the authority and impartiality which are necessary to inspectors in their relations with employers and workers.

II. NATURE OF THE FUNCTIONS AND POWERS OF INSPECTORS.

A. *General.*

3. That inspectors provided with credentials should be empowered by law:

(a) to visit and inspect, at any hour of the day or night, places where

they may have reasonable cause to believe that persons under the protection of the law are employed, and to enter by day any place which they may have reasonable cause to believe to be an establishment, or part thereof, subject to their supervision; provided that, before leaving, inspectors should, if possible, notify the employer or some representative of the employer of their visit;

(b) To question, without witnesses, the staff belonging to the establishment, and, for the purpose of carrying out their duties, to apply for information to any other persons whose evidence they may consider necessary, and to require to be shown any registers or documents which the laws regulating conditions of work require to be kept.

4. That inspectors should be bound by oath, or by any method which conforms with the administrative practice or customs in each country, not to disclose, on pain of legal penalties or suitable disciplinary measures, manufacturing secrets, and working processes in general, which may come to their knowledge in the course of their duties.

5. That, regard being had to the administrative and judicial systems of each country, and subject to such reference to superior authority as may be considered necessary, inspectors should be empowered to bring breaches of the laws, which they ascertain, directly before the competent judicial authorities;

That in countries where it is not incompatible with their system and principles of law, the reports drawn up by the inspectors shall be considered to establish the facts stated therein in default of proof to the contrary.

6. That the inspectors should be empowered, in cases where immediate action is necessary to bring installation or plant into conformity with laws and regulations, to make an order (or, if that procedure should not be in accordance with the administrative or judicial systems of the country, to apply to the competent authorities for an order) requiring such alterations to the installation or plant to be carried out within a fixed time as may be necessary for securing full and exact observance of the laws and regulations relating to the health and safety of the workers.

That in countries where the inspector's order has executive force of itself, its execution should be suspended only by appeal to a higher administrative or judicial authority, but in no circumstances should provisions intended to protect employers against arbitrary action prejudice the taking of measures with a view to the prevention of imminent danger which has been duly shown to exist.

B. *Safety.*

7. Having regard to the fact that, while it is essential that the inspectorate should be invested with all the legal powers necessary for the performance of its duties, it is equally important, in order that inspection may progressively become more effective, that, in accordance with the tendency manifested in the oldest and most experienced countries, inspection should be increasingly directed towards securing the adoption of the most suitable safety methods for preventing accidents and diseases with a view to rendering work less dangerous, more healthy, and even less exhausting, by the intelligent understanding, education, and co-operation of all concerned, it would appear that the following methods are calculated to promote this development in all countries:

(a) that all accidents should be notified to the competent authorities, and that one of the essential duties of the inspectors should be to investigate accidents, and more especially those of a serious or recurring char-

INTERNATIONAL LABOR ORGANIZATION

acter, with a view to ascertaining by what measures they can be prevented;

(b) that inspectors should inform and advise employers respecting the best standards of health and safety;

(c) that inspectors should encourage the collaboration of employers, managing staff and workers for the promotion of personal caution, safety methods, and the perfecting of safety equipment;

(d) that inspectors should endeavour to promote the improvement and perfecting of measures of health and safety, by the systematic study of technical methods for the internal equipment of undertakings, by special investigations into problems of health and safety, and by any other means;

(e) that in countries where it is considered preferable to have a special organisation for accident insurance and prevention completely independent of the inspectorate, the special officers of such organisations should be guided by the foregoing principles.

III. Organisation of Inspection.

A. *Organisation of the Staff.*

8. That, in order that the inspectors may be as closely as possible in touch with the establishments which they inspect and with the employers and workers, and in order that as much as possible of the inspectors' time may be devoted to the actual visiting of establishments, they should be localised, when the circumstances of the country permit, in the industrial districts.

9. That, in countries which for the purposes of inspection are divided into districts, in order to secure uniformity in the application of the law as between district and district and to promote a high standard of efficiency of inspection, the inspectors in the districts should be placed under the general supervision of an inspector of high qualifications and experience. Where the importance of the industries of the country is such as to require the appointment of more than one supervising inspector, the supervising inspectors should meet from time to time to confer on questions arising in the divisions under their control in connection with the application of the law and the improvement of industrial conditions.

10. That the inspectorate should be placed under the direct and exclusive control of a State authority and should not be under the control of or in any way responsible to any local authority in connection with the execution of any of their duties.

11. That, in view of the difficult scientific and technical questions which arise under the conditions of modern industry in connection with processes involving the use of dangerous materials, the removal of injurious dust and gases, the use of electrical plant and other matters, it is essential that experts having competent medical, engineering, electrical or other scientific training and experience should be employed by the State for dealing with such problems.

12. That, in conformity with the principle contained in Article 427 of the Treaty of Peace, the inspectorate should include women as well as men inspectors; that, while it is evident that with regard to certain matters and certain classes of work inspection can be more suitably carried out by men as in the case of other matters and other classes of work inspection can be more suitably carried out by women, the women inspectors should in general have the same powers and duties and exercise the same authority as the men inspectors, subject to their having had the necessary training and experience, and should have equal opportunity of promotion to the higher ranks.

B. *Qualifications and Training of Inspectors.*

13. That, in view of the complexity of modern industrial processes and machinery, of the character of the executive and administrative functions entrusted to the inspectors in connection with the application of the law and of the importance of their relations to employers and workers and employers' and workers' organisations and to the judicial and local authorities, it is essential that the inspectors should in general possess a high standard of technical training and experience, should be persons of good general education, and by their character and abilities be capable of acquiring the confidence of all parties.

14. That the inspectorate should be on a permanent basis and should be independent of changes of Government; that the inspectors should be given such a status and standard of remuneration as to secure their freedom from any improper external influences and that they should be prohibited from having any interest in any establishment which is placed under their inspection.

15. That inspectors on appointment should undergo a period of probation for the purpose of testing their qualifications and training them in their duties, and that their appointment should only be confirmed at the end of that period if they have shown themselves fully qualified for the duties of an inspector.

16. That, where countries are divided for the purposes of inspection into districts, and especially where the industries of the country are of a varied character, it is desirable that inspectors, more particularly during the early years of their service, should be transferred from district to district at appropriate intervals in order to obtain a full experience of the work of inspection.

C. *Standard and Methods of Inspection.*

17. That, as under a system of State inspection the visits of the inspectors to any individual establishment must necessarily be more or less infrequent, it is essential:

(a) That the principle should be laid down and maintained that the employer and the officials of the establishment are responsible for the observance of the law, and are liable to be proceeded against in the event of deliberate violation of or serious negligence in observing the law, without previous warning from the inspector;

It is understood that the foregoing principle does not apply in special cases where the law provides that notice shall be given in the first instance to the employer to carry out certain measures.

(b) That, as a general rule, the visits of the inspectors should be made without any previous notice to the employer.

It is desirable that adequate measures should be taken by the State to ensure that employers, officials and workers are acquainted with the provisions of the law and the measures to be taken for the protection of the health and safety of the workers, as, for example, by requiring the employer to post in his establishment an abstract of the requirements of the law.

18. That, while it is recognized that very wide differences exist between the size and importance of one establishment and another, and that there may be special difficulties in countries or areas of a rural character where factories are widely scattered, it is desirable that, as far as possible, every establishment should be visited by an inspector for the purposes of general inspection not less frequently than once a year, in addition to any special visits that may be made for the purpose of investigating a particular com-

plaint or for other purposes; and that large establishments and establishments of which the management is unsatisfactory from the point of view of the protection of the health and safety of the workers, and establishments in which dangerous or unhealthy processes are carried on, should be visited much more frequently. It is desirable that, when any serious irregularity has been discovered in an establishment, it should be revisited by the inspector at an early date with a view to ascertaining whether the irregularity has been remedied.

D. *Co-operation of Employers and Workers.*

19. That it is essential that the workers and their representatives should be afforded every facility for communicating freely with the inspectors as to any defect or breach of the law in the establishment in which they are employed; that every such complaint should as far as possible be investigated promptly by the inspector; that the complaint should be treated as absolutely confidential by the inspector and that no intimation even should be given to the employer or his officials that the visit made for the purpose of investigation is being made in consequence of the receipt of a complaint.

20. That, with a view to securing full co-operation of the employers and workers and their respective organisations in promoting a high standard in regard to the conditions affecting the health and safety of the workers, it is desirable that the inspectorate should confer from time to time with the representatives of the employers' and workers' organisations as to the best measures to be taken for this purpose.

IV. INSPECTORS' REPORTS.

21. That inspectors should regularly submit to their central authority reports framed on uniform lines dealing with their work and its results, and that the said authority should publish an annual report as soon as possible and in any case within one year after the end of the year to which it relates, containing a general survey of the information furnished by the inspectors; that the calendar year should be uniformly adopted for these reports.

22. That the annual general report should contain a list of the laws and regulations relating to conditions of work made during the year which it covers.

23. That this annual report should also give the statistical tables necessary in order to provide all information on the organisation and work of the inspectorate and on the results obtained. The information supplied should as far as possible state:

(a) The strength and organisation of the staff of the inspectorate;

(b) The number of establishments covered by the laws and regulations, classified by industries and indicating the number of workers employed (men, women, young persons, children);

(c) The number of visits of inspection made for each class of establishment with an indication of the number of workers employed in the establishments inspected (the number of workers being taken to be the number employed at the time of the first visit of the year), and the number of establishments inspected more than once during the year;

(d) The number of and nature of breaches of the laws and regulations brought before the competent authorities and the number and nature of the convictions by the competent authority;

(e) The number, nature and the cause of accidents and occupational diseases notified, tabulated according to class of establishment.

THE INTERNATIONAL PROTECTION OF LABOR

SIXTH SESSION

(Geneva, 16 June - 5 July 1924).

Recommendation [No. 21] concerning the development of facilities for the utilisation of workers' spare time.

Whereas in adopting at its First Session, held at Washington, a Convention on hours of work, the General Conference of the International Labour Organisation had as one of its principal aims to secure for workers, beyond the necessary hours for sleep, an adequate period during which such workers could do as they please, or, in other words, an adequate period of spare time; and

Whereas during such spare time workers have the opportunity of developing freely, according to their individual tastes, their physical, intellectual and moral powers, and such development is of great value from the point of view of the progress of civilisation; and

Whereas a well-directed use of this spare time, by affording to the worker the means for pursuing more varied interests, and by securing relaxation from the strain placed upon him by his ordinary work, may even increase the productive capacity of the worker and increase his output, and may thus help to obtain a maximum of efficiency from the eight-hour day; and

Whereas while giving full weight to the customs prevalent in the different countries and to local circumstances, it may nevertheless be useful to lay down the principles and methods which at the present time seem generally best adapted to secure the best use of periods of spare time, and it may also be instructive to make known for the benefit of all countries what has been done in this direction; and

Whereas the value of this information is particularly great at the moment when the ratification of the Convention on hours of work is being considered by the Members of the International Labour Organisation:

The General Conference makes the recommendations hereinafter appearing:

I. *Preservation of Spare Time.*

Whereas it is agreed that in countries where limitations have been placed on hours of work by law, by collective agreement or otherwise, if all the benefits which may be expected from such measures are to be secured both for the wage-earners and for the community, steps must be taken to ensure that the workers shall have the undiminished enjoyment of the hours of spare time so secured to them as aforesaid; and

Whereas it is important that, on the one hand, the workers should fully appreciate the value of the periods of spare time which have been secured to them and should do their utmost, in all circumstances, to prevent this spare time from being encroached upon, and, on the other hand, that employers should always aim at establishing wages corresponding sufficiently with the needs of the workers to make it unnecessary for them to have recourse during their periods of spare time to additional hours of paid work; and

Whereas prohibitions against the continuance of paid work in their own occupation, for the same or another employer, in excess of the legal working day, are recognised as being difficult to enforce, and may even, at times, seem to infringe the workers' right of using their periods of spare time as they choose, the Conference nevertheless considers that attention should be drawn to the steps which have been taken in this direction in a number of countries;

The Conference recommends that Governments should encourage and facilitate the conclusion of collective agreements which will ensure a normal standard of living to workers in exchange for the legal hours of work, and which will determine, by voluntary agreement between employers and workers, the measures to be taken to prevent workers from having recourse to additional paid work.

And whereas it is agreed that every facility should be given to the workers to enable them to make the best use of their periods of spare time so secured to them as aforesaid, the Conference recommends:

(a) That each Member, whilst having due regard to the requirements of different industries, local customs, and the varying capacities and habits of the different kinds of workers, should consider the means of so arranging the working day as to make the periods of spare time as continuous as possible;

(b) That by means of a well-conceived transport system and by affording special facilities in regard to fares and time-tables, workers should be enabled to reduce to the minimum the time spent in travelling between their homes and their work, and that employers' and workers' organisations should be extensively consulted by public transport authorities or private transport undertakings as to the best means of securing such a system.

II. *Spare Time and Social Hygiene.*

Whereas the utilisation of the workers' periods of spare time cannot be separated from the general measures adopted by the community for promoting the health and welfare of all classes of society, the Conference, without attempting to examine in detail each of the great welfare problems, the solution of which would contribute to improving the workers' status, recommends to the Members:

(a) The encouragement of individual hygiene by the provision of public baths, swimming pools, etc.;

(b) Legislative or private action against the misuse of alcohol, against tuberculosis, venereal disease and gambling.

III. *Housing Policy.*

Whereas it is of advantage to the workers and to the whole community to encourage everything tending to the harmonious development of the workers' family life; and

Whereas the most effective means of protecting the workers from the aforesaid dangers is to place within their reach a proper home;

The Conference recommends the increase in number, if necessary in co-operation with the national or local authorities concerned, of healthy dwellings at low rentals in garden cities or urban communities, under proper conditions of health and comfort.

IV. *Institutions for the Utilisation of Spare Time.*

Without attempting to differentiate between the innumerable institutions which afford to the workers opportunities for the free exercise of their personal tastes, the development of which is dependent on the manners and customs of each country or district, the Conference nevertheless draws the attention of the Members to the necessity of avoiding misplaced activities resulting from the establishment of institutions not called for by some well-defined need. The Conference desires to emphasize the importance of taking into account in the establishment and development of these institutions, the desires, the tastes and the special requirements of the workers for whose use they are designed;

At the same time, among the institutions which may both assist full and harmonious development of the individual and of the family and contribute to the general progress of the community, the Conference recommends those schemes which have for their object:

(a) the improvement of the workers' domestic economy and family life (gardens, allotments, poultry keeping, etc.) which combine the benefits of recreation with the feeling that some addition, however slight, is being made to the family resources;

(b) the development of the physical health and strength of the workers by means of games and sports which enable young workers who are working under the highly specialised conditions prevalent in modern industry to give free play to their energies in a manner which encourages initiative and the spirit of emulation;

(c) the extension of technical, domestic and general education (libraries, reading-rooms, lectures, technical and general courses, etc.) which meets one of the workers' most keenly felt needs and affords the best means of progress to industrial communities;

The Conference further recommends that Members should encourage these forms of activity by the grant of subventions to organisations concerned with the moral, intellectual and physical development of the workers.

V. *Free Use of Institutions and Co-ordination of Local Action.*

Whereas for many years past the workers in the great industrial countries have always sought to ensure that they may live their lives outside the factory or workshop in complete freedom and independence, and they particularly resent any outside interference in their private affairs, and this feeling is so strong as to provoke opposition to any attempts to deal, either nationally or internationally, with the question of the use of spare time for fear that it may possibly restrain their liberty; and

Whereas the Conference, while expressing appreciation of the motives which have led to the creation of institutions for the encouragement of the wise use of the spare time of the workers, suggests that Members should draw the attention of the promotors of such institutions to the necessity of safeguarding the individual freedom of the workers against any system or scheme which has any tendency towards compelling the workers directly or indirectly to use any particular institution; and

Whereas the most practical and successful institutions are those which have been started and developed by the beneficiaries themselves, the Conference, while recognising that in many cases where public authorities or employers lend financial or other assistance for the encouragement of allotments, games or educational institutions, and consequently have a legitimate claim to take part in their management, recommends that every care should be taken to avoid any encroachment on the liberty of those for whose use such institutions are intended.

While not contemplating any systematic organisation of spare time occupations, but having in mind a number of successful efforts made to assist them, the Conference further recommends that each Member should consider the possibility of promoting the formation of district or local committees, composed of representatives of the public authorities, of employers' and workers' organisations, and of co-operative associations, for

INTERNATIONAL LABOR ORGANIZATION

co-ordinating and harmonising the activities of the various institutions providing means of recreation.

The Conference further recommends to the Members that an active and effective propaganda should be undertaken in each country for the purpose of educating opinion in favour of the proper use of the spare time of the workers.

SEVENTH SESSION

(Geneva, 19 May - 10 June 1925).

Draft Convention [No. 17] concerning workmen's compensation for accidents.

The General Conference of the International Labour Organisation of the League of Nations,

> Having been convened at Geneva by the Governing Body of the International Labour Office, and having met in its Seventh Session on 19 May 1925, and
>
> Having decided upon the adoption of certain proposals with regard to workmen's compensation for accidents, which is included in the first item of the agenda of the Session, and
>
> Having determined that these proposals shall take the form of a draft international convention,

adopts, this tenth day of June of the year one thousand nine hundred and twenty-five, the following Draft Convention for ratification by the Members of the International Labour Organisation, in accordance with the provisions of Part XIII of the Treaty of Versailles and of the corresponding Parts of the other Treaties of Peace:

ARTICLE 1.

Each Member of the International Labour Organisation which ratifies this Convention undertakes to ensure that workmen who suffer personal injury due to an industrial accident, or their dependants, shall be compensated on terms at least equal to those provided by this Convention.

ARTICLE 2.

The laws and regulations as to workmen's compensation shall apply to workmen, employees and apprentices employed by any enterprise, undertaking or establishment of whatsoever nature, whether public or private.

It shall nevertheless be open to any Member to make such exceptions in its national legislation as it deems necessary in respect of:

(a) persons whose employment is of a casual nature and who are employed otherwise than for the purpose of the employer's trade or business;

(b) out-workers;

(c) members of the employer's family who work exclusively on his behalf and who live in his house;

(d) non-manual workers whose remuneration exceeds a limit to be determined by national laws or regulations.

ARTICLE 3.

This Convention shall not apply to

(1) seamen and fishermen for whom provision shall be made by a later Convention;

(2) persons covered by some special scheme, the terms of which are not less favorable than those of this Convention.

Article 4.

This Convention shall not apply to agriculture, in respect of which the Convention concerning workmen's compensation in agriculture adopted by the International Labour Conference at its Third Session remains in force.

Article 5.

The compensation payable to the injured workman, or his dependants, where permanent incapacity or death results from the injury, shall be paid in the form of periodical payments: provided that it may be wholly or partially paid in a lump sum, if the competent authority is satisfied that it will be properly utilised.

Article 6.

In case of incapactiy, compensation shall be paid not later than as from the fifth day after the accident, whether it be payable by the employer, the accident insurance institution, or the sickness insurance institution concerned.

Article 7.

In cases where the injury results in incapacity of such a nature that the injured workman must have the constant help of another person, additional compensation shall be provided.

Article 8.

The national laws or regulations shall prescribe such measures of supervision and methods of review as are deemed necessary.

Article 9.

Injured workmen shall be entitled to medical aid and to such surgical and pharmaceutical aid as is recognised to be necessary in consequence of accidents. The cost of such aid shall be defrayed either by the employer, by accident insurance institutions, or by sickness or invalidity insurance institutions.

Article 10.

Injured workmen shall be entitled to the supply and normal renewal, by the employer or insurer, of such artificial limbs and surgical appliances as are recognised to be necessary: provided that national laws or regulations may allow in exceptional circumstances the supply and renewal of such artificial limbs and appliances to be replaced by the award to the injured workman of a sum representing the probable cost of the supply and renewal of such appliances, this sum to be decided at the time when the amount of compensation is settled or revised.

National laws or regulations shall provide for such supervisory measures as are necessary, either to prevent abuses in connection with the renewal of appliances, or to ensure that the additional compensation is utilised for this purpose.

Article 11.

The national laws or regulations shall make such provision as, having regard to national circumstances, is deemed most suitable for ensuring in all circumstances, in the event of the insolvency of the employer or insurer, the payment of compensation to workmen who suffer personal injury due to industrial accidents, or in case of death, to their dependants.

Article 12.

The formal ratifications of this Convention under the conditions set forth in Part XIII of the Treaty of Versailles and in the corresponding

Parts of the other Treaties of Peace shall be communicated to the Secretary-General of the League of Nations for registration.

ARTICLE 13.

This Convention shall come into force at the date on which the ratifications of two Members of the International Labour Organisation have been registered by the Secretary-General.

It shall be binding only upon those Members whose ratifications have been registered with the Secretariat.

Thereafter, the Convention shall come into force for any Member at the date on which its ratification has been registered with the Secretariat.

ARTICLE 14.

As soon as the ratifications of two Members of the International Labour Organisation have been registered with the Secretariat, the Secretary-General of the League of Nations shall so notify all the Members of the International Labour Organisation. He shall likewise notify them of the registration of ratifications which may be communicated subsequently by other Members of the Organisation.

ARTICLE 15.

Subject to the provisions of Article 13, each Member which ratifies this Convention agrees to bring the provisions of Articles 1, 2, 3, 4, 5. 6. 7. 8, 9, 10 and 11 into operation not later than 1 January 1927 and to take such action as may be necessary to make these provisions effective.

ARTICLE 16.

Each Member of the International Labour Organisation which ratifies this Convention engages to apply it to its colonies, possessions and protectorates, in accordance with the provisions of Article 421 of the Treaty of Versailles and of the corresponding Articles of the other Treaties of Peace.

ARTICLE 17.

A Member which has ratified this Convention may denounce it after the expiration of five years from the date on which the Convention first comes into force, by an act communicated to the Secretary-General of the League of Nations for registration. Such denunciation shall not take effect until one year after the date on which it is registered with the Secretariat.

ARTICLE 18.

At least once in ten years, the Governing Body of the International Labour Office shall present to the General Conference a report on the working of this Convention and shall consider the desirability of placing on the agenda of the Conference the question of its revision or modification.

ARTICLE 19.

The French and English texts of this Convention shall both be authentic.

Recommendation [No. 22] concerning the minimum scale of workmen's compensation.

The General Conference recommends that each Member of the International Labour Organisation should take the following principles and rules into consideration:

I.

Where the incapacity for work results from the injury, the national laws or regulations should provide for the payment of compensation at rates not lower than those hereinafter indicated:

(1) In the case of permanent total incapacity, a periodical payment equivalent to two-thirds of the workman's annual earnings;

(2) In case of permanent partial incapacity, a proportion of the periodical payment due in the event of permanent total incapacity calculated in reference to the reduction of earning power caused by the injury;

(3) In case of temporary total incapacity, a daily or weekly payment equivalent to two-thirds of the workman's basic earnings as calculated for purposes of compensation;

(4) In case of temporary partial incapacity, a proportion of the daily or weekly payment payable in the case of temporary total incapacity calculated in reference to the reduction of earning power caused by the injury.

Where compensation is paid in a lump sum, the sum should not be less than the capitalised value of the periodical payment which would be payable under the foregoing paragraphs.

II.

Where the injury is such that the workman requires the constant help of another person, additional compensation should be paid to the workman, which should not be less than half the amount payable in the case of permanent total incapacity.

III.

Where death results from the injury, those entitled to be regarded as dependants for purposes of compensation should include at least the following:

(1) deceased's husband or wife;

(2) deceased's children under eighteen years of age, or above that age if, by reason of physical or mental infirmity, they are incapable of earning;

(3) deceased's ascendants (parents or grandparents), provided that they are without means of subsistence and were dependent on the deceased, or the deceased was under an obligation to contribute towards their maintenance;

(4) deceased's grandchildren and brothers and sisters, if below eighteen years of age, or above that age if, by reason of physical or mental infirmity, they are incapable of earning, and if they are orphans, or if their parents, though still living, are incapable of providing for them.

Where compensation is paid by means of periodical payments, the maximum total of the yearly sum payable to all the dependants should not be less than two-thirds of the deceased's annual earnings.

Where compensation is paid in a lump sum, the maximum sum payable to all the dependants should not be less than the capitalised value of periodical payments equivalent to two-thirds of the deceased's annual earnings.

IV.

The vocational re-education of injured workmen should be provided by such means as the national laws or regulations deem most suitable.

Governments should encourage institutions which undertake such re-education.

INTERNATIONAL LABOR ORGANIZATION

Recommendation [No. 23] concerning jurisdiction in disputes on workmen's compensation.

Whereas disputes on workmen's compensation turn not only on the interpretation of laws and regulations, but also on questions of an occupational character requiring a thorough knowledge of working conditions, for example, questions as to the nature of the undertaking, the kind of risk inherent in it, the relation betwen the workman's employment and the accident, the method of computing earnings, the degree of incapacity for work, the possibility of the workman's adapting himself to some other occupation,

And whereas workmen and employers have the necessary knowledge and experience on these questions, and disputes on compensation matters might be more equitably settled if they were members of or associated with the courts which have to decide such disputes,

And whereas it is possible in many countries to secure the association of employers and workmen with such courts, as members or otherwise, without departing radically from the existing judicial system,

The General Conference recommends that each Member of the International Labour Organisation should take the following principles and rules into consideration:

I.

That every dispute relating to workmen's compensation should preferably be dealt with by a special court or board of arbitration comprising, with or without the addition of regular judges, an equal number of employers' and workmen's representatives appointed to act as adjudicators by their respective organisations or on the nomination of such organisations or comprising employers' and workmen's representatives drawn from other social institutions or elected by separate electoral bodies of employers and workmen.

That, where disputes relating to workmen's compensation are dealt with by the ordinary courts of law, such courts shall be required, on the request of either of the parties concerned, to hear employers' and workmen's representatives as experts in any case where the dispute involves a question of an occupational character, and in particular the question of the degree of incapacity for work.

Draft Convention [No. 18] concerning workmen's compensation for occupational diseases.

ARTICLE 1.

Each Member of the International Labour Organisation which ratifies this Convention undertakes to provide that compensation shall be payable to workmen incapacitated by occupational diseases, or, in case of death from such diseases, to their dependants, in accordance with the general principles of the national legislation relating to compensation for industrial accidents.

The rates of such compensation shall be not less than those prescribed by the national legislation for injury resulting from industrial accidents. Subject to this provision, each Member, in determining in its national law or regulations the conditions under which compensation for the said diseases shall be payable, and in applying to the said diseases its legislation in regard to compensation for industrial accidents, may make such modifications and adaptations as it thinks expedient.

ARTICLE 2.

Each Member of the International Labour Organisation which ratifies this Convention undertakes to consider as occupational diseases those diseases and poisonings produced by the substances set forth in the Schedule appended hereto, when such diseases or such poisonings affect workers engaged in the trades or industries placed opposite in the said Schedule, and result from occupation in an undertaking covered by the said national legislation.

SCHEDULE.

List of diseases and toxic substances.	*List of corresponding industries and processes.*
Poisoning by lead, its alloys or compounds and their sequelae.	Handling of ore containing lead, including fine shot in zinc factories. Casting of old zinc and lead in ingots. Manufacture of articles made of cast lead or of lead alloys. Employment in the polygraphic industries. Manufacture of lead compounds. Manufacture and repair of electric accumulators. Preparation and use of enamels containing lead. Polishing by means of lead files or putty powder with a lead content. All painting operations involving the preparation and manipulation of coating substances, cements or colouring substances containing lead pigments.
Poisoning by mercury, its amalgams and compounds and their sequelae.	Handling of mercury ore. Manufacture of mercury compounds. Manufacture of measuring and laboratory apparatus. Preparation of raw material for the hat-making industry. Hot gilding. Use of mercury pumps in the manufacture of incandescent lamps. Manufacture of fulminate of mercury primers.
Anthrax infection.	Work in connection with animals infected with anthrax. Handling of animal carcasses or parts of such carcasses including hides, hoofs and horns. Loading and unloading or transport of merchandise.

(*For the Standard Articles, see Draft Convention No. 17*)

INTERNATIONAL LABOR ORGANIZATION

Recommendation [No. 24] concerning workmen's compensation for occupational diseases.

Whereas it is recognized that each State is free to establish under its national legislation a more complete list than that embodied in the Schedule appended to Article 2 of the Convention concerning workmen's compensation for occupational diseases,

The Conference recommends that

Each Member of the International Labour Organisation should adopt, where such procedure does not already exist, a simple procedure by which the list of diseases considered occupational in its national legislation may be revised.

Draft Convention [No. 19] concerning equality of treatment for national and foreign workers as regards workmen's compensation for accidents.

ARTICLE 1.

Each Member of the International Labour Organisation which ratifies this Convention undertakes to grant to the nationals of any other Member which shall have ratified the Convention, who suffer personal injury due to industrial accidents happening in its territory, or to their dependents, the same treatment in respect of workmen's compensation as it grants to its own nationals.

This equality of treatment shall be guaranteed to foreign workers and their dependents without any condition as to residence. With regard to the payments which a Member or its nationals would have to make outside that Member's territory in the application of this principle, the measures to be adopted shall be regulated, if necessary, by special arrangements between the Members concerned.

ARTICLE 2.

Special agreements may be made between the Members concerned to provide that compensation for industrial accidents happening to workers whilst temporarily or intermittently employed in the territory of one Member on behalf of an undertaking situated in the territory of another Member shall be governed by the laws and regulations of the latter Member.

ARTICLE 3.

The Members which ratify this Convention and which do not already possess a system, whether by insurance or otherwise, of workmen's compensation for industrial accidents agree to institute such a system within a period of three years from the date of their ratification.

ARTICLE 4.

The Members which ratify this Convention further undertake to afford each other mutual assistance with a view to facilitating the application of the Convention and the execution of their respective laws and regulations on workmen's compensation and to inform the International Labour Office, which shall inform the other Members concerned, of any modifications in the laws and regulations in force on workmen's compensation.

(*For other Standard Articles, see Draft Convention No. 17*)

ARTICLE 10.

A Member which has ratified this Convention may denounce it after the expiration of ten years from the date on which the Convention first comes into force, by an act communicated to the Secretary-General of the

League of Nations for registration. Such denunciation shall not take effect until one year after the date on which it is registered with the Secretariat.

Recommendation [No. 25] concerning equality of treatment for national and foreign workers as regards workmen's compensation for accidents.

I.

In order to facilitate the application of the Convention concerning equality of treatment for national and foreign workers as regards workmen's compensation for accidents the Conference recommends that:

(*a*) When a person to whom compensation is due under the laws and regulations of one Member resides in the territory of another Member, the necessary measures be taken to facilitate the payment of such compensation and to ensure the observance of the conditions governing such payment laid down by the said laws and regulations;

(*b*) In case of dispute concerning the non-payment, cessation of payment, or reduction of the compensation due to a person residing elsewhere than in the territory of the Member where his claim to compensation originated, facilities be afforded for taking proceedings in the competent courts of law in such territory without requiring the attendance of the person concerned;

(*c*) Any advantage in respect of exemption from duties and taxes, free issue of official documents or other privileges granted by the law of any Member for purposes connected with workmen's compensation, be extended under the same conditions to the nationals of the other Members which shall have ratified the afore-mentioned Convention.

II.

The Conference recommends that, where in any country there exists no system, whether by insurance or otherwise, of workmen's compensation for industrial accidents, the Government shall, pending the institution of such a system, afford facilities to alien workers enabling them to benefit by the laws and regulations on workmen's compensation in their own countries.

Draft Convention [No. 20] concerning night work in bakeries.

ARTICLE 1.

Subject to the exceptions hereinafter provided, the making of bread, pastry or other flour confectionery during the night is forbidden.

This prohibition applies to the work of all persons, including proprietors as well as workers, engaged in the making of such products; but it does not apply to the making of such products by members of the same household for their own consumption.

This Convention has no application to the wholesale manufacture of biscuits. Each Member may, after consultation with the employers' and workers' organisations concerned, determine what products are to be included in the term "biscuits" for the purpose of this Convention.

ARTICLE 2.

For the purpose of this Convention, the term "night" signifies a period of at least seven consecutive hours. The beginning and end of this period shall be fixed by the competent authority in each country after consultation with the organisations of employers and workers concerned, and the period shall include the interval between eleven o'clock in the evening and five o'clock in the morning. When it is required by the climate or season, or when it is agreed between the employers' and workers' organisations concerned, the interval between ten o'clock in the evening and four o'clock in the morning may be substituted for the interval between eleven o'clock in the evening and five o'clock in the morning.

Article 3.

After consultation with the employers' and the workers' organisations concerned, the competent authority in each country may make the following exceptions to the provisions of Article 1:

(a) The permanent exceptions necessary for the execution of preparatory or complementary work as far as it must necessarily be carried on outside the normal hours of work, provided that no more than the strictly necessary number of workers and that no young persons under the age of eighteen years shall be employed in such work;

(b) The permanent exceptions necessary for requirements arising from the particular circumstances of the baking industry in tropical countries;

(c) The permanent exceptions necessary for the arrangement of the weekly rest;

(d) The temporary exceptions necessary to enable establishments to deal with unusual pressure of work or national necessities.

Article 4.

Exceptions may also be made to the provisions of Article 1 in case of accident, actual or threatened, or in case of urgent work to be done to machinery or plant, or in case of *force majeure*, but only so far as may be necessary to avoid serious interference with the ordinary working of the undertaking.

Article 5.

Each Member which ratifies this Convention shall take appropriate measures to ensure that the prohibition prescribed in Article 1 is effectively enforced, and shall enable the employers, the workers, and their respective organisations to co-operate in such measures, in conformity with the Recommendation adopted by the International Labour Conference at its Fifth Session (1923).

Article 6.

The provisions of this Convention shall not take effect until 1 January 1927.

Article 7.

The formal ratifications of this Convention under the conditions set forth in Part XIII of the Treaty of Versailles and in the corresponding Parts of the other Treaties of Peace shall be communicated to the Secretary-General of the League of Nations for registration.

Article 8.

This Convention shall come into force at the date on which the ratifications of two Members of the International Labour Organisation have been registered by the Secretary-General.

It shall be binding only upon those Members whose ratifications have been registered with the Secretariat.

Thereafter, the Convention shall come into force for any Member at the date on which its ratification has been registered with the Secretariat.

Article 9.

As soon as the ratifications of two Members of the International Labour Organisation have been registered with the Secretariat, the Secretary-General of the League of Nations shall so notify all the Members of the International Labour Organisation. He shall likewise notify them of the registration of ratifications which may be communicated subsequently by other Members of the Organisation.

Article 10.

Each Member of the International Labour Organisation which ratifies this Convention engages to apply it to its colonies, possessions and protectorates, in accordance with the provisions of Article 421 of the Treaty of Versailles and of the corresponding Articles of the other Treaties of Peace.

Article 11.

A Member which has ratified this Convention may denounce it after the expiration of ten years from the date on which the Convention first comes into force, by an act communicated to the Secretary-General of the League of Nations for registration. Such denunciation shall not take effect until one year after the date on which it is registered with the Secretariat.

Article 12.

At least once in ten years, the Governing Body of the International Labour Office shall present to the General Conference a report on the working of this Convention and shall consider the desirability of placing on the agenda of the Conference the question of its revision or modification

Article 13.

The French and English texts of this Convention shall both be authentic.

EIGHTH SESSION

(Geneva, 26 May - 5 June 1926).

Draft Convention [No. 21] concerning the simplification of the inspection of emigrants on board ship.

Article 1.

For the purposes of application of this Convention the terms "emigrant vessel" and "emigrant" shall be defined for each country by the competent authority in that country.

Article 2.

Each Member which ratifies this Convention undertakes to accept the principle that, save as hereinafter provided, the official inspection carried out on board an emigrant vessel for the protection of emigrants shall be undertaken by not more than one Government.

Nothing in this Article shall prevent another Government from occasionally and at their own expense placing a representative on board to accompany their nationals carried as emigrants in the capacity of observer, and on condition that he shall not encroach upon the duties of the official inspector.

Article 3.

If an official inspector of emigrants is placed on board an emigrant vessel he shall be appointed as a general rule by the Government of the country whose flag the vessel flies. Such inspector may, however, be appointed by another Government in virtue of an agreement between the Government of the country whose flag the vessel flies and one or more other Governments whose nationals are carried as emigrants on board the vessel.

ARTICLE 4.

The practical experience and the necessary professional and moral qualifications required of an official inspector shall be determined by the Government responsible for his appointment.

An official inspector may not be in any way either directly or indirectly connected with or dependent upon the shipowner or shipping company.

Nothing in this Article shall prevent a Government from appointing the ship's doctor as official inspector by way of exception and in case of absolute necessity.

ARTICLE 5.

The official inspector shall ensure the observance of the rights which emigrants possess under the laws of the country whose flag the vessel flies, or such other law as is applicable, or under international agreements, or the terms of their contracts of transportation.

The Government of the country whose flag the vessel flies shall communicate to the official inspector, irrespective of his nationality, the text of any laws or regulations affecting the condition of emigrants which may be in force, and of any international agreements or any contracts relating to the matter which have been communicated to such Government.

ARTICLE 6.

The authority of the master on board the vessel is not limited by this Convention. The official inspector shall in no way encroach upon the master's authority on board, and shall concern himself solely with ensuring the enforcement of the laws, regulations, agreements, or contracts directly concerning the protection and welfare of the emigrants on board.

ARTICLE 7.

Within eight days after the arrival of the vessel at its port of destination the official inspector shall make a report to the Government of the country whose flag the vessel flies, which Government shall transmit a copy of the report to the other Governments concerned, where such Governments have previously requested that this shall be done.

A copy of this report shall be transmitted to the master of the vessel by the official inspector.

ARTICLE 8.

The formal ratifications of this Convention under the conditions set forth in Part XIII of the Treaty of Versailles and in the corresponding Parts of the other Treaties of Peace shall be communicated to the Secretary-General of the League of Nations for registration.

ARTICLE 9.

This Convention shall come into force at the date on which the ratifications of two Members of the International Labour Organisation have been registered by the Secretary-General.

It shall be binding only upon those Members whose ratifications have been registered with the Secretariat.

Thereafter, the Convention shall come into force for any Member at the date on which its ratification has been registered with the Secretariat.

Article 10.

As soon as the ratifications of two Members of the International Labour Organisation have been registered with the Secretariat, the Secretary-General of the League of Nations shall so notify all the Members of the International Labour Organisation. He shall likewise notify them of the registration of ratifications which may be communicated subsequently by other Members of the Organisation.

Article 11.

Subject to the provisions of Article 9, each Member which ratifies this Convention agrees to bring the provisions of Articles 1, 2, 3, 4, 5, 6 and 7 into operation not later than 1 January 1928, and to take such action as may be necessary to make these provisions effective.

Article 12.

Each Member of the International Labour Organisation which ratifies this Convention engages to apply it to its colonies, possessions and protectorates, in accordance with the provisions of Article 421 of the Treaty of Versailles and of the corresponding Articles of the other Treaties of Peace.

Article 13.

A Member which has ratified this Convention may denounce it after the expiration of ten years from the date on which the Convention first comes into force, by an act communicated to the Secretary-General of the League of Nations for registration. Such denunciation shall not take effect until one year after the date on which it is registered with the Secretariat.

Article 14.

At least once in ten years, the Governing Body of the International Labour Office shall present to the General Conference a report on the working of this Convention and shall consider the desirability of placing on the Agenda of the Conference the question of its revision or modification.

Article 15.

The French and English texts of this Convention shall both be authentic.

Recommendation [No. 26] concerning the protection of emigrant women and girls on board ship.

The General Conference of the International Labour Organisation of the League of Nations,

> Having been convened at Geneva by the Governing Body of the International Labour Office, and having met in its Eighth Session on 26 May 1926, and

> Having decided upon the adoption of certain proposals with regard to the means to be taken to ensure the protection of emigrant women and girls on board ship, which question is included in the agenda of the Session, and

> Having determined that these proposals shall take the form of a Recommendation,

adopts, this fifth day of June of the year one thousand nine hundred and twenty-six, the following Recommendation, to be submitted to the Members of the International Labour Organisation for consideration with a view to effect being given to it by national legislation or otherwise in accordance with the provisions of Part XIII of the Treaty of Versailles and of the corresponding Parts of the other Treaties of Peace:

Where fifteen or more women or girls unaccompanied by a responsible person are carried as emigrants on board an emigrant vessel a properly qualified woman who has no other duty to fulfill on board shall be appointed to give such emigrants any material or moral assistance of which they may stand in need without in any way encroaching upon the authority of the master of the vessel. She shall report to the authority making the appointment and her report shall be available for the use of the Governments which may be concerned.

NINTH SESSION

(Geneva, 7 - 24 June 1926).

Draft Convention [No. 22] concerning seamen's articles of agreement.

ARTICLE 1.

This Convention shall apply to all seagoing vessels registered in the country of any Member ratifying this Convention, and to the owners, masters and seamen of such vessels.

It shall not apply to:
ships of war,
Government vessels not engaged in trade,
vessels engaged in the coasting trade,
pleasure yachts,
Indian country craft,
fishing vessels,
vessels of less than 100 tons gross registered tonnage or 300 cubic metres, nor to vessels engaged in the home trade below the tonnage limit prescribed by national law for the special regulation of this trade at the date of the passing of this Convention.

ARTICLE 2.

For the purpose of this Convention the following expressions have the meanings hereby assigned to them, viz.:

(a) The term "vessel" includes any ship or boat of any nature whatsoever, whether publicly or privately owned, ordinarily engaged in maritime navigation.

(b) The term "seaman" includes every person employed or engaged in any capacity on board any vessel and entered on the ship's articles. It excludes masters, pilots, cadets and pupils on training ships and duly indentured apprentices, naval ratings, and other persons in the permanent service of a Government.

(c) The term "master" includes every person having command and charge of a vessel except pilots.

(d) The term "home trade vessel" means a vessel engaged in trade between a country and the ports of a neighbouring country within geographical limits determined by the national law.

ARTICLE 3.

Articles of agreement shall be signed both by the shipowner or his representative and by the seaman. Reasonable facilities to examine the articles of agreement before they are signed shall be given to the seaman and also to his adviser.

The seaman shall sign the agreement under conditions which shall be prescribed by national law in order to ensure adequate supervision by the competent public authority.

The foregoing provisions shall be deemed to have been fulfilled if the competent authority certifies that the provisions of the agreement have been laid before it in writing and have been confirmed both by the shipowner or his representative and by the seaman.

National law shall make adequate provision to ensure that the seaman has understood the agreement.

The agreement shall not contain anything which is contrary to the provisions of national law or of this Convention.

National law shall prescribe such further formalities and safeguards in respect of the completion of the agreement as may be considered necessary for the protection of the interests of the shipowner and of the seaman.

ARTICLE 4.

Adequate measures shall be taken in accordance with national law for ensuring that the agreement shall not contain any stipulation by which the parties purport to contract in advance to depart from the ordinary rules as to jurisdiction over the agreement.

This Article shall not be interpreted as excluding a reference to arbitration.

ARTICLE 5.

Every seaman shall be given a document containing a record of his employment on board the vessel. The form of the document, the particulars to be recorded and the manner in which such particulars are to be entered in it shall be determined by national law.

The document shall not contain any statement as to the quality of the seaman's work or as to his wages.

ARTICLE 6.

The agreement may be made either for a definite period or for a voyage or, if permitted by national law, for an indefinite period.

The agreement shall state clearly the respective rights and obligations of each of the parties.

It shall in all cases contain the following particulars:

(1) The surname and other names of the seaman, the date of his birth or his age, and his birthplace;

(2) The place at which and date on which the agreement was completed;

(3) The name of the vessel or vessels on board which the seaman undertakes to serve;

(4) The number of the crew of the vessel, if required by national law;

(5) The voyage or voyages to be undertaken, if this can be determined at the time of making the agreement;

(6) The capacity in which the seaman is to be employed;

(7) If possible, the place and date at which the seaman is required to report on board for service;

(8) The scale of provisions to be supplied to the seaman, unless some alternative system is provided for by national law;

(9) The amount of his wages;

(10) The termination of the agreement and the conditions thereof, that is to say:

(a) if the agreement has been made for a definite period, the date fixed for its expiry;

(b) if the agreement has been made for a voyage, the port of destination and the time which has to expire after arrival before the seaman shall be discharged;

(c) if the agreement has been made for an indefinite period, the conditions which shall entitle either party to rescind it, as well as the required period of notice for rescission; provided that such period shall not be less for the shipowner than for the seaman;

(11) The annual leave with pay granted to the seaman after one year's service with the same shipping company, if such leave is provided for by national law;

(12) Any other particulars which national law may require.

Article 7.

If national law provides that a list of crew shall be carried on board it shall specify that the agreement shall either be recorded in or annexed to the list of crew.

Article 8.

In order that the seaman may satisfy himself as to the nature and extent of his rights and obligations, national law shall lay down the measures to be taken to enable clear information to be obtained on board as to the conditions of employment, either by posting the conditions of the agreement in a place easily accessible from the crew's quarters, or by some other appropriate means.

Article 9.

An agreement for an indefinite period may be terminated by either party in any port where the vessel loads or unloads, provided that the notice specified in the agreement shall have been given, which shall not be less than twenty-four hours.

Notice shall be given in writing; national law shall provide such manner of giving notice as is best calculated to preclude any subsequent dispute between the parties on this point.

National law shall determine the exceptional circumstances in which notice even when duly given shall not terminate the agreement.

Article 10.

An agreement entered into for a voyage, for a definite period, or for an indefinite period shall be duly terminated by:

(a) mutual consent of the parties;
(b) death of the seaman;
(c) loss or total unseaworthiness of the vessel;
(d) any other cause that may be provided in national law or in this Convention.

Article 11.

National law shall determine the circumstances in which the owner or master may immediately discharge a seaman.

Article 12.

National law shall also determine the circumstances in which the seaman may demand his immediate discharge.

Article 13.

If a seaman shows to the satisfaction of the shipowner or his agent that he can obtain command of a vessel or an appointment as mate or engineer or to any other post of a higher grade than he actually holds, or that any other circumstance has arisen since his engagement which renders its essential to his interests that he should be permitted to take his discharge, he may claim his discharge, provided that without increased expense to the shipowner and to the satisfaction of the shipowner or his agent he furnishes a competent and reliable man in his place.

In such case, the seaman shall be entitled to his wages up to the time of his leaving his employment.

Article 14.

Whatever the reason for the termination or rescission of the agreement, an entry shall be made in the document issued to the seaman in accordance with Article 5, and in the list of crew showing that he has been discharged, and such entry shall, at the request of either party, be endorsed by the competent public authority.

The seaman shall at all times have the right, in addition to the record mentioned in Article 5, to obtain from the master a separate certificate as to the quality of his work or, failing that, a certificate indicating whether he has fully discharged his obligations under the agreement.

Article 15.

National laws shall provide the measures to ensure compliance with the terms of the present Convention.

(*For the Standard Articles, see Draft Convention No. 21*)

Draft Convention [No. 23] concerning the repatriation of seamen.

Article 1.

This Convention shall apply to all seagoing vessels registered in the country of any Member ratifying this Convention, and to the owners, masters and seamen of such vessels.

It shall not apply to:

ships of war,
Government vessels not engaged in trade,
vessels engaged in the coasting trade,
pleasure yachts,
Indian country craft,
fishing vessels,
vessels of less than 100 tons gross registered tonnage or 300 cubic metres, nor to vessels engaged in the home trade below the tonnage limit prescribed by national law for the special regulation of this trade at the date of the passing of this Convention.

Article 2.

For the purpose of this Convention the following expressions have the meanings hereby assigned to them, viz.:

(*a*) The term "vessel" includes any ship or boat of any nature whatsoever, whether publicly or privately owned, ordinarily engaged in maritime navigation.

(*b*) The term "seaman" includes every person employed or engaged in any capacity on board any vessel and entered on the ship's articles. It excludes masters, pilots, cadets and pupils on training ships and duly indentured apprentices, naval ratings, and other persons in the permanent service of a Government.

(c) The term "master" includes every person having command and charge of a vessel except pilots.

(d) The term "home trade vessel" means a vessel engaged in trade between a country and the ports of a neighbouring country within geographical limits determined by the national law.

Article 3.

Any seaman who is landed during the term of his engagement or on its expiration shall be entitled to be taken back to his own country, or to the port at which he was engaged, or to the port at which the voyage commenced, as shall be determined by national law, which shall contain the provisions necessary for dealing with the matter, including provisions to determine who shall bear the charge of repatriation.

A seaman shall be deemed to have been duly repatriated if he has been provided with suitable employment on board a vessel proceeding to one of the destinations prescribed in accordance with the foregoing paragraph.

A seaman shall be deemed to have been repatriated if he is landed in the country to which he belongs, or at the port at which he was engaged, or at a neighbouring port, or at the port at which the voyage commenced.

The conditions under which a foreign seaman engaged in a country other than his own has the right to be repatriated shall be as provided by national law or, in the absence of such legal provisions, in the articles of agreement. The provisions of the preceding paragraphs shall, however, apply to a seaman engaged in a port of his own country.

Article 4.

The expenses of repatriation shall not be a charge on the seaman if he has been left behind by reason of

(a) injury sustained in the service of the vessel, or
(b) shipwreck, or
(c) illness not due to his own wilful act or default, or
(d) discharge for any cause for which he cannot be held responsible.

Article 5.

The expenses of repatriation shall include the transportation charges, the accommodation and the food of the seaman during the journey. They shall also include the maintenance of the seaman up to the time fixed for his departure.

When a seaman is repatriated as member of a crew, he shall be entitled to remuneration for work done during the voyage.

Article 6.

The public authority of the country in which the vessel is registered shall be responsible for supervising the repatriation of any member of the crew in cases where this Convention applies, whatever may be his nationality, and where necessary for giving him his expenses in advance.

(*For the Standard Articles, see Draft Convention No. 21*)

Recommendation [No. 27] concerning the repatriation of masters and apprentices.

The Conference recommends that the national Governments shall take steps to provide for the repatriation of masters and duly indentured apprentices, who are not covered by the terms of the Draft Convention on the repatriation of seamen adopted by the General Conference at its Ninth Session.

Recommendation [No. 28] concerning the general principles for the inspection of the conditions of work of seamen.

Whereas among the methods and principles of special and urgent importance for the physical, moral and intellectual welfare of the workers, the Treaty of Versailles and the other Treaties of Peace make it a duty of the International Labour Organisation to devote special attention to the inspection of conditions of work in order to ensure the enforcement of the laws and regulations for the protection of the workers;

Whereas the International Labour Conference at its Fifth Session (October 1923) adopted a "Recommendation concerning the general principles for the organisation of systems of inspection to secure the enforcement of the laws and regulations for the protection of the workers";

Whereas that Recommendation is based essentially on the experience gained in the inspection of industrial establishments and it would be particularly difficult to apply or even to adapt it to the work of seamen, the nature and conditions of which are essentially different from those of work in a factory;

Whereas the inspection of the conditions under which seamen work will increase in importance in proportion as legislation for the protection of seamen is developed in the different countries and as further conventions concerning the working conditions of seamen are adopted by the Conference;

Whereas for the foregoing reasons it is desirable, in order to place the experience already gained at the disposal of the Members with a view to assisting them in the institution or reorganisation of their systems of inspection of the conditions under which seamen work, to indicate the general principles which practice shows to be best calculated to ensure the enforcement of measures for the protection of seamen;

The General Conference therefore recommends that each Member of the Organisation should take the following principles into consideration:

I. SCOPE OF INSPECTION.

1. That the principal duty of the authority or authorities responsible in each country for the inspection of the conditions under which seamen work should be to secure the enforcement of all laws and regulations dealing with such conditions and the protection of seamen in the exercise of their profession;

2. That, in so far as it may be considered desirable and possible, by reason of the experience they gain in carrying out their principal duties, to entrust the inspecting authorities with other secondary duties of a social nature which may vary according to the conceptions, customs, or traditions prevailing in the different countries, such duties may be assigned to them in addition to their principal duties on condition that:

(*a*) they do not in any way interfere with the performance of the inspectors' principal duties;

(*b*) they do not in any way prejudice the authority and impartiality which are necessary to inspectors in their relations with shipowners and seamen.

INTERNATIONAL LABOR ORGANIZATION

II. Organisation of Inspection.

The Conference recommends:

3. That, wherever it is compatible with administrative practice and in order to secure the greatest possible uniformity in the enforcement of the laws and regulations relating to the conditions under which seamen work, the different services or bodies responsible for supervising the enforcement of such laws and regulations should be centralised under a single authority;

4. That, if existing administrative practice will not admit of such centralisation of supervision, the different services or authorities whose functions are wholly or partly concerned with the protection of seamen should be enabled to benefit by one another's experience and to regulate their methods of work according to such common principles as may be considered the most effective;

5. That for this purpose close liaison and constant collaboration should be established between these different services or authorities, so far as is compatible with administrative practice and by the means considered the most suitable in each country (exchange of reports and information, periodical conferences, etc.); and

6. That the different services or authorities responsible for supervising the conditions under which seamen work should keep in touch with the authorities responsible for factory inspection, in matters of mutual concern.

III. Reports of the Inspection Authorities.

The Conference recommends:

7. That an annual general report on the supervision of the conditions under which seamen work should be published by the central authority or by the collaboration of the different authorities responsible for carrying out such supervision;

8. That this annual report should contain a list of the national laws and regulations affecting the conditions under which seamen work and their supervision together with any amendments thereto, which have come into operation during the year;

9. That it should also contain statistical tables with the necessary comments on the organisation and work of inspection and giving information, as far as may be possible and compatible with national administrative practice, on the following points:

(*a*) the number of vessels in commission subject to the various forms of inspection, these vessels being classified according to type (mechanically propelled vessels and sailing vessels) and each category being sub-divided according to the purpose for which these vessels are used;

(*b*) the number of seamen actually engaged on board the vessels of each class;

(*c*) the number of vessels visited by the inspectors, with an indication of the strength of the crews;

(*d*) the number and nature of breaches of the law or regulations ascertained by the inspectors and of the penalties imposed;

(*e*) the number, nature, and causes of accidents occurring to seamen during their work;

(*f*) the means adopted for the enforcement of the provisions of International Labour Conventions which relate to the conditions under which seamen work, and the extent of the compliance with such provisions, either in the form of the annual report transmitted to the International Labour Office under Article 408 of the Treaty of Peace or in some other appropriate form.

IV. Rights, Powers and Duties of Inspectors.

(a) Rights of inspection.

The Conference recommends:

10. That the inspection authorities, on proof of their identity, should be empowered by national law:

(*a*) to visit without previous notice any vessel flying the national flag by day or by night, in national or foreign territorial waters, and, in exceptional cases fixed by national law and by authorisation of the maritime authority, at sea, provided, however, that the time and manner of such visits should in practice be fixed so as to avoid as far as possible any serious inconvenience to the working of the vessel;

(*b*) to question without witnesses the crew and any other persons whose evidence may be considered desirable, to make any enquiries which may be judged necessary, and to require production of any of the ship's papers or documents which the laws or regulations require to be kept in so far as such papers or documents relate to the matters subject to inspection;

11. That national law should provide that the inspectors should be bound by oath, or by any other method which conforms with the administrative practice or customs in each country, not to disclose commercial secrets which may come to their knowledge in the course of their duties, under pain of criminal penalties or appropriate disciplinary measures.

(b) Compulsory powers.

The Conference recommends:

12. That the inspection authorities should be empowered, in serious cases where the health or safety of the crew is endangered, to prohibit by proper authorisation of the maritime authority a vessel from leaving port until the necessary measures have been taken on board to comply with the law, subject to appeal to higher administrative authority or to the court of competent jurisdiction, according to the law in the different countries;

13. That prohibiting a vessel from leaving port should be considered a measure of exceptional gravity, which should only be employed as a last resort when the other legal means at the disposal of the inspection authority to ensure respect for the law have been used without effect;

14. That the inspection authorities should be empowered in special cases to issue orders for securing observance of the laws and regulations governing the conditions under which seamen work, subject to appeal to higher administrative authority or to the court of competent jurisdiction, according to the law in each country;

15. That the central authority should be empowered in special cases to grant exemption from any specified requirement of any law or regulation governing the conditions under which seamen work, if such authority is satisfied that that requirement has been substantially complied with, or that compliance with the requirement is unnecessary in the circumstances of the case, and that the action taken, or provision made, as regards the subject-matter of the requirement is as effective as, or more effective than, actual compliance with the requirement.

INTERNATIONAL LABOR ORGANIZATION

(*c*) *Right to call for an inspection.*

The Conference recommends:

16. That national law should provide that the master of a vessel should be entitled to call for an inspection in all cases where he considers it necessary;

17. That national law should provide that the members of the crew of a vessel should also be entitled, subject to such conditions as may be prescribed, to call for an inspection on any matters relating to health, the safety of the vessel, or the rules affecting the conditions under which seamen work.

(*d*) *Co-operation of shipowners and seamen with the inspection authorities.*

The Conference recommends:

18. That, so far as is compatible with administrative practice in each country, and by such methods as may be considered most appropriate, shipowners and seamen should be called upon to co-operate in the supervision of the enforcement of the laws and regulations relating to the conditions under which seamen work.

In particular, the Conference draws the attention of the different countries to the following methods of co-operation:

(*a*) it is essential that every facility should be afforded to seamen freely to bring to the notice of the inspection authorities either directly or through their duly authorised representatives any infringement of the law on board the vessel on which such seamen are employed, that the inspection authority should as far as possible promptly make an enquiry into the subject-matter of any such complaint, that such complaints should be treated by the inspection authority as absolutely confidential;

(*b*) with a view to ensuring complete co-operation by shipowners and seamen and their respective organisations with the inspection authorities, and in order to improve conditions affecting the health and safety of seamen, it is desirable that the inspection authorities should from time to time consult the representatives of shipowners' and seamen's organisations as to the best means of attaining these ends. It is also desirable that joint committees of shipowners and seamen should be set up, and that they should be enabled to co-operate with the different services responsible for supervising the enforcement of the laws and regulations governing the conditions under which seamen work.

(*e*) *Safeguards.*

The Conference recommends:

19. That only such persons should be appointed inspectors as command the full confidence both of the shipowners and of the seamen, and that such persons should therefore be required to possess:

(*a*) the qualities necessary to ensure absolute impartiality in the performance of their duties;

(*b*) the technical qualifications necessary for the performance of their duties;

It is desirable that the inspection service should include men who have served at sea whose appointment whether in a permanent or temporary capacity should be at the discretion of the administrative authority;

20. That, when necessary, inspectors should be assisted in their duties by competent experts who command the full confidence of the shipowners and seamen;

21. That inspectors should be public servants whose status renders them independent of changes of Government;

22. That they should be prohibited from having any financial interest whatsoever in the undertakings subject to their inspection.

(*f*) *Other duties.*

The Conference recommends:

23. That as, by reason of the nature of their duties, inspectors have special opportunities of observing the practical results of the operation of the laws and regulations governing the conditions under which seamen work, they should be called upon, so far as it is compatible with the administrative methods in each country, to assist in improving legislation for the protection of seamen and to give the most effectual help possible in promoting the prevention of accidents;

24. That, so far as is compatible with administrative practice in each country, they should be called upon to take part in enquiries into shipwrecks and accidents on board ship, and that they should be empowered, where necessary, to submit reports on the results of such enquiries;

25. That, so far as is compatible with the administrative methods in each country, they should be called upon to collaborate in supplying information preparatory to the drafting of laws and regulations for the protection of seamen.

TENTH SESSION
(Geneva, 25 May - 16 June 1927).

Draft Convention [No. 24] concerning sickness insurance for workers in industry and commerce and domestic servants.

ARTICLE 1.

Each Member of the International Labour Organisation which ratifies this Convention undertakes to set up a system of compulsory sickness insurance which shall be based on provisions at least equivalent to those contained in this Convention.

ARTICLE 2.

The compulsory sickness insurance system shall apply to manual and non-manual workers, including apprentices, employed by industrial undertakings and commercial undertakings, out-workers and domestic servants.

It shall, nevertheless, be open to any Member to make such exceptions in its national laws or regulations as it deems necessary in respect of:

(*a*) Temporary employment which lasts for less than a period to be determined by national laws or regulations, casual employment not for the purpose of the employer's trade or business, occasional employment and subsidiary employment;

(*b*) Workers whose wages or income exceed an amount to be determined by national laws or regulations;

(*c*) Workers who are not paid a money wage;

(*d*) Out-workers whose conditions of work are not of a like nature to those of ordinary wage-earners;

(*e*) Workers below or above age-limits to be determined by national laws or regulations;

(*f*) Members of the employer's family.

It shall further be open to exempt from the compulsory sickness insurance system persons who in case of sickness are entitled by virtue of any laws or regulations, or of a special scheme, to advantages at least equivalent on the whole to those provided for in this Convention.

This Convention shall not apply to seamen and sea fishermen for whose insurance against sickness provision may be made by a decision of a later Session of the Conference.

Article 3.

An insured person who is rendered incapable of work by reason of the abnormal state of his bodily or mental health shall be entitled to a cash benefit for at least the first twenty-six weeks of incapacity from and including the first day for which benefit is payable.

The payment of this benefit may be made conditional on the insured person having first complied with a qualifying period and, on the expiry of the same, with a waiting period of not more than three days.

Cash benefit may be withheld in the following cases:

(*a*) Where in respect of the same illness the insured person receives compensation from another source to which he is entitled by law; benefit shall only be wholly or partially withheld in so far as such compensation is equal to or less than the amount of the benefit provided by the present Article;

(*b*) As long as the insured person does not by the fact of his incapacity suffer any loss of the normal product of his labour, or is maintained at the expense of the insurance funds or from public funds; nevertheless, cash benefits shall only partially be withheld when the insured person, although thus personally maintained, has family responsibilities;

(*c*) As long as the insured person while ill refuses, without valid reason, to comply with the doctor's orders, or the instructions relating to the conduct of insured persons while ill, or voluntarily and without authorisation removes himself from the supervision of the insurance institutions.

Cash benefit may be reduced or refused in the case of sickness caused by the insured person's wilful misconduct.

Article 4.

The insured person shall be entitled free of charge, as from the commencement of his illness and at least until the period prescribed for the grant of sickness benefit expires, to medical treatment by a fully qualified medical man and to the supply of proper and sufficient medicines and appliances.

Nevertheless, the insured person may be required to pay such part of the cost of medical benefit as may be prescribed by national laws or regulations.

Medical benefit may be withheld as long as the insured person refuses, without valid reason, to comply with the doctor's orders or the instructions relating to the conduct of insured persons while ill, or neglects to make use of the facilities placed at his disposal by the insurance institution.

Article 5.

National laws or regulations may authorise or prescribe the grant of medical benefit to members of an insured person's family living in his household and dependent upon him, and shall determine the conditions under which such benefit shall be administered.

Article 6.

Sickness insurance shall be administered by self-governing institutions, which shall be under the administrative and financial supervision of the competent public authority and shall not be carried on with a view of profit. Institutions founded by private initiative must be specially approved by the competent public authority.

The insured persons shall participate in the management of the self-governing insurance institutions on such conditions as may be prescribed by national laws or regulations.

The administration of sickness insurance may, nevertheless, be undertaken directly by the State where and as long as its administration is rendered difficult or impossible or inappropriate by reason of national conditions, and particularly by the insufficient development of the employers' and workers' organisations.

ARTICLE 7.

The insured persons and their employers shall share in providing the financial resources of the sickness insurance system.

It is open to national laws or regulations to decide as to a financial contribution by the competent public authority.

ARTICLE 8.

This Convention does not in any respect affect the obligations arising out of the Convention concerning the employment of women before and after childbirth, adopted by the International Labour Conference at its First Session.

ARTICLE 9.

A right of appeal shall be granted to the insured person in case of dispute concerning his right to benefit.

ARTICLE 10.

It shall be open to States which comprise large and very thinly populated areas not to apply the Convention in districts where, by reason of the small density and wide dispersion of the population and the inadequacy of the means of communication, the organisation of sickness insurance, in accordance with this Convention, is impossible.

The States which intend to avail themselves of the exception provided by this Article shall give notice of their intention when communicating their formal ratification to the Secretary-General of the League of Nations. They shall inform the International Labour Office as to what districts they apply the exception and indicate their reasons therefor.

In Europe it shall be open only to Finland to avail itself of the exception contained in this Article.

ARTICLE 11.

The formal ratifications of this Convention under the conditions set forth in Part XIII of the Treaty of Versailles and in the corresponding Parts of the other Treaties of Peace shall be communicated to the Secretary-General of the League of Nations for registration.

ARTICLE 12.

This Convention shall come into force ninety days after the date on which the ratifications of two Members of the International Labour Organisation have been registered by the Secretary-General.

It shall be binding only upon those Members whose ratifications have been registered with the Secretariat.

Thereafter, the Convention shall come into force for any Member ninety days after the date on which its ratification has been registered with the Secretariat.

INTERNATIONAL LABOR ORGANIZATION

Article 13.

As soon as the ratifications of two Members of the International Labour Organisation have been registered with the Secretariat, the Secretary-General of the League of Nations shall so notify all the Members of the International Labour Organisation. He shall likewise notify them of the registration of ratifications which may be communicated subsequently by other Members of the Organisation.

Article 14.

Subject to the provisions of Article 12, each Member which ratifies this Convention agrees to bring the provisions of Articles 1, 2, 3, 4, 5, 6, 7, 8, 9 and 10 into operation not later than 1 January 1929, and to take such action as may be necessary to make these provisions effective.

Article 15.

Each Member of the International Labour Organisation which ratifies this Convention engages to apply it to its colonies, possessions and protectorates, in accordance with the provisions of Article 421 of the Treaty of Versailles and of the corresponding Articles of the other Treaties of Peace.

Article 16.

A Member which has ratified this Convention may denounce it after the expiration of ten years from the date on which the Convention first comes into force, by an act communicated to the Secretary-General of the League of Nations for registration. Such denunciation shall not take effect until one year after the date on which it is registered with the Secretariat.

Article 17.

At least once in ten years, the Governing Body of the International Labour Office shall present to the General Conference a report on the working of this Convention and shall consider the desirability of placing on the Agenda of the Conference the question of its revision or modification.

Article 18.

The French and English texts of this Convention shall both be authentic.

Draft Convention [No. 25] concerning sickness insurance for agricultural workers.

Article 1.

Each Member of the International Labour Organisation which ratifies this Convention undertakes to set up a system of compulsory sickness insurance for agricultural workers, which shall be based on provisions at least equivalent to those contained in this Convention.

Article 2.

The compulsory sickness insurance system shall apply to manual and non-manual workers, including apprentices, employed by agricultural undertakings.

It shall, nevertheless, be open to any Member to make such exceptions in its national laws or regulations as it deems necessary in respect of:

(a) Temporary employment which lasts for less than a period to be determined by national laws or regulations, casual employment not for the purpose of the employer's trade or business, occasional employment and subsidiary employment;

(b) Workers whose wages or income exceed an amount to be determined by national laws or regulations;

(c) Workers who are not paid a money wage;

(d) Out-workers whose conditions of work are not of a like nature to those of ordinary wage-earners;

(e) Workers below or above age-limits to be determined by national laws or regulations;

(f) Members of the employer's family.

It shall further be open to exempt from the compulsory sickness insurance system persons who in case of sickness are entitled by virtue of any laws or regulations, or of a special scheme, to advantages at least equivalent on the whole to those provided for in this Convention.

ARTICLE 3.

An insured person who is rendered incapable of work by reason of the abnormal state of his bodily or mental health shall be entitled to a cash benefit for at least the first twenty-six weeks of incapacity from and including the first day for which benefit is payable.

The payment of this benefit may be made conditional on the insured person having first complied with a qualifying period and, on the expiry of the same, with a waiting period of not more than three days.

Cash benefit may be withheld in the following cases:

(a) Where in respect of the same illness the insured person receives compensation from another source to which he is entitled by law; benefit shall only be wholly or partially withheld in so far as such compensation is equal to or less than the amount of the benefit provided by the present Article;

(b) As long as the insured person does not by the fact of his incapacity suffer any loss of the normal product of his labour, or is maintained at the expense of the insurance funds or from public funds; nevertheless, cash benefit shall only partially be withheld when the insured person, although thus personally maintained, has family responsibilities.

(c) As long as the insured person while ill refuses, without valid reason, to comply with the doctor's orders, or the instructions relating to the conduct of insured persons while ill, or voluntarily and without authorisation removes himself from the supervision of the insurance institutions.

Cash benefit may be reduced or refused in the case of sickness caused by the insured person's wilful misconduct.

ARTICLE 4.

The insured person shall be entitled free of charge, as from the commencement of his illness and at least until the period prescribed for the grant of sickness benefit expires, to medical treatment by a fully qualified medical man and to the supply of proper and sufficient medicines and appliances.

Nevertheless, the insured person may be required to pay such part of the cost of medical benefit as may be prescribed by national laws or regulations.

Medical benefit may be withheld as long as the insured person refuses, without valid reason, to comply with the doctor's orders or the instructions relating to the conduct of insured persons while ill, or neglects to make use of the facilities placed at his disposal by the insurance institution.

INTERNATIONAL LABOR ORGANIZATION

Article 5.

National laws or regulations may authorise or prescribe the grant of medical benefit to members of an insured person's family living in his household and dependent upon him, and shall determine the conditions under which such benefit shall be administered.

Article 6.

Sickness insurance shall be administered by self-governing institutions, which shall be under the administrative and financial supervision of the competent public authority and shall not be carried on with a view of profit. Institutions founded by private initiative must be specially approved by the competent public authority.

The insured persons shall participate in the management of the self-governing insurance institutions on such conditions as may be prescribed by national laws or regulations.

The administration of sickness insurance may, nevertheless, be undertaken directly by the State where and as long as its administration is rendered difficult or impossible or inappropriate by reason of national conditions, and particularly by the insufficient development of the employers' and workers' organisations.

Article 7.

The insured persons and their employers shall share in providing the financial resources of the sickness insurance system.

It is open to national laws or regulations to decide as to a financial contribution by the competent public authority.

Article 8.

A right of appeal shall be granted to the insured person in case of dispute concerning his right to benefit.

Article 9.

It shall be open to States which comprise large and very thinly populated areas not to apply the Convention in districts where, by reason of the small density and wide dispersion of the population and the inadequacy of the means of communication, the organisation of sickness insurance, in accordance with this Convention, is impossible.

The States which intend to avail themselves of the exception provided by this Article shall give notice of their intention when communicating their formal ratification to the Secretary-General of the League of Nations. They shall inform the International Labour Office as to what districts they apply the exception and indicate their reasons therefor.

In Europe it shall be open only to Finland to avail itself of the exception contained in this Article.

(*For the Standard Articles, see Draft Convention No. 24*)

Recommendation [No. 29] concerning the general principles of sickness insurance.

Whereas the maintenance of a healthy and vigorous labour supply is of capital importance not only for the workers themselves, but also for communities which desire to develop their productive capacity; and

Whereas this development is only attainable by constantly and systematically applying provident measures to obviate or make good any loss of the workers' productive efficiency; and

Whereas the best provident measure for these purposes is to establish a system of social insurance which confers clearly defined rights on the persons to whom it applies;

Therefore the General Conference of the International Labour Organisation,

Having adopted Draft Conventions concerning, of the one part, sickness insurance for workers in industry and commerce and domestic servants, and, of the other part, sickness insurance for agricultural workers, drafts which lay down minimum conditions which must be complied with from the beginning by every system of sickness insurance, and

Considering that, in order to put the experience already gained at the disposal of the Members with a view to assisting them in the institution or completion of their sickness insurance services, it is desirable to indicate a number of the general principles which practice shows to be the best calculated to promote a just, effective and appropriate organisation of sickness insurance,

Recommends that each Member should take the following principles and rules into consideration:

I. Scope of Application.

1. Sickness insurance should include within its scope, without discrimination as to age or sex, every person who performs work by way of his occupation and under a contract of service or apprenticeship.

2. If, however, it is considered desirable to fix age-limits by reason of the fact that workers above or below such limits are already protected by law or otherwise, such limits should not apply to young persons who cannot normally be considered as dependent upon their family or to workers who have not reached the old-age pension age; and

if exceptions are made in respect of workers whose earnings or income exceed a specified amount, such exceptions should only apply to workers whose earnings or income are such that they may reasonably be expected to make their own provision for sickness.

II. Benefits.

A. *Cash Benefits.*

3. In order to secure that an insured person who is rendered incapable of work by sickness may recover his health as early as possible, the cash benefit representing compensation for lost wages should be adequate.

For this purpose the statutory scale of benefit should ordinarily be fixed in relation to the normal wage which is taken into account for the purposes of compulsory insurance, and should be a substantial proportion of such wage, regard being had to family responsibilities; but in countries where the workers have adequate facilities, of which they are accustomed to take advantage to procure for themselves additional benefit by other means, a uniform scale of benefit may be appropriate.

4. The statutory benefit should be paid for at least the first twenty-six weeks of incapacity as from and including the first day for which benefit is payable; nevertheless, the period for which benefit is payable should be increased to one year in cases of serious and chronic illness and for insured persons who will not receive any invalidity benefit on the expiry of their right to sickness benefit.

5. An insurance institution which can show that it is in a sound financial position should be authorised:

(*a*) To increase the statutory scale of benefit up to specified amounts either for all insured persons or for certain groups of the same, in particular insured persons with family responsibilities;

(*b*) To prolong the statutory period during which benefit is payable.

6. In countries where burial expenses are not, customarily or by law, covered by some other insurance, sickness insurance institutions should, on the death of an insured person, pay a benefit in respect of the cost of decent burial; they should also be empowered to pay such a benefit in respect of the burial expenses of the insured person's dependants.

B. *Benefits in kind.*

7. Treatment by a fully qualified doctor and the supply of proper and sufficient medicines and appliances should be granted to an insured person from the beginning of his illness and for so long as the state of his health requires it; the insured person should be entitled to these benefits free of charge from the beginning of his illness and at least until the expiry of the period prescribed for the grant of sickness benefit.

8. In addition to treatment by a fully qualified doctor and the supply of proper and sufficient medicines and appliances, there should be available for the insured person, as and when local and financial conditions admit, facilities for specialist services, as well as dental treatment, and for treatment in hospital, where his family circumstances necessitate it or his illness requires a mode of treatment which can only be given in hospital.

9. While an insured person is maintained in hospital, the insurance institution should pay to his dependants the whole or a part of the sickness benefit which would have been payable to him had he not been so maintained.

10. With a view to ensuring good conditions for the maintenance in health of the insured person and his family, members of the insured person's family living in his home and dependent upon him should be furnished with medical benefit, as and when it may be possible and practicable to do so.

11. Insurance institutions should be empowered to avail themselves, on equitable conditions, of the services of such doctors as they need.

In urban centres, and within specified geographical limits, an insured person should be entitled to choose a doctor from among those at the disposal of the insurance institution, unless this would involve considerable extra expense to the institution.

C. *Sickness Prevention.*

12. As most diseases can be prevented, an alert policy of prevention is calculated to avert loss of productive efficiency, to render available for other purposes the financial resources which are absorbed by avoidable illness, and to promote the material, intellectual and moral well-being of the community.

Sickness insurance should assist in inculcating the practice of the rules of hygiene among the workers. It should give preventive treatment and grant the same to as large a number of individuals as possible as soon as the premonitory symptoms of disease appear. It should be capable of contributing towards the prevention of the spread of disease and the improvement of the national health, in pursuance of a general policy co-ordinating all the various activities towards these ends.

III. ORGANISATION OF INSURANCE.

13. Insurance institutions should be administered, under the supervision

of the competent public authority in accordance with the principles of self-government, and shall not be carried on for profit. The insured persons being those who are the most directly interested in the working of the insurance scheme should, through elected representatives, have an important part in the management of the insurance system.

14. A good organisation of medical benefit and, in particular, the efficient provision and utilisation of medical equipment embodying the results of scientific progress can be most easily secured—except in certain special circumstances—by concentrating action on a territorial basis.

IV. FINANCIAL RESOURCES.

15. The financial resources for the insurance scheme should be provided by contributions from the insured persons and contributions from employers. The provision thus jointly made can be supplemented to advantage by contributions from public funds, especially for the purpose of improving the health of the people.

With a view to securing the stability of the insurance system, reserve funds, appropriate to the peculiar circumstances of the system, should be constituted.

V. SETTLEMENT OF DISPUTES.

16. With a view to their being settled rapidly and inexpensively, disputes as to benefits between insured persons and insurance institutions should be referred to special tribunals, the members of which include judges or assessors who are specially cognisant of the purposes of insurance and the needs of insured persons.

VI. EXCEPTION FOR SPARSELY POPULATED TERRITORIES.

17. States which, by reason of the small density of their population or of the inadequacy of the means of communication, cannot organise sickness insurance in certain parts of their territory should:

(a) Establish in such parts of their territory a sanitary service adequate to the local conditions;

(b) Examine periodically whether the conditions required for the introduction of compulsory sickness insurance in the parts of their territory previously excepted from the compulsory scheme are fulfilled.

VII. SEAMEN AND SEA FISHERMEN.

18. This Recommendation shall not apply to seamen and sea fishermen.

ELEVENTH SESSION
(Geneva, 30 May - 16 June 1928).
Draft Convention [No. 26] concerning the creation of minimum wage fixing machinery.

ARTICLE 1.

Each Member of the International Labour Organisation which ratifies this Convention undertakes to create or maintain machinery whereby minimum rates of wages can be fixed for workers employed in certain of the trades or parts of trades (and in particular in home working trades) in which no arrangements exist for the effective regulation of wages by collective agreement or otherwise and wages are exceptionally low.

For the purpose of this Convention the term "trades" includes manufacture and commerce.

Article 2.

Each Member which ratifies this Convention shall be free to decide, after consultation with the organisations, if any, of workers and employers in the trade or part of trade concerned, in which trades or parts of trades, and in particular in which home working trades or parts of such trades, the minimum wage fixing machinery referred to in Article 1 shall be applied.

Article 3.

Each Member which ratifies this Convention shall be free to decide the nature and form of the minimum wage fixing machinery, and the methods to be followed in its operation:

Provided that

(1) Before the machinery is applied in a trade or part of trade, representatives of the employers and workers concerned, including representatives of their respective organisations, if any, shall be consulted as well as any other persons, being specially qualified for the purpose by their trade or functions, whom the competent authority deems it expedient to consult;

(2) The employers and workers concerned shall be associated in the operation of the machinery, in such manner and to such extent, but in any case in equal numbers and on equal terms, as may be determined by national laws or regulations;

(3) Minimum rates of wages which have been fixed shall be binding on the employers and workers concerned so as not to be subject to abatement by them by individual agreement, nor, except with the general or particular authorisation of the competent authority, by collective agreement.

Article 4.

Each Member which ratifies this Convention shall take the necessary measures, by way of a system of supervision and sanctions, to ensure that the employers and workers concerned are informed of the minimum rates of wages in force and that wages are not paid at less than these rates in cases where they are applicable.

A worker to whom the minimum rates are applicable and who has been paid wages at less than these rates shall be entitled to recover, by judicial or other legalised proceedings, the amount by which he has been underpaid, subject to such limitation of time as may be determined by national laws or regulations.

Article 5.

Each Member which ratifies this Convention shall communicate annually to the International Labour Office a general statement giving a list of the trades or parts of trades in which the minimum wage fixing machinery has been applied, indicating the methods as well as the results of the application of the machinery and, in summary form, the approximate numbers of workers covered, the minimum rates of wages fixed, and the more important of the other conditions, if any, established relevant to the minimum rates.

Article 6.

The formal ratifications of this Convention under the conditions set forth in Part XIII of the Treaty of Versailles and in the corresponding Parts of the other Treaties of Peace shall be communicated to the Secretary-General of the League of Nations for registration.

ARTICLE 7.

This Convention shall be binding only upon those Members whose ratifications have been registered with the Secretariat.

It shall come into force twelve months after the date on which the ratifications of two Members of the International Labour Organisation have been registered with the Secretary-General.

Thereafter, this Convention shall come into force for any Member twelve months after the date on which its ratification has been registered.

ARTICLE 8.

As soon as the ratifications of two Members of the International Labour Organisation have been registered with the Secretariat, the Secretary-General of the League of Nations shall so notify all the Members of the International Labour Organisation. He shall likewise notify them of the registration of ratifications which may be communicated subsequently by other Members of the Organisation.

ARTICLE 9.

A Member which has ratified this Convention may denounce it after the expiration of ten years from the date on which the Convention first comes into force, by an act communicated to the Secretary-General of the League of Nations for registration. Such denunciation shall not take effect until one year after the date on which it is registered with the Secretariat.

Each Member which has ratified this Convention and which does not, within the year following the expiration of the period of ten years mentioned in the preceding paragraph, exercise the right of denunciation provided for in this Article, will be bound for another period of five years and, thereafter, may denounce this Convention at the expiration of each period of five years under the terms provided for in this Article.

ARTICLE 10.

At least once in ten years, the Governing Body of the International Labour Office shall present to the General Conference a report on the working of this Convention and shall consider the desirability of placing on the Agenda of the Conference the question of its revision or modification.

ARTICLE 11.

The French and English texts of this Convention shall both be authentic.

Recommendation [No. 30] concerning the application of minimum wage fixing machinery.

A.

The General Conference of the International Labour Organisation,

Having adopted a Draft Convention concerning the creation of minimum wage fixing machinery, and

Desiring to supplement this Draft Convention by putting on record for the guidance of the Members certain general principles which, as present practice and experience show, produce the most satisfactory results,

Recommends that each Member should take the following principles and rules into consideration:

I.

(1) In order to ensure that each Member ratifying the Convention is

in possession of the information necessary for a decision upon the application of minimum wage fixing machinery, the wages actually paid and the arrangements, if any, for the regulation of wages should be ascertained in respect of any trade or part of trade to which employers or workers therein request the application of the machinery and furnish information which shows *prima facie* that no arrangements exist for the effective regulation of wages and that wages are exceptionally low.

(2) Without prejudice to the discretion left to the Members by the Draft Convention to decide in which trades or parts of trades in their respective countries it is expedient to apply minimum wage fixing machinery, special regard might usefully be had to trades or parts of trades in which women are ordinarily employed.

II.

(1) The minimum wage fixing machinery, whatever form it may take (for instance, trade boards for individual trades, general boards for groups of trades, compulsory arbitration tribunals) should operate by way of investigation into the relevant conditions in the trade or part of trade concerned and consultation with the interests primarily and principally affected, that is to say, the employers and workers in the trade or part of trade, whose views on all matters relating to the fixing of the minimum rates of wages should in any case be solicited and be given full and equal consideration.

(2) (*a*) To secure greater authority for the rates that may be fixed, it should be the general policy that the employers and workers concerned, through representatives equal in number or having equal voting strength, should jointly take a direct part in the deliberations and decisions of the wage fixing body; in any case, where representation is accorded to one side, the other side should be represented on the same footing. The wage fixing body should also include one or more independent persons whose votes can ensure effective decisions being reached in the event of the votes of the employers' and workers' representatives being equally divided. Such independent persons should, as far as possible, be selected in agreement with or after consultation with the employers' and workers' representatives on the wage fixing body.

(*b*) In order to ensure that the employers' and workers' representatives shall be persons having the confidence of those whose interests they respectively represent, the employers and workers concerned should be given a voice as far as is practicable in the circumstances in the selection of their representatives, and if any organisations of the employers and workers exist these should in any case be invited to submit names of persons recommended by them for appointment on the wage fixing body.

(*c*) The independent person or persons mentioned in paragraph (*a*) should be selected from among men or women recognised as possessing the necessary qualifications for their duties and as being dissociated from any interest in the trade or part of trade concerned which might be calculated to put their impartiality in question.

(*d*) Wherever a considerable proportion of women are employed, provision should be made as far as possible for the inclusion of women among the workers' representatives and of one or more women among the independent persons mentioned in paragraph (*a*).

III.

For the purpose of determining the minimum rates of wages to be fixed, the wage fixing body should in any case take account of the necessity of enabling the workers concerned to maintain a suitable standard of living. For this purpose regard should primarily be had to the rates of wages being paid for similar work in trades where the workers are adequately organised and have concluded effective collective agreements, or, if no such standard of reference is available in the circumstances, to the general level of wages prevailing in the country or in the particular locality.

Provision should be made for the review of the minimum rates of wages fixed by the wage fixing bodies when this is desired by the workers or employers who are members of such bodies.

IV.

For effectively protecting the wages of the workers concerned and safeguarding the employers affected against the possibility of unfair competition, the measures to be taken to ensure that wages are not paid at less than the minimum rates which have been fixed should include:

(a) arrangements for informing the employers and workers of the rates in force;

(b) official supervision of the rates actually being paid; and

(c) penalties for infringements of the rates in force and measures for preventing such infringements.

(1) In order that the workers, who are less likely than the employers to have their own means of acquainting themselves with the wage fixing body's decisions, may be kept informed of the minimum rates at which they are to be paid, employers might be required to display full statements of the rates in force in readily accessible positions on the premises where the workers are employed, or in the case of home workers on the premises where the work is given out or returned on completion or wages paid.

(2) A sufficient staff of inspectors should be employed, with powers analogous to those proposed for factory inspectors in the Recommendation concerning the general principles for the organisation of systems of inspection adopted by the General Conference in 1923, to make investigations among the employers and workers concerned with a view to ascertaining whether the minimum rates in force are in fact being paid and taking such steps as may be authorised to deal with infringements of the rates.

As a means of enabling the inspectors adequately to carry out these duties, employers might be required to keep complete and authentic records of the wages paid by them, or in the case of home workers to keep a list of the workers with their addresses and provide them with wage books or other similar record containing such particulars as are necessary to ascertain if the wages actually paid correspond to the rates in force.

(3) In cases where the workers are not in general in a position individually to enforce, by judicial or other legalised proceedings, their rights to recover wages due at the minimum rates in force, such other measures should be provided as may be considered effective for preventing infringements of the rates.

B.

The General Conference of the International Labour Organisation thinks it right to call the attention of Governments to the principle affirmed by Article 427 of the Peace Treaty that men and women should receive equal remuneration for work of equal value.

INTERNATIONAL LABOR ORGANIZATION

TWELFTH SESSION

(Geneva, 30 May - 21 June 1929)

Recommendation [No. 31] concerning the prevention of industrial accidents.

The General Conference of the International Labour Organisation of the League of Nations,

Having been convened at Geneva by the Governing Body of the International Labour Office, and having met in its Twelfth Session on 30 May 1929, and

Having decided upon the adoption of certain proposals with regard to the prevention of industrial accidents, which is the first item on the Agenda of the Session, and

Having determined that these proposals shall take the form of a recommendation,

adopts, this twenty-first day of June of the year one thousand nine hundred and twenty-nine, the following Recommendation, to be submitted to the Members of the International Labour Organisation for consideration with a view to effect being given to it by national legislation or otherwise in accordance with the provisions of Part XIII of the Treaty of Versailles and of the corresponding Parts of the other Treaties of Peace;

Whereas the protection of workers against injury arising out of their employment is instanced by the Preamble to Part XIII of the Treaty of Versailles and to the corresponding Parts of the other Treaties of Peace as one of the improvements in industrial conditions which are urgently required;

Whereas industrial accidents not only cause suffering and distress among workers and their families, but also represent an important material loss to society in general;

Whereas the International Labour Conference in 1923 adopted a Recommendation concerning the general principles for the organisation of systems of inspection, in which it is laid down *inter alia* that inspection, in order to become progressively more effective "should be increasingly directed towards securing the adoption of the most suitable safety methods for preventing accidents and diseases with a view to rendering work less dangerous, more healthy, and even less exhausting by the intelligent understanding, education and co-operation of all concerned";

Whereas it is desirable that these measures and methods which experience in the various countries has shown to be most effective in enabling the number of accidents to be reduced and their gravity mitigated should be put on record for the mutual advantage of the Members;

Whereas a Resolution was adopted at the 1928 Session of the International Labour Conference in which the Conference declared its opinion that the time had come to attempt to reach a higher standard of safety by the development of new methods and that the greatest advance could be made on the lines of the Safety First Movement, although it could not supersede the action of the State in prescribing and enforcing regulations for the prevention of accidents;

Considering that it is of the highest importance that all persons or bodies, including employers, workers, employers' and workers' organisations, Governments and the general public, should use their best endeavours and every means in their power to help to prevent industrial accidents;

The General Conference recommends that each Member of the International Labour Organisation should take the following principles and rules into consideration for the prevention of accidents in industrial undertakings. The following in particular are considered as such:

(a) Mines, quarries, and other works for the extraction of minerals from the earth;

(b) Industries in which articles are manufactured, altered, cleaned, repaired, ornamented, finished, adapted for sale, broken up or demolished, or in which materials are transformed; including shipbuilding and the generation, transformation, and transmission of electricity or motive power of any kind;

(c) Construction, reconstruction, maintenance, repair, alteration or demolition of any building, railway, tramway, harbour, dock, pier, canal, inland waterway, road, tunnel, bridge, viaduct, sewer, drain, well, telegraphic or telephonic installation, electrical undertaking, gas work, waterwork or other work of construction, as well as the preparation for or laying the foundations of any such work or structure;

(d) Transport of passengers or goods by road, rail, sea or inland waterway, including the handling of goods at docks, quays, wharves or warehouses, but excluding transport by hand.

The Conference, considering further that the prevention of accidents is as necessary in agriculture as in industrial establishments, recommends that each Member of the International Labour Organisation should apply the Recommendation to agriculture, taking into account the special conditions of agricultural work.

I.

1. Whereas the foundations of the study of accident prevention are

(a) enquiry into the causes and circumstances of accidents,

(b) the study, by means of statistics of accidents in each industry as a whole, of the special dangers which exist in the several industries, the "laws" determining the incidence of accidents and, by comparison over a series of years, the effect of measures taken to avoid them;

The Conference recommends that each Member should take the necessary steps, by means of legislative or administrative action, effectively to ensure the collection and utilisation of the above information.

The Conference also recommends that methodical investigation should be carried out in each country by public services assisted, where it appears desirable, by institutions or committees set up by individual branches of industry.

The public services should have recourse to the collaboration of the industrial organisations of employers and workers and of the services responsible for the supervision of accident prevention, as well as, where desirable, of technical associations and accident insurance institutions or companies.

It is also desirable that industrial associations of employers and workers should collaborate in the institutions for accident prevention in the individual branches of industry.

2. As experience and research have shown that the incidence and gravity of accidents do not depend merely upon the dangers inherent in the work or in the kind of equipment or the various appliances in use, but also on physical, physiological and psychological factors, the Conference recommends that in addition to the investigations mentioned in

paragraph 1 in connection with material factors, these other factors should also be investigated.

3. Since the suitability of the worker for his work and the interest which he takes in his work are factors of primary importance for the promotion of safety, it is important that the Members should encourage scientific research into the best methods of vocational guidance and selection and their practical application.

4. Since it is important for the furtherance of accident prevention that the results of the investigations referred to in paragraphs 1 and 2 should be made known as widely as possible and since it is also desirable that the International Labour Office should be in possession of the information necessary to enable its work in connection with accident prevention to be extended, the Conference recommends that the more important results of the investigations should be communicated to the International Labour Office for use in its work and publications.

It is also desirable that there should be international consultation and exchange of results between the research institutions or organisations in the several industrial countries.

5. The Members should establish central departments to collect and collate statistics relating to industrial accidents and should communicate to the International Labour Office all available statistics on industrial accidents in their respective countries. They should also, with a view to the subsequent preparation of a Draft Convention, keep in touch with the International Labour Office in framing and developing their industrial accident statistics, with a view to arriving at uniform bases which would as far as possible allow of a comparative study of the statistics of the different countries.

II.

6. In view of the satisfactory results which experience in different countries has shown to follow from co-operation between all parties interested in the prevention of industrial accidents, particularly between employers and workers, it is important that the Members should do all in their power to develop and encourage such co-operation, as recommended in the Recommendation on systems of inspection adopted in 1923.

7. It is recommended that in every industry or branch of industry, so far as circumstances require, periodical conferences should be held between the State inspection service, or other competent bodies, and the representative organisations of employers and workers concerned: *(a)* to consider and review the position in the industry as regards the incidence and gravity of accidents, the working and effectiveness of the measures laid down by law, or agreed upon between the State or other competent bodies and representatives of the industry, or tried by individual employers, and *(b)* to discuss proposals for further improvement.

8. It is further recommended that the Members should actively and continuously encourage the adoption of measures for the promotion of safety, in particular *(a)* the establishment in the works of a safety organisation which should include arrangements for a works investigation of every accident occurring in the works, and the consideration of the methods to be adopted for preventing a recurrence; the systematic supervision of the works, machinery and plant for the purpose of ensuring safety, and in particular of seeing that all safeguards and other safety appliances are maintained in proper order and position; the explanation to new, and especially young, workers of the possible dangers of the work or the machinery or plant connected with their work; the organisation of first

aid and transport for injured workers; and the encouragement of suggestions from the persons employed for rendering work safer; *(b)* co-operation in the promotion of safety between the management and the workers in individual works, and of employers' and workers' organisations in the industry with each other and with the State and with other appropriate bodies by such methods and arrangements as may appear best adapted to the national conditions and aptitudes. The following methods are suggested as examples for consideration by those concerned: appointment of a safety supervisor for the works, establishment of works safety committees.

9. It is recommended that the Members should do all in their power to awaken and maintain the interest of the workers in the prevention of accidents and ensure their co-operation by means of lectures, publications, cinematograph films, visits to industrial establishments, and by such other means as they may find most appropriate.

10. It is recommended that the State should establish or promote the establishment of permanent safety exhibitions where the best appliances, arrangements and methods for preventing accidents and promoting safety can be seen (and in the case of machinery, seen in action) and advice and information given to employers, works officials, workers, students in the engineering and technical schools, and others.

11. In view of the fact that the workers, by their conduct in the factory, can and should contribute to a large extent to the success of protective measures, the State should use its influence to secure *(a)* that employers should do all in their power to improve the education of their workers in regard to the prevention of accidents, and *(b)* that the workers' organisations should by using their influence with their members co-operate in this work.

12. The Conference recommends that, in addition to measures taken in pursuance of the preceding paragraphs, the State should arrange for monographs on accident causation and prevention in particular industries or branches of industry or particular processes to be prepared by the State inspection service or other competent authorities, embodying the experience obtained as to the best measures for preventing accidents in the industry or process, and to be published by the State for the information of employers, works officials and workers in the industry and of employers' and workers' organisations.

13. In view of the importance of the work of education referred to in the preceding paragraph, and as a foundation for such education, the Conference recommends that the Members should arrange for the inclusion in the curricula of the elementary schools of lessons designed to inculcate habits of carefulness, and in the curricula of continuation schools lessons in accident prevention and first aid. Instruction in the prevention of industrial accidents should be given in vocational schools of all grades, where the importance of the subject both from the economic and moral standpoints should be impressed upon the pupils.

14. In view of the great value of immediate first-aid treatment in lessening the gravity of the consequences of accidents, measures should be taken to ensure that the necessary material for first aid should be kept ready for use in all undertakings and that first aid by properly trained persons should be given. It is also desirable that arrangements should be made to ensure that in case of serious accidents the services of a doctor are available as soon as possible. Arrangements should also be made for

providing ambulance services for the rapid transport of injured persons to hospital or to their homes.

Special attention should also be paid to the theoretical and practical training of doctors in the treatment of injuries due to accidents.

III.

15. As any effective system of accident prevention should rest on a basis of statutory requirements the Conference recommends that each Member should prescribe by law the measures required to ensure an adequate standard of safety.

16. It should be provided by law that it is the duty of the employer to equip and manage his undertaking in such a way that the workers are adequately protected, regard being had to the nature of the undertaking and the state of technical progress, as well as to see that the workers in his employment are instructed as to the dangers, if any, of their occupation and in the measures to be observed by them in order to avoid accidents.

17. It is in general desirable that plans for the construction or substantial alteration of industrial establishments should be submitted in due time to the competent authority, in order that it may be ascertained whether the plans are such as to satisfy the statutory requirements referred to above. The plans should be examined as rapidly as possible in order not to delay the execution of the work.

18. So far as the administrative and legal systems of each country allow, officials of the inspection service or other body responsible for supervising the enforcement of the statutory resuirements for the protection of workers against accidents should be empowered to give orders in particular cases to the employer as to the steps to be taken by him to fulfil his obligations, subject to a right of appeal to a higher administrative authority or to arbitration.

In case of imminent danger the supervising authority should be empowered to require immediate compliance with the orders, notwithstanding the right of appeal.

19. In view of the importance of the conduct of the worker in connection with accident prevention, the law should provide that it is the duty of the worker to comply with the statutory requirements on accident prevention and particularly to refrain from removing safety devices without permission and to use them properly.

20. It is recommended that before administrative orders or regulations for the prevention of accidents in any industry are finally issued by the competent authority, opportunity should be given to the representative organisations of employers and workers concerned to submit their views for the consideration of the competent authority.

21. Statutory or administrative provision should be made enabling the workers to collaborate in securing the observance of the safety regulations by the methods best suited to each country; for example, the appointment of qualified workers to positions in the official inspection service; regulations authorising the workers to call for a visit from an official of the inspection service or other competent body when they consider such a course desirable, or requiring the employer to give workers or their representatives an opportunity of seeing the inspector when he is visiting the undertaking; inclusion of workers' representatives in safety committees for securing the enforcement of the regulations and establishing the causes of accidents.

IV.

22. The Conference recommends that the State should endeavour to secure that accident insurance institutions or companies take into account, in assessing the premium for an undertaking, the measures taken therein for the protection of the workers, in order to encourage the development of safety measures by employers.

23. The State should use its influence with accident insurance institutions and companies to co-operate in the work of accident prevention by such means as the following: communication of information on causes and consequences of accidents to the inspection service or other supervising authorities concerned; co-operation in the institutions and committees referred to in paragraph 1 and in the Safety First Movement in general; advances to employers for the adoption or improvement of safety appliances; the award of prizes to workmen, engineers and others who, by their inventions or ideas, contribute substantially to the avoidance of accidents; propaganda among employers and the public; advice on safety measures, contributions to safety museums and institutions for instruction in accident prevention.

Draft Convention [No. 27] concerning the marking of the weight on heavy packages transported by vessels.

ARTICLE 1.

Any package or object of one thousand kilograms (one metric ton) or more gross weight consigned within the territory of any Member which ratifies this Convention for transport by sea or inland waterway shall have had its gross weight plainly and durably marked upon it on the outside before it is loaded on a ship or vessel.

In exceptional cases where it is difficult to determine the exact weight, national laws or regulations may allow an approximate weight to be marked.

The obligation to see that this requirement is observed shall rest solely upon the Government of the country from which the package or object is consigned, and not on the Government of a country through which it passes on the way to its destination.

It shall be left to national laws or regulations to determine whether the obligation for having the weight marked as aforesaid shall fall on the consignor or on some other person or body.

ARTICLE 2.

The formal ratifications of this Convention under the conditions set forth in Part XIII of the Treaty of Versailles and in the corresponding Parts of the other Treaties of Peace shall be communicated to the Secretary-General of the League of Nations for registration.

ARTICLE 3.

This Convention shall be binding only upon those Members whose ratifications have been registered with the Secretariat.

It shall come into force twelve months after the date on which the ratifications of two Members of the International Labour Organisation have been registered with the Secretary-General.

Thereafter, this Convention shall come into force for any Member twelve months after date on which its ratification has been registered.

INTERNATIONAL LABOR ORGANIZATION

Article 4.

As soon as the ratifications of two Members of the International Labour Organisation have been registered with the Secretariat, the Secretary-General of the League of Nations shall so notify all the Members of the International Labour Organisation. He shall likewise notify them of the registration of ratifications which may be communicated subsequently by other Members of the Organisation.

Article 5.

A Member which has ratified this Convention may denounce it after the expiration of ten years from the date on which the Convention first comes into force, by an Act communicated to the Secretary-General of the League of Nations for registration. Such denunciation shall not take effect until one year after the date on which it is registered with the Secretariat.

Each Member which has ratified this Convention and which does not, within the year following the expiration of the period of ten years mentioned in the preceding paragraph, exercise the right of denunciation provided for in this Article, will be bound for another period of ten years and, thereafter, may denounce this Convention at the expiration of each period of ten years under the terms provided for in this Article.

Article 6.

At the expiration of each period of ten years after the coming into force of this Convention, the Governing Body of the International Labour Office shall present to the General Conference a report on the working of this Convention and shall consider the desirability of placing on the Agenda of the Conference the question of its revision in whole or in part.

Article 7.

Should the Conference adopt a new Convention revising this Convention in whole or in part, the ratification by a Member of the new revising Convention shall *ipso jure* involve denunciation of this Convention without any requirement of delay, notwithstanding the provisions of Article 5 above, if and when the new revising Convention shall have come into force.

As from the date of the coming into force of the new revising Convention, the present Convention shall cease to be open to ratification by the Members.

Nevertheless, this Convention shall remain in force in its actual form and content for those Members which have ratified it but have not ratified the revising Convention.

Article 8.

The French and English texts of this Convention shall both be authentic.

Recommendation [No. 32] concerning responsibility for the protection of power-driven machinery.

I.

In order more effectively to ensure, in the interest of the safety of the workers, that the requirements prescribed by national laws or regulations for the protection of power-driven machinery used in the country concerned are properly complied with, and without prejudice to the responsibility which should in any case rest and remain on the employer for seeing that any machinery used in his undertaking is protected in accordance with national laws or regulations,

THE INTERNATIONAL PROTECTION OF LABOR

The Conference recommends that each Member adopt and apply to as great an extent as possible the principle that it should be prohibited by law to supply or install any machine intended to be driven by mechanical power and to be used within its territory, unless it is furnished with the safety appliances required by law for the operation of machines of that type.

The previous paragraph applies to any electrical equipment forming part of such a machine.

II.

Each Member should keep the International Labour Office informed of the measures taken by it to apply the above-mentioned principle and of the result of its application.

Draft Convention [No. 28] concerning the protection against accidents of workers employed in loading or unloading ships.

ARTICLE 1.

For the purpose of this Convention:

(1) the term "processes" means and includes all or any part of the work performed on shore or on board ship of loading or unloading any ship whether engaged in maritime or inland navigation, excluding ships of war, in, on, or at any maritime or inland port, harbour, dock, wharf, quay or similar place at which such work is carried on; and

(2) the term "worker" means any person employed in the processes.

ARTICLE 2.

Any regular approach over a dock, wharf, quay or similar premises which workers have to use for going to or from a working place at which the processes are carried on and every such working place on shore shall be maintained with due regard to the safety of the workers using them.

In particular,

(1) every said working place on shore and any dangerous parts of any said approach thereto from the nearest highway shall be safely and efficiently lighted;

(2) wharves and quays shall be kept sufficiently clear of goods to maintain a clear passage to the means of access referred to in Article 3;

(3) where any space is left along the edge of any wharf or quay, it shall be at least 3 feet (90 cm.) wide and clear of all obstruction other than fixed structures, plant and appliances in use; and

(4) so far as is practicable having regard to the traffic and working,

(a) all dangerous parts of the said approaches and working places (e.g. dangerous breaks, corners and edges) shall be adequately fenced to a height of not less than 2 feet 6 inches (75 cm.);

(b) dangerous footways over bridges, caissons and dock gates shall be fenced to a height of not less than 2 feet 6 inches (75 cm.) on each side, and the said fencing shall be continued at both ends to a sufficient distance which shall not be required to exceed 5 yards (4m. 50).

ARTICLE 3.

(1) When a ship is lying alongside a quay or some other vessel for the purpose of the processes, there shall be safe means of access for the use of the workers at such times as they have to pass to or from the ship,

unless the conditions are such that they would not be exposed to undue risk if no special appliance were provided.

(2) The said means of access shall be:

(a) where reasonably practicable, the ship's accommodation ladder, a gangway or a similar construction;

(b) in other cases a ladder.

(3) The appliance specified in paragraph (2) (a) of this Article shall be at least 22 inches (55 cm.) wide, properly secured to prevent their displacement, not inclined at too steep an angle, constructed of materials of good quality and in good condition, and securely fenced throughout to a clear height of not less than 2 feet 9 inches (82 cm.) on both sides, or in the case of the ship's accommodation ladder securely fenced to the same height on one side, provided that the other side is properly protected by the ship's side.

Provided that any appliances as aforesaid in use at the date of the ratification of this Convention shall be allowed to remain in use:

(a) until the fencing is renewed if they are fenced on both sides to a clear height of at least 2 feet 8 inches (80 cm.);

(b) for one year from the date of ratification if they are fenced on both sides to a clear height of at least 2 feet 6 inches (75 cm.).

(4) The ladders specified in paragraph (2) (b) of this Article shall be of adequate length and strength, and properly secured.

(5) (a) Exceptions to the provisions of this Article may be allowed by the competent authorities when they are satisfied that the appliances specified in the Article are not required for the safety of the workers.

(b) The provisions of this Article shall not apply to cargo stages or cargo gangways when exclusively used for the processes.

(6) Workers shall not use, or be required to use, any other means of access than the means specified or allowed by this Article.

Article 4.

When the workers have to proceed to or from a ship by water for the processes, appropriate measures shall be prescribed to ensure their safe transport, including the conditions to be complied with by the vessels used for this purpose.

Article 5.

(1) When the workers have to carry on the processes in a hold the depth of which from the level of the deck to the bottom of the hold exceeds 5 feet (1 m. 50), there shall be safe means of access from the deck to the hold for their use.

(2) The said means of access shall ordinarily be by ladder, which shall not be deemed to be safe unless it complies with the following conditions:

(a) leaves sufficient free space behind the rungs, which in the case of ladders on bulkheads and in trunk hatchways shall not be less than 4½ inches (11½ cm.), or has throughout rungs of proper width for firm foothold and handhold;

(b) is not recessed under the deck more than is reasonably necessary to keep it clear of the hatchway;

(c) is continued by and is in line with arrangements for secure handhold and foothold on the coamings (e.g. cleats or cups);

(d) the said arrangements on the coamings stand out not less than 4½ inches (11½ cm.) for a width of 10 inches (25 cm.); and *(e)* if separate ladders are provided between the lower decks, the said ladders are as far as practicable in line with the ladder from the top deck.

Where, however, owing to the construction of the ship, the provision of a ladder would not be reasonably practicable, it shall be open to the competent authorities to allow other means of access, provided that they comply with the conditions laid down in this Article for ladders so far as they are applicable.

(3) Sufficient free passage to the means of access shall be left at the coamings.

(4) Shaft tunnels shall be equipped with adequate handhold and foothold on both sides.

(5) When a ladder is to be used in the hold of a vessel which is not decked it shall be the duty of the contractor undertaking the processes to provide such ladder. It shall be equipped at the top with hooks for fastening it on to the coamings or with other means for firmly securing it.

(6) The workers shall not use, or be required to use, other means of access than the means specified or allowed by this Article.

(7) Ships existing at the date of ratification of this Convention shall be exempt from compliance with the measurements in paragraph 2 *(a)* and *(d)* and from the provisions of paragraph 4 of this Article for a period not exceeding four years from the date of ratification of this Convention.

Article 6.

While the workers are on a ship for the purpose of the processes, no hatchway of a cargo hold which exceeds 5 feet (1 m. 50) in depth from the level of the deck to the bottom of the hold and which is accessible to the workers shall be left open and unprotected, but every such hatchway which is not protected to a clear height of 2 feet 6 inches (75 cm.) by the coamings shall either be securely fenced to a height of 3 feet (90 cm.) if the processes at that hatchway are not impeded thereby or be securely covered.

Similar measures shall be taken when necessary to protect any other openings in a deck which might be dangerous to the workers.

Provided that the requirements of this Article shall not apply when a proper and sufficient watch is being kept.

Article 7.

When the processes have to be carried on on a ship, the means of access thereto and all places on board at which the workers are employed or to which they may be required to proceed in the course of their employment shall be efficiently lighted.

The means of lighting shall be such as not to endanger the safety of the workers nor to interfere with the navigation of other vessels.

Article 8.

In order to ensure the safety of the workers when engaged in removing or replacing hatch coverings and beams used for hatch coverings,

(1) hatch coverings and beams used for hatch coverings shall be maintained in good condition;

(2) hatch coverings shall be fitted with adequate hand grips, having regard to their size and weight;

(3) beams used for hatch coverings shall have suitable gear for re-

moving and replacing them of such a character as to render it unnecessary for workers to go upon them for the purpose of adjusting such gear;

(4) all hatch coverings and fore and aft and thwart-ship beams shall, in so far as they are not interchangeable, be kept plainly marked to indicate the deck and hatch to which they belong and their position therein;

(5) hatch coverings shall not be used in the construction of cargo stages or for any other purpose which may expose them to damage.

Article 9.

Appropriate measures shall be prescribed to ensure that no hoisting machine, or gear, whether fixed or loose, used in connection therewith, is employed in the processes on shore or on board ship unless it is in a safe working condition.

In particular,

(1) before being taken into use, the said machines, fixed gear on board ship accessory thereto as defined by national laws or regulations, and chains and wire ropes used in connection therewith, shall be adequately examined and tested, and the safe working load thereof certified, in the manner prescribed and by a competent person;

(2) after being taken into use, every hoisting machine, whether used on shore or on board ship, and all fixed gear on board ship accessory thereto as defined by national laws or regulations shall be thoroughly examined or inspected as follows:

(a) to be thoroughly examined every four years and inspected every twelve months: derricks, goose necks, mast bands, derrick bands, eyebolts, spans and any other fixed gear the dismantling of which is specially difficult;

(b) to be thoroughly examined every twelve months: all hoisting machines (e.g. cranes, winches), blocks, shackles and all other accessory gear not included in *(a)*.

All loose gear (e.g. chains, wire ropes, rings, hooks) shall be inspected on each occasion before use unless they have been inspected within the previous three months.

Chains shall not be shortened by tying knots in them and precautions shall be taken to prevent injury to them from sharp edges.

A thimble or loop splice made in any wire rope shall have at least three tucks with a whole strand of rope and two tucks with one half of the wires cut out of each strand; provided that this requirement shall not operate to prevent the use of another form of splice which can be shown to be as efficient as the form hereby prescribed.

(3) Chains and such similar gear as is specified by national laws or regulations (e.g. hooks, rings, shackles, swivels) shall, unless they have been subjected to such other sufficient treatment as may be prescribed by national laws or regulations, be annealed under the supervision of a competent person as follows:

(a) In the case of chains and the said gear carried on board ship:

(i) half inch (12½ mm.) and smaller chains or gear in general use once at least in every six months;

(ii) all other chains or gear (including span chains but excluding bridle chains attached to derricks or masts) in general use once at least in every twelve months:

Provided that in the case of such gear used solely on cranes and other hoisting appliances worked by hand, twelve months shall be substituted for six months in sub-paragraph (i) and two years for twelve months in sub-paragraph (ii);

Provided also that, if the competent authority is of opinion that owing to the size, design, material or infrequency of use of any of the said gear other than chains the requirements of this paragraph as to annealing are not necessary for the protection of the workers, it may, by certificate in writing (which it may at its discretion revoke) exempt such gear from the said requirements subject to such conditions as may be specified in the said certificate.

(b) In the case of chains and the said gear not carried on board ship:

Measures shall be prescribed to secure the annealing of the said chains and gear.

(c) In the case of the said chains and gear whether carried on board ship or not, which have been lengthened, altered or repaired by welding, they shall thereupon be tested and re-examined.

(4) Such duly authenticated records as will provide sufficient *prima facie* evidence of the safe condition of the machines and gear concerned shall be kept, on shore or on the ship as the case may be, specifying the safe working load and the dates and results of the tests and examinations referred to in paragraphs (1) and (2) of this Article and of the annealings or other treatment referred to in paragraph (3).

Such records shall, on the application of any person authorised for the purpose, be produced by the person in charge thereof.

(5) The safe working load shall be kept plainly marked on all cranes, derricks and chain slings and on any similar hoisting gear used on board ship as specified by national laws or regulations. The safe working load marked on chain slings shall either be in plain figures or letters upon the chains or upon a tablet or ring of durable material attached securely thereto.

(6) All motors, cogwheels, chain and friction gearing, shafting, live electric conductors and steam pipes shall (unless it can be shown that by their position and construction they are equally safe to every worker employed as they would be if securely fenced) be securely fenced so far as is practicable without impeding the safe working of the ship.

(7) Cranes and winches shall be provided with effective appliances to prevent the accidental descent of a load while in process of being lifted or lowered.

(8) Appropriate measures shall be taken to prevent exhaust steam from and, so far as practicable, live steam to any crane or winch obscuring any part of the working place at which a worker is employed.

Article 10.

Only sufficiently competent and reliable persons shall be employed to operate lifting or transporting machinery whether driven by mechanical power or otherwise, or to give signals to a driver of such machinery, or to attend to cargo falls on winch ends or winch drums.

Article 11.

(1) No load shall be left suspended from any hoisting machine unless there is a competent person actually in charge of the machine while the load is so left.

(2) Appropriate measures shall be prescribed to provide for the em-

INTERNATIONAL LABOR ORGANIZATION

ployment of a signaller where this is necessary for the safety of the workers.

(3) Appropriate measures shall be prescribed with the object of preventing dangerous methods of working in the stacking, unstacking, stowing and unstowing of cargo, or handling in connection therewith.

(4) Before work is begun at a hatch the beams thereof shall be removed, unless the hatch is of sufficient size to preclude danger to the workers from a load striking against the beams; provided that when the beams are not removed they shall be securely fastened to prevent their displacement.

(5) Precautions shall be taken to facilitate the escape of the workers when employed in a hold or on 'tween decks in dealing with coal or other bulk cargo.

(6) No stage shall be used in the processes unless it is substantially and firmly constructed, adequately supported and where necessary securely fastened.

No truck shall be used for carrying cargo between ship and shore on a stage so steep as to be unsafe.

Stages shall where necessary be treated with suitable material to prevent the workers slipping.

(7) When the working space in a hold is confined to the square of the hatch, hooks shall not be made fast in the bands or fastenings of bales of cotton, wool, cork, gunny bags or other similar goods (nor canhooks on barrels), except for the purpose of breaking out or making up slings.

(8) No gear of any description shall be loaded beyond the safe working load, except on special occasions expressly authorised by the owner or his responsible agent of which a record shall be kept.

(9) In the case of shore cranes with varying capacity (e.g. raising and lowering jib with load capacity varying according to the angle) an automatic indicator or a table showing the safe working loads at the corresponding inclinations of the jib shall be provided on the crane.

Article 12.

National laws or regulations shall prescribe such precautions as may be deemed necessary to ensure the proper protection of the workers, having regard to the circumstances of each case, when they have to deal with or work in proximity to goods which are in themselves dangerous to life or health by reason either of their inherent nature or of their condition at the time, or work where such goods have been stowed.

Article 13.

At docks, wharves, quays and similar places which are in frequent use for the processes, such facilities as having regard to local circumstances shall be prescribed by national laws or regulations shall be available for rapidly securing the rendering of first-aid and in serious cases of accident removal to the nearest place of treatment. Sufficient supplies of first-aid equipment shall be kept permanently on the premises in such a condition and in such positions as to be fit and readily accessible for immediate use during working hours. The said supplies shall be in charge of a responsible persons or persons, who shall include one or more persons competent to render first-aid, and whose services shall also be readily available during working hours.

At such docks, wharves, quays and similar places as aforesaid appropriate provision shall also be made for the rescue of immersed workers from drowning.

ARTICLE 14.

Any fencing, gangway, gear, ladder, life-saving means or appliance, light, mark, stage or other thing whatsoever required to be provided under this Convention shall not be removed or interfered with by any person except when duly authorised or in case of necessity, and if removed shall be restored at the end of the period for which its removal was necessary.

ARTICLE 15.

It shall be open to each Member to grant exemptions from or exceptions to the provisions of this Convention in respect of any dock, wharf, quay or similar place at which the processes are only occasionally carried on or the traffic is small and confined to small ships, or in respect of certain special ships or special classes of ships or ships below a certain small tonnage, or in cases where as a result of climatic conditions it would be impracticable to require the provisions of this Convention to be carried out.

The International Labour Office shall be kept informed of the provisions in virtue of which any exemptions and exceptions as aforesaid are allowed.

ARTICLE 16.

Except as herein otherwise provided, the provisions of this Convention which affect the construction or permanent equipment of the ship shall apply to ships the building of which is commenced after the date of ratification of the Convention, and to all other ships within four years after that date, provided that in the meantime the said provisions shall be applied so far as reasonable and practicable to such other ships.

ARTICLE 17.

In order to ensure the due enforcement of any regulations prescribed for the protection of the workers against accidents,

(1) The regulations shall clearly define the persons or bodies who are to be responsible for compliance with the respective regulations;

(2) Provision shall be made for an efficient system of inspection and for penalties for breaches of the regulations;

(3) Copies or summaries of the regulations shall be posted up in prominent positions at docks, wharves, quays and similar places which are in frequent use for the processes.

(*For the other Standard Articles, see Draft Convention No. 27.*)

ARTICLE 21.

A Member which has ratified this Convention may denounce it after the expiration of ten years from the date on which the Convention first comes into force, by an act communicated to the Secretary-General of the League of Nations for registration. Such denunciation shall not take effect until one year after the date on which it is registered with the Secretariat.

Each member which has ratified this Convention and which does not, within the year following the expiration of the period of ten years mentioned in the preceding paragraph, exercise the right of denunciation provided for in this Article, will be bound for another period of five years and, thereafter, may denounce this Convention at the expiration of each period of five years under the terms provided for in this Article.

INTERNATIONAL LABOR ORGANIZATION

Recommendation [No. 33] concerning reciprocity as regards the protection against accidents of workers employed in loading or unloading ships.

The Conference,

Recognising that the Convention concerning the protection against accidents of workers employed in loading or unloading ships, while having as its main object the protection against accidents of the said workers, at the same time affords an opportunity for regulations being prepared and issued by the Members which should secure reasonable uniformity on the basis of the Convention and for extension of the principle of reciprocity in the mutual recognition of certificates of inspection and examination; and

Recalling in this connection the principles laid down in the Copenhagen Convention of 28 January 1926 on the seaworthiness and equipment of ships as modified by the Declaration of 11 June 1928:

Strongly recommends that, following the ratification of, and issuing of regulations as aforesaid based upon, the Convention concerning the protection against accidents of workers employed in loading or unloading ships, the Members which have ratified the said Convention should enter into conference for the purpose of securing agreement for reciprocity, subject to all such agreements making secure the main object of the Convention, namely the safety of the persons employed.

Recommendation [No. 34] concerning the consultation of workers' and employers' organisations in the drawing up of regulations dealing with the safety of workers employed in loading or unloading ships.

The Conference,

Having adopted a Draft Convention concerning the protection against accidents of workers employed in loading or unloading ships, and

Desiring to indicate for the guidance of the Members a method of bringing the Convention into operation in their respective countries,

Supplements this Draft Convention by the following Recommendation:

That the authorities responsible for the making of regulations for the protection against accidents of workers employed in loading or unloading ships should, either directly or through any special joint machinery recognised for the purpose, consult the workers' and employers' organisations concerned, if any, in their respective countries in the drawing up of new regulations under the above-mentioned Draft Convention.

FOURTEENTH SESSION

(Geneva, 10-28 June 1930).

Draft Convention [No. 29] concerning forced or compulsory labour.

ARTICLE 1.

Each Member of the International Labour Organisation which ratifies this Convention undertakes to suppress the use of forced or compulsory labour in all its forms within the shortest possible period.

With a view to this complete suppression, recourse to forced or compulsory labour may be had, during the transitional period, for public purposes only and as an exceptional measure, subject to the conditions and guarantees hereinafter provided.

At the expiration of a period of five years after the coming into force of this Convention, and when the Governing Body of the International Labour Office prepares the report provided for in Article 31 below, the said Governing Body shall consider the possibility of the suppression of forced or compulsory labour in all its forms without a further transitional period and the desirability of placing this question on the Agenda of the Conference.

ARTICLE 2.

For the purposes of this Convention the term "forced or compulsory labour" shall mean all work or service which is exacted from any person under the menace of any penalty and for which the said person has not offered himself voluntarily.

Nevertheless, for the purposes of this Convention, the term "forced or compulsory labour" shall not include:

(a) any work or service exacted in virtue of compulsory military service laws for work of a purely military character;

(b) any work or service which forms part of the normal civic obligations of the citizens of a fully self-governing country;

(c) any work or service exacted from any person as a consequence of a conviction in a court of law, provided that the said work or service is carried out under the supervision and control of a public authority and that the said person is not hired to or placed at the disposal of private individuals, companies or associations;

(d) any work or service exacted in cases of emergency, that is to say, in the event of war or of a calamity or threatened calamity, such as fire, flood, famine, earthquake, violent epidemic or epizootic diseases, invasion by animal, insect or vegetable pests, and in general any circumstance that would endanger the existence or the well-being of the whole or part of the population;

(e) minor communal services of a kind which, being performed by the members of the community in the direct interest of the said community, can therefore be considered as normal civic obligations incumbent upon the members of the community, provided that the members of the community or their direct representatives shall have the right to be consulted in regard to the need for such services.

ARTICLE 3.

For the purposes of this Convention the term "competent authority" shall mean either an authority of the metropolitan country or the highest central authority in the territory concerned.

ARTICLE 4.

The competent authority shall not impose or permit the imposition of forced or compulsory labour for the benefit of private individuals, companies or associations.

Where such forced or compulsory labour for the benefit of private individuals, companies or associations exists at the date on which a Member's ratification of this Convention is registered by the Secretary-General of the League of Nations, the Member shall completely suppress such forced or compulsory labour from the date on which this Convention comes into force for that Member.

ARTICLE 5.

No concession granted to private individuals, companies or associations shall involve any form of forced or compulsory labour for the production or the collection of products which such private individuals, companies or associations utilise or in which they trade.

Where concessions exist containing provisions involving such forced or compulsory labour, such provisions shall be rescinded as soon as possible, in order to comply with Article 1 of this Convention.

ARTICLE 6.

Officials of the administration, even when they have the duty of encouraging the populations under their charge to engage in some form of labour, shall not put constraint upon the said populations or upon any individual members thereof to work for private individuals, companies, or associations.

ARTICLE 7.

Chiefs who do not exercise administrative functions shall not have recourse to forced or compulsory labour.

Chiefs who exercise administrative functions may, with the express permission of the competent authority, have recourse to forced or compulsory labour, subject to the provisions of Article 10 of this Convention.

Chiefs who are duly recognised and who do not receive adequate remuneration in other forms may have the enjoyment of personal services, subject to due regulation and provided that all necessary measures are taken to prevent abuses.

ARTICLE 8.

The responsibility for every decision to have recourse to forced or compulsory labour shall rest with the highest civil authority in the territory concerned.

Nevertheless, that authority may delegate powers to the highest local authorities to exact forced or compulsory labour which does not involve the removal of the workers from their place of habitual residence. That authority may also delegate, for such periods and subject to such conditions as may be laid down in the regulations provided for in Article 23 of this Convention, powers to the highest local authorities to exact forced or compulsory labour which involves the removal of the workers from their place of habitual residence for the purpose of facilitating the movement of officials of the administration, when on duty, and for the transport of Government stores.

ARTICLE 9.

Except as otherwise provided for in Article 10 of this Convention, any authority competent to exact forced or compulsory labour shall, before deciding to have recourse to such labour, satisfy itself:

(a) that the work to be done or the service to be rendered is of important direct interest for the community called upon to do the work or render the service;

(b) that the work or service is of present or imminent necessity;

(c) that it has been impossible to obtain voluntary labour for carrying out the work or rendering the service by the offer of rates of wages and conditions of labour not less favourable than those prevailing in the area concerned for similar work or service; and

(d) that the work or service will not lay too heavy a burden upon the present population, having regard to the labour available and its capacity to undertake the work.

ARTICLE 10.

Forced or compulsory labour exacted as a tax and forced or compulsory labour to which recourse is had for the execution of public works by chiefs who exercise administrative functions shall be progressively abolished.

Meanwhile, where forced or compulsory labour is exacted as a tax, and where recourse is had to forced or compulsory labour for the execution of public works by chiefs who exercise administrative functions, the authority concerned shall first satisfy itself:

(a) that the work to be done or the service to be rendered is of important direct interest for the community called upon to do the work or render the service;

(b) that the work or the service is of present or imminent necessity;

(c) that the work or service will not lay too heavy a burden upon the present population, having regard to the labour available and its capacity to undertake the work;

(d) that the work or service will not entail the removal of the workers from their place of habitual residence;

(e) that the execution of the work or the rendering of the service will be directed in accordance with the exigencies of religion, social life and agriculture.

Article 11.

Only adult able-bodied males who are of an apparent age of not less than 18 and not more than 45 years may be called upon for forced or compulsory labour. Except in respect of the kinds of labour provided for in Article 10 of this Convention, the following limitations and conditions shall apply:

(a) whenever possible prior determination by a medical officer appointed by the administration that the persons concerned are not suffering from any infectious or contagious disease and that they are physically fit for the work required and for the conditions under which it is to be carried out;

(b) exemption of school teachers and pupils and of officials of the administration in general;

(c) the maintenance in each community of the number of adult able-bodied men indispensable for family and social life;

(d) respect for conjugal and family ties.

For the purposes of sub-paragraph *(c)* of the preceding paragraph, the regulations provided for in Article 23 of this Convention shall fix the proportion of the resident adult able-bodied males who may be taken at any one time for forced or compulsory labour, provided always that this proportion shall in no case exceed 25 per cent. In fixing this proportion the competent authority shall take account of the density of the population, of its social and physical development, of the seasons, and of the work which must be done by the persons concerned on their own behalf in their locality, and, generally, shall have regard to the economic and social necessities of the normal life of the community concerned.

Article 12.

The maximum period for which any person may be taken for forced or compulsory labour of all kinds in any one period of twelve months shall not exceed sixty days including the time spent in going to and from the place of work.

Every person from whom forced or compulsory labour is exacted shall be furnished with a certificate indicating the periods of such labour which he has completed.

ARTICLE 13.

The normal working hours of any person from whom forced or compulsory labour is exacted shall be the same as those prevailing in the case of voluntary labour, and the hours worked in excess of the normal working hours shall be remunerated at the rates prevailing in the case of overtime for voluntary labour.

A weekly day of rest shall be granted to all persons from whom forced or compulsory labour of any kind is exacted and this day shall coincide as far as possible with the day fixed by tradition or custom in the territories or regions concerned.

ARTICLE 14.

With the exception of the forced or compulsory labour provided for in Article 10 of this Convention, forced or compulsory labour of all kinds shall be remunerated in cash at rates not less than those prevailing for similar kinds of work either in the district in which the labour is employed or in the district from which the labour is recruited, whichever may be the higher.

In the case of labour to which recourse is had by chiefs in the exercise of their administrative functions, payment of wages in accordance with the provisions of the preceding paragraph shall be introduced as soon as possible.

The wages shall be paid to each worker individually and not to his tribal chief or to any other authority.

For the purpose of payment of wages the days spent in travelling to and from the place of work shall be counted as working days.

Nothing in this Article shall prevent ordinary rations being given as a part of wages, such rations to be at least equivalent in value to the money payment they are taken to represent, but deductions from wages shall not be made either for the payment of taxes or for special food, clothing or accommodation supplied to a worker for the purpose of maintaining him in a fit condition to carry on his work under the special conditions of any employment, or for the supply of tools.

ARTICLE 15.

Any laws or regulations relating to workmen's compensation for accidents or sickness arising out of the employment of the worker and any laws or regulations providing compensation for the dependants of deceased or incapacitated workers which are or shall be in force in the territory concerned shall be equally applicable to persons from whom forced or compulsory labour is exacted and to voluntary workers.

In any case it shall be an obligation on any authority employing any worker on forced or compulsory labour to ensure the subsistence of any such worker who, by accident or sickness arising out of his employment, is rendered wholly or partially incapable of providing for himself, and to take measures to ensure the maintenance of any persons actually dependent upon such a worker in the event of his incapacity or decease arising out of his employment.

ARTICLE 16.

Except in cases of special necessity, persons from whom forced or compulsory labour is exacted shall not be transferred to districts where the food and climate differ so considerably from those to which they have been accustomed as to endanger their health.

In no case shall the transfer of such workers be permitted unless all measures relating to hygiene and accommodation which are necessary to adapt such workers to the conditions and to safeguard their health can be strictly applied.

When such transfer cannot be avoided, measures of gradual habituation to the new conditions of diet and of climate shall be adopted on competent medical advice.

In cases where such workers are required to perform regular work to which they are not accustomed, measures shall be taken to ensure their habituation to it, especially as regards progressive training, the hours of work and the provision of rest intervals, and any increase or amelioration of diet which may be necessary.

ARTICLE 17.

Before permitting recourse to forced or compulsory labour for works of construction or maintenance which entail the workers remaining at the workplaces for considerable periods, the competent authority shall satisfy itself:

(1) that all necessary measures are taken to safeguard the health of the workers and to guarantee the necessary medical care, and, in particular, *(a)* that the workers are medically examined before commencing the work and at fixed intervals during the period of service, *(b)* that there is an adequate medical staff, provided with the dispensaries, infirmaries, hospitals and equipment necessary to meet all requirements, and *(c)* that the sanitary conditions of the workplaces, the supply of drinking water, food, fuel, and cooking utensils, and, where necessary, of housing and clothing, are satisfactory;

(2) that definite arrangements are made to ensure the subsistence of the families of the workers, in particular by facilitating the remittance, by a safe method, of part of the wages to the family, at the request or with the consent of the workers;

(3) that the journeys of the workers to and from the workplaces are made at the expense and under the responsibility of the administration, which shall facilitate such journeys by making the fullest use of all available means of transport;

(4) that in case of illness or accident causing incapacity to work of a certain duration, the worker is repatriated at the expense of the administration;

(5) that any worker who may wish to remain as a voluntary worker at the end of his period of forced or compulsory labour is permitted to do so without, for a period of two years, losing his right to repatriation free of expense to himself.

ARTICLE 18.

Forced or compulsory labour for the transport of persons or goods, such as the labour of porters or boatmen, shall be abolished within the shortest possible period. Meanwhile the competent authority shall promulgate regulations determining, *inter alia*, *(a)* that such labour shall only be employed for the purpose of facilitating the movement of officials of the administration, when on duty, or for the transport of Government stores, or in cases of very urgent necessity, the transport of persons other than officials, *(b)* that the workers so employed shall be medically certified to be physically fit, where medical examination is possible, and that where such medical examination is not practicable the person employing such workers shall be held responsible for ensuring that they are physically fit and not suffering from any infectious or contagious disease, *(c)* the maximum load which these workers may carry, *(d)* the maximum distance from their homes to which they may be taken, *(e)* the maximum number of days per month or other period for which they may be taken, including the days spent in returning to their homes, and *(f)* the persons entitled to demand this form of forced or compulsory labour and the extent to which they are entitled to demand it.

In fixing the maxima referred to under *(c), (d) and (e)* in the foregoing paragraph, the competent authority shall have regard to all relevant factors, including the physical development of the population from which the workers are recruited, the nature of the country through which they must travel and the climatic conditions.

The competent authority shall further provide that the normal daily journey of such workers shall not exceed a distance corresponding to an average working day of eight hours, it being understood that account shall be taken not only of the weight to be carried and the distance to be covered, but also of the nature of the road, the season and all other relevant factors, and that, where hours of journey in excess of the normal daily journey are exacted, they shall be remunerated at rates higher than the normal rates.

ARTICLE 19.

The competent authority shall only authorise recourse to compulsory cultivation as a method of precaution against famine or a deficiency of food supplies and always under the condition that the food or produce shall remain the property of the individuals or the community producing it.

Nothing in this Article shall be construed as abrogating the obligation on members of a community, where production is organised on a communal basis by virtue of law or custom and where the produce or any profit accruing from the sale thereof remain the property of the community, to perform the work demanded by the community by virtue of law or custom.

ARTICLE 20.

Collective punishment laws under which a community may be punished for crimes committed by any of its members shall not contain provisions for forced or compulsory labour by the community as one of the methods of punishment.

ARTICLE 21.

Forced or compulsory labour shall not be used for work underground in mines.

ARTICLE 22.

The annual reports that Members which ratify this Convention agree to make to the International Labour Office, pursuant to the provisions of Article 408 of the Treaty of Versailles and of the corresponding Articles of the other Treaties of Peace, on the measures they have taken to give effect to the provisions of this Convention, shall contain as full information as possible, in respect of each territory concerned, regarding the extent to which recourse has been had to forced or compulsory labour in that territory, the purposes for which it has been employed, the sickness and death rates, hours of work, methods of payment of wages and rates of wages, and any other relevant information.

ARTICLE 23.

To give effect to the provisions of this Convention the competent authority shall issue complete and precise regulations governing the use of forced or compulsory labour.

These regulations shall contain, *inter alia*, rules permitting any person from whom forced or compulsory labour is exacted to forward all complaints relative to the conditions of labour to the authorities and ensuring that such complaints will be examined and taken into consideration.

ARTICLE 24.

Adequate measures shall in all cases be taken to ensure that the regulations governing the employment of forced or compulsory labour are strictly applied, either by extending the duties of any existing labour inspectorate which has been established for the inspection of voluntary labour to cover the inspection of forced or compulsory labour or in some other appropriate manner. Measures shall also be taken to ensure that the regulations are brought to the knowledge of persons from whom such labour is exacted.

ARTICLE 25.

The illegal exaction of forced or compulsory labour shall be punishable as a penal offence, and it shall be an obligation on any Member ratifying this Convention to ensure that the penalties imposed by law are really adequate and are strictly enforced.

ARTICLE 26.

Each Member of the International Labour Organisation which ratifies this Convention undertakes to apply it to the territories placed under its sovereignty, jurisdiction, protection, suzerainty, tutelage or authority, so far as it has the right to accept obligations affecting matters of internal jurisdiction; provided that, if such Member may desire to take advantage of the provisions of Article 421 of the Treaty of Versailles and of the corresponding Articles of the other Treaties of Peace, it shall append to its ratification a declaration stating:

(1) the territories to which it intends to apply the provisions of this Convention without modification;

(2) the territories to which it intends to apply the provisions of this Convention with modifications, together with details of the said modifications:

(3) the territories in respect of which it reserves its decision.

The aforesaid declaration shall be deemed to be an integral part of the ratification and shall have the force of ratification. It shall be open to any Member, by a subsequent declaration, to cancel in whole or in part the reservations made, in pursuance of the provisions of sub-paragraphs (2) and (3) of this Article, in the original declaration.

(*For the other Standard Articles, see Draft Convention No. 27*)

ARTICLE 30.

A Member which has ratified this Convention may denounce it after the expiration of ten years from the date on which the Convention first comes into force, by an act communicated to the Secretary-General of the League of Nations for registration. Such denunciation shall not take effect until one year after the date on which it is registered with the Secretariat.

Each Member which has ratified this Convention and which does not, within the year following the expiration of the period of ten years mentioned in the preceding paragraph, exercise the right of denunciation provided for in this Article, will be bound for another period of five years and, thereafter, may denounce this Convention at the expiration of each period of five years under the terms provided for in this Article.

INTERNATIONAL LABOR ORGANIZATION

ARTICLE 31.

At the expiration of each period of five years after the coming into force of this Convention, the Governing Body of the International Labour Office shall present to the General Conference a report on the working of this Convention and shall consider the desirability of placing on the Agenda of the Conference the question of its revision in whole or in part.

Recommendation [No. 35] concerning indirect compulsion to labour.

Having adopted a Draft Convention concerning forced or compulsory labour and

Desiring to supplement this Draft Convention by a statement of the principles which appear best fitted to guide the policy of the Members in endeavoring to avoid any indirect compulsion to labour which would lay too heavy a burden upon the populations of territories to which the Draft Convention may apply,

The Conference recommends that each Member should take the following principles into consideration:

I.

The amount of labour available, the capacities for labour of the population, and the evil effects which too sudden changes in the habits of life and labour may have on the social conditions of the population, are factors which should be taken into consideration in deciding questions connected with the economic development of territories in a primitive stage of development, and, in particular, when deciding upon:

(a) increases in the number and extent of industrial, mining and agricultural undertakings in such territories;

(b) the non-indigenous settlement, if any, which is to be permitted;

(c) the granting of forest or other concessions, with or without the character of monopolies.

II.

The desirability of avoiding indirect means of artificially increasing the economic pressure upon populations to seek wage-earning employment, and particularly such means as:

(a) imposing such taxation upon populations as would have the effect of compelling them to seek wage-earning employment with private undertakings;

(b) imposing such restrictions on the possession, occupation, or use of land as would have the effect of rendering difficult the gaining of a living by independent cultivation;

(c) extending abusively the generally accepted meaning of vagrancy;

(d) adopting such pass laws as would have the effect of placing workers in the service of others in a position of advantage as compared with that of other workers.

III.

The desirability of avoiding any restrictions on the voluntary flow of labour from one form of employment to another or from one district to another which might have the indirect effect of compelling workers to take employment in particular industries or districts, except where such restrictions are considered necessary in the interest of the population or of the workers concerned.

Recommendation [No. 36] concerning the regulation of forced or compulsory labour.

Having adopted a Draft Convention concerning forced or compulsory labour, and

Desiring to give expression to certain principles and rules relating to forced or compulsory labour which appear to be of a nature to render the application of the said Draft Convention more effective,

The Conference recommends that each Member should take the following principles and rules into consideration:

I.

Any regulations issued in application of the Draft Convention concerning forced or compulsory labour, as well as any other legal provisions or administrative orders, existing at the time of the ratification of the said Draft Convention or thereafter enacted, governing the employment of forced or compulsory labour, including any laws or administrative orders concerning compensation or indemnification for sickness, injury to, or death of workers taken for forced or compulsory labour, should be printed by the competent authority in such one or more native languages as will convey their import to the workers concerned and to the population from which the workers are to be drawn. Such printed texts should be widely exhibited and, if necessary, arrangements made for their oral communication to the workers and to the population concerned; copies should also be made available to the workers concerned and to others at cost price.

II.

Recourse to forced or compulsory labour should be so regulated as not to imperil the food supply of the community concerned.

III.

When recourse is had to forced or compulsory labour all possible measures should be taken to ensure that the imposition of such labour in no case leads indirectly to the illegal employment of women and children on forced or compulsory labour.

IV.

All possible measures should be taken to reduce the necessity for recourse to forced or compulsory labour for the transport of persons or goods. Such recourse should be prohibited when and where animal or mechanical transport is available.

V.

All possible steps should be taken to see that no alcoholic temptations are placed in the way of workers engaged in forced or compulsory labour.

Draft Convention [No. 30] concerning the regulation of hours of work in commerce and offices.

ARTICLE 1.

1. This Convention shall apply to persons employed in the following establishments, whether public or private:

(a) commercial or trading establishments, including postal, telegraph and telephone services and commercial or trading branches of any other establishments;

(b) establishments and administrative services in which the persons employed are mainly engaged in office work;

(c) mixed commercial and industrial establishments, unless they are deemed to be industrial establishments.

The competent authority in each country shall define the line which separates commercial and trading establishments, and establishments in which the persons employed are mainly engaged in office work, from industrial and agricultural establishments.

2. The Convention shall not apply to persons employed in the following establishments;

(a) establishments for the treatment or the care of the sick, infirm, destitute, or mentally unfit;

(b) hotels, restaurants, boarding-houses, clubs, cafés and other refreshment houses;

(c) theatres and places of public amusement.

The Convention shall nevertheless apply to persons employed in branches of the establishments mentioned in *(a), (b) and (c)* of this paragraph in cases where such branches would, if they were independent undertakings, be included among the establishments to which the Convention applies.

3. It shall be open to the competent authority in each country to exempt from the application of the Convention:

(a) establishments in which only members of the employer's family are employed;

(b) offices in which the staff is engaged in connection with the administration of public authority;

(c) persons occupying positions of management or employed in a confidential capacity;

(d) travellers and representatives, in so far as they carry on their work outside the establishment.

ARTICLE 2.

For the purpose of this Convention the term "hours of work" means the time during which the persons employed are at the disposal of the employer; it does not include rest periods during which the persons employed are not at the disposal of the employer.

ARTICLE 3.

The hours of work of persons to whom this Convention applies shall not exceed forty-eight hours in the week and eight hours in the day, except as hereinafter otherwise provided.

ARTICLE 4.

The maximum hours of work in the week laid down in Article 3 may be so arranged that hours of work in any day do not exceed ten hours.

ARTICLE 5.

In case of a general interruption of work due to *(a)* local holidays, or *(b)* accidents or *force majeure* (accidents to plant, interruption of power, light, heating or water, or occurrences causing serious material damage to the establishments), hours of work in the day may be increased for the purpose of making up the hours of work which have been lost, provided that the following conditions are complied with:

(a) hours of work which have been lost shall not be allowed to be made up on more than thirty days in the year and shall be made up within a reasonable lapse of time;

(b) the increase in hours of work in the day shall not exceed one hour;

(c) hours of work in the day shall not exceed ten.

2. The competent authority shall be notified of the nature, cause and date of the general interruption of work, of the number of hours of work which have been lost, and of the temporary alterations provided for in the working time-table.

ARTICLE 6.

In exceptional cases where the circumstances in which the work has to be carried on make the provisions of Articles 3 and 4 inapplicable, regulations made by public authority may permit hours of work to be distributed over a period longer than the week, provided that the average hours of work over the number of weeks included in the period do not exceed forty-eight hours in the week and that hours of work in any day do not exceed ten hours.

ARTICLE 7.

Regulations made by public authority shall determine:

1. The permanent exceptions which may be allowed for:

(a) certain classes of persons whose work is inherently intermittent, such as caretakers and persons employed to look after working premises and warehouses;

(b) classes of persons directly engaged in preparatory or complementary work which must necessarily be carried on outside the limits laid down for the hours of work of the rest of the persons employed in the establishment;

(c) shops and other establishments where the nature of the work, the size of the population or the number of persons employed render inapplicable the working hours fixed in Articles 3 and 4.

2. The temporary exceptions which may be granted in the following cases:

(a) in case of accident, actual or threatened, *force majeure*, or urgent work to machinery or plant, but only so far as may be necessary to avoid serious interference with the ordinary working of the establishment;

(b) in order to prevent the loss of perishable goods or avoid endangering the technical results of the work;

(c) in order to allow for special work such as stocktaking and the preparation of balance sheets, settlement days, liquidations, and the balancing and closing of accounts;

(d) in order to enable establishments to deal with cases of abnormal pressure of work due to special circumstances, in so far as the employer cannot ordinarily be expected to resort to other measures.

3. Save as regards paragraph 2 *(a)*, the regulations made under this Article shall determine the number of additional hours of work which may be allowed in the day and, in respect of temporary exceptions, in the year.

4. The rate of pay for the additional hours of work permitted under paragraph 2 *(b), (c)* and *(d)* of this Article shall not be less than one-and-a-quarter times the regular rate.

ARTICLE 8.

The regulations provided for in Articles 6 and 7 shall be made after consultation with the workers' and employers' organisations concerned, special regard being paid to collective agreements, if any, existing between such workers' and employers' organisations.

ARTICLE 9.

The operation of the provisions of this Convention may be suspended in any country by the Government in the event of war or other emergency endangering national safety.

ARTICLE 10.

Nothing in this Convention shall affect any custom or agreement whereby shorter hours are worked or higher rates of remuneration are paid than those provided by this Convention.

Any restrictions imposed by this Convention shall be in addition to and not in derogation of any other restrictions imposed by any law, order or regulation which fixes a lower maximum number of hours of employment or a higher rate of remuneration than those provided by this Convention.

ARTICLE 11.

For the effective enforcement of the provisions of this Convention:

1. The necessary measures shall be taken to ensure adequate inspection;
2. Every employer shall be required:

(a) to notify, by the posting of notices in conspicuous positions in the establishment or other suitable place, or by such method as may be approved by the competent authority, the times at which hours of work begin and end, and, where work is carried on by shifts, the times at which each shift begins and ends;

(b) to notify in the same way the rest periods granted to the persons employed which, in accordance with Article 2, are not included in the hours of work;

(c) to keep a record in the form prescribed by the competent authority of all additional hours of work performed in pursuance of paragraph 2 of Article 7 and of the payments made in respect thereof.

3. It shall be made an offence to employ any person outside the times fixed in accordance with paragraph 2 *(a)* or during the periods fixed in accordance with paragraph 2 *(b)* of this Article.

ARTICLE 12.

Each Member which ratifies this Convention shall take the necessary measures in the form of penalties to ensure that the provisions of the Convention are enforced.

(*For other Standard Articles, see Draft Convention No. 27.*)

ARTICLE 16.

A Member which has ratified this Convention may denounce it after the expiration of ten years from the date on which the Convention first comes into force, by an act communicated to the Secretary-General of the League of Nations for registration. Such denunciation shall not take effect until one year after the date on which it is registered with the Secretariat.

Each Member which has ratified this Convention and which does not, within the year following the expiration of the period of ten years mentioned in the preceding paragraph, exercise the right of denunciation provided for in this Article, will be bound for another period of five years and, thereafter, may denounce this Convention at the expiration of each period of five years under the terms provided for in this Article.

(b) In open coal mines, any person employed directly or indirectly in the extraction of coal, except persons engaged in supervision or management who do not ordinarily perform manual work.

ARTICLE 3.

Hours of work in underground hard coal mines shall mean the time spent in the mine calculated as follows:

1. Time spent in an underground mine shall mean the period between the time when the worker enters the cage in order to descend and the time when he leaves the cage after re-ascending.

2. In mines where access is by an adit the time spent in the mine shall mean the period between the time when the worker passes through the entrance of the adit and the time of his return to the surface.

3. In no underground hard coal mine shall the time spent in the mine by any worker exceed seven hours and forty-five minutes in the day.

ARTICLE 4.

The provisions of this Convention shall be deemed to be complied with if the period between the time when the first workers of the shift or of any group leave the surface and the time when they return to the surface is the same as that laid down in paragraph 3 of Article 3. The order of and the time required for the descent and ascent of a shift and of any group of workers shall, moreover, be approximately the same.

ARTICLE 5.

Subject to the provisions of the second paragraph of this Article, the provisions of this Convention shall be deemed to be complied with if the national laws or regulations prescribe that for calculating the time spent in the mine the descent or ascent of the workers is to be calculated according to the weighted average duration of the descent or ascent of all shifts of workers in the whole country. In this case, the period between the time when the last worker of the shift leaves the surface and the time when the first worker of the same shift returns to the surface shall not in any mine exceed seven hours and fifteen minutes; provided that no method of regulation shall be permitted by which the hewers as a class of workers would on the average work longer hours than the other classes of underground workers in the same shift.

Any Member which, having applied the method laid down in this Article, subsequently applies the provisions of Article 3 and 4 shall make the change simultaneously for the whole country and not for any part thereof.

ARTICLE 6.

1. Workers shall not be employed on underground work in coal mines on Sundays and legal public holidays. National laws or regulations may, however, authorise the following exceptions for workers over 18 years of age:

(a) For work which, owing to its nature, must be carried on continuously;

(b) For work in connection with the ventilation of the mine and the prevention of damage to the ventilation apparatus, safety work, work in connection with first aid in the case of accident and sickness, and the care of animals;

(c) For survey work in so far as this cannot be done on other days without interrupting or disturbing the work of the undertaking;

special regard being paid to collective agreements, if any, existing between such workers' and employers' organisations.

Article 9.

The operation of the provisions of this Convention may be suspended in any country by the Government in the event of war or other emergency endangering national safety.

Article 10.

Nothing in this Convention shall affect any custom or agreement whereby shorter hours are worked or higher rates of remuneration are paid than those provided by this Convention.

Any restrictions imposed by this Convention shall be in addition to and not in derogation of any other restrictions imposed by any law, order or regulation which fixes a lower maximum number of hours of employment or a higher rate of remuneration than those provided by this Convention.

Article 11.

For the effective enforcement of the provisions of this Convention:

1. The necessary measures shall be taken to ensure adequate inspection;
2. Every employer shall be required:

(a) to notify, by the posting of notices in conspicuous positions in the establishment or other suitable place, or by such method as may be approved by the competent authority, the times at which hours of work begin and end, and, where work is carried on by shifts, the times at which each shift begins and ends;

(b) to notify in the same way the rest periods granted to the persons employed which, in accordance with Article 2, are not included in the hours of work;

(c) to keep a record in the form prescribed by the competent authority of all additional hours of work performed in pursuance of paragraph 2 of Article 7 and of the payments made in respect thereof.

3. It shall be made an offence to employ any person outside the times fixed in accordance with paragraph 2 *(a)* or during the periods fixed in accordance with paragraph 2 *(b)* of this Article.

Article 12.

Each Member which ratifies this Convention shall take the necessary measures in the form of penalties to ensure that the provisions of the Convention are enforced.

(For other Standard Articles, see Draft Convention No. 27.)

Article 16.

A Member which has ratified this Convention may denounce it after the expiration of ten years from the date on which the Convention first comes into force, by an act communicated to the Secretary-General of the League of Nations for registration. Such denunciation shall not take effect until one year after the date on which it is registered with the Secretariat.

Each Member which has ratified this Convention and which does not, within the year following the expiration of the period of ten years mentioned in the preceding paragraph, exercise the right of denunciation provided for in this Article, will be bound for another period of five years and, thereafter, may denounce this Convention at the expiration of each period of five years under the terms provided for in this Article.

Recommendation [No. 37]
concerning the regulation of hours of work in hotels, restaurants and similar establishments.

Having adopted a Draft Convention concerning the regulation of hours of work in commerce and offices, and

Wishing to extend subsequently the application of the rules laid down in the said Draft Convention to as many classes of establishments as possible, including hotels, restaurants and similar establishments,

The Conference recommends:

1. That those Members in which no statutory regulation yet exists of the hours of work of persons employed in hotels, restaurants, boarding houses, clubs, cafés and similar establishments which are exclusively or mainly engaged in providing board and lodging or supplying refreshments for consumption on the premises, should make special investigations into the conditions obtaining in these establishments, in the light of the rules laid down in the above-mentioned Draft Convention.

2. That those Members in which statutory regulation of the hours of work of the said persons already exists should make special investigations into the application of the regulations, in the light of the rules laid down in the Draft Convention in question; and

3. That in both cases the Members should, within four years of the adoption of this Recommendation, communicate to the International Labour Office, on a uniform plan to be approved by the Governing Body, full information as to the results of the investigations, so that a special report may be prepared by the Office as a basis for considering the desirability of placing the question of the hours of work of persons employed in the establishments concerned on the Agenda of a subsequent Session of the Conference, with a view to the adoption of a Draft Convention.

Recommendation [No. 38] concerning the regulation of hours of work in theatres and other places of public amusement.

Having adopted a Draft Convention concerning the regulation of hours of work in commerce and offices, and

Wishing to extend subsequently the application of the rules laid down in the said Draft Convention to as many classes of establishments as possible, including theatres and other places of public amusement,

The Conference recommends:

1. That those Members in which no statutory regulation yet exists of the hours of work of persons employed in theatres, music halls, cinemas and places of public amusement generally, whether indoor or outdoor, should make special investigations into the conditions obtaining in these establishments, in the light of the rules laid down in the above-mentioned Draft Convention.

2. That those Members in which statutory regulation of the hours of work of the said persons already exists should make special investigations into the application of the regulations, in the light of the rules laid down in the Draft Convention in question; and

3. That in both cases the Members should, within four years of the adoption of this Recommendation, communicate to the International Labour Office, on a uniform plan to be approved by the Governing Body, full information as to the results of the investigations, so that a special report

may be prepared by the Office as a basis for considering the desirability of placing the question of the hours of work of persons employed in the establishments concerned on the Agenda of a subsequent Session of the Conference, with a view to the adoption of a Draft Convention.

Recommendation [No. 39] concerning the regulation of hours of work in establishments for the treatment or the care of the sick, infirm, destitute or mentally unfit.

Having adopted a Draft Convention concerning the regulation of hours of work in commerce and offices, and

Wishing to extend such regulations to as many classes of establishments as possible, including establishments for the treatment or the care of the sick, infirm, destitute or mentally unfit,

The Conference recommends:

1. That those Members in which no statutory regulations yet exist on the hours of work of persons employed in establishments for the treatment or the care of the sick, infirm, destitute or mentally unfit, should make special investigations into the conditions obtaining in these establishments, in the light of the rules laid down in the above-mentioned Draft Convention;

2. That those Members in which statutory regulation of the hours of work of the said persons already exists should make special investigations into the application of the regulations, in the light of the rules laid down in the Draft Convention in question; and

3. That in both cases the Members should, within four years of the adoption of this Recommendation, communicate to the International Labour Office, on a uniform plan to be approved by the Governing Body, full information as to the results of the investigations, so that a special report may be prepared by the Office as a basis for considering the desirability of placing the question of the hours of work of persons employed in the establishments concerned on the Agenda of a subsequent Session of the Conference, with a view to the adoption of a Draft Convention.

FIFTEENTH SESSION

(Geneva, 30 May - 18 June 1931).

Draft Convention [No. 31] limiting hours of work in coal mines.

ARTICLE 1.

This Convention shall apply to all coal mines, that is to say, to any mine from which only hard coal or lignite, or principally hard coal or lignite together with other minerals, is extracted.

For the purpose of this Convention, the term "lignite mine" shall mean any mine from which coal of a geological period subsequent to the carboniferous period is extracted.

ARTICLE 2.

For the purpose of this Convention, the term "worker" shall mean:

(a) In underground coal mines, any person occupied underground, by whatever employer and on whatever kind of work he may be employed, except persons engaged in supervision or management, who do not ordinarily perform manual work;

(b) In open coal mines, any person employed directly or indirectly in the extraction of coal, except persons engaged in supervision or management who do not ordinarily perform manual work.

ARTICLE 3.

Hours of work in underground hard coal mines shall mean the time spent in the mine calculated as follows:

1. Time spent in an underground mine shall mean the period between the time when the worker enters the cage in order to descend and the time when he leaves the cage after re-ascending.

2. In mines where access is by an adit the time spent in the mine shall mean the period between the time when the worker passes through the entrance of the adit and the time of his return to the surface.

3. In no underground hard coal mine shall the time spent in the mine by any worker exceed seven hours and forty-five minutes in the day.

ARTICLE 4.

The provisions of this Convention shall be deemed to be complied with if the period between the time when the first workers of the shift or of any group leave the surface and the time when they return to the surface is the same as that laid down in paragraph 3 of Article 3. The order of and the time required for the descent and ascent of a shift and of any group of workers shall, moreover, be approximately the same.

ARTICLE 5.

Subject to the provisions of the second paragraph of this Article, the provisions of this Convention shall be deemed to be complied with if the national laws or regulations prescribe that for calculating the time spent in the mine the descent or ascent of the workers is to be calculated according to the weighted average duration of the descent or ascent of all shifts of workers in the whole country. In this case, the period between the time when the last worker of the shift leaves the surface and the time when the first worker of the same shift returns to the surface shall not in any mine exceed seven hours and fifteen minutes; provided that no method of regulation shall be permitted by which the hewers as a class of workers would on the average work longer hours than the other classes of underground workers in the same shift.

Any Member which, having applied the method laid down in this Article, subsequently applies the provisions of Article 3 and 4 shall make the change simultaneously for the whole country and not for any part thereof.

ARTICLE 6.

1. Workers shall not be employed on underground work in coal mines on Sundays and legal public holidays. National laws or regulations may, however, authorise the following exceptions for workers over 18 years of age:

(a) For work which, owing to its nature, must be carried on continuously;

(b) For work in connection with the ventilation of the mine and the prevention of damage to the ventilation apparatus, safety work, work in connection with first aid in the case of accident and sickness, and the care of animals;

(c) For survey work in so far as this cannot be done on other days without interrupting or disturbing the work of the undertaking;

(d) For urgent work in connection with machinery and other appliances which cannot be carried out during the regular working time of the mine, and in other urgent or exceptional cases which are outside the control of the employer.

2. The competent authorities shall take appropriate measures for ensuring that no work is done on Sundays and legal public holidays except as authorised by this Article.

3. Work permitted under paragraph 1 of this Article shall be paid for at not less than one-and-a-quarter times the regular rate.

4. Workers who are engaged to any considerable extent on work permitted under paragraph 1 of this Article shall be assured either a compensatory rest period or an adequate extra payment in addition to the rate specified in paragraph 3 of this Article. The detailed application of this provision shall be regulated by national laws or regulations.

ARTICLE 7.

Lower maxima than those specified in Articles 3, 4 and 5 shall be laid down by regulations made by public authority for workers in workplaces which are rendered particularly unhealthy by reason of abnormal conditions of temperature, humidity or other cause.

ARTICLE 8.

1. Regulations made by public authority may provide that the hours specified in Articles 3, 4, 5 and 7 may be exceeded:

(a) In case of accident, actual or threatened, in case of *force majeure*, or in case of urgent work to be done to machinery, plant or equipment on the mine as a result of a break-down of such machinery, plant or equipment, even if coal production is thereby incidentally involved, but only so far as may be necessary to avoid serious interference with the ordinary working of the mine;

(b) For workers employed on operations which by their nature must be carried on continuously or on technical work, in so far as their work is necessary for preparing or terminating work in the ordinary way or for a full resumption of work on the next shift, provided, however, that this shall not refer to the production or transport of coal. The additional time authorised by this paragraph shall not exceed half an hour on any day for any individual worker, and in the case of all mines in normal operation the number of workers concerned shall at no time exceed 5 per cent. of the total number of persons employed at the mine.

2. Overtime worked in accordance with the provisions of this Article shall be paid for at not less than one-and-a-quarter times the regular rate.

ARTICLE 9.

Regulations made by public authority may, in addition to the provisions of Article 8, put not more than sixty hours' overtime in the year at the disposal of undertakings throughout the country as a whole.

This overtime shall be paid for at not less than one-and-a-quarter times the regular rate.

ARTICLE 10.

The regulations mentioned in Articles 7, 8 and 9 shall be made by public authority after consultation with the organisations of employers and workers concerned.

ARTICLE 11.

The annual Reports to be submitted under Article 408 of the Treaty of Versailles and the corresponding Articles of the other Treaties of

Peace shall contain all information as to the action taken to regulate the hours of work in accordance with the provisions of Articles 3, 4 and 5. They shall also furnish complete information concerning the regulations made under Articles 7, 8, 9, 12, 13 and 14 and concerning their enforcement.

ARTICLE 12.

In order to facilitate the enforcement of the provisions of this Convention, the management of every mine shall be required:

(a) To notify by means of notices conspicuously posted at the pithead or in some other suitable place, or by such other method as may be approved by the public authority, the hours at which the workers of each shift or group shall begin to descend and shall have completed the ascent.

These hours shall be approved by the public authority and be so fixed that the time spent in the mine by each worker shall not exceed the limits prescribed by this Convention. When once notified, they shall not be changed except with the approval of the public authority and by such notice and in such manner as may be approved by the public authority.

(b) To keep a record in the form prescribed by national laws or regulations of all additional hours worked under Articles 8 and 9.

ARTICLE 13.

In underground lignite mines Articles 3 and 4 and Articles 6 to 12 of this Convention shall apply subject to the following provisions:

(a) In accordance with such conditions as may be prescribed by national laws or regulations, the competent authority may permit collective breaks involving a stoppage of production not to be included in the time spent in the mine, provided that such breaks shall in no case exceed thirty minutes for each shift. Such permission shall only be given after the necessity for such a system has been established by official investigation in each individual case, and after consultation with the representatives of the workers concerned.

(b) The number of hours overtime provided for in Article 9 may be increased to not more than seventy-five hours a year.

In addition, the competent authority may approve collective agreements which provide for not more than seventy-five hours further overtime a year. Such further overtime shall likewise be paid for at the rate prescribed in Article 9, paragraph 2. It shall not be authorised generally for all underground lignite mines, but only in the case of individual districts or mines where it is required on account of special technical or geological conditions.

ARTICLE 14.

In open hard coal and lignite mines Articles 3 to 13 of this Convention shall not be applicable. Nevertheless, Members which ratify this Convention undertake to apply to these mines the provisions of the Washington Convention of 1919 limiting the hours of work in industrial undertakings to eight in the day and forty-eight in the week, provided that the amount of overtime which may be worked in virtue of Article 6, paragraph *(b)*, of the said Convention shall not exceed one hundred hours a year. Where special needs so require, and only in such cases, the competent authority may approve collective agreements which provide for an increase of the aforesaid one hundred hours by not more than a further hundred hours a year.

ARTICLE 15.

Nothing in this Convention shall have the effect of altering national laws or regulations with regard to hours of work so as to lessen the guarantees thereby afforded to the workers.

ARTICLE 16.

The operation of the provisions of this Convention may be suspended in any country by the Government in the event of emergency endangering the national safety.

ARTICLE 17.

The formal ratifications of this Convention under the conditions set forth in Part XIII of the Treaty of Versailles and in the corresponding Parts of the other Treaties of Peace shall be communicated to the Secretary-General of the League of Nations for registration.

ARTICLE 18.

This Convention shall be binding only upon those Members of the International Labour Organisation whose ratifications have been registered with the Secretariat.

It shall come into force six months after the date on which the ratifications of two of the following Members have been registered by the Secretary-General of the League of Nations: Belgium, Czechoslovakia, France, Germany, Great Britain, Netherlands and Poland.

Thereafter the Convention shall come into force for any Member six months after the date on which its ratification has been registered.

ARTICLE 19.

As soon as the ratifications of two of the Members mentioned in the second paragraph of Article 18 have been registered with the Secretariat, the Secretary-General of the League of Nations shall so notify all the Members of the International Labour Organisation. He shall likewise notify them of the registration of ratifications which may be communicated subsequently by other Members of the Organisation.

ARTICLE 20.

A Member which has ratified this Convention may denounce it after the expiration of five years from the date on which the Convention first comes into force, by an act communicated to the Secretary-General of the League of Nations for registration. Such denunciation shall not take effect until one year after the date on which it is registered with the Secretariat.

Each Member which has ratified this Convention and which does not, within the year following the expiration of the period of five years mentioned in the preceding paragraph, exercise the right of denunciation provided for in this Article, will be bound for another period of five years and, thereafter, may denounce this Convention at the expiration of each period of three years under the terms provided for in this Article.

ARTICLE 21.

At the latest within three years from the coming into force of this Convention the Governing Body of the International Labour Office shall place on the Agenda of the Conference the question of the revision of this Convention on the following points:

(a) The possibility of a further reduction in the hours of work provided for in paragraph 3 of Article 3;

(b) The right to have recourse to the exceptional method of calculation laid down in Article 5;

(c) The possibility of modifying the provisions of Article 13, paragraphs *(a)* and *(b)*, in the direction of a reduction of the hours of work;

(d) The possibility of a reduction in the amount of overtime provided for in Article 14.

Moreover, at the expiration of each period of ten years after the coming into force of this Convention, the Governing Body of the International Labour Office shall present to the General Conference a report on the working of this Convention and shall consider the desirability of placing on the Agenda of the Conference the question of its revision in whole or in part.

ARTICLE 22.

Should the Conference adopt a new Convention revising this Convention in whole or in part, the ratification by a Member of the new revising Convention shall *ipso jure* involve denunciation of this Convention without any requirement of delay, notwithstanding the provisions of Article 20 above, if and when the new revising Convention shall have come into force.

As from the date of the coming into force of the new revising Convention, the present Convention shall cease to be open to ratification by the Members.

Nevertheless, this Convention shall remain in force in its actual form and content for those Members which have ratified it but have not ratified the revising Convention.

ARTICLE 23.

The French and English texts of this Convention shall both be authentic.

SIXTEENTH SESSION
(Geneva, 12-30 April 1932)
Draft Convention [No. 32]
concerning the protection against accidents of workers employed in loading or unloading ships (revised 1932).

The General Conference of the International Labour Organisation of the League of Nations,

Having been convened at Geneva by the Governing Body of the International Labour Office, and having met in its Sixteenth Session on 12 April 1932, and

Having decided upon the adoption of certain proposals with regard to the partial revision of the Convention concerning the protection against accidents of workers employed in loading or unloading ships adopted by the Conference at its Twelfth Session, which is the fourth item on the Agenda of the Session, and

Considering that these proposals must take the form of a Draft International Convention,

adopts, this twenty-seventh day of April of the year one thousand nine hundred and thirty-two, the following Draft Convention for ratification by the Members of the International Labour Organisation, in accordance with the provisions of Part XIII of the Treaty of Versailles and of the corresponding Parts of the other Treaties of Peace:

ARTICLE 1.

For the purpose of this Convention:

(1) the term "processes" means and includes all or any part of the

INTERNATIONAL LABOR ORGANIZATION

work performed on shore or on board ship of loading or unloading any ship whether engaged in maritime or inland navigation, excluding ships of war, in, on, or at any maritime or inland port, harbour, dock, wharf, quay or similar place at which such work is carried on; and

(2) the term "worker" means any person employed in the processes.

Article 2.

Any regular approach over a dock, wharf, quay or similar premises which workers have to use for going to or from a working place at which the processes are carried on and every such working place on shore shall be maintained with due regard to the safety of the workers using them.

In particular,

(1) every said working place on shore and any dangerous parts of any said approach thereto from the nearest highway shall be safely and efficiently lighted;

(2) wharves and quays shall be kept sufficiently clear of goods to maintain a clear passage to the means of access referred to in Article 3;

(3) where any space is left along the edge of any wharf or quay, it shall be at least 3 feet (90 cm.) wide and clear of all obstructions other than fixed structures, plant and appliances in use; and

(4) so far as is practicable having regard to the traffic and working,

(a) all dangerous parts of the said approaches and working places (e.g. dangerous breaks, corners and edges) shall be adequately fenced to a height of not less than 2 feet 6 inches (75 cm.);

(b) dangerous footways over bridges, caissons and dock gates shall be fenced to a height of not less than 2 feet 6 inches (75 cm.) on each side, and the said fencing shall be continued at both ends to a sufficient distance which shall not be required to exceed 5 yards (4 m. 50).

(5) The measurement requirements of paragraph (4) of this Article shall be deemed to be complied with, in respect of appliances in use at the date of the ratification of this Convention, if the actual measurements are not more than 10 per cent. less than the measurements specified in the said paragraph (4).

Article 3.

(1) When a ship is lying alongside a quay or some other vessel for the purpose of the processes, there shall be safe means of access for the use of the workers at such times as they have to pass to or from the ship, unless the conditions are such that they would not be exposed to undue risk if no special appliance were provided.

(2) The said means of access shall be:

(a) where reasonably practicable, the ship's accommodation ladder, a gangway or a similar construction;

(b) in other cases a ladder.

(3) The appliances specified in paragraph (2) *(a)* of this Article shall be at least 22 inches (55 cm.) wide, properly secured to prevent their displacement, not inclined at too steep an angle, constructed of materials of good quality and in good condition, and securely fenced throughout to a clear height of not less than 2 feet 9 inches (82 cm.) on both sides, or in the case of the ship's accommodation ladder securely fenced to the same height on one side, provided that the other side is properly protected by the ship's side.

Provided that any appliances as aforesaid in use at the date of the ratification of this Convention shall be allowed to remain in use:

(a) until the fencing is renewed if they are fenced on both sides to a clear height of at least 2 feet 8 inches (80 cm.);

(b) for two years from the date of ratification if they are fenced on both sides to a clear height of at least 2 feet 6 inches (75 cm.).

(4) The ladders specified in paragraph (2) *(b)* of this Article shall be of adequate length and strength, and properly secured.

(5) *(a)* Exceptions to the provisions of this Article may be allowed by the competent authorities when they are satisfied that the appliances specified in the Article are not required for the safety of the workers.

(b) The provisions of this Article shall not apply to cargo stages or cargo gangways when exclusively used for the processes.

(6) Workers shall not use, or be required to use, any other means of access than the means specified or allowed by this Article.

Article 4.

When the workers have to proceed to or from a ship by water for the processes, appropriate measures shall be prescribed to ensure their safe transport, including the conditions to be complied with by the vessels used for this purpose.

Article 5.

(1) When the workers have to carry on the processes in a hold the depth of which from the level of the deck to the bottom of the hold exceeds 5 feet (1 m. 50), there shall be safe means of access from the deck to the hold for their use.

(2) The said means of access shall ordinarily be by ladder, which shall not be deemed to be safe unless it complies with the following conditions:

(a) provides foothold of a depth, including any space behind the ladder, of not less than 4½ inches (11½ cm.) for a width of not less than 10 inches (25 cm.) and a firm handhold;

(b) is not recessed under the deck more than is reasonably necessary to keep it clear of the hatchway;

(c) is continued by and is in line with arrangements for secure handhold and foothold on the coamings (e.g. cleats or cups);

(d) the said arrangements on the coamings provide foothold of a depth, including any space behind the said arrangements, of not less than 4½ inches (11½ cm.) for a width of not less than 10 inches (25 cm.);

(e) if separate ladders are provided between the lower decks, the said ladders are as far as practicable in line with the ladder from the top deck.

Where, however, owing to the construction of the ship, the provision of a ladder would not be reasonably practicable, it shall be open to the competent authorities to allow other means of access, provided that they comply with the conditions laid down in this Article for ladders so far as they are applicable.

In the case of ships existing at the date of the ratification of this Convention the measurement requirements of sub-paragraphs *(a)* and *(d)* of this paragraph shall be deemed to be complied with, until the ladders and arrangements are replaced, if the actual measurements are not more than 10 per cent. less than the measurements specified in the said sub-paragraphs *(a)* and *(d)*.

INTERNATIONAL LABOR ORGANIZATION

(3) Sufficient free passage to the means of access shall be left at the coamings.

(4) Shaft tunnels shall be equipped with adequate handhold and foothold on both sides.

(5) When a ladder is to be used in the hold of a vessel which is not decked it shall be the duty of the contractor undertaking the processes to provide such ladder. It shall be equipped at the top with hooks or with other means for firmly securing it.

(6) The workers shall not use, or be required to use, other means of access than the means specified or allowed by this Article.

(7) Ships existing at the date of ratification of this Convention shall be exempt from compliance with the measurements in paragraph (2) *(a)* and *(d)* and from the provisions of paragraph (4) of this Article for a period not exceeding four years from the date of ratification of this Convention.

Article 6.

(1) While the workers are on a ship for the purpose of the processes, every hatchway of a cargo hold accessible to the workers which exceeds 5 feet (1 m. 50) in depth from the level of the deck to the bottom of the hold, and which is not protected to a clear height of 2 feet 6 inches (75 cm.) by the coamings, shall, when not in use for the passage of goods, coal or other material, either be securely fenced to a height of 3 feet (90 cm.) or be securely covered. National laws or regulations shall determine whether the requirements of this paragraph shall be enforced during meal times and other short interruptions of work.

(2) Similar measures shall be taken when necessary to protect all other openings in a deck which might be dangerous to the workers.

Article 7.

When the processes have to be carried on on a ship, the means of access thereto and all places on board at which the workers are employed or to which they may be required to proceed in the course of their employment shall be efficiently lighted.

The means of lighting shall be such as not to endanger the safety of the workers nor to interfere with the navigation of other vessels.

Article 8.

In order to ensure the safety of the workers when engaged in removing or replacing hatch coverings and beams used for hatch coverings,

(1) hatch coverings and beams used for hatch coverings shall be maintained in good condition;

(2) hatch coverings shall be fitted with adequate hand grips, having regard to their size and weight, unless the construction of the hatch or the hatch coverings is of a character rendering the provision of hand grips unnecessary;

(3) beams used for hatch coverings shall have suitable gear for removing and replacing them of such a character as to render it unnecessary for workers to go upon them for the purpose of adjusting such gear;

(4) all hatch coverings and fore and aft and thwart-ship beams shall, in so far as they are not interchangeable, be kept plainly marked to indicate the deck and hatch to which they belong and their position therein;

(5) hatch coverings shall not be used in the construction of cargo stages or for any other purpose which may expose them to damage.

ARTICLE 9.

Appropriate measures shall be prescribed to ensure that no hoisting machine, or gear, whether fixed or loose, used in connection therewith, is employed in the processes on shore or on board ship unless it is in a safe working condition.

In particular,

(1) before being taken into use, the said machines, fixed gear on board ship accessory thereto as defined by national laws or regulations, and chains and wire ropes used in connection therewith, shall be adequately examined and tested, and the safe working load thereof certified, in the manner prescribed and by a competent person acceptable to the national authorities;

(2) after being taken into use, every hoisting machine, whether used on shore or on board ship, and all fixed gear on board ship accessory thereto as defined by national laws or regulations shall be thoroughly examined or inspected as follows:

(a) to be thoroughly examined every four years and inspected every twelve months: derricks, goose necks, mast bands, derrick bands, eyebolts, spans and any other fixed gear the dismantling of which is specially difficult;

(b) to be thoroughly examined every twelve months: all hoisting machines (e.g. cranes, winches), blocks, shackles and all other accessory gear not included in (a).

All loose gear (e.g. chains, wire ropes, rings, hooks) shall be inspected on each occasion before use unless they have been inspected within the previous three months.

Chains shall not be shortened by tying knots in them and precautions shall be taken to prevent injury to them from sharp edges.

A thimble or loop splice made in any wire rope shall have at least three tucks with a whole strand of rope and two tucks with one half of the wires cut out of each strand; provided that this requirement shall not operate to prevent the use of another form of splice which can be shown to be as efficient as the form hereby prescribed.

(3) Chains and such similar gear as is specified by national laws or regulations (e.g. hooks, rings, shackles, swivels) shall, unless they have been subjected to such other sufficient treatment as may be prescribed by national laws or regulations, be annealed as follows under the supervision of a competent person acceptable to the national authorities:

(a) In the case of chains and the said gear carried on board ship:

(i) half inch (12½ mm.) and smaller chains or gear in general use once at least in every six months;

(ii) all other chains or gear (including span chains but excluding bridle chains attached to derricks or masts) in general use once at least in every twelve months;

Provided that in the case of such gear used solely on cranes and other hoisting appliances worked by hand, twelve months shall be substituted for six months in sub-paragraph (i) and two years for twelve months in sub-paragraph (ii);

Provided also that, if the competent authority is of opinion that owing to the size, design, material or infrequency of use of any of the said gear the requirements of this paragraph as to annealing are not necessary for the protection of the workers, it may, by certificate in writing (which it may at its discretion revoke), exempt such gear from the said requirements subject to such conditions as may be specified in the said certificate.

(b) In the case of chains and the said gear not carried on board ship: Measures shall be prescribed to secure the annealing of the said chains and gear.

(c) In the case of the said chains and gear whether carried on board ship or not, which have been lengthened, altered or repaired by welding, they shall thereupon be tested and re-examined.

(4) Such duly authenticated records as will provide sufficient *prima facie* evidence of the safe condition of the machines and gear concerned shall be kept, on shore or on the ship as the case may be, specifying the safe working load and the dates and results of the tests and examinations referred to in paragraphs (1) and (2) of this Article and of the annealings or other treatment referred to in paragraph (3).

Such records shall, on the application of any person authorised for the purpose, be produced by the person in charge thereof.

(5) The safe working load shall be kept plainly marked on all cranes, derricks and chain slings and on any similar hoisting gear used on board ship as specified by national laws or regulations. The safe working load marked on chain slings shall either be in plain figures or letters upon the chains or upon a tablet or ring of durable material attached securely thereto.

(6) All motors, cogwheels, chain and friction gearing, shafting, live electric conductors and steam pipes shall (unless it can be shown that by their position and construction they are equally safe to every worker employed as they would be if securely fenced) be securely fenced so far as is practicable without impeding the safe working of the ship.

(7) Cranes and winches shall be provided with such means as will reduce to a minimum the risk of the accidental descent of a load while in process of being lifted or lowered.

(8) Appropriate measures shall be taken to prevent exhaust steam from and, so far as practicable, live steam to any crane or winch obscuring any part of the working place at which a worker is employed.

(9) Appropriate measures shall be taken to prevent the foot of a derrick being accidentally lifted out of its socket or support.

ARTICLE 10.

Only sufficiently competent and reliable persons shall be employed to operate lifting or transporting machinery whether driven by mechanical power or otherwise, or to give signals to a driver of such machinery, or to attend to cargo falls on winch ends or winch drums.

ARTICLE 11.

(1) No load shall be left suspended from any hoisting machine unless there is a competent person actually in charge of the machine while the load is so left.

(2) Appropriate measures shall be prescribed to provide for the employment of a signaller where this is necessary for the safety of the workers.

(3) Appropriate measures shall be prescribed with the object of preventing dangerous methods of working in the stacking, unstacking, stowing and unstowing of cargo, or handling in connection therewith.

(4) Before work is begun at a hatch the beams thereof shall either be removed or be securely fastened to prevent their displacement.

(5) Precautions shall be taken to facilitate the escape of the workers when employed in a hold or on 'tween decks in dealing with coal or other bulk cargo.

(6) No stage shall be used in the processes unless it is substantially and firmly constructed, adequately supported and where necessary securely fastened.

No truck shall be used for carrying cargo between ship and shore on a stage so steep as to be unsafe.

Stages shall where necessary be treated with suitable material to prevent the workers slipping.

(7) When the working space in a hold is confined to the square of the hatch, and except for the purpose of breaking out or making up slings,

(a) hooks shall not be made fast in the bands or fastenings of bales of cotton, wool, cork, gunny-bags, or other similar goods;

(b) can-hooks shall not be used for raising or lowering a barrel when, owing to the construction or condition of the barrel or of the hooks, their use is likely to be unsafe.

(8) No gear of any description shall be loaded beyond the safe working load save in exceptional cases and then only in so far as may be allowed by national laws or regulations.

(9) In the case of shore cranes with varying capacity (e.g. raising and lowering jib with load capacity varying according to the angle) an automatic indicator or a table showing the safe working loads at the corresponding inclinations of the jib shall be provided on the crane.

ARTICLE 12.

National laws or regulations shall prescribe such precautions as may be deemed necessary to ensure the proper protection of the workers, having regard to the circumstances of each case, when they have to deal with or work in proximity to goods which are in themselves dangerous to life or health by reason either of their inherent nature or of their condition at the time, or work where such goods have been stowed.

ARTICLE 13.

At docks, wharves, quays and similar places which are in frequent use for the processes, such facilities as having regard to local circumstances shall be prescribed by national laws or regulations shall be available for rapidly securing the rendering of first-aid and in serious cases of accident removal to the nearest place of treatment. Sufficient supplies of first-aid equipment shall be kept permanently on the premises in such a condition and in such positions as to be fit and readily accessible for immediate use during working hours. The said supplies shall be in charge of a responsible person or persons, who shall include one or more persons competent to render first-aid, and whose services shall also be readily available during working hours.

At such docks, wharves, quays and similar places as aforesaid appropriate provision shall also be made for the rescue of immersed workers from drowning.

INTERNATIONAL LABOR ORGANIZATION

Article 14.

Any fencing, gangway, gear, ladder, life-saving means or appliance, light, mark, stage or other thing whatsoever required to be provided under this Convention shall not be removed or interfered with by any person except when duly authorised or in case of necessity, and if removed shall be restored at the end of the period for which its removal was necessary.

Article 15.

It shall be open to each Member to grant exemptions from or exceptions to the provisions of this Convention in respect of any dock, wharf, quay or similar place at which the processes are only occasionally carried on or the traffic is small and confined to small ships, or in respect of certain special ships or special classes of ships or ships below a certain small tonnage, or in cases where as a result of climatic conditions it would be impracticable to require the provisions of this Convention to be carried out.

The International Labour Office shall be kept informed of the provisions in virtue of which any exemptions and exceptions as aforesaid are allowed.

Article 16.

Except as herein otherwise provided, the provisions of this Convention which affect the construction or permanent equipment of the ship shall apply to ships the building of which is commenced after the date of ratification of the Convention, and to all other ships within four years after that date, provided that in the meantime the said provisions shall be applied so far as reasonable and practicable to such other ships.

Article 17.

In order to ensure the due enforcement of any regulations prescribed for the protection of the workers against accidents,

(1) The regulations shall clearly define the persons or bodies who are to be responsible for compliance with the respective regulations;

(2) Provision shall be made for an efficient system of inspection and for penalties for breaches of the regulations;

(3) Copies or summaries of the regulations shall be posted up in prominent positions at docks, wharves, quays and similar places which are in frequent use for the processes.

Article 18.

Each Member undertakes to enter into reciprocal arrangements on the basis of this Convention with the other Members which have ratified this Convention, including more particularly the mutual recognition of the arrangements made in their respective countries for testing, examining and annealing and of certificates and records relating thereto;

Provided that, as regards the construction of ships and as regards plant used on ships and the records and other matters to be observed on board under the terms of this Convention, each Member is satisfied that the arrangements adopted by the other Member secure a general standard of safety for the workers equally effective as the standard required under its own laws and regulations;

Provided also that the Governments shall have due regard to the obligations of paragraph (11) of Article 405 of the Treaty of Versailles and of the corresponding Articles of the other Treaties of Peace.

(*For other Standard Articles, see Draft Convention No. 27*)

ARTICLE 22.

A Member which has ratified this Convention may denounce it after the expiration of ten years from the date on which the Convention first comes in to force, by an act communicated to the Secretary-General of the League of Nations for registration. Such denunciation shall not take effect until one year after the date on which it is registered with the Secretariat.

Each Member which has ratified this Convention and which does not, within the year following the expiration of the period of ten years mentioned in the preceding paragraph, exercise the right of denunciation provided for in this Article, will be bound for another period of five years and, thereafter, may denounce this Convention at the expiration of each period of five years under the terms provided for in this Article.

Recommendation [No. 40] for expediting reciprocity as provided for in the Convention, adopted in 1932, concerning the protection against accidents of workers employed in loading or unloading ships.

The Conference,

Seeing that the revised Convention concerning the protection against accidents of workers employed in loading or unloading ships contains an Article concerning reciprocity between Members which ratify the said Convention,

Recommends that the following steps shall be taken to expedite the reciprocity provided for in the said Article:

(1) As soon as practicable after the adoption of the revised Convention, arrangements shall be made by the Governments of the principal countries concerned to confer with a view to securing reasonable uniformity in the application of the Convention, including more particularly the matters specially mentioned in the said Article, and the preparation of common forms of certificates for international use.

(2) Reports shall be furnished annually to the International Labour Office as to steps taken in accordance with the previous paragraph.

Draft Convention [No. 33] concerning the age for admission of children to non-industrial employment.

ARTICLE 1.

(1) This Convention shall apply to any employment not dealt with in the following Conventions adopted by the International Labour Conference at its First, Second and Third Sessions respectively:

Convention fixing the minimum age for admission of children to industrial employment (Washington, 1919);

Convention fixing the minimum age for admission of children to employment at sea (Genoa, 1920);

Convention concerning the age for admission of children to employment in agriculture (Geneva, 1921).

The competent authority in each country shall, after consultation with the principal organisations of employers and workers concerned, define the line of division which separates the employments covered by this Convention from those dealt with in the three aforesaid Conventions.

(2) This Convention shall not apply to:

(*a*) employment in sea-fishing;

INTERNATIONAL LABOR ORGANIZATION

(b) work done in technical and professional schools, provided that such work is essentially of an educative character, is not intended for commercial profit, and is restricted, approved and supervised by public authority.

(3) It shall be open to the competent authority in each country to exempt from the application of this Convention:

(a) employment in establishments in which only members of the employer's family are employed, except employment which is harmful, prejudicial or dangerous within the meaning of Articles 3 and 5 of this Convention;

(b) domestic work in the family performed by members of that family.

Article 2.

Children under fourteen years of age, or children over fourteen years who are still required by national laws or regulations to attend primary school, shall not be employed in any employment to which this Convention applies except as hereinafter otherwise provided.

Article 3.

(1) Children over twelve years of age may, outside the hours fixed for school attendance, be employed on light work:

(a) which is not harmful to their health or normal development;

(b) which is not such as to prejudice their attendance at school or their capacity to benefit from the instruction there given; and

(c) the duration of which does not exceed two hours per day on either school days or holidays, the total number of hours spent at school and on light work in no case to exceed seven per day.

(2) Light work shall be prohibited:

(a) on Sundays and legal public holidays;

(b) during the night, that is to say during a period of at least twelve consecutive hours comprising the interval between 8 p. m. and 8 a. m.

(3) After the principal organisations of employers and workers concerned have been consulted, national laws or regulations shall:

(a) specify what forms of employment may be considered to be light work for the purpose of this Article;

(b) prescribe the preliminary conditions to be complied with as safeguards before children may be employed in light work.

(4) Subject to the provisions of sub-paragraph (a) of paragraph (1) above,

(a) national laws or regulations may determine work to be allowed and the number of hours per day to be worked during the holiday time of children referred to in Article 2 who are over fourteen years of age;

(b) in countries where no provision exists relating to compulsory school attendance, the time spent on light work shall not exceed four and a half hours per day.

Article 4.

In the interests of art, science or education, national laws or regulations may, by permits granted in individual cases, allow exceptions to the provisions of Articles 2 and 3 of this Convention in order to enable children to appear in any public entertainment or as actors or supernumeraries in the making of cinematographic films;

Provided that:

(*a*) no such exceptions shall be allowed in respect of employment which is dangerous within the meaning of Article 5, such as employment in circuses, variety shows or cabarets;

(*b*) strict safeguards shall be prescribed for the health, physical development and morals of the children, for ensuring kind treatment of them, adequate rest, and the continuation of their education;

(*c*) children to whom permits are granted in accordance with this Article shall not be employed after midnight.

ARTICLE 5.

A higher age or ages than those referred to in Article 2 of this Convention shall be fixed by national laws or regulations for admission of young persons and adolescents to any employment which, by its nature, or the circumstances in which it is to be carried on, is dangerous to the life, health or morals of the persons employed in it.

ARTICLE 6.

A higher age or ages than those referred to in Article 2 of this Convention shall be fixed by national laws or regulations for admission of young persons and adolescents to employment for purposes of itinerant trading in the streets or in places to which the public have access, to regular employment at stalls outside shops or to employment in itinerant occupations, in cases where the conditions of such employment require that a higher age should be fixed.

ARTICLE 7.

In order to ensure the due enforcement of the provisions of this Convention, national laws or regulations shall:

(*a*) provide for an adequate system of public inspection and supervision;

(*b*) provide suitable means for facilitating the identification and supervision of persons under a specified age engaged in the employments and occupations covered by Article 6;

(*c*) provide penalties for breaches of the laws or regulations by which effect is given to the provisions of this Convention.

ARTICLE 8.

There shall be included in the annual reports to be submitted under Article 408 of the Treaty of Versailles and the corresponding Articles of the other Treaties of Peace full information concerning all laws and regulations by which effect is given to the provisions of this Convention, including:

(*a*) a list of the forms of employment which national laws or regulations specify to be light work for the purpose of Article 3;

(*b*) a list of the forms of employment for which, in accordance with Articles 5 and 6, national laws or regulations have fixed ages for admission higher than those laid down in Article 3;

(*c*) full information concerning the circumstances in which exceptions to the provisions of Articles 2 and 3 are permitted in accordance with the provisions of Article 4.

INTERNATIONAL LABOR ORGANIZATION

ARTICLE 9.

The provisions of Articles 2, 3, 4, 5, 6 and 7 of this Convention shall not apply to India, but in India:

(1) the employment of children under ten shall be prohibited:

Provided that in the interests of art, science or education, national laws or regulations may, by permits, granted in individual cases, allow exceptions to the above provision in order to enable children to appear in any public entertainment or as actors or supernumeraries in the making of cinematographic films.

Provided also that should the age for the admission of children to factories not using power which are not subject to the Indian Factories Act be fixed by national laws or regulations at an age exceeding ten, the age so prescribed for admission to such factories shall be substituted for the age of ten for the purpose of this paragraph.

(2) Persons under fourteen years of age shall not be employed in any non-industrial employment which the competent authority, after consultation with the principal organisations of employers and workers concerned, may declare to involve danger to life, health or morals.

(3) An age above ten shall be fixed by national laws or regulations for admission of young persons and adolescents to employment for purposes of itinerant trading in the streets or in places to which the public have access, to regular employment at stalls outside shops or to employment in itinerant occupations, in cases where the conditions of such employment require that a higher age should be fixed.

(4) National laws or regulations shall provide for the due enforcement of the provisions of this Article and in particular shall provide penalties for breaches of the laws or regulations by which effect is given to the provisions of this Article.

(5) The competent authority shall, after a period of five years from the date of passing of legislation giving effect to the provisions of this Convention, review the whole position with a view to increasing the minimum age prescribed in this Convention, such review to cover the whole of the provisions of this Article.

Should legislation be enacted in India making attendance at school compulsory until the age of fourteen this Article shall cease to apply, and Articles 2, 3, 4, 5, 6 and 7 shall thenceforth be applicable to India.

(For other Standard Articles, see Draft Convention No. 27)

ARTICLE 13.

A Member which has ratified this Convention may denounce it after the expiration of ten years from the date on which the Convention first comes into force, by an act communicated to the Secretary-General of the League of Nations for registration. Such denunciation shall not take effect until one year after the date on which it is registered with the Secretariat.

Each Member which has ratified this Convention and which does not, within the year following the expiration of the period of ten years mentioned in the preceding paragraph, exercise the right of denunciation provided for in this Article, will be bound for another period of five years and, thereafter, may denounce this Convention at the expiration of each period of five years under the terms provided for in this Article.

THE INTERNATIONAL PROTECTION OF LABOR

Recommendation [No. 41] concerning the age for admission of children to non-industrial employment.

The Conference,

Having adopted a Draft Convention concerning the age for admission of children to non-industrial employment, with a view to completing the international regulations laid down by the three Conventions adopted at previous Sessions concerning the age for admission of children to industrial employment, employment at sea and employment in agriculture; and

Desiring to ensure as uniform application as possible of the new Draft Convention which leaves certain details of application to national laws or regulations;

Considers that, in spite of the variety of employments covered by the Draft Convention and the need of making allowance for the adoption of practical methods of application varying with the climate, customs, national tradition and other conditions peculiar to individual countries, account should be taken of certain methods which have been found to give satisfactory results, and which may accordingly be a guide to the Members of the Organisation.

The Conference therefore recommends the Members to take the following rules and methods into consideration:

I. *Light work.*

(1) In order that children may derive full benefit from their education and that their physical, intellectual and moral development may be safeguarded, it is desirable that so long as they are required to attend school their employment should be restricted to as great an extent as possible.

(2) In determining the categories of employment in light work to which children may be admitted outside the hours of school attendance, such occupations and employments as running errands, distribution of newspapers, odd jobs in connection with the practice of sport or the playing of games, and picking and selling flowers or fruits might be taken into consideration.

(3) For the admission of children to employment in light work the competent authorities should require the consent of parents or guardians, a medical certificate of physical fitness for the employment contemplated, and, where necessary, previous consultation with the school authorities.

(4) The limitations on the hours of work per day of children employed in light work outside school hours should be adapted to the school time-table on the one hand, and to the age of the child on the other. Where instruction is given both in the morning and in the afternoon, the child should be ensured a sufficient rest before morning school, in the interval between morning and afternoon school, and immediately after the latter.

II. *Employment in public entertainments.*

(5) Employment in any public entertainment, or as actors or supernumeraries in the making of cinematographic films, should in principle be prohibited for children under twelve years of age, and exceptions to this rule should be kept within the narrowest limits and only allowed in so far as the interests of art, science or education may require.

The permits to be granted by the competent authorities in individual cases should only be issued if the competent authorities are satisfied as to the nature and the particular type of the employment contemplated, if the parents' or guardians' consent has been obtained, and if the physical fitness of the child for the employment has been established. In the case of cinematographic films, measures should be taken to ensure that the children employed shall be under the supervision of a medical eye specialist. The child should also be assured of receiving good treatment and of being able to continue his education.

Each permit should specify the number of hours during which the child may be employed, with special regard to night work and work on Sundays and legal public holidays. It should be delivered for a particular entertainment, or for a limited period, and may be renewed.

III. *Dangerous employments.*

(6) The competent authorities should consult the principal organisations of employers and workers concerned before determining the employments which are dangerous to the life, health or morals of the persons employed, and before fixing the higher age or ages of admission to be prescribed for such employments by national laws or regulations.

Among employments of the kind referred to might be included, for example, certain employments in public entertainments such as acrobatic performances; in establishments for the cure of the sick such as employment involving danger of contagion or infection; and in establishments for the sale of alcoholic liquor such as serving customers.

Different ages for particular employments should be fixed in relation to their special dangers and in some cases the age required for girls might be higher than the age for boys.

IV. *Prohibition of employment of children by certain persons.*

(7) With a view to safeguarding the moral interests of children persons who have been condemned for certain serious offences or who are notorious drunkards should be prohibited from employing children other than their own, even if such children live in the same household with these persons.

V. *Enforcement.*

(8) In order to facilitate the enforcement of the provisions of the Draft Convention, it is desirable to institute a public system of registration and of employment or identity books for children admitted to employment.

These documents should contain, in particular, indications of the age of the child, the nature of his employment, the number of hours of work authorised, and the dates when the child began and finished his employment. In the case of street trading the wearing of special badges should be prescribed.

In the case of children employed in public entertainments, supervising or inspecting officials should have the right of access to premises in which such entertainments are prepared or performed.

THE INTERNATIONAL PROTECTION OF LABOR

SEVENTEENTH SESSION
(Geneva, 8-30 June 1933)

Draft Convention [No. 34]
concerning fee-charging employment agencies.

ARTICLE 1.

1. For the purpose of this Convention the expression "fee-charging employment agency" means:

(a) employment agencies conducted with a view to profit, that is to say, any person, company, institution, agency or other organisation which acts as an intermediary for the purpose of procuring employment for a worker or supplying a worker for an employer with a view to deriving either directly or indirectly any pecuniary or other material advantage from either employer or worker; the expression does not include newspapers or other publications unless they are published wholly or mainly for the purpose of acting as intermediaries between employers and workers;

(b) employment agencies not conducted with a view to profit, that is to say, the placing services of any company, institution, agency or other organisation which, though not conducted with a view to deriving any pecuniary or other material advantage, levies from either employer or worker for the above services an entrance fee, a periodical contribution or any other charge.

2. This Convention does not apply to the placing of seamen.

ARTICLE 2.

1. Fee-charging employment agencies conducted with a view to profit as defined in paragraph 1 (a) of the preceding Article shall be abolished within three years from the coming into force of this Convention for the Member concerned.

2. During the period preceding abolition

(a) there shall not be established any new fee-charging employment agency conducted with a view to profit;

(b) fee-charging employment agencies conducted with a view to profit shall be subject to the supervision of the competent authority and shall only charge fees and expenses on a scale approved by the said authority.

ARTICLE 3.

1. Exceptions to the provisions of paragraph 1 of Article 2 of this Convention may be allowed by the competent authority in exceptional cases, but only after consultation of the organisations of employers and workers concerned.

2. Exceptions may only be allowed in virtue of this Article for agencies catering for categories of workers exactly defined by national laws or regulations and belonging to occupations placing for which is carried on under special conditions justifying such an exception.

3. The establishment of new fee-charging employment agencies shall not be allowed in virtue of this Article after the expiration of the period of three years referred to in Article 2.

4. Every fee-charging employment agency for which an exception is allowed under this Article

INTERNATIONAL LABOR ORGANIZATION

(*a*) shall be subject to the supervision of the competent authority;

(*b*) shall be required to be in possession of a yearly license renewable at the discretion of the competent authority during a period which shall not exceed ten years;

(*c*) shall only charge fees and expenses on a scale approved by the competent authority; and

(*d*) shall only place or recruit workers abroad if authorised so to do by its license and if its operations are conducted under an agreement between the countries concerned.

Article 4.

Fee-charging employment agencies not conducted with a view to profit as defined in paragraph 1 (*b*) of Article 1

(*a*) shall be required to have an authorisation from the competent authority and shall be subject to the supervision of the said authority;

(*b*) shall not make any charge in excess of the scale of charges fixed by the competent authority with strict regard to the expenses incurred; and

(*c*) shall only place or recruit workers abroad if permitted so to do by the competent authority and if their operations are conducted under an agreement between the countries concerned.

Article 5.

Fee-charging employment agencies as defined in Article 1 of this Convention and every person, company, institution, agency or other private organisation habitually engaging in placing shall, even though making no charge, make a declaration to the competent authority stating whether their placing services are given gratuitously or for remuneration.

Article 6.

National laws or regulations shall prescribe appropriate penalties, including the withdrawal when necessary of the licenses and authorisations provided for by this Convention, for any violation of the above Articles or of any laws or regulations giving effect to them.

Article 7.

There shall be included in the annual reports to be submitted under Article 408 of the Treaty of Versailles and the corresponding Articles of the other Treaties of Peace all necessary information concerning the exceptions allowed under Article 3.

Article 8.

The formal ratifications of this Convention under the conditions set forth in Part XIII of the Treaty of Versailles and in the corresponding Parts of the other Treaties of Peace shall be communicated to the Secretary-General of the League of Nations for registration.

Article 9.

This Convention shall be binding only upon those Members whose ratifications have been registered with the Secretariat.

It shall come into force twelve months after the date on which the ratifications of two Members of the International Labour Organisation have been registered with the Secretary-General.

Thereafter, this Convention shall come into force for any Member twelve months after the date on which its ratification has been registered.

ARTICLE 10.

As soon as the ratifications of two Members of the International Labour Organisation have been registered with the Secretariat, the Secretary-General of the League of Nations shall so notify all the Members of the International Labour Organisation. He shall likewise notify them of the registration of ratifications which may be communicated subsequently by other Members of the Organisation.

ARTICLE 11.

A Member which has ratified this Convention may denounce it after the expiration of ten years from the date on which the Convention first comes into force, by an act communicated to the Secretary-General of the League of Nations for registration. Such denunciation shall not take effect until one year after the date on which it is registered with the Secretariat.

Each Member which has ratified this Convention and which does not, within the year following the expiration of the period of ten years mentioned in the preceding paragraph, exercise the right of denunciation provided for in this Article, will be bound for another period of ten years and, thereafter, may denounce this Convention at the expiration of each period of ten years under the terms provided for in this Article.

ARTICLE 12.

At the expiration of each period of ten years after the coming into force of this Convention, the Governing Body of the International Labour Office shall present to the General Conference a report on the working of this Convention and shall consider the desirability of placing on the Agenda of the Conference the question of its revision in whole or in part.

ARTICLE 13.

Should the Conference adopt a new Convention revising this Convention in whole or in part, then, unless the new Convention otherwise provides,

(*a*) the ratification by a Member of the new revising Convention shall *ipso jure* involve the immediate denunciation of this Convention, notwithstanding the provisions of Article 11 above, if and when the new revising Convention shall have come into force;

(*b*) as from the date when the new revising Convention comes into force, this Convention shall cease to be open to ratification by the Members.

This Convention shall in any case remain in force in its actual form and content for those Members which have ratified it but have not ratified the revising Convention.

ARTICLE 14.

The French and English texts of this Convention shall both be authentic.

Recommendation [No. 42] **concerning employment agencies.**

The Conference,

Having adopted a Draft Convention concerning fee-charging employment agencies intended to supplement the provisions of the Convention and Recommendation concerning unemployment which it adopted at its First Session;

INTERNATIONAL LABOR ORGANIZATION

Considering it to be desirable to ensure within as short a time as possible the complete abolition of fee-charging employment agencies conducted with a view to profit;

Considering that, for certain occupations, the abolition of such agencies may nevertheless involve certain difficulties in countries in which the free public employment offices are not in a position completely to take the place of the agencies abolished;

Considering that features other than placing fees may give a profit-making character to placing operations and may lead to abuses;

Recommends the Members to take the following rules and methods into consideration:

I.

1. Measures should be taken to adapt the free public employment offices to the needs of the occupations in which recourse is often had to the services of fee-charging employment agencies.

2. The principle of having specialised public employment offices for particular occupations should be applied and in so far as possible persons familiar with the characteristics, usages and customs of the occupations concerned should be attached to such offices.

3. Representatives of the organisations most representative of workers and employers in the occupations concerned should be invited to collaborate in the working of the public employment offices.

II.

1. Persons and undertakings which either directly or through any intermediary derive any profit from certain activities such as the keeping of public houses, hotels, secondhand clothes shops, pawn shops or money-changing should be forbidden to engage in placing.

2. Placing operations should be prohibited on all premises or in all outhouses and annexes of such premises where any of the above-mentioned trades are carried on.

Draft Convention [No. 35] concerning compulsory old-age insurance for persons employed in industrial or commercial undertakings, in the liberal professions, and for outworkers and domestic servants.

ARTICLE 1.

Each Member of the International Labour Organisation which ratifies this Convention undertakes to set up or maintain a scheme of compulsory old-age insurance which shall be based on provisions at least equivalent to those contained in this Convention.

ARTICLE 2.

1. The compulsory old-age insurance scheme shall apply to manual and non-manual workers, including apprentices, employed in industrial or commercial undertakings or in the liberal professions, and to out-workers and domestic servants:

2. Provided that any Member may in its national laws or regulations make such exceptions as it deems necessary in respect of

(a) workers whose remuneration exceeds a prescribed amount and, where national laws or regulations do not make this exception general in its application, any non-manual workers engaged in occupations which are ordinarily considered as liberal professions;

(b) workers who are not paid a money wage;

(c) young workers under a prescribed age and workers too old to become insured when they first enter employment;

(d) outworkers whose conditions of work are not of a like nature to those of ordinary wage earners;

(e) members of the employer's family;

(f) workers whose employment is of such a nature that, its total duration being necessarily short, they cannot qualify for benefit, and persons engaged solely in occasional or subsidiary employment;

(g) invalid workers and workers in receipt of an invalidity or old-age pension;

(h) retired public officials employed for remuneration and persons possessing a private income, where the retirement pension or private income is at least equal to the old-age pension provided by national laws or regulations;

(i) workers, who, during their studies, give lessons or work for remuneration in preparation for an occupation corresponding to such studies;

(j) domestic servants employed in the households of agricultural employers.

3. Provided also that there may be exempted from liability to insurance persons who, by virtue of any law, regulations or special scheme, are or will become entitled to old-age benefits at least equivalent on the whole to those provided for in this Convention.

4. This Convention does not apply to seamen and sea fishermen.

ARTICLE 3.

National laws or regulations shall, under conditions to be determined by them, either entitle persons formerly compulsorily insured who have not attained the pensionable age to continue their insurance voluntarily or entitle such persons to maintain their rights by the periodical payment of a fee for the purpose, unless the said rights are automatically maintained or, in the case of married women, the husband, if not liable to compulsory insurance, is permitted to insure voluntarily and thereby to qualify his wife for an old-age or widow's pension.

ARTICLE 4.

An insured person shall be entitled to an old-age pension at an age which shall be determined by national laws or regulations but which, in the case of insurance schemes for employed persons, shall not exceed sixty-five.

ARTICLE 5.

The right to a pension may be made conditional upon the completion of a qualifying period, which may involve the payment of a minimum number of contributions since entry into insurance and during a prescribed period immediately preceding the happening of the event insured against.

ARTICLE 6.

1. An insured person who ceases to be liable to insurance without being entitled to a benefit representing a return for the contributions credited to his account shall retain his rights in respect of these contributions:

2. Provided that national laws or regulations may terminate rights in

respect of contributions on the expiry of a term which shall be reckoned from the date when the insured person so ceased to be liable to insurance and which shall be either variable or fixed:—

(a) where the term is variable, it shall not be less than one-third (less the periods for which contributions have not been credited) of the total of the periods for which contributions have been credited since entry into insurance.

(b) where the term is fixed, it shall in no case be less than eighteen months and rights in respect of contributions may be terminated on the expiry of the term unless, in the course thereof, a minimum number of contributions prescribed by national laws or regulations has been credited to the account of the insured person in virtue of either compulsory or voluntarily continued insurance.

ARTICLE 7.

1. The pension shall, whether or not dependent on the time spent in insurance, be a fixed sum or a percentage of the remuneration taken into account for insurance purposes or vary with the amount of the contributions paid.

2. Where the pension varies with the time spent in insurance and its award is made conditional upon the completion by the insured person of a qualifying period, the pension shall, unless a minimum rate is guaranteed, include a fixed sum or fixed portion not dependent on the time spent in insurance; where the pension is awarded without any condition as to the completion of a qualifying period, provision may be made for a guaranteed minimum rate of pension.

3. Where contributions are graduated according to remuneration, the remuneration taken into account for this purpose shall also be taken into account for the purpose of computing the pension, whether or not the pension varies with the time spent in insurance.

ARTICLE 8.

1. The right to benefits may be forfeited or suspended in whole or in part if the person concerned has acted fraudulently towards the insurance institution.

2. The pension may be suspended in whole or in part while the person concerned

(a) is in employment involving compulsory insurance;

(b) is entirely maintained at the public expense; or

(c) is in receipt of another periodical cash benefit payable by virtue of any law or regulations concerning compulsory social insurance, pensions or workmen's compensation for accidents or occupational diseases.

ARTICLE 9.

1. The insured persons and their employers shall contribute to the financial resources of the insurance scheme.

2. National laws or regulations may exempt from liability to pay contributions

(a) apprentices and young workers under a prescribed age;

(b) workers who are not paid a money wage or whose wages are very low.

3. Contributions from employers may be dispensed with under laws or

regulations concerning schemes of national insurance not restricted in scope to employed persons.

4. The public authorities shall contribute to the financial resources or to the benefits of insurance schemes covering employed persons in general or manual workers.

5. National laws or regulations which, at the time of the adoption of this Convention, do not require contributions from insured persons may continue not to require such contributions.

Article 10.

1. The insurance scheme shall be administered by institutions founded by the public authorities and not conducted with a view to profit, or by State insurance funds:

2. Provided that national laws or regulations may also entrust its administration to institutions founded on the initiative of the parties concerned or of their organisations and duly approved by the public authorities.

3. The funds of insurance institutions and State insurance funds shall be administered separately from the public funds.

4. Representatives of the insured persons shall participate in the management of insurance institutions under conditions to be determined by national laws or regulations, which may likewise decide as to the participation of representatives of employers and of the public authorities.

5. Self-governing insurance institutions shall be under the administrative and financial supervision of the public authorities.

Article 11.

1. The insured person or his legal representatives shall have a right of appeal in any dispute concerning benefits.

2. Such disputes shall be referred to special tribunals which shall include judges, whether professional or not, who are specially cognisant of the purposes of insurance and the needs of insured persons or are assisted by assessors chosen as representative of insured persons and employers respectively.

3. In any dispute concerning liability to insurance or the rate of contribution, the employed person and, in the case of schemes providing for an employer's contribution, his employer shall have a right of appeal.

Article 12.

1. Foreign employed persons shall be liable to insurance and to the payment of contributions under the same conditions as nationals.

2. Foreign insured persons and their dependants shall be entitled under the same conditions as nationals to the benefits derived from the contributions credited to their account.

3. Foreign insured persons and their dependants shall, if nationals of a Member which is bound by this Convention and the laws or regulations of which therefore provide for a State subsidy towards the financial resources or benefits of the insurance scheme in conformity with Article 9, also be entitled to any subsidy or supplement to or fraction of a pension which is payable out of public funds:

4. Provided that national laws or regulations may restrict to nationals the right to any subsidy or supplement to or fraction of a pension which is payable out of public funds and granted solely to insured persons who

have exceeded a prescribed age at the date when the laws or regulations providing for compulsory insurance come into force.

5. Any restrictions which may apply in the event of residence abroad shall only apply to pensioners and their dependants who are nationals of any Member bound by this Convention and reside in the territory of any Member bound thereby to the extent to which they apply to nationals of the country in which the pension has been acquired: Provided that any subsidy or supplement to or fraction of a pension which is payable out of public funds may be withheld.

ARTICLE 13.

1. The insurance of employed persons shall be governed by the law applicable at their place of employment.

2. In the interest of continuity of insurance exceptions may be made to this rule by agreement between the Members concerned.

ARTICLE 14.

Any Member may prescribe special provisions for frontier workers whose place of employment is in its territory and whose place of residence is abroad.

ARTICLE 15.

In countries which, at the time when this Convention first comes into force, have no laws or regulations providing for compulsory old-age insurance, an existing non-contributory pension scheme which guarantees an individual right to a pension under the conditions defined in Articles 16 to 22 hereinafter shall be deemed to satisfy the requirements of this Convention.

ARTICLE 16.

Pensions shall be awarded at an age which shall be determined by national laws or regulations but which shall not exceed sixty-five.

ARTICLE 17.

The right to a pension may be made conditional upon the claimant's having been resident in the territory of the Member for a period immediately preceding the making of the claim. This period shall be determined by national laws or regulations but shall not exceed ten years.

ARTICLE 18.

1. A claimant shall be entitled to a pension if the annual value of his means does not exceed a limit which shall be fixed by national laws or regulations with due regard to the minimum cost of living.

2. Means up to a level which shall be determined by national laws or regulations shall be exempted for the purpose of the assessment of means.

ARTICLE 19.

The rate of pension shall be an amount which, together with any means of the claimant in excess of the means exempted, is at least sufficient to cover the essential needs of the pensioner.

ARTICLE 20.

1. A claimant shall have a right of appeal in any dispute concerning the award of a pension or the rate thereof.

2. The appeal shall lie to an authority other than the authority which gave the decision in the first instance.

ARTICLE 21.

1. Foreigners who are nationals of a Member bound by this Convention shall be entitled to pensions under the same conditions as nationals:

2. Provided that national laws or regulations may make the award of a pension to foreigners conditional upon their having been resident in the territory of the Member for a period which shall not exceed by more than five years the period of residence prescribed for nationals.

ARTICLE 22.

1. The right to a pension may be forfeited or suspended in whole or in part if the person concerned

(a) has been sentenced to imprisonment for a criminal offence;

(b) has obtained or attempted to obtain a pension by fraud; or

(c) has persistently refused to earn his living by work compatible with his strength and capacity.

2. The pension may be suspended in whole or in part while the person concerned is entirely maintained at the public expense.

ARTICLE 23.

Subject to the provisions of paragraph 5 of Article 12, this Convention does not refer to the maintenance of pension rights in the event of residence abroad.

(*For the Standard Articles, see Draft Convention No. 34*)

Draft Convention [No. 36]
concerning compulsory old-age insurance for persons employed in agricultural undertakings.

ARTICLE 1.

Each Member of the International Labour Organisation which ratifies this Convention undertakes to set up or maintain a scheme of compulsory old-age insurance which shall be based on provisions at least equivalent to those contained in this Convention.

ARTICLE 2.

1. The compulsory old-age insurance scheme shall apply to manual and non-manual workers, including apprentices, employed in agricultural undertakings, and to domestic servants employed in the households of agricultural employers:

2. Provided that any Member may in its national laws or regulations make such exceptions as it deems necessary in respect of

(a) workers whose remuneration exceeds a prescribed amount and, where national laws or regulations do not make this exception general in its application, any non-manual workers engaged in occupations which are ordinarily considered as liberal professions;

(b) workers who are not paid a money wage;

(c) young workers under a prescribed age and workers too old to become insured when they first enter employment;

(d) outworkers whose conditions of work are not of a like nature to those of ordinary wage earners;

(e) members of the employer's family;
(f) workers whose employment is of such a nature that, its total duration being necessarily short, they cannot qualify for benefit, and persons engaged solely in occasional or subsidiary employment;
(g) invalid workers and workers in receipt of an invalidity or old-age pension;
(h) retired public officials employed for remuneration and persons possessing a private income, where the retirement pension or private income is at least equal to the old-age pension provided by national laws or regulations;
(i) workers who, during their studies, give lessons or work for remuneration in preparation for an occupation corresponding to such studies.

3. Provided also that there may be exempted from liability to insurance persons who, by virtue of any law, regulations or special scheme, are or will become entitled to old-age benefits at least equivalent on the whole to those provided for in this Convention.

ARTICLE 3.

National laws or regulations shall, under conditions to be determined by them, either entitle persons formerly compulsorily insured who have not attained the pensionable age to continue their insurance voluntarily or entitle such persons to maintain their rights by the periodical payment of a fee for the purpose, unless the said rights are automatically maintained or, in the case of married women, the husband, if not liable to compulsory insurance, is permitted to insure voluntarily and thereby to qualify his wife for an old-age or widow's pension.

ARTICLE 4.

An insured person shall be entitled to an old-age pension at an age which shall be determined by national laws or regulations but which, in the case of insurance schemes for employed persons, shall not exceed sixty-five.

ARTICLE 5.

The right to a pension may be made conditional upon the completion of a qualifying period, which may involve the payment of a minimum number of contributions since entry into insurance and during a prescribed period immediately preceding the happening of the event insured against.

ARTICLE 6.

1. An insured person who ceases to be liable to insurance without being entitled to a benefit representing a return for the contributions credited to his account shall retain his rights in respect of these contributions:

2. Provided that national laws or regulations may terminate rights in respect of contributions on the expiry of a term which shall be reckoned from the date when the insured person so ceased to be liable to insurance and which shall be either variable or fixed:—

(a) where the term is variable, it shall not be less than one-third (less the periods for which contributions have not been credited) of the total of the periods for which contributions have been credited since entry into insurance.

(b) where the term is fixed, it shall in no case be less than eighteen months and rights in respect of contributions may be terminated on the expiry of the term unless, in the course thereof, a minimum number of contributions prescribed by national laws or regulations has been credited to the account of the insured person in virtue of either compulsory or voluntarily continued insurance.

ARTICLE 7.

1. The pension shall, whether or not dependent on the time spent in insurance, be a fixed sum or a percentage of the remuneration taken into account for insurance purposes or vary with the amount of the contributions paid.

2. Where the pension varies with the time spent in insurance and its award is made conditional upon the completion by the insured person of a qualifying period, the pension shall, unless a minimum rate is guaranteed, include a fixed sum or fixed portion not dependent on the time spent in insurance; where the pension is awarded without any condition as to the completion of a qualifying period, provision may be made for a guaranteed minimum rate of pension.

3. Where contributions are graduated according to remuneration, the remuneration taken into account for this purpose shall also be taken into account for the purpose of computing the pension, whether or not the pension varies with the time spent in insurance.

ARTICLE 8.

1. The right to benefits may be forfeited or suspended in whole or in part if the person concerned has acted fraudulently towards the insurance institution.

2. The pension may be suspended in whole or in part while the person concerned

(a) is in employment involving compulsory insurance;

(b) is entirely maintained at the public expense; or

(c) is in receipt of another periodical cash benefit payable by virtue of any law or regulations concerning compulsory social insurance, pensions or workmen's compensation for accidents or occupational diseases.

ARTICLE 9.

1. The insured persons and their employers shall contribute to the financial resources of the insurance scheme.

2. National laws or regulations may exempt from liability to pay contributions

(a) apprentices and young workers under a prescribed age;

(b) workers who are not paid a money wage or whose wages are very low;

(c) workers in the service of an employer who pays contributions assessed on a basis which is not dependent on the number of workers employed.

3. Contributions from employers may be dispensed with under laws or regulations concerning schemes of national insurance not restricted in scope to employed persons.

4. The public authorities shall contribute to the financial resources or to the benefits of insurance schemes covering employed persons in general or manual workers.

5. National laws or regulations which, at the time of the adoption of this Convention, do not require contributions from insured persons may continue not to require such contributions.

INTERNATIONAL LABOR ORGANIZATION

ARTICLE 10.

1. The insurance scheme shall be administered by institutions founded by the public authorities and not conducted with a view to profit, or by State insurance funds:

2. Provided that national laws or regulations may also entrust its administration to institutions founded on the initiative of the parties concerned or of their organisations and duly approved by the public authorities.

3. The funds of insurance institutions and State insurance funds shall be administered separately from the public funds.

4. Representatives of the insured persons shall participate in the management of insurance institutions under conditions to be determined by national laws or regulations, which may likewise decide as to the participation of representatives of employers and of the public authorities.

5. Self-governing insurance institutions shall be under the administrative and financial supervision of the public authorities.

ARTICLE 11.

1. The insured person or his legal representatives shall have a right of appeal in any dispute concerning benefits.

2. Such disputes shall be referred to special tribunals which shall include judges, whether professional or not, who are specially cognisant of the purposes of insurance and the needs of insured persons or are assisted by assessors chosen as representative of insured persons and employers respectively.

3. In any dispute concerning liability to insurance or the rate of contribution, the employed person and, in the case of schemes providing for an employer's contribution, his employer shall have a right of appeal.

ARTICLE 12.

1. Foreign employed persons shall be liable to insurance and to the payment of contributions under the same conditions as nationals.

2. Foreign insured persons and their dependants shall be entitled under the same conditions as nationals to the benefits derived from the contributions credited to their acocunt.

3. Foreign insured persons and their dependants shall, if nationals of a Member which is bound by this Convention and the laws or regulations of which therefore provide for a State subsidy towards the financial resources or benefits of the insurance scheme in conformity with Article 9, also be entitled to any subsidy or supplement to or fraction of a pension which is payable out of public funds:

4. Provided that national laws or regulations may restrict to nationals the right to any subsidy or supplement to or fraction of a pension which is payable out of public funds and granted solely to insured persons who have exceeded a prescribed age at the date when the laws or regulations providing for compulsory insurance come into force.

5. Any restrictions which may apply in the event of residence abroad shall only apply to pensioners and their dependants who are nationals of any Member bound by this Convention and reside in the territory of any Member bound thereby to the extent to which they apply to nationals of the country in which the pension has been acquired: Provided that any subsidy or supplement to or fraction of a pension which is payable out of public funds may be withheld.

Article 13.

1. The insurance of employed persons shall be governed by the law applicable at their place of employment.

2. In the interest of continuity of insurance, exceptions may be made to this rule by agreement between the Members concerned.

Article 14.

Any Member may prescribe special provisions for frontier workers whose place of employment is in its territory and whose place of residence is abroad.

Article 15.

In countries which, at the time when this Convention first comes into force, have no laws or regulations providing for compulsory old-age insurance, an existing non-contributory pension scheme which guarantees an individual right to a pension under the conditions defined in Articles 16 to 22 hereinafter shall be deemed to satisfy the requirements of this Convention.

Article 16.

Pensions shall be awarded at an age which shall be determined by national laws or regulations but which shall not exceed sixty-five.

Article 17.

The right to a pension may be made conditional upon the claimant's having been resident in the territory of the Member for a period immediately preceding the making of the claim. This period shall be determined by national laws or regulations but shall not exceed ten years.

Article 18.

1. A claimant shall be entitled to a pension if the annual value of his means does not exceed a limit which shall be fixed by national laws or regulations with due regard to the minimum cost of living.

2. Means up to a level which shall be determined by national laws or regulations shall be exempted for the purpose of the assessment of means.

Article 19.

The rate of pension shall be an amount which, together with any means of the claimant in excess of the means exempted, is at least sufficient to cover the essential needs of the pensioner.

Article 20.

1. A claimant shall have a right of appeal in any dispute concerning the award of a pension or the rate thereof.

2. The appeal shall lie to an authority other than the authority which gave the decision in the first instance.

Article 21.

1. Foreigners who are nationals of a Member bound by this Convention shall be entitled to pensions under the same conditions as nationals:

2. Provided that national laws or regulations may make the award of a pension to foreigners conditional upon their having been resident in the territory of the Member for a period which shall not exceed by more than five years the period of residence prescribed for nationals.

INTERNATIONAL LABOR ORGANIZATION

Article 22.
1. The right to a pension may be forfeited or suspended in whole or in part if the person concerned
(a) has been sentenced to imprisonment for a criminal offence;
(b) has obtained or attempted to obtain a pension by fraud; or
(c) has persistently refused to earn his living by work compatible with his strength and capacity.

2. The pension may be suspended in whole or in part while the person concerned is entirely maintained at the public expense.

Article 23.
Subject to the provisions of paragraph 5 of Article 12, this Convention does not refer to the maintenance of pension rights in the event of residence abroad.

(*For the Standard Articles, see Draft Convention No. 34*)

Draft Convention [No. 37] concerning compulsory invalidity insurance for persons employed in industrial or commercial undertakings, in the liberal professions, and for outworkers and domestic servants.

Article 1.
Each Member of the International Labour Organisation which ratifies this Convention undertakes to set up or maintain a scheme of compulsory invalidity insurance which shall be based on provisions at least equivalent to those contained in this Convention.

Article 2.
1. The compulsory invalidity insurance scheme shall apply to manual and non-manual workers, including apprentices employed in industrial or commercial undertakings or in the liberal professions, and to outworkers and domestic servants:

. Provided that any Member may in its national laws or regulations make such exceptions as it deems necessary in respect of

(a) workers whose remuneration exceeds a prescribed amount and, where national laws or regulations do not make this exception general in its application, any non-manual workers engaged in occupations which are ordinarily considered as liberal professions;

(b) workers who are not paid a money wage;

(c) young workers under a prescribed age and workers too old to become insured when they first enter employment;

(d) outworkers whose conditions of work are not of a like nature to those of ordinary wage earners;

(e) members of the employer's family;

(f) workers whose employment is of such a nature that, its total duration being necessarily short, they cannot qualify for benefit, and persons engaged solely in occasional or subsidiary employment;

(g) invalid workers and workers in receipt of an invalidity or old-age pension;

(h) retired public officials employed for remuneration and persons possessing a private income, where the retirement pension or private income is at least equal to the invalidity pension provided by national laws or regulations;

(i) workers who, during their studies, give lessons or work for remuneration in preparation for an occupation corresponding to such studies;

(j) domestic servants employed in the households of agricultural employers.

3. Provided also that there may be exempted from liability to insurance persons who, by virtue of any law, regulations or special scheme, are or will become entitled to invalidity benefits at least equivalent on the whole to those provided for in this Convention.

4. This Convention does not apply to seamen and sea fishermen.

ARTICLE 3.

National laws or regulations shall, under conditions to be determined by them, either entitle persons formerly compulsorily insured who are not in receipt of a pension to continue their insurance voluntarily or entitle such persons to maintain their rights by the periodical payment of a fee for the purpose, unless the said rights are automatically maintained or, in the case of married women, the husband, if not liable to compulsory insurance, is permitted to insure voluntarily and thereby to qualify his wife for an old-age or widow's pension.

ARTICLE 4.

1. An insured person who becomes generally incapacitated for work and thereby unable to earn an appreciable remuneration shall be entitled to an invalidity pension:

2. Provided that national laws or regulations which secure to insured persons medical treatment and attendance throughout invalidity and, if invalidity terminates in death, secure pensions at the full rate to widows without any conditions as to age or invalidity and to orphans, may make the award of an invalidity pension conditional upon the insured person's being unable to perform remunerative work.

3. In the case of special schemes for non-manual workers, an insured person who suffers from incapacity which renders him unable to earn an appreciable remuneration in the occupation in which he was ordinarily engaged or in a similar occupation shall be entitled to an invalidity pension.

ARTICLE 5.

1. Notwithstanding the provisions of Article 6, the right to a pension may be made conditional upon the completion of a qualifying period, which may involve the payment of a minimum number of contributions since entry into insurance and during a prescribed period immediately preceding the happening of the event insured against.

2. The duration of the qualifying period shall not exceed 60 contribution months, 250 contribution weeks or 1,500 contribution days.

3. Where the completion of the qualifying period involves the payment of a prescribed number of contributions during a prescribed period immediately preceding the happening of the event insured against, periods for which benefit has been paid in respect of temporary incapacity for work or of unemployment shall be reckoned as contribution periods to such extent and under such conditions as may be determined by national laws or regulations.

INTERNATIONAL LABOR ORGANIZATION

ARTICLE 6.

1. An insured person who ceases to be liable to insurance without being entitled to a benefit representing a return for the contributions credited to his account shall retain his rights in respect of these contributions:

2. Provided that national laws or regulations may terminate rights in respect of contributions on the expiry of a term which shall be reckoned from the date when the insured person so ceased to be liable to insurance and which shall be either variable or fixed:—

(a) where the term is variable, it shall not be less than one-third (less the periods for which contributions have not been credited) of the total of the periods for which contributions have been credited since entry into insurance.

(b) where the term is fixed, it shall in no case be less than eighteen months and rights in respect of contributions may be terminated on the expiry of the term unless, in the course thereof, a minimum number of contributions prescribed by national laws or regulations has been credited to the account of the insured person in virtue of either compulsory or voluntarily continued insurance.

ARTICLE 7.

1. The pension shall, whether or not dependent on the time spent in insurance, be a fixed sum or a percentage of the remuneration taken into account for insurance purposes or vary with the amount of the contributions paid.

2. Where the pension varies with the time spent in insurance and its award is made conditional upon the completion by the insured person of a qualifying period, the pension shall, unless a minimum rate is guaranteed, include a fixed sum or fixed portion not dependent on the time spent in insurance.

3. Where contributions are graduated according to remuneration, the remuneration taken into account for this purpose shall also be taken into account for the purpose of computing the pension, whether or not the pension varies with the time spent in insurance.

ARTICLE 8.

Insurance institutions shall be authorised, under conditions which shall be determined by national laws or regulations, to grant benefits in kind for the purpose of preventing, postponing, alleviating or curing invalidity to persons who are in receipt of or may be entitled to claim a pension on the ground of invalidity.

ARTICLE 9.

1. The right to benefits may be forfeited or suspended in whole or in part if the person concerned

(a) has brought about his invalidity by a criminal offence or wilful misconduct; or

(b) has acted fraudulently towards the insurance institution.

2. The pension may be suspended in whole or in part while the person concerned

(a) is entirely maintained at the public expense or by a social insurance institution;

(b) refuses without valid reason to comply with the doctor's orders or the instructions relating to the conduct of invalids or voluntarily and without authorisation removes himself from the supervision of the insurance institution;

(c) is in receipt of another periodical cash benefit payable by virtue of any law or regulations concerning compulsory social insurance, pensions or workmen's compensation for accidents or occupational diseases; or

(d) is in employment involving compulsory insurance or, in the case of special schemes for non-manual workers, is in receipt of remuneration exceeding a prescribed rate.

ARTICLE 10.

1. The insured persons and their employers shall contribute to the financial resources of the insurance scheme.

2. National laws or regulations may exempt from liability to pay contributions

(a) apprentices and young workers under a prescribed age;

(b) workers who are not paid a money wage or whose wages are very low.

3. Contributions from employers may be dispensed with under laws or regulations concerning schemes of national insurance not restricted in scope to employed persons.

4. The public authorities shall contribute to the financial resources or to the benefits of insurance schemes covering employed persons in general or manual workers.

5. National laws or regulations which, at the time of the adoption of this Convention, do not require contributions from insured persons may continue not to require such contributions.

ARTICLE 11.

1. The insurance scheme shall be administered by institutions founded by the public authorities and not conducted with a view to profit or by State insurance funds:

2. Provided that national laws or regulations may also entrust its administration to institutions founded on the initiative of the parties concerned or of their organisations and duly approved by the public authorities.

3. The funds of insurance institutions and State insurance funds shall be administered separately from the public funds.

4. Representatives of the insured persons shall participate in the management of insurance institutions under conditions to be determined by national laws or regulations, which may likewise decide as to the participation of representatives of employers and of the public authorities.

5. Self-governing insurance institutions shall be under the administrative and financial supervision of the public authorities.

ARTICLE 12.

1. The insured person or his legal representative shall have a right of appeal in any dispute concerning benefits.

2. Such disputes shall be referred to special tribunals which shall include judges, whether professional or not, who are specially cognisant of the purposes of insurance and the needs of insured persons or are assisted by assessors chosen as representative of insured persons and employers respectively.

3. In any dispute concerning liability to insurance or the rate of contribution, the employed person and, in the case of schemes providing for an employer's contribution, his employer shall have a right of appeal.

ARTICLE 13.

1. Foreign employed persons shall be liable to insurance and to the payment of contributions under the same conditions as nationals.

2. Foreign insured persons and their dependants shall be entitled under the same conditions as nationals to the benefits derived from the contributions credited to their account.

3. Foreign insured persons and their dependants shall, if nationals of a Member which is bound by this Convention and the laws or regulations of which therefore provide for a State subsidy towards the financial resources or benefits of the insurance scheme in conformity with Article 10, also be entitled to any subsidy or supplement to or fraction of a pension which is payable out of public funds:

4. Provided that national laws or regulations may restrict to nationals the right to any subsidy or supplement to or fraction of a pension which is payable out of public funds and granted solely to insured persons who have exceeded a prescribed age at the date when the laws or regulations providing for compulsory insurance come into force.

5. Any restrictions which may apply in the event of residence abroad shall only apply to pensioners and their dependants who are nationals of any Member bound by this Convention and reside in the territory of any Member bound thereby to the extent to which they apply to nationals of the country in which the pension has been acquired: Provided that any subsidy or supplement to or fraction of a pension which is payable out of public funds may be withheld.

ARTICLE 14.

1. The insurance of employed persons shall be governed by the law applicable at their place of employment.

2. In the interest of continuity of insurance, exceptions may be made to this rule by agreement between the Members concerned.

ARTICLE 15.

Any Member may prescribe special provisions for frontier workers whose place of employment is in its territory and whose place of residence is abroad.

ARTICLE 16.

In countries which, at the time when this Convention first comes into force, have no laws or regulations providing for compulsory invalidity insurance, an existing non-contributory pension scheme which guarantees an individual right to a pension under the conditions defined in Articles 17 to 23 hereinafter shall be deemed to satisfy the requirements of this Convention.

ARTICLE 17.

A person who becomes generally incapacitated for work and thereby unable to earn an appreciable remuneration shall be entitled to a pension.

ARTICLE 18.

The right to a pension may be made conditional upon the claimant's having been resident in the territory of the Member for a period immediately preceding the making of the claim. This period shall be determined by national laws or regulations but shall not exceed five years.

ARTICLE 19.

1. A claimant shall be entitled to a pension if the annual value of his means does not exceed a limit which shall be fixed by national laws or regulations with due regard to the minimum cost of living.

2. Means up to a level which shall be determined by national laws or regulations shall be exempted for the purpose of the assessment of means.

ARTICLE 20.

The rate of pension shall be an amount which, together with any means of the claimant in excess of the means exempted, is at least sufficient to cover the essential needs of the pensioner.

ARTICLE 21.

1. A claimant shall have a right of appeal in any dispute concerning the award of a pension or the rate thereof.

2. The appeal shall lie to an authority other than the authority which gave the decision in the first instance.

ARTICLE 22.

1. Foreigners who are nationals of a Member bound by this Convention shall be entitled to pensions under the same conditions as nationals:

2. Provided that national laws or regulations may make the award of a pension to foreigners conditional upon their having been resident in the territory of the Member for a period which shall not exceed by more than five years the period of residence prescribed for nationals.

ARTICLE 23.

1. The right to a pension may be forfeited or suspended in whole or in part if the person concerned
(a) has brought about his invalidity by a criminal offence or wilful misconduct;
(b) has obtained or attempted to obtain a pension by fraud;
(c) has been sentenced to imprisonment for a criminal offence; or
(d) has persistently refused to earn his living by work compatible with his strength and capacity.

2. The pension may be suspended in whole or in part while the person concerned is entirely maintained at the public expense.

ARTICLE 24.

Subject to the provisions of paragraph 5 of Article 13, this Convention does not refer to the maintenance of pension rights in the event of residence abroad.

(*For the Standard Articles, see Draft Convention No. 34*)

Draft Convention [No. 38] concerning compulsory invalidity insurance for persons employed in agricultural undertakings.

ARTICLE 1.

Each Member of the International Labour Organisation which ratifies this Convention undertakes to set up or maintain a scheme of compulsory invalidity insurance which shall be based on provisions at least equivalent to those contained in this Convention.

INTERNATIONAL LABOR ORGANIZATION

Article 2.

1. The compulsory invalidity insurance scheme shall apply to manual and non-manual workers, including apprentices, employed in agricultural undertakings, and domestic servants employed in the households of agricultural employers:

2. Provided that any Member may in its national laws or regulations make such exceptions as it deems necessary in respect of

(a) workers whose remuneration exceeds a prescribed amount and, where national laws or regulations do not make this exception general in its application, any non-manual workers engaged in occupations which are ordinarily considered as liberal professions;

(b) workers who are not paid a money wage;

(c) young workers under a prescribed age and workers too old to become insured when they first enter employment;

(d) outworkers whose conditions of work are not of a like nature to those of ordinary wage earners;

(e) members of the employer's family;

(f) workers whose employment is of such a nature that, its total duration being necessarily short, they cannot qualify for benefit, and persons engaged solely in occasional or subsidiary employment;

(g) invalid workers and workers in receipt of an invalidity or old-age pension;

(h) retired public officials employed for remuneration and persons possessing a private income, where the retirement pension or private income is at least equal to the invalidity pension provided by national laws or regulations;

(i) workers who, during their studies, give lessons or work for remuneration in preparation for an occupation corresponding to such studies.

3. Provided also that there may be exempted from liability to insurance persons who, by virtue of any law, regulations or special scheme, are or will become entitled to invalidity benefits at least equivalent on the whole to those provided for in this Convention.

Article 3.

National laws or regulations shall, under conditions to be determined by them, either entitle persons formerly compulsorily insured who are not in receipt of a pension to continue their insurance voluntarily or entitle such persons to maintain their rights by the periodical payment of a fee for the purpose, unless the said rights are automatically maintained or, in the case of married women, the husband, if not liable to compulsory insurance, is permitted to insure voluntarily and thereby to qualify his wife for an old-age or widow's pension.

Article 4.

1. An insured person who becomes generally incapacitated for work and thereby unable to earn an appreciable remuneration shall be entitled to an invalidity pension:

2. Provided that national laws or regulations which secure to insured persons medical treatment and attendance throughout invalidity and, if invalidity terminates in death, secure pensions at the full rate to widows without any condition as to age or invalidity and to orphans, may make

the award of an invalidity pension conditional upon the insured person's being unable to perform remunerative work.

3. In the case of special schemes for non-manual workers, an insured person who suffers from incapacity which renders him unable to earn an appreciable remuneration in the occupation in which he was ordinarily engaged or in a similar occupation shall be entitled to an invalidity pension.

Article 5.

1. Notwithstanding the provisions of Article 6, the right to a pension may be made conditional upon the completion of a qualifying period, which may involve the payment of a minimum number of contributions since entry into insurance and during a prescribed period immediately preceding the happening of the event insured against.

2. The duration of the qualifying period shall not exceed 60 contribution months, 250 contribution weeks or 1,500 contribution days.

3. Where the completion of the qualifying period involves the payment of a prescribed number of contributions during a prescribed period immediately preceding the happening of the event insured against, periods for which benefit has been paid in respect of temporary incapacity for work or of unemployment shall be reckoned as contribution periods to such extent and under such conditions as may be determined by national laws or regulations.

Article 6.

1. An insured person who ceases to be liable to insurance without being entitled to a benefit representing a return for the contributions credited to his account shall retain his rights in respect of these contributions:

2. Provided that national laws or regulations may terminate rights in respect of contributions on the expiry of a term which shall be reckoned from the date when the insured person so ceased to be liable to insurance and which shall be either variable or fixed:—

(*a*) where the term is variable, it shall not be less than one-third (less the periods for which contributions have not been credited) of the total of the periods for which contributions have been credited since entry into insurance.

(*b*) where the term is fixed, it shall in no case be less than eighteen months and rights in respect of contributions may be terminated on the expiry of the term unless, in the course thereof, a minimum number of contributions prescribed by national laws or regulations has been credited to the account of the insured person in virtue of either compulsory or voluntarily continued insurance.

Article 7.

1. The pension shall, whether or not dependent on the time spent in insurance, be a fixed sum or a percentage of the remuneration taken into account for insurance purposes or vary with the amount of the contributions paid.

2. Where the pension varies with the time spent in insurance and its award is made conditional upon the completion by the insured person of a qualifying period, the pension shall, unless a minimum rate is guaranteed, include a fixed sum or fixed portion not dependent on the time spent in insurance.

3. Where contributions are graduated according to remuneration, the

remuneration taken into account for this purpose shall also be taken into account for the purpose of computing the pension, whether or not the pension varies with the time spent in insurance.

ARTICLE 8.

Insurance institutions shall be authorised, under conditions which shall be determined by national laws or regulations, to grant benefits in kind for the purpose of preventing, postponing, alleviating or curing invalidity to persons who are in receipt of or may be entitled to claim a pension on the ground of invalidity.

ARTICLE 9.

1. The right to benefits may be forfeited or suspended in whole or in part if the person concerned
(a) has brought about his invalidity by a criminal offence or wilful misconduct; or
(b) has acted fraudulently towards the insurance institution.

2. The pension may be suspended in whole or in part while the person concerned
(a) is entirely maintained at the public expense or by a social insurance institution;
(b) refuses without valid reason to comply with the doctor's orders or the instructions relating to the conduct of invalids or voluntarily and without authorisation removes himself from the supervision of the insurance institution;
(c) is in receipt of another periodical cash benefit payable by virtue of any law or regulations concerning compulsory social insurance, pensions or workmen's compensation for accidents or occupational diseases; or
(d) is in employment involving compulsory insurance or, in the case of special schemes for non-manual workers, is in receipt of remuneration exceeding a prescribed rate.

ARTICLE 10.

1. The insured persons and their employers shall contribute to the financial resources of the insurance scheme.

2. National laws or regulations may exempt from liability to pay contributions
(a) apprentices and young workers under a prescribed age;
(b) workers who are not paid a money wage or whose wages are very low;
(c) workers in the service of an employer who pays contributions assessed on a basis which is not dependent on the number of workers employed.

3. Contributions from employers may be dispensed with under laws or regulations concerning schemes of national insurance not restricted in scope to employed persons.

4. The public authorities shall contribute to the financial resources or to the benefits of insurance schemes covering employed persons in general or manual workers.

5. National laws or regulations which, at the time of the adoption of this Convention, do not require contributions from insured persons may continue not to require such contributions.

Article 11.

1. The insurance scheme shall be administered by institutions founded by the public authorities and not conducted with a view to profit, or by State insurance funds:

2. Provided that national laws or regulations may also entrust its administration to institutions founded on the initiative of the parties concerned or of their organisations and duly approved by the public authorities.

3. The funds of insurance institutions and State insurance funds shall be administered separately from the public funds.

4. Representatives of the insured persons shall participate in the management of insurance institutions under conditions to be determined by national laws or regulations, which may likewise decide as to the participation of representatives of employers and of the public authorities.

5. Self-governing insurance institutions shall be under the administrative and financial supervision of the public authorities.

Article 12.

1. The insured person or his legal representatives shall have a right of appeal in any dispute concerning benefits.

2. Such disputes shall be referred to special tribunals which shall include judges, whether professional or not, who are specially cognisant of the purposes of insurance and the needs of insured persons or are assisted by assessors chosen as representative of insured persons and employers respectively.

3. In any dispute concerning liability to insurance or the rate of contribution, the employed person and, in the case of schemes providing for an employer's contribution, his employer shall have a right of appeal.

Article 13.

1. Foreign employed persons shall be liable to insurance and to the payment of contributions under the same conditions as nationals.

2. Foreign insured persons and their dependants shall be entitled under the same conditions as nationals to the benefits derived from the contributions credited to their account.

3. Foreign insured persons and their dependants shall, if nationals of a Member which is bound by this Convention and the laws or regulations of which therefore provide for a State subsidy towards the financial resources or benefits of the insurance scheme in conformity with Article 10, also be entitled to any subsidy or supplement to or fraction of a pension which is payable out of public funds:

4. Provided that national laws or regulations may restrict to nationals the right to any subsidy or supplement to or fraction of a pension which is payable out of public funds and granted solely to insured persons who have exceeded a prescribed age at the date when the laws or regulations providing for compulsory insurance come into force.

5. Any restrictions which may apply in the event of residence abroad shall only apply to pensioners and their dependants who are nationals of any Member bound by this Convention and reside in the territory of any Member bound thereby to the extent to which they apply to nationals of the country in which the pension has been acquired: Provided that any subsidy or supplement to or fraction of a pension which is payable out of public funds may be withheld.

ARTICLE 14.

1. The insurance of employed persons shall be governed by the law applicable at their place of employment.

2. In the interest of continuity of insurance exceptions may be made to this rule by agreement between the Members concerned.

ARTICLE 15.

Any Member may prescribe special provisions for frontier workers whose place of employment is in its territory and whose place of residence is abroad.

ARTICLE 16.

In countries which, at the time when this Convention first comes into force, have no laws or regulations providing for compulsory invalidity insurance, an existing non-contributory pension scheme which guarantees an individual right to a pension under the conditions defined in Articles 17 to 23 hereinafter shall be deemed to satisfy the requirements of this Convention.

ARTICLE 17.

A person who becomes generally incapacitated for work and thereby unable to earn an appreciable remuneration shall be entitled to a pension.

ARTICLE 18.

The right to a pension may be made conditional upon the claimant's having been resident in the territory of the Member for a period immediately preceding the making of the claim. This period shall be determined by national laws or regulations but shall not exceed five years.

ARTICLE 19.

1. A claimant shall be entitled to a pension if the annual value of his means does not exceed a limit which shall be fixed by national laws or regulations with due regard to the minimum cost of living.

2. Means up to a level which shall be determined by national laws or regulations shall be exempted for the purpose of the assessment of means.

ARTICLE 20.

The rate of pension shall be an amount which, together with any means of the claimant in excess of the means exempted, is at least sufficient to cover the essential needs of the pensioner.

ARTICLE 21.

1. A claimant shall have a right of appeal in any dispute concerning the award of a pension or the rate thereof.

2. The appeal shall lie to an authority other than the authority which gave the decision in the first instance.

ARTICLE 22.

1. Foreigners who are nationals of a Member bound by this Convention shall be entitled to pensions under the same conditions as nationals:

2. Provided that national laws or regulations may make the award of a pension to foreigners conditional upon their having been resident in the territory of the Member for a period which shall not exceed by more than five years the period of residence prescribed for nationals.

Article 23.

1. The right to a pension may be forfeited or suspended in whole or in part if the person concerned
(a) has brought about his invalidity by a criminal offence or wilful misconduct;
(b) has obtained or attempted to obtain a pension by fraud;
(c) has been sentenced to imprisonment for a criminal offence; or
(d) has persistently refused to earn his living by work compatible with his strength and capacity.

2. The pension may be suspended in whole or in part while the person concerned is entirely maintained at the public expense.

Article 24.

Subject to the provisions of paragraph 5 of Article 13, this Convention does not refer to the maintenance of pension rights in the event of residence abroad.

(*For the Standard Articles, see Draft Convention No. 34*)

Draft Convention [No. 39] concerning compulsory widows' and orphans' insurance for persons employed in industrial or commercial undertakings, in the liberal professions, and for outworkers and domestic servants.

Article 1.

Each Member of the International Labour Organisation which ratifies this Convention undertakes to set up or maintain a scheme of compulsory widows' and orphans' insurance which shall be based on provisions at least equivalent to those contained in this Convention.

Article 2.

1. The compulsory widows' and orphans' insurance scheme shall apply to manual and non-manual workers, including apprentices, employed in industrial or commercial undertakings or in the liberal professions, and to outworkers and domestic servants:

2. Provided that any Member may in its national laws or regulations make such exceptions as it deems necessary in respect of
(a) workers whose remuneration exceeds a prescribed amount and, where national laws or regulations do not make this exception general in its application, any non-manual workers engaged in occupations which are ordinarily considered as liberal professions;
(b) workers who are not paid a money wage;
(c) young workers under a prescribed age and workers too old to become insured when they first enter employment;
(d) outworkers whose conditions of work are not of a like nature to those of ordinary wage earners;
(e) members of the employer's family;
(f) workers whose employment is of such a nature that, its total duration being necessarily short, they cannot qualify for benefit and persons engaged solely in occasional or subsidiary employment;
(g) invalid workers and workers in receipt of an invalidity or old-age pension;

(h) retired public officials employed for remuneration and persons possessing a private income, where the retirement pension or private income is at least equal to the invalidity pension provided by national laws or regulations;

(i) workers who, during their studies, give lessons or work for remuneration in preparation for an occupation corresponding to such studies;

(j) domestic servants employed in the households of agricultural employers.

3. Provided also that there may be exempted from liability to insurance persons whose survivors will, by virtue of any law, regulations or special scheme, become entitled to benefits at least equivalent on the whole to those provided for in this Convntion.

4. This Convention does not apply to seamen and sea fishermen.

Article 3.

National laws or regulations shall, under conditions to be determined by them, either entitle persons formerly compulsorily insured who are not in receipt of a pension to continue their insurance voluntarily or entitle such persons to maintain their rights by the periodical payment of a fee for the purpose, unless the said rights are automatically maintained or, in the case of married women, the husband, if not liable to compulsory insurance, is permitted to insure voluntarily and thereby to qualify his wife for an old-age or widow's pension.

Article 4.

1. Notwithstanding the provisions of Article 5, the right to a pension may be made conditional upon the completion of a qualifying period, which may involve the payment of a minimum number of contributions since entry into insurance and during a prescribed period immediately preceding the happening of the event insured against.

2. The duration of the qualifying period shall not exceed 60 contribution months, 250 contribution weeks or 1,500 contribution days.

3. Where the completion of the qualifying period involves the payment of a prescribed number of contributions during a prescribed period immediately preceding the happening of the event insured against, periods for which benefit has been paid in respect of temporary incapacity for work or of unemployment shall be reckoned as contribution periods to such extent and under such conditions as may be determined by national laws or regulations.

Article 5.

1. An insured person who ceases to be liable to insurance without being entitled to a benefit representing a return for the contributions credited to his account shall retain his rights in respect of these contributions:

2. Provided that national laws or regulations may terminate rights in respect of contributions on the expiry of a term which shall be reckoned from the date when the insured person so ceased to be liable to insurance and which shall be either variable or fixed:—

(a) where the term is variable, it shall not be less than one-third (less the periods for which contributions have not been credited) of the total of the periods for which contributions have been credited since entry into insurance.

(b) where the term is fixed, it shall in no case be less than eighteen months and rights in respect of contributions may be terminated on the expiry of the term unless, in the course thereof, a minimum number of contributions prescribed by national laws or regulations has been credited to the account of the insured person in virtue of either compulsory or voluntarily continued insurance.

Article 6.

The widows' and orphans' insurance scheme shall as a minimum confer pension rights on widows who have not remarried and the children of a deceased insured or pensioned person.

Article 7.

1. The right to a widow's pension may be reserved to widows who are above a prescribed age or are invalid.

2. The provisions of paragraph 1 shall not apply in the case of special schemes for non-manual workers.

3. The right to a widow's pension may be restricted to cases where the marriage has lasted for a prescribed period and was contracted before the insured or pensioned person had reached a prescribed age or become invalid.

4. The right to a widow's pension may be withheld if, at the time of the death of the insured or pensioned person, the marriage had been dissolved or if a separation had been pronounced in proceedings in which the wife was found solely at fault.

5. Where there are several claimants to a widow's pension, the amount payable may be limited to that of one pension.

Article 8.

1. Any child who has not reached a prescribed age which shall not be less than fourteen shall be entitled to a pension in respect of the death of either parent:

2. Provided that the right to a pension in respect of the death of an insured or pensioned mother may either be made conditional upon the mother's having contributed to the support of the child or be made conditional upon her having been a widow at the time of her death.

3. National laws or regulations shall determine the cases in which a child other than a legitimate child shall be entitled to a pension.

Article 9.

1. The pension shall, whether or not dependent on the time spent in insurance, be a fixed sum or a percentage of the remuneration taken into account for insurance purposes or vary with the amount of the contributions paid.

2. Where the pension varies with the time spent in insurance and its award is made conditional upon the completion by the insured person of a qualifying period, the pension shall, unless a minimum rate is guaranteed, include a fixed sum or fixed portion not dependent on the time spent in insurance; where the pension is awarded without any condition as to the completion of a qualifying period, provision may be made for a guaranteed minimum rate of pension.

3. Where contributions are graduated according to remuneration, the remuneration taken into account for this purpose shall also be taken into

account for the purpose of computing the pension, whether or not the pension varies with the time spent in insurance.

Article 10.

Insurance institutions shall be authorised, under conditions which shall be determined by national laws or regulations, to grant benefits in kind for the purpose of preventing, postponing, alleviating or curing invalidity to persons who are in receipt of or may be entitled to claim a pension on the ground of invalidity.

Article 11.

1. The right to benefits may be forfeited or suspended in whole or in part

(*a*) if death has been caused by a criminal offence committed by or the wilful misconduct of the insured person or any person who may become entitled to a survivor's pension; or

(*b*) if the insured person or any person who may become entitled to a survivor's pension has acted fraudulently towards the insurance institution.

2. The pension may be suspended in whole or in part while the person concerned

(*a*) is entirely maintained at the public expense or by a social insurance institution;

(*b*) refuses without valid reason to comply with the doctor's orders or the instructions relating to the conduct of invalids or voluntarily and without authorisation removes herself from the supervision of the insurance institution;

(*c*) is in receipt of another periodical cash benefit payable by virtue of any law or regulations concerning compulsory social insurance, pensions or workmen's compensation for accidents or occupational diseases;

(d) having been awarded a widow's pension without any condition as to age or invalidity, is living with a man as his wife; or

(*e*) in the case of special schemes for non-manual workers, is in receipt of remuneration exceeding a prescribed rate.

Article 12.

1. The insured persons and their employers shall contribute to the financial resources of the insurance scheme.

2. National laws or regulations may exempt from liability to pay contributions

(*a*) apprentices and young workers under a prescribed age;

(*b*) workers who are not paid a money wage or whose wages are very low.

3. Contributions from employers may be dispensed with under laws or regulations concerning schemes of national insurance not restricted in scope to employed persons.

4. The public authorities shall contribute to the financial resources or to the benefits of insurance schemes covering employed persons in general or **manual workers.**

5. National laws or regulations which, at the time of the adoption of

this Convention, do not require contributions from insured persons may continue not to require such contributions.

ARTICLE 13.

1. The insurance scheme shall be administered by institutions founded by the public authorities and not conducted with a view to profit, or by State insurance funds:

2. Provided that national laws or regulations may also entrust its administration to institutions founded on the initiative of the parties concerned or of their organisations and duly approved by the public authorities.

3. The funds of insurance institutions and State insurance funds shall be administered separately from the public funds.

4. Representatives of the insured persons shall participate in the management of insurance institutions under conditions to be determined by national laws or regulations, which may likewise decide as to the participation of representatives of employers and of the public authorities.

5. Self-governing insurance institutions shall be under the administrative and financial supervision of the public authorities.

ARTICLE 14.

1. The survivors of a deceased insured or pensioned person shall have a right of appeal in any dispute concerning benefits.

2. Such disputes shall be referred to special tribunals which shall include judges, whether professional or not, who are specially cognisant of the purposes of insurance or are assisted by assessors chosen as representative of insured persons and employers respectively.

3. In any dispute concerning liability to insurance or the rate of contribution, the employed person and, in the case of schemes providing for an employer's contribution, his employer shall have a right of appeal.

ARTICLE 15.

1. Foreign employed persons shall be liable to insurance and to the payment of contributions under the same conditions as nationals.

2. The survivors of foreign insured or pensioned persons shall be entitled under the same conditions as nationals to the benefits derived from the contributions credited to their account.

3. The survivors of foreign insured or pensioned persons shall, if nationals of a Member which is bound by this Convention and the laws or regulations of which therefore provide for a State subsidy towards the financial resources or benefits of the insurance scheme in conformity with Article 12, also be entitled to any subsidy or supplement to or fraction of a pension which is payable out of public funds:

4. Provided that national laws or regulations may restrict to nationals the right to any subsidy or supplement to or fraction of a pension which is payable out of public funds and granted solely to the survivors of insured persons who have exceeded a prescribed age at the date when the laws or regulations providing for compulsory insurance come into force.

5. Any restrictions which may apply in the event of residence abroad shall only apply to pensioners who are nationals of any Member bound by this Convention and reside in the territory of any Member bound thereby to the extent to which they apply to nationals of the country in which the pension has been acquired: Provided that any subsidy or supplement to

or fraction of a pension which is payable out of public funds may be withheld.

ARTICLE 16.

1. The insurance of employed persons shall be governed by the law applicable at their place of employment.

2. In the interest of continuity of insurance exceptions may be made to this rule by agreement between the Members concerned.

ARTICLE 17.

Any Member may prescribe special provisions for frontier workers whose place of employment is in its territory and whose place of residence is abroad.

ARTICLE 18.

In countries which, at the time when this Convention first comes into force, have no laws or regulations providing for compulsory widows' and orphans' insurance, an existing non-contributory pension scheme which guarantees an individual right to a pension under the conditions defined in Articles 19 to 25 hereinafter shall be deemed to satisfy the requirements of this Convention.

ARTICLE 19.

1. The following shall be entitled to a pension:—
(a) every widow who has not remarried and who has at least two dependent children;
(b) every orphan, that is to say, every child who has lost both parents.

2. National laws or regulations shall define
(a) the cases in which a child other than a legitimate child shall be deemed to be the child of a widow for the purpose of entitling her to a pension;
(b) the age until which a child shall be considered dependent upon a widow or shall be entitled to an orphan's pension: Provided that this age shall in no case be less than fourteen.

ARTICLE 20.

1. The right to a widow's pension may be made conditional upon the residence in the territory of the Member
(a) of the deceased husband during a period immediately preceding his death; and
(b) of the widow during a period immediately preceding the making of her claim for a pension.

2. The right to an orphan's pension may be made conditional upon the residence, in the territory of the Member during a period immediately preceding death, of whichever of the parents died the more recently.

3. The period of residence in the territory of the Member to have been completed by a widow or a deceased parent shall be prescribed by national laws or regulations but shall not exceed five years.

ARTICLE 21.

1. A claimant shall be entitled to a widow's or orphan's pension if the annual value of the claimant's means, including any means of dependent children or orphans, does not exceed a limit which shall be fixed by national laws or regulations with due regard to the minimum cost of living.

2. Means up to a level which shall be determined by national laws or regulations shall be exempted for the purpose of the assessment of means.

ARTICLE 22.

The rate of pension shall be an amount which, together with any means of the claimant in excess of the means exempted, is at least sufficient to cover the essential needs of the pensioner.

ARTICLE 23.

1. A claimant shall have a right of appeal in any dispute concerning the award of a pension or the rate thereof.

2. The appeal shall lie to an authority other than the authority which gave the decision in the first instance.

ARTICLE 24.

1. Foreign widows and orphans shall, if nationals of a Member bound by this Convention, be entitled to pensions under the same conditions as nationals:

2. Provided that national laws or regulations may make the award of a pension to foreigners conditional upon the completion of a period of residence in the territory of the Member which shall not exceed by more than five years the period of residence provided for in Article 20.

ARTICLE 25.

1. The right to a pension may be forfeited or suspended in whole or in part if the widow or the person who has undertaken responsibility for the care of the orphan has obtained or attempted to obtain a pension by fraud.

2. The pension may be suspended in whole or in part while the person concerned is entirely maintained at the public expense.

ARTICLE 26.

Subject to the provisions of paragraph 5 of Article 15, this Convention does not refer to the maintenance of pension rights in the event of residence abroad.

(For the Standard Articles, see Draft Convention No. 34)

Draft Convention [No. 40] concerning compulsory widows' and orphans' insurance for persons employed in agricultural undertakings.

ARTICLE 1.

Each Member of the International Labour Organisation which ratifies this Convention undertakes to set up or maintain a scheme of compulsory widows' and orphans' insurance which shall be based on provisions at least equivalent to those contained in this Convention.

ARTICLE 2.

1. The compulsory widows' and orphans' insurance scheme shall apply to manual and non-manual workers, including apprentices, employed in agricultural undertakings, and to domestic servants employed in the households of agricultural employers:

2. Provided that any Member may in its national laws or regulations make such exceptions as it deems necessary in respect of

(*a*) workers whose remuneration exceeds a prescribed amount and, where national laws or regulations do not make this exception general in its application, any non-manual workers engaged in occupations which are ordinarily considered as liberal professions;

(*b*) workers who are not paid a money wage;

(*c*) young workers under a prescribed age and workers too old to become insured when they first enter employment;

(*d*) outworkers whose conditions of work are not of a like nature to those of ordinary wage earners;

(*e*) members of the employer's family;

(*f*) workers whose employment is of such a nature that, its total duration being necessarily short, they cannot qualify for benefit and persons engaged solely in occasional or subsidiary employment;

(*g*) invalid workers and workers in receipt of an invalidity or old-age pension;

(*h*) retired public officials employed for remuneration and persons possessing a private income, where the retirement pension or private income is at least equal to the invalidity pension provided by national laws or regulations;

(*i*) workers who, during their studies, give lessons or work for remuneration in preparation for an occupation corresponding to such studies.

3. Provided also that there may be exempted from liability to insurance persons whose survivors will, by virtue of any law, regulations or special scheme, become entitled to benefits at least equivalent on the whole to those provided for in this Convention.

Article 3.

National laws or regulations shall, under conditions to be determined by them, either entitle persons formerly compulsorily insured who are not in receipt of a pension to continue their insurance voluntarily or entitle such persons to maintain their rights by the periodical payment of a fee for the purpose, unless the said rights are automatically maintained or, in the case of married women, the husband, if not liable to compulsory insurance, is permitted to insure voluntarily and thereby to qualify his wife for an old-age or widow's pension.

Article 4.

1. Notwithstanding the provisions of Article 5, the right to a pension may be made conditional upon the completion of a qualifying period, which may involve the payment of a minimum number of contributions since entry into insurance and during a prescribed period immediately preceding the happening of the event insured against.

2. The duration of the qualifying period shall not exceed 60 contribution months, 250 contribution weeks or 1,500 contribution days.

3. Where the completion of the qualifying period involves the payment of a prescribed number of contributions during a prescribed period immediately preceding the happening of the event insured against, periods for which benefit has been paid in respect of temporary incapacity for work or of unemployment shall be reckoned as contribution periods to such extent and under such conditions as may be determined by national laws or regulations.

Article 5.

1. An insured person who ceases to be liable to insurance without being entitled to a benefit representing a return for the contributions credited to his account shall retain his rights in respect of these contributions:

2. Provided that national laws or regulations may terminate rights in respect of contributions on the expiry of a term which shall be reckoned from the date when the insured person so ceased to be liable to insurance and which shall be either variable or fixed:—

(a) where the term is variable, it shall not be less than one-third (less the periods for which contributions have not been credited) of the total of the periods for which contributions have been credited since entry into insurance.

(b) where the term is fixed, it shall in no case be less than eighteen months and rights in respect of contributions may be terminated on the expiry of the term unless, in the course thereof, a minimum number of contributions prescribed by national laws or regulations has been credited to the account of the insured person in virtue of either compulsory or voluntarily continued insurance.

Article 6.

The widows' and orphans' insurance scheme shall as a minimum confer pension rights on widows who have not remarried and the children of a deceased insured or pensioned person.

Article 7.

1. The right to a widow's pension may be reserved to widows who are above a prescribed age or are invalid.

2. The provisions of paragraph 1 shall not apply in the case of special schemes for non-manual workers.

3. The right to a widow's pension may be restricted to cases where the marriage has lasted for a prescribed period and was contracted before the insured or pensioned person had reached a prescribed age or become invalid.

4. The right to a widow's pension may be withheld if, at the time of the death of the insured or pensioned person, the marriage had been dissolved or if a separation had been pronounced in proceedings in which the wife was found solely at fault.

5. Where there are several claimants to a widow's pension, the amount payable may be limited to that of one pension.

Article 8.

1. Any child who has not reached a prescribed age which shall not be less than fourteen shall be entitled to a pension in respect of the death of either parent:

2. Provided that the right to a pension in respect of the death of an insured or pensioned mother may either be made conditional upon the mother's having contributed to the support of the child or be made conditional upon her having been a widow at the time of her death.

3. National laws or regulations shall determine the cases in which a child other than a legitimate child shall be entitled to a pension.

Article 9.

1. The pension shall, whether or not dependent on the time spent in insurance, be a fixed sum or a percentage of the remuneration taken into account for insurance purposes or vary with the amount of the contributions paid.

2. Where the pension varies with the time spent in insurance and its award is made conditional upon the completion by the insured person of a qualifying period, the pension shall, unless a minimum rate is guaranteed, include a fixed sum or fixed portion not dependent on the time spent in insurance; where the pension is awarded without any condition as to the completion of a qualifying period, provision may be made for a guaranteed minimum rate of pension.

3. Where contributions are graduated according to remuneration, the remuneration taken into account for this purpose shall also be taken into account for the purpose of computing the pension, whether or not the pension varies with the time spent in insurance.

Article 10.

Insurance institutions shall be authorised, under conditions which shall be determined by national laws or regulations, to grant benefits in kind for the purpose of preventing, postponing, alleviating or curing invalidity to persons who are in receipt of or may be entitled to claim a pension on the ground of invalidity.

Article 11.

1. The right to benefits may be forfeited or suspended in whole or in part

(*a*) if death has been caused by a criminal offence committed by or the wilful misconduct of the insured person or any person who may become entitled to a survivor's pension; or

(*b*) if the insured person or any person who may become entitled to a survivor's pension has acted fraudulently towards the insurance institution.

2. The pension may be suspended in whole or in part while the person concerned

(*a*) is entirely maintained at the public expense or by a social insurance institution.

(*b*) refuses without valid reason to comply with the doctor's orders or the instructions relating to the conduct of invalids or voluntarily and without authorisation removes herself from the supervision of the insurance institution;

(*c*) is in receipt of another periodical cash benefit payable by virtue of any law or regulations concerning compulsory social insurance, pensions or workmen's compensation for accidents or occupational diseases;

(*d*) having been awarded a widow's pension without any condition as to age or invalidity, is living with a man as his wife; or

(*e*) in the case of special schemes for non-manual workers, is in receipt of remuneration exceeding a prescribed rate.

Article 12.

1. The insured persons and their employers shall contribute to the financial resources of the insurance scheme.

2. National laws or regulations may exempt from liability to pay contributions
(*a*) apprentices and young workers under a prescribed age;
(*b*) workers who are not paid a money wage or whose wages are very low;
(c) workers in the service of an employer who pays contributions assessed on a basis which is not dependent on the number of workers employed.

3. Contributions from employers may be dispensed with under laws or regulations concerning schemes of national insurance not restricted in scope to employed persons.

4. The public authorities shall contribute to the financial resources or to the benefits of insurance schemes covering employed persons in general or manual workers.

5. National laws or regulations which, at the time of the adoption of this Convention, do not require contributions from insured persons may continue not to require such contributions.

ARTICLE 13.

1. The insurance scheme shall be administered by institutions founded by the public authorities and not conducted with a view to profit, or by State insurance funds:

2. Provided that national laws or regulations may also entrust its administration to institutions founded on the initiative of the parties concerned or of their organisations and duly approved by the public authorities.

3. The funds of insurance institutions and State insurance funds shall be administered separately from the public funds.

4. Representatives of the insured persons shall participate in the management of insurance institutions under conditions to be determined by national laws or regulations, which may likewise decide as to the participation of representatives of employers and of the public authorities.

5. Self-governing insurance institutions shall be under the administrative and financial supervision of the public authorities.

ARTICLE 14.

1. The survivors of a deceased insured or pensioned person shall have a right of appeal in any dispute concerning benefits.

2. Such disputes shall be referred to special tribunals which shall include judges, whether professional or not, who are specially cognisant of the purposes of insurance or are assisted by assessors chosen as representative of insured persons and employers respectively.

3. In any dispute concerning liability to insurance or the rate of contribution, the employed person and, in the case of schemes providing for an employer's contribution, his employer shall have a right of appeal.

ARTICLE 15.

1. Foreign employed persons shall be liable to insurance and to the payment of contributions under the same conditions as nationals.

2. The survivors of foreign insured or pensioned persons shall be entitled under the same conditions as nationals to the benefits derived from the contributions credited to their account.

3. The survivors of foreign insured or pensioned persons shall, if nationals of a Member which is bound by this Convention and the laws

or regulations of which therefore provide for a State subsidy towards the financial resources or benefits of the insurance scheme in conformity with Article 12, also be entitled to any subsidy or supplement to or fraction of a pension which is payable out of public funds:

4. Provided that national laws or regulations may restrict to nationals the right to any subsidy or supplement to or fraction of a pension which is payable out of public funds and granted solely to the survivors of insured persons who have exceeded a prescribed age at the date when the laws or regulations providing for compulsory insurance come into force.

5. Any restrictions which may apply in the event of residence abroad shall only apply to pensioners who are nationals of any Member bound by this Convention and reside in the territory of any Member bound thereby to the extent to which they apply to nationals of the country in which the pension has been acquired: Provided that any subsidy or supplement to or fraction of a pension which is payable out of public funds may be withheld.

ARTICLE 16.

1. The insurance of employed persons shall be governed by the law applicable at their place of employment.

2. In the interest of continuity of insurance exceptions may be made to this rule by agreement between the Members concerned.

ARTICLE 17.

Any Member may prescribe special provisions for frontier workers whose place of employment is in its territory and whose place of residence is abroad.

ARTICLE 18.

In countries which, at the time when this Convention first comes into force, have no laws or regulations providing for compulsory widows' and orphans' insurance, an existing non-contributory pension scheme which guarantees an individual right to a pension under the conditions defined in Articles 19 to 25 hereinafter shall be deemed to satisfy the requirements of this Convention.

ARTICLE 19.

1. The following shall be entitled to a pension:—

(a) every widow who has not remarried and who has at least two dependent children;

(b) every orphan, that is to say, every child who has lost both parents.

2. National laws or regulations shall define

(a) the cases in which a child other than a legitimate child shall be deemed to be the child of a widow for the purpose of entitling her to a pension;

(b) the age until which a child shall be considered dependent upon a widow or shall be entitled to an orphan's pension: Provided that this age shall in no case be less than fourteen.

ARTICLE 20.

1. The right to a widow's pension may be made conditional upon the residence in the territory of the Member

(a) of the deceased husband during a period immediately preceding his death; and

(b) of the widow during a period immediately preceding the making of her claim for a pension.

2. The right to an orphan's pension may be made conditional upon the residence, in the territory of the Member during a period immediately preceding death, of whichever of the parents died the more recently.

3. The period of residence in the territory of the Member to have been completed by a widow or a deceased parent shall be prescribed by national laws or regulations but shall not exceed five years.

ARTICLE 21.

1. A claimant shall be entitled to a widow's or orphan's pension if the annual value of the claimant's means, including any means of dependent children or orphans, does not exceed a limit which shall be fixed by national laws or regulations with due regard to the minimum cost of living.

2. Means up to a level which shall be determined by national laws or regulations shall be exempted for the purpose of the assessment of means.

ARTICLE 22.

The rate of pension shall be an amount which, together with any means of the claimant in excess of the means exempted, is at least sufficient to cover the essential needs of the pensioner.

ARTICLE 23.

1. A claimant shall have a right of appeal in any dispute concerning the award of a pension or the rate thereof.

2. The appeal shall lie to an authority other than the authority which gave the decision in the first instance.

ARTICLE 24.

1. Foreign widows and orphans shall, if nationals of a Member bound by this Convention, be entitled to pensions under the same conditions as nationals:

2. Provided that national laws or regulations may make the award of a pension to foreigners conditional upon the completion of a period of residence in the territory of the Member which shall not exceed by more than five years the period of residence provided for in Article 20.

ARTICLE 25.

1. The right to a pension may be forfeited or suspended in whole or in part if the widow or the person who has undertaken responsibility for the care of the orphan has obtained or attempted to obtain a pension by fraud.

2. The pension may be suspended in whole or in part while the person concerned is entirely maintained at the public expense.

ARTICLE 26.

Subject to the provisions of paragraph 5 of Article 15, this Convention does not refer to the maintenance of pension rights in the event of residence abroad.

(*For the Standard Articles, see Draft Convention No. 34*)

INTERNATIONAL LABOR ORGANIZATION

Recommendation [No. 43]
concerning the general principles of invalidity, old-age and widows' and orphans' insurance.

The Conference,

Having adopted Draft Conventions concerning compulsory invalidity, old-age and widows' and orphans' insurance for persons employed in industrial or commercial undertakings, in the liberal professions, and for outworkers and domestic servants and concerning compulsory invalidity, old-age and widows' and orphans' insurance for persons employed in agricultural undertakings, and

Considering that these Draft Conventions lay down the minimum conditions to be complied with from the beginning by every scheme of compulsory invalidity, old-age and widows' and orphans' insurance, and

Considering that it is desirable to indicate a number of general principles which practice shows to be best calculated to promote a just, effective and appropriate organisation of invalidity, old-age and widows' and orphans' insurance;

Recommends that each Member should take the following principles and rules into consideration:

I.
SCOPE.

1. *(a)* Compulsory invalidity, old-age and widows' and orphans' insurance for employed persons should include, irrespective of age, sex or nationality, every person who is ordinarily engaged in employment for remuneration.

(b) Where economic, social and administrative conditions permit, national laws or regulations should provide that invalidity, old-age and widows' and orphans' insurance should also include persons of small means working on their own account in industry, commerce and agriculture.

2. If, however, it is considered advisable to fix a minimum age for entry into insurance, such age should be as close as possible to the age at which compulsory school attendance ceases and at which the choice of an occupation is made.

3. The fixing of a maximum age for entry into insurance is only justified in insurance schemes which make the right to a pension conditional upon the completion of a qualifying period and then only for workers who, when they take up employment for remuneration as their ordinary occupation, are too old to be able to complete the qualifying period before the normal pensionable age.

4. Where it is considered advisable to fix (apart from the limitation, inherent in social insurance, of the remuneration taken into account for insurance purposes) a maximum remuneration as a criterion of liability to insurance, only such workers should thereby be excluded as, by reason of the fact that their remuneration is considerably in excess of the general level of wages, may be deemed to be capable of making provision by themselves against invalidity, old-age and death.

II.
PENSIONS.

A. *Qualifying Period and Insurance Periods.*

5. The qualifying period prescribed by insurance schemes which provide for awarding all pensioners a pension at a fixed rate or varying with the

remuneration taken into account for insurance purposes should be restricted to a contribution period which shall not be longer than is strictly necessary to preclude persons from entering insurance with intent to take undue advantage of it and to ensure some consideration for the benefits afforded.

6. The qualifying period for the purpose of an invalidity or survivor's pension should in no case exceed 60 contribution months, 250 contribution weeks or 1,500 contribution days, and the qualifying period for the purpose of an old-age pension should not exceed twice this maximum.

7. Periods during which the insured person is incapable of work by reason of sickness, is not available for work by reason of childbirth or is involuntarily unemployed should, within limits to be prescribed, count towards the qualifying period, even where no contributions are paid for such periods by sickness or maternity insurance or by an unemployment fund.

8. (a) Insurance schemes which place limitations on the retention of rights in respect of contributions which have been paid should guarantee retention of such rights for a term of at least eighteen months reckoned from the last contribution payment, this term being prolonged, in schemes in which contributions are graduated according to remuneration, up to at least one-third (less the periods for which contributions have not been credited) of the total of the periods for which contributions have been credited since entry into insurance. In reckoning this term, periods during which the insured person was incapable of work by reason of sickness, was not available for work by reason of childbirth or was involuntarily unemployed or engaged in military service, should not be considered as periods for which contributions have not been credited.

(b) Any further retention of rights in respect of contributions may be made conditional either upon resumption of payment of contributions in virtue of compulsory or voluntarily continued insurance or upon the payment of a moderate fee for this purpose; in insurance schemes in which contributions are graduated according to remuneration and which provide for pensions varying with the time spent in insurance, resumption of payment of contributions should operate to increase the value of the rights in course of acquisition.

9. A person formerly insured should be able to recover rights already expired, by the payment of a prescribed number of contributions in virtue of compulsory or voluntarily continued insurance; where the pension varies with the number or amount of the contributions credited to the account of the insured person, the number of contributions so prescribed should be less than the number required for the initial qualifying period.

10. Sums required to be paid for maintaining the rights in course of acquisition of insured persons who are unemployed for a long time should—in view of the impossibility of putting the expense of such payments solely on the insured persons in employment—be obtained through the financial assistance of the public authorities; and the same principle should apply to payments for the purpose of consolidating and enhancing the rights of such unemployed persons.

B. *Old-Age Pensions.*

11. For insurance schemes which fix the pensionable age above sixty it is recommended, as a means of relieving the labour market and of ensuring rest for the aged, that the pensionable age should be reduced to sixty, in so far as the demographic, economic and financial situation of the country permits and, if necessary, by stages.

12. Insured persons who have for many years been engaged in a par-

ticularly arduous or unhealthy occupation should be enabled to claim a pension at a less advanced age than workers in other occupations.

13. (*a*) In order to ensure that workers in their old age shall not suffer privations, the pension should be sufficient to cover essential needs. The pension provided for all pensioners who have completed a certain qualifying period should accordingly be fixed with due regard to the cost of living.

(*b*) In insurance schemes in which contributions are graduated according to remuneration, insured persons to the account of whom have been credited contributions corresponding to the normal duration of working life should be awarded a pension commensurate with their economic condition during their working life. To this end the pension provided for insured persons who have completed thirty years of actual contribution should not be less than half the remuneration taken into account for insurance purposes either since entry into insurance or over a prescribed period immediately preceding the award of the pension.

14. A bonus should be paid to a pensioner:

(*a*) for each dependent child who is of school age or, being under the age of seventeen, is continuing his general or vocational education, or who cannot by reason of infirmity earn his living;

(*b*) when his wife is aged or infirm and is not herself on this account entitled to a pension.

15. A pensioner who needs the constant attendance of another person should be awarded a special supplement.

C. *Invalidity Pensions.*

16. (*a*) A pension should be awarded to an insured person who by reason of sickness or infirmity is unable to earn an appreciable remuneration by work suited to his strength and ability and his training; remuneration which is less than one-third of the ordinary remuneration of a fit worker of similar training and experience should not be deemed to be appreciable.

(*b*) Nevertheless, in special insurance schemes set up on behalf of manual or non-manual workers in certain occupations, reduction of capacity for work should be assessed solely with reference to the occupation hitherto followed or to a similar occupation.

17. (*a*) In order to fulfil its purpose, an insurance scheme should provide for every insured person who becomes invalid after having completed the qualifying period a pension sufficient to cover his essential needs. The minimum pension provided for every pensioner should accordingly be fixed with due regard to the cost of living.

(*b*) In insurance schemes in which the minimum pension is fixed in terms of the remuneration taken into account for insurance purposes, the minimum should not be less than 40 per cent. of such remuneration. The same result should be aimed at by schemes in which the pension includes a fixed portion which is the same for every pensioner and a portion varying with the number and amount of the contributions credited to his account.

18. A bonus should be paid to a pensioner for each dependent child who is of school age or, being under the age of seventeen, is continuing his general or vocational education or who cannot by reason of infirmity earn his living.

19. A pensioner who needs the constant attendance of another person should be awarded a special supplement.

D. *Survivor's Pensions.*

20. (*a*) If a pensioner or insured person dies after completing the qualifying period and leaves a widow, the widow should be entitled to a pension as long as she does not remarry.

(*b*) If, however, the award of the pension is subject to the fulfillment of other conditions, pensions should nevertheless be awarded to widows unable to earn their living by reason of age or invalidity and to widows with a dependent child who is of school age or who, being under the age of seventeen, is continuing his general or vocational education.

21. A pension should also be awarded to an invalid widower who by reason of his invalidity was dependent on an insured woman who died after completing the qualifying period.

22. (*a*) The pension awarded to a widow (or invalid widower) should represent a substantial contribution towards covering essential needs. Whatever may be the method of computing it, the minimum pension should be fixed with due regard to the cost of living.

(*b*) In insurance schemes in which contributions are graduated according to the remuneration of the deceased, the widow's (or invalid widower's) pension should not be less than half the pension to which the deceased was entitled or would have been entitled if at the date of his death he had been awarded an invalidity or old-age pension. Nevertheless, where such schemes determine the rights of survivors without regard to the rate of the pension to which the deceased was or would have been entitled, a widow's (or invalid widower's) pension should not be less than 20 per cent. of the remuneration of the deceased taken into account for the purposes of his insurance either since entry into insurance or over a prescribed period immediately preceding his death.

23. (*a*) Every child of school age who was dependent on a pensioner or insured person who died after completing the qualifying period should be entitled to a child's pension and the pension should continue to be paid until the age of seventeen if the child is continuing his general or vocational education and even beyond this age if the child cannot by reason of infirmity earn his living.

(*b*) A child's pension may be paid in the form of a supplement to the pension of his widowed mother.

24. (*a*) The minimum pension provided for every child should represent a substantial contribution towards the cost of maintaining and educating him; such minimum should be higher in the case of an orphan child.

(*b*) In insurance schemes in which contributions are graduated according to the remuneration of the deceased, a child's pension should not be less than one-quarter or in the case of orphans one-half of the pension to which the deceased was entitled or would have been entitled if at the date of his death he had been awarded an invalidity or old-age pension. Nevertheless, where such schemes determine the rights of survivors without regard to the rate of the pension to which the deceased was or would have been entitled, a child's pension should not be less than 10 per cent. or in the case of orphans 20 per cent. of the remuneration of the deceased as taken into account for the purposes of his insurance either since entry into insurance or over a prescribed period immediately preceding his death.

25. If it is considered advisable to fix a maximum for the total of the

survivors' pensions which may be awarded in respect of one deceased person, such maximum should not, where survivors' pensions vary with the pension of the deceased, be less than the pension, including bonuses for family responsibilities, to which the deceased was or would have been entitled, or, where survivors' pensions vary with the remuneration of the deceased taken into account for the purposes of his insurance, be less than half such remuneration.

26. Survivors not eligible for a pension because the qualifying conditions have not been fulfilled should (provided that a minimum number of payments has been credited to the account of the deceased) be granted a lump sum which will enable them to adapt themselves to the change in their circumstances caused by the death of the head of the family.

27. In countries where burial expenses are not, by law or custom, covered by some other insurance, and in particular by sickness insurance, a benefit in respect of the cost of decent burial should be paid by widows' and orphans' insurance on the death of an insured person.

E. *Provisions for the Suspension or Reduction of Pensions.*

28. Where provision is made for the suspension or reduction of invalidity, old-age or survivors' pensions in cases where a concurrent title exists to a pension acquired under another scheme of social insurance or a scheme of pensions or workmen's compensation for accidents or occupational diseases, the provisions concerning suspension or reduction should be such as to enable the pensioner to receive in its entirety whichever of the pensions is the higher and in any case he should be paid that part of the invalidity, old-age or survivor's pension which corresponds to the insured person's own contributions.

29. Where an invalidity or old-age pension is suspended for reason other than the existence of a concurrent title to another pension, the dependent family of the person whose pension is suspended should be awarded a maintenance allowance equal to the whole or to a part of the pension.

III.
Financial Resources.

30. (*a*) The financial resources of the insurance scheme should be provided by contributions from the insured persons and contributions from their employers.

(*b*) The public authorities should contribute to the insurance scheme.

31. As a general rule the contribution of the insured person should not be higher than the contribution of his employer.

32. The employer should be responsible for the whole or the greater part of the joint contribution in respect of workers who are remunerated only in kind, outworkers and apprentices whose remuneration does not exceed a prescribed amount.

33. The State should be responsible for the contributions in respect of periods of compulsory military service performed by persons who were insured before beginning their military service.

IV.
Amdinistration.

34. National laws or regulations should provide that insured women are adequately represented on the administrative bodies of invalidity, old-age and widows' and orphans' insurance.

EIGHTEENTH SESSION
(Geneva, 4-23 June 1934)

Draft Convention [No. 41] concerning employment of women during the night (revised 1934).

ARTICLE 1.

1. For the purpose of this Convention, the term "industrial undertaking" includes particularly:

(a) Mines, quarries, and other works for the extraction of minerals from the earth;

(b) Industries in which articles are manufactured, altered, cleaned, repaired, ornamented, finished, adapted for sale, broken up or demolished, or in which materials are transformed; including shipbuilding, and the generation, transformation, and transmission of electricity or motive power of any kind;

(c) Construction, reconstruction, maintenance, repair, alteration, or demolition of any building, railway, tramway, harbour, dock, pier, canal, inland waterway, road, tunnel, bridge, viaduct, sewer, drain, well, telegraphic or telephonic installation, electrical undertaking, gas work, water work, or other work of construction, as well as the preparation for or laying the foundations of any such work or structure.

2. The competent authority in each country shall define the line of division which separates industry from commerce and agriculture.

ARTICLE 2.

1. For the purpose of this Convention, the term "night" signifies a period of at least eleven consecutive hours, including the interval between ten o'clock in the evening and five o'clock in the morning:

2. Provided that, where there are exceptional circumstances affecting the workers employed in a particular industry or area, the competent authority may, after consultation with the employers' and workers' organisations concerned, decide that in the case of women employed in that industry or area, the interval between eleven o'clock in the evening and six o'clock in the morning may be substituted for the interval between ten o'clock in the evening and five o'clock in the morning.

3. In those countries where no Government regulation as yet applies to the employment of women in industrial undertakings during the night, the term "night" may provisionally, and for a maximum period of three years, be declared by the Government to signify a period of only ten hours, including the interval between ten o'clock in the evening and five o'clock in the morning.

ARTICLE 3.

Women without distinction of age shall not be employed during the night in any public or private industrial undertaking, or in any branch thereof, other than an undertaking in which only members of the same family are employed.

ARTICLE 4.

Article 3 shall not apply:

(a) In cases of *force majeure*, when in any undertaking there occurs an interruption of work which it was impossible to foresee, and which is not of a recurring character.

(b) In cases where the work has to do with raw materials or materials in course of treatment which are subject to rapid deterioration, when such night work is necessary to preserve the said materials from certain loss.

ARTICLE 5.

In India and Siam, the application of Article 3 of this Convention may be suspended by the Government in respect to any industrial undertaking, except factories as defined by the national law. Notice of every such suspension shall be filed with the International Labour Office.

ARTICLE 6.

In industrial undertakings which are influenced by the seasons and in all cases where exceptional circumstances demand it, the night period may be reduced to ten hours on sixty days of the year.

ARTICLE 7.

In countries where the climate renders work by day particularly trying to the health, the night period may be shorter than prescribed in the above articles, provided that compensatory rest is accorded during the day.

ARTICLE 8.

This Convention does not apply to women holding responsible positions of management who are not ordinarily engaged in manual work.

ARTICLE 9.

The formal ratifications of this Convention shall be communicated to the Secretary-General of the League of Nations for registration.

ARTICLE 10.

1. This Convention shall be binding only upon those Members of the International Labour Organisation whose ratifications have been registered with the Secretary-General.

2. It shall come into force twelve months after the date on which the ratifications of two Members have been registered with the Secretary-General.

3. Thereafter, this Convention shall come into force for any Member twelve months after the date on which its ratification has been registered.

ARTICLE 11.

As soon as the ratifications of two Members of the International Labour Organisation have been registered with the Secretariat, the Secretary-General of the League of Nations shall so notify all the Members of the International Labour Organisation. He shall likewise notify them of the registration of ratifications which may be communicated subsequently by other Members of the Organisation.

ARTICLE 12.

1. A Member which has ratified this Convention may denounce it after the expiration of ten years from the date on which the Convention first comes into force, by an act communicated to the Secretary-General of the League of Nations for registration. Such denunciation shall not take effect until one year after the date on which it is registered with the Secretariat.

2. Each Member which has ratified this Convention and which does not, within the year following the expiration of the period of ten years mentioned in the preceding paragraph, exercise the right of denunciation

provided for in this Article, will be bound for another period of ten years and, thereafter, may denounce this Convention at the expiration of each period of ten years under the terms provided for in this Article.

ARTICLE 13.

At the expiration of each period of ten years after the coming into force of this Convention, the Governing Body of the International Labour Office shall present to the General Conference a report on the working of this Convention and shall consider the desirability of placing on the Agenda of the Conference the question of its revision in whole or in part.

ARTICLE 14.

1. Should the Conference adopt a new Convention revising this Convention in whole or in part, then, unless the new Convention otherwise provides,
    (a) the ratification by a Member of the new revising Convention shall *ipso jure* involve the immediate denunciation of this Convention, notwithstanding the provisions of Article 12 above, if and when the new revising Convention shall have come into force;
    (b) as from the date when the new revising Convention comes into force, this Convention shall cease to be open to ratification by the Members.

2. This Convention shall in any case remain in force in its actual form and content for those Members which have ratified it but have not ratified the revising Convention.

ARTICLE 15.

The French and English texts of this Convention shall both be authentic.

Draft Convention [No. 42] concerning workmen's compensation for occupational diseases (revised 1934).

The General Conference of the International Labour Organisation of the League of Nations,

Having been convened at Geneva by the Governing Body of the International Labour Office, and having met in its Eighteenth Session on 4 June 1934, and

Having decided upon the adoption of certain proposals with regard to the partial revision of the Convention concerning workmen's compensation for occupational diseases adopted by the Conference at its Seventh Session, which is the fifth item on the Agenda of the Session, and

Considering that these proposals must take the form of a Draft International Convention,

adopts, this twenty-first day of June of the year one thousand nine hundred and thirty-four, the following Draft Convention which may be cited as the Workmen's Compensation (Occupational Diseases) Convention (Revised), 1934.

ARTICLE 1.

1. Each Member of the International Labour Organisation which ratifies this Convention undertakes to provide that compensation shall be payable to workmen incapacitated by occupational diseases, or, in case of death from such diseases, to their dependants, in accordance with the general principles of the national legislation relating to compensation for industrial accidents.

INTERNATIONAL LABOR ORGANIZATION

2. The rates of such compensation shall be not less than those prescribed by the national legislation for injury resulting from industrial accidents. Subject to this provision, each Member, in determining in its national law or regulations the conditions under which compensation for the said diseases shall be payable, and in applying to the said diseases its legislation in regard to compensation for industrial accidents, may make such modifications and adaptations as it thinks expedient.

ARTICLE 2.

Each Member of the International Labour Organisation which ratifies this Convention undertakes to consider as occupational diseases those diseases and poisonings produced by the substances set forth in the Schedule appended hereto, when such diseases or such poisonings affect workers engaged in the trades, industries or processes placed opposite in the said Schedule, and result from occupation in an undertaking covered by the said national legislation.

SCHEDULE

List of diseases and toxic substances.	List of corresponding trades, industries or processes.
Poisoning by lead, its alloys or compounds and their sequelae.	Handling of ore containing lead, including fine shot in zinc factories. Casting of old zinc and lead in ingots. Manufacture of articles made of cast lead or of lead alloys. Employment in the polygraphic industries. Manufacture of lead compounds. Manufacture and repair of electric accumulators. Preparation and use of enamels containing lead. Polishing by means of lead files or putty powder with a lead content. All painting operations involving the preparation and manipulation of coating substances, cements or colouring substances containing lead pigments.
Poisoning by mercury, its amalgams and compounds and their sequelae.	Handling of mercury ore. Manufacture of mercury compounds. Manufacture of measuring and laboratory apparatus. Preparation of raw material for the hatmaking industry. Hot gilding. Use of mercury pumps in the manufacture of incandescent lamps. Manufacture of fulminate of mercury primers.

Anthrax infection.	Work in connection with animals infected with anthrax. Handling of animal carcasses or parts of such carcasses including hides, hoofs and horns. Loading and unloading or transport of merchandise.
Silicosis with or without pulmonary tuberculosis, provided that silicosis is an essential factor in causing the resultant incapacity or death.	Industries or processes recognised by national law or regulations as involving exposure to the risk of silicosis.
Phosphorus poisoning by phosphorus or its compounds, and its sequelae.	Any process involving the production, liberation or utilisation of phosphorus or its compounds.
Arsenic poisoning by arsenic or its compounds, and its sequelae.	Any process involving the production, liberation or utilisation of arsenic or its compounds.
Poisoning by benzene or its homologues, their nitro- and amido-derivatives, and its sequelae.	Any process involving the production, liberation or utilisation of benzene or its homologues, or their nitro- and amido-derivatives.
Poisoning by the halogen derivatives of hydrocarbons of the aliphatic series.	Any process involving the production, liberation or utilisation of halogen derivatives of hydrocarbons of the aliphatic series designated by national laws or regulations.
Pathological manifestations due to: (*a*) radium and other radio-active substances; (*b*) X-rays.	Any process involving exposure to the action of radium, radioactive substances, or X-rays.
Primary epitheliomatous cancer of the skin.	Any process involving the handling or use of tar, pitch, bitumen, mineral oil, paraffin, or the compounds, products or residues of these substances.

(*For other Standard Articles, see Draft Convention No. 41*)

ARTICLE 6.

1. A Member which has ratified this Convention may denounce it after the expiration of five years from the date on which the Convention first comes into force, by an act communicated to the Secretary-General of the League of Nations for registration. Such denunciation shall not take effect until one year after the date on which it is registered with the Secretariat.

INTERNATIONAL LABOR ORGANIZATION

2. Each Member which has ratified this Convention and which does not, within the year following the expiration of the period of five years mentioned in the preceding paragraph, exercise the right of denunciation provided for in this Article, will be bound for another period of five years and, thereafter, may denounce this Convention at the expiration of each period of five years under the terms provided for in this Article.

Draft Convention [No. 43] for the regulation of hours of work in automatic sheet-glass works.

Article 1.

1. This Convention applies to persons who work in successive shifts in necessarily continuous operations in sheet-glass works which manufacture by automatic machines sheet-glass or other glass of the same characteristics which only differs from sheet-glass in thickness and other dimensions.

2. By necessarily continuous operations are meant all operations which, on account of the automatic and continuous character of the feeding of the molten glass to the machines and the working of the machines, are necessarily carried on without a break at any time of the day, night or week.

Article 2.

1. The persons to whom this Convention applies shall be employed under a system providing for at least four shifts.

2. The hours of work of such persons shall not exceed an average of forty-two per week.

3. This average shall be calculated over a period not exceeding four weeks.

4. The length of a spell of work shall not exceed eight hours.

5. The interval between two spells of work by the same shift shall not be less than sixteen hours: Provided that this interval may where necessary be reduced on the occasion of the periodical change-over of shifts.

Article 3.

1. The limits of hours prescribed in paragraphs 2, 3 and 4 of Article 2 may be exceeded and the interval prescribed in paragraph 5 reduced, but only so far as may be necessary to avoid serious interference with the ordinary working of the undertaking,

(*a*) in case of accident, actual or threatened, or in case of urgent work to be done to machinery or plant, or in case of *force majeure*; or

(*b*) in order to make good the unforeseen absence of one or more members of a shift.

2. Adequate compensation for all additional hours worked in accordance with this Article shall be granted in such manner as may be determined by national laws or regulations or by agreement between the organisations of employers and workers concerned.

Article 4.

In order to facilitate the effective enforcement of the provisions of this Convention every employer shall be required:

(*a*) to notify, by the posting of notices in conspicuous positions in the works or other suitable place or by such other method as may be

approved by the competent authority, the hours at which each shift begins and ends;
(b) not to alter the hours so notified except in such manner and with such notice as may be approved by the competent authority; and
(c) to keep a record in the form prescribed by the competent authority of all additional hours worked in pursuance of Article 3 of this Convention and of the compensation granted in respect thereof.

(*For the Standard Articles, see Draft Convention No. 41*)

Draft Convention [No. 44] ensuring benefit or allowances to the involuntarily unemployed.

Article 1.

1. Each Member of the International Labour Organisation which ratifies this Convention undertakes to maintain a scheme ensuring to persons who are involuntarily unemployed and to whom this Convention applies:

(a) benefit, by which is meant a payment related to contributions paid in respect of the beneficiary's employment whether under a compulsory or a voluntary scheme; or

(b) an allowance, by which is meant provision being neither benefit nor a grant under the ordinary arrangements for the relief of destitution, but which may be remuneration for employment on relief works organised in accordance with the conditions laid down in Article 9; or

(c) a combination of benefit and an allowance.

2. Subject to this scheme ensuring to all persons to whom this Convention applies the benefit or allowance required by paragraph 1, the scheme may be

(a) a compulsory insurance scheme;

(b) a voluntary insurance scheme;

(c) a combination of compulsory and voluntary insurance schemes; or

(d) any of the above alternatives combined with a complementary assistance scheme.

3. The conditions under which unemployed persons shall pass from benefit to allowances, if the occasion arises, shall be determined by national laws or regulations.

Article 2.

1. This Convention applies to all persons habitually employed for wages or salary:

2. Provided that any Member may in its national laws or regulations make such exceptions as it deems necessary in respect of:

(a) persons employed in domestic service;

(b) homeworkers;

(c) workers whose employment is of a permanent character in the service of the government, a local authority or a public utility undertaking;

(d) non-manual workers whose earnings are considered by the competent authority to be sufficiently high for them to ensure their own protection against the risk of unemployment;

(e) workers whose employment is of a seasonal character, if the season is normally of less than six months' duration and they are not

ordinarily employed during the remainder of the year in other employment covered by this Convention;
(*f*) young workers under a prescribed age;
(*g*) workers who exceed a prescribed age and are in receipt of a retiring or old-age pension;
(*h*) persons engaged only occasionally or subsidiarily in employment covered by this Convention;
(*i*) members of the employer's family;
(*j*) exceptional classes of workers in whose cases there are special features which make it unnecessary or impracticable to apply to them the provisions of this Convention.

3. Members shall state in the annual reports submitted by them upon the application of this Convention the exceptions which they have made under the foregoing paragraph.

4. This Convention does not apply to seamen, sea fishermen, or agricultural workers as these categories may be defined by national laws or regulations.

Article 3.

In cases of partial unemployment, benefit or an allowance shall be payable to unemployed persons whose employment has been reduced in a way to be determined by national laws or regulations.

Article 4.

The right to receive benefit or an allowance may be made subject to compliance by the claimant with the following conditions:
(*a*) that he is capable of and available for work;
(*b*) that he has registered at a public employment exchange or at some other office approved by the competent authority and, subject to such exceptions and conditions as may be prescribed by national laws or regulations, attends there regularly; and
(*c*) that he complies with such other requirements as may be prescribed by national laws or regulations for the purpose of showing whether he fulfils the conditions for the receipt of benefit or an allowance.

Article 5.

The right to receive benefit or an allowance may be made subject to other conditions and disqualifications, in particular those provided for in Articles 6, 7, 8, 9, 10, 11 and 12. Any conditions or disqualifications other than those provided for in the said Articles shall be indicated in the annual reports submitted by Members upon the application of this Convention.

Article 6.

The right to receive benefit or an allowance may be made conditional upon the completion of a qualifying period, involving:
(*a*) the payment of a prescribed number of contributions within a prescribed period preceding the claim to benefit or preceding the commencement of the period of unemployment;
(*b*) employment covered by this Convention for a prescribed period preceding the claim to benefit or an allowance or preceding the commencement of a period of unemployment; or
(*c*) a combination of the above alternatives.

Article 7.

The right to receive benefit or an allowance may be made conditional upon the completion of a waiting period the duration and conditions of application of which shall be prescribed by national laws or regulations.

Article 8.

The right to receive benefit or an allowance may be made conditional upon attendance at a course of vocational or other instruction.

Article 9.

The right to receive benefit or an allowance may be made conditional upon the acceptance, under conditions prescribed by national laws or regulations, of employment on relief works organised by a public authority.

Article 10.

1. A claimant may be disqualified for the receipt of benefit or of an allowance for an appropriate period if he refuses an offer of suitable employment. Employment shall not be deemed to be suitable:
   (*a*) if acceptance of it would involve residence in a district in which suitable accommodation is not available;
   (*b*) if the rate of wages offered is lower, or the other conditions of employment are less favorable:
   (*i*) where the employment offered is employment in the claimant's usual occupation and in the district where he was last ordinarily employed, than those which he might reasonably have expected to obtain, having regard to those which he habitually obtained in his usual occupation in that district or would have obtained if he had continued to be so employed;
   (*ii*) in all other cases, than the standard generally observed at the time in the occupation and district in which the employment is offered;
   (*c*) if the situation offered is vacant in consequence of a stoppage of work due to a trade dispute;
   (*d*) if for any other reason, having regard to all the considerations involved including the personal circumstances of the claimant, its refusal by the claimant is not unreasonable.

2. A claimant may be disqualified for the receipt of benefit or of an allowance for an appropriate period:
   (*a*) if he has lost his employment as a direct result of a stoppage of work due to a trade dispute;
   (*b*) if he has lost his employment through his own misconduct or has left it voluntarily without just cause;
   (*c*) if he has tried to obtain fraudulently any benefit or allowance; or
   (*d*) if he fails to comply with the instructions of a public employment exchange or other competent authority with regard to applying for employment, or if it is proved by the competent authority that he has failed or neglected to avail himself of a reasonable opportunity of suitable employment.

3. A claimant who on leaving his employment has received from his employer in virtue of his contract of service compensation for and substantially equal to his loss of earnings for a certain period may be disqualified for the duration of that period for the receipt of benefit or of

an allowance. A discharge allowance provided for by national laws or regulations shall not be deemed to be such compensation.

Article 11.

The right to receive benefit or an allowance may be limited in duration to a period which shall not normally be less than 156 working days per year, and shall in no case be less than 78 working days per year.

Article 12.

1. Benefit shall be payable irrespective of the needs of the claimant.

2. The right to receive an allowance may be made conditional upon the need of the claimant being proved in such manner as may be prescribed by national laws or regulations.

Article 13.

1. Benefit shall be payable in cash, but supplementary grants to facilitate the reemployment of an insured person may be in kind.

2. Allowances may be in kind.

Article 14.

There shall be constituted in accordance with national laws or regulations tribunals or other competent authorities for the purpose of determining questions arising on applications for benefit or an allowance made by persons to whom this Convention applies.

Article 15.

1. The claimant may be disqualified for the receipt of benefit or of an allowance in respect of any period during which he is resident abroad.

2. Special provisions may be prescribed for frontier workers employed in one country and resident in another.

Article 16.

Foreigners shall be entitled to benefit and allowances upon the same conditions as nationals: Provided that any Member may withhold from the nationals of any Member or State not bound by this Convention equality of treatment with its own nationals in respect of payments from funds to which the claimant has not contributed.

(*For other Standard Articles, see Draft Convention No. 41*)

Article 20.

1. A Member which has ratified this Convention may denounce it after the expiration of five years from the date on which the Convention first comes into force, by an act communicated to the Secretary-General of the League of Nations for registration. Such denunciation shall not take effect until one year after the date on which it is registered with the Secretariat.

2. Each Member which has ratified this Convention and which does not, within the year following the expiration of the period of five years mentioned in the preceding paragraph, exercise the right of denunciation provided for in this Article, will be bound for another period of five years and, thereafter, may denounce this Convention at the expiration of each period of five years under the terms provided for in this Article.

ARTICLE 21.

At the expiration of each period of five years after the coming into force of this Convention, the Governing Body of the International Labour Office shall present to the General Conference a report on the working of this Convention and shall consider the desirability of placing on the Agenda of the Conference the question of its revision in whole or in part.

Recommendation [No. 44] concerning unemployment insurance and various forms of relief for the unemployed.

The Conference,

Having adopted a Draft Convention ensuring benefit or allowances to the involuntarily unemployed;

Considering that this Draft Convention lays down the minimum conditions to be complied with by every scheme of unemployment insurance or assistance;

Considering that it is desirable to indicate a number of general principles which practice shows to be best calculated to promote a satisfactory organisation of unemployment insurance and assistance;

Recommends that each Member should take the following principles and rules into consideration:

1. In countries where compulsory insurance against unemployment is not in operation, steps should be taken to create such a system as soon as possible.

2. In countries in which compulsory or voluntary unemployment insurance is in operation, a complementary assistance scheme should be maintained to cover persons who have exhausted their right to benefit and in certain cases those who have not yet acquired the right to benefit; this scheme should be on a different basis from the ordinary arrangements for the relief of destitution.

3. All schemes for the payment of unemployment benefit or allowances should cover not only persons who are wholly unemployed, but also persons who are partially unemployed.

4. (*a*) Unemployment insurance and assistance schemes should be applied as soon as possible to all persons who are employed under a contract of service, and to persons employed under a contract of apprenticeship with money payment. If, however, exceptions are considered necessary, they should be confined within the narrowest possible limits.

(*b*) Such persons should be covered either by insurance or assistance until they reach the age at which they are entitled to an old-age pension.

(*c*) If circumstances make it difficult to apply the general provisions relating to unemployment insurance to a particular class of workers, special arrangements should be made for the insurance of such workers. These special arrangements should aim in particular at ensuring adequate proof of unemployment and at adapting the benefit to the normal earnings of the workers concerned.

(*d*) Whenever possible, and in particular whenever satisfactory measures of supervision can be applied, special provision should be made for the relief in case of unemployment of persons of comparatively small means who work on their own account.

5. Where it is considered advisable to fix a maximum remuneration as a criterion of liability to insurance, only such workers should thereby

be excluded as are in receipt of remuneration sufficiently high for them to ensure their own protection against the risk of unemployment, the ultimate object being to include all workers manual and non-manual irrespective of income.

6. The qualifying period permitted by the Draft Convention should not exceed 26 weeks' employment in an occupation covered by the scheme, or the payment of 26 weekly contributions or the equivalent, within twelve months preceding the claim for benefit, or alternatively 52 weeks' such employment, or 52 weekly contributions or the equivalent, within twenty-four months preceding the claim for benefit.

7. The period during which benefit is payable under national laws or regulations should be as long as is consistent with the solvency of the scheme; and every effort should be made to pay allowances as long as claimants are in need of them.

8. Subject to the provisions concerning partially unemployed persons, of Articles 3 and 7 of the Draft Convention, and of paragraph 3 of the present Recommendation, the waiting period permitted by the Draft Convention should not exceed eight days per spell of unemployment.

9. In deciding whether employment in an occupation other than that in which a claimant has previously been engaged is "suitable employment" for the purpose of the disqualification permitted by the Draft Convention, account should be taken of the length of the claimant's service in the previous occupation, his chances of obtaining work in it, his vocational training, and his suitability for the work.

10. Disqualification for the receipt of benefit or allowances on the ground that a claimant has lost his employment by reason of a stoppage of work due to a trade dispute should be confined to cases in which the claimant is directly interested in the dispute, and should in all cases cease when the stoppage of work ceases.

11. (a) The obligation to attend a course of vocational or other instruction permitted by the Draft Convention as a condition for the receipt of benefit or allowances should be imposed only if the unemployed person will derive an advantage therefrom either from the point of view of physical or mental well-being or of vocational or general capabilities.

(b) When imposing on an unemployed person an obligation to accept employment on relief works, account should be taken of his age, health, previous occupation and suitability for the employment in question.

(c) Only works of an exceptional and temporary character, organised by the public authority by means of funds specially allocated for the relief of the unemployed, should be considered as relief works.

12. Part of the money allocated to the relief of unemployment should be available for the purpose of facilitating the return of unemployed persons to employment, such as vocational and other training, and the payment of fares to unemployed persons who find employment in a district other than that in which they have been residing.

13. There should be a periodical review by the competent authority of the financial position of insurance funds in order that they may be kept as far as possible solvent and self-supporting. The financial arrangements should so far as possible include provisions to enable the scheme to surmount changes of short duration in the level of unemployment without change of the conditions governing the scheme.

14. An emergency fund should be created for the purpose of ensuring the payment, during periods of particularly severe unemployment, of the allowances provided for under national laws or regulations.

15. Provision should be made for the participation of representatives of the contributors in the administration of insurance schemes.

16. Equality of treatment should be applied in appropriate cases not only to the nationals of Members bound by the Convention but also to those of Members and States which, without having ratified the Convention, effectively apply its provisions.

17. States should regulate by means of bilateral agreements with neighboring States the conditions under which benefit or allowances shall be paid to unemployed workers in frontier zones who have their residence in one country and who work in another.

Date Due

APR 1 2 1949			
JAN 24 1950			
DE 15 69			